THE ROUTLEDGE HANDBOOK ON RESPONSIBILITY IN INTERNATIONAL RELATIONS

What does responsibility mean in International Relations (IR)? This handbook brings together cutting-edge research on the critical debates about responsibility that are currently being undertaken in IR theory.

This handbook both reflects upon an emerging field based on an engagement in the most crucial theoretical debates and serves as a foundational text by showing how deeply a discussion of responsibility is embedded in broader questions of IR theory and practice. Contributions cover the way in which responsibility is theorized across different approaches in IR and relevant neighboring disciplines and demonstrate how responsibility matters in different policy fields of global governance. Chapters with an empirical focus zoom in on particular actor constellations of (emerging) states, international organizations, political movements, or corporations, or address how responsibility matters in structuring the politics of global commons, such as oceans, resources, or the Internet.

Providing a comprehensive overview of IR scholarship on responsibility, this accessible and interdisciplinary text will be a valuable resource for scholars and students in many fields including IR, international law, political theory, global ethics, science and technology, area studies, development studies, business ethics, and environmental and security governance.

Hannes Hansen-Magnusson is Senior Lecturer in International Relations at Cardiff University and Director of the International Studies Research Unit.

Antje Vetterlein is Professor of Global Governance at the University of Münster and Associate Professor at Copenhagen Business School.

THE ROUTLEDGE HANDBOOK ON RESPONSIBILITY IN INTERNATIONAL RELATIONS

Edited by
Hannes Hansen-Magnusson
and Antje Vetterlein

LONDON AND NEW YORK

First published 2022
by Routledge
2 Park Square, Milton Park, Abingdon, Oxon OX14 4RN

and by Routledge
52 Vanderbilt Avenue, New York, NY 10017

Routledge is an imprint of the Taylor & Francis Group, an informa business

© 2022 selection and editorial matter, Hannes Hansen-Magnusson and Antje Vetterlein; individual chapters, the contributors

The right of Hannes Hansen-Magnusson and Antje Vetterlein to be identified as the authors of the editorial material, and of the authors for their individual chapters, has been asserted in accordance with sections 77 and 78 of the Copyright, Designs and Patents Act 1988.

All rights reserved. No part of this book may be reprinted or reproduced or utilised in any form or by any electronic, mechanical, or other means, now known or hereafter invented, including photocopying and recording, or in any information storage or retrieval system, without permission in writing from the publishers.

Trademark notice: Product or corporate names may be trademarks or registered trademarks, and are used only for identification and explanation without intent to infringe.

British Library Cataloguing-in-Publication Data
A catalogue record for this book is available from the British Library

Library of Congress Cataloging-in-Publication Data
Names: Hansen-Magnusson, Hannes, editor. | Vetterlein, Antje, editor.
Title: The Routledge handbook on responsibility in international relations / edited by Hannes Hansen-Magnusson and Antje Vetterlein.
Other titles: Handbook on responsibility in international relation
Description: Abingdon, Oxon; New York, NY: Routledge, 2021. | Includes bibliographical references and index.
Identifiers: LCCN 2020055895 (print) | LCCN 2020055896 (ebook) | ISBN 9780367218195 (hardback) | ISBN 9780429266317 (ebook)
Subjects: LCSH: International relations—Moral and ethical aspects. | International relations—Moral and ethical aspects—Case studies.
Classification: LCC JZ1306 .R684 2021 (print) | LCC JZ1306 (ebook) | DDC 172/.4—dc23
LC record available at https://lccn.loc.gov/2020055895
LC ebook record available at https://lccn.loc.gov/2020055896

ISBN: 978-0-367-21819-5 (hbk)
ISBN: 978-1-032-00422-8 (pbk)
ISBN: 978-0-429-26631-7 (ebk)

Cover image: "As It Was", from the series "Solid Shapes" by Angela Dwyer, 2020 (oil on canvas)

Typeset in Bembo
by KnowledgeWorks Global Ltd.

CONTENTS

List of figures and tables — ix
List of contributors — x
Acknowledgements — xxi
Abbreviations — xxiii

1 Responsibility in International Relations theory and practice: Introducing the handbook — 1
  Hannes Hansen-Magnusson and Antje Vetterlein

PART I
Theories of responsibility in International Relations — **29**

2 A plural theory of responsibility — 31
  Ilan Zvi Baron

3 The emergence of responsibility as a global scheme of governance — 43
  Tomer Shadmy

4 Human rights approach(es) to responsibility — 58
  Brooke Ackerly

5 Political responsibility in a globalized but fractured age — 71
  Richard Beardsworth

6 Moral irresponsibility in world politics — 84
  Peter Sutch

7 Rationalization, reticence, and the demands of global social and economic justice *Mark Busser*	96
8 Responsibility and authority in global governance *Jelena Cupać and Michael Zürn*	114
9 Responsibility and the English School *Viktor Friedmann*	125

PART II
Mapping responsibility relations across policy fields — 137

10 The assigning and erosion of responsibility for the global environment *Steven Bernstein*	139
11 Moral geographies of responsibility in the global agrifood system *Tobias Gumbert and Doris Fuchs*	153
12 State responsibilities and international nuclear politics *Laura Considine and James Souter*	164
13 Delegating moral responsibility in war: Lethal autonomous weapons systems and the responsibility gap *Elke Schwarz*	177
14 Negotiating protection through responsibility *Erna Burai*	192
15 From Lisbon to Sendai: Responsibilities in international disaster management *Marco Krüger and Friedrich Gabel*	203

PART III
Responsibility relations: Subjects, objects and speakers of responsibility — 217

16 Responsible diplomacy: Judgments, wider national interests and diplomatic peace *Markus Kornprobst*	219
17 Rising powers and responsibility *Johannes Plagemann and Amrita Narlikar*	231

18 Responsibility as an opportunity: China's water
    governance in the Mekong region   242
    Yung-Yung Chang

19 Responsibility as practice: Implications of UN Security
    Council responsibilization   257
    Holger Niemann

20 Rebel with a cause: Rebel responsibility in intrastate
    conflict situations   271
    Mitja Sienknecht

21 What responsibility for international organisations?
    The independent accountability mechanisms of the
    multilateral development banks   288
    Susan Park

22 The international labour organization's role to ensure decent
    work in a globalized economy: A contested responsibility?   301
    Julia Drubel

23 Business and responsibility for human rights in
    global governance   318
    David Jason Karp

24 Social media actors: Shared responsibility 3.0?   331
    Gabi Schlag

PART IV
Global commons as responsibility objects   **345**

25 Responsibility on the high seas   347
    J. Samuel Barkin and Elizabeth R. DeSombre

26 The role of humanity's responsibility towards biodiversity:
    The BBNJ treaty   358
    *Rachel Tiller, Elizabeth Nyman, Elizabeth Mendenhall
    and Elizabeth De Santo*

27 A responsibility to freeze? The Arctic as a complex object
    of responsibility   369
    Mathias Albert and Sebastian Knecht

28 Shareholders, supervisors, and stakeholders: Practices of financial
    responsibility and their limits   380
    Michael C. Sardo and Erin Lockwood

29 Diplomacy and responsibilities in the transnational governance
    of the cyber domain   394
    Andrea Calderaro

PART V
Critical reflections and theoretical debates   **407**

30 Framing responsibility research in International Relations   409
    Antje Wiener

31 Academic responsibility in the face of climate change   423
    Patrick Thaddeus Jackson

32 Responsibility as political beauty? Derrida's ethics of decision
    and the politics of responding to others   436
    Stephan Engelkamp

33 On potential and limits of the concept of responsibility as a
    reference point for the use of practical reason   449
    Sergio Dellavalle

Index   464

FIGURES AND TABLES

Figures

1.1	The field of responsibilization	8
8.1	From responsibility to authority	119
8.2	From authority to responsibility	121
20.1	Responsibility triangles	274
20.2	Conflicting responsibility triangles in intrastate conflict	277
20.3	Conflicting responsibility triangles in Iraq in the 1990s	283
30.1	Cycle-grid model: sites of contestation and practices of validation	412
31.1	Orientations towards politics	430

Tables

15.1	Dimensions of responsibility	204
22.1	People affected by forced labor in millions	306
23.1	What constitutes responsibility approaches to global ethics?	320
23.2	Moral, political, and legal responsibility of businesses for human rights across four models	323
26.1	Stages and subsections in regime creation processes	363
30.1	Three segments of norms	414
30.2	The norm typology	414
30.3	Two ontologies: Community versus diversity	418

CONTRIBUTORS

The Editors

Hannes Hansen-Magnusson is Senior Lecturer in International Relations at Cardiff University and Director of the International Studies Research Unit. He was awarded an Early Career Researcher Grant by the British International Studies Association (2017). His research draws on hermeneutic philosophy and praxiographic methodology in order to understand micro-practices of interaction processes and their relation to macro structures. He is interested in the role of norms, ideas, and cultural practices in global politics, focusing on oceans and the Arctic. His research has been published in *Cooperation & Conflict*, *The Cambridge Review of International Affairs*, the *Journal of International Relations and Development*, and the *Journal of Common Market Studies*. He is co-editor of "The Rise of Responsibility in World Politics" (Cambridge University Press 2020, with Antje Vetterlein) and is the author of "International Relations as Politics among People – Hermeneutic Encounters and Global Governance" (Routledge 2020).

Antje Vetterlein is Professor of Global Governance at the University of Münster and Associate Professor in the Department of Organization at Copenhagen Business School. Her research is located within international political economy with particular interests in global governance, the politics of development and the relationship between economy and society focusing on political actors and practices at the transnational level and the role of ideas and norms in international politics. Specifically, she studies international organizations and multinational corporations and questions of legitimacy and responsibility in international politics. Her work often draws upon sociological approaches and methodology in order to understand the micro-foundations of political processes and formations on a macro scale. Her work is published in journals such as *Global Governance*, *New Political Economy*, *European Political Science Review*, *Business & Politics*, *Journal of International Relations and Development*, and *Politische Vierteljahresschrift*. She has edited special issues in *Contemporary Politics* and *Journal of International Relations and Development*, as well as "The Rise of Responsibility in World Politics" (Cambridge University Press 2020, with Hannes Hansen-Magnusson) and "Owning Development. Creating Policy Norms in the IMF and World Bank" (Cambridge University Press 2010, with Susan Park).

Contributors

Brooke Ackerly is Professor of Political Science at Vanderbilt University. She is co-Editor-in-Chief of the *International Feminist Journal of Politics* (2018–2021). In her research, teaching, and collaborations, she works to clarify without simplifying the most pressing problems of global justice, including human rights and climate change. She is currently working on the intersection of global economic, environmental, and gender justice in their material and epistemic dimensions. She is the founder of the Global Feminisms Collaborative, a group of scholars and activists developing ways to collaborate on applied research for social justice. Using feminist methodologies, she integrates into her theoretical work empirical research on activism and the experiences of those affected by injustice (Grounded Normative Theory). Her monographs include "Political Theory and Feminist Social Criticism" (Cambridge University Press 2000), "Universal Human Rights in a World of Difference" (Cambridge University Press 2008), "Doing Feminist Research" (with Jacqui True, Palgrave Macmillan 2010), and most recently, "Just Responsibility: A Human Rights Theory of Global Justice" (Oxford University Press 2018).

Mathias Albert is Professor of Political Science at Bielefeld University. He works on various aspects of international relations and world society theory in a historical-sociological perspective and the politics of the polar regions. In addition, he is also active in research on youth (Shell youth studies). His research has been published in journals such as *European Journal of International Relations, Cooperation and Conflict, Journal of International Relations and Development, Review of International Studies, Geopolitics, International Political Sociology*, and *Zeitschrift für Internationale Beziehungen*. Recent books include "A Theory of World Politics" (Cambridge University Press 2016), "What in the World?" (ed. With Tobias Werron, Bristol University Press 2021), and "Envisioning the World Mapping and Making the Global" (ed. With Sandra Holtgreve and Karlson Preuß, transcript 2021).

J. Samuel Barkin is Professor of Global Governance and Human Security at the University of Massachusetts Boston. His research addresses International Relations theory and international organization, with particular attention to global environmental politics, international monetary politics, theories of sovereignty, and constructivist theory. His work has been published in *International Organization, International Studies Quarterly, International Studies Review, Foreign Policy Analysis, American Journal of International Law, Global Environmental Politics, Global Governance, Millennium*, and *Environmental Politics*, among other journals, as well as in numerous edited volumes. Recent books include "The Sovereignty Cartel" (Cambridge University Press 2021), "International Relations' Last Synthesis? Decoupling Constructivisms and Critical Approaches", co-authored with Laura Sjoberg (Oxford University Press 2019), as well as "Fish" (Polity 2011) and "Saving Global Fisheries: Reducing Capacity to Promote Sustainability" (MIT Press 2013), both co-authored with Elizabeth R. DeSombre.

Ilan Zvi Baron is Professor in International Political Theory at Durham University. He has held visiting appointments at the University of British Columbia and the Hebrew University of Jerusalem. His research explores different ways that we experience international politics in our everyday lives. To date, he has written on post-truth politics, the Jewish Diaspora's relationship with Israel, and the international cultural politics of Israeli cuisine. In addition, he has written on violence, the ethics of war, identity and security, and International Relations theory. He is currently working on a long-term research project about political responsibility and dystopian novels. His monographs include "How to Save Politics in a Post-Truth Era: Thinking through Difficult Times" (Manchester University Press 2018) and "Obligation in Exile: The Jewish Diaspora, Israel and Critique" (Oxford University Press 2015).

Richard Beardsworth is Professor of International Politics and Head of School at the University of Leeds. He is also research associate at the *Institut des Etudes Politiques (SciPo)*, Paris. His research interests lie in global politics, statecraft, and long-term policy-formation regarding global challenges, particularly climate change and sustainability. He co-directs research projects on state responsibility towards global challenges and the rehearsal of plausible norms in international politics. Two major questions in these projects are: How can we understand state responsibilities at the intersection of non-territorial challenges? What is the relation between normative change and political judgment? His own work increasingly focuses on establishing political narratives around climate change responsibility and the possibility of systemic change. His IR research has been published in *International Relations, Journal of International Political Theory*, and *Ethics & International Affairs*.

Steven Bernstein is Distinguished Professor of Global Environmental and Sustainability Governance at the University of Toronto. He is a Professor in the Department of Political Science and Co-Director of the Environmental Governance Lab at the Munk School of Global Affairs and Public Policy. He also co-edits the journal *Global Environmental Politics* and is a lead faculty member of the Earth Systems Governance Project. His research spans the areas of global governance and institutions, global environmental politics, non-state forms of governance, international political economy, and policy studies. He is the author or co-editor of several books and author of over 75 scholarly articles and book chapters, including in *Science, Nature Climate Change, European Journal of International Relations, Review of International Political Economy, Comparative Political Studies, Journal of International Economic Law, International Affairs, Canadian Journal of Political Science, Policy Sciences, Regulation and Governance*, and *Global Environmental Politics*.

Erna Burai is Postdoctoral Researcher at the Global Governance Centre at The Graduate Institute Geneva. Her research focuses on norm contestation in humanitarian interventions and the responsibility to protect, and the politics of responsibility in general. She is currently working on the research project "To Save and to Defend: Global Norm Ambiguity and Regional Order", with Stephanie C. Hofmann, where she covers African regional and sub-regional organizations. Before joining the Graduate Institute, she held visiting fellowships at the European University Institute (EUI) in Florence, the Montréal Centre for International Studies (CÉRIUM), and the School of Slavonic and East European Studies (SSEES) at University College London. Her article "Parody as Norm Contestation: Russian Normative Justifications in Georgia and Ukraine and their Implications for Global Norms" was published in *Global Society* (2016).

Mark Busser teaches at the Department of Political Science and in the Faculty of Social Sciences at McMaster University in Hamilton, Canada, where he is Manager of Experiential Education. His research and teaching are focused on international relations, global ethics, gender, and the politics of conspiracism and misinformation. He is the author of "Ethics, Obligations and the Responsibility to Protect" (Routledge 2019), which examines the role of power relationships of accountability and answerability in the international debates over the humanitarian Responsibility to Protect.

Contributors

Andrea Calderaro is Senior Lecturer in International Relations at Cardiff University and the director of the Centre for Internet and Global Politics. His research centers on transnational governance of the cyber domain, with a focus on cybersecurity and cyber diplomacy. He has conducted research and supported cyber capacity-building initiatives in Africa, Asia, Middle East, Central America, in EU institutions, and he serves as a member of the Research Committee of the Global Forum of Cyber Expertise (GFCE). He was visiting fellow at California Institute of Technology, Robert Schumann Centre for Advanced Studies/EUI, University of Oslo, LUISS Guido Carli, Humboldt University, and he holds his PhD from the European University Institute.

Yung-Yung Chang holds a PhD from Free University Berlin. Currently she works as Research Fellow for the International Consortium for Research in the Humanities at Friedrich-Alexander-Universität Erlangen-Nürnberg. Her research interests include regional integration in East Asia, comparative regionalism, global governance, China's external relations and politics, economics and security of the Indo-Pacific region. At present, she is working on the topics concerning China's narrative power in the international arena and China's rising "responsible" role in global governance and international cooperation, such as the Belt and Road Initiative or the Digital Silk Road. She will participate in the book project "China under Xi Jinping: interdisciplinary assessment". She has published in journals such as the *Journal of Chinese Political Science* and the *European Journal of East Asian Studies*.

Laura Considine is a Lecturer in International Relations at the University of Leeds and co-Director of the Centre for Global Security Challenges. She was a Junior Fellow at the Kluge Center at the United States Library of Congress in Washington DC in 2011. Her current work focuses on conceptualizing nuclear weapons in international politics, feminist approaches to nuclear weapons and nuclear disarmament. Her work has been published in journals such as *International Affairs*, the *European Journal of International Relations*, and *Millennium: Journal of International Studies*.

Jelena Cupać is Postdoctoral Research Fellow at the Global Governance research unit at the WZB Berlin Social Science Centre. She holds a PhD from the European University Institute. Her research has been published in *CEU Political Science Journal* and the *Journal of Regional Security*. Her article "The personal is global political: The antifeminist backlash in the United Nations" was published in *The British Journal of Politics and International Relations* (2020, with Irem Ebetürk).

Sergio Dellavalle is Professor of Public Law and State Theory at the University of Turin and Senior Research Affiliate at the Max Planck Institute of Comparative Public Law and International Law in Heidelberg. An expert on the philosophy of G.W.F. Hegel, among his monographs is "Paradigmi dell'ordine" (Paradigms of Social Order, Palgrave Macmillan 2011), while his recent research has been published in *Zeitschrift für ausländisches öffentliches Recht und Völkerrecht*, *Theoretical Inquiries in Law*, *Göttinger Journal of International Law*, *Oxford Journal of Legal Studies*.

Elizabeth De Santo is Associate Professor of Environmental Studies and Chair of the Environmental Studies Program at Franklin & Marshall College. Her research focuses on marine conservation and environmental governance, critically examining (i) the efficacy of spatial approaches to conserving marine species and habitats, and (ii) mechanisms for improving the science-policy interface in environmental decision-making. She is particularly interested in the challenges of effectively implementing Marine Protected Areas and biodiversity conservation worldwide. Her research has been published, *inter alia*, in *Marine Policy*, *Ocean and Coastal Management*, *Earth System Governance*, *Environmental Science & Policy*, and *Journal of Geography*.

Elizabeth R. DeSombre is the Camilla Chandler Frost Professor of Environmental Studies at Wellesley College. Her research focuses on environmental politics, international environmental law, ocean and atmospheric issues, and the protection of the global commons. Recent projects have involved the impact of flag-of-convenience shipping, the regulation of international fisheries, protection of the ozone layer, and global environmental institutions generally. Her first book, "Domestic Sources of International Environmental Policy: Industry, Environmentalists, and U.S. Power" (MIT Press 2000) won the 2001 Chadwick F. Alger Prize for the best book published in the area of international organization, and the 2001 Lynton Caldwell Award for the best book published on environmental policy. Other recent books include "Why Good People Do Bad Environmental Things" (Oxford University Press 2018) and "What is Environmental Politics?" (Polity Press 2000).

Julia Drubel is Postdoctoral Researcher at the University of Gießen. Her research focuses on theories of International Relations and Global Political Economy as well as global social and economic governance. She has completed her doctoral thesis, which examined the effectiveness of the ILO's prohibition of forced labor with a special emphasis on norms research. Previously she has been working as a research associate at the DFG-funded project *Interreligious Dialogue and the Global Norm of Freedom of Religion*. She is currently working on the Sustainable Development Goals and decent work as an associated researcher at the Max Planck Research Group MAGGI (*The Multiplication of Authorities in Global Governance Institutions*). Her research has been published in *Global Social Policy*.

Stephan Engelkamp is Lecturer in International Relations at King's College London. His main research interests are global security governance and processes of normalization in global and European politics, critical approaches to peace and conflict, international relations theory (especially critical norms research and post-colonial approaches), and political anthropology. His research has appeared in journals such as *Alternatives*, *International Studies Perspectives* and *European Review of International Studies*. He is the co-editor of a volume on critical norms research in Germany, titled "Kritische Normenforschung in Deutschland" (with Katharina Glaab and Antonia Graf, Nomos 2021).

Viktor Friedmann is an Associate Professor at Budapest Metropolitan University and Program Director for International Relations. His main research interests are the history of global governance, great power management, the history of ideas in China's foreign relations, and the history of international political thought. His current research focuses on China's self-conception of greatness and on the role of virtues in international society. He is further interested in the global governance of climate migration, in combining classical realist, English School and Foucauldian approaches to International Relations, in the impact of technological change on global politics. His research has been published, inter alia, in *The Palgrave Encyclopedia of Global Security Studies*, the *Corvinius Journal of International Relations*, and *Acta Oeconomica*.

Contributors

Doris Fuchs is Professor of International Relations and Sustainable Development and Speaker of the Center for Interdisciplinary Sustainability Research at the University of Münster. Her research concentrates on questions of sustainability governance with a particular focus on sustainable consumption and power, as well as normative questions of justice, legitimacy, and responsibility. She is the co-author of "Consumption Corridors: Living a Good Life within Sustainable Limits" (2021), and co-editor of "The Routledge Handbook of Global Sustainability Governance" (2020) and has published in *Global Environmental Politics, Environmental Values, Social Sciences, Journal of Sustainable Development,* and *Business and Politics,* among others.

Friedrich Gabel is a research associate at the International Center for Ethics in the Sciences and Humanities at the University of Tübingen, and a PhD candidate at the Karlsruhe Institute of Technology. His dissertation is supported by the Heinrich Böll Foundation. His research focuses on questions of disaster ethics, justice in crisis management, as well as security and inclusion (of persons with disabilities). His research has been published in the *International Journal of Disaster Risk Reduction* and in *Disasters*.

Tobias Gumbert is Postdoctoral Researcher at the University of Münster, focusing on environmental politics and governance, with a particular focus on food policy, waste policy, sustainable consumption, and democratic innovations. His research has been published in *Politics and Governance, The Routledge Handbook of Global Sustainability Governance, Sustainability: Science, Practice & Policy,* and *The Routledge Handbook of Transnational Studies,* among others.

Patrick Thaddeus Jackson is Professor of International Studies in the School of International Service at American University Washington, DC. His book "The Conduct of Inquiry in International Relations: Philosophy of Science and its Implications for the Study of World Politics" (Routledge 2011; second edition 2016) received the ISA-Northeast's Yale H. Ferguson Book Award and the ISA Theory Section's Best Book of the Year Award. He is presently working on a book about explanation and a book about Max Weber.

David Jason Karp is Senior Lecturer at the University of Sussex. His research is at the intersection of global ethics, human rights and international theory. He is co-director of the Sussex Rights and Justice Research Centre; co-convenor of the BISA Ethics & World Politics working group; and member of the Management Committee for the Centre for Advanced International Theory. His research has been published in *International Theory, Global Responsibility to Protect, Review of International Studies, International Studies Review,* and *Global Governance,* among others. He has co-edited "Human Rights Protection in Global Politics: Responsibilities of States and Non-State Actors" (Palgrave Macmillan 2015, with Kurt Mills) and is the author of "Responsibility for Human Rights: Transnational Corporations in Imperfect States" (Cambridge University Press 2014).

Markus Kornprobst is Professor of Political Science International Relations at the Vienna School of International Studies. His research appears in leading journals in the field such as the *European Journal of International Relations International Affairs, International Organization* and *International Theory.* He has co-edited five books, co-authored "Understanding International Diplomacy" and authored "Irredentism in European Politics" as well as "Co-managing International Crises". He is co-editor of the *Routledge New Diplomacy Series,* serves on the board of the *Hague Journal of Diplomacy,* leads the Peaceful Change Working Group at the Austrian Research Association, and serves as Regional Director Africa of the *Global Research Network on Peaceful Change.* His current research projects deal with processes of global and regional ordering, peaceful change, arms control, digital international relations and global health.

Sebastian Knecht was a Postdoctoral Researcher at the University of Bielefeld between April 2019 and December 2020. His research was primarily concerned with international cooperation in the polar regions, the design and stratification of membership systems in international organizations, and science-policy interactions. He has published widely in peer-reviewed journals, including *Cooperation and Conflict*, *Polar Record*, *The Polar Journal*, and *Zeitschrift für Internationale Beziehungen*. He is further co-author of the German-language textbook *Internationale Politik und Governance in der Arktis: Eine Einführung* (Springer 2018, with Kathrin Stephen and Golo Bartsch) and co-editor of *Governing Arctic Change: Global Perspectives* (Palgrave Macmillan 2017, with Kathrin Keil).

Marco Krüger is a research associate at the International Center for Ethics in the Sciences and Humanities at the University of Tübingen. He coordinates a transdisciplinary research project on the disaster resilience of the ambulatory care infrastructure in Germany (AUPIK). His research focusses on the conception of resilience and the societal construction of notions of normality in the realm of security as well as on security ethics. He is the co-editor of "Disaster resilience: Concepts for strengthening care recipients and people in need of help" (Transcript 2019, with Matthias Max, in German). His research has been published in the *Disaster*, *International Political Sociology*, and *Security Dialogue*, among others.

Erin Lockwood is Assistant Professor of Political Science at University of California, Irvine. Her research interests encompass international political economy; global financial politics; financial derivatives; regulation; risk and uncertainty; power, authority, and legitimacy in international politics; and global inequality. Her current book project examines the financial market practices through which both the market for over-the-counter derivatives and the authority of private financial actors were constructed. Her research has been published, inter alia, in *Review of International Political Economy*, *New Political Economy* and *Theory and Society*.

Elizabeth Mendenhall is Assistant Professor of Marine Affairs at the University of Rhode Island. Her research centers on the progressive development of the ocean governance regime, especially the Law of the Sea Convention. Recent work addresses artificial island building, sea level rise, marine plastic debris, strategic nuclear submarines, and the "Biodiversity Beyond National Jurisdiction" negotiations. She has published in *Marine Policy*, *Journal of Military and Strategic Studies*, *Astropolitics*, *Marine Pollution Bulletin*, *Strategic Studies Quarterly*, and *Current History*, among others.

Amrita Narlikar is President of the German Institute of Global and Area Studies (GIGA), Professor at the University of Hamburg, and non-resident Senior Fellow at the Observer Research Foundation. Prior to moving to Hamburg, she held the position of Reader in International Political Economy at the University of Cambridge and a Fellowship at Darwin College. She was also Senior Research Associate at the Centre for International Studies at the University of Oxford from 2003 to 2014. Amrita has authored/edited eleven books. Her most recent book has been published by Cambridge University Press ("Poverty Narratives in International Trade Negotiations and Beyond"). Her previous books include:

"Bargaining with a Rising India: Lessons from the Mahabharata (co-authored, Oxford University Press 2014); "The Oxford Handbook on the World Trade Organization (co-edited, 2012); "Deadlocks in Multilateral Negotiations: Causes and Solutions (edited, Cambridge University Press 2010).

Holger Niemann is a postdoctoral researcher at the Institute for Peace Research and Security Policy (IFSH) at the University of Hamburg. His research focusses on the norms and practices of global governance, the legitimation of international organizations, and an international political sociology of the United Nations. Currently, he is working on the structural, organizational, and programmatic transformation of the UN Security Council, the normativity of international practices, and the relationship between science and society. His research has been published in *Review of International Studies*, *Palgrave Encyclopedia of Peace and Conflict Studies*, and *Zeitschrift für Internationale Beziehungen*. He is the author of "The Justification of Responsibility in the UN Security Council. Practices of Normative Ordering in International Relations" (Routledge 2019).

Elizabeth Nyman is Assistant Professor at Texas A&M University, Galveston. Her research focuses on international maritime conflict, piracy, and environmental issues, and has been published in a variety of academic venues. She is particularly interested in oceanic resources, such as fish or offshore oil and gas, and how those impact state desires to control ocean spaces. She has conducted research in a variety of locations, from Iceland to Barbados to Canada, focusing on maritime issues such as the Cod Wars between Britain and Iceland and the flying fish dispute between Barbados and Trinidad and Tobago. Her research has been published in, inter alia, *Games Culture*, *Ocean and Coastal Management*, *International Journal of Maritime History*, *Marine Policy*, *International Interactions*, and *Antipode*.

Susan Park is Professor of Global Governance in the Department of Government and International Relations at the University of Sydney. She focuses on how international organizations and global governance can become greener and more accountable. Her most recent books are: "Environmental Recourse at the Multilateral Development Banks" (2020); "Global Environmental Governance and the Accountability Trap" (2019, with Teresa Kramarz), and "International Organisations: Theories and Explanations" (2018). She is an Associate Editor of the journal *Global Environmental Politics* and is Co-Convenor with Dr Kramarz (University of Toronto) of the Earth Systems Governance (ESG) Task Force *Accountability in Global Environmental Governance*. She is a Senior Hans Fischer Fellow at the Technical University of Munich (2019-2022), a Senior Research Fellow of the ESG, an affiliated Faculty member of the Environmental Governance Lab at the University of Toronto, and an external associate at Warwick University.

Johannes Plagemann is a political scientist and research fellow at the German Institute of Global and Area Studies (GIGA) where he acts as the spokesperson of the research team *Ideas, Actors and Global Politics* and coordinates the research project *Legitimate* Multipolarity (2018-2022). He works on rising powers in international politics and Indian foreign policy in particular. In his latest research he focusses on (1) how populism affects foreign policy and (2) the legitimacy of international organizations in a multipolar world. His research has been published in *Foreign Policy Analysis*, *International Studies Review*, *Review of International Studies*, *International Relations of the Asia Pacific*, and *The Pacific Review*.

Michael Christopher Sardo is Non-Tenure Track Assistant Professor in Politics at Occidental College. He is a political theorist with research and teaching interests in the history of political thought, contemporary democratic theory, and environmental political theory. His current research projects include a book project on political theory and the Anthropocene through the lens of Nietzsche's thought as well as article-length projects on the challenges of political responsibility in global politics. His article "Political Responsibility for Climate Justice: Political not Moral" is being published in *European Journal of Political Theory*.

Gabi Schlag is Senior Lecturer at the Institute of Political Science at the University of Tübingen. She serves as a member in the Governing Board of the European International Studies Association (EISA). Her research interests include Critical Security Studies; discourse and practice theories; social media and visual IR; political violence and emotions; gender and bodies. Her research is published in peer-reviewed journals like *Zeitschrift für Internationale Beziehungen*, *European Journal of International Relations*, *Journal of International Relations and Development*, as well as *Critical Studies on Terrorism*. She co-edited "Visualität und Weltpolitik" (Springer 2020, with Axel Heck), "Transformations of Security Studies" (Routledge 2016, with Julian Junk and Christopher Daase) as well as a special issue in *Global Disccourse* on "Visualizing violence: aesthetics and ethics in international politics" (2017, with Anna Geis).

Elke Schwarz is Senior Lecturer in Political Theory at Queen Mary University of London. Her research focuses on the political and ethical implications of new technologies, with a focus on digital technologies and autonomous systems. In 2018, she published her monograph "Death Machines: The Ethics of Violent Technologies" (Manchester University Press). Her work has been published in *Thesis Eleven*, *Security Dialogue*, *Millennium: Journal of International Studies*, the *Journal of International Political Theory*, and other journals. She has been awarded a BA/Leverhulme Small Grant for a project titled "Moral Agency and Meaningful Human Control: Exploring Military Ethical Values for Alignment in the Use of Autonomous Weapons Systems". She is co-founder of the BISA Ethics and World Politics Working Group and an RSA Fellow.

Tomer Shadmy is research fellow at The Federmann Cyber Center, at Hebrew University of Jerusalem, and the Institute for National Security Studies. Additionally she is an Adjunct Professor for Computer Science Law and Ethics at Tel Aviv University, the Hebrew University of Jerusalem and The Interdisciplinary Center, Herzliya. Her scholarship is situated at the intersection of digital technologies, global law, and ethics. She investigates the legal, ethical, social, and political challenges associated with the governance of emerging technologies such as Artificial Intelligence (AI). At the center of her research stands the question of how data-driven technologies challenge, transform, or require a transformation of basic legal and civic concepts and institutions. She is interested in both sides of the algorithm: How to regulate emerging technologies and how do emerging technologies regulate us? Her research has been published in the *Boston University International Law Journal* and *North Carolina Journal of International Law and Commercial Regulation*.

Mitja Sienknecht is Postdoctoral Researcher at the University of Münster. Previously, she was a researcher at the Global Governance research unit at the Berlin Social Science Centre (WZB) and at the "B/Orders in Motion" project at the Viadrina European University, Frankfurt (Oder). Her research addresses the fields of peace and conflict studies, systems theory and world society, border and boundary studies, international organizations, and the transgression of intrastate conflicts beyond borders. Her research has been published in *Zeitschrift für Internationale Beziehungen* and *Politische Vierteljahresschrift*. She is the author of the monograph "Delimited Conflicts in World Society. On the Inclusion of International Organizations in Intrastate Conflicts" (in German, SpringerVS 2018).

James Souter is a Lecturer in International Relations at the University of Leeds. He is interested in understanding states' responsibilities to address pressing global issues, and has written on this topic in relation to human rights, the responsibility to protect, and nuclear responsibility. However, much of his work focuses on asylum and states' responsibilities to protect refugees. His book, entitled "Asylum as Reparation: Refuge and Responsibility for the Harms of Displacement", is forthcoming with Palgrave Macmillan. James has also published work in journals such as *Political Studies*, *International Affairs*, *Politics*, the *British Journal of Politics and International Relation*, and the *Journal of Social Philosophy*.

Peter Sutch is Professor of Politics at Cardiff University. His main research area explores questions of international justice, in particular questions relating to international law. He is particularly interested in normative or moral questions and their impact on, and relation to, questions of politics and law. He has been concerned with questions of how we should conceive of the relation between ethics and international politics ("Ethics Justice and International Relations", Routledge 2001) and has published "The Politics of International Law and International Justice" (Edinburgh University Press 2013, with Edwin Egede). He also has broader interests in contemporary political theory and the history of political thought and along with colleagues in the political theory research unit, has recently collaborated on projects on multiculturalism ("Multiculturalism, Identity and Rights", Routledge 2003) and questions of justification in moral theory ("Principles and Political Order: The Challenge of Diversity", Routledge 2006) and the nature of evil in contemporary political theory (Edinburgh University Press 2011, with Bruce Haddock and Peri Roberts). He is currently working on questions of just war theory, global law and distributive justice in the global commons.

Rachel Tiller is Senior Research Scientist at SINTEF Trondheim. Her research focus is on interdisciplinary marine research, especially looking at multilevel governance and stakeholder interaction and co-production of knowledge. She was the Fulbright Arctic Chair at Texas A&M University at Galveston and Rice University in Houston, Texas in 2018, working on plastics governance and the Arctic Ocean as an area beyond national jurisdiction. She currently works on, among others, the EU project GoJelly on finding a gelatinous solution to plastic pollution (www.gojelly.eu) and she is Project Manager of the Smartfish H2020 project on innovations in fisheries technology (www.smartfishh2020.eu). She also follows the BBNJ negotiations towards a new treaty for biodiversity protection in areas beyond national jurisdiction, doing observation studies, coding statements and holding in-depth interviews with delegates and NGOs. Her research has been published in international journals such *Marine Policy*, *Journal of Environmental Management*, *Maritime Studies*, *Ocean and Coastal Management*, *Global Environmental Politics*, and *Ocean Development and International Law*.

Antje Wiener is Professor of Global Governance at the University of Hamburg, elected By-Fellow of Hughes Hall, University of Cambridge, and Fellow of the UK's Academy of Social Sciences. Her research and teaching centers on International Relations (IR) theory, especially norms research and contestation theory. Current projects include contested climate justice (Cluster of Excellence, CLICCS, Hamburg), democratizing security (Graduate College, funded by the State of Hamburg), and multiplicity and international order/s (Lauterpacht Centre for International Law, Cambridge). With James Tully, she is co-founding editor of Global Constitutionalism (Cambridge University Press, since 2012). She also edits the Norm Research in International Relations Series (Springer). She currently serves on several Committees of the Academy of Social Sciences, as well as of the International Studies Association, and she has been re-appointed to the ESRC's Global Challenges Research Fund Peer Review College in 2019. In 2018, she was elected to the Executive Committee of the German Political Science Association in 2018. Her most recent book "Contestation and Constitution of Norms in Global International Relations" (Cambridge University Press 2018) was awarded the International Studies Association's International Law Section's Book Prize in 2020.

Michael Zürn is Director at the WZB Berlin Social Science Center and Professor of International Relations at the Free University Berlin. He is the Founding Rector of the Hertie School of Governance and is Spokesperson of the Cluster of Excellence "Contestations of the Liberal Script (SCRIPTS)". His most recent books are "A Theory of Global Governance. Authority, Legitimacy, and Contestation" (Oxford University Press 2018) and "Die Demokratische Regression" (Suhrkamp 2021, with Armin Schäfer).

ACKNOWLEDGEMENTS

Responsibility is a cross-cutting concept which raises questions at multiple levels of analysis. It is also increasingly invoked in political debates as many challenges of our time are characterized by insecurities when responsibilities cannot easily be attributed. The questions of who should be responsible and what for are embedded in a broader normative context that points towards issues of authority and legitimacy, which in turn can have legal, social and/or material dimensions. Similarly, those who invoke responsibility in the first place can also become subject to analytic scrutiny. With so many dimensions simultaneously at play, addressing the different analytical questions around responsibility requires a calibrated compass and an up-to-date map in order not to get lost. The objective to provide such compass is expressed in the artwork we selected for the cover of this handbook. In characterizing her work, the artist Angela Dwyer writes, "While in my previous work I was looking for an abstract way to make visible the conflicts between man and nature [...] the new series I call 'Solid Shapes' is looking for a more manifest representation of where we are – in this particular place, in this particular moment. [...] This period of general insecurity and the impact of changes in human interaction has created a strong need to hold on to our core values, while at the same time there is a shift in priorities. I refer, among other things, to a line from the poem 'The Second Coming' by W.B. Yeats: 'the centre will not hold' or to the thoughts of Levi-Strauss/Lacan on the myth of the individual as a basis of subjective structure." We considered this characterization a fitting description for our undertaking in two ways. First, this Handbook originated from the desire to provide guidance and orientation to the growing community of scholars whose work engages with some or all of the different analytical levels that the concept of responsibility entails. Second, politically it might also be a time of insecurities which requires rethinking our values and reconsidering our priorities.

Initially, we had sketched some of these dimensions that informed the Handbook during a brainstorming coffee break with Antje Wiener at the 2014 ISA conference in Toronto. Beginning to work on some issues around responsibility for a different book project at an ISA Venture Workshop in New Orleans in 2015, we recognized the wealth of work on responsibility and thus the need for a more comprehensive compendium on that topic. We hence set out to develop a proposal to map and discuss the various strands of research on responsibility in International Relations as well as neighboring disciplines. Helpful feedback was provided by Peter Hall, John Ruggie, and Kathryn Sikkink when Antje was Visiting Fellow for one year at the Minda de Gunzburg Center for European Studies at Harvard University in 2015/2016. Our intention was to deliver clarifications and a comprehensive overview across the various ways in which responsibility has come to matter as a core concept of world politics in the discipline of International Relations. While responsibility is being discussed in neighboring disciplines such as philosophy or legal theory, the Handbook seeks to complement and connect to these debates through contributions from the vantage point of International Relations, broadly perceived.

Our initial question of "what is IR-responsibility?" opened a number of avenues for inquiry – and puns – which we discussed at a workshop in Münster in May 2019. This event was generously supported by the Fritz-Thyssen-Foundation and the University of Münster. In addition, the invitation by the City of Münster to a reception at the town hall – birthplace of the Westphalian Peace – and to signing the city's guestbook made this a truly memorable occasion. The workshop was tremendously well organized by Kate Backhaus and Julian Ermann. The event greatly benefitted from papers and contributions to the discussion from Mathias Albert, Sam Barkin, Steven Bernstein, Jelena Cupać, Joachim Delventhal, Beth DeSombre, Stephan Engelkamp, Doris Fuchs, Tobias Gumbert, Patrick Jackson, David Karp, Sebastian Knecht, Markus Kornprobst, Susan Park, Tobias Schmidtke, Tomer Shadmy, Mitja Sienknecht, Pete Sutch, and Antje Wiener.

Contributions to that workshop form the core of this Handbook. In addition, we solicited further chapters through an open call across our networks which we had previously established by organizing sections and panels at international conferences hosted by the European International Studies Association, the International Studies Association, the European Consortium for Political Research, and the British International Studies Association. We are grateful for the numerous papers presented at these events and the stimulating discussions we have had with colleagues from across the world and a diverse range of IR subdisciplines. They provided us with valuable ideas for our own theorizing and empirical work, as well as plans for the structure of this Handbook. About half of the chapters in this volume were presented previously as conference papers and this volume greatly benefitted from all our encounters as they helped sharpen the overall conceptual focus. Likewise, the anonymous feedback we received for single chapters and the Handbook's structure was extremely supportive of our project and we would like to convey our thanks to Rob Sorsby at Routledge for setting up the process of producing this Handbook.

Providing a map for others based on a project of this size is no easy feat. The editors themselves are not immune against losing sight of the track, especially if there is no beaten path to follow, while administrative burdens and all sorts of organizational obstacles emanating from the COVID-19 crisis needed to be overcome. We would therefore like to thank Julian Ermann for editorial help with this text. We are ever so grateful for the patience our authors have shown with the publication process. Not least, we are thankful to our families to recalibrate our focus from time to time. We would like to dedicate this book to Selma, Eni, Piet, and Jonna.

Münster & Cardiff, summer 2020

ABBREVIATIONS

AAC	Arctic Athabaskan Council
ABNJ	areas beyond national jurisdiction
ADB	Asian Development Bank
AfDB	African Development Bank
AI	artificial intelligence
AIA	Aleut International Association
ATLAS	Advanced Targeting and Lethality Automated System program
ATS	Antarctic Treaty System
AU	African Union
BASIC	British American Security Information Council
BBNJ	biodiversity in areas beyond national jurisdiction
BIMSTEC	Bay of Bengal Initiative for Multi-Sectoral Technical and Economic Cooperation
BRICS	so-called rising powers Brazil, Russia, India, China, and South Africa
CAO	Compliance Advisor/Ombudsman
CAOF Agreement	Agreement to Prevent Unregulated High Seas Fisheries in the Central Arctic Ocean
CAS	Conference Committee on the Application of Standards
CBDR	Common but Differentiated Responsibilities
CCAMLR	Convention for the Conservation of Antarctic Marine Living Resources
CCW	UN Convention on Conventional Weapons
CEACR	Committee of Experts on the Application of Conventions and Recommendations
CEO	Chief Executive Officer
CFO	Chief Financial Officer
CLS	core labor standards
CSR	Corporate Social Responsibility
DNS	Domain Name System
DoD	US Department of Defence
DWA	Decent Work Agenda
EBRD	European Bank for Reconstruction and Development

ECOWAS	Economic Community of West African States
EEZ	exclusive economic zone
EPR	extended producer responsibility
ES	English School
EU	European Union
FAO	Food and Agriculture Organization
FCIC	Financial Crisis Inquiry Commission
FOC	Freedom Online Coalition
FPRW	Declaration on Fundamental Principles and Rights at Work
FSA	Fish Stock Agreement
GAC	Global Advisory Committee
GATT	Global Agreement on Trade and Tariffs
GCA	grocery code adjudicator
GCI	Gwich'in Council International
GDPR	General Data Protection Regulation
HINW	Humanitarian Initiative on Nuclear Weapons
IAEA	International Atomic Energy Agency
IAMs	Independent Accountability Mechanisms
IANA	Internet Assigned Number Authority
IBRD	International Bank for Reconstruction and Development
ICAN	International Campaign to Abolish Nuclear Weapons
ICANN	Internet Corporation for Assigned Names and Numbers
ICISS	International Commission on Intervention and State Sovereignty
ICRW	International Convention for the Regulation of Whaling
ICSID	International Centre for Settlement of Investment Disputes
ICT	Internet communication technology
IFC	International Finance Corporation
IHL	International Humanitarian Law
IHRL	international humanitarian rights law
ILC	International Labour Conference
ILO	International Labour Organization
IMF	International Monetary Fund
IMO	International Maritime Organization
IONS	Indian Ocean Naval Symposium
IOs	international organizations
IP	Internet Protocol
IPT	International Political Theory
ISA	International Seabed Authority
ITU	International Telecommunication Union
ITUC	International Trade Union Confederation
IUU	illegal, unregulated and unreported fishing
KDP	Kurdistan Democratic Party
KLA	Kosovo Liberation Army
KRG	Kurdish Regional Government
LAWS	lethal autonomous weapons systems
LTTE	Liberian Tigers of Tamil Eelam

Abbreviations

MARPOL	International Convention for the Protection of Marine Pollution from Ships
MDBs	Multilateral Development Banks
MDGs	Millennium Development Goals
MIGA	Multilateral Investment Guarantee Agency
MRM	Monitoring and Reporting Mechanism
NATO	North Atlantic Treaty Organization
NGOs	non-governmental organizations
NIEO	New International Economic Order
NNWS	Non-nuclear Weapon States
NPT	Treaty on the Non-Proliferation of Nuclear Weapons, or Non-Proliferation Treaty
NTIA	National Telecommunications and Information Administration
OECD	Organisation for Economic Cooperation and Development
OEWG	UN Open-ended Working Group
OPRC	International Convention on Oil Pollution Preparedness, Response and Co-Operation
R2P	Responsibility to Protect
RAIPON	Russian Association of Indigenous Peoples of the North
RCO	responsible corporate officer
RFMO	Regional Fisheries Management Organization
RtoP	Responsibility to Protect
RwP	Responsibility while Protecting
SALW	small arms and light weapons
SC	Saami Council
SCAR	Science Committee on Antarctic Research
SDGs	Sustainable Development Goals
SFDRR	Sendai Framework for Disaster Risk Reduction of the UN
SNM	Somali National Movement
SOLAS	International Convention for the Safety of Life at Sea
SRI	socially responsible investment
TFAMC	Task Force on Arctic Marine Cooperation
TNC	transnational corporation
TPNW	Treaty on the Prohibition of Nuclear Weapons
UDHR	Universal Declaration of Human Rights
UN	United Nations
UNCLOS	United Nations Convention on the Law of the Sea
UNDP	UN Development Program
UNDRO	United Nations Disaster Relief Office
UNESCO	United Nations Educational, Scientific and Cultural Organization
UNFCCC	UN Framework Convention on Climate Change
UNGA	UN General Assembly
UNGGE	UN Group of Governmental Experts
UNGPs	UN Guiding Principles on Business and Human Rights
UNHCR	UN High Commissioner for Refugees
UNSC	UN Security Council
WGIG	World Group on Internet Governance

Abbreviations

WPS	UN resolution on Women, Peace, and Security
WSIS	World Summit on the Information Society
WSOD	World Summit Outcome Document
WTO	World Trade Organization

1
RESPONSIBILITY IN INTERNATIONAL RELATIONS THEORY AND PRACTICE

Introducing the handbook

Hannes Hansen-Magnusson and Antje Vetterlein

Introduction

Why do we need a handbook on the concept of responsibility in International Relations (IR)? We claim that many of the most pressing political challenges of our time, such as climate change, humanitarian crises, migration, financial crises, the implications of artificial intelligence or advances in science and technology to mention but a few, evoke questions of responsibility. They present us with political problems that do not lend themselves to simple and clear-cut answers regarding the identification of whose fault it is and who should take action. Many current challenges cannot easily be solved through a reallocation of resources, enforcing existing regulations or designing new ones. Debates around these challenges rather seem to get stuck and end in political conflicts about who is responsible, for what or to whom and on what basis. Thus, we seem to observe an increased moralization in negotiating political problems. The recent EU migration pact is a case in question where most actors agree that something needs to be done with regard to the migrants and refugees at the EU external borders and states who have the economic and political capacity should lead the way. Yet, others argue that for states the responsibility towards their own people comes first, signified by domestic resistance framed not only in the language of distributional conflict and justice but also increasingly related to argumentations of values and identities. Often, such initiatives end in declarations of intent from a few actors but lead to no action as actors cannot agree on one strategy. If one cannot solve political problems through compensating, sanctioning or finding consensus for new binding regulation, all what is left, it seems, is calling on the morality of actors to behave responsibly.

The observation of increased references to responsibility in political discourse (see Hansen-Magnusson and Vetterlein 2020) has prompted us to consider it more closely as a concept to be studied in IR theory and its relations to other key concepts, such as authority, power, accountability and legitimacy, and how these play out in practice. Two interlinked developments are of importance with regard to the rise of responsibility: first, the changes in the role of the nation-state and the nature of the relationship between state, market and society, and second, at the same time the shifting reference frame of rights towards a global scale, in particular with regard to human rights. Specifically, the changing system of global governance, in particular since the 1990s (Zürn 2018), has impacted actor constellations, their power relations and practices of responsibility and accountability, and the nature of broader questions of justice and legitimacy in world politics (Vetterlein 2018). Global governance comes about with a different allocation of authority and responsibilities across an increased variety of actors and with new modes of governing that go beyond the democratic mechanisms of participation and delegation. As a consequence, we observe new questions and challenges with regard to organizing relations at the individual, organizational, national, regional and international level, often related to a lack of appropriate regulation and/or a lack of legitimate actors willing and/or able to adopt and enforce appropriate regulation. Some scholars perceive global governance as exposing 'regulatory gaps' (Doh 2005; Palazzo and Scherer 2006). At the same time, it is not possible or even desirable to regulate everything (Ruggie 2004). What we observe empirically then is an increase in calls for more responsibility, and, as we argue, an emerging new system of negotiated governance (Vetterlein 2018). References to responsibility resemble semantic struggles which revolve around normative expectations about who should be doing what and to whose benefit. They manifest as responsibilized governance practices across a number of policy areas.

IR scholarship has begun to pick up on such observations, and an increasing amount of research and commentary has emerged that investigates responsibility more explicitly. Yet, since the concept of responsibility is a cross-cutting theme, the scholarship is far from being united and work is mainly scattered across disciplines and policy fields. Many empirical studies exist, in particular on explicit policy tools such as the responsibility to protect or corporate responsibility (Carroll 1999; Bellamy 2006; Rajamani 2006; Wheeler 2006; Honkonen 2009; Brunnée and Toope 2010) or on the responsibility of specific powerful states and institutions (Lang 1999; Lebow 2003; Erskine 2008; Bukovansky, Clark et al. 2012; Gaskarth 2017). At the same time, theoretical work has appeared that takes up crucial dimensions that the concept of responsibility evokes such as the possibility and limitations of moral agency, the location of moral agency as well as questions of community for which moral values are valid or the link between responsibility and accountability and processes of constitutionalization of political spheres (Campbell 1996; Grant and Keohane 2005; Ainley 2008; Vetterlein and Wiener 2013). These brief considerations show how deeply a discussion of responsibility is embedded in broader questions of IR theory. At the same time, they also signify the interdisciplinarity of the topic as questions of responsibility in world politics relate to political theory and global ethical studies, international law as well as area/development studies, let alone the many existing sub-fields such as governance or welfare state studies, among others (Daase, Junk et al. 2017; Debiel, Finkenbusch et al. 2018; Bazargan-Forward and Tollefsen 2020).

Given the multidimensionality of the concept, it is not possible to offer a text that would be able to claim coherence and consistency across all chapters in using the precise same understandings of responsibility and related terms such as duty, obligation or accountability as there are disciplinary differences and differential theoretical approaches. Nor was this the objective of the Handbook. Rather to the contrary, what we offer here is a broad overview of research on responsibility across a variety of subfields in IR, zooming in on specific angles of responsibility relations, levels of analysis and policy fields.[1] Nevertheless, there is an overall structure to this Handbook because what all responsibility research has in common is to focus on one of the following elements of established responsibility relations more specifically, these are the subject of responsibility or who should take responsibility, the object of responsibility or who/what for should responsibility be taken, and finally based on what normative framework are claims of responsibility being invoked. Taking on or ascribing responsibility between a subject and an object referring to agreed-upon norms and regulations we argue is a contextualized and political activity, which we refer to as 'responsibilization'.

We understand responsibilization as a political and normative struggle taking place in specific policy fields with the attempt to negotiate who is responsible for what. The Handbook's structure follows this conceptualization and after the introduction and Part I, which introduces theoretical approaches to responsibility in IR, Part II sheds special light on specific policy fields with the aim to show how responsibility came to matter with regard to a specific policy and to map the emergence of responsibility relations between key actors (subject and object) and how they position themselves in that particular field. Part III then turns to relations between responsibility stakeholders, which are 'subject', 'object' and 'speaker', to capture the contestation of responsibility statements, claims and social practices. We have identified different actors, individual and collective, whose relations instantiate responsibility and who have core stakes in global governance policies. These actors range from individual states (e.g., China, see Chapter 18) to international organizations such as regional development banks (Chapter 21) or private sector actors (Chapter 24). Part IV then turns to the objects of stakeholders' engagement. Here, the focus is on global commons which more or less explicitly form part of the common heritage of humankind and how their meaning and significance has changed over time. Part V closes the volume with an overview of different normative discussions and debates of how responsibility 'works' or should be made to work in world politics.

With such a broad ambition, a handbook on responsibility in International Relations provides an extraordinary opportunity to present an encompassing and cross-disciplinary discussion of the concept itself as well as its impact in various governance areas. Three objectives guide this Handbook. First of all, it brings together scholarship and maps work on responsibility that is currently undertaken in International Relations as well as in the above-mentioned neighbouring disciplines. The Handbook thus offers a way to shed light on different theoretical approaches towards responsibility, to bridge disciplinary divides and to show how responsibility matters in different policy fields of global governance. Existing work is diverse and covers several policy-fields without a coherent link and without the opportunity to compare fields side by side – the proposed handbook stands to correct this shortcoming.

Second, the Handbook thereby offers the opportunity to reflect on current scholarship on the topic by engaging with the most crucial theoretical debates in the field and state-of-the-art research in policy areas in which responsibility has become an institutionalized part of normative order. It aims to make existing knowledge accessible in a comprehensive manner. Third, the Handbook is the first of its kind that provides a comprehensive overview of IR scholarship on responsibility and thus will serve as the foundational text for this interdisciplinary and multi-policy field. By doing so, the volume not only provides a state-of-the-art text on research on responsibility in world politics that brings together existing knowledge in an encompassing manner. As a consequence, it also advances the field since such a mapping provides the opportunity to open up a dialogue among theoretical approaches, disciplines and policy fields that in turn allows for comparison and synergies.

In what follows, we will first outline the rise of the responsibility concept in global politics in order to show the need for a deeper engagement with this topic. In a second step, we outline relations among political actors that arise when actors invoke responsibility. In particular, we address the subject and object of responsibility, the normative basis and questions of authority that responsibilization raises, as well as the speaker who initiates the process of responsibilization in the first place. This sets the readers up for the structure of this Handbook and the many different ways in which our authors approach responsibility, which we detail in the brief overview of the Handbook in the final section.

The rise of responsibility in world politics

The concept of responsibility, as we use it today, with its moral and ethical implications has only been introduced to philosophical debates in the 19th century (Bayertz 1995). It received increased attention in a variety of academic disciplines after World War II. Some authors emphasize that it is traditionally an individualist concept (Loh 2017, 40), as it relies on three preconditions which are predominantly characteristics of individual actors; these are causality, freedom and rationality (Nida-Rümelin, 2011). Actors can be perceived as responsible if they have had the chance to intervene in situations and change the outcome of an event (causality), had the freedom to decide which intervention they would like to choose and had the rationality to reason about this decision. Hence, people usually can take responsibility or be made responsible for their actions, based on socially defined criteria, which usually involve criteria of age, soundness of mind and competency. This perspective paves the way for inquiries into the relations between an individual and his/her social context and also opens up debates for political theory concerning the responsibility of individuals in the setting of a particular community. This latter approach was taken by Hannah Arendt (1958), for example, who held that individuals are responsible for the doings of the community or society of which they are a part. In contrast to such individualist approaches, other authors investigate the role of collective or corporate moral agency (Erskine 2003), shared responsibility (Nollkaemper 2018) as well as systemic or global responsibility (Loh 2017, 40), for instance with regard to the responsibility for particular weather phenomena triggered by climate change, and the impact of these on communities.

References to responsibility have increased in political discourses and this is not only the case for policy fields where the term responsibility already found its way into specific policy norms, such as corporate responsibility or the responsibility to protect. We argue here that this has to do with changes in the institutional and normative structure of world politics (Weiss 2013; Zürn 2018). On the one hand, global governance is characterized as an exercise of authority across a variety of actors whose power relations and accountability practices vary significantly according to the specific context. Over the past three decades, new institutional modes of governance have developed, such as soft law arrangements, public–private partnerships or the like, which do not only shift around power positions across actors but also open up new answers to questions of who is responsible for specific outcomes/events, for what and on what basis. On the other hand, and tied to this first point, we can observe an increased pluralism in interests and values; and with an accompanying discourse on rights, this leads to an increase in situations of equally correct, yet opposing fundamental values. This in turn means that not every problem can be solved by designing and implementing the 'correct' regulation but that we can expect increased contestation and negotiation when it comes to asserting one value over the other. Here, responsibility comes into play, as it is often attributed but also taken by actors in political debates when force or sanctions are not possible. The references to responsibility that different actors make may be difficult to reconcile as the semantic engagements may rest on normative foundations that are not easily commensurable. Responsible corporate behaviour is one example where the decrease of state control over corporations is countered by calling on their ethics to *voluntarily* step up for this institutional void (Ruggie 2011). What corporate responsibility, however, is supposed to mean is often left open and subject for debate. One could therefore argue that the rise of responsibility in public debates signifies a move towards a global governance system characterized by negotiation and debate (Vetterlein 2018).

Over the past few decades, the literature on global governance has provided us with excellent descriptive as well as analytical work regarding the institutional changes of global political structures with increased globalization processes (amongst many, Dingwerth and Pattberg 2006; Mattli and Woods 2009; Karns and Mingst 2010; Ougaard and Leander 2010; de Burca, Keoahne et al. 2013; Abbott 2014; Weiss and Wilkinson 2018; Zürn 2018). Not only do we observe a pluralization of governance actors and their influence in political processes at a global scale but also shifts in political processes and modes of governance towards more hybridity (Biermann, Pattberg et al. 2009; Armitage, de Loë et al. 2012; Leander 2012). Governance is not just governing without government. Zürn (2018, 4) for instance distinguishes between governance by government, governance with governments or governance without governments. The focus in this literature has been on questions regarding which actor has the legitimate authority and capacity to regulate specific issue areas according to consented norms and rules and beyond national borders. Regulatory gaps (Doh 2005; Palazzo and Scherer 2006) or 'unregulated spaces' (Clunan and Trinkunas 2010) have been identified which open up room for contestation in which rules, regulations and norms are being negotiated and where arguments and justifications are brought forward in form of responsibility claims, based on conflicting interests as well as different sets of values about how social, political and economic relations should be organized.

The degree of contestation over the meaning of responsibility claims, however, varies according to the nature of the problem in question, that is, the degree of an existing regulatory context, the presence of a legitimate actor with the capacity to regulate, and the level of value pluralism. We might for instance face situations where rules and regulations do exist but are contested based on different interests involved. Examples could be distributional conflicts in welfare states regarding social benefits where some people would call on the state as the responsible actor to intervene while others would argue for more self-responsibility. A second type of situation can be described as cases where regulation exists but is not enforced by the responsible actor(s). Tax breaks for big corporations can be an example, or the Diesel scandal around Volkswagen and some other automobile companies can serve as a case in question. Such situations are often perceived as unfair and thus can cause a significant amount of criticism and resistance. A third situation is cases in which regulatory spaces are fragmented. Take the example of multinational corporations (MNCs) for instance that have their headquarters in one country and are active in others. Legally, the subsidiaries of an MNC fall under the jurisdiction of the country in which the company has invested. If that country cannot or will not punish the company for its wrong-doings, the home country has no legal power beyond political/moral pressure.

In contrast to these situations that highlight the limits or shortcomings of law and regulation are instances that describe conflicts where value-based arguments might become more prominent. The fourth case is a situation where we face outcomes that are legal but not legitimate. Most of the financial practices of bankers and other financial experts leading up to the last financial crisis was legal but their legitimacy can be questioned. The same goes for MNC investment in countries that do not abide to human rights. A last prominent example is UNSC resolutions not to intervene in potential cases of genocide (see Rwanda). The question here is whether a number of actors (states) who do have the capacity to intervene would have the moral responsibility to do so despite the outcome of a legal procedure, i.e. non-intervention (Erskine 2014). This last case also serves as an example for the fifth scenario, that is, a situation of opposing regulations and/or fundamental values. In the example of the responsibility to protect specific groups of people from harm caused by their own government or because that government cannot protect them, the rivalling principles are those of state sovereignty versus individual human rights. Finally, we also observe unregulated spaces, that is, global challenges that are characterized by complexity where it is difficult to identify responsible actors and hold them accountable or problems that refer to outcomes lying in the future and thus require prospective action and positive responsibility. Environmental issues such as climate change serve as an example. Responsibility here is about more general goals to be reached in the future where exact action cannot necessarily be defined a priori.

These institutional changes that have led to an increase in references to responsibility are accompanied by normative changes too. Elsewhere we argue that the rise of the human rights discourse has enabled a turn to responsibility (Vetterlein and Hansen-Magnusson, 2020). Researchers have long since shown how human rights came to matter within particular countries

(Risse, Ropp et al. 1999) following the establishment of specific rights such as the provision covered by the International Covenant on Civil and Political Rights, the International Covenant on Economic, Social and Cultural Rights as well as the Universal Declaration of Human Rights. In this regard, we argue that the link to human rights provides argumentative clout for global actors to hold others to account or to shame/blame them into engaging in particular behaviour, while it also provides enabling conditions. In other words, because human rights are well established as a normative principle, speaking of responsibilities of someone and for something commands attention and seems to be key in the attempt to induce a sense of appropriateness.

Human rights have enjoyed a special legal status over the past decades (D'Amato 1982). In many policy fields, they have changed normative contexts with the consequence that the allocation of responsibilities has been shifted around. The argumentative push to consider security in terms of *human* security rather than from a national point of view is a famous example. Specifically, the human dimension and the well-being of individuals or groups stand in direct opposition to the value of state sovereignty. Here, the concept of responsibility, as in the responsibility to protect (R2P), was introduced as a compromise to reconcile individual rights and state sovereignty as it is demanding responsible behaviour, yet open enough to allow for non-intervention (de Carvalho 2020). Other examples can be found with regard to climate change, for instance. The fact that a German court accepted to hear a case of a Peruvian farmer against the energy company RWE for its responsibility of the impact of climate change is writing legal history. While RWE is not active in Peru, Saul Luciano Lluiya sued the company for contributing to a melting glacier in the Andes Mountains because of its carbon emissions which in turn increases the likelihood of flooding the city of Huaraz, the farmer's home (Wang 2017). UN Special Rapporteur on Human Rights and the Environment John H. Knox says that '[t]his case is part of a growing trend to try to hold corporations responsible in their home jurisdictions for human rights abuses and environmental harm that they cause elsewhere. There are difficult legal and factual issues to overcome, of course'.[2] Also, the OHCHR has established that climate change affects the full set of human rights, that is, a right to life, adequate food and housing, health and self-determination. But still, courts have rejected holding states accountable for their contribution to global warming, such as attempted by the Circumpolar Conference in front of the Inter-American Commission on Human Rights regarding the United States' role.[3]

The link to human rights made it much more explicit what it is that an actor is responsible for and who such an actor might be in the first place. We can further observe an increased formalization of responsibility across different policy fields (Vetterlein and Hansen-Magnusson 2020). On the one hand, once it has become clear that people have rights to clean water or air, those whose activities impact on it have a moral as well as a legal obligation to ensure its provision. Human rights are increasingly embraced by MNCs (Favotto and Kollman 2020) because they are interested in leaving a positive imprint of their doings by engaging with local communities and in philanthropy (Thompson 2020). These activities signal a growing sense of obligation towards providing the communities in which they operate with access to resources, education, etc., which can be viewed as strengthening the human rights provisions entailed in both the International Covenant on Civil and Political Rights and the International Covenant on Economic, Social and Cultural Rights. On the other hand, R2P for instance was fully enacted for the first time in combination with Chapter VII of the UN Charter in UN Security Council Resolution 1973 in 2011. However, while formalized, the actual application remains contested following the way the mandate was enacted. Brazil for instance has proposed its own understanding of the role of the international community in this constellation as 'Responsibility while Protecting'. This signals disagreement on the legal side of responsibility regarding accountability and obligation while in principle acknowledging the ethical dimension. In fact, the debate over the formal constitutionalization of R2P is on-going (Welsh and Banda 2010). Tomer Shadmy (2018), however, shows how formalizing responsibility works positively for the case of business and human rights. Human rights norms increasingly conceptualize obligations as responsibilities, which indicate the voluntary character of such action. Yet, she argues that these developments indicate the emergence of a new jurisprudential order, opening up for new forms of non-democratic authority and power, signifying new ways of theorizing global governance.

Overall, this combination of institutional and normative changes in the structure of global governance leads to a situation where responsibility is referred to as a compromise solution in order to tackle regulatory gaps. To be more precise, a pluralization of actors in the global sphere combined with new modes of governance results in changes in the allocation of power and legitimacy of actors. We witness situations where regulation reaches its limits mainly due to conflicting or sometimes even incommensurable rights (see sovereignty versus human rights in the case of R2P). Given an additional increase in fundamental rights that actors can refer to in order to justify responsibility claims we observe an increase in value pluralism, that is, currently resolved through the introduction of the vague concept of responsibility. While we also note an increased formalization of responsibility in world politics in guidelines, treaties and laws over the course of the last decades starting with the 1987 Brundtland Report (Vetterlein and Hansen-Magnusson 2020), responsibility often remains a deliberately ambiguous concept, legally non-binding and open for interpretation and debate. This is not to say that we end up in weak governance regimes. Yet, the strength of the evocation of responsibility varies and depends on different constellations between the subject, object, addressee, authority and normative basis of responsibility.

Responsibility relations: the positioning of subject, object and speaker in policy fields

Just as there is more than one way to skin a cat, there are numerous ways to define responsibility and approach it analytically. The semantic struggle over responsibility paves the way for a variety of possible different emphases on who should be responsible and what for, as does its instantiation in practice. Similarly, customary or legal understandings of responsibility create structural links between subjects and objects, thereby further differentiating the ways in which responsibility can be characterized.

While the historical development of the concept and its connection to agency were already noted, references to responsibility come with a range of – often – dichotomous characteristics related to the quality of the action itself. In this regard, responsibility can be future-oriented, or prospective (Cowley 2014; Heidbrink 2017), or oriented on past action, that is retrospective. This distinction partly overlaps with positive versus negative responsibility, yet with the difference that positive responsibility does not only refer to the time-dimension but also to an action that explicitly enhances the status quo of a situation, while negative responsibility connotes a passive take and refers to the avoidance of harm. Retrospective, or 'ex post', responsibility raises the question whether those who brought something about, and thereby have 'causal responsibility', should also deal with the results, which describes 'remedial responsibility'. Other authors have found different ways to classify responsibility. Hart (1968) for instance distinguishes between four types of responsibility, these are causal responsibility concerning the question who has caused an outcome, role responsibility with regard to a specific task that needs to be addressed, capability in terms of who has the ability to take on responsibility and finally liability referring to legal responsibility. Other commentators perceive responsibility as a relation of an actor to his/her community/society, to a higher authority (such as the law, god or nature) and to his/herself (Baran 1990).

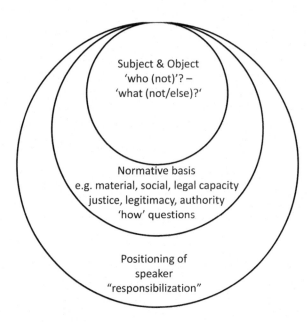

Figure 1.1 The field of responsibilization

Throughout this volume, authors will refer to one or more of these ways of defining and describing responsibility. Yet, the basic elements of responsibility are present in every situation of calling for or taking on responsibility: these are the responsibility subject (who), the responsibility object (who/what for), and the responsibility authority (against whom/based on what), which marks the normative basis of the relation between subject and object. Taking on or attributing responsibility is a contextualized and political activity, which we can refer to as 'responsibilization'. Responsibilizing is a political struggle as well as a practical phenomenon, enacted by a speaker, which linguists may understand in terms of a constant tension between illocutionary and perlocutionary force, that is, the speaker's intent and the effect of this speech act on the speaker or the audience, respectively. 'Who' may be responsible and 'what' they may be responsible for points to a broader set of normative foundations that underpin the arrangement, all of which may be subject to critique by others who may engage in countering claims. Responsibilization thereby gives rise to a set of questions which are related and can be represented in terms of different layers, as expressed in Figure 1.1.

Responsibilizing creates a set of relations between actors – the subjects of responsibility – and that which they are responsible for – the objects of responsibility, invoked by a speaker, and thereby circumscribing a specific field of responsibility. Responsibilizing is not a neutral process as it contains assumptions about the basis upon which, or reasons why, someone is or should be responsible for something. In a similar manner, responsibilizing delineates the object of responsibility in particular ways by defining its boundaries and differentiating it from other objects that someone could be responsible for. Questions of 'who is responsible?', 'what are they responsible for?' and 'how does this responsibility come about?' are contextually embedded, as responsibilizing happens in relation to a – given or imagined – community that is somehow affected by this action. This setting gets further complicated if we, as researchers, step back from the scene: from an observer's position we can also point at the political dimension of responsibilizing, because who attempts to define 'who?', 'what?' and 'how?' reveals actual or idealized constellations of a global society. This is to say that a speaker holding someone responsible or assigning responsibility for something draws on or refers to normative understandings of how things should be, which may be quite different from the status quo.

This political character of responsibilizing becomes even more apparent if we pose the questions in the negative form of 'who not?' and 'what not?' and also inquire into who is able to and raises them in the first instance and who does not, which concerns questions of legitimacy and authority. As argued above, references to subjects and objects of responsibility do not necessarily come with an agreed set of norms, nor with a clearly demarcated field within which responsibility is taken or assigned, nor with a given locus of authority. These components are being (re-)arranged in the practices of responsibilizing. Looking at the four issues of (1) 'who?', (2) 'what?', (3) the normative basis of responsibilizing as well as the (4) position of the speaker provides scholars with plenty of scope for analysis, which we will briefly discuss in the following paragraphs as our Handbook is structured around those.

The subject of responsibility

Who, the subject, is the central focus when responsibility is claimed or assigned. The subject designates the actor or actors that is or are tied in various ways to the object of responsibility. By virtue of this exposed status and the connection to the object, the subject is elevated into a privileged position in comparison to other (potential) subjects in the process of responsibilizing. The subject of responsibility need not necessarily be the speaker who raises the issue of responsibility.

There are two issues with regard to the subject, when taking responsibility to the realm of world politics: First, the default position in International Relations used to be that the state takes precedence over other actors, which can be explained by the vantage point of particular approaches, such as Realism. This is still the case when we approach responsibility through the angle of International Law, given that states occupy a central position in its making. However, recent years have seen a shift of responsibility towards non-state actors, such as MNCs, especially in the context of business and human rights (Karp 2014). Second, an important question in political theory is whether and to what extent collective actors, rather than individuals, are even able to or should be assigned responsibility (Erskine 2003; Bazargan-Forward and Tollefsen 2020). Besides states, there are therefore multiple foci of analysis, including individuals, civil society, corporations and international organizations.

This shift in or diversification of the subject of responsibility reveals that 'who?' is intimately connected to the empirical context and the 'how?' question that is at the heart of the normative basis of responsibilizations. An awareness of this shift brings to our attention that material capacities are only one of at least three ways identified by researchers in which subjects come to a position of responsibility. After all, some corporations command considerably more resources than some states and are therefore in a better position to take responsibility for the well-being, livelihood and life of their employees (O'Neill 2005). A similar focus on material capacity is advanced by English School scholars, who hold that so-termed 'great powers' hold special managerial responsibility for global affairs based on the resources they command (Bull 2002 (1977), 196). The discourse usually involves prospective responsibility such as ensuring particular working conditions or peace.

A second way in which 'who?' and 'how?' are connected becomes plain when we consider that, in practice, material capacity is contextually bound up with social expectations. Material capacity does not possess inherent qualities that give rise to responsibility. Rather, social expectations refer to the ways in which those who *can* command resources *should* put them to use (Nolan 2005; Heupel 2013), to either avoid harm or do good. In addition to the normative question of how resources are or should be put into use, it is also crucial to see who is raising the issue in the first place. Both the *content* of social expectations in terms of negative and/or positive responsibility, and the *practice* of responsibilizing with a focus on actors and sites are likely to contain pointers towards what kind of global society the speaker envisages in the present and what they would like to move towards in the future. It is thus prime material for International Relations scholarship.

Next to material capacity and social expectations, legal settings mark a third way in which the 'how?' question is linked to the subject of responsibility.[4] Conventionally, legal structures give rise to expectations that a particular role entails responsibility for an object. Such role-related expectations can be investigated with a view to ex ante responsibility in either positive or negative variance. The question thus becomes, 'what (not) should actor X do, given their role in a particular setting?'. In its purer form, the discussion of legal responsibility is often framed as 'accountability' (Slaughter 2004; Grant and Keohane 2005; Bovens, Goodin et al. 2014), but often at the detriment of the broader contextual vision (Vetterlein 2018): the answer to the question of who caused or did not prevent something is not necessarily the same as the answer to the question who should do something about it. In International Relations this has been discussed extensively in terms of the legality and legitimacy of actions of so-termed 'coalitions of the willing' and their responsibility for peace and security (Erskine 2014). Governance arrangements may rest on some kind of legal foundation, but they are subject to discussions of legitimacy that reach beyond purely legal aspects. These discussions are further complicated by the growing plurality of actors in world politics that we mentioned earlier.

Overall, we can see from the discussion that questions pertaining to the subject of responsibility cannot be conclusively answered without engaging a set of further questions that relate to the context in which responsibility is claimed or assigned, by whom and in what manner. In the process of responsibilizing, different aspects of the 'how?' issue overlap and form a dynamic, multi-layered web of responsibility (Hansen-Magnusson 2019) within which we can inquire retrospectively in terms of who brought something about and with what kinds of consequences for them or others, as well as prospectively in terms of what should happen in the future. Given that the discipline of International Relations neither needs to privilege the perspective and role of states nor addresses a unified global order, research concerning how responsibility matters in world politics can arrange the questions introduced above in various constellations of actors and contextual focus.

The object of responsibility

The object of responsibility can be understood not only as an action but also as a person, thing or event (Loh 2017). The object of responsibility is inseparable from the process of its emergence – it is not simply given but the product of the kinds of responsibilizing practices described above. This means that the object can be invoked by a subject of responsibility, who actively seeks responsibility for something with a view to past or future action, or a third party in the process of responsibilization (the speaker, see below), who ascribes responsibility for something – negative or positive, ex post or ex ante – to someone else. How objects of responsibility are framed and by whom usually has implications on the subject(s) involved and their roles concerning responsible action (Jasanoff 1999, 2005), which is even more true if the object is a person or group advocating being responsibilized. But regardless of whether the object is actively involved in the process, like the subject, it is embedded in a normative context.

Discussing objects of responsibility, rather than subjects, puts a different emphasis on the inquiry and is linked with other and additional sets of questions. These questions concern, first, not only the boundaries of the object as a general matter but also more specifically in terms of global public goods. Second, they concern questions of retrospective and prospective responsibility. With regard to the first issue, it is for instance not always clear whether a policy issue of positive responsibility, such as investment in infrastructure, concerns aspects of human security or economic development. Responsibilizing an object may therefore resonate differently with different communities that are affected, raising the issue of underlying normative bases of responsibility claims and questions about the speaker (see below). At other times, the boundaries of the object may be fuzzy because a subject may need to handle competing responsibilities simultaneously, such as during war when responsibility for the well-being of one's soldiers (and citizens) needs to be reconciled with the responsibility to protect civilians in another state while also avoiding harm to them (Hansen-Magnusson 2019). In both instances, the debate over the boundary of the object is likely to touch on the role of a particular subject and their actions, especially whose concerns should prevail and how they should be handled. In a context of war, but also world politics more generally, there may be structural constraints for parties to address responsibility issues because a procedure of arbitration may not exist or may not be accessible.

Another question on the boundaries of objects of responsibility is addressed in discussions about the emergence and nature of global public goods, with which the object is associated (Zürn 2018). The benefit of taking or ascribing someone responsibility ex ante usually takes place within a discourse of benefits to humanity and human well-being which transcends national boundaries and interests (regardless of whether this is de facto the case). For instance, BRICS countries are demanding, by way of offering, to take on additional responsibility for global trade and finance (Narlikar 2011). But in consequence this may mean that neither human rights nor the norms of environmental governance are implemented in a universal manner.

With regard to the second issue, the question of 'what is the object of responsibility?' can be addressed both retrospectively as well as prospectively, while also requiring an engagement with normative discussions. Concerning the retrospective approach, it appears that the object already exists but it is not clear if a subject with causal responsibility should also bear remedial responsibility or whether this should be delegated to someone else. A case in point is the debate about climate change and whether the countries and corporations that caused climate change historically should engage in particular activities to mitigate further damage in the future, and whether present contributions and capabilities should be treated in a differentiated manner. Interesting for International Relations, this debate raises questions about present and future global order, possibilities and obligations of participation in institutions, and the normative foundations thereof institutions. Prospectively, an engagement with the object of responsibility is also embedded in such normative questions, because it concerns the direction of travel as a global community, who is part of it and in what ways. Institutionalizing responsibility with regard to the future is not without challenges, though, if we look at the institutionalization of responsibility for peace in the UN system, for example. What seemed to be a workable solution in the aftermath of World War II is not necessarily the right design for all times.

Normative basis, authority and legitimacy

These last examples show that the context of human activity changes over time and may thereby alter the boundaries of an object. We may investigate changes in discourses, such as in the emergence of a responsibility to protect to 'save strangers' (Wheeler 2002; Brunnée and Toope 2005; Bellamy 2006; Evans 2008; Welsh 2011), as well as material factors, such as climate change or the arrival of new technologies, be they nuclear energy or different means of communication, that influence life on the planet (Jonas 1984; Falkner 2007; Pal 2009; Manjikian 2010). Pressing issues for International Relations that arise from discursive and/or material changes are 'how and in what ways should an object of responsibility be dealt with?', 'who is included or excluded in its definition as well as managerial and administrative practices?', and 'how can the set-up ensure sufficient flexibility to account for changes in the object's boundaries or the general context?' (Bernstein and Coleman 2009; Wiener 2018; Zürn 2018). The involvement of the 'how?' question with regard to subjects and objects of responsibility points to the normative basis upon which subject and object come into being as well as the ways in which world politics should work (differently), which touches on questions of authority and legitimacy.

In this regard, avenues for research are opened up by inquiring into the normative basis that responsibilization offers because the process of how responsibility is taken or assigned contains notions of justice and fairness, and the ways in which world politics *should* be organized more broadly. This aspect can be linked to questions of authority, such as who can or should make decisions, and to questions of legitimacy, such as how this decision-making process is or should be embedded in the wider structures of world politics. Philosophical debates have advanced the distinction between internal authority, which can denote one's moral consciousness, and external authority, such as a court, as the arbiter of the normative basis of responsibility (Loh 2017, 44). Yet the realities of world politics, in which the audience of responsibility claims is often diffuse as well as cross- or transnational, and in which legal accountability may be difficult to establish, are likely to escape such clarity. However, by drawing on political theory, researchers *can* inquire how the contours of an object of responsibility are shaped, what claims are made concerning the organization of a particular governance field, and whether there are consented norms underlying this process.

Christian Barry has identified four general normative principles that may be used to characterize responsibilization and help describe such a debate. The so-termed 'capacity principle', as has been discussed previously, holds that 'capacity to bring remedy to serious deprivations entails the responsibility to do so' (Barry 2003, 230). It resonates particularly well with positive responsibility, which sets it apart from the 'contribution principle', which is mostly about negative responsibility that is mainly causal and retrospective and holds agents responsible 'when, and to the extent that, they have contributed to bringing (…particular) situations about' (Ibid. 228). As a third type, he puts forward the 'beneficiary principle', which 'asserts that the strength of one's ethical reason to alleviate some hardship or unfair social rules depends on the extent to which one has benefited from its injustice' (Ibid. 229). This principle is also primarily backward-looking, as those who responsibilize interpret how a particular historical trajectory would have been different in the absence of a specific social arrangement. A well-known example in this context is the debate over the legacy of colonialism. Finally, the 'connectedness principle' (Ibid. 229) focuses on links between subject and object of responsibility, which may involve a shared history or institutions, but also membership in solidaristic communities or a social connection to the unjust action (see Young 2011). This principle expresses how closer ties of some kind allocate more responsibility to remedy a situation. Historically, sovereignty strongly linked a state and its citizens, but the debate over R2P since the beginning of the century has highlighted that this is no longer the case. And as the example of the Peruvian farmer's case against RWE shows, it may not necessarily require territorial proximity to express connectedness.[5]

These principles are ideal-types, which can appear in mixed form when we talk about responsibility. They designate the connections between subject and object in different ways and with different emphases on how authority and legitimacy are (supposedly) established. Heuristically, they inform research and reflection on responsibility, for if we perceive of world politics as a subject of International Relations that may defy boundaries and may work in multiple sites and at different scales, assumptions about actors and their characteristics as well as about actual and tentative loci of authority *may guide* inquiries, but they *should not prevent* debates about designs of institutions of global governance that are different to the ones established in the latter half of the 20th century (Rengger 2003).

Position of speaker

The speaker is the central agent in the process of responsibilizing because subject and object of responsibility, the ways in which they are connected, and the normative basis upon which the connection rests upon do not come into being on their own. The issue of who evokes responsibility may involve an actor who is part of an existing governance field, but also one who is not (yet), but may strive to be admitted to it, as in the above-mentioned case of BRICS states. But while the BRICS states speak from a position of strength, motivated by aspiration to become recognized as a leading power, speakers may invoke responsibility from a marginalized position, highlighting their own vulnerability.[6] Discursive interventions may reveal particular claims concerning authority and legitimacy as well as questions of inclusion and exclusion, which the speaker supports, would like to alter, or build from scratch. While the speakers may position themselves in an authoritative role that assigns responsibility, this need not be the case as they may merely advocate for particular institutional arrangements to be set up.

Statements about why particular institutional arrangements are necessary and should follow certain normative principles are likely to involve arguments of shared benefits of global goods (Zürn 2018), because foregrounding national interests has hardly been a successful strategy in building global institutions in the past. Yet, of course the question remains whether that is an honest intention or merely a disguise of interests. That the position of the speaker during responsibilization matters also with regard to particular audiences can be inferred from the observation that, in recent years, unilateral and national agendas score well with some domestic audiences. An example of this is the development of the United States' foreign policy since 2016.

In sum, it cannot be understated that the relation between subject and object of responsibility is one that is constantly evolving because responsibilization is embedded in normatively charged institutional structures. Not every academic discussion of responsibility in world politics will weigh questions of 'who?', 'what?' and 'how?' equally, nor will they necessarily balance issues such as causal vs. remedial responsibility, or retrospective and prospective views. But from the stock-taking of the status quo in different governance fields and by shedding light on the role of different actors, we can gain valuable insights into the workings of contemporary world politics. In addition, we can employ the range of theories of International Relations to pave the way for normative discussions about the ways in which world politics works better, fairer or more sustainable in the future.

Structure of the handbook

The idea for this Handbook arose from the observation of an increased reference to responsibility in world politics. As this volume documents, there is also an enormous body of literature in International Relations that has captured this development. This scholarship is very diverse not only when it comes to the variety of policy fields and thematic issues for which investigations of responsibility relations are being conducted but also with regard to theoretical inclinations and the engagement with neighbouring disciplines as well as methodological approaches. The main objective of this volume was to display this diversity and by doing so to offer the first handbook that provides a comprehensive overview of IR scholarship on responsibility and thus will serve as the foundational text for this interdisciplinary and multi-policy field. As a consequence, the volume not only provides a state-of-the-art text on research on responsibility in world politics that brings together existing knowledge in an encompassing manner. In addition, it also advances the field since such a mapping provides the opportunity to open up a dialogue among theoretical approaches, disciplines and policy fields that in turn allows for comparison and synergies.

Despite this diversity, the previous section outlined the main elements all responsibility research is concerned with (see also Figure 1.1), these are who is responsible, what/whom for, on what normative basis and who invoked the responsibility claims. We described the process of responsibilization as taking place in specific policy fields in which the actors form responsibility relations and take on positions as subject(s) and speaker(s) of responsibility around specific responsibility objects. This understanding is resembled in the structure of this Handbook. Part II will provide a mapping of policy fields and the positionings different actors have assumed around a certain object. Part III then zooms in on those responsibility relations and captures the ways in which actors contest and argue about responsibility, ascribe it to others or also claim it for certain objects. Finally, part IV sheds light on some global commons, such as the ocean or the Arctic, as responsibility objects. The aim here is to follow the object and the emergence, contestation and transformation of responsibility around it. This core of the Handbook is bracketed by the first part on different theoretical approaches to responsibility and the final part which offers critical reflections and alternative debates currently ongoing in responsibility research. While the chapters each fit to their part, they are not meant to be read sequentially. Cross-references in the chapters will guide the reader to related themes and discussions elsewhere in the Handbook.

The first section provides an overview of theoretical perspectives when it comes to responsibility research. We have selected authors who have explicitly engaged with questions of responsibility covering different theoretical approaches and also disciplines. In different ways, they touch upon the issues of how responsibility became a point of conceptual discussion, how it is currently understood, and what other concepts responsibility relates to. Ilan Baron's chapter (Chapter 2) discusses responsibility in terms of its ontological and phenomenological dimensions, highlighting its contextual embeddedness. For him, responsibility is a form of activity, which means that our understanding of responsibility changes according to the different conditions we find ourselves in. He distinguishes five different accounts of responsibility, which echo throughout subsequent chapters in various forms and guises. The first relates to causality and liability, and treats responsibility as a combination of agency and accountability. The second explains how one is responsible because of membership in various but specific communities. The third account refers to what he terms the political responsibility of identity. The fourth one is ontological and frames responsibility as an ethical consequence of our being as opposed to our not-being. The fifth account unfolds political responsibility as political ethics.

Taking a socio-legal approach, Tomer Shadmy discusses the emergence of responsibility as a global regulative concept (Chapter 3). The chapter recounts how over the last decades various human rights instruments have been established in order to bridge the transnational accountability gap and impose human rights norms on non-state actors and on extraterritorial relations. Many of these instruments describe transnational obligations as responsibilities. Shadmy argues in the chapter that the use of the term 'responsibility' implies an emergence of a new scheme of governance for regulation of transnational relationships and influences that traditional law fails to recognize. Her in-depth inquiry into the jurisprudential features of the responsibility-based scheme of governance finds that this scheme has many progressive elements that enable to oblige strong global entities to take into consideration the interests and voices of those affected by them. At the same time, Shadmy reveals that this scheme of governance could ultimately foster un-democratic modes of authority of those powerful entities.

The following chapter continues the sociological and legal perspective, and the potential ambiguity inherent in the use of 'responsibility', which it combines with a critical, normative approach. Drawing on the practice of human rights law, advocacy and struggles, Brooke Ackerley's chapter provides a grounded normative theory of global responsibility (Chapter 4). Recognizing the cognitive and other limitations to understanding the scope, dynamics and complexity of global injustice, the author argues in the chapter that the basis for responsibility for injustice is not in conventional moral and legal notions of duty, but rather in political notions of human rights. The chapter distinguishes between rights as entitlement and rights as enjoyment in order to discuss how these two notions give rise to different kinds of struggle over responsibility and human rights. Ultimately, the chapter concludes, when making arguments for the political, social and economic transformations necessary to take on the structural aspects of injustice, the enjoyment approach to human rights is a better partner.

Turning towards global politics, Richard Beardsworth advances the concept of political responsibility to address the issue of fragmented objects, actors and practices (Chapter 5). He argues that at this current historical moment – structured politically by material and ideological decline of the West and the emergence of new powers, populism, and the sustainable development agenda – it is important to rehearse the idea of political responsibility towards global concerns, threats and challenges. The chapter focuses on the gap between these concerns and the state system, arguing that, in a globalized but fractured age, a Weberian and pragmatic understanding of political responsibility towards one's own citizenry may release most effectively practices of global responsibility.

This theme is discussed from different angles in the following two chapters. Peter Sutch holds that the relationship between moral responsibility and political/legal responsibility is a vital element of a general conception of responsibility in world politics (Chapter 6). Importantly, for him, this entails moving beyond an account of the moral failure of the international system to an exploration of how that system might become an agent of our moral responsibility. In the contemporary literature, this goal is pursued through an engagement with institutional concepts such as the Responsibility to Protect (R2P), the humanization of international law, common or community interest, and human rights that appear to share the moral foundations of cosmopolitanism. Here, his chapter argues, lies the problem. Appearances can be deceiving, and we need to reconsider the claim that a plausible account of moral responsibility, grounded in an accessible account of political/legal responsibility, can have cosmopolitan foundations.

This scepticism is shared by Mark Busser who examines ongoing debates about the 'remedial' obligations the world's more fortunate people might have to help the most vulnerable. In Chapter 7, he suggests that emergent social, cultural and political movements that explicitly reject cosmopolitanism should perhaps be understood as reactions to the prevalence of compelling arguments in favour of responsibility that make unwelcome practical demands. Busser explores the role of motivated moral reasoning in these movements in the context of longstanding academic and theoretical debates over the various principles governing international responsibility. Even prominent scholarly arguments about 'global responsibility', he holds, have sometimes conflated various facets of the power relations of obligation, answerability and accountability, as when obligations in a 'bystander' mode are emphasized at the expense of the demands that would come with acknowledging 'consequential' duties that flow from culpabilities. For Busser, connecting responsibility debates from international theory to their practical personal and political stakes raises questions about the role that motivated moral reasoning might play, not only in reactionary and conspiracist subcultures but also in the sober and high-minded theorizing of the academy.

Moving away from a discussion of principles and towards IR theorizing, Jelena Cupać and Michael Zürn use the expansion of responsibility and authority of international organizations to reflect on the relationship between these two concepts (Chapter 8). Their theoretical sketch of the relationship starts by discussing the concepts separately, thereby identifying their major differences. In a second step, they focus on their relationship. They observe that IO responsibility and authority are not co-constitutive: there are cases in which responsibility comes without authority and cases in which authority is exercised in the absence of responsibility. Cupać and

Zürn then move to a detailed discussion of two other possibilities: that responsibility precedes and is causally prior to authority, and that authority precedes and is causally prior to responsibility. They also discuss the possibility of IO authority and responsibility being withdrawn as a consequence of the vertical relationship between the two.

Continuing with IR theory, Viktor Friedman draws on English School concepts to show how responsibilities as moral and legal standards, norms or obligations are attached to specific actors as participants in the social realm of international politics and are defined in relation to various relevant moral communities – the nation, the society of states, humankind or even the planet (Chapter 9). Further, he argues how the English School regards responsibilities not as causes of behaviour but as standards of human conduct that actors draw on to make and justify situated decisions about how to apply general rules within the confines of specific contexts. To do this well, practitioners must exhibit responsibility as a set of political virtues. Finally, Friedman shows how in emphasizing conduct rather than behaviour, the English School rejects the separation between normative and empirical inquiry. This implies that responsible scholarship requires grounding normative theorizing in the empirical study of the rules and standards that constitute the practices of international and world politics.

Themes and issues discussed in these opening chapters are elaborated upon or put into perspective in the subsequent parts. In part II, the Handbook turns to policy fields. The authors of this section provide an overview of how responsibility plays out in practice. Some of them take a more historical approach, outlining since when and through which developments responsibility has come to matter in a particular policy field. Others primarily address the question of how responsibility is institutionalized in a particular field with regard to the main actors involved and their relations, practices of formalization as well as how the field operates as a whole. The six chapters thus map responsibility relations across policy fields either in terms of how the responsibility object started to matter or in terms of the actor constellations and their positionings in the field.

Steven Bernstein discusses the assigning and erosion of responsibility for the environment as international norms assign common responsibilities to states for environmental protection while carving out sovereign responsibility for use and protection of domestic resources, with some liability for external harms (Chapter 10). He shows how the 1970s/1980s saw attempts to create greater shared responsibility by applying notions such as the 'common heritage of [hu]mankind' to resources deemed part of the global commons to enshrine responsibilities for access, benefit sharing, and to limit harms like climate change. However, Bernstein argues, major economies resisted such notions and specific obligations they implied. Contestation over the appropriate distribution of responsibilities led to new norms such as 'common but differentiated responsibility and respective capabilities' as a guide. It too came under increasing strain as debates intensified over relative historical and current contributions to environmental harms, and principled debates over distributive and historical justice and liability. The result has been further erosion of common responsibility, viewing differentiation as more about capabilities than justice, the diffusion of responsibility among states and non-state (including corporate) actors and weakening of overall responsibility, and a shift from external to internal responsibility of states for addressing environmental problems. Bernstein closes on a more upbeat note, presenting proposals to counter these trends, which include building support for environmental rights and novel proposals such as for an environmental 'responsibility to protect' or transitional justice processes to address global environment concerns.

The differentiated nature of responsibility is a theme that is also addressed in the chapter by Tobias Gumbert and Doris Fuchs discussing the global agri-food system (Chapter 11). They speak of 'moral geographies' to describe varying responsible attitudes as the result of expectations that link geographical ordering with morally adequate behaviours. Their chapter details the governance issue of food waste and explores the roles and responsibilities of transnationally operating retail companies within this particular field. The authors argue that the scrutiny of retailers' practices of responsibility reveals their spatial differentiation: sharing responsibility for the generation of food waste downstream on the distribution and consumption stage in European countries, while continuing to shift responsibilities for waste upstream to weaker producers and suppliers along food supply chains in Non-European contexts. Gumbert and Fuchs suggest that adopting a relational ontology as well as paying close attention to power differentials in the food system may help to generate a clearer picture of varying responsibility attitudes and attributions.

Turning to the high stakes of nuclear weapons, Laura Considine and James Souter outline prominent policy debates surrounding state nuclear responsibilities in Chapter 12, identifying the standards of responsibility formalized in the 1968 Nuclear Nonproliferation Treaty, which was recently challenged by the Treaty on the Prohibition of Nuclear Weapons. The authors also provide an overview of different academic models of nuclear responsibility and their critics before moving on to examine some of the issues that nuclear weapons raise for normative political and International Relations theory. While a body of earlier theoretical work argued that practices of nuclear deterrence involve taking an immoral posture towards other states, some scholars have questioned the compatibility of nuclear weapons with the responsibilities of liberal democratic states, and others have understood the possession of nuclear weapons as generating moral conflicts between different state responsibilities. Considine and Souter also point to an emerging line of argument, inspired by republican political theory, which claims that nuclear deterrence irresponsibly dominates the world's population by subjecting it to arbitrary power, even if nuclear weapons are never used.

Staying with the theme of warfare, but moving into the 21st century, Elke Schwarz's chapter engages with the complexities of assigning and taking responsibility in the use of lethal autonomous weapons systems (LAWS) (Chapter 13). At stake in the debates is the issue of whether the human can exert adequate levels of meaningful human control over weapons systems that are capable of selecting and engaging targets autonomously. Schwarz shows how the advent of new complex and distributed technologies of autonomy, especially those that employ advanced modes of machine learning and deep neural networks, challenges conceptions of the human as knowledgeable and free moral agent, acting with intent in the conduct of warfare. This challenge to human agency and control has consequences not only for legal responsibility and accountability in war, she argues, but also changes parameters for taking moral responsibility for lethal acts in warfare. In consequence, characteristics of the technology itself pose a considerable challenge to conventional understandings of lines of responsibility for actions in the context of conflict warfare.

Erna Burai focuses on the Responsibility to Protect (RtoP) in the field of security as an eminent example where 'responsibility' became an institutionalized part of normative order, not only in practice but also in name (Chapter 14). In the chapter, she asks how the introduction of responsibility contributed to negotiating the protection of populations from war crimes, crimes against humanity, genocide and ethnic cleansing and what we can learn about responsibility in world politics through the case of RtoP. The chapter starts from the dilemmas of protecting populations as they arose by the end of the 1990s, and asks how introducing responsibility to the debate responded to these conundrums on four levels: the level of discourse, the level of institutionalization, the level of collective expectations and that of public justifications for state action. Burai argues that on all four levels responsibility facilitated negotiating protection, i.e. it led to a better specification of what protection is and who should carry it out. It did so by providing politically viable terms of the debate on the level of discourse, facilitating institutionalized knowledge on mass atrocities in policy-making and in practices such as peacekeeping. On the levels of collective expectations and public justifications for action, R2P ignited debates on specific responsibilities and understandings of protection.

The final of this section provides a historical overview of responsibility for disaster management (Chapter 15). Marco Krüger and Friedrich Gabel identify the 1755 Lisbon earthquake as the point of origin of the debate. Much later, the increasing institutionalization of disaster management within the framework of the United Nations has spurred a more nuanced discussion of different aspects of responsibility. The authors draw from a multidimensional theoretical approach to trace the complexity of responsibility by distinguishing four dimensions. These are the subject, object, quality and the normative basis of responsibility. Through these dimensions, Krüger and Gabel demonstrate that the understanding of responsibility has changed in all four dimensions. First, the allocation of responsibility has become fuzzier. They argue that while the state has remained the main subject of responsibility, additional actors have been responsibilized. Second, the object of responsibility has shifted from the affected state to the affected individuals. Third, the enactment of responsibility has become proactive and moved from a narrative of protection to a resilience approach. Finally, the quality of responsibility has altered from protecting vulnerable groups to mitigating situational vulnerability. The authors close with a discussion of the question of how to assess the legitimacy of the distribution of responsibility.

Part III zooms in on the responsibility relations amongst the actors we have discussed above, subject, object and speaker. This approach allows contributions to highlight how these relations work in practice and thus to capture the contestation of responsibility. While chapters obviously talk about specific policies, the primary focus lies on different actors, individual and collective, whose relations instantiate responsibility and who have core stakes in global governance policies. Authors were asked to address whether there are specific ways in which an actor is engaged in global politics and whether there are particular historical trajectories through which they came to matter and shape world politics. Other issues addressed in this section concern what an actor is supposedly responsible for, and how the process of assigning or taking responsibility works, including how they negotiate, shape or adopt norms relating to specific policy problems or objects of responsibility.

Diplomats are a key type of actor in this regard as it is through them that the state's interest and position in the world is instantiated. In Chapter 16, Markus Kornprobst raises the question of what responsible diplomacy ought to be. He proceeds in four steps. First, he borrows the terms *raison d'état*, and *raison de système* from the literature on diplomacy and discusses to what extent they map onto related ones such as *Realpolitik* and *Idealpolitik*. Second, he identifies basic principles of public international law that help specify what raison d'état and raison de système ought to be. In a third step, he elaborates on the clues provided by the diplomacy literature and in international law, conceptualizing the raison d'état as wider national interests and the raison de système as diplomatic peace. Finally, he assembles the pieces from the previous steps, arguing that responsible diplomacy is about judgments that balance wider national interests and diplomatic peace.

The issue of balancing national interests and the wider interests of the global community is a recurring theme, of course, and an issue that comes to the fore whenever scholars address the changing world order. Accordingly, the responsibility of so-called rising powers is at the centre of Johannes Plagemann and Amrita Narlikar's chapter (Chapter 17). Throughout the 2000s, rising powers such as China and India have greatly increased their economic, military, and political capabilities as actors in the global realm. It is not surprising that these gains have gone hand in hand with calls by western leaders and International Relations scholars alike for those powers to take on more 'responsibility' in the provision of public goods and to contribute their 'fair share' to the solution of global and regional challenges such as climate change, global health, piracy, and free trade. With particular reference to India, Plagemann and Narlikar's chapter reviews rising powers' trajectories since the advent of multipolarity in the early 2000s. They show how rising powers continuously redefine their roles and responsibilities. Often, established narratives of North-South conflict and post-colonialism are employed, as they provide well-developed reference points widely shared amongst both rising powers and developing countries. Moreover, the authors argue, rising powers tend to prioritize their regional environment over global engagements, especially when it comes to areas of high politics and when they are situated in zones of potential or actual conflict. Plagemann and Narlikar also see some important points of difference between the rising powers, contra the common tendency to lump them together as a group. Their chapter concludes by highlighting the different limits to rising powers' willingness – individually as well as collectively – to accept responsibility in global governance and its consequences for the resolution of collective action problems in a multipolar world.

The next chapter adds to this discussion but highlighting China's role as a hydro-hegemon in the Mekong region. In Chapter 18, Yung-Yung Chang shows how the country pursues geopolitical aims albeit with a diplomatic and cooperative approach, which comes close to the English School's understanding of responsibility. Along the Mekong, riparian states have been engaging in various cooperations over the years, but it was not until China engaged more fully with neighbouring countries, following a withdrawal of the USA and Japan from earlier organizations, that these succeeded. The chapter provides a genealogy of projects and could be used as a framework for further investigation in other regions that might have a similar constellation in terms of power hierarchy between upstream and downstream states.

The primary location for solving such collective problems, of course, is the UN Security Council, which holds primary responsibility for the maintenance of international peace. Holger Niemann works out the current predicament of this arrangement in Chapter 19: for while the UNSC holds authority and power as a result of its special responsibility, there has been a profound shift in the meaning of responsibility since the 1990s. The UNSC has widened its remit from a traditional state-centred focus on country-level crises by claiming responsibility for a growing number of transnational topics, such as counter-terrorism and climate change. The Council has also claimed responsibility for groups of vulnerable people, such as civilians and children. Niemann argues that these processes of responsibilization have the effect of changing Council discourses and decision-making, arguing that responsibilization leads to new interpretations about practices and objects of Council responsibility. His chapter provides insights into the empirical developments of such new topics, objects and practices of Security Council responsibility. It also discusses their implications, most notable the segmentation of responsibility objects, the rise of routinized practices, the establishment of accountability mechanisms and the role of anticipation for evoking Security Council responsibility. As he argues, responsibilization expands the Security Council's authority, but also leads to entanglements and creates stakeholder expectations. Responsibilization, Niemann concludes, can be understood as a non-linear process pointing to the concurrence of traditional and no-traditional understandings of Security Council responsibility.

While the UNSC is arguably the prime site of state-led top-down politics, others aspire to be integrated into the system of global state politics. Mitja Sienknecht focuses on rebel groups that claim responsibility for ethnic groups in intrastate conflicts (Chapter 20). This move pitches them against a state's government that holds responsibility for citizens, her prime example being the struggle of the Kurds in a number of countries. Sienknecht's chapter thereby contributes to a nuanced understanding of different subjects of responsibility and their (conflictive) relations to each other. The Kurdish conflict over recognition and responsibility for their own people is embedded in a broader global context, of course, which is why Sienknecht further differentiates between claims of responsibility internal to a particular polity, on the one hand, and external recognition of responsibility, on the other.

The array of actors and stakeholders in world politics is wider than states or aspiring state groups, which the remaining chapters in this section deal with. Susan Park raises the question whether international organizations are responsible given their general immunity under international law, and investigates the case of Multilateral Development Banks (Chapter 21). These have taken on 'democratic' norms like accountability, including establishing the Independent Accountability mechanisms (IAMs) that assess whether they have contributed to environmental and social harm. Her chapter distinguishes responsibility from accountability, where the former is part of accountability, but has been understood by IOs in a negative compliance sense. Park argues that the IAM process is delinked from positive understandings of responsibility, because IOs operate as bureaucracies with preferences for efficiency and meeting contractual obligations. The chapter provides an example of how a typical 'mega-loan for a mega-project', the IFC financed Pangue Dam in Chile, led protestors to make a claim to the World Bank Inspection Panel to demand accountability. Given the Inspection Panel had no remit over the IFC, this in turn led to the creation of the Compliance Advisor/Ombudsman (CAO). In this intriguing case, Park shows how the IFC's CAO went beyond its mandate to take responsibility to provide redress for the people harmed by the project. The case demonstrates that IAMs can hold the IFC to account but that responsibility requires positive actions that go beyond bureaucratic incentives and contractual obligations.

The International Labour Organization (ILO) provides further ways to redress harm to people. While sixteen million people are affected by forced labour within the private economy for the purpose of exploiting their labour power, Julia Drubel focuses on the ILO as the competent international organization to realize decent work in a globalized economy (Chapter 22). It does so mainly via the formulation and monitoring of normative standards. While forced labour is prohibited by the respective ILO Conventions that are legally binding for ratifying states, labour is increasingly organized within transnational labour markets in which also abusive labour relations like forced labour and modern slavery are prevalent. Drubel shows how under these changed contexts the ILO and its members assign responsibilities with regard to forced labour, including states and corporations passing it on between them. Characterizing this development in terms of a topology of responsibility, the chapter demonstrates a mismatch between ILO regulations and the practical conditions under which forced labour is reproduced within a globalized economy.

Continuing with the theme, David Karp's chapter situates contemporary developments in the policy and practice of business and human rights within a broader theorization of the concept of responsibility in world politics (Chapter 23). The chapter adopts a periodization that stretches back to the colonial era, thereby challenging common assumptions about what is truly new and/or 'rising' within this field of practice. To this end, Karp first develops a theoretical distinction between discretionary and non-discretionary responsibility; relates this distinction to questions of authority; and shows how responsibility can be viewed as simultaneously moral, political and legal. Second, he historicizes the practice of business and human rights across four governance models: colonial, sovereignty-based, neo-liberal and 'global governance'. Third, the chapter uses the conclusions of the first two sections to analyze the most significant contemporary policy initiative in this field: the UN Guiding Principles on Business and Human Rights (UNGPs). Karp concludes that the UNGPs are consequentialist and assign responsibilities that are both legal and moral in nature, but they under-emphasize political responsibility.

The final chapter of the section focuses on the ongoing debate over the responsibility of public and private actors concerning common goods online where policies of content moderation have to balance the freedom of expression on the one hand, and the safety of users on the other hand. Gabi Schlag argues that being responsible and acting responsibly in the field of social media is a shared enterprise (Chapter 24). Shared responsibility implies that not one but many actors hold responsibility. She argues that the flipside of shared responsibility, however, often results in diffusion where nobody seems to be in charge. As the Facebook case illustrates, the dualism of shared and diffused responsibility is not a contradiction but shows the negotiated and contested character of acting responsibly in social media. Therefore, Schlag's chapter has two main goals. First, it asks what it means to hold responsibility for the content uploaded and shared on social media platforms like Facebook. Second, it discusses how Facebook addresses challenges of responsibility, accountability and liability as the policies and practices of reviewing, moderating and deleting harmful content often remain opaque. Finally, Schlag shows that Facebook's approach to content regulations is shaped both by shared responsibility and its diffusion.

Part IV then discusses the objects of responsibility contestation. Here, the focus is on global commons, broadly understood. The main questions addressed in this section concern how responsibility is being defined in particular policy fields, and how boundaries around these fields are contested or demarcated, and whether the current responsibility arrangement is viable for the future.

Samuel Barkin and Elizabeth DeSombre examine the development of what responsibility means in the context of the oceans as a global common (Chapter 25). Their focus lies primarily, but not exclusively on legal responsibility. Barkin and DeSombre's examination begins with a discussion of the common pool resource characteristics of ocean governance. It centres on the historical evolution of state responsibility in the management of that commons in the last century, in a context that worked to carve out sections of the formerly common areas of the ocean that states control, separating those from a newly evolving high norm of collective responsibility for resources on the high seas. The authors demonstrate how this norm has evolved in the context of management of marine living resources (e.g., fisheries), pollution, and minerals at the same time that a norm of responsibility for environmental effects of state behaviour was developing more generally in international environmental law. They argue that the limitations of this developing norm of responsibility in the context of the commons characteristics of the high seas form a counterpoint to this evolution; norms require matching mechanisms for implementation to have the intended effect on commons resources. Barkin and DeSobre conclude both by lauding the shift from norms of open access to those of responsible management, and by calling for better mechanisms of implementation to back up those norms.

Staying with the theme of oceans, the chapter by Rachel Tiller, Elizabeth Nyman, Elizabeth Mendenhall and Elizabeth De Santo focuses on so-called 'areas beyond national jurisdiction' (ABNJ) which make up more than half of the global ocean area (Chapter 26). Within these, there exists merely a patchwork of uncoordinated governance efforts that is subject to joint responsibility between states and non-state actors. Scientific discoveries have identified seamounts, hydrothermal vents and cold-water corals in rare and vulnerable ecosystems, as well as the potentials of marine genetic resources that could be used in the biotechnology industry, which leads to a concern over contradictions in terms of sustainable development and conservation efforts to preserve the biodiversity that have been increasingly vocalized in global politics. To address such concerns the UNGA has called for an intergovernmental negotiation process towards a new multilateral treaty in Resolution 69/292, adopted in June 2015, on biodiversity in areas beyond national jurisdiction (BBNJ). The resultant treaty will act both as a conservation and governance mechanism, meant to establish methods to protect marine biodiversity and provide guidelines to regulate it in the ABNJ. The chapter discusses human interactions and explores the responsibility of actors within the context of biodiversity protection in areas with little or no governance, where unknown potentials for exploitation exist. In doing so, the authors ask questions about processes of regime formation, the design of effective regimes, and interaction with other regimes and thereby analyze the institutional articulation humanity's responsibility towards biodiversity, within the framework of complex institutional dynamics, and how this could lead to adequate governance of our common heritage in this new frontier.

Although geographically on the margins of the planet, the polar regions play an important role in the global climate system. The Arctic is home to several million people whose culture and socio-economic well-being is closely intertwined with the environment. The chapter by Mathias Albert and Sebastian Knecht provides an overview over the institutional context for Arctic governance in order to lay the ground for discussing what (or who) could be, or in fact are, the subjects and objects of responsibility that play a role in the Arctic governance system and in the various discourses on the present and future development of the region (Chapter 27). In addition, the chapter scrutinizes the difficulties associated with Arctic issues that stem from the fact that 'the Arctic' cannot but be seen as a highly complex regional representation of many interlocked social and natural systems. For Albert and Knecht, this leads to the question of whether the 'bazaar governance', that has been identified as a peculiar feature of handling Arctic affairs, points to a somewhat 'deficient' mode of governance, or could not rather be seen as an appropriate form of governance under the conditions mentioned. In their conclusion, the authors discuss whether responsibilities in and towards the Arctic could be regarded as holding lessons for thinking about the future of responsibility in IR more broadly.

While the Arctic may appear abstract not least because of its remoteness, global financial markets as a responsibility object are often considered elusive as well, but arguably are of crucial systemic importance too. Michael Christopher Sardo and Erin Lockwood explore the deep relationships between global financial markets and responsibility, demonstrating both how ordinary financial practices are constituted and shaped by relationships of responsibility and how financial crises, and their severe distributional consequences, reveal the inadequacies of traditional conceptions of individual responsibility (Chapter 28). Sardo and Lockwood begin their chapter with an overview of how responsibility is traditionally conceived of, practiced, and institutionalized in financial markets, focusing on fiduciary responsibility and shareholder value, fraud regulation and the responsible corporate officer doctrine, as well as corporate social responsibility and socially responsible investing. They then turn to narratives of responsibility in the wake of the 2008 financial crisis, before showing how the structural dynamics of global finance undermine the onto-political assumptions underpinning traditional conceptions of responsibility. The authors conclude with a discussion of the conceptual and normative implications of this disconnect. Because traditional conceptions of individual and moral responsibility risk displacing and obscuring responsibility for the effects of global finance, Sardo and Lockwood outline the need for a fundamental rethinking of the concepts and practices of responsibility to move beyond the reliance on individualistic causal attribution.

The final chapter of this section addresses the internet as an object of responsibility. Given its transnational nature and impact on key aspects of our economy, politics and society worldwide, internet governance has become a critical issue in global politics. Andrea Calderaro demonstrates how negotiations on how to spread responsibilities among actors playing a crucial role in its functioning have emerged as one of the relevant challenges for global diplomacy (Chapter 29). The debate is characterized by the traditional contention between stakeholders' negotiation priorities, competencies and questions of accountability in governing a decentred issue area. Calderaro argues that if the industry is seen to be responsible for developing connectivity infrastructure and digital services, state actors play a critical role in creating regulations influencing citizens' access to the internet. His chapter unfolds this debate by looking at the evolution of the governance of the internet since its origins, characterized by the existing tensions among state actors, civil society and industry for the control of the internet domain name system, until till the more recent increasing priority in international diplomacy agenda on cybersecurity with which, he concludes, we are witnessing to a return to the state.

Part V closes the volume with an overview of different normative discussions of how responsibility 'works' or should be made to work in world politics. Authors address conceptual questions, ask why and how IR scholarship should engage in questions of responsibility, and what issues should be raised concerning the institutional design of world politics and governance practices.

Antje Wiener addresses responsibility research from the vantage point of critical norms research (Chapter 30). Her chapter presents a framework based on the ethics of knowledge production as well as the contestedness of norms research in global society. For her, these two aspects account for the dynamics of reflexive theorizing as a process which involves value-based critical analysis of everyday practice in International Relations and its reflection in IR theory-building. After introducing the two central tools of the framework, the norm-typology and the cycle-grid model, the chapter turns to the use of the norm-typology with reference to the R2P norm. The final section of the chapter addresses the empirical mapping and staging of contestations with reference to the R2P norm. The summary argument holds that using the framework offers an interface for reflexive research engagement that helps avoiding responsibility researchers to talk past each other despite taking distinct and often mutually exclusive epistemological standpoints on responsibility.

Patrick Jackson's chapter picks up themes that are discussed at various other parts of the Handbook, arguing that the question of academic responsibility is intimately linked with the question of what political responsibility is (Chapter 31). After all, he holds, the point of a responsible academic intervention in ongoing political contests would necessarily be the production of a more responsible political outcome. To him, this is especially significant in the case of an issue like human-induced climate change, which is well established as a scientific claim that is indisputable within the scientific community, yet how such a claim should figure in the political sphere is far from obvious. To explore this question, Jackson looks first to Max Weber's treatment of a politics of responsibility, and then to John Dewey's account of how publics are constituted and the role of academic knowledge in that process. He argues that the figure of the public intellectual, rather than the figure of the expert, provides an especially compelling route for bringing the results of scholarly inquiry into politics in a way that does not result in the politicization of factual claims.

The final two chapters discuss possibilities and limits of responsibility. Stephan Engelkamp's contribution starts from the assumption that 'acting responsibly' towards others presents one with an impossible problem (Chapter 32). Given constrained time and resources, Engelkamp problematizes the questions to whom do 'we' respond and how? Which issues and who merit 'our' responsibility, and whose questions may (necessarily) be neglected? Based on Jacques Derrida's writings on ethics and responsibility, Engelkamp's chapter enquires the moral underpinnings of taking responsibility towards the other as an ethical and political concept. It critically engages ethical accounts of making a decision in International Relations and the moral implications of the concept of aporia for responsible politics. Following a theoretical discussion of the relationship between responsibility, decision and sacrifice, the chapter illustrates the specific aporias of responding to others through the example of European immigration policy. For Engelkamp, the German performative art group Center for Political Beauty highlights ethical dilemmas of making a responsible decision vis-à-vis the refugee crisis. While the artists' performances aim at formulating a utopian alternative to neglecting the suffering of others, the chapter argues that they also demonstrate the limits of sustaining responsible politics. As he shows, this dilemma became visible in the actual German response to the so-called refugee crisis in 2015.

Similarly discussing the limits of responsibility, Sergio Dellavalle offers a historical account before turning to implications in practice (Chapter 33). He sets off by arguing that according to the individualistic paradigm of the Modern Ages, true knowledge and just action are exclusively based on the correct use of reason made by the individual agent. Against the background of the deficits deriving from the individualistic concept of the use of reason, Dellavalle holds that an alternative idea was developed, according to which action should essentially focus on considerations regarding the effects that action may have. This is the intellectual atmosphere in which the concept of responsibility was developed. Besides allowing to take the consequences of action into due account, the focus on responsibility had a further advantage. As he shows, by distinguishing between the subjects of obligations and the objects of obligations and by extending the range of the latter ensemble much farther than the former, the concept of responsibility makes it possible to concentrate on the impact of action on entities such as non-human animals, the biosphere, the global environment, as well as historically or aesthetically significant landscapes. However, Dellavalle holds, the problems that may arise from the substitution of the individualistic perspective on moral action with the focus on responsibility are at least as important as its possible advantages. Accordingly, his contribution explores the way in which the advantages that can be drawn from referring to responsibility could be maintained while preserving the main tenets of modern philosophy.

Notes

1. We also do not claim exhaustion of policy topics or responsibility objects in this volume.
2. Source: https://www.climatedocket.com/2017/11/30/germany-rwe-peru-farmer-saul-luciano-lliuya/ (accessed 21 July 2020).
3. See here: https://www.inuitcircumpolar.com/press-releases/inuit-petition-inter-american-commission-on-human-rights-to-oppose-climate-change-caused-by-the-united-states-of-america/ (accessed 15 October 2020).
4. This dimension may overlap with social expectations, as legal philosophers have made abundantly clear, e.g. Hart (1968), Honoré (1999) and Miller (2007), but it is worth considering in its own right, if only as an ideal type.
5. https://www.climatedocket.com/2017/11/30/germany-rwe-peru-farmer-saul-luciano-lliuya/ (accessed 21 July 2020).
6. This is the case when communities in the Pacific Ocean highlight the danger of their states drowning, see Munoz (2019).

References

Abbott, K.W., ed. (2014). *International Organizations as Orchestrators*. Cambridge: Cambridge University Press.

Ainley, K. (2008). "Individual Agency and Responsibility for Atrocity." In Jeffrey, R., ed., *Confronting Evil in International Relations*: 37–70. New York: Palgrave.

Arendt, H. (1958). *The Human Condition*. Chicago: University of Chicago Press.

Armitage, D., de Loë, R., and Plummer, R. (2012). "Environmental Governance and Its Implications for Conservation Practice." *Conservation Letters*, 5(4): 245–255.

Baran, P. (1990). "Verantwortung." In Sandkühler, H. J., ed., *Europäische Enzyklopädie zu Philosophie und Wissenschaften*: 690–694. Hamburg: Meiner.

Barry, C. (2003). "Global Justice: Aims, Arrangements, and Responsibilities." In Erskine, T., ed., *Can Institutions Have Responsibilities? Collective Moral Agency and International Relations*: 218–237. Houndmills and New York: Palgrave Macmillan.

Bayertz, K. (1995). "Eine kurze Geschichte der Verantwortung." In Bayertz, K., ed., *Verantwortung: Prinzip oder Problem*. Darmstadt: Wissenschaftliche Buchgesellschaft.

Bazargan-Forward, S., and Tollefsen, D., eds. (2020). *The Routledge Handbook of Collective Responsibility*. New York: Routledge.

Bellamy, A. J. (2006). "Whither the Responsibility to Protect? Humanitarian Intervention and the 2005 World Summit." *Ethics & International Affairs*, 20(2): 143–169.

Bernstein, S., and Coleman, D. W. (2009). "Introduction: Autonomy, Legitimacy, and Power in an Era of Globalization." In Bernstein, S., and Coleman, D. W., eds., *Unsettled Legitimacy. Political Community, Power, and Authority in a Global Era*: 1–29. Vancouver: UBC Press.

Biermann, F., Pattberg, P., van Asselt, H., and Zelli, F. (2009). "The Fragmentation of Global Governance Architectures: A Framework for Analysis." *Global Environmental Politics*, 9(4): 14–40.

Bovens, M. A. P., Goodin, R. E., and Schillemans, T. (2014). *The Oxford Handbook of Public Accountability*. Oxford and New York: Oxford University Press.

Brunnée, J. and Toope, S. J. (2005). "Norms, Institutions and UN Reform: The Responsibility to Protect." *Journal of International Law & International Relations*, 2(1): 121–137.

Brunnée, J., and Toope, S. J. (2010). *Legitimacy and Legality in International Law*. Cambridge: Cambridge University Press.

Bukovansky, M., Clark, I., Eckersley, R., Price, R. M., Reus-Smit, C., and Wheeler, N. J. (2012). *Special Responsibilities: Global Problems and American Power*. Cambridge and New York: Cambridge University Press.

Bull, H. (2002 (1977)). *The Anarchical Society: A Study of Order in World Politics*. Basingstoke, Macmillan.

Campbell, D. (1996). "Violent Performances: Identity, Sovereignty, Responsibility." In Lapid, A., and Kratochwil, F., eds., *The Return of Culture and Identity in IR Theory*: 163–180. Boulder and London: Lynne Rienner.

Carroll, A. B. (1999). "Corporate Social Responsibility." *Business and Society*, 3(38): 268–294.

Clunan, A., and Trinkunas, H., eds. (2010). *Ungoverned Spaces: Alternatives to State Authority in an Era of Softened Sovereignty*. Stanford: Stanford University Press.

Cowley, C. (2014). *Moral Responsibility*. London: Routledge.

Daase, C., Junk, J., Kroll, S., and Rauer, V. (2017). "Politik und Verantwortung. Analysen zum Wandel politischer Entscheidungs- und Rechtfertigungspraktiken." *Politische Vierteljahresschrift*, (Special Issue 53): 3–11.

D'Amato, A. (1982). "The Concept of Human Rights in International Law." *Columbia Law Review*, 82(6): 1110–1159.

Debiel, T., Finkenbusch, P., Sondermann, E., and Ulbert, C., eds. (2018). *Moral Agency and the Politics of Responsibility*. London and New York, Routledge.

De Burca, G., Keohane, R. O., and Sabel, C. (2013). "New Modes of Global Governance." *New York University Journal of International Law and Politics*, 45(1): 723–786.

De Carvalho, B. (2020). "Twisting Sovereignty: Security and Human Rights in the 'Invention' and Promotion of the Responsibility to Protect." In Hansen-Magnusson, H., and Vetterlein, A., eds., *The Rise of Responsibility in World Politics*: 35–54. Cambridge: Cambridge University Press.

Dingwerth, K., and Pattberg, P. (2006). "Global Governance as a Perspective on World Politics." *Global Governance*, 12(2): 185–203.

Doh, J. P. (2005). "Offshore Outsourcing: Implications for International Business and Strategic Management Theory and Practice." *Journal of Management Studies*, 42(3): 695–704.

Erskine, T., ed. (2003). *Can Institutions Have Responsibilities? Collective Moral Agency and International Relations*. Basingstoke and New York: Palgrave Macmillan.

Erskine, T. (2008). "Locating Responsibility: The Problem of Moral Agency in International Relations." In Reus-Smit, C., and Snidal, D., eds., *The Oxford Handbook of International Relations*: 699–707. Oxford: Oxford University Press.

Erskine, T. (2014). "Coalitions of the Willing and Responsibilities to Protect: Informal Associations, Enhanced Capacities, and Shared Moral Burdens." *Ethics & International Affairs*, 28(1): 115–145.

Evans, G. J. (2008). *The Responsibility to Protect – Ending Mass Atrocity Crimes Once and for All*. Washington, DC: Brookings Institution Press.

Falkner, R. (2007). "The Political Economy of 'Normative Power' Europe: EU Environmental Leadership in International Biotechnology Regulation." *Journal of European Public Policy*, 14(4): 507–526.

Favotto, A., and Kollman, K. (2020). "An Expanding Conception of Social Responsibility? Of Global Norms and Changing Corporate Perceptions." In Hansen-Magnusson, H., and Vetterlein, A., eds., *The Rise of Responsibility in World Politics*: 188–212. Cambridge: Cambridge University Press.

Gaskarth, J. (2017). "Rising Powers, Responsibility, and International Society." *Ethics & International Affairs*, 31(3): 287–311.

Grant, R. W., and Keohane, R. O. (2005). "Accountability and Abuses of Power in World Politics." *American Political Science Review*, 99(1): 29–43.

Hansen-Magnusson, H. (2019). "The Web of Responsibility in and for the Arctic." *Cambridge Review of International Affairs*, 32(2): 132–158.

Hansen-Magnusson, H., and Vetterlein, A., eds. (2020). *The Rise of Responsibility in World Politics*. Cambridge: Cambridge University Press.

Hart, H. L. A. (1968). *Punishment and Responsibility. Essays in the Philosophy of Law*. Oxford and London: Clarendon Press.

Heidbrink, L. (2017). "Definitionen und Voraussetzungen der Verantwortung." In Heidbrink, L., Langbehn, C., and Loh, L., eds., *Handbuch Verantwortung*: 3–34. Wiesbaden: Springer VS.

Heupel, M. (2013). "With Power Comes Responsibility: Human Rights Protection in United Nations Sanctions Policy." *European Journal of International Relations*, 19(4): 771–795.

Honkonen, T. (2009). *The Common but Differentiated Responsibility Principle in Multilateral Environmental Agreements: Regulatory and Policy Aspects*. Alphen aan den Rijn: Kluwer Law International.

Honoré, T. (1999). *Responsibility and Fault*. Oxford and Portland: Hart Publishing.

Jasanoff, S. (1999). "STS and Public Policy: Getting Beyond Deconstruction." *Science Technology & Society*, 4(1): 59–72.

Jasanoff, S., ed. (2005). *States of Knowledge: the Co-Production of Science and Social Order*. London: Routledge.

Jonas, H. (1984). *The Imperative of Responsibility – In Search of an Ethics for the Technological Age*. Chicago and London: The University of Chicago Press.

Karns, M., and Mingst, K. (2010). *International Organizations: The Politics and Processes of Global Governance*. Boulder: Lynne Rienner.

Karp, D. (2014). *Responsibility for Human Rights: Transnational Corporations in Imperfect States*. Cambridge: Cambridge University Press.

Lang, A. F. (1999). "Responsibility in the International System: Reading US Foreign Policy in the Middle East." *European Journal of International Relations*, 5(1): 67–107.

Leander, A. (2012). "What Do Codes of Conduct Do? Hybrid Constitutionalization and Militarization in Military Markets." *Global Constitutionalism*, 1(1): 91–119.

Lebow, R. N. (2003). *The Tragic Vision of Politics: Ethics, Interest and Orders*. Cambridge: Cambridge University Press.

Loh, J. (2017). "Strukturen und Relata der Verantwortung." In Heidbrink, L., Langbehn, C., and Loh, L., eds., *Handbuch Verantwortung*: 35–56. Wiesbaden: Springer VS.

Manjikian, M. M. (2010). "From Global Village to Virtual Battlespace: The Colonizing of the Internet and the Extension of Realpolitik." *International Studies Quarterly*, 54(2): 381–401.

Mattli, W., and Woods, N., eds. (2009). *The Politics of Global Regulation*. Princeton: Princeton University Press.

Miller, D. (2007). *National Responsibility and Global Justice*. Oxford and New York: Oxford University Press.

Munoz, S. M. (2019). "What Happens When a Country Drowns?" *The Conversation*, https://theconversation.com/what-happens-when-a-country-drowns-118659.

Narlikar, A. (2011). "Is India a Responsible Great Power?" *Third World Quarterly*, 32(9): 1607–1621.

Nida-Rümelin, J. (2011). *Verantwortung*. Stuttgart: Reclam.

Nolan, J. (2005). "With Power Comes Responsibility: Human Rights and Corporate Accountability." *University of New South Wales Law Journal*, 28(3): 581–613.

Nollkaemper, A. (2018). "The Duality of Shared Responsibility." *Contemporary Politics*, 24(5): 524–544.

O'Neill, O. (2005). "Agents of Justice." In Kuper, A., ed., *Global Responsibilities – Who Must Deliver on Human Rights?*: 37–52. New York and London: Routledge.

Ougaard, M., and Leander, A. (2010). *Business and Global Governance*. London: Routledge.

Pal, L. A. (2009). "Governing the Electronic Commons: Globalization, Legitimacy, Autonomy, and the Internet." In Bernstein, S., and Coleman, D. W., eds., *Unsettled Legitimacy. Political Community, Power, and Authority in a Global Era*: 280–299. Vancouver: UBC Press.

Palazzo, G., and Scherer, A. G. (2006). "Corporate Legitimacy as Deliberation: A Communicative Framework." *Journal of Business Ethics*, 66(1): 71–88.

Rajamani, L. (2006). *Differential Treatment in International Environmental Law*. Oxford and New York: Oxford University Press.

Rengger, N. (2003). "On 'Good Global Governance', Institutional Design and the Practices of Moral Agency." In Erskine, T., eds., *Can Institutions have Responsibilities? Collective Moral Agency and International Relations*: 207–217. Houndmills and New York: Palgrave Macmillan.

Risse, T., Ropp, S. C., and Sikkink, K., eds. (1999). *The Power of Human Rights. International Norms and Domestic Change*. Cambridge: Cambridge University Press.

Ruggie, J. G. (2004). "Reconstituting the Global Public Domain – Issues, Actors, and Practices." *European Journal of International Relations*, 10(4): 499–531.

Ruggie, J. G. (2011). "Guiding Principles on Business and Human Rights: Implementing the United Nations 'Protect, Respect and Remedy' Framework." *Netherlands Quarterly of Human Rights*, 29(2): 224–252.

Shadmy, T. (2018). "Superheroes' Regulation: Human Rights Responsibilities As a Source of Transnational Authority." *North Carolina Journal of International Law and Commercial Regulation*, 43(1): 1–52.

Slaughter, A.-M. (2004). "Disaggregated Sovereignty: Towards the Public Accountability of Global Government Networks." *Government and Opposition*, 39(2): 159–190.

Thompson, G. (2020). "Can Corporations be Held 'Responsible'?." In Hansen-Magnusson, H., and Vetterlein, A., eds., *The Rise of Responsibility in World Politics*: 213–229. Cambridge: Cambridge University Press.

Vetterlein, A. (2018). "Responsibility is More Than Accountability: From Regulatory Towards Negotiated Governance." *Contemporary Politics*, 24(5): 545–567.

Vetterlein, A., and Wiener, A. (2013). "Gemeinschaft Revisited: Die sozialen Grundlagen internationaler Ordnung." *Leviathan*, 41(28): 78–103.

Vetterlein, A., and Hansen-Magnusson, H. (2020). Introduction: The Rise of Responsibility in World Politics. In Hansen-Magnusson, H., and Vetterlein, A., eds., *The Rise of Responsibility in World Politics*: 3–31. Cambridge: Cambridge University Press.

Wang, U. (2017). "German Court OKs Potentially Groundbreaking Climate Lawsuit." *Climate Liability News*, https://www.climateliabilitynews.org/2017/2011/2030/germany-rwe-peru-farmer-saul-luciano-lliuya/.

Weiss, T. G. (2013). *Global Governance: What? Why? Whither?* Cambridge: Polity.

Weiss, T. G., and Wilkinson, R. (2018). *International Organization and Global Governance*. London: Routledge.

Welsh, J. (2011). "Civilian Protection in Libya: Putting Coersion and Controversy Back into RtoP." *Ethics & International Affairs*, 25(3): 255–262.

Welsh, J. M., and Banda, M. (2010). "International Law and the Responsibility to Protect: Clarifyingv or Expanding State's Responsibility." *Global Responsibility to Protect*, 2(3): 213–231.

Wheeler, N. J. (2002). *Saving Strangers – Humanitarian Intervention in International Society*. Oxford and New York: Oxford University Press.

Wheeler, N. J. (2006). "The Humanitarian Responsibility of Sovereignty: Explaining the Development of a New Norm of Military Intervention for Humanitarian Purposes in International Society." In Welsh, J. M., ed., *Humanitarian Intervention and International Relations*, 29–51. Oxford and New York: Oxford University Press.

Wiener, A. (2018). *Constitution and Contestation of Norms in Global International Relations*. Cambridge: Cambridge University Press.

Young, I. M. (2011). *Responsibility for Justice*. Oxford: Oxford University Press.

Zürn, M. (2018). *A Theory of Global Governance – Authority, Legitimacy & Contestation*. Oxford: Oxford University Press.

PART I

Theories of responsibility in International Relations

2
A PLURAL THEORY OF RESPONSIBILITY
Ilan Zvi Baron

Introduction

Political responsibility is both a central feature in, and it is often absent from politics. What some might see as the height of irresponsibility others may view as being responsible. Evidence of this simultaneous presence and absence can be seen in the United Kingdom's debacle during and after the EU referendum with many on the Leave side promoting blatant falsehoods (Baron 2018), in Brazil with the election of Jair Bolsanaro, in Hungary under Viktor Orbán, in Israel with Prime Minister Benjamin Netanyahu, with President Donald Trump in the United States, and the list goes on. However, no doubt others would contest this selection. Aren't these really illustrations of political irresponsibility? The answer will depend in part on the values we hold. There is no single measure by which we can identify what constitutes political responsibility, as doing so invokes values that are external to the idea of responsibility itself.

Responsibility is not something that someone has like rights, for example. Rather responsibility is what someone does and who someone is. One *is* responsible. You *are* responsible. One *acts* responsibly. Responsibility, as I approach it in this chapter, is ontological and phenomenological. Responsibility is a form of activity, and as such our understanding of what being responsible means changes according to the different conditions we find ourselves needing to act. This characteristic is one of its great strengths as a normative category: that responsibility can change while still remaining the same.

In the following, I develop an outline for a plural theory of responsibility. A plural theory is important because the very idea of responsibility is central to the functioning of any legitimate political order, but what responsibility means is often unclear. For example, the 2001 International Commission on Intervention and State Sovereignty (International Commission on Intervention and State Sovereignty et al. 2001) used responsibility as a signifier for legitimacy and as a critique of sovereignty. Responsibility as a normative concept tends to refer to something outside of itself that provides the reasons for what is or is not responsible. Adding further room for confusion is how the concept of responsibility is also often used in such a way that overlaps with other concepts such as duty and obligation.[1] This begs the question of what is unique about responsibility, or at least, what is special about it? Part of what makes responsibility unique is how in theorizing responsibility we reveal normative structures that characterize our being in the world.

In what follows, I offer a critique of the concept of political responsibility by building on this idea that responsibility functions as a signifier and that responsibility often means very different things in practice. In my outline of a plural theory I offer five accounts. The first is about causality and liability and treats responsibility as a combination of agency and accountability. The second account is the non-causal model we find the works of Hannah Arendt, Iris Marion Young, and Jade Schiff. In this account we are responsible because of our membership in various but specific communities. Our belonging to these communities places a demand upon ourselves for being responsible for what is done "in our name" as members of a community, even though we do not directly cause that which we have some responsibility for.

The third account is the political responsibility of identity, is influenced by the works of Hannah Arendt, Charles Taylor and William Connolly, and is based on our conditions of plurality and intersubjectivity. The Political responsibility of identity is a responsibility to the world of meaning in which we live in, and how who we are is always part of our belonging to a world of difference. The fourth account is ontological and frames responsibility as an ethical consequence of our being as opposed to our not-being. This account is advanced by Hans Jonas, although related ethical arguments are present in the philosophy of Emmanuel Lévinas, and Martin Buber. Finally, there is political responsibility as political ethics. This is the account we see with Max Weber and Hans Morgenthau, and provides a useful reminder of how important context is for understanding what our political responsibilities are. But the ethic of responsibility we find in their work also contributes to my general claim that political responsibility is best understood phenomenologically.

Responsibility as a signifier

Finding meaning can be surprisingly difficult. Looking up a word in a dictionary offers only one mechanism by which we discover the meaning of words. Meaning is a product of the way words are used. As Wittgenstein (2009, 693) shouts in *Philosophical Investigations*, "And nothing is more wrong-headed than to call meaning something of a mental activity!" We cannot find meaning outside of the language we use (Gunnell 2014). To understand the meaning of responsibility we should consider how the term is used and what this usage signifies. In this section I demonstrate that the way the term responsibility is deployed demonstrates that what we mean by responsibility is not especially clear.

The concept of responsibility is an interesting one because it is both immensely important and also potentially devoid of any specific content. What I mean by devoid of content is that the meaning of responsibility is often assumed in such a way that the content of what being responsible means can be difficult to specify. To briefly return to the original Responsibility to Protect document, responsibility is about what sovereignty involves, which includes an emphasis on protecting human security. When a state fails in this duty, the international community has a responsibility to prevent, react and rebuild. My point is that when we use responsibility in this context we are ultimately referring to the normative principles of sovereignty, and acting responsibly becomes a reference to the norms of the international community. None of this actually explains what responsibility means.

Toni Erskine, a leading scholar of responsibility in international politics, offers a systematic critique of who can be considered to be a moral agent in international relations. For her, the matter of responsibility in international politics is a moral one, and the application of responsibility requires that we are able to identify which types of agents can be held responsible. This identification is, she points out, not obvious. As she writes, "Claims to moral responsibility are ubiquitous in world politics" (Erskine 2014, 117).[2] However, this ubiquity is despite the paradox of how, "Theorizing about international relations …[assumes] that though states are actors (often the actors) in international relations, they are not capable of specifically moral action" (Erskine 2001, 67). The point being that there can be no responsibility if we cannot hold specific agents in international politics to be moral agents. Erskine seeks to resolve this paradox by arguing that there is a type of collective responsibility that can be applied in international politics, and the way she makes this argument is to focus on the agent. Serena Parekh (2011, 673) makes a similar move by focusing on the state as being able to "assume political responsibility."

A difficulty with this approach, however, is that instead of explaining how we are responsible, the focus becomes on what types of agents we can apply the concept of responsibility onto. Hence Erskine (2018) notes that responsibility refers to a combination of agency and freedom. She also argues (Erskine 2014, 117) that there are two different types of judgements that characterize responsibility:

> Prospective moral responsibility involves *ex ante* judgments regarding acts that ought to be performed, or forbearances that must be observed. Retrospective moral responsibility entails *ex post facto* assessments of a particular event or set of circumstances for which an agent's acts or omissions were such that the agent is the object of praise or blame. The forward-looking variation is heard in assertions of duty and obligation; the backward-looking variation emerges most often in charges of blame and accountability.

By focusing on the agent, Erskine reveals an interesting complexity. Responsibility is ontological (hence the focus on what types of agents can be held to *be* responsible), but it is also temporal insofar as responsibility is both forward and backward looking, and it is also deontological as a means to apply an ethical standard to various situations. What this explanation suggests is not just that there is a temporal dimension to what responsibility means (I will return to this dimension later), but that the way we judge what is responsible always refers to something outside of responsibility itself: blame, praise, duty, obligation and accountability.

Treating responsibility as a signifier is evident in a range of approaches. In *Men in Groups: Collective Responsibility for Rape*, Larry May and Robert Strikwerda (1994, 148) argue that, "in western societies, rape is deeply embedded in a wider culture of male socialization. Those who have the most to do with sustaining that culture must also recognize that they are responsible for the harmful aspects of that culture." In that paper, they represent responsibility as a combination of complicity (they are not arguing "that all men are responsible for the prevalence of rape" (May and Strikwerda 1994, 148)), and of benefiting from outcomes that emerge from this complicity. Responsibility in this context is something that is widely shared. Responsibility also involves a relationship between identifiable agents and a specific outcome, even if the agents did not directly cause this outcome. Their argument is structurally similar to Farid Abdel-Nour's (2003, 713), who writes that, "where there is national pride, there is national responsibility." The shared point being that we are implicated and thus responsible for conditions, circumstances or events that affirm a position of benefit, be it political, economic, cultural or emotional. Responsibility refers to how complicity enables a benefit. Inaction matters. By casting complicity and inaction with benefit, these concepts carry a normative character that makes them evidence of responsibility. Responsibility signifies this normative character.

The signifying character of responsibility is perhaps most clearly presented by Bernard Williams (1993, 55), who in *Shame and Necessity* writes that "we might label [the] four elements [of responsibility] cause, intention, state [of mind], and response. These are the basic elements of any conception of responsibility." Responsibility functions as a normative pointer towards features that characterize particular actions. The definition of responsibility appears to be a structural one first, and a normative one second. Central to this structural character of responsibility is its causal dimension.

For example, Sarah Clark Miller (2011) proposes that responsibility is a form of the ethics of care, and others have addressed or responded to the causal character of responsibility (Braham and VanHees 2011; Parekh 2011; Reiff 2008; Richman 1969; Rosen 2004). Importantly, however, even when framed causally, responsibility is not a normative example of rigorism, where "certain duties (principles, rules, or whatever one calls them) are exceptionless or absolute" (Frey 1978, 106) – which might appear relevant in the cause of causal rules.

Responsibility does not necessarily tell you what to do (i.e. do not lie). Responsibility refers to outcomes that emerge because of a previous action or choice, or in some cases simply by virtue of our membership in a particular community. It is not necessary that the agent produces the responsibility so much as responsibility presents itself as a response to specific situations. Responsibility emerges out of our participation in the world.

This relational and structural dimension of responsibility is consistent with its etymology. The word responsibility comes from the Latin *respondeo*, which translates as I answer (Lucas 1993, 5). However, *respondeo* has its own etymology, as it is a combination of *re-* and *spondeo*. *Re* is a Latin prefix that not only refers generally to a past action or a backward motion but is also forwarding looking as it means to repeat something. *Spondeo* mean promise, guarantee or pledge. *Re-spondeo* can be translated as "I promise." Thus, the idea of responsibility is more than just to answer. Responsibility is to commit yourself in some way. It is something that we do in response to a question, call or challenge and is relational or reactive to a past event or action but is forward looking. It is a reaction to a situation in which our action binds ourselves in some way. To define responsibility in a meaningful sense is to explain the character of this structural relationship, so that as agents we can determine what types of actions *become* or *are* responsible. Responsibility is always something we *do* because it is a part of who we *are*. Our responsibilities change in different contexts because responsibility is "a social practice" in which people "rely on their (conflicting) values and beliefs and on their best interpretations of the facts and of social conventions" (Goodhart 2017, 21, 22). To put this differently, because responsibility emerges out of specific conditions, there will always be different types of responsibility because there is always a multiplicity of conditions we will face in our lives.

Responsibility appears to require a reference to something external to itself, such as agency, causality, accountability, etc. None of these are by themselves moral terms, and one function of the concept of responsibility as a normative category is partly to transform them into ones. What we need is a kind of map in which we frame the different ways in which responsibility is meaningful. This map would help reveal how the concept of responsibility works to impart a normative dimension to choices and actions.

The plural theory

The following five accounts of responsibility are intended to collectively contribute to mapping out the terrain in which responsibility carries meaning. They are all political because they all respond in some measure to the human condition of plurality, which, to paraphrase Hannah Arendt (1958, 7), is that women and men, not woman or man, inhabit the earth. A consequence of this condition is that our public choices have consequences that we are unable to witness directly. Political responsibility involves decisions and practices that shape the lives of people that we do not know (Beardsworth 2015). What we need is a mechanism by which it is possible to understand the role of our actions and choices in our collective lives as members of multiple communities. This mechanism is political responsibility (compare Beardsworth in this volume). What the following five-point account also demonstrates is that political responsibility functions as a normative structure in a phenomenological sense.

Causal or liable

The causal or liable account states that I can be held accountable for a particular outcome that emerged as a direct consequence of my actions or choices. There are, of course, different causal relations in any account of responsibility. R. G. Frey (1978) notes that there are contributory causes as well as necessary and sufficient ones. A decade later, Shelly Kagan (1988, 293), queried how responsibility is causal, writing "I want to try to understand the view that having caused harm generates a special obligation to aid the victim of that harm." Kagan (1988, 301) is specifically interested in why "*causing* harm… is the offensive relation… that generates the special obligation." Her point is to highlight that there is something specifically different between allowing and doing. This is an important insight. Any account of responsibility needs to understand that to be responsible is to recognize that our actions and choices do create outcomes, and that because we contributed to creating these outcomes, we bear a responsibility for them. The law works in this way, this is an important part of responsibility, and it must play an important part in politics. Political leaders and political activists should be held responsible for their decisions and actions.

However, the causal account is limiting, or as Kagan acknowledges, confusing. A limitation of the causal account is evident in how it is not clear how responsibility is transmitted. If my inaction contributes to an outcome did I cause that outcome? What if I acted with a clear intention to make X happen, but Y did instead? Am I responsible for Y? What about complicity? Am I responsible for something I did not directly cause but somehow through my actions contributed towards? Whatever the answers to these questions, the point is that causality functions as a "vehicle" for responsibility (Sartorio 2004, 328). Thus, whether it is inaction, action, or intent, in the responsibility literature they often fall on how the different types of causal relations work to transmit responsibility. The causal model of responsibility refers to such conditions, where we can be held to account for what our choices lead to. But the complexity (intent, inaction, action, are clearly very different) means that we cannot rely exclusively on a causal account of responsibility (and not only because it would require a clear exposition on what is causality).

Non-causal/non-liable (membership)

Political choices are about not keeping silent and in recognizing that as members of a diverse society it is incumbent upon us all to appreciate how our own actions have consequences that may not be directly causal. Political responsibility requires that we take the first kind of responsibility not only in regard to our own actions (being accountable for our decisions and behavior) as members in a society but also that our choices implicate us in a wider range of societal and political effects. In this sense, who we align ourselves with, that which we tolerate without speaking against, and the actions of complicity all contribute to being politically responsible that is not directly causal (compare chapter by Shadmy in this volume).

Reflecting on the Holocaust, Hannah Arendt came to the conclusion that one of its enabling conditions was that good people did not speak out or stand up when they had the chance to. Later writers, notably Iris Marion Young (2013) and Jade Schiff (2014) have taken up this argument by exploring how to foster an account of responsibility that does not require liability. Arendt opens her essay, *Collective Responsibility*, stating that "There is such a thing as being responsible for things one has not done" (Arendt 2003, 147). Arendt, who is also concerned with distinguishing guilt from political responsibility, is making an important point, that: "Every government assumes responsibility for the deeds of its predecessors and every nation for the deeds and misdeeds of the past" (Arendt 2003, 149). The only mechanism for escaping our political responsibility is to leave our community, but because we "cannot live without belonging to some community" (Arendt 2003, 150) we are always faced with our fair share of political responsibility.

Our political responsibility emerges from the condition of membership, but we are not all responsible in the same way. This is why Arendt is at pains to distinguish guilt from political responsibility. Her concern is that if we are all equally guilty, then it is not possible to differentiate the guilt of someone like Eichmann from any other German at that time. We can see here how Arendt is making a distinction that still allows for a causal account of responsibility which is legally necessary, but that there remain other forms of responsibility.

Nevertheless, Arendt appears to be suggesting that our political responsibility emerges purely out of membership in the political community regardless of what we may do (or not do). Iris Marion Young notes that this is deeply unsatisfying because of how Arendt appears to focus on membership to the exclusion of what people actually do (Young 2013, 79). Young argues that although Arendt sticks in part to this account in *Eichmann in Jerusalem*, in that book she also provides some modifications. Indeed, it is unlikely that Arendt would be dismissive of action as a component of responsibility. How we act as members is what I take Arendt to be getting at; that our membership incurs a special responsibility. This membership creates choices for its members that others may not have. Membership may not make all its members legally liable for the actions of the state, for example, but it does mean that all members have a special stake in the future of the community, and are burdened by its past. As such, membership does create specific contexts for political responsibility that non-members may not have.

A non-liable model of responsibility is especially important in international politics. Injustices are rarely exclusively national. For Schiff, political responsibility is about how to respond to situations where we are implicated in the suffering of others. Political responsibility arises when our conduct involves implicating ourselves because of our actions or choices in the suffering of other people. Choices such as deciding what products to buy (where were they made, and in what working conditions?), where to buy them (what are the employment practices of that company?), what foods we consume (did they come from sustainable farming?) and so on reveal that our everyday choices can carry far reaching consequences that each of us, individually, cannot be held liable for.

Identity and intersubjectivity

Intersubjectivity is an ontological basis for understanding the processes of interpreting the world. In explaining intersubjectivity, Charles Taylor (1971, 27) writes:

> It is not just that the people in our society all or mostly have a given set of ideas in their heads and subscribe to a given set of goals. The meanings and norms implicit in these practices are not just in the minds of the actors but are out there in the practices themselves, practices which cannot be conceived as a set of individual actions, but which are essentially modes of social relations, of mutual action.

Intersubjectivity emphasizes how we come into contact with a world of meaning. The world is not made up of empty vessels into which we impart meaning (like filling a glass). We are never faced with objects that are empty or bare of meaning, that are inherently meaningless (Heidegger 2013). As we come into contact with this world of meaning, one that shapes our experiences, interpretations and understanding of this world, we also contribute to this world of meaning. A consequence of this intersubjective condition is that what I know is never authentically mine.

It is also always someone else's. Our ability to make sense of the world depends upon our participating in a world of meaning where this meaning is not solely produced by ourselves as isolated individual minds. Because we do not produce a meaningful world by ourselves, we depend on a world of plurality.

This condition of plurality means that the knowledge I have of the world – knowledge that enables my functioning in this world – is never only mine, this knowledge is shared in a world of others. The world of plurality has significance for our identity as well. There is, as William Connolly argues, an ethic to identity. He writes that, "You need identity to act and to be ethical…" (Connolly 2002, xix) and, "To be ethical is to put identity, to some degree, at risk." (Connolly 2002, xix). In that work, Connolly is not concerned with political responsibility, but the connection between identity and ethics that he proposes can be applied to political responsibility. By making a claim to belonging we are always making a normative commitment that aligns who we are with the values of that community which we belong to. Hence, the famous Groucho Marx joke about not wanting to join a club that would have him as a member. The punchline being that belonging is a sign of shared values (*I* would not want *me* in *their* club!). Membership of this sort (of any, for that matter) is always also a claim to identity. But more than that, anytime we make a claim to identity we do so in an intersubjective way. We cannot make a claim to identity without also appreciating the world of difference that makes our claims to identity meaningful and possible.

Political responsibility functions in a similar regard. Not as a joke, but as a signpost to how political responsibility is always also a claim to identity. Political responsibility emerges as a response, and as such it is also a risk of sorts. Responsibility is, remember, an answer. To answer responsibly is to recognize that there is a choice that involves the risk of irresponsibility. We never know for sure what our choices will lead to. St. Augustine knew as much, which is why he writes that, "ignorance is unavoidable, and … judgment is also unavoidable…." (Augustine 1998, 927 (Book XIX 6)). Uncertainty is always a feature of our political choices. Political responsibly reflects this uncertainty because to be responsible is to take a risk. It is to reveal yourself in the face of a difficult situation, and to live with the consequences. It is also to be responsible to this world that enables us to make claims to identity.

This account of political responsibility is based in an ontological claim about our being, and that this claim is always an uncertain one, uncertain insofar as our knowledge is never our own and because of how difference and plurality are necessary for any claim to identity. One consequence of this twofold condition of intersubjectivity and plurality is that to be responsible is to recognize our own fallibility, because what we know is never only ours, and is never certain.

Ontological

Responsibility is always both backwards and forwards looking. We are responsible for that which we have done or been complicit in and also for the future outcomes of our choices. In this sense, responsibility is about who we are across time and space. Responsibility is a meaningful relation that conditions our being across time in specific places that informs our identities and opportunities (or lack thereof) for action. Responsibility is thus always also to some extent, ontological.

There is, to the best of my knowledge, only one theory of political responsibility that is explicitly ontological, and it is provided by Hans Jonas.

To explain the ontological account, I need to make a brief clarification. I am using (hermeneutic) phenomenology in the Heideggerian (Heidegger 2013) sense insofar as political responsibility is ontological by it functioning as a meaningful structure in the relations of our being. Heidegger is infamous for his political choices, and of the possible linkage between his politics and his philosophy (Faye 2009). This is not a debate I will engage with here, but needless to say, it is curious that in *Being and Time* Heidegger does not engage in any political discussions.[3] It is *Heidegger's Children* (Wolin 2015) who do – perhaps in spite of him. For example, The Jewish philosopher Emmanuel Lévinas can be read as an ethical critique of Heidegger, and Hans Jonas's argument about political responsibility is another such attempt.

In *The Imperative of Responsibility*, Jonas argues that we have a responsibility to the future of humanity, and that this responsibility functions in the same way that being a parent does. Responsibility is, for him, a duty for the future existence and conditions of humanity. While this might appear to be some kind of social contract with the future, it is not. That is because Jonas' argument is not contractual, it is ontological.

It is ontological because of how it approaches the condition of our being. Heidegger, in *Being and Time*, develops a philosophical language for making sense of the structures of the world that make it meaningful to us in its being. What this means is that the essence of a hammer, for example, is hammering. Jonas turns this question onto the character of being itself, and, similar to Heidegger, asks what the being of our Being (our existence) is. To put this crudely, they want to know what our beingness entails. Jonas argues that because of our being, as opposed to our not-being, there is an imperative for being. Thus, the very first imperative, he states, is that there is humankind. As he writes, "The first rule, is therefore, that no condition of future descendants of humankind should be permitted to arise which contradict the reason why the existence of mankind is mandatory" (Jonas 1979, 43). This imperative creates an ontological responsibility: "With this imperative we are, strictly speaking, not responsible to the future of human individuals but to the *idea* of man" (Jonas 1979, 43). Our being, he suggests is not just a question of what it means *to be*, but rather, what it means that we "ought-to-be" (Jonas 1979, 50). He writes, "In every purpose, being declares itself for itself and against nothingness… the fact that being is not indifferent toward itself makes its differences from nonbeing the basic value of all values, the first 'yes'" (Jonas 1979, 81). However, it is not just the "what" of our being that matters, but the "'how' of acting" (Jonas 1979, 88).

He proceeds to develop a theory of responsibility. There is more to this theory than our existence. His concern is in part inspired by the human ability to develop technologies that threaten our very existence. Thus, he notes that the first condition of responsibility is a causal one. The causal dimension here is that "acting makes an impact on the world, and … that such acting is under the agent's control" (Jonas 1979, 20). Responsibility is something that we do, and it has consequences, consequences that this agent can "foresee… to some extent" (Jonas 1979, 90–91). However, Jonas points out that the responsibility under these three conditions (impact/causal, agency/control, and foreseeable/temporal) can be different. We can be responsible *for* something – formal responsibility. But we can also *be* a responsible person – substantive responsibility.

Jonas is formulating responsibility phenomenologically in a Heideggerian sense. Responsibility is something that we *are*, or can be. But it is also a framework for action, and actions happen in time as evidence by one action leading to future consequences, and this action being in some sense fashioned by what came before. We *are* always responsible *in* time.

The formal conception of responsibility is, nevertheless, in practical terms, effectively the same as the liability model already discussed (Jonas 1979, 90). It is the substantive one where Jonas develops the ontological dimension. The point he is making here is that the "ought-to-be" leads to an "ought-to-do" and this second ought pertains to the care that we have for our being and to the future. Responsibility is not a reciprocal relation because responsibility is different from, for example, solidarity because it is unconditional and involves a vertical relation. The model he uses, indeed the model that he describes as the "archetype of all responsibility" is that of the parent (Jonas 1979, 101). There are a few reasons he gives for making this claim, but the main ones pertain to continuity and the future, that the relation is a vertical one (at least for a time), and that it is unconditional and does not demand a reciprocal relation. While it is unlikely that *The Imperative of Responsibility* is about to become a best-selling parenting book, and I am not going to comment on how Jonas frames parenthood, his insight here is that being responsible does not require reciprocity, that it has a temporal dimension, that it follows from the normative question of our being, and that it is both causal (liable) and ontological.

Political ethics

The fifth account of political responsibility treats political responsibility as political ethics. This reading of responsibility relies heavily on the thought of Machiavelli, Weber and Morgenthau. But I am not suggesting that this is a "realist" account of political responsibility. Rather, the point here is that there exists a kind of political responsibility that is specific to those who hold public office, and who must make decisions for the general welfare or benefit of the country.

It might appear that political responsibility of this kind is distinct from any moral considerations. Indeed, in Morgenthau's (early) writings, foreign policy should always be based on the national interest and not moral considerations. As he wrote in 1949, "A foreign policy which is guided primarily by moral considerations is not only threatened with failure; it can be successful only by accident" (Morgenthau 1949, 210). National interest was what ought to guide the responsible statesperson. What precisely characterizes the national interest may change, but the point he is making is to distinguish a particular kind of political ethics – in which political and moral considerations are separate (Morgenthau 1949, 210).

The Vietnam War, however, changed his mind. Morgenthau's opposition to the Vietnam War compelled him to become something of an activist, or at least to exercise what he felt to be the political responsibility that comes with academic freedom (Molloy 2019), and he regularly spoke out against the War. The Vietnam War,

> led Morgenthau to expand his notion of the national interest, which he had promoted as the supreme guide to realist decision-making in foreign affairs. In his revised view, serving the national interest came to mean more than ensuring American security in the Western Hemisphere and maintaining a balance of power in Europe and Asia. He argued that the United States must uphold its exceptional moral stature as a model of integrity for the rest of the world.
>
> *(Rafshoon 2001, 57)*

This War transformed "Morgenthau, the jaded Central European, [into] a moralist" (Rafshoon 2001, 71). Morgenthau still adhered to the principle of national interest, but he came to recognize that this interest includes a moral component, and was not simply about balancing.

Morgenthau, however, realizes along with Machiavelli and Weber, that morality in politics is of a particular variety. Part of the reason for this is, as Hannah Arendt notes, "politics is not like the nursery" (Arendt 1994, 279). Both her and Weber share the conviction that politics involves recognizing the consequences of one's choices. This is the brunt of the ethic of responsibility that Weber develops in his essay *The Vocation of Politics*. It does not matter what intentions are, what matters are outcomes. This is why Weber quotes Fichte who in turn is citing Machiavelli, writing about the ethic of responsibility that, "He does not feel that he is in a position to shift the consequences of his actions, where they are foreseeable, onto others. He will say, 'These consequences are to be ascribed to my actions'" (Weber 2004, 84).

From Weber's perspective, politics may very well involve the use of violence, regardless of one's convictions. Political responsibility includes a particular type of (political) ethics. Such ethics may mean that, as Machiavelli (1988, 59) writes, "It is desirable to be both loved and feared, but it is difficult to achieve both and, if one of them has to be lacking, it is much safer to be feared than loved." Or, as Weber (Weber 2004, 59) put it in one especially chilling passage,

> Anyone who wishes to engage in politics at all, and particularly, anyone who wishes to practice it as a profession, must become conscious of these ethical paradoxes and of his own responsibility for what may become *of him* under the pressure they exert. For, I repeat, he is entering into relations with the satanic powers that lurk in every act of violence.

For Weber, political responsibility is always about outcomes and the recognition that the outcomes may not be moral ones in any Kantian sense. Consequences are the crux of responsibility, but there is also an ontological dimension insofar as what happens to the person who makes political choices is a part of the ethic of responsibility.

Weber is emphasizing something particularly important, and easily missed. Political responsibility is not just about consequences and outcomes, it is about uncertainty. It is in not knowing what our choices will lead to – nobody has such predictive powers – that characterizes responsibility. This characterization is in contrast to the ethic of conviction in which ideology overcomes the potential of any lingering doubt from not knowing. To be responsible is to embrace that we do not know for sure what our actions will produce in politics, but that intention is not the measure of our responsibility. As David Owen and Tracy Strong (Weber 2004, xii) write an introductory essay about Weber's vocation essays, "it does no good in politics to say that you did not intend the (unfortunate) consequences of your actions." This uncertainty and the divorce of responsibility from intention are key features in responsibility – what makes it political in a Weberian sense is the underlying possibility of violence or force of some kind. But political responsibility is not really about violence. Rather, political responsibility is about recognizing this twofold character of uncertainty and outcome.

It is not, however, obviously clear how uncertainty and outcome correspond to how political responsibility means acting in the national interest. Morgenthau, nevertheless, did share with Weber a concern about distinguishing an ethic of conviction from an ethic of responsibility. This distinction is clear when Morgenthau challenges the architects of the Vietnam War as ideologically driven and prone to revisionist assessments that support the war (Morgenthau 1968; Rafshoon 2001). There is, then, some synergy across these thinkers vis-à-vis how to conceptualize what responsibility means without then identifying the content of being responsible. This synergy is further evidence that the idea of responsibility functions not as a moral rule as such, but as a normative structure. Political responsibility is about understanding what the right thing to do is, under the circumstances.

Conclusion: "What has the future ever done for me?"[4]

In this chapter I have suggested that responsibility functions phenomenologically. To be responsible or to act responsibly is to recognize that our being carries within it some normative characteristics that pertain to the world(s) in which we live. What I have not argued for is what the content of responsibility is. In other words, what it means to recognize our responsibility for climate change, for example, will mean different things to different people, and different people will have different conditions of opportunity in which to respond to climate change responsibly.

Responsibility is a normative framework that attributes a moral or ethical dimension to our being. If responsibility is to be simplified in a way that draws on the five accounts developed here, it is that political responsibility is about our being across time, and that responsibility may be backward looking, but it is concerned with the future.

Notes

1. See, for example, Mapel (1998), May (1989), Miller (2007), Striblen (2007) and Walzer (1970). Duty is sometimes used in political theory as a vehicle for obedience (Rawls 1999), whereas (political) obligation is generally restricted to the obligation that citizens have to obey the law (Horton 2010; Simmons 1980).
2. See also, Erskine (2001, 67).
3. For an opposing view see Olafson (1998).
4. See Jonas (1979, 39).

References

Abdel-Nour, F. (2003). "National Responsibility", *Political Theory* 31(5): 693–719.
Arendt, H. (1958). *The Human Condition*. London and Chicago: Chicago University Press.
Arendt, H. (1994). *Eichmann in Jerusalem: A Report on the Banality of Evil*. Rev. and enl. New York; London: Penguin Books.
Arendt, H. (2003). *Responsibility and Judgment*. New York: Schoken Books.
Augustine. (1998). *The City of God Against the Pagans*. Cambridge; New York: Cambridge University Press.
Baron, I. Z. (2018). *How to Save Politics in a Post-Truth Era: Thinking through Difficult Times*. Manchester: Manchester University Press.
Beardsworth, R. (2015). "From Moral to Political Responsibility in a Globalized Age." *Ethics & International Affairs*, 29(1): 71–92.
Braham, M. & Van Hees, M. (2011). "Responsibility Voids." *The Philosophical Quarterly*, 61(242): 6–15.
Connolly, W. E. (2002). *Identity, Difference: Democratic Negotiations of Political Paradox*. Expanded. Minneapolis, MN; London: University of Minnesota Press.
Erskine, T. (2001). "Assigning Responsibilities to Institutional Moral Agents: The Case of States and Quasi-States." *Ethics & International Affairs*, 15(2): 67–85.
Erskine, T. (2014). "Coalitions of the Willing and Responsibilities to Protect: Informal Associations, Enhanced Capacities, and Shared Moral Burdens." *Ethics & International Affairs*, 28(1): 115–145.
Erskine, T. (2018). "The Oxford Handbook of International Political Theory." In *Moral Responsibility—and Luck?—In International Politics*, Brown, C. & Eckersley, R., eds., Oxford: Oxford University Press, 130–142. http://oxfordhandbooks.com/view/10.1093/oxfordhb/9780198746928.001.0001/oxfordhb-9780198746928-e-8 (March 17, 2019).
Faye, E. (2009). *Heidegger, the Introduction of Nazism into Philosophy in Light of the Unpublished Seminars of 1933–1935*. New Haven: Yale University Press.
Frey, R. G. (1978). "Causal Responsibility and Contributory Causation." *Philosophy and Phenomenological Research*, 39(1): 106–119.
Goodhart, M. (2017). "Interpreting Responsibility Politically." *Journal of Political Philosophy*, 25(2): 173–195.
Gunnell, John G. 2014. *Social Inquiry after Wittgenstein & Kuhn: Leaving Everything as It Is*. New York: Columbia University Press.
Heidegger, M. (2013). *Being and Time*. 35. reprint. Malden: Blackwell.
Horton, J. (2010). *Political Obligation*. Basingstoke: Palgrave Macmillan.
International Commission on Intervention and State Sovereignty, Evans, G. J., Sahnoun, M., & International Development Research Centre (Canada), eds. (2001). *The Responsibility to Protect: Report of the International Commission on Intervention and State Sovereignty*. Ottawa: International Development Research Centre.
Jonas, H. (1979). *The Imperative of Responsibility: In Search of an Ethics for the Technological Age*. Chicago, IL: The University of Chicago Press.
Kagan, S. (1988). "Causation and Responsibility." *American Philosophical Quarterly*, 25(4): 293–302.
Lucas, J. R. (1993). *Responsibility*. Repr. Oxford: Clarendon Press.
Machiavelli, N. (1988). *The Prince*. Cambridge: Cambridge University Press.

Mapel, D. R. (1998). "Coerced Moral Agents? Individual Responsibility for Military Service." *The Journal of Political Philosophy*, 6(2): 171–189.
May, L. (1989). "Philosophers and Political Responsibility." *Social Research*, 56(4): 877–901.
May, L. & Strikwerda, R. (1994). "Men in Groups: Collective Responsibility for Rape." *Hypatia*, 9(2): 134–151.
Miller, D. (2007). *National Responsibility and Global Justice*. Oxford: Oxford University Press.
Miller, S. C. (2011). "A Feminist Account of Global Responsibility." *Social Theory and Practice*, 37(3): 391–412.
Molloy, S. (2020). "Realism and Reflexivity: Morgenthau, Academic Freedom and Dissent." *European Journal of International Relations*, 26(2): 321–343.
Morgenthau, H. J. (1949). "The Primacy of the National Interest." *The American Scholar*, 18(2): 207–212.
Morgenthau, H. J. (1968). "Bundy's Doctrine of War without End." *The New Republic*. https://newrepublic.com/article/92235/george-bundy-vietnam-war (June 4, 2019).
Olafson, F. A. (1998). *Heidegger and the Ground of Ethics: A Study of Mitsein*. Cambridge, UK; New York: Cambridge University Press.
Parekh, S. (2011). "Getting to the Root of Gender Inequality: Structural Injustice and Political Responsibility." *Hypatia*, 26(4): 672–689.
Rafshoon, E. G. (2001). "A Realist's Moral Opposition to War: Han J. Morgenthau and Vietnam." *Peace and Change*, 26(1): 55–77.
Rawls, J. (1999). *Theory of Justice*. Oxford: Oxford University Press.
Reiff, M. R. (2008). "Terrorism, Retribution, and Collective Responsibility." *Social Theory and Practice*, 34(2): 209–242.
Richman, R. J. (1969). "Responsibility and the Causation of Actions." *American Philosophical Quarterly*, 6(3): 186–197.
Rosen, G. (2004). "Skepticism about Moral Responsibility." *Philosophical Perspectives*, 18(1): 295–313.
Sartorio, C. (2004). "How to Be Responsible for Something without Causing It." *Philosophical Perspectives*, 18(1): 315–336.
Schiff, J. (2014). *Burdens of Political Responsibility: Narrative and the Cultivation of Responsiveness*. New York, NY: Cambridge University Press.
Simmons, A. J. (1980). *Moral Principles and Political Obligation*. Princeton: Princeton University Press.
Striblen, C. (2007). "Guilt, Shame, and Shared Responsibility." *Journal of Social Philosophy*, 38(3): 469–485.
Taylor, C. (1971). "Interpretation and the Sciences of Man." *The Review of Metaphysics*, 25(1): 3–51.
Walzer, M. (1970). *Obligations: Essays on Disobedience, War and Citizenship*. Cambridge: Harvard University Press.
Weber, M. (2004). In David, S. O., and Strong, T. B., eds., *The Vocation Lectures*. Indianapolis: Hackett Pub.
Williams, B. A. O. (1993). *Shame and Necessity*. Berkeley, CA: University of California Press.
Wittgenstein, L. (2009). *Philosophical Investigations*. Rev. 4th ed. Chichester; Malden, MA: Wiley-Blackwell.
Wolin, R. (2015). *Heidegger's Children*. Princeton University Press. http://public.eblib.com/choice/publicfullrecord.aspx?p=2028327 (June 4, 2019).
Young, I. M. (2013). *Responsibility for Justice*. New York, NY: Oxford University Press.

3
THE EMERGENCE OF RESPONSIBILITY AS A GLOBAL SCHEME OF GOVERNANCE

Tomer Shadmy

Introduction

After the "Cambridge Analytica" data scandal plagued Facebook and slashed its stock value, the social media giant's founder and CEO, Mark Zuckerberg, wrote in a statement posted to his Facebook page, "We have a responsibility to protect your data, and if we can't then we don't deserve to serve you". The next day, in a special speech to the press, he repeated the word "responsibility" no less than 17 times. A few months later during his testimony to the US Congress Zuckerberg have continued with this line of expressions and said: "Now we have to go through every part of our relationship with people and make sure we're taking a broad enough view of our responsibility" (Frenkel and Roose 2018). Zuckerberg's frequent use of the concept of responsibility is not coincidental and does not derive solely from public relations efforts (compare the chapter by Schlag in this volume). As I demonstrate in this chapter, the reuse of the term also implies an emergence of a new scheme of governance that regulates relations between powerful entities and individuals in the global arena. This scheme of governance provides a normative ground for regulation of transnational relationships and influences that traditional law fails to recognize. At the same time, I argue that this scheme has potential to transform the power held by transnational "superheroes", like the giant internet company, into political authority.

The repetition of the use of the term *responsibility* in the context of the trust crisis between the internet giant and the public, joins a growing use of the term in the public discourse and in various legal initiatives, standards, code of ethical conduct and frameworks, which impose social obligations on non-state actors and on foreign countries. One can mention in this context various Corporate Social Responsibility mechanisms, the Responsibility to Protect paradigm in international relations, and initiatives for Responsible Innovation in the technological field (see the respective chapters by Park, Karp, Claderaro, Schwarz, and Burai in this volume). There can be various explanations for the explosion in the use of the concept of responsibility in the current global arena, beyond the cynical claim that the use of the word "responsibility" can be a litmus test for detecting areas of irresponsibility – areas in which modern state legislation fails to regulate power relations and to protect human rights in the global arena. The current literature tends to understand this extensive use of the term *responsibility* as indicative of the voluntarily, non-binding character of some new regulative instruments (Howen 2005; Parker and Howe 2012) On this basis, human rights advocates criticize the responsibility-based norms and argue that their amorphous character enables powerful entities to evade real legal obligations (Meier 2007). In contrast to the tendency to interpret some of the new norms as non-legal norms, I argue here that the responsibility-based instruments actually present a shift into a new form of quasi-legal norms, which serves to regulate transnational relationships.

This chapter frames different instruments as part of a new responsibility-based jurisprudential paradigm. By combining the analytical study of the philosophical and conceptual roots of the concept of responsibility, together with tracing the social and political context of the contemporary rise of the concept, the chapter offers a unique characterization of an emerging regulative transnational paradigm. This perspective enables us to see in a new light current legal developments in the global transnational space and to discuss not only the new possibilities it opens but also the inherent limitations that come with the reliance on the concept of responsibility as a leading normative and regulatory concept.

According to the philosophical and jurisprudential distinctions between the terms *responsibility*, *duty* and *obligation* when they all describe a demand or a task one should perform, *duty* and *obligation* refer to a mission with fixed content and time duration, whereas responsibility is a dynamic, relational, ongoing mission involving broad discretion and authority (Feinberg, 1966; Hart 1968; Long 1999). While liberal law uses *duty* to describe the structure of the majority of individuals' and corporations' legal obligations, it uses *responsibility* to describe the special structure of role-based tasks and relationships: tasks carried out by parents for their children, by doctors for their patients, by executives for their shareholders, and by states for their citizens. Therefore, responsibility-based demands in liberal law are usually relational demands, which involve hierarchical power relations and offer the responsible party broad discretion in deciding how to act, while demanding from her a specific kind of effort. In these cases, the responsibility has dual functions: it constitutes authority and at the same time restricts and shapes the authority. Therefore, responsibility-based norms are not non-legal norms, but could be understood as the most fundamental legal norms: the norms that determine who has the authority over whom.

In the absence of a global "adult in-charge", so to speak, who determines concrete content of global obligations, their allocations, and their sanctions, the concept of responsibility, based upon dynamic discretions and constant dialogue, becomes slowly but surely a major player in the global legal drama. In the next sections, I argue that some new regulative instruments borrow the jurisprudential structure of future-oriented responsibility and use it (with some important adjustments) to establish transnational responsibilities. I demonstrate that this scheme of governance, established in order to bridge the global accountability gap and to diffuse human rights norms into transnational relations, could equip already powerful entities with a new form of power: political authority.

Responsibility-based regulatory instruments

It is fair to observe that in the last two decades, the term "responsibility" has become a key concept in many transnational legal documents and mechanisms. Many contemporary legal instruments seek to impose new kinds of human rights, social and environmental obligations on entities such as multinational corporations and foreign states. In this chapter, I will discuss samples of these instruments that include *The Guiding Principles on Business and Human Rights: Implementing the United Nations 'Protect, Respect and Remedy'* Framework (Ruggie 2011; "The Guiding Principles"); the *ISO Standards on Social Responsibility* (ISO 2010; "ISO Standard"); and *The Responsibility to Protect Doctrine*.

These instruments use the term *responsibility*, rather than equivalent terms, such as *duties*, to describe these obligations. *The Guiding Principles* describe demands imposed on states as "obligations", and demands made of corporations as "responsibilities". *The ISO Standard* defines the requirements made of an organization as "responsibilities". And *The Responsibility to Protect Doctrine* uses the concept of responsibility, instead of the parallel concepts of duties and obligations, to describe the requirements made of states (International Commission on Intervention, State Sovereignty and International Development Research Centre (Canada) 2001). The use of "responsibility" as a central term in these documents is both rhetorical and substantive. Rhetorically, the concept can frequently be found in the titles and text of normative documents. Fundamentally, these documents give a unique and far-reaching meaning to the concept.

The Responsibility to Protect Doctrine is one of the most interesting and extensive efforts to expand the requirements imposed on states, also beyond their borders (Hamilton 2006). It focuses on the responsibility to protect humans from war crimes. The doctrine determines that when a state fails to provide protection for its inhabitants, the responsibility transfers to the international community. Thus, the doctrine goes beyond the traditional model of human rights obligations, as it deals with a given state's responsibilities towards citizens of foreign states. Many scholars and practitioners have criticized the doctrine from various perspectives, but in a relatively short time the doctrine has become part of the international legal, political, and moral discourse.

Other main mechanisms which use the term *responsibility* as their organizing principle deal with the relationship between corporations and human rights. Published in 2011, *The Guiding Principles* are the UN's latest initiative regarding corporations and human rights, and set the current international policies in this field (Alston and Goodman 2013). *The ISO Standard* is one of the important soft-law mechanisms in this arena. This non-governmental standard, which was published in 2010, offers broad and detailed views on Corporate Social Responsibility, as well as its connection to human rights, and has significant influence on other norms in the field (Ward 2012). *The Responsibility to Protect Doctrine* and the Corporate Social Responsibility mechanisms are very different, at first glance. They developed in different contexts and they regulate different actors with different tools. However, I argue that both mechanisms use the term responsibility and approach it similarly.

The jurisprudential interpretations of the concept of responsibility

In order to analyze the way in which the new mechanisms use the term responsibility, we must first explore the interpretation of the concept in the existing legal and philosophical discourses. Responsibility is among the most important concepts in the modern legal, political, and moral vocabularies, and one of the most confusing concepts in these discourses. It can assume radically diverse meanings and serve different purposes in varied contexts (Lenk 2006). An element that is central to the confusion surrounding the concept of responsibility is its dual usage as both a retrospective, past-oriented concept and a prospective, future-oriented demand.

In the legal arena, the term *responsibility* is usually used retrospectively (Raz 2011). It identifies the subject of a legal proceeding—*the responsible party*. In this context responsibility is a combination between accountability, causation, and capability. To say one is legally responsible means that she should be accountable for a certain previous act or a state of affairs; that she is capable of being party to the proceedings (i.e., she is legally competent); and also that there is a causal relationship between the party's activity and the harm. In human rights law and in international law, the meaning of the term "responsibility" is similar. Responsibility is usually used as a secondary rule that determines who is obliged to obey the primary rule, the demand itself, and the allocation of the demands (Hart 1968). The primary rule is usually represented by the word *duty* or *obligation* (Crawford and James 2002; Nollkaemper and Jacobs 2013).

This traditional role of the term *responsibility* encourages many to understand its contemporary extensive use as part of ongoing discussions about the proper allocation of human rights obligations and the need to rethink international law's secondary rules (Bichta 2003). It is assumed that the term responsibility represents today the same stable meaning it used to represent in the legal vocabulary, i.e. a secondary rule, which determines the attribution of legal obligations (Eshleman 2014). Other scholars rely on the fact that usually *legal* demands themselves are conceptualized through the terms *duties* and *obligations*, so they argue that the goal of the instruments' reliance on the term *responsibility* is to declare clearly that while states' domestic human rights obligations are legal obligations, corporate demands and statist exterritorial demands are different and more voluntary. Therefore, some critical scholars claim that using the term *responsibility*, as opposed to *duty* or *obligation*, is sufficiently vague to grant powerful agents legitimacy without imposing real constraints upon them. They argue that the concept of responsibility is incorporated within those instruments for that reason (Sanders 2014).

By contrast, I argue that the role of the term *responsibility* in the novel instruments can be understood not only as a tool for changing the allocation of obligations or for cementing the non-legal charter of the demands but also as a way to establish a new form of obligations and a new model of power relations. The key source for this interpretation is hiding in covert references to the role of the concept of responsibility in the liberal jurisprudence literature.

In general, as we have observed, the concept of *responsibility* is used in the legal arena as a secondary rule to allocate obligations, while the concepts of *duty* and *obligation* are used as primarily rules to describe the content of the demand. Yet, the liberal jurisprudence tends to conceptualize certain special prospective demands and tasks as *responsibilities* rather than *duties* or *obligations*. In this context, the concepts *duty* and *responsibility* both describe a situation in which a command is imposed on an agent, thereby restricting the agent's freedom (Simmons 1981). While that similarity lies at the heart of each concept's meaning, there are also important differences between the terms when they both describe a task. While *duty* refers to a mission with fixed content and time duration, *responsibility* is a dynamic, ongoing mission based upon relationships and offering broad discretion to the responsible party.

Responsibilities that are like demands usually result from ongoing relationships with inherited power differences. This kind of demand is called "role responsibility" and usually represents the responsibility of officers, parents, or custodians. H.L.A. Hart claims that role responsibility is a general concept within which are "varieties of duties of care" (Hart 1968, 212–214). These "duties of care", taken together, establish a "sphere of responsibility". Simple "do" or "do-not-do" duties are not part of this sphere. Roderick Long names these commitments *prospective responsibility* and claims that this responsibility is a function of authority and that a duty to act is part of this authority (Long 1999, 124). Joel Feinberg claims that responsibility as a task is, like a duty, both a burden and a liability, but unlike a duty, it carries with it considerable discretion (Feinberg 1966). A goal is assigned, and the means of implementing that goal are left to the independent judgment of the responsible party. Duty, by contrast, demands a specific defined action.

One can also find similar distinctions between duties and responsibilities in philosophical literature. Robert Goodin argues that duties dictate actions, while responsibilities dictate outcomes (Goodin 1986). Being a duty-carrier entails performing a concrete action, while being a responsibility-carrier entails striving to achieve a result. Therefore, while a *duty* prescribes a specific and unchanging action, a *responsibility* allows for varied ways and means to achieve the task and grants discretion to the responsible party. Furthermore, while a *duty* can be located at a specific point on the timeline, a *responsibility* usually represents a long, continuous mission. Garrath Williams adds an additional layer to this distinctive understanding of responsibility, claiming that *responsibility* governs ongoing relationships (Williams 2008). It therefore has a prospective, dynamic, and ever-changing character. It deals with the need to live together with others as they are and as they constantly change and become. Hence, responsibility is a response to ever-changing, different, and contradictory normative demands.

Therefore, duty-based demands generate individual missions, in which the duty bearer is required to perform (or to refrain from performing) a fixed and predefined task. The behavior or responses of the potential beneficiaries do not influence the content of the *duty*. In contrast, responsibility-based demands establish a new future-oriented normative relationship between the responsible party and the beneficiary. It is not possible to perform well a responsibility-based demand, without taking into consideration and responding to the beneficiary's positions. Consider the differences between the *duty* of a dog-walker to take a dog for a walk every morning at 9 a.m. and give it one can of dogs' food, as opposed to the dog owner's *responsibility* for the dog's well-being: while the dog-walker should perform a fixed duty, which does not involve discretion or serious need to take into real consideration the dog's responses, the *responsibility* of the dog owner to the dog is a normative framework for the relationship between the two. Responsibility therefore includes duties, whereas duties do not necessarily involve responsibilities.

The liberal jurisprudence, in which individual autonomy is one of the central rationales, seeks to minimize areas of interpersonal dependency and subordination of one to the discretion of the other, and therefore, the use of responsibility-based demands is very rare (White 2017). Furthermore, liberal jurisprudence assumes that concrete do/do-not duties, which are byproducts of democratic legislative proceedings, are better suited to the rule-of-law principles of equality before the law and the law generality and certainty. Therefore, in very few cases do liberal jurisdictions prefer to shape demands as *responsibilities* rather than default to *duties* (Simmons 1981, 12), and only when there are very strong policy-oriented or moral justifications for the interpersonal subordination.

Conceptually, there is no impediment that responsibility will form the basis of the relationship between equal individuals. For example, mutual responsibility between equal citizens can serve as a justification for the welfare state. However, the difficulty of liberal law, which presupposes the existence of separate individuals and has difficulty recognizing dependency relationships, leads to the fact that law recognizes responsibility as a legal basis for relationships, mainly when one of the parties is in a distinctly inferior position. Therefore, the responsibility-based demands usually regulate hierarchical relationships like the relationships between parents and children, guardian and custodian, rulers and ruled, doctors and patients. The responsibility-based demands are thus described and at the same time establish at the normative-level hierarchical relationships of dependency—between the responsible party in power and the weaker subordinate beneficiary. In this sense, responsibility-based demand is actually the legal mechanism for the creation of authority, even if limited.

One more important characteristic of responsibility-based demands, in the liberal interpretation of the concept, is its circular nature. On the one hand, this interpretation presumes that some hierarchical relationships are given, inevitable, and necessary; thus, framing the demands as *responsibilities* could help to mitigate their risks. On the other hand, the responsibility-based demands do not just regulate existing relationships but also constitute another layer in the hierarchy, a normative layer, which is best described as *authority*. Therefore, the responsibility-based demands describe existing power relations but at the same time constitute them and give them normative and legal significance (Walker 2007). It is maybe justified with regard to certain relationships (such as parent–child relationships) that many believe that authority is an essential component in the relationships, but when this normative structure is adopted in other fields, as I will demonstrate later, it is important to consider the full implications of this imposition.

The *transnational responsibilities*, according to my interpretation, adopt the existing structure of responsibility-based demands, which usually represents the responsibility of states, officers, parents, or custodians, and use this structure to regulate transnational relationships. Designing the transnational demands as responsibilities rather than concrete duties has the potential to make some important contributions. In the absence of a global authority, it is allegedly difficult to impose concrete duties on transnational actors. In this state of affairs, responsibility-based demands could be a reasonable solution for creating transnational regulative frameworks. Such demands facilitate a response to the anomaly of modern-day transnational arenas. The transnational structure of economic relations has created legal lacunas and a legal "no-man's land". These are spaces and interactions that are either uncontrolled by any legal system or controlled by many parallel legal systems (Fischer-Lescano and Teubner 2019; Koskenniemi 2007a, b). Such legal construction enables powerful actors to evade regulations. The transnational responsibilities directly govern these relationships between powerful actors and the affected entities and make it possible to offer a normative response in these legal "no-man's land" spaces. Therefore, on the one hand, in the absence of a clear and structured global authority, the responsibility-based demands could be a reasonable solution. On the other hand, my analysis reveals that the responsibility-based framework is not just a framework of demands, but the seed of an undemocratic new form of legal authority—the authority of multinational corporations and foreign super powers. In the next section, I will elaborate on the unique jurisprudential features of the new responsibility-based norms.

The transnational responsibility scheme of governance

According to this analysis, several seemingly unrelated new legal instruments use a similar structure for conceptualizing transnational demands. Those demands aim to protect basic human interests and have special jurisprudential characteristics. Using the term *responsibility* to describe the demand shapes the demand as dynamic, prospective, and dialogical. These demands include negative and positive elements alike, and they have a preventive quality. Furthermore, these norms rely on special rules on the allocation of demands, in which the power to influence others entails responsibility. In this section, I will outline the main characteristics of the transnational responsibilities.

Prospective responsibility

Most of the demands that the examined instruments establish are prospective, future-oriented requirements that are of an ongoing nature. In contrast to concrete duties, which can be located at a certain point on a timeline, these requirements apply both at the present and in the future and refer to a long period of time during which the responsibility exists. The norms grant the responsible entities broad discretion to decide precisely how to act in order to achieve some required result or state of affairs. The responsible entities must act in order to achieve a certain goal, but it is up to them to decide in what way the goal will be achieved.

The text on which the *Responsibility to Protect Doctrine* is founded, namely, the 2001 report entitled *The Responsibility to Protect* (International Commission on Intervention, State Sovereignty and International Development Research Centre (Canada) 2001) explicitly mentions the purposes of changing the name of the practice of intervention from *Right of Humanitarian Intervention to Responsibility to Protect*. In one of the explanations, the authors of the report point out that the concept of *responsibility* allows for the conceptualization of ongoing demands—not just a response to a war crime but also the prevention of future war crimes and the rehabilitation of its victims after the act. In this regard, *responsibility* is understood as a general term that includes a variety of different duties having an ongoing quality: crime prevention, responses to the crime, and rehabilitation of its victims. The transition from *right* to *responsibility* is not very surprising, because in both the intervention is voluntary. *Responsibility* is indeed more demanding than *right*, but contrary to *duty*, it allows a margin of discretion for the intervening party. Protecting civilians from war crimes does not require the structure of responsibility and maybe could have been more effective if there was a clear legal duty. But the establishment of a *duty* would have required a clear definition of the intervention, of the conditions for it, and would have required the existence of a sovereign or consensus that would define the conditions and enforce that duty. However, the structure of responsibility offers a normative response for the protection of war crimes, but allows for a broad definition of the timeline of efforts to prevent them.

Expression of this idea can be found in Article 38 of the 2005 *World Summit Outcome Document*, which adopts the doctrine as a formal UN tool (UN General Assembly 2005). According to this article, the international community has a responsibility to make use of various measures, as it deems fit, to help protect foreign populations, even before a crisis erupts (measures that may include helping the state build the capability to protect itself from serious war crimes) and also after the crisis ends.

Dialogical responsibility

Responsibility, even in its etymologic origins, is first and foremost about response, about the need to communicate with the other. The dialogical dimension of the norms obliges the powerful side to listen to the weak side's voice and to act in accordance with this dialogue. The responsible party is obliged to stay in constant communication with the party that benefits from the exercise of responsibility and to hear their particular voices and needs. The dialogical dimension of the transnational responsibility-based norms, if interpreted and enforced properly, can help to reduce the risk of endowing already powerful actors with an even greater power—the power to design their own responsibility. However, this channel of involvement could enable the powerful actors to gain a new mode of legitimation for their acts and decisions, while their commitments are abstract and flexible, and there is no guarantee that the voices of those affected will truly be heard and influence decisions (compare the respective chapters in this volume by Kornprobst, Sienknecht, Bernstein, and Wiener).

The dialogical dimension of the responsibilities is expressed through requirements to hear the affected persons, in the emphasis on the dynamic character of the norms, and by requiring the responsible party to respond to the changing needs and situations of the affected people. In the field of business and human rights, one can find some important examples of the dialogical dimension (compare the respective chapters by Drubel and Karp in this volume). Engaging in direct dialogical relationships with the affected persons is almost the core of a corporation's responsibility, according to the Guiding Principles (Mares 2012). A corporation should base its human rights behavior upon consultation and continual meaningful dialogue with those whose rights may be affected (Guiding Principles 13-16). That dialogue should take place before any violation of human rights has occurred or before the corporation establishes relationships with an entity that can violate rights. Furthermore, the dialogue should occur during the violation of rights (if inflicted) and after the violation. The corporation has the discretion to decide whether to end relationships with potential human rights violators or to try to amend the violations, but it must be committed to the creation of dialogical communication channels with the victims.

Positive responsibility

The use of the concept of *responsibility*, instead of *duty*, frees the norms from some basic jurisprudential distinctions—among them the distinction between negative and positive duties.[1] The traditional liberal perspective, based on rights and their correlative duties, obliges states, corporations, and individuals to avoid causing harm to others (Sanders 2014, 4). Other duties that deviate from this are seen sometimes as an illegitimate intervention and coercion of free will. Individuals and corporations are expected to act to better their own condition, yet usually they are not required to bear positive duties toward others. Western law defines very clearly and sharply a few kinds of relationships that do involve positive legal duties; these are mainly relationships that are shaped by the concept of responsibility: for example, the relationship between a state and its citizens, between a corporation and its shareholders, and between parents and their children (Simmons 1981). The transnational responsibilities norms also include not only general negative commands—the duty to do no harm—but also general positive responsibility—the responsibility to do good, to help others.

According to the human rights responsibilities norms corporations and states are obliged in particular circumstances to help others and to better their conditions in regard to specific issues and not just to refrain from hurting them. The bearer of responsibility is required to assist a particular other, to contribute to his development and prosperity, and to better his condition by action or by omission.

The whole idea of the *Responsibility to Protect Doctrine* is to establish a positive demand on the part of the international community to assist populations that are in danger and not simply to avoid perpetrating war crimes. The doctrine's innovation is its establishment of a responsibility to help other countries to take actions in their territories. Article 38 of the 2005 *World Summit Outcome Document* concerning the *Responsibility to Protect Doctrine* formulates the international community's responsibility to make use of various measures to help protect foreign populations (UN General Assembly 2005).

The language of responsibility in its future-oriented meaning expresses and captures this notion of ex-ante prevention. The responsibility, in the examined norms, is sometimes understood as preemptive and proactive. These norms were designed as a behavioral guide that, in relation to certain risks, imposes the responsibility to act or to refrain from acting in order to prevent a substantial risk from being actualized. The norms presuppose that there are some risks that lead to enormous and unexpected consequences and that an actor should therefore do all he can to prevent them from happening (International Commission on Intervention, State Sovereignty and International Development Research Centre (Canada) 2001).

For example, in the 2005 UN General Assembly decision on the *Responsibility to Protect Doctrine*, the international community is requested to assist states so that they refrain from committing serious war crimes, even before a conflict arises (UN General Assembly 2005, para. 139). The 2014 Report of the UN Secretary-General states that preference should be given to prevention of serious war crimes, even when only the risk of a war crime exists (Ban 2014) The Report also lists indicators for the future risk of war crimes and states that these indicators can be grounds for intervention. This intervention can be encouraged through "Preventive Diplomacy", among other things. In addition, the 2013 Secretary-General's Report is wholly concerned with the ways in which states can prevent war crimes from the start in their territories (Ban 2013).

Positive responsibility can be traced also in the business and human rights mechanisms. For example, the primary rule regarding the content of the responsibility in the ISO standard establishes that responsibility is not limited to negative commitments—to avoid causing harms—but includes positive commitments to protect and assist others. For example, organizations should take "positive actions to provide for the protection and advancement of vulnerable groups", even if the organizations did not contribute to the group's vulnerability (ISO 2010, 6.3.10.3).

The principles for attributing responsibility

The responsibility-based mechanisms adopt a new principle for the attribution of responsibility that is different from modern rules. According to this alternative approach, responsibility is not attributed merely to direct causation of harms but also to other kinds of connections and relationships and in accordance with one entity's ability to influence and help others. Furthermore, there is no preliminary division of responsibilities in accordance with the entity's identity and function in society. Rather, the allocation of responsibility is determined according to the relationships between the entities and the capacity of every entity. Additionally, responsibility in this logic is not a zero-sum game, but a shared responsibility: the responsibility of one entity does not exempt others from their relative responsibility, depending on their degree of influence (Nollkaemper and Jacobs 2013).

These additional rationales could be described perfectly through the slogan of Stan Lee's *Spiderman*: "[W]ith great power there must also come great responsibility!" (Lee and Ditko 1962) According to this principle, responsibility is attributed to the powerful entity, not as punishment for being so powerful, but rather as an expression of the power itself and of the particular ability of that entity to influence others. This is, of course, not a novel legal idea. It can be seen as one of the guiding principles of international law after World War II. The assumption then was that states are the most powerful actors and thus also the most responsible ones. Furthermore, this principle is also the rationale behind many of the current legal doctrines in both private law and public law, among them the responsibility-based demands mentioned in the previous section.

Nowadays, however, this idea is taking on new meaning. In the absence of a constitutionally established, centralized global system to impose a global division of powers and duties, human rights responsibilities norms establish that within the existing division of power, privilege must carry with it responsibility. Therefore, power itself, or more precisely the ability to influence others significantly, together with a particular relationship or connection to those others, is the litmus test for assigning responsibility. In the global justice literature, there are lively debates on the need to redesign the allocation of responsibilities for global wrongs. In these debates, the principles of influence or as it is called there the capability principle, and the relational principle (the connectedness principle) are mentioned as criteria for determining responsibility, in addition to causing the damage itself (Barry 2003; Milman-Sivan and Lerner et al. 2013; Young 2008). A similar conceptualization of the relationships that should establish responsibility discusses in relation to states responsibility for human rights abuses outside their borders. The functional approach to extraterritorial human rights applicability determines responsibility in accordance with two key notions: the intensity of power relations or, alternatively, special legal relations—relations of power that put the state in a unique legal position to afford responsibility (Shany 2013).

Drawing on this literature and on empirical analysis of the responsibility-based mechanisms, I propose the "significant influence test" for assigning responsibility. It can accordingly be understood as a combination of two conditions: A is responsible for B if and only if A has the power to influence B, and A has a special connection to B (such as participating in a joint project, benefiting from harm somebody else caused B, or causing B harm).

As an example, the ISO standard sees a corporation's ability to influence others as a source of its responsibility. The standard explicitly mentions the "Sphere of Influence Principle".[2] This principle determines that an organization has responsibility when it has influence (ISO 2010, 2.12).

According to this principle, an organization is linked to other actors via networks of relationships through which it can influence actions and outcomes outside its own organizational boundaries, and its social responsibility extends also into this zone. Thus, the ability of an organization to influence others is the source of its demands. The principle is part of the standard definition of social responsibility, and it is also included in some Articles that provide, for example, that an organization should "act to improve its own [environmental] performance, as well as the performance of others within its sphere of influence" (ISO 2010, 6.5.2.1.).

One can also read the *Responsibility to Protect Doctrine* in light of this principle. According to this reading, when countries have connections to other countries and have the ability to influence and assist citizens from those countries who have suffered or are likely to suffer from serious war crimes, they have a responsibility to them. It is important to note that this is not the common interpretation of the norms. According to the traditional reading, the responsibility does not necessarily stem from relational sources, but rather from an overall equal cosmopolitan humanitarian duty. I suggest reading these norms differently: they can be understood to indicate that responsibility stems from "real-world" relationships with citizens of other countries and from the power to influence them. I argue that this reading is supported in light of the language of the text itself.

The annual reports of the UN Secretary-General on the doctrine determine that states in the same geographic area have priority in intervention in their neighbor's war crimes. This suggests that a closer relationship creates a more significant responsibility, and that cosmopolitan duties have relational aspects and sources. This responsibility does not stem from causing harms or contributing directly to the war crimes, but from the existence of relationships and influences. The norms, therefore, do not create new relationships between states, but only give normative meaning to the already existing relationships. The network of contacts and economic/diplomatic/environmental cross-border influences between states and other states' citizens existed before the establishment of the norms. The norms only give these connections normative significance—the responsibility to prevent, protect, and rehabilitate the victims of war crimes through these relationships.

Therefore, transnational human rights responsibilities norms, according to the suggested interpretation, do not impose responsibility merely due to harm that was caused in the past or due to a constitutional division of labor. Rather, the norms impose responsibility as a result of a relationship and the power to influence, creating a dependency of one entity on the other.

The proposed description of the jurisprudential structure of responsibility-based norms makes it possible to read the norms not necessarily as "non-legal" norms, but as a new form of legal norms that change the legal game. This structure is much more amorphous, dynamic, agent-relative, and relational than the duty structure. It changes in accordance with ongoing dialog and according to the agents involved; it contains both negative and positive demands and serves more as a preventive ex-anta guide than ex-post coercive tool. Together, all these components suggest a distinct understanding of transnational obligations that undermines common jurisprudential dichotomies.

The implications of designing transnational obligations as responsibilities

As I argued above *duties* and *obligations* are byproducts of pre-existing authority, which is expressed by the power of the state to impose concrete duties on its citizens. *Responsibilities*, by contrast, also constitute the authority. *Responsibility*, in this sense, renders authority as the conceptual meeting point between power and obligation. In the state system, the state itself has a *responsibility* to respect, protect, and fulfil human rights in its territory, while individuals and other entities have concrete obligations which the state clearly defines. These obligations stem from the already existing authority of states to impose rules, while states' responsibilities legitimize and establish this authority. The imaginary social contract and the real constitutive moments are the moment of birth of both elements—the state's powers and the state's responsibilities. They are established together, and together constitute the state's authority. Power, in this case, means responsibilities and vice versa. State responsibilities actually establish and certainly legitimize the power relations, the hierarchy.

The central implication of shaping the transnational demands through the language of responsibility is therefore the addition of another layer to the already existing transnational hierarchy—it creates the authority of multinational corporations and of powerful foreign states over human beings. Therefore, as I see it, the serious concern here is not that these demands are non-legal and could not be legal, as some human rights advocates argue. Consider that similar kinds of demands exist in the case of states and parents and that these demands are completely legal. Rather, the central concern here is the legal authority that those entities could gain through this jurisprudential structure. Furthermore, unlike state authority, the new form of the transnational authority is not accompanied by democracy.

In the case of the democratic state, the justification for the hierarchy, for the authority inherent in the state's responsibility, is the consent of the citizens, which is established in the social contract. The popular sovereignty model and democracy as an institution of self-rule justify the authoritarian statutes of the state.[3] Additionally, in states there are many public institutions and legal arrangements that guarantee and construct the responsibility. Even in the absence of powerful international mechanisms for supervision of the state's responsibility, the running assumption is that state democratic institutions, among them the legal system and the democratic elections, could supervise the state from within. With regard to multinational corporations and foreign states, we do not have even justification for the authority, and we do not have any legal and democratic institutional arrangements that guarantee and construct those responsibilities. Imposing responsibility, which as I have shown here means authority, without democracy could lead to restoration of colonial-like and even feudal-like relationships[4], in which some powerful entities take responsibility for the wellbeing of some individuals. But they do so without treating these individuals as full sovereign subjects. Therefore, this form of responsibility could grant the already powerful entities normative and new political powers over humans and could allow unjust relationships of interdependency and subordination to obtain legitimacy.

The absence of institutions and arrangements of democratic "self-rule", which regulate the transnational responsibility, have not just substantive implications but also functional implications. The unique structure of the norms raises difficult questions concerning their enforcement and their institutional structure. Who will enforce the norms? Who will monitor whether the responsible entity is performing its task? How can one determine whether the responsible entity has acted correctly, if it has such broad discretion? Do the norms set a result-based or behavior-based standard of review? It is impossible to locate the answers to these questions in the norms. Powerful actors may take advantage of the open structure of the norms and use them to gain legitimacy without taking meaningful action to further their responsibility. In the absence of a concrete prescribed rule, the broad discretion of the responsible actor could lead to situations in which similar circumstances yield different results. Formal equality is challenged in this ad hoc regime, as well as the expectations of the actors.

Putting the spotlight on these jurisprudential features of responsibility-based norms demonstrates the far-reaching implications of shaping human rights demands through the term responsibility. While framing human rights as responsibilities could oblige such entities as corporations to really take into consideration individuals' basic interests, it could also simultaneously establish non-democratic authoritarian relations between the transnational superpowers and humans. Whereas in the cases of parent–child and state–citizen relations the authority is well justified and protected by democratic supervisions (at least "in books"), the new transnational superheroes' authority lacks justification and democratic supervisions.

The concerns mentioned above are very serious, but the transnational human rights responsibilities, if interpreted and developed properly, could also provide opportunities to rethink basic concepts and adjust them to current needs. The suggested framework allows responsibility-based moral perceptions to be embedded into human rights theories. The open structure of the norms and its dialogical dimension could be interpreted in light of some "post-liberal" theories of morality that see moral norms as a byproduct of social and bilateral engagement and dialogue, rather than as predetermined, unchangeable rules (Tronto 1998). In a different but not entirely separate vein, the philosopher Emanuel Levinas sees morality not as a matrix of predefined and abstract rules but as an endless engagement in a set of responsibilities to a particular other, whose particular face and needs are disposable (Levinas 1981). Relying on such contributions, the dialogical dimension of the norms could be understood as signposts for adjusting the legal discourse to a "brave new world" in which morality and its manifestation in law are composed not just of universal rules but also of mutual channels of dialogue, communication, and care.

Additionally, the norms represent an opportunity to reconnect human rights with democracy at the global level. The dialogical demand that the framework identifies can offer a new channel for deliberation and an opportunity to involve in the decision-making process those who will be affected by decisions. It could recreate the global missing link between human rights and political participation and serve as a new channel of democratic participation. The task here is to develop methods and institutions that will enable substantive and equal dialogue, obliging the powerful actors to really consider, respond to, and act in accordance with the affected persons' voice.[5]

Lastly, many human rights abuses and social problems today result from complex relations between agents and structures, which in the end cause severe harm to an overwhelming number of victims around the world. Often, there is no one entity with exclusive control over those harms and their possible remedies (Ashford 2006). In such circumstances, it is hard to use the traditional human rights instruments to find and sue guilty parties. Responsibility-based norms, however, do not pinpoint one responsible actor, but instead enable the division of responsibility among many appropriate actors, illuminating a variety of connections to the harms inflicted and thus also providing an array of possible solutions to alleviate the situation, rectify the injustice, or repair the damage. Thus, responsibility-based norms actually make it possible for remedial responsibilities to be shared by an assortment of parties. This is a point of departure for rethinking the problem of complicity and the complex causational relationships that characterize today's world (Kutz 2007).

Conclusion

The development of transnational responsibilities can be viewed as a result of neoliberal logic (Shamir 2008) and at the same time as a result of its critique and subsequent attempt to overcome it. On the one hand, this form of demands enables the most powerful economic global entities to evade "hard" domestic and international law and to gain new modes of authority. On the other hand, responsibility-based norms make it possible to frame human rights and social obligations in a novel way and provide a normative ground for regulation of transnational relationships and influences that traditional human rights law fails to recognize. Therefore, transnational responsibilities norms are in fact a new arena in the struggle for meaning and for determining the normative significance of cross-border relations.

This new arena in the struggle for meaning invites a theoretical challenge and begs the following questions: Is the liberal connection between responsibility and authority inevitable? Could responsibility be adopted as a general standard of behavior, circumventing the legitimization and prompting of the hierarchal existing power relations? Can we imagine a world in which we are responsible to others for the environment and not just for ourselves? These are all open theoretical questions that deserve further elaboration.

This study identifies an initial linguistic change, which has not yet stabilized or grown institutional mechanisms that support and enable it. But, law is not philosophy. The institutional aspects stand at the heart of the legal arena. Therefore, future studies should investigate and develop the institutionalization of the norms through court systems and other institutional practices that support this unique form of human rights obligations.

Notes

1 One significant difference between the concept of *duty* and the concept of *responsibility* lies in the particular way in which the history of ideas has evolved. The liberal tradition connected the concept of *duty*, unlike *responsibility*, to the concept of rights. All rights, according to this understanding, have correlative duties. This tradition attached supplementary distinctions to the rights/duty connection: the distinction between duties of justice and duties of benevolence; and the distinction between negative and positive duties. Perfect negative duties of justice are the main justification for coercion in liberal thinking; imperfect positive duties of benevolence are hardly mentioned in liberal law. In regard to the connection between rights and duties, consider Emmanuel Kant and Joseph Raz who presumed that a right is the justification for a perfect duty (See Feinberg 2014; Raz 1984; Hohfeld 1913). For the complex historical relationships between rights and duties see Samuel Moyn (2016). For the distinction between duties of justice and duties of benevolence, and the distinction between negative and positive duties see, Richard B. Brandt (1959) and Goodin (1986).
2 The concept of sphere of influence was introduced into the discourse by the United Nations Global Compact, which calls on signatory companies to embrace, support and enact the Compact's ten principles *"within their sphere of influence."* The United Nations Global Compac is available at www.unglobalcompact.org/. The ISO standard mentioned the principle despite heavy external pressures to remove this principle when last-minute drafting changes were adopted. Ruggie tried to prevent the inclusion of the sphere of influence principle in the ISO standard. Despite this opposition, finally the standard adopted a limited version of the principle. For the debate on the principle see Stefan Wood (2011).
3 See Locke (1967), Beran (2019), Hart (1955). For a critique of the consent principle see Simmons (1981). For other justifications for political obligation see, for instance, the "Fair play" argument: Hart (1955) and Rawls (1964). The natural duty of justice argument is expanded in Rawls (1971); and the sovereign's expertise argument in Raz (1984).
4 For a future-oriented historical perspective on the way that the idea of responsibility can be used to legitimize colonialism and can be deployed to justify expansionism in the name of humanitarianism, as it has done for hundreds of years, see Fitzmaurice (2015). For the way that corporate governance mechanisms could lead to colonialism, see Banerjee (2003).
5 On the need to establish new channels of discussions and justifications see Forst (2014), Fraser (2009), Fung (2013).

References

Alston, P., and Goodman, R. (2013). *International Human Rights*. Oxford: Oxford University Press.
Ashford, E. (2006). "The Inadequacy of Our Traditional Conception of the Duties Imposed by Human Rights." *Canadian Journal of Law & Jurisprudence*, 19(2): 217–235.
Banerjee, S. B. (2003). "The Practice of Stakeholder Colonialism: National Interest and Colonial Discourses in the Management of Indigenous Stakeholders." In Prasad, A., ed., *Postcolonial Theory and Organizational Analysis*: 255–275. Basingstoke and New York: Palgrave.
Barry, C. (2003). "Global Justice: Aims, Arrangements, and Responsibilities." In Erskine, T., ed., *Can Institutions Have Responsibilities?*: 218–237. Basingstoke: Palgrave Macmillan.

Ban, Ki-Moon. (2013). "*Responsibility to Protect: State Responsibility and Prevention.*" Report of the Secretary General. UN Doc. A/67/929-S/2013/399.
Ban, Ki-Moon. (2014). "*Fulfilling our Collective Responsibility: International Assistance and the Responsibility to Protect*" Report of the Secretary General. UNGA 68th Session. https://digitallibrary.un.org/record/754122; https://digitallibrary.un.org/record/775455
Beran, H. (2019). *The Consent Theory of Political Obligation*. London: Routledge.
Bichta, C. (2003). *Corporate Social Responsibility: A Role in Government Policy and Regulation?* University of Bath School of Management: Centre for the study of Regulated Industries.
Brandt, R. B. (1959). *Ethical Theory the Problems of Normative and Critical Ethics*. Englewood Cliff NJ: Prentice Hall.
Crawford, J., and James, C. (2002). *The International Law Commission's Articles on State Responsibility: Introduction, Text and Commentaries*. Cambridge: Cambridge University Press.
Eshleman, A. (2014). *Moral Responsibility*. Philosophy Faculty Publications and Presentations. http://pilotscholars.up.edu/phl_facpubs/1
Feinberg, J. (1966). "Duties, Rights, and Claims." *American Philosophical Quarterly*, 3(2): 137–144.
Feinberg, J. (2014). *Rights, Justice, and the Bounds of Liberty: Essays in Social Philosophy*. Princeton: Princeton University Press.
Fischer-Lescano, A., and Teubner, G. (2019). Regime-Collisions: The Vein Search for Legal Unity in the Fragmentation of Global Law. In Teubner, G., ed., *Critical Theory and Legal Autopoiesis*. Manchester: Manchester University Press.
Fraser, N. (2009). *Scales of Justice: Reimagining Political Space in a Globalizing World*. New York: Columbia University Press.
Fitzmaurice, A. (2015). "Sovereign Trusteeship and Empire." *Theoretical Inquiries in Law*, 16(2): 447–472.
Forst, R. (2014). *Justice, Democracy and the Right to Justification: Rainer Forst in Dialogue*. London: Bloomsbury.
Frenkel, S., and Roose, K. (2018). "Zuckerberg, Facing Facebook's Worst Crisis Yet." *New York Times*. https://www.nytimes.com/2018/03/21/technology/facebook-zuckerberg-data-privacy.html
Fung, A. (2013). "The Principle of Affected Interests: An Interpretation and Defense." In Nagel, J., and Smith, R., eds., *Representation: Elections and Beyond*: 236–268. Philadelphia: University of Philadelphia Press.
Goodin, R. E. (1986). "Responsibilities." *The Philosophical Quarterly*, 36(142): 50–56.
Hamilton, R. J. (2006). "The Responsibility to Protect: From Document to Doctrine – But What of Implementation?" *Harvard Human Rights Law Journal*, 19: 289–297.
Hart, H. L. A. (1955). "Are There any Natural Rights?" *The Philosophical Review*, 64(2): 175–191.
Hart, H. L. A. (1968). *Punishment and Responsibility: Essays in the Philosophy of Law*. Oxford: Oxford University Press.
Hohfeld, W. N. (1913). "Some Fundamental Legal Conceptions as Applied in Judicial Reasoning." *Yale Law Journal*, 23: 16–58.
Howen, N. (2005). "'Voluntary or Mandatory: That is (Not) the Question'. A Comment." *Zeitschrift für Wirtschafts-und Unternehmensethik*, 6(3): 321–323.
International Commission on Intervention, State Sovereignty and International Development Research Centre (Canada). 2001. *The Responsibility to Protect: Report of the International Commission on Intervention and State Sovereignty*. https://undocs.org/pdf?symbol=en/a/57/303
ISO. (2010). *Guidance on Social Responsibility*. ISO 26000:2010(E). https://www.iso.org/standard/42546.html
Koskenniemi, M. (2007a). "Formalism, Fragmentation and Freedom: Kantian Themes in Today's International Law." *Revista Internacional Pensamiento Politico*, 2: 209–226.
Koskenniemi, M. (2007b). "The Fate of Public International Law: between Technique and Politics." *The Modern Law Review*, 70(1): 1–30.
Kutz, C. (2007). *Complicity: Ethics and Law for a Collective Age*. Cambridge: Cambridge University Press.
Lee, S., and Ditko, S. (1962). *Spiderman*. New York: Marvel Comics.
Lenk, H. (2006). "What is Responsibility?" *Philosophy Now*, (56): 29–32.
Levinas, E. (1981). *Otherwise Than Being or Beyond Essence*. Dordrecht: Springer.
Locke, J. (1967). *Locke: Two Treatises of Government*. Cambridge: Cambridge University Press.
Long, R. T. (1999). "The Irrelevance of Responsibility." *Social Philosophy and Policy*, 16(2): 118–145.
Mares, R., ed. (2012). *The UN Guiding Principles on Business and Human Rights*. Leiden: Brill.
Meier, B. M. (2007). "Advancing Health Rights in a Globalized World: Responding to Globalization Through a Collective Human Right to Public Health." *The Journal of Law, Medicine & Ethics*, 35(4): 545–555.

Milman-Sivan, F., Lerner, H., and Dahan, Y. (2013). "Labor Rights, Associate Duties, and Transnational Production Chains." *Cornell Human Rights Review*, Available online. https://digitalcommons.ilr.cornell.edu/chrr/60/.

Moyn, S. (2016). Rights vs. Duties. *Boston Review*, Available online. http://bostonreview.net/books-ideas/samuel-moyn-rights-duties.

Nollkaemper, A., and Jacobs, D. (2013). "Shared Responsibility in International Law: A Conceptual Framework." *Michigan Journal of International Law*, 34(2): 359–438.

Parker, C. and Howe, J. (2012). "Ruggie's diplomatic project and its missing regulatory infrastructure." In Mares, R., ed., *The UN Guiding Principles on Business and Human Rights*: 273–301. Leiden: Brill.

Rawls, J. (1964). "Legal Obligation and the Duty of Fair Play." In Hook, S., ed., *Law and Philosophy*: 3–18. New York: New York University Press.

Rawls, J. (1971). *A Theory of Justice*. Harvard, MA: Bellknap.

Raz, J. (1984). "Hart on Moral Rights and Legal Duties." *Oxford Journal of Legal Studies*, 4(1): 123–131.

Raz, J. (2011). *From Normativity to Responsibility*. Oxford: Oxford University Press.

Ruggie, J. (2011). "Report of the Special Representative of the Secretary-General on the Issue of Human Rights and Transnational Corporations and Other Business Enterprises: Guiding Principles on Business and Human Rights: Implementing the United Nations 'Protect, Respect and Remedy' Framework." *Netherlands Quarterly of Human Rights*, 29(2): 224–253.

Sanders, A. (2014). "The Impact of the 'Ruggie Framework' and the United Nations Guiding Principles on Business and Human Rights on Transnational Human Rights Litigation." In Martin, J., and Bravo, K. E., eds., *The Business and Human Rights Landscape: Moving Forward, Looking Back*. Cambridge: Cambridge University Press.

Shamir, R. (2008). "The Age of Responsibilization: On Market-Embedded Morality." *Economy and Society*, 37(1): 1–19.

Shany, Y. (2013). "Taking Universality Seriously: A Functional Approach to Extraterritoriality in International Human Rights Law." *Law & Ethics of Human Rights*, 7(1): 47–71.

Simmons, A. J. (1981). *Moral Principles and Political Obligations*. Princeton: Princeton University Press.

Tronto, J. C. (1998). "An Ethic of Care." *Generations: Journal of the American Society on Aging*, 22(3): 15–20.

UN General Assembly (2005). 2005 World Summit Outcome. United Nations, Report A/60/L, 1. Walker, M. U. (2007). *Moral Understandings: A feminist Study in Ethics*. Oxford: Oxford University Press.

Ward, H. (2012). *ISO 26000 and Global Governance for Sustainable Development*. London: International Institute for Environment and Development.

White, M. D. (2017). *The Decline of the Individual: Reconciling Autonomy with Community*. London: Palgrave.

Williams, G. (2008). "Responsibility as a virtue." *Ethical Theory and Moral Practice*, 11(4): 455–470.

Wood, S. (2011), "The Meaning of 'Sphere of Influence' in ISO 26000" In Henriques, A., ed., *Understanding ISO 26000: A Practical Approach to Social Responsibility*: 115–130. London: British Standards Institution.

Young, I. M. (2008). "Responsibility and Global Justice: A Social Connection Model." In Scherrer, A.G., and Palazzo, G., eds., *Handbook of Research on Global Corporate Citizenship*: 137–165. Cheltenham: Edward Elgar.

4
HUMAN RIGHTS APPROACH(ES) TO RESPONSIBILITY

Brooke Ackerly

Introduction

What does it mean to take responsibility for human rights if what these rights are, who has the right to make rights claims, and what responsibility for human rights requires are always philosophically and politically contested? In this essay, I disaggregate two broad approaches to human rights and their corresponding notions of responsibility. The first focuses on the philosophical reasons for human rights and for responsibility for human rights. The second focuses on the political challenges to human rights and responsibility for human rights. Thus, these are in fact two distinguishable human rights approaches to responsibility based on two complementary constellations of concepts. Like the Little Dipper and the Big Dipper which seem to pour into each other in the night sky, they are two complementary constellations of concepts that though distinct can be mutually reinforcing. I will explain these approaches and conclude by arguing that the second is essential for the notion of human rights to be meaningful at all. This argument comes with a caution that the first can be used to undermine the second as well as optimism that it can and has been used to complement the second. Moreover, we can see in international conventions, advocacy, and the struggles of rights activists that this is the theory of human rights and responsibility that those in struggle deploy.

Generally, a theory of human rights entails the following key elements. First, the *subject*; a human rights theory specifies to whom it applies. It needs to specify whether rights are born by individuals, groups, and/or a legal person like a corporation. It needs to clarify whether this specification of the subject is true everywhere and always, that is, culturally and temporally universal. Second, the *substance*; a human rights theory of responsibility specifies what is meant by a right: are these pieces of a whole (indivisible) or can a right be recognized while others violated? Are all rights known now for always or might we recognize new rights as we become aware of them? Third, their *legitimacy*; a theory identifies the source of the moral and political legitimacy of rights, sometimes called the "basis" or "justification" of rights. Fourth, the *responsibility*; a theory clarifies the nature of responsibility for human rights.

This chapter provides both an exposition of two ways of framing a human rights approach to responsibility and an argument about the relationship of these two theories in theory and practice. As an exposition, it provides a basic account of these four elements for two approaches to human rights and responsibility: the entitlement and the enjoyment approaches. As an argument it provides an important distinction between them and an argument for why the entitlement approach, unmodified by the enjoyment approach, is a view of human rights that potentially undermines the legitimacy of human rights.

To foreshadow the argument, if the source of the legitimacy of human rights is the basis or justification of rights, then the philosophical, moral, and political arguments about the basis and justification of human rights, such as those waged in the name of cultural difference, can be used to undermine the political legitimacy of rights. However, if as in the enjoyment approach, the political legitimacy of human rights provides the basis and justification for taking responsibility for human rights, then people can use human rights to argue that they are the kind of people who get to make rights claims and that their claims are legitimate claims. This does not alleviate the need for political struggle for rights recognition, but it shifts attention to where it needs to be: the politics of struggle (compare also the respective chapters by Baron, Wiener, Karp, and Dellavalle in this volume).

Entitlement and enjoyment approaches to human rights[1]

As I began, generically, a theory of human rights and responsibility needs to provide an account of the subject, substance, legitimacy, and responsibility of and for human rights. Each of the basic approaches interprets these differently and further, within each approach, among the adherents to the general approach, there is variability in how they specify the subject, substance, legitimacy, and responsibility of and for human rights. In this section, I set out the two broad approaches and some of the variations within each.

Rights as entitlements

The entitlement approach to human rights and responsibility focuses on the moral reasons for why we have responsibility for human rights. This approach is common in legal philosophy (Buchanan 2013), analytic philosophy (Talbott 2005), and ideal moral theory. It is used by those who seek to assign responsibility for human rights, as well as by those who seek to delimit responsibilities for human rights. In this view, human rights are entitlements with corresponding responsibilities which are duties.

The entitlement approach entails notions of rights and duties that are complementary. As Dunne and Wheeler set it out:

> Historically, the idea of rights has embodied two foundational claims. First, that there is an identifiable subject who has entitlements; and secondly, that to possess a right presupposes the existence of a duty-bearer against whom the right is claimed. (1999, 3)

Ian Shapiro clarifies the nature of the entitlement:

> [a] claim about rights generally involves a fourfold assertion about the *subject* of entitlement, the *substance* of entitlement, the *basis* for entitlement, and the *purpose* of entitlement.
> *(Shapiro 1986, 14)*

and associates it with liberal theory. To understand what this means for responsibility, we might refer to R. J. Vincent's framing:

> A right in this sense can be thought of as consisting of five main elements: a right-holder (the subject of a right) has a claim to some substance (the object of a right), which he or she might assert, or demand, or enjoy, or enforce (exercising a right) against some individual or group (the bearer of the correlative duty), citing in support of his or her claim some particular ground (the justification of a right). (1986, 8)[2]

Although this account may seem decisive in this schematic framing, each of the pieces of the definition can be nuanced and provide rich terrain for debate. Within the entitlement approach, people may debate whether the basis of human rights are universal or relative (Donnelly 1985; Donnelly 2007; Donnelly 2008; Goodhart 2008). They may contest whether the justification for responsibility is liability or social connectedness (Adler 2007; Caney 2010; Bukovansky et al. 2012; Eckersley 2016; Feinberg and Gross 1975; Young 2006).

In short, in the entitlement approach: the subject is a rights bearer who may be individual, group, or corporate individual;[3] the substance of rights are indivisible and interrelated rights, but that nonetheless may be enumerated; the basis of legitimacy must be determined (bases may include the divinity within each person,[4] human rationality, birth right regardless of citizenship, international law, international practice (Ackerly 2017; Buchanan 2013)); and responsibility is based on being tied to the entitlement or its violation through the liability model of responsibility familiar in legal and moral philosophy[5] or the social connectedness model, developed by feminists (Tronto 1993; Young 2006; Young 2010). In order to provide unambiguous guidance on what human rights entitlements require of duty-bearers both the liability and social connectedness models require very specific information. In this sense, the entitlement approach can be morally rigorous and yet politically conservative because it provides political exceptions everywhere there is moral contestation.

Rights as enjoyment

The enjoyment approach to human rights and responsibility focuses on the political reasons for responsibility for human rights. It is a political theory for revealing and challenging the power politics that undermine or block rights enjoyment for some and therefore all. It is a human rights theory of responsibility in contexts of political contestation even when that contestation is attributed to moral difference (cf. Ackerly 2008; Donnelly 2008; Goodhart 2008).

What is the difference between the entitlement-centered view of*** rights and the enjoyment-centered view of rights? It is the difference between having an ice cream cone and eating it. If you don't actually eat the ice cream, all you have is a mess on your hand. It is in the eating of the ice cream, it is in the exercise of your rights, that the ice cream and the rights attain their intended purpose.

The enjoyment approach to human rights is common among critical, feminist, and decolonial theorists, grassroots human rights activists, the negotiators of the Universal Declaration of Human Rights (Goodhart 2013; Liu 2014; Maritain 1949), many participants in the negotiations of the subsequent Conventions and the United Nations meetings of the 1990s (Chen 1995; Friedman 2003; Merry 2006), and those philanthropists and states who integrate human rights into their development aid plans. The enjoyment approach is articulated in the Preamble of the Universal Declaration of Human rights which I cite at length (emphasis added):

> ...*recognition* of the inherent dignity and of the equal and inalienable rights of all members of the human family is the foundation of freedom, justice and peace in the world, ...
>
> *(United Nations 1948, Preamble)*

Note it is the *recognition* of human dignity and of the human family and not the *basis* of that recognition that is the foundation of the Declaration.

> …disregard and contempt for human rights have resulted in barbarous acts which have outraged the conscience of mankind, and the advent of a world in which human beings shall *enjoy* freedom of speech and belief and freedom from fear and want has been proclaimed as the highest aspiration of the common people, …

Note the Declaration declares the *enjoyment* of rights is the "highest aspiration of the common people."

> …it is essential, if man is not to be compelled to have recourse, as a last resort, to rebellion against tyranny and oppression, that human rights should be protected by the rule of law,

Note the intent is for the rule of law within states to secure rights so that people do not need to rebel against oppression.

> … it is essential to promote the development of friendly relations between nations,

Rights are expected to keep peace between states as well. This is a political consequence of rights enjoyment.

> … the peoples of the United Nations have in the Charter reaffirmed *their faith in fundamental human rights, in the dignity and worth of the human person and in the equal rights of men and women* and have determined to promote social progress and better standards of life in larger freedom,

There is no agreement as to the basis of the nations' affirming their faith in rights dignity and equality.

> … Member States have pledged themselves to achieve, in co-operation with the United Nations, the promotion of *universal respect for and observance of* human rights and fundamental freedoms,

Again, the commitment is to respect and observance of rights on a *common* not on a universal basis for that respect and observance.

> … a *common understanding* of these rights and freedoms is of the greatest importance for the full *realization* of this pledge,

Finally, they agree that they need a common understanding of the realization of rights not merely a common commitment to them in the abstract. In sum, in the Preamble, the Nations take political responsibility for human rights without agreeing on the foundational basis of human rights. The UDHR does articulate an entitlement theory of human rights and responsibility. Instead, the Nations agreeing to the UDHR take up their common political responsibilities by committing to fostering the structural conditions of human rights enjoyment within nations and among nations (see also Ackerly 2008; 2011).

To this end, these nations and practitioners of the enjoyment approach more generally center not only the harms of rights violations but also the political, social, and economic conditions that may cause as well as obfuscate those harms. Politically, they focus on making visible human rights violations and on understanding the contexts that contribute to or impede their being lived out in our lives. The Convention on the Rights of Persons with Disabilities (CRPD), makes explicit the multiple forces – political, social, and economic – that determine rights enjoyment.

> The purpose of the present Convention is to *promote, protect and ensure the full and equal enjoyment* of all human rights and fundamental freedoms by all persons with disabilities, and to promote respect for their inherent dignity.
>
> Persons with disabilities include those who have long-term physical, mental, intellectual or sensory impairments which **in interaction with various barriers** may hinder their full and effective participation in society on an equal basis with others.
>
> *(Article 1; emphasis added)*

Historically, each Convention has been used to clarify and specify the political, social, and economic conditions necessary for rights enjoyment for individuals,[6] migrant workers,[7] women,[8] children,[9] Indigenous people,[10] and persons with disabilities[11] and to delegitimize barriers including the racialized colonial legacies[12] to addressing these.

In short, the enjoyment approach to the subject of rights worries when political claims to the universal application of a law inhibits the enjoyment of rights for all by not attending to the differences among people (e.g. Charlesworth and Chinkin 1993). It worries about the exclusion of some from the benefits of group membership when rights are secure through membership, whether broadly as in citizenship rights or more narrowly as in group rights within multicultural states. As with the entitlement approach, the substance of rights are indivisible and interrelated rights; yet, their enumeration is insufficient for their full recognition, hence the further clarifications of formal and informal institutional requirements within the Conventions and the Platforms for Action of the UN meetings (e.g. United Nations 1995). The basis of the *legitimacy* of human rights is the political agreement that these are the rights necessary for human life, peace within states, and peace among states; the enjoyment of rights may not be curtailed except with their exercise infringes on those of others (UDHR Article 29 (2)). However, the qualifier of UDHR Article 29(2) is worrisome for those attentive to the politics of rights enjoyment:

> (2) In the exercise of his rights and freedoms, everyone shall be subject only to such limitations as are determined by law solely for the purpose of securing due recognition and respect for the rights and freedoms of others and *of meeting the just requirements of morality, public order and the general welfare in a democratic society*. (emphasis added)

This last clause might be interpreted as giving democratic societies license to oppress the rights enjoyment of those who wish to exercise their freedom of expression to protest legal constraints under the guise of "*morality, public order and the general welfare.*" In the entitlement approach, responsibility is not based on either the liability or the social connectedness model, though it welcomes those who take responsibility for human rights conditions under either of those normative auspices. Rather, the enjoyment approach takes the commitment to human rights as a call to attend to their violation and their potential violation even when we are not fully aware of their threat or of all of the dimensions of the sources of that threat (Ackerly 2018, Chapters 2 and 3).

This approach has answers to the puzzles of the entitlement approach, but it has its own nuances and debates. If enjoyment requires transformative change in political, social, and economic conditions and barriers, some of which are as deeply rooted as racism and misogyny, can such change come at the hands of American foreign policy, donor-funded activities more broadly, or political movements? (Liu 2014; Moyn 2010; Incite! Women of Color Against Violence 2007) This approach does not evade or answer as much as signal a different way of answering the question of whether notions of rights are laden with "western," "secular," "religious," or otherwise culturally particular values (Chan 1997; Dalai Lama 1999; Dallmayr 2002; de Bary 1998; Englehart 2000; Johnson 2001). Third, the enjoyment approach allows for an ever expanding and transforming notion of rights such that the idea may seem meaningless or to serve particular interests?

Differences and debates

While the entitlement approach reflects in its very account that there has been moral disagreement with political import about each element of its definition, the enjoyment approach focuses on the political contestation at stake in such competing moral claims. What does it mean to identify a subject who is entitled to human rights? For some[13] the foundation of such identification is its *basis* in human nature or human dignity.[14] This can have a secular or religious *justification*[15] and has been used to justify different treatment by group and struggles for justice against differences in status. The discussion about the moral basis of human rights is well suited to the entitlement framing; the debate about the justification calls for the enjoyment account of human rights. The Universal Declaration of Human Rights provides a politically negotiated list, not a list based on a moral basis. As Jacques Maritain reports, at a UNESCO meeting, "someone expressed astonishment that certain champions of violently opposed ideologies had agreed on a list of those rights. 'Yes', they said, 'we agree about the rights *but on condition that no one ask us why.*' That 'why' is were argument begins" (emphasis in original) (Maritain 1949, I).

From the enjoyment approach, the focus is less on assigning *responsibility* for human rights violations and more on taking responsibility for the political, social, and economic conditions that enable them to happen and persist. The advantage of this approach is that even if all are not agreed on the subject, substance, basis, and justification of human rights, there is political agreement on their political legitimacy and this political legitimacy enables those in struggle to make their claims and rally their allies to take responsibility for change with them.

The entitlement approach is challenged to wrestle with the question of whether individuals and groups can be the *subject* of human rights. This question was at the heart of whether human rights are a useful tool with which to conceive of and argue for the rights of Indigenous peoples particularly with reference to displacement, exploitation, and sovereignty (Berger 2011; Cohen 1998; Deveaux 2000; Jacob 2010; Mackey 2005; Speed and Collier 2000; Spivak 2005; United Nations 2007a). In the entitlement approach, the question of whether individuals or groups can be the subject of rights poses a tension for the substance of rights: group rights cannot provide a justification for suppressing individual rights, but if a group wants to do so in the name of group rights, the group rights claim is in tension with the rights of individuals within the group. By contrast, even if all are not agreed as to the boundaries of responsibility by individuals and groups, the entitlement framework does not put the two in tension but rather in context. Thinking about rights as entitlements seems to invite discrimination by implying that there are certain people who are not the kinds of people who get to make rights claims.[16]

In the entitlement approach, those rights that are human rights (the *substance* of rights) are those that are consistent with the basis and justification of rights. Yet, there are two ways to understand the list of human rights. One is as finite and fixed. Another is as part of the practice of human rights. For example, is the right to enjoy one's sexuality a universal human rights entitlement to health and well-being (Article 25)? Or does such sexual freedom amount to undermining the "morality, public order and the general welfare"? The entitlement approach would have us argue over the list. The enjoyment approach recognizes that the meaning of health and well-being is undermined if exercising healthy sexuality is denied by social norms or laws. Incorporating this recognition into subsequent rights documents and ensuring their enjoyment at home has required political struggle and this struggle (Merry 2006; Petchesky 2003; Rothschild, Long, and Fried 2005).

More generally, if specific rights were not enumerated within the Universal Declaration of Human Rights or clarified in any subsequent Conventions, are they "new" rights? (Bob 2009; Nelson and Dorsey 2008; Perry 2009) If so, are there any constraints on what could be claimed as a human right? I am picturing an advertisement for Kohler in which the copy asserted that "everyone has a right to a designer faucet." Neither rights-based approach to responsibility that I have been describing requires that we take responsibility for all to have a fancy faucet if we agree that all should have a right to water. The "right" to a faucet is divisible from other rights (such as to water, to leisure, or to participate in the arts). All of these can be enjoyed without a faucet. By contrast, sexuality rights cannot be divisible from the right to health and thus is a human right, not a "new" right. If an articulation of a right is not divisible from an already acknowledged right, then it is not a "new" right, but rather a new articulation made necessary by context or politics.

The focus of the politics of responsibility for rights is also different between the two approaches. To exercise a right in the entitlement model, the subject gets to assert, demand, enjoy, and enforce their rights. What are the corresponding responsibilities of duty-bearers and who are they? Are they individual or collective? Those whose actions or inactions caused the rights violation? Those of this generation or past generations? And are they responsible only retrospectively for rights violations that have occurred? If we have a chronic problem with domestic violence (for example), are duty-bearers prospectively responsible? (Bunch 1990; Merry and Shimmin 2011; Sweet 2015) Are duty-bearers responsible for all of their actions and inactions or only those for which they did not know or could not anticipate the rights violations that might ensue from their actions as might be claimed with regard to toxic waste? (Bullard 2005; Campbell et al. 2016; Carmin and Agyeman 2011; Hancock 2003; Wright 2005) In the enjoyment model, the focus is not on the politics of the rights demand and assigning responsibility. Rather the enjoyment approach focuses on the political transformations in social, economic, and political structures that enable rights enjoyment for all.[17]

The entitlement approach works comfortably within the liability model of responsibility that is familiar in the law and moral philosophy of liberal democracies (Buchanan 2013; Feinberg and Gross 1975). However, this comfort should give us pause. Much of the history of injustice during the development of liberal democracies – the history that gives rise to the struggles for human rights within those liberal democracies – has taken place in the shadow of the liability model of responsibility. That is, the entitlement approach to human rights and the liability model of responsibility are conservative on the questions above (Ackerly 2018, esp Chapters 2 and 3).

The kinds of politics that are central to the enjoyment approach are not so much assigning responsibility when prosecuting human rights or genocide cases as taking up responsibility in development, health, peace, and security. The focus is on the taking up of responsibility and on the best ways of sharing responsibility (see Ackerly 2018, esp Chapter 7).

From the standpoint of assigning responsibility for human rights, the advantage of the entitlement approach is that if all are agreed on the basis, justification, subject, and substance of human rights and all are agreed as to the boundaries of responsibility by individuals and groups, across generations (or not),[18] for intended or unintended (or just intended) harms, for harms known and unknown (or just known), and if responsible parties can be identified, the account provides an argument for doing so and for their taking responsibility or being held responsible. The disadvantage is that if an entitlement is not clearly identified, an entitlement holder identified, and the duty for that entitlement not assigned, then the right is not protected *and has no basis for being protected.*

As noted, this mode of supporting human rights accountability is powerful in the courtroom when the violation is of a right that is not politically disputed, of a person whose right to have rights in this context is unquestioned, when the actions that caused the violation are undisputed in both their content and their consequence, and the violator is likewise clearly identifiable. In that, its political import is limited.

The enjoyment approach is differently historical. It requires that we understand political, social, and economic formal and informal institutions as a consequence of historical processes that include processes of oppression and liberation. Therefore, it is not bound by generations and calls us to take responsibility for past harms and harms for which we are not visibly causally implicated by recognizing that the systems that have contributed to these harms are systems of oppression. This idea which fits well within feminist, decolonial, and critical analysis (Ackerly 2018) is also recognized in the United Nations negotiations on climate change, specifically the Warsaw International Mechanism for Loss and Damage associated with Climate Change Impacts (Eckersley 2015; Eckersley 2016). In that agreement the parties disaggregated to notions of duty to take responsibility for harm caused by climate change and instead supported burden sharing. Climate mitigation and adaptation would be guided by two principles: "equity and common but differentiated responsibilities and respective capabilities."[19] This approach, as Robyn Eckersley (2016) and Parks and Roberts (2010) argue, increases the likelihood of political agreement on addressing climate change while leaving unaddressed the deep inequalities of our world which are in part responsible for the climate crisis (Eckersley 2016; Parks and Roberts 2010).

Historical injustices can be both known and unknown. For example, in the United States, slavery was a known injustice that expropriated the labor of African Americans and shortened their lives. Both the entitlement and enjoyment approaches consider slavery a human rights violation. And both approaches could understand the human rights violations of less visible but damaging effects of Jim Crow, segregation, redlining, and discriminatory lending practices as violating many of the same rights violated by slavery (Alexander 2010). Both approaches enable us to understand responsibility for intended or unintended harms (or just intended harms) and for harms known and unknown (or just known). If responsible parties can be identified, the account provides an argument for doing so and for their taking responsibility or being held responsible. Both support seeking reparations from insurance companies and banks that supported the slave economy by accepting slaves as collateral for loans, etc.

However, the entitlement approach can go no further. If an entitlement is not clearly identified, an entitlement holder identified, and the duty for that entitlement not assigned, then the right is not protected *and has no basis for being protected.* Since identifying the entitlements, holders, and duty-bearers are political processes, taking responsibility for human rights violations means being engaged (or mired) in these political processes.

The enjoyment approach takes on the politics of these questions and treats them as part of the human rights approach to responsibility.

Conclusion: A human rights theory of responsibility for human rights as a political project

Human rights are a political project. People make rights claims because they experience injustice. The idea itself is necessary because we have human rights violations and those in struggle seek recognition of their struggle from those who oppress them and those who are outside the struggle but whose political support may strengthen their cause. They demand that their claims be seen as politically legitimate regardless of the particular politics of those making the claims.

The entitlement approach can undermine these politics, particularly when paired with the liability model of responsibility. As I argued above with respect to the liability model, an approach to human rights that requires the assent of the oppressor is not a source of recognition and freedom. However, the entitlement approach does not require the liability model of responsibility. Legal and moral theorists do pair it with the liability model of responsibility because it works in the court room and specific cases. Since identifying the entitlements, holders, and duty bearers are political processes, taking responsibility for human rights violations means being engaged (or mired) in these political processes. When making arguments for the political, social, and economic transformations necessary to take on the structural aspects of injustice, the enjoyment approach to human rights is a better partner.

I conclude by returning to Jacques Maritain's Introduction to the work of UNESCO on the Universal Declaration of Human Rights. The question he put to himself and his audience turns us toward the practice of human rights:

> How…can we imagine an agreement of minds between men who are gathered together precisely in order to accomplish a common intellectual task, men who come from the four corners of the globe and who not only belong to different cultures and civilizations, but are of antagonistic spiritual associations and schools of thought…? Because…the goal of UNESCO is a practical goal, agreement between minds can be reached spontaneously, not on the basis of common speculative ideas, but on common practical ideas. Not on the affirmation of one and the same conception of the world, of man and of knowledge, but upon the affirmation of a single body of beliefs for guidance in action.
>
> *(Maritain 1949, II)*

In the enjoyment approach to responsibility for human rights, responsibility is not assigned but taken up. The enjoyment approach can rely on the entitlement model to hold to account those who are assigned duties, but does not require agreement as to why we have human rights in order to take responsibility for them. Further, it can take up the forms of injustice that manifest in the power inequalities of human society.

Thus, the enjoyment approach focuses instead on how to take responsibility for human rights in a just way. In world politics, there is no site in which we can be confident that justice will always prevail. The enjoyment approach reminds us to be vigilant.

Notes

1. The discussion in this part of the paper draws substantiall from Ackerly (2008), cf. Miller (2010).
2. Also cited by Dunne and Wheeler (1999, 4).
3. Though arguing this is well beyond the scope of this chapter, in its most liberal manifestations, it is most conducive to treating individuals as rights-bearers (see French 1984).
4. On this view, human rights would not extend to groups or corporate individuals.
5. Iris Marion Young provides a thorough theoretical review and critique of this approach and its family of stakeholders before putting forward the social connectedness model (Young 2006, 2010). Goodhart argues that theorizing in this vein shares an approach he calls ideal moral theory which prohibits taking up the difficult political questions of responsibility for injustice (Goodhart 2018). Ackerly argues that the nature of political life inhibits even acting as if we could reason about responsibility in this way and thus proposes a political approach to responsibility (Ackerly 2018).

6 International Covenant on Civil and Political Rights, G.A. Res. 2200A (XXI), U.N. GAOR, Supp. No. 16 at 52, U.N. Doc. A/6316 (1966); International Covenant on Economic, Social and Cultural Rights, G.A. Res. 2200A (XXI), U.N. GAOR, Supp. No. 16, U.N. Doc. A/6316 (1966); Convention against Torture and Other Cruel, Inhuman or Degrading Treatment or Punishment, G.A. Res. 39/46, U.N. GAOR, 39th Sess., Annex, Supp. No. 51 at 197, U.N. Doc. A/39/51 (1984); International Convention for the Protection of All Persons from Enforced Disappearance, G.A. Res., 20 December 2007 (adopted, but not entered into force).
7 International Convention on the Protection of the Rights of All Migrant Workers and Members of their Families, G.A. res. 45/158 of 18 December 1990 (2003).
8 United Nations (1979). Convention on the Elimination of All Forms of Discrimination against Women, G.A. Res. 34/180, U.N. GAOR, 34th Sess., Supp. No. 46, at 193, U.N. Doc. A/34/46 (1981).
9 United Nations (1989). Convention on the Rights of the Child, G.A. Res. 44/25, U.N. GAOR, 44th Sess., Supp. No. 49, at 161, U.N. Doc. A/44/49 (1989).
10 See United Nations (2007a).
11 See United Nations (2007b). Convention on the Rights of Persons with Disabilities, G.A. Res. 61/106 (2007).
12 International Convention on the Elimination of All Forms of Racial Discrimination, G.A. Res. 2106 (XX), U.N. GAOR, Supp. No. 14, at 47, U.N. Doc. A/6014 (1966).
13 This view is associated with natural law theorists. For a nice typology see Dunne and Wheeler (1999: 4).
14 "Human rights are closely tied to notions of justice and human dignity that are as old as human society" (Goodhart 2016, 2).
15 On the secular view see Rawls et al. On the religious view across religions, see Sobrino Sj (2001) and Sachedina (2009).
16 See discussions of Arendt's formulation of the right to have rights (Benhabib 2002; Ingram 2008; Oman 2010; Benhabib 2011; D'Costa 2012; Gündogdu 2015).
17 See Ackerly (2018) for an argument for taking responsibility for injustices grounded in activists account of their agency and Hoover (2012) for an argument for taking responsibility for injustices grounded in John Dewey.
18 For an intergenerational justice argument using human rights to think about climate change, see Caney (2008; Caney 2014).
19 UNFCCC 2013 (see Articles 3(1), 4(1), and 4(3)).

References

Ackerly, B.A. (2008). *Universal Human Rights in a World of Difference*. Cambridge: Cambridge University Press.
Ackerly, B.A. (2011). "Human Rights Enjoyment in Theory and Activism." *Human Rights Review*, 12(2): 221–239.
Ackerly, B.A. (2017). "Interpreting the Theory in the Practice of Human Rights." *Law and Philosophy*, 36(2): 135–153.
Ackerly, B.A. (2018). *Just Responsibility: A Human Rights Theory of Global Justice*. Oxford: Oxford University Press.
Adler, M.D. (2007). "Corrective Justice and Liability for Global Warming." *University of Pennsylvania Law Review*, 155(6): 1859–1867.
Alexander, M. (2010). *The New Jim Crow: Mass Incarceration in the Age of Colorblindness*. New York: New Press.
Benhabib, S. (2002). "Political Geographies in a Global World: Arendtian Reflections." *Social Research*, 69(2): 539–566.
Benhabib, S. (2011). *Dignity in Adversity: Human Rights in Troubled Times*. Cambridge: Polity.
Berger, B.R. (2011). "The Anomaly of Citizenship for Indigenous Rights." In Hertel, S., and Libal, K., eds. *Human Rights in the United States: Beyond Exceptionalism*: 217–233. Cambridge: Cambridge University Press.
Bob, C. (2009). *The International Struggle for New Human Rights*. Philadelphia: University of Pennsylvania Press.
Buchanan, A.E. (2013). *The Heart of Human Rights*. Oxford: Oxford University Press.
Bukovansky, M., Clark, I., Eckersley, R., Price, R., Reus-Smit, C., and Wheeler, N.J. (2012). *Special Responsibilities: Global Problems and American Power*. Cambridge: Cambridge University Press.
Bullard, R.D., ed. (2005). *The Quest for Environmental Justice: Human Rights and the Politics of Pollution*. San Francisco, CA: Sierra Club Books.

Bunch, C. (1990). "Women's Rights as Human Rights: Toward a Re-Vision of Human Rights." *Human Rights Quarterly*, 12(4): 486–498.
Campbell, C., Greenberg, R., Mankikar, D., and Ross, R.D. (2016). "A Case Study of Environmental Injustice: The Failure in Flint." *International Journal of Environmental Research and Public Health*, 13(10): 951–962.
Caney, S. (2008). "Human Rights, Climate Change, and Discounting." *Environmental Politics*, 17(4): 536–555.
Caney, S. (2010). "Climate Change and the Duties of the Advantaged." *Critical Review of International Social and Political Philosophy*, 13(1): 203–228.
Caney, S. (2014). "Climate Change, Intergenerational Equity and the Social Discount Rate." *Politics, Philosophy & Economics*, 13(4): 320–342.
Carmin, J., and Agyeman, J., eds. (2011). "*Environmental Inequalities Beyond Borders Local Perspectives on Global Injustices.*" Cambridge, MA: MIT Press.
Chan, J. (1997). "An Alternative View." *Journal of Democracy*, 8(2): 35–48.
Charlesworth, H. and Chinkin, C. (1993). "The Gender of Jus Cogens." *Human Rights Quarterly*, 15(1): 63–76.
Chen, M.A. (1995). "Engendering World Conferences: The International Women's Movement and the United Nations." *Third World Quarterly*, 16(3): 477–494.
Cohen, C.P. (1998). *The Human Rights of Indigenous Peoples.* Ardsley, NY: Transnational Publishers.
D'Costa, B. (2012). "The Humanitarian Frontline: Rohingya Refugees and the 'Right to Have Rights'." Forum Monthly, the Daily Star. https://archive.thedailystar.net/forum/2012/August/rohingyas.htm
Dalai Lama (1999). "Buddhism, Asian Values, and Democracy." *Journal of Democracy*, 10(1): 3–7.
Dallmayr, F. (2002). ""Asian Values" and Global Human Rights." *Philosophy East and West*, 52(2): 173–189.
de Bary, W.T. (1998). *Asian Values and Human Rights: A Confucian Communitarian Perspective*. Cambridge, MA: Harvard University Press.
Deveaux, M. (2000). "Conflicting Equalities? Cultural Group Rights and Sex Equality." *Political Studies*, 48(3): 522–539.
Donnelly, J. (1985). *The Concept of Human Rights*. New York: St. Martin's Press.
Donnelly, J. (2007). "The Relative Universality of Human Rights." *Human Rights Quarterly*, 29(2): 281–306.
Donnelly, J. (2008). "Human Rights: Both Universal and Relative (a Reply to Michael Goodhart)." *Human Rights Quarterly*, 30(1): 194–204.
Dunne, T., and Wheeler, N.J. (1999). "Introduction: Human Rights and the Fifty Years' Crisis." In Dunne, T., and Wheeler, N.J., eds. *Human Rights in Global Politics*: 1–28. Cambridge: Cambridge University Press.
Eckersley, R. (2015). "The Common but Differentiated Responsibilities of States to Assist and Receive 'Climate Refugees'." *European Journal of Political Theory*, 14(4): 481–500.
Eckersley, R. (2016). "Responsibility for Climate Change as a Structural Injustice." In Gabrielson, T., ed. *Oxford Handbook of Environmental Political Theory*: 347–361. Oxford: Oxford University Press.
Englehart, N.A. (2000). "Rights and Culture in the Asian Values Argument: The Rise and Fall of Confucian Ethics in Singapore." *Human Rights Quarterly*, 22(2): 548–568.
Feinberg, J., and Gross, H. (1975). *Responsibility*. Encino, CA: Dickenson Pub. Co.
French, P.A. (1984). *Collective and Corporate Responsibility*. New York: Columbia University Press.
Friedman, E.J. (2003). "Gendering the Agenda: The Impact of the Transnational Women's Rights Movement at the UN Conferences of the 1990s." *Women's Studies International Forum*, 26(4): 313–331.
Goodhart, M. (2008). "Neither Relative nor Universal: A Response to Donnelly." *Human Rights Quarterly*, 30(1): 183–193.
Goodhart, M. (2013). "Human Rights and the Politics of Contestation." In Goodale, M., ed. *Human Rights at the Crossroads*: 31–44. Oxford: Oxford University Press.
Goodhart, M. (2016). "Introduction." In Goodhart, M., ed. *Human Rights in Politics and Practice*: 1–8. Oxford: Oxford University Press.
Goodhart, M. (2018). *Injustice: Political Theory for the Real World*. Oxford: Oxford University Press.
Gündogdu, A. (2015). *Rightlessness in an Age of Rights: Hannah Arendt and the Contemporary Struggles of Migrants*. Oxford: Oxford University Press.
Hancock, J. (2003). *Environmental Human Rights: Power, Ethics, and Law*. Burlington, VT: Ashgate.
Hoover, J. (2012). "Reconstructing Responsibility and Moral Agency in World Politics." *International Theory*, 4(2): 233–268.
Incite! Women of Color against Violence (2007). *The Revolution Will Not Be Funded: Beyond the Non-Profit Industrial Complex*. Cambridge, MA: South End Press.

Ingram, J. (2008). "What Is a "Right to Have Rights"? Three Images of the Politics of Human Rights." *The American Political Science Review*, 102(4): 401–416.

Jacob, M.M. (2010). "Claiming Health and Culture as Human Rights." *International Feminist Journal of Politics*, 12(3–4): 361–380.

Johnson, M.G. (2001). "Human Rights and Asian Values: Contesting National Identities and Cultural Representations in Asia; Jacobsen, Michael, and Ole Bruun, Eds." *Perspectives on Political Science*, 30(3): 182.

Liu, L.H. (2014). "Shadows of Universalism: The Untold Story of Human Rights around 1948." *Critical Inquiry*, 40(Summer): 385–417.

Mackey, E. (2005). "Universal Rights in Conflict: 'Backlash' and 'Benevolent Resistance' to Indigenous Land Rights." *Anthropology Today*, 21(2): 14–20.

Maritain, J. (1949). "Introduction." In *Human Rights: Comments and Interpretations*. New York: Columbia University Press, 9–17.

Merry, S.E. (2006). "Transnational Human Rights and Local Activism – Mapping the Middle." *American Anthropologist*, 108(1): 38–51.

Merry, S.E., and Shimmin, J. (2011). "The Curious Resistance to Seeing Domestic Violence as a Human Rights Violation in the United States." In Hertel, S., and Libal, K., eds. *Human Rights in the United States: Beyond Exceptionalism*: 113–131. Cambridge: Cambridge University Press.

Miller, H. (2010). "From Rights-Based to Rights-Framed Approaches: A Social Constructionist View of Human Rights Practice." *The International Journal of Human Rights*, 14(6): 915–931.

Moyn, S. (2010). *The Last Utopia: Human Rights in History*. Cambridge, MA: Belknap Press of Harvard University Press.

Nelson, P.J., and Dorsey, E. (2008). *New Rights Advocacy: Changing Strategies of Development and Human Rights NGOs*. Washington, DC: Georgetown University Press.

Oman, N. (2010). "Hannah Arendt's "Right to Have Rights": A Philosophical Context for Human Security." *Journal of Human Rights*, 9(3): 279–302.

Parks, B.C., and Roberts, J.T. (2010). "Climate Change, Social Theory and Justice." *Theory, Culture & Society*, 27(2–3): 134–166.

Perry, E.J. (2009). "A New Rights Consciousness?" *Journal of Democracy*, 20(3): 17–20.

Petchesky, R.P. (2003). *Global Prescriptions: Gendering Health and Human Rights*. New York: Zed Books.

Rothschild, C., Long, S., and Fried, S.T., eds. (2005). *Written Out: How Sexuality Is Used to Attack Women's Organizing*. New York: International Gay and Lesbian Human Rights Commission & The Center for Women's Global Leadership.

Sachedina, A.A. (2009). *Islam and the Challenge of Human Rights*. Oxford: Oxford University Press.

Shapiro, I. (1986). *The Evolution of Rights in Liberal Theory*. Cambridge: Cambridge University Press.

Sobrino Sj, J. (2001). "Human Rights and Oppressed Peoples: Historical-Theological Reflections." In Hayes, M. and Tomb, D., eds. *Truth and Memory: The Church and Human Rights in El Salvadore and Guatemala*: 134–158. Gloucester: Gracewing.

Speed, S., and Collier, J.F. (2000). "Limiting Indigenous Autonomy in Chiapas, Mexico: The State Government's Use of Human Rights." *Human Rights Quarterly*, 22(4): 877–905.

Spivak, G.G. (2005). "Use and Abuse of Human Rights." *Boundary 2*, 32(1): 131–189.

Sweet, P.I. (2015). "Chronic Victims, Risky Women: Domestic Violence Advocacy and Medicalization of Abuse." *Signs*, 41(1): 81–106.

Talbott, W.J. (2005). *Which Rights Should Be Universal?* New York: Oxford University Press.

Tronto, J.C. (1993). *Moral Boundaries: A Political Argument for an Ethic of Care*. New York: Routledge.

United Nations (1948). "Universal Declaration of Human Rights." http://www.unhchr.ch/udhr/lang/eng.htm

United Nations (1979). "Convention on the Elimination of All Forms of Discrimination against Women, Declarations, Reservations and Objections." United Nations, Division for the Advancement of Women: http://www.un.org/womenwatch/daw/cedaw/text/econvention.htm.

United Nations (1989). "Convention on the Rights of the Child." *Annex GA Res. 44/25 Doc. A/Res/4425. Adopted November 20, 1989.* http://www.unhchr.ch/html/menu3/b/k2crc.htm.

United Nations (1995). "Fourth World Conference on Women, Beijing Platform for Action." In *United Nations Fourth World Conference on Women*. Beijing, China.

United Nations (2007a). "Declaration on the Rights of Indigenous Peoples." ed. General Assembly: September 13, 2007. http://www.un.org/esa/socdev/unpfii/en/declaration.html

United Nations (2007b). "Convention on the Rights of Persons with Disabilities, G.A. Res. 61/106." https://www.un.org/development/desa/disabilities/convention-on-the-rights-of-persons-with-disabilities.html

Vincent, R.J. (1986). *Human Rights and International Relations*. Cambridge: Cambridge University Press.

Wright, B. (2005). "Living and Dying in Louisiana's "Cancer Alley"." In Bullard, R.D., ed. *The Quest for Environmental Justice: Human Rights and the Politics of Pollution*: 87–107. San Francisco, CA: Sierra Club Books.

Young, I.M. (2006). "Responsibility and Global Justice: A Social Connection Model." *Social Philosophy and Policy*, 23(1): 102–130.

Young, I.M. (2010). *Responsibility for Justice*. New York: Oxford University Press.

5
POLITICAL RESPONSIBILITY IN A GLOBALIZED BUT FRACTURED AGE

Richard Beardsworth

Introduction: Some background to foregrounding political responsibility

With the end of the Cold War in 1989, theories, practices, and objects of international responsibility greatly expanded. Prior to the end of the Cold War the overall problematic of international responsibility was embedded in the state system and was predominantly linked to state responsibility toward the maintaining of international order. Its objects were, in turn, practiced and theorized either through the lens of legal responsibility and international law or through the Realist/English School lens of the responsibility of "great powers" and hegemonic orders/international society (Bull 1977; Claude 1986; Crawford 2002; Gilpin 1981; Hurrell 2008). With the end of the Cold War and the global re-ordering that ensued, the problematic of international responsibility widened considerably (Tardif 2020). Normatively, the human rights framework now stood at the foreground of international politics; empirically, processes of globalization accelerated following the decline of both ideological and economic borders. As a result, other actors, to one side of the state, became objects of international law (individuals, marginalized groups, and corporations); more issues came to be included in the "international responsibility" agenda (humanitarian aid, gender, post-conflict resolution, food and water security, the climate, etc.); and international actors themselves proliferated (in particular, NGOs and INGOs working across state borders in partnership with international organizations like the UN).

This widening of the international responsibility problematic came to be couched during the 1990s and 2000s in the terms of "global governance," "global public goods," and "global collective action" (Kahler and Lake 2003; Kaul 1999; Sandler 2010). Indeed, with the widening of the objects, issues, and agents of international responsibility beyond the state and its traditional international responsibilities, it appeared as if the practices of international responsibility were moving "up" from the dilemmas of international order to those of addressing "global problems"; or better put, problems of order and justice in a globalizing world were considered to be best understood through a global lens or from a global/human perspective. This post-Cold War transformation of the problematic of international responsibility elicits three immediate remarks that constitute an important background to the chapter's focus on political responsibility.

First, the transformation was primarily theorized and practiced in normative, if not, at times, exclusively moral terms (Beardsworth 2015). This normative turn should be considered both positively and negatively. It was a positive thing that, with wider objects and agents, the problematic of international responsibility was taken out of the traditionally limited and limiting box of state behavior and, as the IR ethicist Ariel Colonomos has put it, "moralized" (Colonomos 2008). The normative principles of the doctrine of the "Responsibility to Protect" (RtoP) are probably the best-known example of this "moralization of international relations." The moralization encouraged states to consider their cosmopolitan responsibilities toward the protection of human beings in an age of increasing interdependence of populations below and above the unit of the state (ICISS 2001). However, this moralization of international relations had also an immediate negative effect. As the diversely schooled critics of military intervention in the name of humanity have emphasized over the last decade, the moralization of state behavior led to perverse consequences (for example: Bacevich 2008, Hehir 2012; Menon 2016; Smith 2010; Vilmer 2012). The most common has been non-western perception of new forms of imperial domination under the cover of moral interest. In the first fifteen years of the twenty-first century the moralization of state behavior also disguised a fundamental lack of political will on the part of states to tackle global issues. The constant refrain, for example, on the part of states (not only civil society leaders) that politics assume "its moral responsibility" to address climate change or the structural failings of the global capitalist economy this refrain, pitched eloquently in moral terms, betrayed in essence a *political deficit* on a global scale (Beardsworth 2015). As a result, the post-Cold War transformation of legal and hegemonic notions of international responsibility has proved ambivalent for progressive state behavior.[1]

Second, this transformation of the actors and objects of international responsibility (again, widening the international landscape to encompass more issues, more types of behavior from states, and more actors under processes of globalization) offered the *promise* of a different international order. The promise was again best captured by the doctrine of RtoP with its concept of "sovereignty as responsibility" (ICISS 2001; Glanville 2014). No longer to consider sovereignty as a principle of independence within the state system, but to deepen the outward-facing obligations of sovereign states toward rights and responsibilities that ultimately lay above them— the concept of "sovereignty as responsibility" necessarily looked forward to a new world order, one in which individuals and groups as well as states were the essential objects of global security and justice. To one side of the ambivalence of state behavior indicated above, the concept of "sovereignty as responsibility" promised, in other words, an end to the state system as understood and practiced from its modern beginnings to its post-1945 settlements (Jackson, 2007).[2]

Third, and following both remarks above, the post-Cold War transformation of international responsibility constituted an attempt to *bridge the gap between global/human issues and the state system*. The widening of the problematic of international responsibility was never, to this author's knowledge at least, explicitly envisaged in these terms. That said, the widening could be usefully understood as an attempt to mend this "gap" under the name of global governance strategies (Beardsworth 2017). With accelerating processes of globalization following the end of the Cold War, both material reality and the western liberal imagination leapt ahead of the state system. Under this light the formulation of international responsibilities amidst a wide array of actors constituted an attempt to plug the gap between a world-order-in-waiting attuned to global/human concerns and a system of states unable institutionally and politically to address the new realities.[3] In essence, the post-Cold War transformation of international responsibility was (and is) attempting to confront the increasing *political irresponsibility* of the state system in response to global (and now "planetary") matters.

The attempt has proved problematic, as the political fates of RtoP over the last twenty years have demonstrated, underscoring the following structural dilemma. *Without the capacity and responsibilities of the state, a global politics cannot be conducted; with these capacities, the material requirements and responsibilities of a global politics become necessarily compromised by state and nation-state interests.*

This political dilemma has become all the clearer with two changing realities of both national and international politics since the 2007/8 global financial crisis. International liberalism has, first, declined with the emergence of non-western powers and the relative decline of the western powers. The decline has been accompanied, second, by a populist backlash against the neo-liberal and technocratic dimensions of globalization and, together with the digital fragmentation of the liberal public sphere, by the consequent weakening of the major pillars of liberal (and social) democracy (Müller 2016). These challenges to national and international forms of liberalism are inseparable. With them global threats and challenges like climate catastrophe, nuclear proliferation and an unstable, deeply hierarchical global capitalist economy continue to escalate.[4] The said "gap" between global problems/human concerns, on the one hand, and the state system, on the other, has widened again after thirty years of international liberal endeavor, an endeavor through which the problematic of international responsibility looked to make the state a responsible post-national actor.

For many, particularly those on the left critical of liberalism, the present predicaments of domestic and international liberalism may well have condemned "responsibility talk" to post-Cold War history. As intimated, the project of deepening and of widening the agenda of international responsibility formed part of "the liberal moment" of post-Cold War politics. With this moment at an end, the responsibility project appears heavily compromised as well. One hears a lot today, for example, of the "retreat" of RtoP, just as Russian and Chinese promotion of the principle of the sovereign independence of states no longer constitutes a rearguard action against processes of interdependence (as it still did at the time of the 2007/8 financial crisis). The principle is again a major norm of world politics whatever the realities of both global interdependence and recent atrocity crimes in Myanmar, Syria, and Yemen (Human Rights Watch Report 2019). Both the retreat of "RtoP" and the brazen return of the principle of sovereign independence to world politics constitute signs of a new period of history, a period whose symbolic origins can be taken back, at the very least, to the western financial crisis and its neo-liberal origins as well as the contested "humanitarian intervention" in Libya in 2011. Rather, however, than give up on "responsibility talk" in this context, I consider it important to make the argument for *political responsibility* in the ongoing historical gap between global/human threats and challenges, on the one hand, and the system of states within which all present politics must take place, on the other.

My argument is Weberian (Weber 1965) and pragmatic (compare chapter by Jackson in this volume). Weberian, it understands political responsibility in terms of the state and its powers and considers that the state remains, whatever present criticisms of it, a responsible agent of change. Choosing the state as an agent of change within contemporary world politics (and not an obstacle, bound to an antiquated system) is also a pragmatic argument. The latter is time-bound and context-specific. At this historical juncture, the state, with its monopoly of violence and ensuing capacities, is the only political agent that can make a concerted and comprehensive effort to effect change on global issues. Of course, many states—particularly those in the south of the world—have neither the capacity nor power to effect change; and powerful states that can effect change can only do so through strategies of cooperation with other states and with other international actors (the EU, IOs, NGOs, corporations, civil society). These two points on the state's structural incapacities in a globalized, hierarchical, and fractured world are important. That said, in the terms of a Weberian, pragmatic argument, I suggest that the state remains today the principle actor among international actors to organize and effect concerted political action.

The remainder of the chapter considers from this perspective what political responsibility means with regard to a globalized, fractured world. The first section considers how political responsibility is thought in terms of responsible government. I use basic principles of liberal and republican theory to do this. The second section then places this account of political responsibility in the context of global threats and challenges and international responsibility, and it considers the "stretch" between these two scales of responsibility. The third section steps beyond the analysis of governmental power and duty in order to consider political responsibility as responsive/responsible political leadership. The conclusion summarizes the major moves of my argument, ending with a final comment on why renewed focus on the state as an agent of change does not run the risk of a revived "state-centric" focus. My basic point throughout the article is the pragmatic need, at this historical juncture, to embed the recent normative problematic of "international responsibility" within the dynamics of the political responsibilities of the state to its own citizenry.[5]

Political responsibility as responsible government

To understand the concept and practice of "responsibility" in general from a pragmatic perspective is to understand responsibility relationally (see Introduction to this volume). An agent (x) is responsible to some entity (y) and for something (z), but the terms of each instance x, y, and z depend on context, circumstance, and decision. With my Weberian focus on the state at this historical juncture, I understand political responsibility, therefore, as the agency of *responsible government*. This choice is neither to dismiss other international/global actors nor to ignore the effects of these actors on state behavior in world politics: especially, civil society pressure on state agendas and state accountability (Colonomos 2008; Hayden 2005; Young 2013, 146, 151). To repeat, it is to advance at a moment of liberal internationalist retreat and renewed claims to state sovereigntism the central importance of the state and, at the same time, the central importance of the capacities of the state and its responsibilities regarding global issues, threats and challenges. The following argument draws from liberal, republican, and realist political theories (respectively: Deudney 2007; Geuss 2008; Green 2007; Hobbes 1977; Mitrany 1946; Pettit 1997; 2014, Rosanvallon 2015; Skinner 1998; Slaughter 2005; Williams 2005).

Under general conditions of modernity, responsible government—in the widest sense of the combination of legislative, judiciary, and executive instances and of the separation of their powers for collective effect—is primarily responsible *to* its citizens and responsible *for* their freedom from external and internal threats—what the republican literature calls "domination" (Pettit 1997, 59–66). This responsibility connotes both accountability to its principles (the citizenry) and liability in respect of actions taken for the sake of their freedom from threats. If government shows neither primary responsibility to its citizens nor the will to secure their basic interests, it is correctly accused of being "irresponsible." A state's refusal, for example, to subordinate global financial markets to the requirements of a self-determining polity is considered by most of us as "irresponsible government." Its inability to do so is considered as part of an ongoing transformation of power away from the state under processes of globalization (Strange 1996). In the first situation, a state is willfully irresponsible because it could do otherwise according to rule-bound norms; in the second, a state is structurally irresponsible because these rule-bound norms are no longer effective at scale. What is critical, then, to the very idea of political responsibility, as against other forms of responsibility, is the fundamental nature of the relation between x and y—understood here as agent and principal, governors, and governed. This relation, as the contemporary political historian Pierre Rosanvallon has put it, is "structural" (2015, 254). If the structure is broken, political irresponsibility necessarily follows (experienced by citizenry y as mistrust, anger, resentment, frustration, etc.). This structure of responsible government *qua* political responsibility can be best understood in terms of *efficacy* and *legitimacy*. These are analytically separate forms of power-justification, but as I will argue in the next section, they should ultimately be placed as two moments on a continuous spectrum of protection.

A concise way to understand the efficacy argument particular to political responsibility is provided by the philosopher Leslie Green. Green understands domestic state responsibility in terms of the "duty to govern" (Green 2007). He justifies this primary duty neither in terms of legitimacy nor in terms of obligation, but in terms of *effective capacity* (under conditions of the common good). The duty to govern, he writes, is "called forth by the needs of the common good [...]. Those who have the effective capacity to solve it bear the responsibility of doing so" (Green 2007, 166–167). In other words, regarding the primary duty of government, it is capacity that triggers responsibility. Political authority is exercised where there is a certain kind of problem to be solved and *should be exercised by those who have the effective capacity to solve it*. Understood in these terms of task efficacy, political responsibility entails government as the management of political, social, and economic events in order to maintain the "basic goods" of a people (Green 2007, 168). Responsible government implies that the primary needs of a people—or, in liberal parlance, the fundamental rights of a people—are satisfied.

Green does not address the question of legitimacy in the same group of justificatory arguments.[6] But, if, as Green argues, political responsibility is concerned with the basic "needs of the common good," failure to be task-efficacious cannot fail to lead to de-legitimization. Those who accept the duty to govern with efficacy must constantly deal with the status of their own political authority, whether through contractarian consensus building (democracies), offensive populism (failing democracies and non-democratic regimes), or overt repression of dissatisfaction (authoritarian regimes). The modern "duty to govern" must be considered, therefore, in two inextricably related stages of efficacy *and* legitimacy.

I consider the terms of legitimacy best suited to understanding the structural relation between governors and governed to be that of republicanism. In distinction to liberalism, it emphasizes the critical role of the state in securing and protecting the freedoms of its citizenry in a modern world. For the intellectual historian Quentin Skinner, for example, freedom from arbitrary interference or domination can only be secured by the (countervailing) powers of the state (Skinner 1998). Political freedom, as argued from Machiavelli, through Rousseau and Kant, to the Founding Fathers of the American Republic, is not a contract between individuals but one between individuals and the state (a contract for and to *citizens*). How, then, can this modern understanding of political responsibility be re-articulated in terms of the above-mentioned gap between global/human threats and challenges, on the one hand, and the state system, on the other? Or rather, on what terms can this understanding of political responsibility stretch from the domestic level to that of international responsibilities so that it can provide us with a functional, accountable politics of the state that responds to international, global, and planetary threats and challenges?

Political responsibility: Bridging the gap between the national and the international/global

This section takes, first, the two arguments around efficacy and legitimacy and, then, brings them together under a canopy-theory of security, protection and freedom.

Regarding the duty to govern *qua* task-efficacy, I have argued that the fulfillment of need is a primary political duty or a duty of government. Needs are now systemically determined by threats and challenges beyond the borders of the governed polity. It therefore follows that—within the very concept of political duty—those states that are affected (and able to respond) have a responsibility to do so *in order to answer their peoples' needs in the first place*. In short, it is the responsibility of government to understand and demonstrate that "global responsibility" (ultimately, response to global threats in the name of human interests) constitutes the *very condition* of securing its citizens" interests in the first place. Government cannot responsibly protect its own citizens without working responsibly at a global level. In an interdependent world a state must go abroad to come home. To secure one's home first *before* stepping abroad—in the extreme, sovereigntism—puts the cart before the horse given the material realities of the twenty-first century (Beardsworth 2017, 12).

There is a necessary consequence to this point concerning the primary duty of government. Those states that are both affected by trans-border threats and have the capacity to respond will find themselves increasingly responding to the needs of the peoples of *other* states in order to answer their own peoples' needs. Given the material realities of the twenty-first century government cannot responsibly protect its own citizens without responding to the needs, also, of non-citizens. I return to this consequence in a moment. The extension of the logic of the primary duty of government to the international/global scale means the following. If states can only respond effectively to trans-border threats and challenges by cooperating with other states—at the limit, ceding issue-specific domestic sovereignty to supranational control—then according to their primary duty of protection, they have an associated or consequent duty to cooperate. If, as we are frequently told by liberal-minded politicians and diplomats, not co-operating is "politically irresponsible," it is precisely because citizenship requires fulfillment of the state's primary political duty.

The willingness of governments to pool some of their unilateral decision-making power among themselves through international institutions demonstrates that governments do see the benefits to their own populations of "pooling sovereignty." This is clear in the areas of maritime law, international trade standards and communication systems where governments delegate powers to an external authority over which they have no veto (see the respective chapters by Bernstein, Sado and Lockwood, and Tiller et al. in this volume). The most evident example is the World Trade Organization with its appellate body: hence the attempt on the part of contemporary populist politics to undermine the organization's essentially supranational remit. That governments do see the benefit of cooperation and pooling sovereignty is also the case, to varying extent, with regard to regional and global security networks that tackle intelligence issues, cyber-security, terrorism and the international crimes of human trafficking, sex trafficking and money laundering. My argument regarding political responsibility is therefore simple and understandable. Cooperation and pooling of sovereignty should happen also when dealing with major issues that affect in an interdependent world the physical and social integrity of a state's people: not because pooling sovereignty is morally right regarding peoples as a whole (a strong cosmopolitan argument), but because pooling sovereignty is, precisely, the responsibility of the state toward its own citizenry (a strong political argument).

Regarding the legitimacy of political authority, I have suggested that the primary political duty of government entails over time the legitimacy of power wielded. Addressing threats and challenges of a trans-border nature by delegating some powers sideways or upwards, the state not only answers the needs of its people. It also ensures their freedom from empirical and structural forms of threat (domination). One can think of these forms of domination in non-human and/or human terms: the concrete events of climate change (precipitation, drought, sea-level rises, consequential breaks in the food chain, etc.), the empirical consequences of capital accumulation (financial runs, sudden food price hikes or pharmaceutical cartels) and/or the structural logic of nuclear arms (the domination of peoples by fear and anxiety).[7] The political duty to govern these empirical and structural forms of threat must be made, in terms exceeding the basic need of citizens, in the name of citizenry's freedom from domination. The duty to govern at global scale is consequently justified in terms of securing citizens' freedom from threats and, therefore, securing an environment of non-domination for its citizens. The argument for governmental task-efficacy slides into one regarding the legitimacy of governmental power.

One sees here how a formulation of political responsibility that bridges the gap between the national and the global works along a continuous spectrum of security and freedom. Regarding the above-rehearsed structural understanding of political responsibility, I consider this more dynamic point important. A la Hobbes basic security of life is, at one end of the spectrum, the primary political action of the state (what I have called up to now fulfillment of basic need). The guarantee of survival by government is however only the first step in security (Booth 2007, 95ff.; Williams 2005, 1–27). The more secure a polity becomes, the more possibilities of *what security means* emerge. On one end of the spectrum a highly vulnerable state rejects or loses the capacity to offer *physical security*, as is the case today for island states under the existential threat of climate change. Moving along the spectrum, a resilient state will go on to offer *social security* and, according to the nature of its political regime, institutionalize *equality of opportunity* across the public realm. At the far end of the spectrum, a resilient state with high capacity and legitimacy incorporates the moral values of freedom from threat into its very conception of "national interest" and "national security," as is the case with powers that assume the cosmopolitan responsibilities of threatened populations.[8] Following the important, prescient work of Ken Booth on world security (Booth 2007), I would argue that this sliding scale of security and freedom frames much of the horizon of contemporary and future world politics (and will include the future principles of global ordering). In the context of climate change adaptation, the human ability to govern global health, rising populations, migratory displacements, resource conflict and post-conflict peace building, as well as the set of decisions required concerning the parameters of artificial intelligence, are all matters of security from threat so that a life free from domination is made possible. It is therefore the duty of government to ensure, within a virtuous/vicious circle of increasing/decreasing human "resilience," the security of its peoples.[9]

This last point is perhaps most pertinent regarding the normative horizon of sustainable development. The contemporary example of sustainable development draws together the various arguments of this section, so I will conclude with it. The Sustainable Development Agenda is often considered as an extension of the Millennium Development Goals, with an enlarged remit (United Nations 2015). The agenda no longer deals with poverty reduction alone, but with the three pillars of the economic, the social and the environmental. This approach to the Sustainable Development Agenda misses a critical point, however: a point that becomes self-evident when the agendas of sustainable development and climate change adaptation converge. Under the threat of climate change, sustainable development concerns the developed countries as much as the developing countries. Every government has become duty-bound to protect its people(s) so that *freedom from threat is sustainable*. What does this canopy vision of sustainability imply for the question of political responsibility?

First, the binary distinction between developed and developing states, "North" and "South" can no longer be an organizing one (despite massive differences of equality and quality of life in the two geographical regions of the world). There are large pockets of the "North" that are already at risk of underdevelopment and that certainly risk under-development in the coming years unless concerted political action is taken. The return of populism within liberal democracy can be considered a clear call, for example, for governments to address growing inequality at home, not abroad (against my general argument). And yet this action must be taken in concert with the "South" since threats to underdeveloped areas of the "North" will rapidly increase with the effects of climate change in the South (migration patterns north- and westwards, most obviously). The sustainable development agenda can only work appropriately if both "developed" and "developing" states work responsibly together. This is an urgent matter of state political responsibility.

Second, if the binary distinction between developed and developing countries is undone by the realities of climate change and sustainability, then all states can be measured in terms of the spectrum of security and freedom from threat/domination. States may progress and regress along this spectrum. At the very least the Sustainable Development Agenda allows people to fight for an age in which the distinction between North and South is obsolete—not because the South has caught up with the North (far from it), but because the world as a whole must move to a new understanding of modernization processes if the planet is to remain sustainable (Latour 2018). Due to "development" now (re-)affecting all states, state responsibility to its own citizenry is necessarily caught up in a set of global responsibilities that will increasingly gain momentum. The astute move at this moment of history is not only to make these global responsibilities internationally accountable but to embed them in domestic political efficacy and legitimacy.

Third, it is here where my previous comments on the consequences for non-citizens of state responsibility toward its own citizenry make proper sense. In order for a state to provide for the needs of its people, it must at the same time respond to the needs of other peoples so that these other needs *do not come to dominate its own polity and rid its citizenry of their freedom from threat*.[10] The argument is amoral from the deontological perspective of intention. Its dialectic between self and other is nevertheless critical to the present political imperative to bridge the national concern of social and economic equality, on the one hand, and the global concern of sustainable development, on the other. Helping non-citizens in need beyond the borders of the state maintains freedom from threat for citizens within the borders of the state. Government must increasingly go abroad to be able to respond, sustainably, to matters at home.

Fourth and finally, if the sustainable development agenda is correctly considered to address all states of the world across a spectrum of resilience toward climate change and its effects, then "best practices" of resilience in one country can be scaled up to the global level and become an example to other countries. Scaling-up and scaling-down are of course already happening in the food, water and energy sectors and depend on multiple partnerships at state, municipal and market levels of activity. I do not wish to go into detail here. The theoretical point I want to make is that under the banner of general sustainability in a world of increasing threats, political responsibility toward the security and freedom of one's own peoples can be considered to enhance the security and freedoms of other peoples. It is, at the very least, not the case that such *political* responsibility *necessarily* puts up borders between citizens and non-citizens—a fundamental issue in cosmopolitan literature concerning the relation between political community, on the one hand, and human interests, on the other (Beardsworth, Brown, and Shapiro 2019, 1–14; Brock 2009; Caney 2006; Cabrera 2010; Linklater 1998; Tan 2010). I spoke earlier of the dilemma between an effective global politics and state interests: without the capacity and responsibilities of the state, a global politics cannot be conducted; with these capacities, the material requirements and responsibilities of a global politics become compromised by state and nation-state interests. The latter interests include those of its citizens. The logic of political responsibility, as I have rehearsed it, transcends in principle this dilemma.

To conclude this pragmatic analysis of responsibility from the Weberian perspective of the state: The agency x (who is responsible?) is government; the addressee y (to whom?) is the citizen and the referent z (for what?) is the citizen's freedom from threats. If the pragmatics of responsibility lies primarily in these political terms, it is possible to argue that these terms bridge the gap between national and global responsibilities.

Political responsibility as responsible leadership

Michael Zürn argues in his excellent *A Theory of Global Governance: Authority, Legitimacy and Contestation* that global governance will remain issue specific for the imminent future given its dual political deficit: lack of power to provide sufficient coordination among policies and lack of a separation of powers that would give it legitimate political infrastructure (Zürn 2018, 220–224). The Weberian perspective on political responsibility is obviously important in these respects. The concerted political action that is required to respond to the global threat of climate change means that the power of the state—"its legitimate monopoly of violence" in Weberian language—remains a critical means by which to finance, mainstream and coordinate diverse activities and markets underpinning sustainable development. In the gap between planetary sustainability and the state system, the state remains the only agent in world politics with such legitimate capacity.[11] The last two sections have theorized this legitimate capacity in terms of the task efficacy and legitimacy of responsible government. I suggested at the end of the last section that the dilemma between an effective global politics and state interests could be addressed. Addressing this dilemma in the way that I have produces another paradox however.

I have argued that it is within the concept of political duty to cooperate with other states, pool sovereignty with other states and indeed cede sovereignty to supranational control where necessary if the duty to govern entails fulfilling the needs of a state's citizens. I have also argued that this logic of duty is required not only by most challenges to security in an interdependent world but also by the very idea of freedom to which democratic governments, at least, subscribe. The paradox is therefore the following: to maintain sovereignty with regard to global threats, the state must at the least pool it and at most cede it. *Retaining sovereign control requires letting go of sovereign control* (Beardsworth 2017, 2019a, 2019b). Reconfiguring the duty to govern and equating political responsibility with the duty to govern cannot resolve this paradox theoretically (as this chapter has up to this point). It requires a qualitatively different understanding of political responsibility, one no longer of responsible government, but one of *responsible leadership* from within government.

The former American foreign policy expert and IR scholar C.B. Marshall wrote in 1952 in the context of the emerging thermonuclear age: "We can serve our national interest in these times only by a policy which transcends our national interest. That is the meaning of responsibility" (Marshall 1952). Serving the demands of sovereignty by transcending sovereignty should be equally considered, I suggest, an act of responsibility. This act has to be assumed; it cannot be deduced logically from the concept of governmental duty. Put differently, the bridge between the national and global may be settled theoretically by the concept of political responsibility, but it needs the responsibility of leadership to initiate it practically; it needs responsible statecraft.

By announcing in October 2014 that the US was cutting CO_2 emissions by 20% by 2025, on the base line of 2005, and that China was increasing its use of renewable energies to a minimum of 20% of its energy mix by 2030, Presidents Barack Obama and Xi Jinping undid the gridlock which climate change negotiations had fallen into at the UN Conference of the Parties in Copenhagen 2009. The two leaders also rerouted the climate change regime by making the Paris Climate Agreement of 2015 possible and by brokering lines of potential reciprocity between developed and developing countries. October 2014 presented a strong moment in political responsibility, aligned with the sustainable development agenda.

Both presidencies have of course moved on since 2014, with Xi Jinping seeking long-term global hegemony for China and Donald Trump associating political responsibility with a specific, if important domestic constituency (the "losers of globalization"). The deepening gap between global concerns and the state system that has followed their acts is deeply troubling at both domestic and global scales, but the greater reality of this gap today does not negate Marshall's argument. The gap simply points to the fact that it is an ideological and political struggle to *assume* political responsibility *qua* the duty to govern: an act of responsiveness before duty as such.[12]

The material realities of an interdependent world can determine what effective and legitimate government should be (as this chapter has argued). These realities cannot determine, however, that this kind of government will take place. I suggest that much of the post-Cold War liberal hope was predicated on this determinism. The return of populism to the underbelly of liberal democracies is important on many levels. Most importantly here, this return demonstrates that the notions of task efficacy and legitimacy particular to governmental duty have to be fought for. This fight involves leadership from civil society, as the young climate activist Greta Thunberg, Climate School strikes and Extinction Rebellion have again recently shown (see the chapter by Jackson in this volume). That said, it also requires an act of political leadership at the wheel of government that serves state sovereignty by transcending it. *The doctrine of RtoP never took us through these political waters*, pitched understandably but unilaterally at the moral and normative level. Contemporary populism has reminded us of the importance of these waters. As the present difficulties of global governance regimes attest, a global politics can only be achieved first through new acts of interest, responsibility and sovereignty—acts that, by transcending the dilemma of global politics and state interest, bridge the gap between global threats and challenges and the state system. Assuming these acts is the contemporary meaning of responsible political leadership.

Conclusion

This chapter started with comments on the post-Cold War problematic of international responsibility, a problematic that avoided the problem of political will and the specificity of political responsibility. I also suggested that with the end of this liberal moment of international history from, broadly speaking, 2007/8 (the western-induced global financial crisis) and 2011 (the intervention in Libya), both this political deficit and the deepening gap between global concerns and the state system came to the fore in the decline of international liberalism and the return of populism to liberal democracies. The chapter has maintained as a result the need to focus on political responsibility as the bridge between global concerns and the state system and has rehearsed a Weberian, pragmatic understanding of political responsibility to do this. The major argument has been that attention to the needs of a state's own citizenry necessarily requires attention to global matters. The consequence is twofold: first, states must cooperate with other states and pool or, at the limit, cede their sovereignty if they are to remain in control of their own borders and satisfy their citizens; and second, that helping one's own citizens therefore means helping as well the populations of other states. This logic of responsible government has been made in terms of task efficacy and the legitimacy of political authority. Reframing the content of these terms with regard to global threats and challenges embeds international responsibility in the domestic polity without raising borders around this polity. This is, I consider, the importance of this chapter's argument. To reframe the concepts of political responsibility and political duty accordingly may go a long way in bridging the gap between the national and the global (theoretically at least). As the chapter finally argued, however, bridging this gap requires from the first responsibility as leadership in order that acts of national interest, security and sovereignty are considered to be those that, precisely, transcend territorially determined notions of security, interest and sovereignty. These are the forward-looking meanings of political responsibility in our globalized, fractured age, and they structure the political challenges to come. The fact that this renewed Weberian focus on the state as an agent of change is not another form of state-centrism from the discipline of International Relations follows: without the state, no systemic change toward a wider-conceived planetary politics is possible in the first place.

Notes

1. On the relation between responsibility and progressive state leadership see Beardsworth (2019c).
2. This is not to underestimate the importance of the state regarding the protection of its own citizens (something emphasized later). It is simply to note that the principle of sovereignty as responsibility places responsibility above the post-1945 principle of sovereign independence.
3. Hedley Bull articulated this problem long ago in terms of the tension between 'world order' (the value of which is individuals) and 'international order' (the value of which is states). A system of states instituting world order creates international disorder (Bull 1977, 85–89).
4. The first systematic use of the term "global threats and challenges" began with Kofi Annan's launch of the "High Level Panel on Threats, Challenges and Change" in December 2003. The report was published by the Secretary General's Office a year later (United Nations 2004) and critiqued by the General Assembly for inadequate treatment of economic development for global collective security in February 2005.
5. This does not discount a strong argument regarding the state and its cosmopolitan responsibilities (see Beardsworth, Brown, and Shapiro 2019). A state-focused cosmopolitanism and my Weberian argument can work in tandem theoretically. The latter position does argue, however, for a political route to systemic change that is based on enlightened self-interest rather than altruism.
6. Leslie Green only concludes with a consent-based theory of governance (Green 2007,183).
7. The distinction here between the human and non-human is ultimately precarious: climate change is human-induced, etc.
8. As classical realists from George Kennan (1984) to Barack Obama (2011) have maintained. The fate of the Libyan intervention proves the difficulty of this moral projection within a system of states. Libya's fate does not disprove, however, its possibility (as realists argue).
9. I have assumed in this chapter a liberal republican approach to security. The projection of non-domination onto the global scale will necessarily imply negotiations of principles of security on the world stage in the coming decades. In this context, the relation between democratic and non-democratic states will be negotiated in terms of this spectrum of security.
10. Philip Pettit makes a strong republican case for this kind of political logic in *Just Freedom* (2014); see also Skinner (2010). From the perspective rehearsed here the point is political. It does *not* entail the consequence that a state will refuse to intervene to aid foreigners in need *unless* it is in its national interest to do so. Rather, it contends that, to one side of the moral argument, it is politically appropriate to help foreigners in need because, without doing so, one's own freedom is jeopardized in an interdependent world. My point is that with the sustainable development agenda political and moral interests of more resilient states can converge.
11. Whatever one's particular politics around relations between the state and the market, and however unrealistic in detail, the 2019 Labour Party Manifesto (UK Labour Party 2019) addressed squarely the need for concerted political action in order to address the challenges of our age.
12. The act of responsiveness has often been considered 'ethical' over the last forty years of political theorizing (Beardsworth 1996; Jonas 1984; Levinas 1961). I consider it an essentially political act of leadership.

References

Bacevich, A. (2008). *The Limits of Power: The End of American Exceptionalism*. New York: Metropolitan Books.
Beardsworth, R. (1996). *Derrida and the Political*. London: Routledge.
Beardsworth, R. (2015). "From Moral to Political Responsibility in a Globalized Age." *Ethics & International Affairs*, 29(1): 71–92.
Beardsworth, R. (2017). "Our Political Moment: Political Responsibility and Leadership in a Globalized, Fragmented Age." *Journal of International Relations*, 32(4): 1–19.
Beardsworth, R. (2019a). *What is Progressive State Leadership Today?* https://www.openaccessgovernment.org/progressive-state-leadership/61425/ (accessed November 07, 2019).
Beardsworth, R. (2019b). *Progressive State Leadership Today: Part 2*. https://www.openaccessgovernment.org/?s=Progressive+state+leadership+Part+2 (accessed November 07, 2019).
Beardsworth, R. (2019c). *Progressive State Leadership and the Rise of Populist Nationalism*. https://www.openaccessgovernment.org/progressive-state-leadership-populist-nationalism/76559/ (accessed November 20, 2019).

Beardsworth, R., Brown, G.W., and Shapiro, R. (2019). *The State and Cosmopolitan Responsibilities*. Oxford: Oxford University Press.
Booth, K. (2007). *Theory of World Security*. Cambridge: Cambridge University Press.
Brock, G. (2009). *Global Justice: A Cosmopolitan Account*. Oxford: Oxford University Press.
Bull, H. (1977). *The Anarchical Society: A Study of Order in World Politics*. New York: Columbia University Press.
Cabrera, L. (2010). *The Practice of Global Citizenship*. Cambridge, UK: Cambridge University Press.
Caney, S. (2006). *Justice Beyond Borders: A Global Political Theory*. Oxford: Oxford University Press.
Claude, I. (1986). "Common Defense and Great Power Responsibilities." *Political Science Quarterly*, 101(5): 719–732.
Colonomos, A. (2008). *Moralizing International Relations*. New York: Palgrave Macmillan.
Crawford, J. (2002). *The International Law Commission's Articles on State Responsibility: Introduction, Text and Commentaries*. Cambridge, UK: Cambridge University Press.
Deudney, D. (2007). *Bounding Power: Republican Security Theory from the Polis to the Global Village*. Princeton, NJ: Princeton University Press.
Geuss, R. (2008). *Philosophy and Real Politics*. Princeton, NJ: Princeton University Press.
Gilpin, R. (1981). *War and Change in World Politics*. Cambridge, UK: Cambridge University Press.
Glanville, L. (2014). *Sovereignty and the Responsibility to Protect: A New History*. Chicago, IL: Chicago University Press.
Green, L. (2007). "The Duty to Govern." *Legal Theory*, 13(3–4): 165–185.
Hayden, P. (2005). *Cosmopolitan Global Politics*. Aldershot: Ashgate.
Hehir, A. (2012). *The Responsibility to Protect: Rhetoric, Reality and the Future of Humanitarian Intervention*. Basingstoke, UK: Palgrave Macmillan.
Hobbes, T. (1977). *Leviathan*. London: Penguin.
Human Rights Watch Report (2019). *Atrocities as the New Normal*. https://www.hrw.org/world-report/2019/essay/atrocities-as-the-new-normal (accessed November 07, 2019).
Hurrell, A. (2008). *On Global Order: Powers, Values and the Constitution of International Society*. Oxford: Oxford University Press.
ICISS (2001). *Report of the International Commission on Intervention and State Sovereignty*. Ottawa: International Development Research Centre.
Jackson, R. (2007). *Sovereignty*. Cambridge: Polity.
Jonas, H. (1984). *The Imperative of Responsibility*. Chicago: Chicago University Press.
Kahler, M., and Lake, D.A. (2003). *Governance in a Global Economy: Political Authority in Transition*. Princeton, NJ: Princeton University Press.
Kennan, G. (1984). *American Diplomacy*. Chicago, IL: Chicago University Press.
Kaul, I. (1999). *Global Public Goods: International Cooperation in the 21st Century*. Oxford: Oxford University Press.
Latour, B. (2018). *Down to Earth: Politics in the New Climate Regime*. Cambridge, UK: Polity Press.
Levinas, E. (1961). *Totality and Infinity: An Essay on Exteriority*. Dordrecht, NL: Kluewer Associated Publishers.
Linklater, A. (1998). *The Transformation of Political Community* Cambridge: Polity Press.
Marshall (1952). "National Interest and National Responsibility." *Annual of the American Academy of Political and Social Science*, 282(1): 84–90.
Menon, R. (2016). *The Conceit of Humanitarian Intervention*, New York: Oxford University Press.
Mitrany, D. (1946). *A Working Peace System: An Argument for the Functional Development of International Organization Organization*. London: Royale Institute of International Affairs.
Müller, J.-W. (2016). *What is Populism?*. Philadelphia: University of Pennsylvania Press.
Obama, B. (2011). *Remarks by the President to the Nation on Libya*. https://obamawhitehouse.archives.gov/the-press-office/2011/03/28/remarks-presidentaddress-nation-libya (accessed November 15, 2019).
Pettit, P. (1997). *Republicanism: A Theory of Freedom and Government*. New York: Oxford University Press.
Pettit, P. (2014). *Just Freedom: A Moral Case for a Complex World*. New York: W.W. Norton and Co.
Rosanvallon, P. (2015). *Le bon gouvernement*. Paris: Editions du Seuil.
Sandler, T. (2010). *Global Collective Action*. Cambridge, UK: Cambridge University Press.
Skinner, Q. (1998). *Liberty before Liberalism*. Cambridge: Cambridge University Press.
Skinner, Q. (2010). "On the Slogans of Republican Political Theory." *European Journal of Political Theory*, 9(1): 95–102.
Slaughter, S. (2005). *Liberty Beyond Neo-Liberalism: A Republican Critique of Liberal Governance in A Globalizing Age*. Basingstoke, UK: Palgrave Macmillan.

Smith, T. (2010). "From 'fortunate vagueness' to 'democratic globalism': American democracy promotion as imperialism", *Paper Presented at the International Studies Association Annual Conference*, New Orleans, February 2010.
Strange, S. (1996). *The Retreat of the State: The Diffusion of Power in the World Economy*. Cambridge: Cambridge University Press.
Tardif, M (2020). *The International Responsibility Project: An Examination of State Practice in Relation to the Concept of International Responsibility in the Post-Cold War Period*, PhD Thesis. Department of International Politics: University of Aberystwyth.
Tan, K.-K. (2010). *Justice without Borders: Cosmopolitanism, Nationalism, and Patriotism*. Cambridge, UK: Cambridge University Press.
Vilmer, J.-P. (2012). *La Guerre au Nom de l'Humanite: Tuer ou Laisser Mourir*. Paris: Presses Universitaires Françaises.
Weber, M. (1965). *Politics as a Vocation*, Transl. H. Gerth and C. Wright Mills. Philadelphia, PA: Fortress Press.
Williams, B. (2005). *In the Beginning Was the Deed: Realism and Moralism in Political Argument*. Princeton, NJ: Princeton University Press.
Young, I.M. (2013). *Responsibility for Justice*. New York: Oxford University Press.
UK Labour Party (2019). *It's Time for Real Change*. https://labour.org.uk/manifesto/ (accessed November 22, 2019).
United Nations (2004). *A More Secure World: Our Shared Responsibility*. https://www.un.org/en/events/pastevents/a_more_secure_world.shtml (accessed November 07, 2019).
United Nations (2015). *Transforming Our World: The Sustainable Development Agenda for 2030*. https://sustainabledevelopment.un.org/post2015/transformingourworld/publication (accessed November 07, 2019).
Zürn, M. (2018). *A Theory of Global Governance: Authority, Legitimacy and Contestation*. Oxford: Oxford University Press.

6
MORAL IRRESPONSIBILITY IN WORLD POLITICS

Peter Sutch

Introduction

The relationship between moral responsibility and political/legal responsibility is a vital element of a general conception of responsibility in world politics. Without a sense of moral responsibility it is impossible to comprehend the idea that the intervention in Kosovo might be properly described as 'illegal yet legitimate' (Independent International Commission on Kosovo 2000) or that failure to reach a binding and effective agreement on climate change might be thought of as irresponsible. Without a conception of political/legal responsibility, we lack any sense of the political agency or of the practical means of realising the goals set by the international community or demanded by morality. The argument of this chapter is not simply that we need to think about moral responsibility as well as political and legal responsibility. Rather, the chapter argues that we need to focus on the relationship between them and that the most influential scholarship that does so is problematic in important respects. It is not unusual to see moral claims (concerning a responsibility to alleviate humanitarian suffering or to mitigate environmental degradation) flounder on a lack of political agency or to see attempts to overcome this institutional deficit defeated by a lack of state-consent to new institutions (like the International Criminal Court) or practical buy-in to new concepts (like the Responsibility to Protect (RtoP)). The apparent disjuncture between accounts of moral and political responsibility has prompted international political theory to engage with the practical. Importantly, this entails moving beyond an account of the moral failure of the international system to an exploration of how that system might become an agent of our moral responsibility. The putative 'our' in the phrase 'our moral responsibility' rests on the cosmopolitan claim that all human beings have moral duties to all others (including future generations). Cosmopolitanism has enjoyed such success in the debates in international political thought that Michael Blake's claim that 'we are all cosmopolitans now' (Blake 2013), an argument grounded on the claim that any moral argument worthy of the name rests on a baseline commitment to egalitarianism, is, on the face of it, plausible.[1] Thus, the relationship between a cosmopolitan account of morality and the international legal order (historically seen as pursuing distinct and incompatible ends) becomes central to thinking about responsibility. In the contemporary literature, this goal is pursued through an engagement with institutional concepts such as Responsibility to Protect (RtoP) (Beardsworth et al. 2019), the humanisation of international law (Meron 2006; Teitel 2011), Common or Community interest (Benvenista and Nolte 2018), and human rights (Beitz 2009b;

Buchanan 2010; Pogge 2002) that appear to share the moral foundations of cosmopolitanism. Here, this chapter argues, lies the problem. Appearances can be deceiving, and we need reconsider the claim that a plausible account of moral responsibility, grounded in an accessible account of political/legal responsibility, can have cosmopolitan foundations.

The nexus between the normative and the empirical has been the locus for some of the most ground-breaking work in IR (Erskine 2012; Hurrell and Macdonald 2013; Price 2008). In ethical and political theory, the search for institutional traction has pushed scholars towards a practical or institutional approach (Beitz 2009b; Buchanan 2004, 2013; Hurrell 2007). However, the dominant tradition pursuing questions of global justice in International Political Theory (IPT) is cosmopolitan, whereas the scholarship pursuing questions of global constitutionalism, legitimacy and justice in IR is communitarian, in the sense adopted by Adler (2005) and in the broader sense described in the IPT literature by, e.g. Brown (1992). The distinction between cosmopolitan and communitarian political thought was never the caricatured distinction between universalist and moral egalitarian cosmopolitans and parochial, statist communitarians. Rather, it was a deep theoretical divide over how moral universals arise and how that alters the ways we think about how to institutionalise moral responsibility (Sutch 2018). Despite making some extraordinary accommodations to the practical, and developing a research agenda that mirrors the central element of that found in constructivist norm research, cosmopolitan IPT has not yet sufficiently rethought the relationship between the moral and the practical/legal and this, I contend, can lead to moral irresponsibility that has dangerous political consequences. It is a moral irresponsibility that fundamentally undermines the rule of law. What this means is that cosmopolitan moral demands not only challenge specific rules and regimes in international law (challenging for example the right of states to refuse to consent to rules or institutional practises that advance morally vital humanitarian concerns) but that they go deeper to the very constitutive principles that govern the nature of the legal order and the questions of who makes the law and how and how hegemony is limited by the system.

The chapter is going to look particularly at some standard but ambitious cosmopolitan claims about our moral responsibility to reform the law (or to flout it) to achieve a more morally satisfying outcome. Encouraging the use of force to promote humanitarian ends or prevent terrorist strikes in contravention of customary and treaty norms, or arguments urging us to reform or abandon institutions and legal regimes that don't live up to moral principles are common in the literature. The underlying thought is that moral imperatives have a clear priority over legal and political norms—an idea that has survived two vital moves in IPT. The first of these is the move away from foundationalist political theory to constructivist and interpretivist political theory (Hurrell and Macdonald 2013, 63–4). The second is a move towards a practical approach—one that gives practises 'authority' in guiding ethical theorising (Beitz 2009b, 10; Buchanan 2010, 91). Both moves should reopen the question of how we should conceive of the relationship between a legal injunction and a moral one but, in cosmopolitan IPT at least, this does not appear to be the case. This chapter will focus on the second of these moves (the first being a well-explored aspect of contemporary IPT since Rawls). IPT has recently drawn inspiration from legal theorists thinking about the evolution of the international community. It is now quite commonplace to see political theorists relying on the power of *jus cogens* norms, *erga omnes* obligations, and non-derogable human rights to point to the ways that international law is becoming more receptive to and more fertile for cosmopolitan ideas. However, it is vital that scholars are extremely careful when evaluating the moral ambition of this 'common language' or when interpreting the moral and political potential of apparently cosmopolitan developments in international law (compare chapter by Wiener in this volume). The identification of cosmopolitan moral aims in legal norms that arise in the discourse of public international law and arguing that they signal a decisive move away from a state-based order to an egalitarian and individual-based order strains the empirical and therefore the moral credibility of the argument (compare the respective chapters by Busser, Baron, and Dellavalle in this volume). This last point forms the core of the chapter. The important move to the practical approach entails an account of how the empirical relates to our construction of the moral and so misrepresenting the nature of human rights or community obligations fundamentally undermines the arguments about responsibility in play.

Cosmopolitans and the practical approach

The practical approach is shared by a small subset of cosmopolitan scholars, but their place in the debate, as well as the richness of their argument, merits serious attention. Thomas Pogge, Allen Buchanan, and Charles Beitz first rose to prominence in the field as they criticised Rawls for not seeing the full cosmopolitan implications of his political liberalism. As a deeper, and more secure, cosmopolitanism came to be associated with liberal IPT all three of these scholars began, in different ways, to rely on principles inherent in the existing international legal order, rather than principles drawn directly from their cosmopolitan political theory, to ground their moral and political claims. This trend, beginning with Pogge's claim that articles 25 and 28 of the UDHR give cosmopolitanism all the purchase necessary to ground reformist political and moral demands and further developed in the more recent work of Buchanan and Beitz, captures a trend towards a practical approach to cosmopolitan justice.

The basic argument is that the moral commitments inherent in IHRL are incompatible with other aspects of international law and practise. Pogge, for example, argues that the commitment to a social and international order in which human rights can be realised (article 28 UDHR) demands reforms to existing institutions. In 2002 Pogge, exploring developments associated with the evolution of international human rights law, noted that an 'historic transformation of our moral norms has mostly produced cosmetic rearrangements' (Pogge 2002, 5). His work, then and since, was intended to highlight the full extent of our moral obligations that underpinned, but were not fully met in, our institutional and legal undertakings. Our moral irresponsibility, he argued, lay in failing to fully understand the ways our moral principles should alter our practises. He shows, for example, that the international borrowing privilege, conferred on the governments of a sovereign state, regardless of their human rights record, is both a cause of severe poverty in their country and an institution sustained by international law (Pogge 2002, 13–15). Here the argument is not that human rights law demands reform of the borrowing privilege but that any plausible interpretation of the moral commitment to human rights does so. This is a complex and fascinating argument that addresses the nature of human rights norms, their relation to other legal norms, and the relationship between our moral and legal responsibilities (Sutch 2019). Pogge argues that IHRL explicitly rests on a shared set of moral commitments found in the preamble to the UDHR and other human rights instruments. The document does appear to echo this. Its opening lines include the idea that the 'recognition of the inherent dignity and of the equal and inalienable rights of all members of the human family is the foundation of freedom, justice and peace in the world'. Yet, there is evidence in the history of the drafting of the UDHR, in the legal practise of not treating the preamble to a treaty as a part of the normative body of the text, and in subsequent state practice that a shared, defined moral commitment cannot be inferred from the mere existence of IHRL. Buchanan (2004, 2013) and Beitz (2009b) both explicitly build on a critique of Pogge's argument here to deepen a commitment to a practical approach.

Cosmopolitanism has a long-standing fascination for human rights. Yet, the 'practical' approach employed by Beitz and Buchanan is distinct within it and the ambition to link the work being done in the practise of international politics, particularly in international law, to normative debates is the key to this distinctiveness. Each theorist offers an argument that consists of three crucial features. The first is a description of the practise itself. Each sees the practise as an international legal-institutional order, and each describes the place of human rights as being significant to the constitution of that order. The second crucial feature is a claim to justificatory modesty, something that entails at least putting aside (if not rejecting) orthodox, philosophical accounts of normativity in favour of deriving values from practices. Each, in distinct ways, argues that the moral claims that they make are modest enough to make the task of moral critique and prescription accessible to all participants in the practise and by doing so they feed into the third crucial feature of the practical approach—institutionally plausible reform. These three features of the argument combine to argue that a plausibly modest moral argument must allow the practise some authority over the moral argument in order to achieve the institutional traction required for cosmopolitanism to become practical (Beitz 2009b, 10, 102, 212; Buchanan 2004, 38; 2010, 91; 2013, 21). These features intend to provide a moral argument that is accessible to, and motivational for, actors engaged in an existing practise as well as developing a practically achievable set of institutional refinements that can realise those moral goals.

In describing the practise of contemporary international politics, these cosmopolitans recognise the significance of international law to that practise. In describing the international legal order, they derive moral principles that require reform of existing laws and institutions in order to more fully realise the values that are already explicit in the practise. More specifically, each argues that the normative force of human rights claims generates a moral obligation to ignore or reform the law. In both cases, the description of the practise, searching for its constitutive norms, and understanding the normative and institutional dynamics of their evolution are crucial. It is crucial for understanding the moral basis of the international legal order (whether we present these as shared understandings (Brunée and Toope 2010), constitutional principles (Reus Smit 2004), or institutionalised moral reasons (Buchanan 2004)).

Human rights law and cosmopolitan responsibilities

In cosmopolitan thought, it is individual rights claims that underpin the critical claims concerning legal reform. Unsurprisingly, perhaps, the development of international human rights law (IHRL) since 1948 is the focus of attention for those seeking to ground normative claims about individual rights in the practises of the international legal order. A brief look at how Beitz and Buchanan push the argument found in Pogge to a more complete practical theory shows just how serious they are about grounding their moral claims in legal practices.

Pogge's turn to IHRL is, he argues, a shortcut. The shortcut is significant not just because it draws on the power of a socially constituted discourse but because it is modest in that it 'indicates a reorientation of the sort for which Rawls has coined the phrase "political not metaphysical"' (Pogge 2002, 57). The word human in human rights is different from the word natural in natural rights in that it does not imply an ontological commitment to human rights beyond the context of the practise he wants to examine. The practise, as he describes it, is neutral among comprehensive moral doctrines, confirms that all human beings have the same and equal rights and focuses our attention on the obligations of official agents (primarily but not only the state) to respect, protect, and fulfil those rights and, in this, it is a moral universalism that arises in a world of states (Pogge 2002, 57–8). Yet Pogge's modest reference to article 28 of the UDHR suggests an urgent need to reform the international legal order from the WTO and the UN to the very idea of state-centred sovereignty.

Pogge recognises the important (but in his view rarely drawn) distinction between moral and legal human rights and states his intention to explicate a moral notion of human rights. But his move to the moral import of IHRL entails what Buchanan calls the 'mirroring view' that human rights law is meant to give effect to preexisting moral rights (Buchanan 2013, 14–23; Pogge 2002, 53).

As noted above, Pogge cites the language of the preamble to the UDHR to substantiate the view that states accept the existence and primacy of preexisting moral rights something Buchanan and Beitz challenge as a misleading declaratory flourish (Beitz 2009b, 72; Buchanan 2013, 21). The power of Pogge's claim, they argue, derives from a false claim about the intentions of the framers and practices of IHRL. Nevertheless, Buchanan and Beitz see further opportunity in the practical approach.

Beitz and Buchanan both seek to harness the promise of IHRL and acknowledge that doing so requires that we 'approach human rights practically, not as the application of an independent philosophical idea to the realm, but as a political doctrine constructed to play a certain role in global political life' (Beitz 2009b, 48–9). There is, both make clear, 'folk' pretheoretical or philosophical theory of moral human rights that enjoys this authoritative status in the practice (Buchanan 2013, 7). Both seek to move beyond description to understand the justification for the practise, drawing on the reasons why IHRL developed to limit the power of the state and to impose duties upon actors (first the state and then the international community) to respect, protect, promote, and fulfil human rights (Beitz 2009b, 209–19; Buchanan 2013, 36).

Here then, we get back to the process of theorising moral responsibility and its relation to existing laws and institutions. For Beitz, human rights have become more than the sum of their parts and:

> are better conceived as background norms or principles – they are widely although not unanimously accepted as publicly available, critical standards to which agents can appeal in justifying and criticizing actions and policies proposed or carried out (or not) by governments.
>
> *(Beitz 2009b, 210)*

Human rights have become a language that helps us reflect on the extent to which the state and the international community effectively protect individuals from standard threats to urgent interests (the predations or failings of the state) (Beitz 2009b, 11). Similarly, Buchanan, in generating a moral justification of the international legal order (Buchanan 2013, 45), argues that when we consider the deepest reasons for having IHRL, we realise that:

> Having a system of international legal human rights is a necessary condition for the existing international order to be justifiable, because without a system of international legal human rights the strong rights of sovereignty that the international order confers on states would be morally unacceptable.
>
> *(Buchanan 2013, 44)*

From here he argues that implicit in the practise is a moral responsibility to reform institutions and norms that do not live up to human rights. His work here, often in a very fruitful partnership with Robert Keohane (Buchanan and Keohane 2004, 2015), he calls institutional moral reasoning (Buchanan 2004). It is necessary, he argues, to conceive of institutions and moral principles as entwined and to adopt a progressive conservatism in our approach to morally guided institutional reform. By this he means:

> that the theory should build upon, or at least not squarely contradict, the more morally acceptable principles of the existing international legal system. The most obvious reason for this requirement is that satisfying it will generally contribute to the accessibility of the theory's proposals…But there is another reason: Where possible the theorist should build upon the moral strengths of the existing system, because it would be irresponsible to advocate, unnecessarily, a disregard for whatever progress has already been achieved in the system.
>
> *(Buchanan 2004, 63)*

Weak institutions cause us to be overly conservative in the creation and implementation of legal rules. As Buchanan explains, the driver for conservatism in international law is what he calls the parochialism objection—the concern that powerful agents will use permissive norms to impose their favoured interpretation of rules to further their own ends. Hence, restrictions on the use of force for humanitarian purposes, sovereign consent as the source of binding law, weak enforcement mechanisms in IHRL, and vetoes for the Permanent Five (P5) of the United Nations Security Council. In each case, Buchanan argues that our moral commitments to human rights require reform of these legal norms. Buchanan argues that in grasping the 'heart' of human rights we should note that:

> the system as I have just formulated it… does not speak to whether such regulation is to be achieved voluntarily, that is through the consent of all states subject to it, or otherwise. It may be true that at the founding of the system of international human rights law, there was no practical alternative to the reliance on the consent of states, that is, to create this law primarily through the making of treaties. But if circumstances changed sufficiently, it might become feasible to take a less voluntary approach. And it would be a mistake to assume that doing so would be morally unacceptable or deprive international human rights law of legitimacy.
>
> *(Buchanan 2013, 28)*

Consent-based law may protect the weaker against the predations of the stronger, but it also provides a legitimacy veto (Buchanan 2010). The use of the P5 veto to restrain UNSC action even in the face of gross breaches of humanitarian law is the most familiar face of such a veto, but the ability of states to refuse to consent to rules and institutions that better protect human rights or to consent with reservations also constitutes a legitimacy veto (Buchanan 2013, 280). Buchanan argues that a more expansive conception of state's responsibilities under human rights is morally mandatory so that it becomes morally required that we develop 'institutional resources that would make a more expansive conception of duties not only feasible but morally acceptable' (Buchanan 2013, 283). The moral power of the justification for human rights law drives arguments including an expanded category of *jus cogens* norms, supermajority ratification of treaties imposing universal obligation, and he points to innovations such as a proposed EU constitution allowing for supermajority voting and the attempt to make the Responsibility to Protect (R2P) a required response to humanitarian wrongdoing as examples of progressive and morally responsible innovations (Buchanan 2013, 282).

Moral irresponsibility and humanitarian military intervention: an example

Both Beitz and Buchanan believe that existing laws restricting the use of force to respond to humanitarian crises are irresponsible. Here I explore this claim to explore the general issue of how they theorise the relationship between morality and law.

Both offer critiques of Michael Walzer's just war theory as a vehicle for their arguments. Beitz engaged with Walzer's *Just and Unjust Wars* in his 1979 book review and a subsequent response to Walzer's now seminal 'The Moral Standing of States' (Beitz 1980; Walzer 1980), a subject to which he returned in 'The Moral Standing of States Revisited' (Beitz 2009a). Buchanan offers a critique of Walzer's conventionalism, arguing that the just war/legalist position is 'methodologically flawed' because it is not empirical enough and that the costs of continued adherence to the just war norm are therefore 'intolerably high' (Buchanan 2004, 264). Its conservatism, he argues, stems from its failure to treat the normative force of human rights with the institutional creativity it demands. The core issue at stake concerns whether the growing normative force of human rights should licence reforms to the laws of war to enable the pursuit of goals including humanitarian protection or the defeat of international terrorism. Both Beitz and Buchanan argue that it should. In making this case, Beitz issues a less demanding set of demands for reform than Buchanan and, in the later work at least, sees more of Walzer's 'developing internationalism' (Beitz 2009a, 325). Nevertheless, Beitz wants to make more of Walzer's argument that the international community 'may have obligations to foster [a type of statehood that protects individual rights] when a state does not' (Walzer 2004, 251 in Beitz 2009a, 344). For both cosmopolitans, the debate is between a restrictionist regime governing the use of force and a progressive one that protects and promotes human rights. For the sake of clarity, I will explore the issue using Buchanan's bolder critique of restrictionism.

We already have the working parts of his argument before us. The first claim is that there has been a 'transition from an international legal system whose constitutive legitimizing aim was peace among states (and before that the regulation of war among states) to one that takes the protection of human rights as one of its central goals' (Buchanan 2010, 72). The second claim is that a conservative approach to this development rests its case on 'the parochialism objection' (Buchanan 2010, 73 above). The danger that powerful states will use rules permitting humanitarian intervention for their own ends has led to restrictionist norms and a veto for the P5 in the UNSC, the consent of which is required to allow humanitarian intervention. However, Buchanan's institutional moral reasoning approach argues it is possible to mitigate this risk by instituting institutional reforms that would enable us to work confidently towards the goals indicated by a commitment to human rights. He writes:

> To put the same point differently, traditional philosophical theorizing about human rights needs to be augmented by social moral epistemology, understood as the systematic comparative evaluation of alternative social institutions and practises as to their effectiveness and efficiency in forming beliefs that are critical for moral judgment and justification.
>
> (Buchanan 2004, 5–6)

The argument is, in brief, that Walzer's restrictionist adherence to the legalist paradigm and war convention is unduly conservative (and thus morally irresponsible) because it does not reimagine institutions in ways that could both guard against parochialism and better serve the promotion and protection of human rights. Buchanan invites us to imagine a reformed UNSC—one where the legitimacy veto owned by the P5 is removed and where *ex-ante* and *ex-post* accountability mechanisms provide confidence in pushing rules of self-defence and humanitarian intervention beyond Charter prohibitions (Buchanan and Keohane 2004). In later work examining the use of drones, Buchanan and Keohane acknowledge the risks associated with the technology (unauthorised violations of sovereignty, over use of the military option encouraged by lower costs, less easily detected violations of the discrimination principle) but argue that a 'drone accountability regime' (DAR) could minimise the risks while allowing access to the attractions of using the technology (it is cheaper, it can kill targets who may otherwise be immune from attack, greater precision in targeting, nonexposure of human operators) (Buchanan and Keohane 2015, 18–19). Importantly, in both cases, the authors are aware that major hurdles to institutional reform exist from the provisions in the Charter relating to UNSC reform to the nonideal nature of the international legal order where the intransigence of major powers meets the requirement of consent. In the face of these challenges, and in both instances, Buchanan and Keohane argue for institutions that can promote the values they derive from the international legal order but that do not work within its structures. In place of reformed UNSC, Buchanan and Keohane argue for a coalition of reasonably democratic states who would implement the accountability mechanisms in order to authorise the legitimate use of force and sanction the illegitimate use of force (Buchanan and Keohane 2004, 20). In the case of the DAR, they propose an 'informal interstate arrangement' between '"first-movers" – in this case states that are already using lethal drone technology' (Buchanan and Keohane 2015, 17, 25).

The core of the argument is that it would be morally irresponsible to accept a restrictionist normative order when these options are available to us. But in what sense are these options really available to morally and legally responsible actors?

Cosmopolitans, communitarians, and moral and legal responsibility

The key claim is that restrictionist norms limiting war to self-defence (with a few limited revisions or rules of disregard) are morally irresponsible. It is morally irresponsible because it pays too little attention to the injunction to promote and protect human rights and to the institutional reforms that could give the international community faith in a system that does so more effectively. Both Beitz and Buchanan argue that Walzer acknowledges the central moral injunction to protect human rights noting that in his work prohibitions on the use of force are premised on individual rights to life and liberty. Given that the arguments start from the same point how is it possible to reach such radically different conclusions?

The key to this conundrum is to note that they are not arguing from shared premises. Despite the shared claim to be deriving the moral argument from established practises and the recognition that individual rights are central to those practises, the ways in which they conceive of moral universalism, and of the relationship between morality and law is distinct and I think we have two main reasons to be wary of the cosmopolitan claims here. These reasons can be explored when we think about 1) whether the account of how moral rules arise in practises is relevantly similar and 2) whether the cosmopolitan account of how moral human rights function in the practise of the international legal order is defensible.

The way that Walzer conceives of individual moral rights is very different from the way that cosmopolitans—even those engaged in this practical approach, conceive of them. Walzer's universalism is 'a non-standard variety, which encompasses, perhaps even helps to explain the appeal of moral particularism' (Walzer 1990, 509). Walzer's 'thin' and 'reiteratively learned' universalism is contrasted to the 'covering law' universalism of liberal universalism and this is a distinction that can still be made. Reiterative universalism is an explanation about how a global system characterised by moral pluralism develops shared moral and legal rules—most importantly humanitarian rules proscribing 'acts that shock the conscience of mankind'. Recognising the rights of men and women in Walzer's work comes hand in hand with respect for pluralism, otherness and, most importantly, the recognition that universal rights are thin. They are urgent and in need of protection but not the basis of a fully elaborated morality. Walzer's ideal global constitution and his just war theory is premised on a set of principles which (when given 'covering law' formulation) sounds like cosmopolitan individual rights but is in fact grounded in the idea of a legalised international society with principles of equality, collective self-determination and international (legal) human rights as an outer limit to toleration (Walzer 1994, 2004). Walzer's conception of universal rights is legalised in ways that go far beyond conservative conventionalism but shares little common ground with cosmopolitanism.

The cosmopolitan account of human rights (as a normative justification derived from the legal practise) still undergoes a process of abstraction from the broader context both of IHRL and of global political practise more broadly. The process of constructing the moral justification they deploy moves ethical theorising away from actors engaged in the practise and back to political theorists who are able to abstract themselves from the constitutive forces of the practise. The move from an account of the egalitarianism inherent in IHRL to the claim that a concern for egalitarianism can reject state consent as a basis for legal obligation or legitimise unilateral uses of force is not theoretically available to Walzer and not attractive to his communitarianism.

If the cosmopolitans are wrong to argue that Walzer shares a premise with them but that he fails to cash it out in a morally satisfying way they might still be able to argue that their account of the normative promise of IHRL is more historically and sociologically satisfying. The fact that Buchanan and Beitz reject Pogge's claim that the declaratory sections of human rights treaties indicates agreement on the moral premises of IHRL is an important step in the right direction. Nevertheless, it is hard to agree, especially given the unlikely prospect of major consent-based reforms to the UNSC or the Vienna Convention on the Law of Treaties, that our commitment to human rights licenses what Reus Smit has called the hierarchisation of international law (Reus Smit 2005). In large part I think this is because, in spite of the institutional/practical focus of this work, these cosmopolitans fail to engage fully with the broader morality of international law. My claim here is not that this scholarship neglects the broader contours of the international legal order (indeed Buchanan's work is world-leading in this respect). Rather I argue that while we might agree that the status-egalitarian function is central to the moral basis of IHRL I do not think the same can be said for international law as a whole. The claim here has to be that the moral commitments that have evolved through the practises of IHRL have trumped the core constitutional principles of contemporary public international law. International law has evolved to ensure sovereign independence to protect peoples from the imposition of rules and practises by the powerful (in his recognition of the parochialism objection (above) Buchanan acknowledges this fact). The idea of sovereign equality, protected by rules of noninterference, state consent, and self-determination are key parts of the legislative account of procedural justice that is at the foundation of modern international law (Reus Smit 1999). As Beitz neatly puts it human rights are 'revisionist appurtenances of a global political order' (Beitz 2009b, 197). They arise as a corrective to one of the great evils that is fostered by this system (state predation on those in its power). But it is not at all clear that in arising a corrective to that system they exist as transcendent principles that ought to move us beyond that system; that if it was a choice between human rights and sovereignty that human rights will always win out. Indeed, Walzer is also critical of the limitations of the international system (Walzer 2004, 179–82) and believes that the moral force of international human rights requires institutional reform. While he advocates a dedicated UN military force, a world court, and new layer of governmental organisation it is one that sacrifices some opportunities for action on behalf of human rights to minimise the risk of global tyranny (Walzer 2004, 187–8).

Legal and sociological scholars exploring the evolution of the international legal order tend to be similarly minded. Teitel's account of the rise of 'humanity law' looks at the centrality of humanitarianism in the rise of the Law of Armed Conflict/International Humanitarian Law, International Criminal Law and Human Rights Law and argues that 'the status of the human is a basis for new and diverse claims, on the part of diverse voices that are new to international law and politics' (Teitel 2011, 31). Nevertheless, she argues that the law is still crisis driven, reparatory, or transitional rather than revolutionary. Ratner argues that peace rather than human rights has priority in his account of 'the thin justice of international law' (Ratner 2015). Brunée and Toope (2010, 324) show why RtoP lacks the interactional (sociological) basis to be seen as a settled norm. Reus Smit (2013) shows how repeated individual rights-based challenges to the international system have strengthened rather than undermined the system of sovereign states. While it is very clear that IHRL arose and evolved to meet the challenges, Beitz and Buchanan describe it is important to note that it is not moral irresponsibility that meant that moral principles were accompanied by relatively limited institutional avenues for unilateral and international remedy in cases of routine or even severe breaches of the legal and moral rules in play. In fact, the international legal order both shares an account of the injustices of humanitarian and human rights violations and a conservative account of the most appropriate institutional tools for the pursuit of justice. For example, the prohibition of genocide may well be the subject of *jus cogens* law, but we learn from in the 2006 judgment of the International Court of Justice in *Armed Activities on the Territory of the Congo (Democratic Republic of Congo v. Rwanda)* (Armed Activities Case) that this does not alter the consent based nature of the jurisdiction of international courts (at paragraph 64). There is little evidence that agreement on the moral significance of, for instance, crimes against humanity comes hand in hand with agreement on what coercive tools are appropriate for the responding to them or that rules making the use of coercive tools difficult in international politics should be weakened. This is not merely a technical issue or a lack of institutional imagination but a morally significant point. Human rights do not capture a thick, universal moral position on how the international order should be organised. They arise, as Beitz rightly notes, to correct moral flaws in the existing legal order. But that order protects other morally significant values and a moral theory of international law has to contend with moral pluralism and weak or thin moral agreements on urgent issues. It has to be administrable in extremely morally and politically complex situations. The fact that it is a theory of law rather than a pure moral theory carries with it a responsibility to recognise the flaws and failings of a system that is susceptible to power. We need, Waldron argues:

> To take account of considerations of legal technicality that may make a norm look arbitrary by the standards of moral philosophers…the relevant norms may have to be administered among people who certainly disagree about justice and guilt…it may be impossible to administer norms using words like 'just' and 'guilty' in their traditional moral senses or to impose tests about whose application there is likely to be irresolvable disagreement.
>
> *(Waldron 2018, 86)*

To fear the parochialism objection is not just to fear the use of law by the powerful to pursue their own ends. It is to fear the corruption of law—the violation of the principle that those subject to the law should make it and that those executing the law should obey its injunctions. It is also to ignore the fact that is a very real and permanent fear in a society characterised by what Rawls termed reasonable pluralism. The egalitarianism in IHRL cannot be the basis for undermining the rule of law itself. It can be the basis for extending our understanding of what standard threats to urgent interests are—but those threats are only manifest and sensible to us in the context of the international legal order as a whole. It is a respect for the rule of law that requires us to resist the argument that a respect for human rights requires that we disobey the law where it is inconvenient for cosmopolitans.

Conclusion

Rather than see the failure to perfectly institutionalise the protection and promotion of human rights as morally irresponsible it seems more convincing to argue that policies that aim to do so at the expense of the broader rule of law are irresponsible. Buchanan's insistence on a progressive conservatism is compelling and there is real substance to Pogge's (2012) claim that international law is 'divided against itself', yet the ways that cosmopolitan political theorists conceive of the relationship between the moral and the practical undermines their insight. In IPT the cosmopolitan/communitarian debate has fallen out of fashion but as IPT reaches out to norm research (and vice-versa) the power of its insight is invaluable. Despite the move from metaphysical to political conceptions of justice and the move to a practical approach to institutionalised moral thinking cosmopolitan theory fails the test of institutional responsibility. Communitarian thought—both normative and norm-oriented is more promising, not least because it is more comfortable with the thought that moral norms arise in the context of practises that are morally significant in themselves.

The project of working on the idea of justice in tandem with institutional reflection is essential, but isolating normative regimes and practises that look promising from a cosmopolitan point of view undermines the relationship between practises and norms. In separating our moral obligations from the constitutive legal order, their arguments threaten to undermine the system of law that is immeasurably better (but not perfect or perfectable) with the corrective that is IHRL.

Note

1 For a recent and comprehensive exploration of this claim, see B. Müller (2019) *Who Is Cosmopolitan Now?* PhD thesis presented at Johannes Gutenburg University Mainz.

References

Adler, E. (2005). *Communitarian International Relations: The Epistemic Foundations of International Relations.* New York: Routledge.
Beardsworth, R., Wallace Brown, G., and Shapcott, R., eds. (2019). *The State and Cosmopolitan Responsibilities.* Oxford: Oxford University Press.
Beitz, C. (1980). "Non-intervention and communal integrity." *Philosophy and Public Affairs*, 9(4): 385–391.
Beitz, C. (2009a). "The Moral Standing of States Revisited." *Ethics and International Affairs*, 23(4): 325–347.
Beitz, C. (2009b). *The Idea of Human Rights.* Oxford: Oxford University Press.
Benvenista, E. and Nolte, G., eds. (2018). *Community Interests Across International Law.* Oxford: Oxford University Press.
Blake, M. (2013) "We are all cosmopolitans now." In Brock, G., ed., *Cosmopolitanism versus Non-Cosmopolitanism: Critiques, Defenses and Reconceptualizations.* Oxford: Oxford University Press.
Brown, C. (1992). *International Relations Theory: New Normative Approaches.* London: Harvester Wheatsheaf.
Brunée, J., and Toope, S. (2010). *Legitimacy and Legality in International Law: An Interactional Approach.* Cambridge: Cambridge University Press.
Buchanan, A. (2004). *Justice, Legitimacy and Self Determination: Moral Foundations for International Law.* Oxford: Oxford University Press.
Buchanan, A. (2010). *Human Rights, Legitimacy and the Use of Force.* Oxford: Oxford University Press.
Buchanan, A. (2013). *The Heart of Human Rights.* Oxford: Oxford University Press.
Buchanan, A., and Keohane, R. (2004). "The Preventative Use of Force: A Cosmopolitan Institutional Proposal." *Ethics & International Affairs*, 18(1): 1–22.
Buchanan, A., and Keohane, R. (2015). "Toward a Drone Accountability Regime." *Ethics & International Affairs*, 29(2): 15–37.
Erskine, T. (2012) "Whose progress, which morals? Constructivism, normative theory and the limits and possibilities of studying ethics in world politics." *International Theory*, 4(3): 449–468.
Hurrell, A. (2007). *On Global Order: The Constitution of International Society.* Oxford: Oxford University Press.
Hurrell, A. and Macdonald, T. (2013). "Ethics and Norms in International Relations." In Carlsnaes, W., Risse, T., and Simmons, B.A., eds., *Handbook of International Relations*: Chapter 3. London: Sage.
Independent International Commission on Kosovo (2000). *The Kosovo Report: Conflict, International Response, Lessons Learned.* Oxford: Oxford University Press.
Meron, T. (2006). *The Humanization of International Law.* Leiden: Brill.
Müller, B. (2019). *Who Is Cosmopolitan Now? Cosmopolitanism as Nonrelationsim*, PhD thesis presented at Johannes Gutenburg University Mainz.

Pogge, T. (2002). *World Poverty and Human Rights*. Oxford: Polity Press.
Pogge, T. (2012). "Divided Against Itself: Aspiration and Reality of International Law." In Crawford., J., and Koskeniemmi, M., eds., *The Cambridge Companion to International Law*: Chapter 17. Cambridge: Cambridge University Press.
Price, R., ed. (2008). *Moral Limit and Possibility in World Politics*. Cambridge: Cambridge University Press.
Ratner, S. (2015) *The thin Justice of International Law: A Moral Reckoning of the Law of Nations*. Oxford: Oxford University Press.
Reus Smit, C. (1999). *The Moral Purpose of the State: Culture, Social Identity and Institutional Rationality in International Relations*. Princeton, NJ: Princeton University Press.
Reus Smit, C. (2004). *The Politics of International Law*. Cambridge University Press.
Reus Smit, C. (2005). "Liberal Hierarchy and the Licence to Use Force." *Review of International Studies*, 31(S.I.): 71–92. Cambridge.
Reus Smit, C. (2013). *Individual Rights and The making of the International System*. Cambridge: Cambridge University Press.
Sutch, P. (2018). "The Slow Normalisation of International Political Theory: Cosmopolitanism and Communitarianism then and now." In Brown, C., and Eckersley, R., eds., *The Oxford Handbook of International Political Theory*: Chapter 3. Oxford: Oxford University Press.
Sutch, P. (2019). "Neo-Kantian Cosmopolitanism and International Law: Modest Practicality." *The Kantian Review*, 24(4): 605–629.
Teitel, R. (2011). *Humanity's Law*. Oxford: Oxford University Press.
Waldron, J. (2018). "Deep Morality and Laws of War." In Lazar, S., and Frowe, H. eds., *The Oxford Handbook of Ethics of War*. 81–99. Oxford: Oxford University Press.
Walzer, M. (1994) *Thick and Thin: Moral Arguments At Home and Abroad*. Notre Dame, Indianapolis; London: University of Notre Dame Press.
Walzer, M. (1980). "The Moral Standing of States: A Response to Four Critics." *Philosophy and Public Affairs*, 9(3): 209–229.
Walzer, M. (1990). "Nation and Universe." In Peterson, G., ed., *The Tanner Lectures on Human Values*. Salt Lake City: University of Utah Press.
Walzer, M. (2004). *Arguing About War*. New Haven: Yale University Press.

7
RATIONALIZATION, RETICENCE, AND THE DEMANDS OF GLOBAL SOCIAL AND ECONOMIC JUSTICE

Mark Busser

Introduction[1]

What do the global rich owe to the global poor? What should the powerful do for the powerless? What obligations do the privileged and comfortable have towards the marginalized and downtrodden? These generic questions are often discussed with reference to particular issue areas:

- Do people in wealthy countries and peoples have a duty to assist poor countries with their economic development? To help feed the hungry? To provide life-saving medicines?
- Do people of rich and powerful states owe it to the most disadvantaged members of the world economy to abandon harmful or unfair practices (e.g. agricultural subsidies) and to refrain from using economic institutions (e.g. the IMF or World Bank) to impose unjust policies ad pressures?
- When genocide or other atrocities are being committed within an ostensibly sovereign state, with disastrous humanitarian consequences, are outsiders obligated to mount costly interventions to stop them? Are they permitted to do so?
- Is there an obligation to participate in and strengthen international criminal law in order to hold world leaders accountable for acts of aggression, invasion, or occupation that destabilize regions and lead to deprivation, destruction, and death?
- Are governments, citizens, and firms culpable if their economic and strategic choices give material support to foreign autocrats who commit abuses or atrocities, and whose corruption or diversion of resources leaves their people impoverished?
- Who is to blame for the environmental degradation that exacerbates poverty, and who should carry the burden of the sacrifices and policy investments that are urgently needed to avoid climate-related disaster?

These various issue areas share the problem of distributing what David Miller (2001) calls 'remedial' responsibilities – the duty to remedy some sort of harm or deprivation.

As the entries in this volume show, the concept of 'responsibility' is becoming more and more prevalent in global politics as trends towards the deterritorialization of ethical sentiments have called into question the traditional understanding of the nation-state boundary as the terminus of ethical relationships. Driven in part by the role of communications technology in making faraway suffering more visible and visceral, calls for responsibility continue to resound against the backdrop of a world not currently structured to facilitate cosmopolitan politics. There is thus what Onora O'Neill calls a 'tension between moral cosmopolitanism and institutional anti-cosmopolitanism' (O'Neill 2016, 99). This incongruity between universalist concern and particularist institutions has complicated ongoing debates and disagreements about the scope and intensity of transnational obligations to protect basic human rights and fulfil basic human needs for the world's worst-off.

The very idea that all people have basic human rights, of which they should not be deprived, has achieved widespread, if nominal, recognition in global politics. In practice, however, it has been quite difficult to ensure that people are guaranteed their rights. Rights, it seems, are only one side of the equation. They need to be complemented with obligations and duties in order to be of any practical value. 'In my view', Onora O'Neill has written, 'we do not take rights seriously unless we seek to show *who* ought to do *what* for *whom*' (O'Neill 2016, 10). This has led many political theorists and activists to switch from a rights-focused paradigm to a 'responsibilities approach' (Kuper 2005) which approaches the problem of guaranteeing rights from a point of view that focuses on corollary obligations and accountabilities.

Yet, we are not all cosmopolitans now. New waves of nationalism and populism have emerged, energized by leaders and followers who explicitly reject both 'globalism', understood in a pejorative way, and some of the core egalitarian values upon which transnational responsibility-talk tends to be premised. Many such critiques of cosmopolitanism are carefully reasoned and rooted in sincere, good-faith scepticism and disagreement. Others, including some of the most popular and accessible anti-globalist narratives, are rooted in cynical or low-effort misrepresentations and exaggerations, often steering into conspiracism and an embrace of so-called 'alternative facts'. In some of their most vulgar forms anti-globalist ideas and arguments are flavoured with exceptionalism, xenophobia, and white supremacy. The social, cultural, and political power of these movements, both at their best and at their worst, countervails against the trends towards the deterritorialization of ethical responsibility that can be detected in so many academic and activist spheres.

In this chapter, I argue that, contrary to claims that thinking and writing about global responsibility have proven ineffectual, the resurgent nationalist and xenophobic movements of the early twenty-first century ought to be considered as backlash against global responsibility claims and a testament to the potency and of their inherent challenge to existing global political and economic structures. While conspiracism and extremism are particularly sensational and alarming instances of anti-globalist recalcitrance, they are only one manifestation of the kinds of narrative coping mechanisms people use to grapple with the moral, political, and practical provocations posed by contemporary calls for increased global responsibility.

This chapter proceeds in four parts. In the first section, I trace some of the core themes in contemporary conversations about remedial responsibility and global relations, and surveys some of the reasons, rationales, and argumentative warrants that underpin claims about who ought to be responsible, to whom, for doing what. Differentiating between the various principles focusing on factors such as causation, proximity, and practical ability helps to show that each principle emphasizes certain empirical factors and prioritizes certain problems and solutions. By their nature the different obligation principles imply different relationships of heroism or culpability – asserting either 'bystander' duties or 'consequential' duties – and thus encourage different orientations towards being accountable and holding accountable. These insights play into the overall analysis in two ways. On the one hand, the various principles can be complementary and additive, forming cumulative layers that add to the intensity of the contemporary 'call' to be more globally responsible. On the other hand, talking about one principle can often be a way of *sidestepping* talking about another principle and its related issues – while still adopting an ostensibly ethical stance.

In the second section, I engage with the concern that global political philosophy and its shift towards responsibility talk have not had significant impact on observable political behaviour. To be sure, moral philosophers' arguments about how core liberal-democratic principles and values ought to translate into engagement with global Others have not yet succeeded in revolutionizing transnational ethical relations. Yet, those same thinkers have thoughtfully scrutinized the cultural, practical, and political challenges that act as bulwarks against substantive change. In particular, I highlight Thomas Nagel's observation that many ostensibly internationalist governments (and their people) would prefer to eschew any new commitments to accountability even while they seek to expand the scope of global governance in the name of human rights and justice. This inconsistency between the abundance of rights-based justifications for contemporary global structures of power and the lack of interest in being actually held responsible is awkward to reconcile, or even acknowledge. Thus, it is worth examining whether debates over the distribution of global responsibilities have been shaped and limited by what we might call motivated moral reasoning – in particular, by a tendency towards particular kinds of principles and themes because of conscious or unconscious bias against the radically transformative demands of cosmopolitan globalism and in favour of extant structures of neo-liberal internationalism, if not reactionary statism or isolationism.

In the third section, I consider the ways in which even 'theoretical' and 'scholarly' arguments and ideas about the distribution of global responsibilities are manifestations of the global power relations of responsibility. I draw briefly on previous work in order to suggest that responsibility is most helpfully framed relationally, in the sense that obligations are borne out in practice when actors hold each other accountable, answerable, and culpable. These relationships are, of course, inevitably shaped by the power of the participants, understood both in physical coercive strength and in other more complex forms of persuasive influence or authoritative standing. Understanding obligation-claims, ethical narratives, and justifications in terms of the power relations of holding-responsible calls attention to the importance of agenda-setting, recognition, and framing. Insofar as being held accountable for one's imputed obligations means being called to give an account, the ability to satisfy or deflect moral scrutiny is a crucial resource. While calls to answerability can be satisfied with principled argumentation, they can also be deflected with obfuscation, or through outright avoidance. A tendency towards these latter options can be observed, I argue, in the tendency of recalcitrant actors to deflect calls to responsibility with alternative narratives rather than explicit rejections. In more benign instances, these narratives take the form of underdeveloped arguments about whether and how a more responsible and accountable form of global politics might be arranged, but in more extreme cases, they can take the form of nationalist ideologies, conspiracy theories, or both.

In the fourth section, I examine whether that contemporary trends towards nationalism, nativism, conspiracism, and xenophobia can be understood, at least in part, as reactions to the increasing pressures of contemporary global politics – in particular, by the overwhelming demands they feel are imposed by various calls to responsibility. Like scholars and diplomats who err on the side of the status quo, populists' and nationalists' argumentative contortions are arguably demonstrate motivated moral reasoning. However, unlike those elites, they are typically less inhibited about rejecting unwelcome facts or evidence head on, embracing questionable conspiracist, pseudo-historical, or fabricated claims. Alternately, they may accept evidence that their actions affect outsiders but reject that this implies some sort of corrective responsibility by refusing to see those outsiders as worthy of moral engagement.

Overall, principled argumentation about the distribution of global obligations presents us all with challenging calls to be answerable and accountable, with often radical implications for how we should live our lives, how we should relate to others, and how our world's political institutions and economic relationships should be arranged. Demands for greater equality and accountability, taken to their logical conclusions, often pose radical implications for how we ought to live, how we ought to organize our world, and how we ought to deal with those outside our state borders. These radical implications can be difficult to reject head-on (as conspiracists and nationalists do), and so in more polite circles, reluctant parties often seem to confront them indirectly instead, by making flimsy arguments or by consciously or unconsciously changing the subject. How we think and talk about global responsibilities, in other words, may be influenced by our conscious or unconscious desires to maintain status quo practices and structures even though we fear we could not *justify* them if we were to be held answerable for them. This raises interesting questions about the political psychology of global justice politics and the role that motivated moral reasoning exceptionalism, apathy, and inaction plays in contemporary debates over global relations – both in 'vulgar' subcultures and in 'serious' mainstream debates.

Principles for distributing obligations

How do proponents of obligation claims related to global inequity justify them argumentatively to interlocutors who demand some reason to believe (and act as if) any duties exist? By examining how arguments about global duties are assembled, presented, and backed with supporting claims, we can more clearly understand why related questions about relationships of accountability are so contested and contentious. Furthermore, as I shall argue, the way in which people with relative global privilege think and talk about the content of our duties has practical effects on how we consequently engage in the politics of accountability – and with whom.

When it comes to remedying troubling situations, discourses of global ethics tend to ground remedial responsibilities in two significantly different ethical impulses. On the one hand, what we might call *bystander* duties stem from 'innocent' factors such as the capacity to prevent or alleviate harm suffered by another. On the other hand, *consequential* duties stem from problematic actions or behaviour, which render certain agents culpable, to some degree or other, because they have contributed to the creation of the problem. This connection generates what Henry Shue (2003) calls 'corrective' obligations.

The division between bystander duties and consequential duties gets at the heart of the matter by gesturing at the core issue of culpability. Yet within each category there is ample room for further nuance and detail. As many of the most prolific theorists of global justice have demonstrated, there are many potential reasons and rationales which might motivate us to attribute remedial responsibilities to a particular actor, whether or not they are culpable. A brief consideration of some key principles, in no particular order, can help to set the stage for a discussion in later sections of how their *content* may shape the *practices* of argumentation in which actors engage – or disengage – about them.

The capacity principle

One of the most intuitive principles holds that remedial duties stem from the practical ability to help. The 'capacity' principle suggests that agents are responsible for addressing problematic situations when the cost to them of doing so is morally negligible. These sorts of duties apply among strangers, even to the agent who is understood as merely 'arriving on the scene'. Still, the question of capacity does not just relate to geographical proximity. It might also consider which actors are most able to bear the costs of action. Similarly, it might be worth asking which actor has the ability, skill, or expertise best suited to make a difference (Miller 2001).

The capacity principle has been asserted most notably by Peter Singer (1972) in his influential essay, 'Famine, Affluence and Morality', and other works. Analyzing the relationship between foreign suffering and domestic priorities, Singer expresses a moral concern with the way states and populations spend only a fraction on foreign assistance relative to what they spend on domestic luxuries. He insists that no substantive moral conceptual scheme can account for the incredibly weak responses the relatively affluent countries offer to the suffering that is known to be occurring in the world. His goal is to show how the logics behind certain arguments that reinforce inaction or insufficient action seem ridiculous when basic situational analogies and comparisons are made.

Singer outlines an ethical responsibility based on three premises. The first is straightforward: that human suffering is inherently negative. The second is equally simple: 'If it is in our power to prevent something very bad from happening, without thereby sacrificing anything morally significant, we ought, morally, to do it' (Singer 1972, 231). Third, he argues: 'If we accept any principle of universalizability, equality, or whatever, we cannot discriminate against someone merely because he is far away from us' (Singer 1972, 232). In essence, Singer concludes that according to a simple moral calculus, people in more privileged countries should forfeit the luxuries and excesses they do not need in order to contribute to the prevention of suffering where it is most severe. Of course, this is an argument commonly borne out in debates and discussions on global disparity. There is a strain of universal utilitarianism in Singer's argument that seems, at its core, fundamentally logical and sensible. What is most interesting about this point of view is that it appears so agreeable that one must wonder why his proposed resetting of priorities has not found root in practice. What is it that stops us from following these assumptions to their logical conclusion? What prevents a tremendous shift in priorities away from lavish excesses and towards greater care for the neediest people in the world?

Singer himself gives some clues as to why this sort of reorientation of resources has not taken place. One explanation is the prevalence of a moral scheme wherein aiding the distant victims of misfortune is considered *supererogatory* in that it is 'an act which it would be good to do, but not wrong not to do' (Singer 1972, 235). Of course, Singer plainly asserts that sacrificing the purchase of more new clothes in order to feed the starving, to use his example, should not be considered a supererogatory act. We must ask ourselves, then, if Singer is correct: Is it indeed morally wrong to buy new clothes when the money could go to help end a famine? More to the point, is it morally wrong for states to spend any resources on domestic luxuries instead of using them to promote universal human rights and security for the world's worst-off people? It may be that this is, as Singer fears, 'too drastic a revision of our moral scheme' (Singer 1972, 232).

The most common critique to Singer's argument is that the universalist urge is necessarily 'brought back to reality' in the face of necessary and natural sources of particularism and communitarianism. His framework is criticized for discounting the importance of nationality, language, tradition, history, race, economy, and other such grouping forces, which prevent a universalist or cosmopolitan international ethical scheme from finding expression. Of course, there is a difference between suggesting that these forces are politically and psychologically potent and suggesting that their exclusionary and effects are ethically consistent with the professed principles (universalizability, equality justice, etc.) that govern relations within communities.

The contribution principle

As Christian Barry (2005a, 103) puts it, the contribution principle holds that agents are responsible for addressing problematic situations 'when they have contributed, or are contributing, to bringing them about'. It has most prominently emphasized by cosmopolitans such as Thomas Pogge (2002). Here remedial obligations are generated because the actions of the duty-bound agent have causally contributed to creating the problem, whether the contribution is made by commission, by omission, by accident or by error. Another prominent proponent of the contribution principle is Henry Shue (2003, 162), who argues that human beings are not 'adrift in space', suggesting that 'the absence of private connections is immaterial if there are deep social connections through the institutional structure of the international system in which all human individuals live'. Thus in contrast to the blameless bystander conception of responsibility, Shue suggests that we ought to consider whether particular actors have corrective responsibilities, meaning obligations stemming from *culpability*.

If there is indeed such a thing as transnational duties, then why are they not as widely accepted as the idea of universal rights? Shue analyzes two arguments which are typically put forth to challenge the idea that duties should reach across oceans and borders. Shue calls these the *thesis of principled communitarianism* and the *thesis of causal ineffectuality* (Shue 2003, 162). Both theses are key to understanding how international responsibility is conceived in traditional global politics. Because the former is so closely linked to the association principle, I shall discuss it below, focusing first on the latter.

The thesis of causal ineffectuality is concerned with the perceived impossibility that one individual's life has impacted the life of each of the billions of other people on the planet. The assumption that I have not affected most of the world is followed by the conclusion that I bear no responsibility towards them. If there is a starving child in a foreign country, one might argue, it cannot be because I did not finish eating the vegetables on my dinner plate. If there is a civil war in a faraway region, I cannot be said to have played a role in igniting the aggression. The thesis of causal ineffectuality simply states that it is not morally imperative that I act as guarantor of the rights of faraway Others, because I had no role in denying them. Shue divides this argument into two sections: the *empirical* claim that 'I have not touched most of humanity' and the *ethical* claim that 'I therefore bear no responsibility toward most of humanity – even granting that they have rights that someone ought to protect' (Shue 2003, 164). These claims, especially the former, are difficult to defend based on the available evidence, and yet they seem play a significant role in rationalizing disengagement from global responsibility politics, as I shall argue.

Contribution can be a tricky concept, especially because of its tenuous links with ideas of causality. It is important to consider forms of contribution which are not always immediately apparent. For example, according to Iris Marion Young (2006), all agents whose actions contribute to *structural* processes that produce injustice have obligations to work to remedy these injustices. For Young, having participated in the behaviours that sustain problematic relations of domination or exploitation translates into the duty to transform those relations. While a single 'contribution' principle could arguably capture all of these nuances on its own, the complications involved with the relationship between structure and responsibility make it worthwhile to briefly emphasize two variants: the 'risk' principle and the 'beneficiary' principle.

The 'risk' principle holds that when bad situations arise, remedial duties fall on those who have contributed to the aggregate risk that a problematic situation will occur (Barry 2005a). This principle is worth closer examination, because it helps to give voice to some people's moral intuitions about cases where the actual causal contribution is difficult to demonstrate. For example, actors might be held culpable for blameworthy behaviour, not because their actions actually *did* have problematic consequences, but because they *risked* them unacceptably. They might consequently be argued to have the obligation to help to remedy a situation of the sort, which their behaviour *risked* even though their contributory role is indeterminate. Thus, Barry argues that agents who are uncertain about whether they contributed to a deprivation should 'err in favour' of assistance (Barry 2005b).

According to the 'beneficiary' principle, those who benefit from a bad situation, or the circumstances that brought it about, have a duty to address it. This might arguably be the case even if the beneficiaries in question are not causally responsible. A particularly challenging issue area here is the question of intergenerational justice. Ought the sins of the parents to be visited upon the children, so to speak? Can culpability be inherited?

Furthermore, as is often the case, this principle may overlap with and reinforce the others. For example, it might make sense to argue that where the benefits that spring from deprivation take the form of resources and empowerment, these give the beneficiary a greater capacity to act. The link between this increase in capacity and its origins is perhaps morally significant – and so reminds us that the analytic division between these principles is heuristic and any clear typological separation is difficult to sustain in actual practice.

The association principle

Another principle given considerable weight in these debates is variously called the 'relationship' principle, the 'communitarian' principle (Miller 2001), or the 'association' principle (Barry 2005a). It is based on the idea that remedial obligations should be imputed to those actors who have a special relationship with the people affected by the situation. This sort of association is usually understood in terms of co-citizenship, friendship, family, national and ethnic ties, and the like. People with relationships of this sort have deep connections of interactions and exchange, leading to meaningful 'communities of shared values' (Walzer 1983). Furthermore, they tend to coordinate action together and then face shared consequences (Rawls 1999), making them what David Held calls 'communities of fate'.

Of course, Held's cosmopolitan perspective argues that human societies form '*overlapping* communities of fate' that are interconnected in meaningful ways (Held 1995, 136). But this emphasis on transnational interconnectedness is not typically the emphasis of those who argue in favour of the association principle. Rather than merely informing the source of particular kinds of obligations, the association principle is often used to establish the comparative *priority* of local connections over global or transnational ones. An example of this sensibility was influentially articulated by international relations theorist E.H. Carr: 'most men's sense of common interest and obligation is keener in respect of family and friends than in respect of their fellow-countrymen, and keener in respect of their fellow-countrymen than of other people' (Carr 1962, 163). Indeed, the association principle is often accompanied, even if implicitly, by the thesis of principled communitarianism. As described by Shue, the thesis of principled communitarianism suggests that the special relationships which define local communities warrant a priority over the expenditure of resources elsewhere. It is not that the rights and welfare of distant strangers are diminished in importance; it is merely that local community responsibilities 'exhaust the resources that anyone can be reasonably expected to devote to the performance of duty' (Shue 2003, 162).

Of course, it is not necessarily morally or politically justifiable to exhaust all or most resources on local community responsibilities if one also has transnational responsibilities. How a society's 'inward' and 'outward' duties ought to be balanced is at the crux of debates over global justice and the transnational politics of responsibility.

Do theories of global justice make a difference?

Decades of political philosophy has enriched the conceptual toolkit at our disposal for analyzing our relationships and the obligations we may arguably have towards global Others. Have contemporary arguments in favour of the contribution principle, for example, succeeding in chipping away at the traditional dominance of the association principle, and pushed participants the power relations of responsibility towards an increasing emphasis on engaged consequential framings obligation rather than bystander framings?

Chris Brown (2017, 359) argues that theories of global justice have had 'more or less no effect on real-world politics'. In trying to assess why, Brown cites Nagel's explanation that theories of global justice 'invariably involve the need to coordinate the activities of large numbers of people, which in turn requires the existence of government (Brown 2017, 360)'. Yet because the political structure of world government seems so unlikely, many theorists advocate for a moral cosmopolitanism that attempts to build a just order from the grass roots by reshaping patterns of individual choice. However, Nagel argues, individuals cannot be expected to work towards transnational justice through voluntary and private initiatives, even if based on mutual recognition of shared values and priorities (cf. Cohen 2000). It will be too difficult for them to sustain their efforts 'without the assurance that their conduct will in fact be part of a reliable and effective system' (Nagel 2005, 116). Justice, put simply, requires policy, law, and enforcement.

In order to grapple with the problem of global justice, Nagel contrasts cosmopolitan conceptions of the relationship between justice and sovereignty with what he terms the 'political' conception exemplified by Rawls' 'Law of Peoples' (Rawls 1999). Cosmopolitans steer towards a unified human community and see territorial states as a temporary phenomenon, which should and will give way to world-federal structures where any special relationships between co-nationals would be nested within the wider and more universal relationships that all humans share. In this view, obligations of justice are shared by human beings in the first place, and the state has merely been one social mechanism we have built in order to fulfil them. The 'political' conception, in contrast, views the fact of territorial sovereignty and government domination as the source and grounding of the relationship of justice. Being subjected to sovereign power creates reciprocal associative obligations between citizens and their governments. Over time, the power dynamics of this existing relationship create pressures and accountabilities. As Nagel (2005, 145) puts it 'sovereignty usually precedes legitimacy'. This, Nagel suggests, is why the effort to build global-level sovereignty on the basis of arguments about justice have failed to have purchase.

However, it is not only *within* sovereign states that people feel the effects of power. As Gillian Brock (2010) notes, Rawls's critics fault his interpretation of relations between societies for drastically underestimating the ways in which local societies are shaped by global forces, power relationships, structures, and even coercion. For example, Rawls's explanation for poverty and deprivation in 'burdened societies' puts the blame on problems with their own traditions, cultures, resources, and leadership (Rawls 1999, 106–108). His account of their situation seems to rely on a version of what Shue called the *thesis of causal ineffectuality,* so his account of justice in the relations between people therefore puts little to no emphasis on the contribution, risk, or beneficiary principles. A politics of holding-accountable, of holding-answerable, is not part of the equation.

Rawls's critics thus argue that he relies on 'outmoded views of relations between states, peoples, and individuals of the outmoded views of relations between states, peoples, and individuals of the world', essentially ignoring interconnectedness and mutual influence (Brock 2010, 88). As Brock notes, there is plenty of room for nuance here, and for Rawls' defenders to redeem his overall arguments. And yet it is also fair to say that his consideration of anything resembling the contribution principle is underdeveloped at best. Nobody is perfect, certainly, but Rawls is often celebrated as one of the greatest political theorists of his era. How could such a competent thinker have such a significant blind spot?

Nardin's discussion of the problem suggests one potential explanation. Even in Rawls's controversial account of transnational relations, relationships between bounded communities may involve certain kinds of shared interests, commitments and duties, such as nonaggression, fulfilling treaties, and helping weak states with development. According to the 'political' conception as described by Nagel, these relationships are different in kind than the relationships between co-citizens, but they may nevertheless encourage the development of institutions and structures. Yet, this creates a dilemma:

> Prosperous nations have reasons to want more governance on a world scale, but they do not want the increased obligations and demands for legitimacy that may follow in its wake. They *do not want to increase the range of those to whom they are obliged* as they are toward their own citizens; and this reflects the convictions of their citizens, not just of their governments.
>
> *(Nagel 2005, 136, emphasis added)*

For this reason, Nagel suspects, we will continue to see privileged global elites continue to expand transnational governance and the exercise of power *without* complementary political structures of accountability. They want to be *permitted* to make the world a better place, but they do not want to be *required* by others to do so. To maintain this awkward balance, one must make certain kinds arguments about rights and justice, but must avoid certain others.

In the same vein, one possible explanation for his underdeveloped engagement with transnational culpability is that Rawls was simply neither prepared nor willing to follow the evidence of global interconnectedness precisely because it would necessarily lead down a path towards discussing the demand for corrective obligations, and thus a reconsideration of whether societies and 'peoples' can really be treated as separate and 'bounded' entities. Could it be that this weak point in Rawls' work is the result of his implicit bias in favour of a state-centric world more consistent with the arguments he had developed so carefully in his previous work on justice *within* bounded societies? Many of Rawls' critics have suggested something to this effect, but this possibility cannot fully be evaluated here. For present purposes it suffices to highlight the intriguing question the topic raises: does motivated reasoning affect even the best of us when we engage in challenging conversations about global rights and culpabilities? In addition to the oft-discussed practical and political barriers, are there cognitive and psychological barriers that prevent us from taking seriously the transformative possibilities of cosmopolitan globalism in favour of a more preservative neoliberal internationalism?

Nagel's suggestion that inconsistencies and unresolved dilemma in political theory might be related to recalcitrance about the possibility of taking on more obligations challenges us to consider the degree to which motivated moral reasoning might explain why people do not embrace the conclusions of contemporary global moral philosophy. Maintaining a status quo built on an unresolved tension between the strategic wielding of responsibility talk and the deficit of responsibility practice (see Chandler 2003) is becoming increasingly difficult as more and more critics politicize and question the inconsistency and demand that it be justified and explained. Indeed, the desire to have effective transnational governance that is not accountable is not typically tenable from the point of view of those actors so often left behind or marginalized by elite decision-making. Furthermore, while the global privileged may refuse to set up formal political and legal structures to accommodate calls to account, this does not prevent those who are or aggrieved dissatisfied from making such calls in their own ways. The politics of holding-accountable, of making responsibility claims and demanding justifications is often practiced against the will of those who do not wish to be held answerable. So what happens when aggrieved or concerned groups make principled claims against those who do not wish to acknowledge them but have few good reasons to reject them?

The power relations of holding-responsible

The descriptions above represent only the barest sketch of the nuanced ways in which these principles have been conceptualized, contrasted, and problematized. As David Miller (2001) rightly argues, it is impossible to select any one of these principles to privilege over the others. It is equally difficult to rank them for the purposes of developing a moral algorithm that we can apply to all cases. It is therefore necessary to explore how these principles apply to actual cases and circumstances, finding some way to sort out their relative significance to the situations and relationships at hand.

So who exactly is responsible, and for what, when it comes to global disparities and the deprivation of faraway strangers? 'Because the problem of distributing responsibilities is so urgent', writes Miller, 'human societies have evolved mechanisms whereby they are formally assigned to individual people or to institutions' (Miller 2001, 454). When institutional mechanisms are in place, the politics of obligation is rendered more predictable because the consistency and regularity of clear roles and expectations helps to give relations of obligation the stable weight of legitimacy. However, as Miller notes, there are often situations in which duties and accountabilities are not formally assigned – especially at the global level. Under these circumstances, he suggests, it is necessary to appeal to the same sorts of principles that underlie formal regimes of responsibility 'in the hopes that they will command widespread agreement' (Miller 2001, 454).

When obligations are relatively formalized, calling actors to account for the fulfilment of their obligations is a straightforward social action because the 'call' will connect well with most of the relevant actors' expectations about roles and lines of authority. Widespread recognition facilitates coordination. However, where obligations are not strongly institutionalized (in either the formal or informal sense), the power relations of responsibility take the form of more complex and energetic forms of contestation. In these settings, calls to account are much more likely to be contested, questioned, and challenged – if not ignored – not only by those who are attributed obligations but also by those who are expected to help reinforce them. Agreement, recognition, and legitimation are much more difficult to attain outside of formal structures because the existence of the duty and its relevant relations of accountability must often be justified 'from the ground up' through debate and argumentation.

It consequently makes sense to understand arguments that grapple with the topic of heretofore-unrecognized global duties as *contributions* to an ongoing social and political process through which obligations and accountabilities are imputed, ascribed, and even shirked. Academic writing, pop philosophy, television punditry, celebrity advocacy – each of these is an important site of the global power relations of responsibility. This debate is far from 'merely academic' since every argument has the potential to be taken up, taken seriously, and translated into the production of norms of obligation. Arguments about duties are rendered actionable in practice because of their intersubjective resonance and, often, performative effects. Thus, argumentation and debate are key components of the power relations of responsibility, and so it is difficult to distinguish theoretical analyses of obligation debates from acts of participation in them.

When faced with deprivations needing remedy, writes Miller, we will want to find an approach that helps us to apply these principles to identify an actor A who will be treated as having a special obligation to act to remedy a bad situation. It is important that some actor A be identified promptly, and '[we] want A to feel that he is responsible, and to act accordingly, and we want everyone else to make the same judgment and therefore to put pressure of various kinds on A if he fails to act' (Miller 2001, 469). By focusing on how principles are invoked and mobilized in order to apply pressure outside of formal structures, Miller shifts in a productive direction.

In previous work (Busser 2019), I have suggested that a focus on the messy power relations[2] of holding-responsible can help to make sense of contestations over who is required – and permitted – to take action in response to mass atrocity crimes under the rubric of the global 'responsibility to protect'. The slipperiness of responsibility-talk often obscures the difference between permission and requirement, just as it elides different conceptions of various modes of responsibility and obligation. There is a significant difference between, on the one hand, transcendental responsibilities imputed to an actor in some sort of metaphysical, way, and relational responsibilities grounded in the grounded, humanistic politics of holding-responsible. Furthermore, the autonomous mode differs from the other two because the actor in question neither looks 'upward' to the cosmos nor 'outward' to others, but 'inward' to the actor's own standards and metrics. When attributing obligation or culpability by invoking responsibility-talk, it matters which of these three modes we are talking about, since they have very different orientations towards accountability both in the sense of account-settling (i.e. how are debts resolved) and account-giving (i.e. to whom must one give justifications) and furthermore towards questions of answerability (i.e. to how much interrogation or 'cross-examination' one must submit, and by whom).

While purely 'ethical' duties in the transcendental mode may (or may not) indeed exist and have meaningful force in people's experiences, and while it is possible that people will somehow be held accountable by the cosmic workings of universe or in the hereafter, politics is about *relational* responsibility. Our own beliefs and the arguments we make to others may gesture at the transcendental, but such invocations are only ultimately given effect in the social world when they have enough argumentative purchase to convince people to feel responsible and to participate in the interpersonal dynamics of holding-accountable, as Miller describes. Similarly, while individual or collective actors may seek to prioritize holding themselves to their own standards, as in the autonomous mode of responsibility, the solipsistic nature of this self-check may not satisfy external Others who want to make claims, demand explanations, or otherwise hold the actor responsible. Self-regulation and principle may align with the norms and pressures of relational interaction, but that alignment is not automatic. Ultimately, I argue, it is most helpful to ground our discussion of contestations of responsibility in a relational framing that emphasizes how transcendental and autonomous claims are mobilized and contested in real interpersonal power relations of holding-obligated, holding-culpable, holding-accountable, and holding-answerable.

When analyzing the power relations of responsibility in its relational form, arguments, beliefs, principles and philosophies certainly do matter in practice. They shape the degree to which actors in any given context are predisposed to participate in the politics of holding accountable and being accountable. The stronger the inclinations felt by the greater number of people, and the clearer the pathways of social pressure through which the power relations of holding-accountable, the more robust will be the regime of responsibility surrounding a particular issue or problem.

So how can the principles discussed in the previous section be used to settle, or even understand, contestations over global remedial duties? Can they help us build more robust regimes of remedial responsibility by distributing responsibilities? Instead of relying on any single principle, or working down a pre-ordered list of the principles, Miller suggests utilizing a *connection* theory to frame the way we distribute remedial obligations. This involves understanding the various principles as specifying different forms of connection that link those who are vulnerable and those who are able to help. The strongest duties are to be imputed to those with the strongest connections to the people in need of help. The connections in question may stem from any or all of the principles outlined above. Where more than one principle applies, weighing and evaluating the strengths of the connections established by the various principles will help to allocate obligations to different actors.

Examining how each of the principles might apply is an appropriate response to the indeterminacy and case-dependency of the politics of responsibility as it plays out in practice. Miller rightly recognizes that our approach to the distribution of responsibility has to make space for inevitable practices of contestation. This underscores the practical importance of argumentation and persuasive power. The sorts of principles and connections we recognize will help us to figure out who is most the most appropriate candidate to pressure into action in a given situation. Which connections ultimately get emphasized, and the direction in which pressure is consequently directed, will depend on the persuasiveness of the arguments made and evidence presented. The power relations of accountability depend on who ends up being persuaded to pressure whom.

The result is that actors whose connections to bad situations are forgotten, obscured, or downplayed will be less likely to experience social pressure and the costs associated with it. Furthermore, even where connections are impossible to deny, the *sorts* of connections that get alleged, discussed, and recognized will have an impact on the nature of the duties and obligations an actor will have to fulfil. This is because there are key practical and *political* differences between consequential duties and bystander duties. Each frames the engagement between the duty-bearers and their counterparts in distinct ways. On the one hand, fulfilling duties of the 'helpful bystander' variety tends to be seen as heroic, charitable, or benevolent. There is no past wrong being rectified, and so the interaction between actors is not structured by a context of atonement or account-settling. Of course, this is not to say that bystander duties are supererogatory. It is still arguably bad *not* to fulfil them. Yet, the relationship between the obligated actor and the people in need of assistance tends to be qualitatively different than when remedial duties are seen as consequential. Bystander duties, once fulfilled, tend to be seen as having restorative effects, leading actors to be freed to carry on with their own business much as before.

On the other hand, consequential duties are, by their nature, more complex than bystander duties due to the fact that they are generated by problematizing risk or harm on the part of the actor called to be responsible. Claims framed in terms of consequential duties are thus very likely to capture a reformative or transformative impulse. Recognition and acknowledgment of culpability and harm has the potential to lead to the creation of new social obligations that reach beyond the immediate question of 'fixing the problem' in the restorative sense, and demand further of actors that they reform or transform the way they act in the future. Once particular acts of commission and omission are acknowledged to be problematic, they cannot be repeated without incurring further social criticism and censure.

To complicate matters, there is always the possibility that it will be determined that it is not the individual actions of careless or unaware actors that have been problematic, but a whole *system* of relations. This harkens back to Iris Marion Young's suggestion that those who contribute to the maintenance of unjust structures processes have a duty to work towards their reform or transformation. In her work on questions related to duties surrounding sweatshop labour, Young (2006, 120) warns against approaches to justice that take the status quo as a moral baseline and seeks to 'restore normality'. Instead, she argues for a model of responsibility that 'brings into question precisely the background conditions that ascriptions of blame or fault assume as normal'. She argues that instead of being taken for granted, problematic background conditions should be subjected to critical scrutiny. Where reform or transformation is seen as appropriate, it will be appropriate to impute transformative duties to all those actors who shared responsibility for maintaining these structures. Most significantly, the recognition of systemic connection underscores the importance of being accountable to those whom our actions affect, because it reminds us that those Others are in a position to point out problems we are not able, or inclined, to notice (Shue 2003).

The exercise of negotiating the distribution of obligations has the potential to serve as a transformational instance of political contestation where the usual flows of power and accountability-holding in global politics are called into question. This is far more likely, however, when the applicability of *consequential* duties is the focus of discussion. Thinking about consequential duties tends to involve an examination of background conditions and actions in a way that thinking about bystander duties does not.

When actors focus on their own obligations as 'bystander' duties, based on principles such as capacity or association, there is less onus to be accountable or answerable to the people who are treated as the mere *object* of assistance. Thus, the 'responsible' actors are more likely to engage as if they know exactly what the problem is, and what needs to be done to address it. This exacerbates the top-down saviour mentality which so often characterizes aid and assistance relationships, and which further marginalize affected peoples and communities (Easterly 2006; Moyo 2009). Furthermore, through exercises of discursive exclusion, which showcase monological justifications but evade dialogical answerability and challenge, the world's more advantaged citizens avoid being burdened with obligations they might be compelled to acknowledge – if more vulnerable peoples could get them to engage, listen, and respond.

Defaulting to an emphasis on bystander duties helps to evade the pressures and burdens that come with being held accountable and answerable for one's actions. This is why the tendency to shifting away from a discussion of the contribution principle in order to refocus attention on the capacity or association principles is such a potent strategy of misdirection. The latter do not negate the former logically, but they do often displace it rhetorically, intentionally, or not. Examining the contribution principle means facing pressure to offer justifications and explanations for one's actions, which can have unwelcome implications because of the consequential duties that such a conversation might arguably ascribe. It is thus tempting to disengage from answerability, from openness to questions, correction, and feedback. However, as Young (2006, 123) suggests, the responsibility that comes with social connection is best lived out as a *political* responsibility. This means that it demands justification understood not as a solitary intellectual exercise but as a social practice, via 'public communicative engagement with others for the sake of organizing our relationship and coordinating our actions most justly'.

Radical implications and anti-globalist recalcitrance

As outlined above, there are many overlapping reasons why people with relative privilege may justifiably be ascribed remedial obligations to assist the global poor and insecure. Yet if, as Brown suggests, political philosophy about global justice has failed to convince people to engage more ethically with the issues at hand, perhaps it is not because of a lack of good and convincing reasons why they ought to feel obliged to take action. Instead, I suggest, perhaps it is precisely because the *abundance* of good reasons to be obliged represents a call to take responsibility that is overwhelming and difficult to live up to in practice.

Again, this tension is captured effectively by Nagel:

> It is not only the fear of tyranny but also the resistance to expanded democracy, expanded demands for legitimacy, and expanded scope for the claims of justice that inhibits the development of powerful supranational institutions. Fortunate nations, at any rate, fear such developments. They therefore face the problem of how to create a global order that will have its own legitimacy, but not the kind of legitimacy that undermines the strict limits on their responsibilities.
>
> *(Nagel 2005, 143)*

Indeed, the recalcitrance towards external obligations may derive from the radical implications which accepting them would have in practice. Principled claims that impute obligation and culpability may be intellectually acceptable in the abstract but psychologically unacceptable for reasons deeply related to privilege and practice. Perhaps, then, a pivot towards political psychology is warranted. How do people with relative global privilege grapple with the fact of severe inequity and the implied demands of global justice? What is the role of rationalization, justification, motivated reasoning, and avoidance in shaping everyday practices of nonresponsibility?

In the broadcast network and newspaper era, the power dynamics of elite ownership and public sentiment tended to impose filters on media content, with one effect being that issues of global inequity, deprivation and culpability were typically covered minimally or avoided altogether (Chomsky and Herman 1988). Yet in the age of social media, claims, and counterclaims are aired and exchanged at great volume and with great speed, with the consequence that claims, grievances, and calls for justice are more difficult to block out of the public conversation. In fact, radical claims about historical injustice and redistribution are often counterintuitively amplified by unsympathetic media outlets and personalities who seek to generate easy content by presenting the assertions as a foil fit for derision or outrage. Indeed, many participants in the so-called culture wars being waged in media and online fora no longer ignore claims of historical inequity, privilege, and colonial inheritance – instead they mock and ridicule those ideas as the loopy ramblings of 'social justice warriors' and 'globalists'.

The conspiratorial demonization of 'globalists' is not a new phenomenon (Hofstadter, 1996; Olmsted 2009; Mulloy 2014), but the cases of Brexit and of the rise to power of the Trump administration have shown how this sort of anti-globalism has been mainlined into the populist political culture of many advanced industrial societies. In the so-called post-truth era, claims about the rights of refugees, the experience of intergenerational injustice related to slavery, and the excesses of militarism and exploitative capitalism are often not directly challenged on their merits but instead shouted down with louder, bolder, and more vulgar counter-narratives. These alternate narratives are promulgated not only by anti-globalist conspiracy theorists but also nationalist militia movements, racist identity groups, military isolationists, and others. To what extent might the revitalized energy of these kinds of groups be explained, in part, as reactions to, and as rejections of, principled calls to be accountable for the well-being of global Others?

The literature on the political psychology of conspiracist belief highlights the role that motivated reasoning may play in the shaping of beliefs and even perceptions. Individuals' ability to filter out unwelcome facts or information in favour of evidence that provides greater 'cognitive ease' by fitting with pre-existing practices and presumptions is well documented (Kahneman 2011). Scholars have connected conspiracy psychology to the kinds of psychological threats we feel when 'our identity, values, community, party, or anything else we happen to cherish is ridiculed, criticized, blamed, or otherwise humbled' (Difonzo 2019, 259). Conspiracy culture may be only one of many forms of cultural coping with unwelcome social changes and political demands, but research investigating whether a 'need for cognitive closure' (Leman and Cinnirella 2013) drives conspiracist belief may be asking the kinds of questions which may also be relevant for a research programme investigating how people deal with empirically persuasive but personally untenable demands to respond to global injustice and unfairness.

While relatively few academic studies of conspiracism have drawn explicit links between the psychology of conspiracy theories and global justice pressures specifically, many observers understand conspiracism and populism as a manifestation of 'economic anxiety' in response to changes posed by the technological, cultural, and economic dimensions of globalization (Goertzel 1994; Gallagher 2000; Kimmel 2013). In addition, some work has been done on the ways in which conspiracy theorists have engaged with several of the global justice issue areas mentioned in at the beginning of this chapter. At the peak of the European migrant crisis in 2015, migrants and asylum-seekers from the Middle East and North Africa were framed by populists and conspiracy theorists as threats to be protected against rather than victims to be assisted. A disproportionate narrative emphasis was placed by conspiracist figures such as Alex Jones on the phenomenon Kelly Greenhill (2010) has called the use of 'refugees as weapons', with some websites suggesting that the migrants were a part of a larger plot by George Soros, Zionists, or the New World Order (Marder 2018, 579). The images and news coverage of the crisis at its height posed tough ethical and political questions and was highly visual and often visceral, perhaps most notably when photographs of the body of 3-year-old migrant Alan Kurdi on a Turkish beach gave the crisis an individualized, personalized incarnation. The call to take responsibility for the well-being of migrants was daunting – it is perhaps unsurprising that many preferred to cope with it by convincing themselves that the migrants were themselves malevolent threats to be guarded against rather than answered. In effect, any potential duties to outsiders based on the capacity principle or the contribution principle are rejected and reframed as *threats* to one's own community, which must be protected under the association principle.

There is similarly a growing literature on the political psychological dimensions of climate change denial, where scholars have investigated the role of motivated reasoning rooted in reticence about accepting the economic and political changes in diet, production, consumption, transportation, and land use suggested by sustainability advocates (Feinberg and Willer 2011; Dunlap 2013; Jolley and Douglas 2014). The scientific evidence of climate change is often depicted by conspiracy theorists and populists as an elite fabrication. The scientists, institutions, leaders, and organizations who take climate change seriously are demonized as insincere globalists perpetuating a ruse whose true purpose is the pacification and transformation of states into cogs in the machine of a New World Order. This alternative narrative has been examined, for instance, in terms of the populist opposition to the United Nations' Agenda 21 plan for sustainable development (Norton 2014; Berry and Portney 2017). When actors understand climate change itself as a globalist ruse, claims about the need for climate justice by outsiders and foreigners are decidedly unwelcome – and may even be taken as evidence of the true purpose of climate-aware movements. Here again, as above, any possibility that there might be duties to outsiders is cancelled out and interpreted as threats to the strength and stability of one's own community. Thus, as Goertzel (1994) suggests, the *content* of conspiracy theories often insulates their believers from engagement with contrary voices or worldview, creating a monological 'echo chamber' that reduces exposure to the potentially corrective or moderating effects of dialogical conversation and contestation.

In sum, despite any number of principled reasons why they may arguably have remedial obligations to respond to injustice, the global privileged are, in practice, able to look away from issues of global injustice, to make token gestures, to make questionable excuses, and even to spin fantasies. The power structures of answerability are changing, but pressures threatening to disrupt the narrative protective shells which shield elites from being held to account seem to be creating newly resistant narratives in an attempt to pursue a form of 'ontological security' (Giddens 1991; Mitzen 2006). As I have suggested, perhaps on some deep level the world's more privileged people 'know' they have no satisfactory justification to offer in answer to contemporary calls to be accountable, but on another level they cannot bring themselves to *believe* it. Given some of the potentially radical implications of calls to address inequity, in the sense of the sacrifices and changes that would be required, they do not want to hold themselves responsible, let alone be held responsible by others. These recalcitrant responses are arguably not justifiable from the perspective of activists nor in the eyes of the world's most impoverished people, but they are worth further scrutiny, perhaps via approaches which complement the political philosophy of injustice with research on the political psychology of inaction.

Conclusion

Understanding obligation and accountability as interpersonal orientations and relations of power underscores the importance of argumentation and contestation to 'responsible' political engagement. Such an outlook raises important questions about the way in which the power to steer conversations about obligation makes it possible to escape and evade being held accountable. If we are truly concerned with interpersonal ethics and responsibility, then we will do well to face the possibility that our discourses of responsibility are themselves *irresponsible* if they permit us illusions of disconnection, which stop us from facing important questions about the duties we might conceivably owe to others. A truly responsible approach to global politics demands that we examine and evaluate *all* of the sorts of social connections we have to others and engage honestly and openly with them in order to negotiate the consequent obligations we may have towards one another. 'It is not even enough to say that we care for others, we must show the politics and the consequences of that caring' (Warner 1996, 126).

As I have suggested, contemporary debates about global responsibilities have the potential to serve as opportunities for radical political contestation and the critique of unjust systems and processes – that is, *if* the conversation is inclusive of the sorts of voices who would level such challenges. The problem with many discourses of responsibility, however, is that they tend to omit these sorts of voices. Furthermore, they tend to treat obligation as if it is a transcendental rather than relational and therefore downplay the importance of relationships of accountability, of real responsiveness. As a result, when it comes to questions about the obligation to fulfil remedial duties, they also tend to emphasize principles based on the helpful-bystander rationale.

The less we focus on the possibility that we have consequential duties, the less inclined we are to be accountable to our global Others – and vice versa. When those of us who see ourselves in a position to remedy problematic situations engage in debates about our duties, we tend to treat obligations as something we have to hold ourselves to. Furthermore, we often frame our own obligations for (not 'to') our 'Others' as if they are the duties of innocent bystanders rather than duties of justice that accrue to us as a consequence of our social actions. By adopting this framing, we fail to consider the complexities of our relationship with our 'Others' and subsequently lose sight of some of the reasons we might have to expand the scope of our accountabilities. We end up being less pressured than we otherwise might be to make ourselves accountable to our global 'Others' for our participation in, and ongoing contribution to the maintenance of, social structures 'they' might want us to recognize as unjust and harmful.

I refer to 'those of us' who debate our duties, because, as I see it, the most serious and sustained conversations about global responsibility tend to exclude the very people who are its subject. For the most part, the debate takes place between relatively privileged academics, journalists, and other advocates in forums that are not accessible to many key stakeholders. Participating in this debate and being able to use it as a medium through which to organize political action is of crucial importance if one wishes to shape the ebbs and flows of the global power relations of responsibility. The format of these debates is a closed one, and the *content* of our debates reinforces this fact, since the way we talk about responsibility shapes the way we act it out. Our debates tend not to emphasize those arguments about the relational politics of justification, answerability, accountability that would prompt us to expand the participatory scope of our debates themselves.

Notes

1 I would like to thank Hannes Hansen-Magnusson, Liam Stockdale, and Andrew Neal for helpful feedback on earlier versions of this chapter.

2 'Power' is understood here in terms that mix moral, ideational, and physical influence, and in which the exercise of power diffused throughout social relations. Influenced by Foucault's (1982, 791) conception of power relations involving "actions upon other actions", I focus on the ways in which people exercise power in their relations with others through argumentation, pressure, and reaction, such that the practices of monitoring, discipline, reward and punishment give responsibility-talk practical relational weight. For an elaboration see Busser (2019, 45–48).

References

Barry, C. (2005a). "Understanding and Evaluating the Contribution Principle." In Føllesdal, A., and Pogge, T., eds., *Real World Justice: Grounds, Principles, Human Rights and Social Institutions*. Dordrecht: Springer.

Barry, C. (2005b). "Applying the Contribution Principle." *Metaphilosophy*, 36(1/2): 210–227.

Berry, J.M., and Portney, K.E. (2017). "The Tea Party versus Agenda 21: Local Groups and Sustainability Policies in U.S. Cities." *Environmental Politics*, 26(1): 118–137.

Brock, G. (2010). "Recent Work on Rawls's *Law of Peoples*: Critics versus Defenders." *American Philosophical Quarterly*, 47(1): 85–101.

Brown, C. (2017). "Poverty Alleviation, Global Justice, and the Real World." *Ethics & International Affairs*, 31(3): 357–365.

Busser, M. (2019). *Ethics, Obligation and the Responsibility to Protect*. New York: Routledge.

Carr, E.H. (1962). *Twenty Years' Crisis: 1919–1939*, Second Edition, New York: St. Martin's Press.

Chandler, D. (2003). "Rhetoric without Responsibility: The Attraction of 'Ethical' Foreign Policy." *British Journal of Politics and International Relations*, 5(3): 295–316.

Chomsky, N., and Herman, E. S. (1988) [2002]. *Manufacturing Consent: The Political Economy of the Mass Media*. New York: Pantheon Books.

Cohen, G.A. (2000). "If You're an Egalitarian, How Come You're So Rich?" *Journal of Ethics*, 4(1–2): 1–26.

Difonzo, N. (2019). "Conspiracy Rumour Psychology." In Uscinski, J., ed., *Conspiracy Theories and the People Who Believe Them*. Oxford: Oxford University Press.

Dunlap, R.E. (2013). "Climate Change Skepticism and Denial: An Introduction." *American Behavioural Scientist*, 57(6): 691–698.

Easterly, W. (2006). *The White Man's Burden: Why the West's Efforts to Aid the Rest Have Done So Much Ill and So Little Good*. Oxford: Oxford University Press.

Feinberg, M., and Willer, R. (2011). "Apocalypse Soon? Dire Messages Reduce Belief in Global Warming by Contradicting Just-World Beliefs." *Psychological Science*, 22(1): 34–38.

Foucault, M. (1982). "The Subject and Power," *Critical Inquiry*, 8(4): 777–795.

Gallagher, C. (2000). "Global Change, Local Angst: Class and the American Patriot Movement." *Environment and Planning D: Society and Space*, 18(6): 667–691.

Giddens, A. (1991). *Modernity and Self-Identity*. Cambridge: Polity Press.

Goertzel, T. (1994). "Belief in Conspiracy Theories." *Political Psychology*, 15(4): 731–742.

Greenhill, K. (2010). *Weapons of Mass Migration: Forced Displacement, Coercion, and Foreign Policy*. Ithaca: Cornell University Press.

Held, D. (1995). *Democracy and the Global Order*. Cambridge: Polity Press.

Hofstadter, R. (1996). "The Paranoid Style in American Politics." in *The Paranoid Style in American Politics and Other Essays*: 3–40. Cambridge, MA: Harvard University Press.

Jolley, D., and Douglas, K.M. (2014). "The Social Consequences of Conspiracism: Exposure to Conspiracy Theories Decreases Intentions to Engage in Politics and to Reduce One's Carbon Footprint." *British Journal of Psychology*, 105: 35–56.

Kahneman, D. (2011). *Thinking Fast and Slow*. New York: Farrar, Straus and Giroux.

Kimmel, M. (2013). *Angry White Men: American Masculinity at the End of an Era*. New York: Nation Books.

Kuper, A. (2005). "Introduction", in Kuper, A., ed., *Global Responsibilities: Who Must Deliver on Human Rights?* New York: Routledge.

Leman, P., and Cinnirella, M. (2013). "Beliefs in Conspiracy Theories and the Need for Cognitive Closure." *Frontiers in Psychology*, 4(378): 1–10.

Marder, L. (2018). "Refugees Are Not Weapons: The 'Weapons of Mass Migration' Metaphor and Its Implications." *International Studies Review*, 20(4): 576–588.

Miller, D. (2001). "Distributing Responsibilities." *Journal of Political Philosophy*, 9(4): 453–471.

Mitzen, J. (2006). "Ontological Security in World Politics: State Identity and Security Dilemma." *European Journal of International Relations*, 12(3): 341–370.

Moyo, D. (2009). *Dead Aid*. New York: Farrar, Straus and Giroux.
Mulloy, D.J. (2014). *The World of the John Birch Society: Conspiracy, Conservatism and the Cold War*. Nashville: Vanderbilt University Press.
Nagel, T. (2005). "The Problem with Global Justice." *Philosophy and Public Affairs*, 33(2): 1113–147.
Norton, R.K. (2014). "Agenda 21 and Its Discontents: Is Sustainable Development a Global Imperative or Globalizing Conspiracy." *Urban Lawyer*, 46(2): 325–360.
Olmsted, K. (2009). *Real Enemies: Conspiracy Theories and American Democracy, World War I to 9/11*. Oxford: Oxford University Press.
O'Neill, O. (2016). *Justice across Boundaries: Whose Obligations?* Cambridge: Cambridge University Press.
Pogge, T. (2002). *World Poverty and Human Rights*. Cambridge: Polity Press.
Rawls, J. (1999). *The Law of Peoples*. Cambridge, MA: Harvard University Press.
Shue, H. (2003). "Global Accountability." In Coicaud, J.-M., Doyle, M.W., and Gardner, A.-M., eds., *The Globalization of Human Rights*. New York: United Nations University Press.
Singer, P. (1972). "Famine, Affluence and Morality." *Philosophy and Public Affairs*, 1(1): 229–243.
Walzer, M. (1983). *Spheres of Justice: A Defense of Pluralism and Equality*. New York: Basic Books.
Warner, D. (1996). "Levinas, Buber, and the Concept of Otherness in International Relations." *Millennium – Journal of International Studies*, 25(1): 111–128.
Young, I.M. (2006). "Responsibility and Global Justice: A Social Connection Model." *Social Philosophy and Policy Foundation*, 23(1): 102–130.

8
RESPONSIBILITY AND AUTHORITY IN GLOBAL GOVERNANCE

Jelena Cupać and Michael Zürn

Introduction

World politics discourse is full of responsibility demands to prevent genocides, to promote democracy, to fight terrorism, to feed the starving, to save the environment, to halt sexual violence against women, to manage economic crises, to contain epidemics, and so forth (Hansen-Magnusson and Vetterlein 2015). Addressees of these demands are various, but international organizations (IOs) have been among the ones most frequently targeted in the realm of global governance. And indeed, IOs have increasingly assumed or have been assigned these responsibilities. At the same time, another trend has emerged: the authority of IOs has increased, especially since the early 1990s. Today's IOs exercise authority in setting agendas, making rules, monitoring their implementation, interpreting norms, enforcing norms and policies, making evaluations, and generating knowledge (Zürn 2018).

There are good reasons not to see these two trends as coincidental. For example, an IO that is assigned responsibility to promote democracy often has the authority to make decisions and interpretations in that respect, for instance, in the monitoring of elections. Despite this evident link between IO responsibility and IO authority, there is little communication between responsibility and authority scholarship on IOs. In this contribution, we, therefore, ask: How are responsibility and authority connected in IOs? Is authority constitutive of responsibility, or the other way around? Is it also possible that they are co-constitutive phenomena?

To answer these questions, we first discuss the use of the concepts of responsibility and authority separately to identify the major differences between them. In a second step, we try to answer the question about the connections between responsibility and authority by discussing different relationships. In all of those, we focus on the relationship in global governance. Therefore, our examples are primarily about the responsibility and authority of IOs. Sometimes, we add examples from other realms to highlight that the relationships we identify are not special for IOs but of general conceptual character. In the conclusion, we summarize our main arguments and sketch areas of further inquiry.

Defining responsibility and authority of international organizations

Responsibility and authority scholarship on IOs are embedded in different theoretical traditions. Responsibility scholars mostly draw on insights from moral philosophy and are often (although not exclusively) interested in normative theorizing (Ainley 2011; Beardsworth 2015;

Erskine 2001; 2003a; 2003b; 2004; 2008; Frost 2003). As a result, they are chiefly concern with whether international institutions can be seen as responsible agents (Erskine 2003a). Authority, on the other hand, is a central though contested concept in political philosophy and empirical social science (Friedman 1990, 56). Authority scholars in International Relations (IR) typically aim at explaining the causes and effects of authoritative institutions and actors. They have thus asked the question of the extent to which international institutions can get states to behave in a way that does not reflect only their short-term interests. Uncovering the social sources of this authority has been one of their primary goals. In what follows, we briefly review both of these scholarships, settling on a particular notion of IO responsibility and authority.

Responsibility

Responsibility refers to the general obligation of social agents towards someone or something. While a specific obligation to do X is usually described as a duty, the concept of responsibility is more broadly geared towards having a general obligation to achieve something. Therefore, duties as specific obligations refer to missions with fixed content and specific assignments, while responsibility refers to missions with dynamic content and broad discretion (see Shadmy this handbook). Responsibility can be understood both as a future-oriented moral obligation and a backward-oriented fulfilment of the criteria for deserving blame or praise. While the backward-oriented meaning of responsibility is often used in legal contexts, we are more interested in the future-oriented meaning as it is prevalent in moral and political contexts (Klein 2005). We, therefore, define *responsibility as an accepted assignment of a general obligation to take care of something or someone*. In this sense, parents have a responsibility for their children, states for their citizens, and the United Nations Security Council for peace. The general character of responsibility makes it hard to create legal accountability, but, in extreme cases, the accepted assignment of responsibilities may nonetheless lead to social or legal punishment.

Whether institutions can hold responsibility, particularly moral responsibility, is a contested issue. Toni Erskine is the most vocal proponent of 'institutional moral agency' among responsibility scholars in IR (Erskine 2003a; 2004; 2008). For her, it is paradoxical that most IR theorists treat states as actors but are reluctant to see them as capable of moral action.[1] For this reason, she proposes criteria that, if fulfilled, should qualify any institution—be it a state, an IO, or a private actor—as a moral agent capable of holding responsibility. These criteria are the capacity for moral deliberation (i.e., understanding and reflecting upon moral requirements), the capacity for moral action (i.e., act to conform to these requirements), and the freedom to act (i.e., to have a degree of independence from other agents and forces) (Erskine 2001, 69). Erskine then goes on to specify features that an institution must have to conform to these criteria. She lists four of them: an identity that is more than the sum of the identities of its constitutive parts (i.e., members); a central decision-making structure and procedures; an identity over time or, more precisely, continuity; and a conception of itself as a unit (Erskine 2001, 71–72). These four features define a moral agent.

Being a moral agent *capable* of having responsibility is one thing; holding responsibility is another. It requires a social process of ascription that requires elements of acceptance and assignment (compare the respective chapters by Shadmy, Busser, and Baron in this volume). David Miller famously, therefore, asks more specifically for the sources of the assignment of authority beyond the moral agency. Discussing the question 'Who has a responsibility to rescue a child who falls into deep water?,' he singles out three sources besides morality: a causal one asking who caused the problem; a communitarian one asking who is socially closest to the child; and a capacity-based one asking who is able to rescue the child. He concludes that capacity is the primary criterion; the other ones are only secondary (Miller 2001). This is in line with IR theory, where many talk about the responsibility of great powers (Bukovansky et al. 2012), while the responsibility of neighbouring or causing states is used in more specific and legal contexts. In sum, responsibility is an obligation to take care, requiring the capacity to do so.

Against this background, we maintain that IOs can be theorized as holders of a prospect-oriented responsibility, understood as a general obligation to take care of something or someone, for instance, international peace, minorities, or the environment. IOs apply for or are assigned this kind of responsibility because, among other things, they have mechanisms for moral deliberation (as argued by Erskine) and capacity for remedial action (as argued by Miller).

Authority

While responsibility refers to a generalized *duty*, authority *refers to the right of certain social agents to make decisions, give orders, and issue commands to subordinates from whom obedience or deference is expected.* Those who recognize authority defer their judgement or choice without being necessarily forced or persuaded to do so (Arendt 1970). In IR, an IO is considered an authority when the direct or indirect addressees recognize, in principle or in practice, that the institution can make competent judgements and binding decisions (Cooper et al. 2008, 555; Zürn et al. 2012, 88).

When it comes to the sources of authority, the debate is complex. Two distinctions seem especially important. For one group of scholars, legitimacy is the source of authority. In this view, authority is legitimate power. Authority is seen here as inseparable from legitimacy, making the term legitimate authority redundant (Hurd 2008, 61, footnote 116; see also Ruggie 2004). Authority then is the approved use of power within some socially constructed system of norms, values, and beliefs. Another perspective acknowledges a close link between authority and legitimation – in the sense that any authority requires legitimation as pointed out by Weber (2013) – but does not assume that all authorities are successful in creating beliefs in legitimacy (Zürn 2018, 66). In this perspective, the belief in a legitimate exercise of authority is necessary to reproduce authority over time (Zürn 2018, 62–88).[2] The initial source of authority, however, must be something else.

This leads us to a debate about the source of IO authority. IR scholars from different theoretical camps argue for different sources, and this leads them to see IO authority differently—as contracted, inscribed, and reflexive (Zürn 2018). The notion of *contracted authority* is proposed by rationalist scholars (see Cooley 2005; Lake 2009, 2010). For them, authority in global governance emerges through contract making between constituencies (most often states) and future authority holders (most often IOs). The most important components of this conception of authority are interests and commands. States are willing to enter authority relations to the extent that they provide them with an opportunity to advance their interests. As David Lake puts it, '[b]oth dominant and subordinate state[s] have to be better off in hierarchic than in strictly anarchic relations for the contract to be fulfilled' (Lake 2009, 93). In other words, authority relations are based on the exchange of values. Therefore, in contracted authority, the authority holders derive their right to command from the interest-based contracts (Hooghe et al. 2017).

Inscribed authority is proposed by constructivists (Adler and Pouliot 2011; Avant et al. 2010; Barnett and Finnemore 2004; Hurd 1999; 2008). It is the kind of authority that does not emerge from autonomous actors pursuing their interests, but from them being socialized into existing contexts and social orders (Barnett and Finnemore 2004, 5). For the proponents of inscribed authority, legitimacy plays an important role. Ian Hurd has most explicitly expressed this by arguing that '[a] rule will become legitimate to an individual (and therefore become behaviorally significant) when the individual internalizes its content and reconfigures his or her interests according to the rule. When this happens, compliance becomes habitual (in the sense of being the default position)…' (Hurd 2008, 31). In this understanding, authority is based on shared beliefs about a legitimate power structure of society and a criterion of appropriateness. When power is exercised along those lines, it is considered as an authority. In other words, the source of authority is socialization.

The notion of *reflexive authority* is rooted neither in interests nor in norms, but in recognition of the constituency and audiences, in our case of states and societies, that an institution or an individual can make competent judgements and binding decisions (Zürn 2018, 45–47). Accordingly, authority is observed because it is seen as a trusted source of orientation. In international relations, states are sometimes willing to defer their judgement and choice to IOs if there is a belief that they may know better (epistemic authority) and/or that there is a need for a third perspective (political authority) (Zürn et al. 2012). The development of such international authorities is based on a relationship between IOs with little resources and states with much more resources. Given that the authority of IOs is rarely internalized, the relationship includes a permanent and ongoing question of the exercise of authority. IOs, therefore, do not often command states but mostly put forward requests. Their source of authority is the self-reflective recognition of the limits of rationality on the side of constituent actors.

In this paper, we opt for the reflexive understanding of IO authority. The notion of contracted authority is too narrow. States do not only defer to IOs because they see them as maximizing their interests. They often look to IOs in the process of interest-definition. They defer to IOs because they bring added value to the table: they are a trusted source of orientation and competent judgement. Also, states do not defer to IOs solely out of appropriateness, habit, or socialization, as suggested by proponents of inscribed authority. States continuously judge, monitor, and question IO authority; in other words, they continuously reflect upon it.

How are responsibility and authority intertwined in global governance

Scholarships on the responsibility and authority of IOs rarely communicate. As a result, we know little about how the two phenomena are connected. Anne Orford's book *International Authority and the Responsibility to Protect* is a notable exception (Orford 2011). Orford sees R2P as embedded in a dilemma of who should assume political authority in times of civil wars and revolutions. This leads her to Thomas Hobbes and Carl Schmidt, who resolve the dilemma by arguing that those who have the capacity and willingness to assume responsibility for people's protection should be granted political authority. Taking their cue, Orford argues that R2P resulted from the UN's attempt to provide a coherent account of its own authority, an account directed towards integrating dispersed protection-oriented responsibilities Secretary-General Dag Hammarskjöld introduced in the wake of decolonization. Therefore, Orford sees the UN's authority as contingent upon its assumption of responsibility. Speaking of IOs more generally, this is also one of the possibilities we envision. However, we are also interested in the reverse possibility—authority being constitutive of responsibility—as well as in the two phenomena being co-constituted.

Regarding the possibility of mutual constitutiveness, it is first important to observe that responsibility and authority can work independently of each other. Unlike authority, responsibility can be exercised without a demand for obedience or deference. This means that an actor can have responsibility without authority. In most cases, however, the assignment of responsibility comes with the right to make some interpretations and decisions. The person who has the responsibility to rescue the child from drowning has some discretion about how to carry out the mission. However, not all discretion amounts to the exercise of authority directed towards another person(s). As for authority, in most cases, it does come with responsibility. An actor exercising authority through decisions, orders, or commands never does so in a vacuum but as part of assumed responsibility to protect someone or something, to produce valid information and appropriate judgements for the collective, or to provide public services. In some cases, however, the authority does not care about the social purpose for which it has been established. It may claim to do so but actually care about more parochial goals. While in these cases, it is likely that legitimacy evaporates quickly, leading to the decline of authority, it still leaves us with a possibility of authority existing without responsibility. One may dare to say that history knows a lot of those cases.

Given that each of the phenomena can exist in the absence of the other, we can exclude the possibility that they are co-constitutive; that is, that whenever we find authority, we inevitably will also find responsibility and vice versa. This leaves us with four remaining relationships to discuss. We will thus examine whether and when responsibility is causally prior to authority and, in turn, whether and when authority is causally prior to responsibility. In addition, we ask about the vertical relationship: Are authorities able to withdraw responsibility and vice versa.

From responsibility to authority

As we already pointed out, in recent decades, the responsibility discourse has proliferated in world politics. Problems and events such as genocides, migration, economic crisis, and environmental degradation are almost exclusively framed as issues of failed or required protective responsibility. Given this ubiquity of the responsibility discourse, Hannes Hansen-Magnusson is right to observe that responsibility might very well be one of the main sources of normativity in today's world politics (Hansen-Magnusson 2019). Since the expansion of IO authority typically requires normative justification with reference to a social purpose, taking responsibility may, therefore, also be a factor that underlines the trend of IOs' rising authority.

A responsibility discourse contains two elements: it is about the designation of referent objects that need protection (e.g., humans, environment, cultures, economic equality) and the actors that can provide this protection (e.g., the international community, states, IOs). Referent objects are usually designated based on shared moral values such as human rights or collective goods such as the climate. Both can serve as social purposes for IOs and other international authorities. In turn, the choice of responsible actors usually depends on their quality. As we already indicated, IOs are seen as fitting responsibility holders in global governance due to their deliberative mechanisms (emphasized by Erskine) and their capacity to organize remedial action (emphasized by Miller). All three—social purpose, deliberative mechanisms, and capacity—have the potential to justify, individually or in combination, the expansion of IO authority. Responsibility to Protect (R2P) is a good case in point. It shows how agreeing on the universal value of human lives led to the UN Security Council being invested with a controversial authority to temporarily suspend state sovereignty if a state failed to protect its citizens from atrocity crimes. But, this development in the Security Council's authority was also dependent on the Council's credentials to deliberate on the issues of peace and security and its capacity to act remedially.[3]

However, the move from a responsibility discourse to an established IO authority is not a direct one. A process of translating societal pressure for responsibility into a specific responsibility of an IO needs to occur first. And this process requires the fulfilment of several conditions (see Figure 8.1). To begin with, an issue for which responsibility discourse is evoked needs to reach an IO's agenda. IO member states and staff then need to agree on the definition of a referent object towards which an IO will orient itself. In ideal-typical terms, they either agree on the definition or they do not. If not, an IO is unlikely to be assigned corresponding responsibilities.

Authority in global governance

A good example of this scenario is the 2015 migration crisis. In many IOs, a debate developed whether to treat forced and voluntary migrants separately or as a single group. By failing to settle the debate, states and other involved agents also failed to assign a single IOs with specific responsibility for the ongoing flows of migration (Kortendiek 2019).

In the next step, again, two scenarios are possible. First, an IO can still choose not to 'apply' for corresponding responsibility. This was the case with human security in the context of the Commission on Security and Cooperation in Europe (CSCE) during the Cold War. Participating states agreed to enshrine the 'respect for human rights and fundamental freedoms, including the freedom of thought, conscience, religion or belief' in the 1975 Helsinki Final Act. However, throughout the Cold War, the CSCE had no responsibility in this domain as it was in contradiction with other rights and principles prioritized at the time, above all the right of each state 'freely to choose and develop its political, social, economic and cultural systems.'[4]

In the second scenario, an IO can 'apply' for responsibility relating to an agreed referent. However, there is still an additional condition that needs to be met for it to become a responsible party: there should be an implicit or explicit act of responsibility assignment. An example of

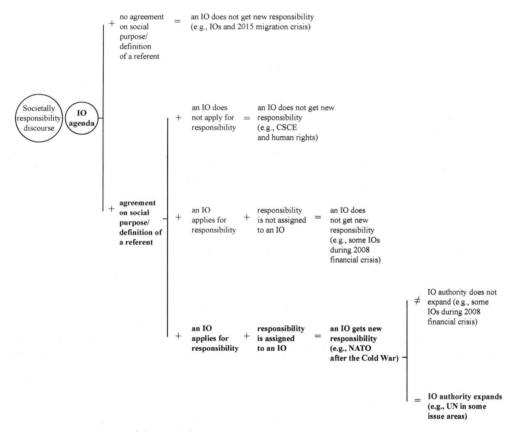

Figure 8.1 From responsibility to authority

both these conditions being met is the post-Cold War NATO. Throughout the 1990s, its member states defined democracy, freedom, and human rights as referents that need to be protected if Europe was to remain peaceful. Simultaneously, they volunteered and assigned NATO with the responsibility to protect these referents, the responsibility that materialized in the Alliance conducting various 'out of area' operations. However, there are situations in which an IO's responsibility application is not met with responsibility assignment. This usually happens when there is a competition among IOs. For instance, in the course of the financial crisis, many IOs displayed a willingness to take over responsibility. Yet, in the end, it was mainly the IMF and the Financial Stability Board that got the responsibility assigned.

Finally, we arrive at IO authority. Once an IO is assigned responsibility, it is essentially endowed with a social purpose that can be evoked as justification for the IO's authority expansion. It can now issue requests and commands via such practices as knowledge-generation, agenda-setting, rule-setting, monitoring, interpretation, and even enforcement. This expansion would not have been possible if the UN was not assigned responsibility for issues as diverse as human rights, state-building, development, and environment protection. Yet, the extension of IO authority does not follow automatically from the assignment of IO responsibility. To look at the example of financial regulation again: While the responsibility for financial stability as the social purpose was established and the major economic powers picked few IO to take the assignment, these IOs remained relatively toothless. Powerful financial actors were successful in limiting the expansion of their international authority.

In sum, while IO responsibility expansion can be seen as a precondition of IO authority expansion, the relationship between the two is not determined. Neither the number nor the type of responsibilities an IO assumes can predictably tell us if that an IO will expand its authority. The assignment of responsibility to an IO only increases its potentiality to expand authority. The process is ultimately a political one, resting on various considerations and power asymmetries, including states constantly monitoring IOs while deferring to them.

Before moving on, let us also ask what can lead to the withdrawal of authority. Can there be a hierarchical relationship between responsible actors and authorities? As hinted in the paragraphs above already, each of the steps requires aggregate social choices, processes, and agreements. The withdrawal of authority requires a reversal of at least one of these steps: either of the agreement on the social purpose and the application for the assignment of responsibility or the agreement to assign responsibility and authority. As a result of each of these reversals, an authority may evaporate. Though only one reversal may suffice, the decline of IO authority is still as much an emerging social process as its rise. Authority in global governance cannot be just taken away by a hierarchical decision.

From authority to responsibility

The story we have so far told suggests that the assignment of responsibility to an IO is prior to the delegation of authority. While the exercise of IO authority thus is often grounded in the societally recognized need for the exercise of responsibility in a specific domain or issue-area, the willingness to take over responsibility neither automatically leads to the delegation of authority nor is the exercise of authority always grounded in responsibility. In this view, authority (sometimes) comes after responsibility. In the remainder, we argue that dynamic feedback effects also are possible. Once an IO is established as an authority, it may, via two paths, widen its responsibilities.

In order to sketch this dynamic, it is useful to distinguish epistemic and political authority (see Zürn 2018; Zürn et al. 2012). Political authority refers to the right to make decisions or behavioural requests. Epistemic authority refers to the right to make impartial and neutral interpretations, either on the basis of expert knowledge or moral standing. Both types of authority are vested in IOs as an issue-area specific authority. It is the right to make interpretations about

Authority in global governance

problems affecting the issue-area that may be used to extend the referent(s) for responsibility. For example, the World Health Organization has authority in the domain of international public health. Over the years, this authority allowed it to take responsibility for specific issues such as pandemic and epidemic diseases, nutrition, food safety, substance abuse, and occupational health. Moreover, the Security Council can be said to have exercised epistemic authority when, in the 1990s, it was assigned protective responsibility for human rights violations as a result of defining these violations as threats to international peace and security.

In these cases, IOs use their issue-area authority to redefine the social purpose (the meaning of the referent) so that either newly emerging issues will be incorporated or existing issues, so far not part of the responsibility, will be claimed to be a necessary part of the responsibility.

The first case may be labelled *mission-adaptation*. In this path, new issues come up over time that arguably need to be taken into account by a responsible actor. If the issue area is global health, for instance, and a new, so far unknown, disease spreads, an IO with epistemic and political authority in this issue area is expected to take care of it. When IO members and staff then exercise political authority by using existing procedures and recipes, it is likely that the extension of responsibility and authority will not be rejected by the constituency. However, when an IO exercises authority regarding new issues in a way that moves beyond existing practices, there is the danger that it will be considered as emergency power that will be rejected at the end of the day (Kreuder-Sonnen 2019).

The second case (old issues are incorporated as part of a redefined social purpose) can be labelled *mission-creeping*. In this case, the authority-holders extend their responsibility by redefining the social purpose so that it covers more issues and more responsibility. The mentioned re-definition of a threat to international peace driven by the General Secretary and some of the Veto-Powers of the UN Security Council during the 1990s is a case in point. The new meaning of a threat to international peace included now the responsibility to prevent atrocity crimes. Over the years, many peacekeeping missions conducted in circumstances where human rights were being violated, thus started taking responsibilities that go beyond the separation of conflicting parties, responsibilities such as civilian protection, promoting economic development, and fostering inclusive political process. The concrete exercise of authority in this regard by orchestrating international interventions established the new responsibility.

One conducive condition for mission-creeping in global governance is the absence of a strong meta-authority. The absence of a meta-authority allows issue-area specific authorities to redefine the underlying issue to broaden the scope of responsibility and authority. The absence of a meta-authority prevents an authoritative decision to limit the authority of specific institutions. To reject mission-creeping, it thus requires a complicated social process leading to a shared understanding that mission-creeping needs to be rejected. Mission-creeping and the process in which authority is prior to assuming new responsibility, therefore, is not rare. Figure 8.2 illustrates this dynamic.

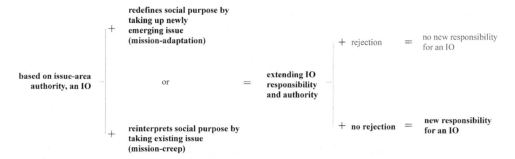

Figure 8.2 From authority to responsibility

Regarding our final conceivable relationship between authority and responsibility, we want to point to an important difference in the vertical relationship between authority and responsibility. Whereas the withdrawal of authority requires an emergent or horizontal process, the withdrawal of responsibility can, in principle, be carried out by a superior authority. The responsibility of parents for their kids can be withdrawn by state authorities in case there are strong indications of the abuse of responsibility. Similarly, the whole construct of responsibility to protect followed the same logic. An international authority can withdraw the responsibility that states claim to have over their citizens. Due to the lack of an established meta-authority, it is very rare that international authorities are circumscribed by other international authorities. Yet, the G-summits as a very rudimentary form of meta-authority have sometimes shifted authorities away from IOs in the past.

Conclusion

We have observed in this chapter that, while significant contributions exist on the responsibility and authority of IOs, there is very little theoretical work on how the two phenomena are connected. In this contribution, we aimed at spelling out the relationships between the concepts after introducing them separately in the first part. We have identified some important differences in the use of concepts in IR. To begin with, responsibility is used mainly in normative debates, while authority is primarily a descriptive concept. Responsibility is a general obligation and does not need to come with specified duties. In turn, the exercise of authority by IOs most often is issue-area specific and based on prescribed procedures. Finally, while the sources of IO responsibility are largely found in features of IOs themselves such as the capacity to deliberate and act, the sources of authority refer mainly to features of the relationship between the authority and its constituency.[5]

In spite of the strong overlap between the two concepts, we do not see them as co-constitutive. There are cases in which responsibility comes without authority and cases in which authority is exercised in the absence of responsibility. With this in mind, we have moved forward and discussed different causal relationships suggesting two possibilities: that responsibility precedes and is causally prior to authority and that authority precedes and is causally prior to responsibility. We proposed that responsibility can, under specific additional conditions, indeed lead to authority. The link between the two thus entails an emergent social process. In turn, the extension of responsibility due to IO authority occurs as a result of an IO exercising its inherent epistemic and political capacities either to tackle new issues within designated social domains or as a result of mission-creeping. At the same time, we argue that the withdrawal of authority in global governance also requires the social processes of de-emergence. By contrast, the withdrawal of responsibility can be exerted by an authority that is hierarchically superior.

This general theoretical sketch of the relationship between responsibility and authority in IOs should, however, be seen as a start. The next necessary step should be an examination of the actual practices through which the translation of responsibility into authority and authority into responsibility occurs.

Notes

1 Erskine mentions two authors in particular: Niebuhr (2013) and Wendt (1999).
2 This, of course, raises the sources-question again, here about anticipation, legality, fairness, knowledge, tradition, and provision of relative gains as the sources of legitimacy.
3 The responsibility to protect case is an interesting one, since it demonstrates that the identification of a social purpose itself can be contested. With the rejection of human security as a reason for external intervention by especially China and Russia, the authority of the UN Security Council was reduced again.

4 See the Helsinki Final Act, adopted at the First CSCE Summit of Heads of States or Governments (Helsinki, 1 August 1975), Declaration on Principles Guiding Relations between Participating States, Section I.
5 This refers to the *debates* about the sources. In the end, the *assignment* of responsibility is also a relational concept.

References

Adler, E., and Pouliot, V., eds. (2011). *International Practices*. Cambridge: Cambridge University Press.
Ainley, K. (2011). "Excesses of Responsibility: The Limits of Law and the Possibilities of Politics." *Ethics & International Affairs*, 25(4): 407–431.
Arendt, H. (1970). *On Violence*. London: Houghton Mifflin Harcourt.
Avant, D.D., Finnemore, M., and Sell, S.K. (2010). *Who Governs the Globe?* Cambridge: Cambridge University Press.
Barnett, M.N., and Finnemore, M. (2004). *Rules for the World: International Organizations in Global Politics*. Ithaca: Cornell University Press.
Beardsworth, R. (2015). "From Moral to Political Responsibility in a Globalized Age." *Ethics & International Affairs*, 29(1): 71–92.
Bukovansky, M., Clark, I., Eckersley, R., Price, R., Reus-Smit, C., and Wheeler, N.J. (2012). *Special Responsibilities: Global Problems and American Power*. Cambridge: Cambridge University Press.
Cooley, A. (2005). *Logics of Hierarchy: The Organization of Empires, States, and Military Occupation*. Ithaca: Cornell University Press.
Cooper, S., Hawkins, D., Jacoby, W., and Nielson, D. (2008). "Yielding Sovereignty to International Institutions: Bringing System Structure Back In." *International Studies Review*, 10(3): 501–524.
Erskine, T. (2001). "Assigning Responsibilities to Institutional Moral Agents: The Case of States and Quasi-States." *Ethics & International Affairs*, 15(2): 67–85.
Erskine, T., ed. (2003a). *Can Institutions Have Responsibilities?: Collective Moral Agency and International Relations*. New York: Palgrave.
Erskine, T. (2003b). "Introduction: Making Sense of 'Responsibility' in International Relations—Key Questions and Concepts." In Erskine, T., ed. *Can Institutions Have Responsibilities?* New York: Palgrave.
Erskine, T. (2004). ""Blood on the UN's Hands"? Assigning Duties and Apportioning Blame to an Intergovernmental Organisation." *Global Society*, 18(1): 21–42.
Erskine, T. (2008). "Locating Responsibility: The Problem of Moral Agency in International Relations." In Reus-Smit, C., and Snidal, D., eds. *The Oxford Handbook of International Relations*. New York: Oxford University Press.
Friedman, R.B. (1990). "On The Concept of Authority in Political Philosophy." In Raz, J., ed. *Authority*. Oxford: Blackwell.
Frost, M. (2003). "Constitutive Theory and Moral Accountability: Individuals, Institutions, and Dispersed Practices." In Erskine, T., ed. *Can Institutions Have Responsibilities?: Collective Moral Agency and International Relations*. New York: Palgrave.
Hansen-Magnusson, H. (2019). "The Web of Responsibility in and for the Arctic." *Cambridge Review of International Affairs*, 32(2): 132–158.
Hansen-Magnusson, H., and Vetterlein, A. (2015). "Framing Responsibility in World Politics." *International Studies Association 56th Annual Convention*. New Orleans.
Hooghe, L., Marks, G., Lenz, T., Bezuijen, J., Ceka, B., and Derderyan, S. (2017). *Measuring International Authority*. Oxford: Oxford University Press.
Hurd, I. (1999). "Legitimacy and Authority in International Politics." *International Organization*, 53(2): 379–408.
Hurd, I. (2008). *After Anarchy: Legitimacy and Power in the United Nations Security Council*. New Jersey: Princeton University Press.
Klein, M. (2005). "Responsibility." In Honderich, T., ed. *The Oxford Companion to Philosophy*. Oxford: Oxford University Press.
Kortendiek, N. (2019). "Experiments in Global Migration Governance – How International Organisations Govern in and through Practice." *ECPR Joint Sessions*. UCL Mons.
Kreuder-Sonnen, C. (2019). *Emergency Powers of International Organizations*. Oxford: Oxford University Press.
Lake, D.A. (2009). *Hierarchy in International Relations*. New York: Cornell University Press.

Lake, D.A. (2010). "Rightful Rules: Authority, Order, and the Foundations of Global Governance." *International Studies Quarterly*, 54(3): 587–613.

Miller, D. (2001). "Distributing Responsibilities." *Journal of Political Philosophy*, 9(4): 453–471.

Niebuhr, R. (2013). *Moral Man and Immoral Society: A Study in Ethics and Politics*. Louisville: Westminster John Knox Press.

Orford, A. (2011). *International Authority and the Responsibility to Protect*. Cambridge: Cambridge University Press.

Ruggie, J.G. (2004). "Reconstituting The Global Public Domain—Issues, Actors, and Practices." *European Journal of International Relations*, 10(4): 499–531.

Weber, M. (2013). "Typen der Herrschaft." In Borchardt, K., Hanke, E., and Schluchter, W., eds. *Max Weber-Gesamtausgabe: Band I/23: Wirtschaft und Gesellschaft. Soziologie. Unvollendet. 1919-1920*. 1st ed. Tübingen: Mohr Siebeck.

Wendt, A. (1999). *Social Theory of International Politics*. Cambridge, UK: Cambridge University Press.

Zürn, M. (2018). *A Theory of Global Governance: Authority, Legitimacy, and Contestation*. Oxford: Oxford University Press.

Zürn, M., Binder, M., and Ecker-Ehrhardt, M. (2012). "International Authority and Its Politicization." *International Theory*, 4(1): 69–106.

9
RESPONSIBILITY AND THE ENGLISH SCHOOL

Viktor Friedmann

Introduction

The English School (ES) is best known for the idea of international society: an anarchical, yet norm-governed set of social relations between states, which is an alternative to both the realist power politics of an international system and the idealist morality of cosmopolitan world society (Bull 2002; Dunne 1998). From the perspective of identifying its characteristic contribution to the study of responsibility in international politics, however, the way ES approaches norms is just as important as the fact that it sees them as central to world politics (Jackson 2000). It rejects the positivist methodology of much of social constructivism, which sees norms as causes of behaviour, in favour of an interpretivist approach that seeks to make intelligible the standards that guide the decisions and actions of the practitioners of international politics (Dunne 1998, 7–10; Jackson 2009; Navari 2009a). Its emphasis on the normativity of norms and its refusal to separate empirical and moral inquiry make it similar to critical constructivism but distinct both from post-positivist takes on norms as hegemonic discourses and from ideal normative theory (Cochran 2009; Jackson 2000, 44–67).

This chapter explores three connected aspects of this approach. First, *responsibilities as moral and legal standards, norms or obligations* are attached to specific actors as participants in the social realm of international politics and are defined in relation to various relevant moral communities – the nation, the society of states, humankind or even the planet (Jackson 2000, 169–78). Many of these are general responsibilities of states, but special responsibilities can also be allocated to specific actors, especially to great powers (Bukovansky et al. 2012), while entities other than states – such as the international community or international organizations – might also be identified as possessing moral agency and thus as adequate bearers of responsibility (Erskine 2008). Second, ES sees the above responsibilities not as causes of behaviour but as standards of human conduct that actors draw on to make and justify situated decisions about how to apply general rules within the confines of specific contexts (Brown 2010b; Jackson 2000, chap. 6). To do this well, practitioners must exhibit *responsibility as a set of political virtues*. Third, in emphasizing conduct rather than behaviour, the ES rejects the separation between normative and empirical inquiry, with implications for *scholarly responsibility* (Cochran 2008; Reus-Smit 2009). Since the activities of the practitioners themselves involve normative reasoning, studying them requires an interpretive, rather than positivist, approach and invites normative assessment. At the same time, normative scholarly judgements must be rooted in the standards of conduct internal to the practices of international politics rather than in abstract, ideal theories. The close links that these three aspects establish between theory and practice, as well as normative and empirical inquiry, pin down the characteristic ES approach to responsibility in International Relations.

Responsibilities as moral and legal standards

The ES conceptualizes international politics as an order constituted by standards of conduct that guide the behaviour and inform the self-conception of states and statespeople (Navari 2009a, 5–6; Jackson 2009). Thus, states do *not* merely form an international system, a world of regular mechanistic interaction that is "sufficient to make the behaviour of each a necessary element in the calculations of the other" (Bull 2002, 9–10). Their practices are "shaped by international norms, regulated by international institutions, and guided by moral purposes" (Dunne 2008, 268). In other words, states and other practitioners of world politics have responsibilities that point beyond their domestic societies. Based on the three traditions of international political thought identified by Wight (1991), it was Jackson (2000, 169–78) who first provided an extensive discussion of responsibilities from an ES perspective, distinguishing between three kinds responsibilities that act as standards of conduct for practitioners of world politics: national responsibilities (realist tradition), international responsibilities (rationalist tradition) and cosmopolitan responsibilities (revolutionary tradition). One of the ES's main strengths is its ability to bring into its analysis simultaneously all three of these competing and often conflicting elements of world order and the responsibilities that constitute them.

General responsibilities: nation, international society, world society and the earth

Although some responsibilities are allocated only to certain states or groups of states, most of them are general, valid equally – although not in an identical manner – for every state. From its beginnings, the ES has argued that such responsibilities go beyond the national interest and are defined by a larger community of which states are a part. Early ES writings identified this community above all as the society of states, with a correspondingly minimalist account of responsibilities circumscribed by the central rule of state sovereignty. Reflecting upon, as well as being shaped by, a shift in standards in world politics by the late 20th century, the ES increasingly incorporated more substantial interstate responsibilities as well as cosmopolitan obligations derived from the idea of a society of humankind, with a recent foray into ecological responsibilities.

ES authors generally agree that today the primary responsibilities of states and statespeople (as office holders acting on behalf of the state) remain the security and well-being of their citizens, and thus the national interest (Jackson 2000, 170–72). This expresses the continuing political reality that domestic societies are better able to provide the kind of moral community that can support a norms-based order than anything beyond their boundaries. A world politics based solely on such national responsibilities would constitute an *international system*, a domain of power politics devoid of morality outside the state, in line with the realist tradition of international political thought.

From the perspective of the ES, however, states also form an *international society* in which their claim towards each other – to political agency as states – has a distinctively moral character that establishes reciprocal rights and duties (Brown 2010a, 127). As a counterpart to the right to sovereign equality, statespeople and diplomats are office holders with responsibilities not only towards their own citizens but also vis-à-vis other states (Jackson 2000, 172–74). Their status as legitimate members of international society – their right to have rights – is linked to the fulfilment of fundamental expectations about their conduct (Clark 2005, 26).

The responsibilities of international society are typically defined in the framework of a minimalist (also called pluralist or rationalist) ethics that makes orderly co-existence between autonomous political units with their own way of life possible. Such responsibilities include adhering to the constitutive rules and fundamental institutions of the society of states, such as mutual recognition of sovereign equality, non-interference in internal affairs, self-determination, diplomacy or international law, all of which serve to make the world safe for diversity (Bull 2002).

As an illustration of the relationship between legitimacy, order and responsibility, consider the institution of the balance of power. From an ES perspective, it should neither be understood as a natural mechanism through which elements of a system adjust their position to maintain equilibrium nor simply as a policy pursued by individual states seeking to counterbalance rising powers and maximize their security. Instead, since the 17th and 18th centuries, balance of power has been understood as an institution of international society: the collective responsibility of states to prevent the emergence of a dominant power and maintain the plural condition of the society of states (Butterfield 1966; Watson 1992, 198–202; Wight 1966a), as well as individual self-restraint, "the responsibility not to upset the balance" (Bull 2002, 102). The legitimacy of states, in turn, is subject to the requirements of this fundamental institution. Clark (2005, 22) argues – based on Watson (1992, 204) – that the idea that the legitimacy of states depends upon recognition by other members of international society emerged with the Peace of Utrecht of 1713, when it was decided that succession based on dynastic legitimacy might be overridden if it threatened the balance of power and thus the independence of European states.

The responsibilities of international society prioritize the maintenance of order over the pursuit of justice and place considerable constraints on the realization of norms of cosmopolitan solidarity (Bull 2002). This does not, however, mean that they have no implications for the internal affairs of states. In the 19th century concert system, responsibility for international stability implied the duty to preserve domestic order and revolutionary states could lose their status as legitimate members of the European state system (Clark 2005, chap. 5). Around the same period, international law's so-called "standards of civilization" distinguished European states with full rights in international society, from the "barbarian" polities that could not enjoy equal status so long as they did not constitute themselves as appropriate political agents (e.g. by setting up foreign ministries, adopting the rules of international law and diplomacy, accepting sovereign equality) (Gong 1984). After the First World War, state legitimacy came to be linked to democratic government and respect for minority rights for the sake of preserving the peace (Clark 2005, chap. 6). The Cold War – dominated as it was by power politics – brought to prominence responsibilities towards sovereignty and non-violence, which are core responsibilities of the ethics of pluralism (Shaw 1992). With the end of the bipolar world, however, the standards of responsible statehood began to shift significantly in the opposite direction: first, towards having a good standing in international institutions, and then later moving towards more substantial solidarist, liberal cosmopolitan values such as liberal democracy, human rights or standards of economic governance (Foot 2001; Gong 2002; Zhang 2016).

ES writings have proposed to make sense of this shift as the rise of the cosmopolitan responsibilities of *world society* (Buzan 2004; Clark 2007). Just as the society of states can be understood as a moral community with its distinctive form of ethics that emphasizes diversity and co-existence, so does world society constitute a moral community that generates responsibilities towards humankind as a whole and towards the rights of individuals outside the state's borders. Vincent (1986), in this manner, explores the impact of the emergence of human rights on the relations between states. Wheeler (2000) examines the degree to which states recognized humanitarian intervention as a norm or at least as a legitimate practice in international society despite its direct clash with the values of sovereignty, non-intervention and non-use of force that underlie the order of international society. In arguing that states that commit massive human rights violations forfeit their sovereignty, this anticipates the development of the norm of sovereignty as responsibility, which makes a state's sovereignty conditional upon the protection of the basic rights of its population and places the responsibility to intervene on the international community in cases where a state fails to do so (Teitt 2017).

Reconstructing the longer historical process behind this transformation, Clark (2007) argues that world society as a transnational social world of non-state actors, began to have a considerable autonomous impact on the norms of legitimacy in the society of states – and hence on state responsibilities – in the early 19th century. He identifies the Congress of Verona's 1822 resolution on preventing slave trade as the starting point of this process. By the early 20th century, the normative preferences of the "public conscience" became incorporated into the fabric of international legitimacy. In the 20th century, substantial issues such as social justice (with the establishment of the International Labour Organization in 1919), human rights (after 1945) and democratic values (after 1989) joined the list of state responsibilities based on the claims of world society.

With national, international and cosmopolitan responsibilities making simultaneous demands on states, many ES authors grappled with the problem of their relationship. Jackson (2000, chaps 10–11), for one, is strongly supportive of sovereignty and non-intervention and opposed to humanitarian interventions and international trusteeship, as he argues for the priority of stability over justice and of the standards of international society over the values of some subset of states. Nevertheless, there are ways in which different responsibilities may be reconciled. Vincent (1986) argues that state responsibility for human rights, rather than threatening the stability of international society, could add to the legitimacy of a society of sovereign states (see also: Linklater 2011a). According to Youde (2018), international society itself has developed a new fundamental institution of moral obligation and responsibility by accepting the cosmopolitan duty to provide assistance beyond the state's borders to vulnerable populations. Linklater (2011b; 2017) draws on Norbert Elias's work on the "civilizing process" to analyze how the historical development of the rules and responsibilities that moderate conflicts within state systems fits into, and has contributed to, a larger movement towards increasing self-restraint and expanding circles of moral solidarity between strangers.

Underlining their evolving nature, Jackson (2000, 175–77) further suggests that responsibilities in contemporary world politics might even extend beyond the human realms of nation, international society and world society. In the context of a deepening and widening environmental crisis, and especially of climate change, states have by the end of the 20th century been recognized as bearing responsibilities towards preserving the global commons or, in other words, Earth as the condition of all life. Falkner (2012) calls this the greening of international society and claims that global environmental responsibility or environmental stewardship has become a new fundamental norm or institution of international society (Falkner and Buzan 2019). Although this development is often considered to have taken place within the framework of world society – given that the state of the environment is an important condition of the preservation and realization of basic human rights – Jackson's formulation suggests the emergence of a moral imaginary that goes beyond the confines of humankind and includes the environment on its own right, with potentially revolutionary implications that have not yet been addressed within the ES.

Special responsibilities and status differentiation

Along with the general responsibilities discussed so far, the ES has also long recognized the existence of special responsibilities attached to a smaller circle of states, most prominently to great powers (Bull 2002, chap. 9; Cui and Buzan 2016). These were originally linked in ES writings, which provided the first extensive discussions of the concept of responsibility within this tradition, to the institution of great power management having as its goal the upholding of the pluralist order of international society. More recently, as many ES scholars moved closer to constructivism, special responsibilities have been reconceived in relation to the special status accorded to certain individual states or hegemonic powers in order to better manage collective problems, thus loosening its connection with restraints on power in favour of its functional deployment.

In Hedley Bull's classical formulation, "great powers are powers recognised by others to have, and conceived by their own leaders and peoples to have, certain special rights and duties" (Bull 2002, 196). Just as general responsibilities are constitutive of legitimate statehood, special responsibilities are constitutive of the legitimacy of the managerial role of great powers, and both are linked to the self-conception of states. Great power management is, in turn, understood as one of the fundamental institutions of international society due to its contribution to the maintenance of international order.

The special responsibilities of the great powers are thought to derive from the inequality of material power, which makes great powers more responsible for certain morally desirable or undesirable outcomes in international politics than lesser ones (Bull 2002, 199). If they want to enjoy the special rights of legitimate managerial powers, they must pay attention to the moral demands that come with their outstanding power. Countries seeking great power status might do so by taking on or claiming responsibilities expected from great powers (Suzuki 2008), considering the interest of other states and of the preservation of international society as a whole when devising their policies (Bull 1980, 437–38).

According to Bull (2002, 200), the duties of great powers include both horizontal and vertical responsibilities. The former concerns managing their relations with each other to preserve the balance of power, and limiting conflicts among themselves with a view to safeguarding the stability of the international system. Great powers further have the vertical responsibility of "exploiting their preponderance in such a way as to impart a degree of central direction to the affairs of international society as a whole" (Bull 2002, 200) This can be achieved by dividing the world into mutually recognized spheres of influence within which great powers are expected to exercise their power unilaterally but in line with the goals of international society. Alternatively, great powers can also practice "joint responsibility" by establishing a concert to promote certain goals throughout the entire international society (Bull 2002, 218–19; Watson 1984, 31). In both cases, they are expected to use force – including the fundamental institution of war – where necessary to enforce the values and goals of international society (Gaskarth 2017; Morris 2004).

As in the case of general responsibilities, historical responsibilities have also undergone historical evolution beyond the demands of the state system. Although Bull conceived of great power management as a fundamental institution of international society, he did not rule out that it might act on cosmopolitan responsibilities. In fact, he connected the legitimacy of great powers to their willingness to respond to the demands of smaller states for just change (Bull 2002, 222). Kopra (2016, 20–44) argues that, today, environmental responsibilities play a major role in a rising China's quest for great power status.

Simpson (2004) analyzed how the special rights and duties of great powers are turned into legal responsibilities with the incorporation of great power management into international law as a form of legalized collective hegemony. The UN Charter, for instance, confers upon its five permanent members a special responsibility for the maintenance of international peace and security as well as the special right to veto decisions they find unacceptable. As Clark (1989, 185) points out, however, the legalization of veto rights effectively removes the central group norm of a shared responsibility of great powers for international order and replaces it with a principle of individualistic, national responsibility, weakening the link between great power management and international society.

As the framework of special responsibilities was adapted to the post-Cold War era of US unipolar dominance, the removal of the horizontal responsibilities of great power management began to feel even more natural. Although Bull (2002, 194) insisted that "there could not be simply one great power" since that would be incompatible with the idea of international society, recently great power management has increasingly been seen as merely a collective version of the more general phenomenon of hegemony, which can just as well be applicable to a single power. Thus, Clark (2011a, 35) defines hegemony as "a status, bestowed by others, and rests on recognition by them […] in return for the bearing of special responsibilities in the management of international order." Whereas the horizontal responsibilities of great powers in relation to each other represented the idea of the pluralistic international society, the hegemony of a single power merely needs to rest upon vertical relations of responsibility, accountability and legitimacy (Clark 2011b; 2017). As Brown (2004) points out, however, without the institutional restraints that great powers as a collective body impose upon one another, a single superpower might in fact take as its responsibility to impose its own conception of the good on the rest of the world. It can, in fact, more generally be said that the downplaying of horizontal responsibilities among the great powers overemphasizes the ability of international society as a whole, instead of the circle of the great powers, to define the criteria of legitimate management.

The separation of the special responsibilities of great powers from the fundamental rules of international order was developed further in Bukovansky et al. (2012). Bringing together ES and social constructivist approaches, special responsibilities are here theorized as "a differentiated set of obligations, the allocation of which is collectively agreed, and they provide a principle of social differentiation for managing collective problems in a world characterised by both formal equality and inequality in material capability" (Bukovansky et al. 2012, 16). This formulation no longer frames special responsibilities in terms of the standards of conduct derived from ES categories of a unitary international society or world society, but instead argues that different actors might be allocated special responsibilities in different functional domains depending on where their power counts. Thus, instead of a clear set of great powers, various states might be allocated special responsibilities in specific social domains according to different logics. For instance, developed and developing countries are recognized to have common but differentiated responsibilities in the climate change regime.

Responsibilities in international society beyond states

This chapter has so far treated states and practitioners of international politics interchangeably as bearers of responsibilities. It can be questioned, however, whether one can talk about the conduct of states in the same way that one can discuss the conduct of individuals. Since the ES operates with an understanding of responsibilities as standards of conduct that enter into the reasoning of actors, rather than as causes of behaviour, it needs – in order to make the case for an analysis of international politics in terms of state responsibilities – to show that states can in fact be reasonably regarded as moral agents, capable of understanding and deliberating about moral imperatives and having the capacity and freedom to act upon them (Erskine 2008). Although ES authors often focus on individual decision-makers (Gaskarth 2013) rather than on the abstract entity of the state, this is clearly neither always realistic, given the collective nature of much of political decision-making, nor practicable in the macro-analysis of international politics.

Despite being collective actors, states can be regarded as sufficiently unitary and stable in terms of their identity, decision-making structure and self-conception to assign them moral agency and the corresponding moral rights and responsibilities. In contrast, failed states or quasi-states, lacking some of the above attributes, might not be properly seen as moral agents (Erskine 2003a). At the same time, collective or institutional actors other than states can in fact meet the criteria and be allocated special responsibilities (Erskine 2003b). With this in mind, it becomes possible to more clearly establish which collective actors can exercise institutional moral agency, and thus to avoid placing responsibilities on agents that cannot discharge them and to hold responsible those that can.

Everyday political discourse, for instance, regularly invokes the responsibility of the "international community" to respond to emergencies or address global problems. But is the location of responsibility appropriately identified in this case? Erskine (2003a) argues that the "international community" should not be regarded as having institutional moral agency because it does not meet the above-listed criteria. Brown (2003), in contrast, is more permissive: he points out that although societies in general do not have agency, international society should rather be viewed as an association, which might have agency. The United Nations Security Council (UNSC) can, at least to a certain extent, be understood as an agent capable of acting on behalf of international society in relation to the primary responsibility for international peace and stability that states have assigned to it. Such occasions, however, can be expected to be rare, since the UNSC does not possess collective agency independent of its member states. Claims by groups of states (such as those that intervened in the Kosovo crisis in 1999) to act on behalf of the "international community" without explicit backing by the UN, remain dubious if we take that community to stand for international society as a whole rather than for a limited circle of states with shared values.

Responsibility as virtue

The responsibilities discussed so far, which Jackson (2000, 151) defines as "procedural responsibilities," only make up one side of the standards of conduct in international politics. They describe, in the form of moral or legal rules and norms, expectations towards an actor of a particular kind, of the holder of a particular office. But such abstract moral rules cannot be directly applied to specific cases. The complexity and uncertainty of political situations and competing moral demands place strict limits on what is possible to achieve (Brown 2010c). The ES tradition identifies a gap that always remains between the rules and the concrete situation in which they should be applied, a space of discretion that requires situated, practical judgement possessing its own standards of conduct. To deny the distinct character of situational ethics, to follow abstract rules without regard to the specific circumstances, is to act irresponsibly.

Jackson (2000, 151, 170) defines as "prudential" or "discretionary" responsibility the standards of conduct adequate for such situational ethics. These are qualities of character a statesperson needs to possess and demonstrate to make the best available choice in a concrete case (Gaskarth 2011). Whereas procedural responsibilities bring into play a vocabulary of moral or legal norms, prudential responsibility evokes a closely connected set of political virtues such as judgement, foresight, circumspection or prudence. Practitioners rely on these qualities to make responsible decisions with a view not only to one's procedural responsibilities but also to the constraints imposed by the situation one finds oneself in.

Prudential responsibility mediates between rules and circumstances, and hence also between morality and political expediency. Wight (1966b, 128–29) identifies prudence as a moral virtue that enables politicians to combine the exigencies of politics with a personal moral sense, thus bringing ethical considerations into political action. Just as the procedural responsibilities of international society offer a middle way between an international system and world society, the situated ethics of practitioners carves out a middle-ground ethics between moral ideals and political realities (Cochran 2009). Here the approach taken by the ES comes close to classical realism's Weberian morality of the ethics of responsibility and its Augustinian emphasis on tragic choice (Murray 1996; Smith 1990). Both schools see political action as inseparable from morality, but from a morality constrained by the tyranny of circumstances.

Where classical realism and the ES part ways is in the nature of the moral rules that need to be reconciled with the constraints of politics. For the former, since there are "no internationally accepted standards of morality" (Kennan 1985, 207), the relevant norms are primarily national responsibilities, with a rather limited role played by the particular nation's moral values. For the latter, in contrast, the reasoning of practitioners also involves judging which of the procedural responsibilities of international and world society are relevant to the concrete situation and how they should be applied. Thus, the ES's conception of responsibility as practical judgement comes closer to the interpretivist form of critical constructivism represented by Kratochwil (1989; 2018).

Making situated judgements in a responsible manner requires the practitioner to exhibit several closely interconnected virtues. First, one needs to exercise good judgement, which enables the discernment of the relevant characteristics of the situation as well as of the relevant procedural responsibilities. Responsible action hence often looks inconsistent from the perspective of the rules of procedural responsibility, and so it should: political decisions require not the application of a single rule for every case, but rather an attempt at discerning the relevant differences between particular cases (Brown 2010b, 245). Second, responsible choices require prudence, the ability to act with caution and foresight, to take into account the foreseeable (and foreseeably unforeseeable) consequences of one's action, so as not to cause more harm than absolutely necessary. This prudential responsibility is other-regarding – it takes into consideration the consequences of a particular decision not only for oneself or for one's state but for international – and perhaps world – society as well (Jackson 2000, 153–54). Finally, since in any concrete case several procedural responsibilities clash and one is likely forced to make tragic choices about which value to sacrifice in the search for the least bad decision, acting upon one's practical judgement requires a certain strength of character (Brown 2010c, 235).

Although prudential responsibility and its connected virtues are central to any political decision, Jackson (2000, 169–78) identifies further virtues that fill in the discretionary gap left by each type of procedural responsibility. For national responsibility, these are patriotism and prudence; for international responsibility, recognition, regard, restraint, reciprocity, reliability and amicability. Cosmopolitan responsibilities are supported by compassion, charity, hospitality and justice, and environmental responsibilities by the virtue of stewardship. All these still require the cardinal virtue of prudential responsibility that allows the practitioner to make the best choice given the relevant moral demands and the circumstances of the decision. Gaskarth (2012) outlines an approach to studying how the virtues of individuals support the responsibilities, rules and values that constitute international society by providing the attitudes and motivation needed to adequately perform them.

Academic responsibility

It follows from the interpretivist perspective of the ES that, in order to make the world of international politics intelligible, the academic must pay attention to the meanings practitioners give to their actions and to the standards of conduct that guide them (Jackson 2009; see also chapter by Jackson in this volume). Since these standards do not cause behaviour as independent variables but instead constitute reality as they are performed in action (Navari 2009a, 5–6), they must be studied by the scholar in such a way as to take their normativity into account (Cochran 2009, 221). On the flipside, in order to avoid empty moralism, international politics can only be adequately assessed from a normative perspective on the basis of the empirically discoverable standards internal to its existing practices. These two directions – from normative theory to empirical analysis and vice versa – taken together set out a form of morality internal to the nature of the inquiry itself and identify the responsibility of the academic studying international politics (Cochran 2008).

The ontology of the ES posits that moral reasoning and the standards of conduct that inform it are constitutive of international politics. Norms function as standards about which practitioners deliberate in order to make practical, moral judgements within the confines of particular circumstances. It is only by employing an interpretivist, participant standpoint methodology that analysts can reach a proper understanding of the workings of international politics. Students of international politics must attempt to enter "vicariously" into the situation of practitioners in order to recover the latter's self-conceptions and the language they use to evaluate, explain and justify their actions (Navari 2009b; Jackson 2000, 144). This means that normativity and scholarly judgement are central to any academic inquiry into international politics as a sphere of human conduct.

The close intertwining of normativity and practice, however, means that this connection also works in the opposite direction. Just as the scientific study of international politics is impossible without considering its normative aspects, normative theorizing must be firmly rooted in the empirical study of international relations (Watson 1998). Inspired by positive international law and defined by Martin Wight and Hedley Bull, the approach that became dominant in the ES sees the responsibility of the academic as always to build ethical arguments on strong empirical foundations (Cochran 2009). What is rejected here is abstract, philosophical inquiry into normative ends detached from the political and social realities of the world. The value of any ethical position is circumscribed by whether there exists a sufficiently developed moral community able to sustain it as a practical standard, which can only be gauged by attending to the empirical reality of human conduct. Practitioners of international politics must therefore be judged by standards internal to the practices they engage in, by rules they themselves have worked out in a history of interaction and political decisions. This can realistically reflect what moral standards are attainable in any situation. Analogous to the case of the situated judgement that practitioners must make, scholarly judgements arrived at without regard to the historical circumstances are condemned as cases of irresponsible moralism (Jackson 2009).

The responsibility of the academic is thus to make intelligible the practices of international politics by providing a disinterested exposition of the norms and standards internal to them (Bull 1975, 284; Jackson 2009). There is space for assessing the decisions of statespeople, and academic works can seek to clarify the implications of existing standards and responsibilities (Aslam 2013), but any such scholarly judgement must be the outcome – rather than the starting point – of the inquiry and should be made from inside the world of the practitioners (Jackson 2009, 26). The standards by which international politics should be judged cannot be identified independently of the concrete, historically evolved practices that they guide, although their evolving nature and the emergence of new practices and standards must therefore also be considered.

This gives the normative inquiry of the ES a somewhat conservative character, as it places limitations on the extent to which existing norms and practices can be critiqued. Jackson (2009, 24–25), for instance, strongly rejects the approach of critical theorists that identifies providing "knowledge in order to change the world for the better" as the primary scholarly responsibility. Others, however, have demonstrated how empirical inquiry into the shifting landscape of practices can make the case for normative critique. Vincent (1986) and Wheeler (2000) identify the impact of emerging norms – including cosmopolitan norms – on the practices of international society. Linklater's (2010) analysis of the progressive aspects of long-term historical processes is conducted with a view to supporting emancipatory cosmopolitan projects. It remains the case, however, that distinctively ES contributions never fully leave behind the academic responsibility to ground normative theorizing in the empirical study of the rules and standards that constitute the practices of international and world politics.

Conclusion

This chapter outlined three interrelated aspects of responsibility that together make up the ES's distinct approach to analyzing international relations as a social reality constituted by standards of human conduct. The conduct of practitioners in the various practices of international politics is guided by moral and legal standards (procedural responsibilities) and political virtues (prudential responsibilities) that they draw upon for making responsible choices in confining circumstances, while knowledge production and scholarly judgement should similarly be grounded in the discernment of standards and constraints internal to the world of practitioners (academic responsibility). While not relinquishing the task of normative judgement, the ES exhibits a much needed openness to, and humility towards, the world of practice. Since normative assessments should be based on responsibilities understood as standards internal to that world, decisions on what and who count as relevant practices and practitioners becomes critical in limiting or expanding the scope of empirical and normative inquiry. Although this poses the danger of unjustified conservativism, the ES's sensitivity to historical change and its emphasis on the centrality of human judgement offer rich resources for discerning and navigating the shifting grounds of responsibility in international politics.

References

Aslam, W. (2013). *The United States and Great Power Responsibility in International Society: Drones, Rendition and Invasion*. London and New York: Routledge.
Brown, C. (2003). "Moral Agency and International Society: Reflections on Norms, the UN, the Gulf War, and the Kosovo Campaign." In Erskine, T., ed., *Can Institutions Have Responsibilities?: Collective Moral Agency and International Relations*: 51–65. Basingstoke and New York: Palgrave Macmillan.
Brown, C. (2004). "Do Great Powers Have Great Responsibilities? Great Powers and Moral Agency." *Global Society*, 18(1): 5–19.
Brown, C. (2010a). "Not My Department? Normative Theory and International Relations." In Brown, C., *Practical Judgement in International Political Theory: Selected Essays*, 125–132. London and New York: Routledge.
Brown, C. (2010b). "Practical Judgment and the Ethics of Preemption." In Brown, C., *Practical Judgement in International Political Theory: Selected Essays*: 236–249. London and New York: Routledge.
Brown, C. (2010c). "Selective Humanitarianism: In Defense of Inconsistency." In Brown, C., *Practical Judgement in International Political Theory: Selected Essays*: 221–235. London and New York: Routledge.
Bukovansky, M., Clark, I., Eckersley, R., Price, R., Reus-Smit, C., and Wheeler, N. J. (2012). *Special Responsibilities: Global Problems and American Power*. Cambridge: Cambridge University Press.
Bull, H. (1975). "New Directions in the Theory of International Relations." *International Studies*, 14(2): 277–287.
Bull, H. (1980). "The Great Irresponsibles? The United States, the Soviet Union, and World Order." *International Journal*, 35(3): 437–447.
Bull, H. (2002). *The Anarchical Society: A Study of Order in World Politics*. London: Palgrave Macmillan.
Butterfield, H. 1966. "The Balance of Power." In Butterfield, H., Weight, M., and Bull, H., eds., *Diplomatic Investigations: Essays in the Theory of International Politics*: 132–148. Cambridge, MA: Harvard University Press.
Buzan, B. (2004). *From International to World Society?* Cambridge and New York: Cambridge University Press.
Clark, I. (1989). *The Hierarchy of States: Reform and Resistance in the International Order*. Cambridge: Cambridge University Press.
Clark, I. (2005). *Legitimacy in International Society*. Oxford: Oxford University Press.
Clark, I. (2007). *International Legitimacy and World Society*. Oxford: Oxford University Press.
Clark, I. (2011a). *Hegemony in International Society*. Oxford: Oxford University Press.
Clark, I. (2011b). "China and the United States: A Succession of Hegemonies?" *International Affairs*, 87(1): 13–28.
Clark, I. (2017). "Hierarchy, Hegemony, and the Norms of International Society." In Dunne, T., and Reus-Smit, C., eds., *The Globalization of International Society*: 248–264. Oxford: Oxford University Press.

Cochran, M. (2008). "The Ethics of the English School." In Reus-Smit, C., and Snidal, D., eds., *The Oxford Handbook of International Relations*: 286–297. Oxford: Oxford University Press.

Cochran, M. (2009). "Charting the Ethics of the English School: What 'Good' Is There in a Middle-Ground Ethics?" *International Studies Quarterly*, 53(1): 203–225.

Cui, S., and Buzan, B. (2016). "Great Power Management in International Society." *The Chinese Journal of International Politics*, 9(2): 181–210.

Dunne, T. (1998). *Inventing International Society: A History of the English School*. Basingstoke: Palgrave Macmillan.

Dunne, T. (2008). "The English School." In Reus-Smit, C., and Snidal, D., eds., *The Oxford Handbook of International Relations*: 267–285. Oxford: Oxford University Press.

Erskine, T. (2003a). "Assigning Responsibilities to Institutional Moral Agents: The Case of States and 'Quasi-States.'" In Erskine, T., ed., *Can Institutions Have Responsibilities?: Collective Moral Agency and International Relations*: 19–40. Basingstoke and New York: Palgrave Macmillan.

Erskine, T. (2003b). "Making Sense of 'responsibility' in International Relations – Key Questions and Concepts." In Erskine, T., ed., *Can Institutions Have Responsibilities?: Collective Moral Agency and International Relations*: 1–18. Basingstoke and New York: Palgrave Macmillan.

Erskine, T. (2008). "Locating Responsibility: The Problem of Moral Agency in International Relations." In Reus-Smit, C., and Snidal, D., eds., *The Oxford Handbook of International Relations*: 699–707. Oxford: Oxford University Press.

Falkner, R. (2012). "Global Environmentalism and the Greening of International Society." *International Affairs*, 88(3): 503–522.

Falkner, R., and Buzan, B. (2019). "The Emergence of Environmental Stewardship as a Primary Institution of Global International Society." *European Journal of International Relations*, 25(1): 131–155.

Foot, R. (2001). "Chinese Power and the Idea of a Responsible State." *The China Journal*, 45(Jan): 1–19.

Gaskarth, J. (2011). "Where Would We Be without Rules? A Virtue Ethics Approach to Foreign Policy Analysis." *Review of International Studies*, 37(1): 393–415.

Gaskarth, J. (2012). "The Virtues in International Society." *European Journal of International Relations*, 18(3): 431–53.

Gaskarth, J. (2013). "Interpreting Ethical Foreign Policy: Traditions and Dilemmas for Policymakers." *The British Journal of Politics and International Relations*, 15(2): 192–209.

Gaskarth, J. (2017). "Rising Powers, Responsibility, and International Society." *Ethics & International Affairs*, 31(3): 287–311.

Gong, G. W. (1984). *The Standard of 'Civilization' in International Society*. Oxford: Clarendon Press.

Gong, G. W. (2002). "Standards of Civilization Today." In Mozaffari, M., ed., *Globalization and Civilizations*: 77–96. London and New York: Routledge.

Jackson, R. H. (2000). *The Global Covenant: Human Conduct in a World of States*. Oxford: Oxford University Press.

Jackson, R. H. (2009). "International Relations as a Craft Discipline." In Navari, C., ed., *Theorising International Society: English School Methods*: 21–38. Basingstoke and New York: Palgrave Macmillan.

Kennan, G. F. (1985). "Morality and Foreign Policy." *Foreign Affairs*, 64(2): 205–218.

Kopra, S. (2016). "Great Power Management and China's Responsibility in International Climate Politics." *Journal of China and International Relations*, 4(1): 20–44.

Kratochwil, F. (1989). *Rules, Norms and Decisions: On the Conditions of Practical and Legal Reasoning in International Relations and Domestic Affairs*. Cambridge: Cambridge University Press.

Kratochwil, F. (2018). "Judgement: A Conceptual Sketch." In Brown, C., and Eckersley, R., eds., *The Oxford Handbook of International Political Theory*: 575–586. Oxford: Oxford University Press.

Linklater, A. (2010). "Global Civilizing Processes and the Ambiguities of Human Interconnectedness." *European Journal of International Relations*, 16(2): 155–178.

Linklater, A. (2011a). "Prudence and Principle in International Society: Reflections on Vincent's Approach to Human Rights." *International Affairs*, 87(5): 1179–1191.

Linklater, A. (2011b). *The Problem of Harm in World Politics: Theoretical Investigations*. Cambridge and New York: Cambridge University Press.

Linklater, A. (2017). *Violence and Civilization in the Western States-Systems*. Cambridge: Cambridge University Press.

Morris, J. (2004). "Normative Innovation and the Great Powers." In Bellamy, A. J., ed., *International Society and Its Critics*: 265–281. Oxford and New York: Oxford University Press.

Murray, A. J. H. (1996). "The Moral Politics of Hans Morgenthau." *The Review of Politics*, 58(1): 81–107.

Navari, C. (2009a). "Introduction: Methods and Methodology in the English School." In Navari, C., ed., *Theorising International Society: English School Methods*: 1–20. Basingstoke and New York: Palgrave Macmillan.

Navari, C. (2009b). "What the Classical English School Was Trying to Explain, and Why Its Members Were Not Interested in Causal Explanation." In Navari, C., ed., *Theorising International Society: English School Methods*: 39–57. Basingstoke and New York: Palgrave Macmillan.

Reus-Smit, C. (2009). "Constructivism and the English School." In Navari, C., ed., *Theorising International Society: English School Methods*, 58–77. Basingstoke and New York: Palgrave Macmillan.

Shaw, M. (1992). "Global Society and Global Responsibility: The Theoretical, Historical and Political Limits of 'International Society'." *Millennium Journal of International Studies*, 21(3): 421–434.

Simpson, G. J. 2004. *Great Powers and Outlaw States: Unequal Sovereigns in the International Legal Order*. Cambridge: Cambridge University Press.

Smith, M. J. 1990. *Realist Thought from Weber to Kissinger*. Baton Rouge: Louisiana State University Press.

Suzuki, S. (2008). "Seeking 'Legitimate' Great Power Status in Post-Cold War International Society: China's and Japan's Participation in UNPKO." *International Relations*, 22(1): 45–63.

Teitt, S. (2017). "Sovereignty as Responsibility." In Dunne, T., and Reus-Smit, C., eds., *The Globalization of International Society*: 325–344. Oxford: Oxford University Press.

Vincent, R. J. (1986). *Human Rights and International Relations*. Cambridge: Cambridge University Press.

Watson, A. (1984). "European International Society and Its Expansion." In Bull, H., and Watson, A., eds., *The Expansion of International Society*: 13–32. Oxford: Clarendon Press.

Watson, A. (1992). *The Evolution of International Society: A Comparative Historical Analysis*. London: Routledge.

Watson, A. (1998). "The Practice Outruns the Theory." In Roberson, B.A., ed., *International Society and the Development of International Relations Theory*: 145–155. London: Pinter Publishers.

Wheeler, N. J. (2000). *Saving Strangers: Humanitarian Intervention in International Society*. Oxford: Oxford University Press.

Wight, M. (1966a). "The Balance of Power." In Butterfield, H., Wight, M., and Bull, H., eds. *Diplomatic Investigations: Essays in the Theory of International Politics*: 159–175. Cambridge, MA: Harvard University Press.

Wight, M. (1966b). "Western Values in International Relations." In Butterfield, H., Wight, M., and Bull, H., eds., *Diplomatic Investigations: Essays in the Theory of International Politics*: 89–131. Cambridge, MA: Harvard University Press.

Wight, A. (1991). *International Theory: The Three Traditions*. Leicester: Leicester University Press for The Royal Institute of International Affairs.

Youde, J. (2018). *Global Health Governance in International Society*. Oxford and New York: Oxford University Press.

Zhang, Y. (2016). "China and Liberal Hierarchies in Global International Society: Power and Negotiation for Normative Change." *International Affairs*, 92(4): 795–816.

PART II

Mapping responsibility relations across policy fields

10
THE ASSIGNING AND EROSION OF RESPONSIBILITY FOR THE GLOBAL ENVIRONMENT

Steven Bernstein

Introduction[1]

International environmental norms have articulated common responsibilities of states toward each other in protecting and sharing access to the global commons and carving out sovereign responsibility for use and protection of their own resources, with some minimal liability for external harms of pollution that affect other states. Early efforts in the 1970s to bring environmental and planetary resource concerns onto the international agenda articulated even bolder visions of general responsibilities, including the notion of "shared responsibility" for the Earth found in the 1972 Stockholm Declaration and the idea of the "common heritage of [human] kind" in treaties such as the Law of the Sea and rules on plant genetic resources. Neither those bolder notions of responsibility nor specific obligations that flowed from them took hold.

By the 1980s, such notions had largely fallen out of favor. Major developed states resisted specific obligations or global schemes for joint responsibility because they sought disproportionate benefits from exploitation of resources given their power positions and economic goals. Meanwhile, developing countries argued for differential responsibilities rooted in arguments around historical injustice, while rising economies such as China and India sought to leverage their political and military power to support differentiation and reinforce their legitimacy and status as leading states among developing countries. Meanwhile, the compromise norm of "common but differentiated responsibility and respective capabilities" (CBDR) that emerged in the late 1980s and early 1990s – particularly in relation to climate change but also more broadly – has come under increasing strain as the international system has become more multipolar along both political and economic dimensions. Rising economies especially, with increasing capabilities and who contribute significantly to global environmental problems, face growing pressure to take on more responsibilities. The result is not only further erosion of notions of "common" responsibility but also a shift in understandings of differentiation to focus less on justice and more on capabilities.

This contribution to the handbook will document these trends. It first examines how responsibility for the environment has been assigned, focusing on norms and international law. This discussion will highlight the ongoing contestation over the meaning and implications of responsibility, how it should be distributed, and its relationship to justice. The second half of the chapter will examine two current trends and their implications for the assigning of responsibility: the diffusion of responsibility not only horizontally among states but to nonstate actors, possibly weakening notions of responsibility overall; and a shift from external to internal responsibility, that is, from a focus on efforts to promote cooperation, collective action, and responsibilities to other states and to address global problems where responsibility cannot easily be assigned to any particular state, to increasingly emphasize states' responsibility for their own environmental and development outcomes. The Paris Agreement on climate change and Sustainable Development Goals (SDGs) are two prominent examples that illustrate these trends, through support of country ownership, nationally determined contributions in the case of the Paris Agreement, voluntary national reviews in the case of the SDGs, and movement toward goals, benchmarks, and best practices generally and away from binding obligations. These sections also explore more radical proposals for redefining responsibility and entrenching new norms, including proposals for an "environmental responsibility to protect" (Conca 2015) and for processes of transitional justice to reconcile notions of justice, accountability, and responsibility, especially in climate governance (e.g., Klinsky 2017; Klinsky and Brankovic 2018).

The assigning of responsibility in global environmental governance

International environmental norms identify states, individually and collectively, as the holders of responsibility and, like in other areas of international law, pair responsibility with external sovereignty understood vis-à-vis other states. Principle 21 of the 1972 Stockholm Declaration on the Human Environment identifies states as the only specific holders of responsibilities, and only vis-à-vis other states (United Nations 1972). Often recognized as the foundational norm of international environmental law, Principle 21 builds on earlier UN resolutions and the historical context of then emerging claims for a New International Economic Order (NIEO). It asserts that states have the "sovereign right to exploit their own resources pursuant to their own environmental policies, and the responsibility to ensure that activities within their jurisdiction or control do not cause damage to the environment of other States or of areas beyond the limits of national jurisdiction." Principle 2 of the 1992 Rio Declaration reproduces this language, adding only that states have a right to exploit their own resources "pursuant to their own environmental *and developmental* policies" (United Nations 1992). In sum, responsibility is framed as "state responsibility" with some limited notion of liability for external environmental harms that directly result from domestic pollution.

In reference to some of the distinctions in this handbook, international environmental responsibility largely targets states as opposed to individuals or corporations. While international law almost exclusively maintains this understanding, various institutional, normative, and legal developments since the 1990s challenge that view by focusing on corporations or individuals in addition to states as holders of responsibility. Some also seek to expand the objects of responsibility, especially via newer rights discourses that invoke responsibilities to individuals or communities – as opposed only to other states – affected by environmental harms as opposed only to other states. Still, attempts to create specific duties or obligations (see Shadmy, this volume) beyond the formalism of state responsibility are limited and often resisted. Meanwhile, the language of responsibility, even in reference to states, mostly takes the form of moral or normative prescriptions rather than legal obligations.

In practice, international environmental law has rarely operationalized, created, or used mechanisms to enforce liability. The reason, legal scholars have argued, is the formalism of state responsibility mechanisms (Brunnée 2005). Hence, even that acknowledgement of responsibility is only weakly linked in practice to accountability mechanisms unless they are formally established within specific legal instruments. As Brunnée (2005, 25) explains, "The law of state responsibility provides for a form of international legal accountability that is limited in several important respects: it is triggered only by breaches of positive international law; it applies only to breaches of international law by or attributable to a state and operates only when responsibility can be invoked by other states...."

Because of these initial framings around state responsibility, subsequent debates and contestation have rarely questioned targets of responsibility, but rather the form, type, justification, and distribution of responsibilities of states to each other in pursuit of environmental goals. One notable shift has been from common responsibility to preserve and share the benefits of areas or resources designated as the "common heritage" of humankind (i.e., areas beyond any state's jurisdiction such as the deep seabed, outer space, oceans beyond national jurisdiction, and plant genetic resources) to differentiated responsibilities.

Part XII of the 1982 UN Convention on Law of the Sea (UNCLOS) marks the highpoint of the articulation of common responsibilities to prevent pollution in the global commons. According to Article 194, "States shall take, individually or jointly as appropriate, all measures consistent with this Convention that are necessary to prevent, reduce and control pollution of the marine environment ...." As Barkin and DeSombre (this volume) highlight, in practice the implementation of this responsibility is through specific positive institutional arrangements, sometimes under the auspices of UNCLOS like the 1995 Straddling Fish Stocks Agreement, and sometimes outside of it. They also observe, however, that "the norm [of collective responsibility] is least institutionalized with respect to pollution and seems to have had a smaller impact on behavior there than with other resources." And, where it is most institutionalized – in the form of the International Seabed Authority to manage mining beyond national jurisdictions – it has moved significantly away from its original 1982 formulation as consistent with the "common heritage" principle.

The 1994 implementation agreement – negotiated in large part as an attempt to respond to US concerns over the perception that the Seabed Authority granted a kind of sovereign power to the Authority with a mandate to impose a new set of rights and obligations to states or corporations acting in the Area designated as part of the common heritage – effectively altered Part XI to be in conformity with market-based norms.[2] For example, Sections 2, 5, and 6, on the Enterprise, Technology Transfer, and Production Policy, make the following provisions: the deep seabed will be mined through joint ventures; technology transfer provisions no longer include active programs for "fair and reasonable" terms of transfer but instead encourages the Enterprise and interested states to "seek" such transfers on "fair and reasonable commercial terms" and "conditions on the open market;" and development of the seabed shall take place according to "sound commercial principles." Consequently, the Seabed Authority must respond to the "right" of states to mine mineral resources in the deep seabed, essentially putting in place an assured access rather than a common heritage regime, severely limiting the ability of the weakened Authority to control access. These provisions effectively put an end to institutional arrangements that implemented norms of common heritage (Payoyo 1997).

While these provisions are not about the environment per se, they signaled a shift to common "concern" from responsibilities for collective management and redistribution. While the language of common concern can imply a positive responsibility of "equitable sharing of the burdens of cooperation and problem solving" (Brunnée 2008, 566), historically the use of the concept marks an explicit movement away from more specific articulations of either responsibility or obligation to jointly act or manage and in opposition to attempts to introduce or support ideas such as common heritage. By the 1992 UN Conference on Environment and Development (or Earth Summit) in Rio de Janeiro, common concern language became dominant and appears in the climate change and biodiversity treaties (Bodansky 1994, 52). Developing countries argued against the idea of common heritage in negotiations on forestry and biodiversity in the lead-up to the Earth Summit, fearing loss of sovereign control. Meanwhile, developed countries opposed it because they associated it with global economic management and redistribution in opposition to market-based principles (see Bernstein and van der Ven 2017a for detailed discussions).[3]

While that shift has multiple dimensions – including a move to open some of those previously designated areas to private commercial use and ownership and general normative shift to market norms and away from collective management – it also set the stage for movement away from undifferentiated "common" responsibilities to special or differentiated responsibilities.

Arising out of North-South bargaining dynamics, this corollary to the shift away from common heritage can be found in Rio Declaration Principle 7, which explicitly turns from the language of common goals, and the implicit idea of collective responsibility to address and manage them, to differentiation. It states that, "In view of the different contributions to global environmental degradation, States have common but differentiated responsibilities. The developed countries acknowledge the responsibility that they bear in the international pursuit of sustainable development in view of the pressures their societies place on the global environment and of the technologies and financial resources they command." Notice, the principle assigns no historical responsibility even though intergenerational equity underpins the notion of sustainable development as promoted in the Brundtland Commission report (World Commission on Environment and Development 1987). The shift is even more explicit in the climate change convention, where differential obligations derive from states' current contributions to the problem and their "respective capabilities" (United Nations Framework Convention on Climate Change 1992, Article 3(1)). Although the argument in negotiations and broader discourse continues to be made on historical grounds for differentiation, there is no language in any multilateral climate change agreement that endorses this justification for differentiation.

The CBDR norm, in line with the doctrine of state responsibility, applies only to states vis-à-vis obligations to one another. Any other holders or targets of responsibilities implied by the norm are stated so generally as to limit any direct application or specific obligation or duties. For example, the first part of Rio Declaration Principle 7 suggests the overall purpose to which CBDR applies is to protect the environment generally, saying that "states shall cooperate in the spirit of global partnership to conserve, protect and restore the health and integrity of the Earth's ecosystem." Twenty years earlier, Principle 1 of the 1972 Stockholm Declaration more explicitly assigned responsibility to "improve the environment," but to no one in particular. Instead, humankind collectively holds responsibility: "Man [sic] has the fundamental right to freedom, equality and adequate conditions of life, in an environment of a quality that permits a life of dignity and well-being, and he bears a solemn responsibility to protect and improve the environment for present and future generations."[4] The wording of both principles vitiates any possibility of accountability other than to states, thus leaving the doctrine of state responsibility primary in practice.

While most of the attention in the literature on the CBDR norm focuses on differentiation, the question of responsibility has been much more politically contentious. The idea of differentiation is opposed more in theory than in practice, while the opposite is true for contestation over responsibility. Whereas the United States, especially, fought against the formalization of differentiation in the 1997 Kyoto Protocol of the UN Framework Convention on Climate Change (UNFCCC), which committed only developed countries to binding emission targets, it has accepted differential obligations (even if obligations are eventually supposed to harmonize as capacities allow), time lags for implementation, and commitments to provide technical or financial assistance to assist countries to meet their obligations in several treaties. For example, the Montreal Protocol and subsequent amendments to combat ozone depletion allowed longer phase-out periods of ozone-depleting chemicals for developing countries and set up a Multilateral Ozone Fund to help fund the transition. The CBDR norm has been increasingly incorporated into multilateral environmental agreements since 1992, including the Biodiversity Convention, Convention to Combat Desertification, Stockholm Convention on Persistent Organic Pollutants, and the Minamata Convention on Mercury. And, despite US rejection of CBDR as the foundation for blanket differentiations of developed and developing commitment categories, its negotiating positions subsequent to its rejection of Kyoto suggest it has accepted the principle but contests its meaning and interpretation (e.g., Brunnée 2011). For example, in the lead-up to the 2009 Copenhagen climate conference, US insistence that developing countries accept emission commitments was phrased as something "that CBDR actually demands, or at least accommodates… suggesting that major developing economies with large emissions must accept some emissions commitments" (Brunnée 2011, 57–58).

The legitimation of differentiation based on level of development extends back much further, at least to the 1972 Stockholm Declaration's statement that most environmental problems in developing countries resulted from underdevelopment. Negotiations then and since have prioritized development, aid, and technology transfer as preconditions to developing countries accepting responsibility for environmental integrity. Not surprisingly, the underlying historical context of differentiation rooted in North/South dynamics has played out in parallel in other issue areas. For example, in trade, the norm of "special and differential treatment" has gradually become entrenched in WTO agreements, although it is controversial when there are attempts to apply it in a blanket way. The practice of special treatment gained traction beginning in 1964 when parties amended the General Agreement on Tariffs and Trade to include a new Part IV on Trade and Development with special provisions for "less developed countries." While it resulted in few commitments in the 1970s and 1980s, the Tokyo Round, completed in 1979, included a so-called "enabling clause" that extended the generalized system of preferences (to favor imports from developing countries) indefinitely and differentiated between obligations for different categories of developing countries. When developing countries were brought fully into the agreement following the creation of the WTO in 1994, it included many special provisions for developing countries based on circumstances and issues. The most recent round of decisions, at the 2015 Nairobi Ministerial Conference, included (nonbinding) texts on preferential rules of origin, duty free quota free market access, and a monitoring mechanism on special and differential treatment (Wilkinson et al. 2016). Even prior to this round, Pauwelyn (2013) counted 145 WTO provisions related to special advantages, technical assistance, phase-in periods and more lenient obligations for developing countries, but no official list of who those countries are, in contrast to what existed under the Kyoto Protocol.

Including "responsibility" in the CBDR norm raises the stakes significantly. First, it implies an obligation "to" act. Second, in the environmental area, various governments and NGOs have tried to link the norm to liability as an accountability mechanism; acknowledging responsibility invokes a legalistic view of accountability that includes obligations to compensate. As a result, the main target of contestation is the notion of differentiation of a specific identifiable group based on its status or history as a basis on which to assign it, or forgive it, responsibility. This interpretation would shift the reading of CBDR to suggest a responsibility "for" an environmental problem as the source of the moral requirement to act, thus invoking "causal" or "remedial" responsibility linked to historical practices that benefited some states but led to a global problem (Introduction, this volume). The resulting debate over liability and compensation are at the heart of the political fight over the idea of "loss and damage" in climate change negotiations. This idea is based on the acknowledgement that there will be unavoidable loss and damage – both economic and noneconomic (culture and ways of life, species loss, landscapes) – from climate change.

Loss and damage made it into the Paris Agreement article 8, but the enabling Conference of the Parties decision states that "Article 8 of the Agreement does not involve or provide a basis for any liability or compensation."[5] While the United States has been most vocal in its opposition to links to liability, several other major powers share this preference and quietly support the US position (Allen et al. n.d.). The United States has held this position consistently through successive administrations from the earliest articulation of the CBDR norm in Rio Declaration Principle 7. A US interpretive statement accompanying the UN resolution adopting the Declaration reads, "The United States does not accept any interpretation of principle 7 that would imply a recognition or acceptance by the United States of any international obligations or liabilities, or any diminution of the responsibilities of developing countries under international law" (United Nations 1993, chap. III, para. 16). Moreover, the United States has consistently resisted any stated or implied linkage between CBDR and obligations or responsibility for additional financing or diminution of common responsibilities for global problems, even as it recognizes differential abilities to address problems. In the case of the Paris Agreement, loss and damage is framed as a problem of risk management, adaptation, promoting sustainable development, but with no specific responsibility assigned or obligation that flows from it.

In sum, the practices of assigning responsibility in the environmental domain depend almost wholly on current contributions to a specific problem and capacity to address it. Meanwhile, responsibility as a principle of historical justice (or culpability) has had no formal traction, and links between historical responsibility as a financial principle or a legal principle of liability are actively resisted. The ability of climate negotiators to successfully link loss and damage to financial compensation depended on *avoiding* any explicit acknowledgement of historical responsibility. Instead, the expectation is increasingly that as emerging economies and rising powers gain capabilities, the distribution of responsibility will rise with them.

Trajectories of environmental responsibility

The formal assigning and distribution of responsibilities, while contested, aligns consistently in practice with a capacity or capabilities reading of CBDR and accountability mechanisms focused on explicit state-based obligations, often codified in treaty law. However, shifting distributions of power and structural positions of states in the political economy and evolving ecological and human rights discourses are increasingly playing out in contestation over environmental responsibility alongside older North-South bargaining dynamics. These tensions are playing out along two dimensions: challenges to the doctrine of state-based responsibility by shifting the focus to individual and community rights and away from an exclusive state responsibility framing; and the diffusion, downloading, and, perhaps, erosion, of state responsibility as governments and international institutions contest understandings of collective responsibility and instead look to more polycentric, diffuse and internal notions of responsibility to replace it.

The de-centering of state responsibility

Recalling that the tension over responsibility to whom has never been fully resolved, there are some who want to link responsibility as a moral principle to protection of individuals and vulnerable communities. Doing so would imply a radical shift in the dominant understandings of responsibility in international society. While a significant departure from current practices, linking environmental protection to human rights has a long tradition dating back to the Stockholm Declaration's Principle 1, which begins with a statement of collective responsibility to uphold human rights. Since then, the relationship between human rights and the environment "has been recognized at every level of the world's legal systems, from domestic courts to multilateral treaties." However, a right to a healthy environment has never been recognized globally and operationalization has been challenging (Knox and Pejan 2018, 1).

Similarly, several attempts to link the environment, development and human rights agendas within the UN system have faced significant institutional barriers (Conca 2015). For example, attempts to address climate change in the Security Council have met with resistance by permanent and nonpermanent members who argue it is not the appropriate institutional setting. The one attempt by a Security Council member (France) to extend the Responsibility to Protect (R2P) doctrine to the environment – for disaster relief when Myanmar refused international aid after Cyclone Nargis in 2008 – was rejected, a position later echoed by a 2012 International Law Commission report that explicitly rejected the extension of R2P's scope (Conca 2015, 196).

To overcome these hurdles, Conca (2015, 197) proposes a positive "environmental responsibility to protect." He cautions against wholly adopting the institutional arrangements of the R2P doctrine, especially the backstop of the UN Security Council owing to the moral contradiction in the Council's current structure where the largest emitters have veto power. Instead, he argues for a layered responsibilities doctrine linking human rights and the environment: "the state's responsibility to protect, the international community's responsibility not to neglect, and the leading emitters' responsibility for the effects." The latter might be operationalized through creating obligations for loss and damage, adaptation financing, or disaster relief and assistance. His proposal builds on contemporary legal, normative, and institutional developments to make a moral and pragmatic case that existing UN human rights machinery could be adapted to support such a doctrine. The main barrier, he argues, is the firewall between the law and development frame that underpins sovereign rights and responsibilities in environment and sustainable development institutional arrangements and the UN human rights and peace and security machinery. If endorsed, however, a responsibility for environmental protection would empower individuals and encourage accountability. It would shift the focus of responsibility onto states not vis-à-vis each other, but for the well-being of people and vulnerable groups such as indigenous communities, whose environmental rights have already been acknowledged in the 2007 UN Declaration on Rights of Indigenous Peoples, or populations displaced by or in regions severely affected by climate change, natural disasters, conflicts, or other environmentally harmful human activities.[6] In practice, an environmental R2P would first require, "defining the responsibilities that correspond to human rights, identifying the parties to whom such responsibilities attach, and highlight the ineffectiveness with which those responsibilities are carried out" (Conca 2015, 195). Like R2P, this new doctrine would put responsibility on states *and* the international community when states are unable or unwilling to fulfill their duties. Operationalizing and gaining support for such a proposal would, however, require significant institutional innovation. It is also possible that attempts to push such a doctrine could cause a backlash, undermining advances in articulating environmental human rights through other forums, such as the Human Rights Council special report on environmental human rights (United Nations 2018).

Other innovative proposals to bypass the stalemate over invoking justice concerns to create greater responsibilities or produce obligations for compensation can be found in the academic literature. One intriguing idea proposed by Klinsky (2017; see also Klinsky and Brankovic 2018) is to draw on experiences in many countries with transitional justice mechanisms such as reparations, truth commissions, amnesties, or new forms of legal accountability. Klinsky argues that the structural context of historical responsibility is similar enough that such processes could be productively adapted in the case of climate change.

Meanwhile, absent governments taking up these more radical, top down, proposals, actors at multiple political levels and scales are attempting to push beyond state responsibility or "common concern" by introducing notions of "causal responsibility" through the legal system. While most climate change litigation is at the domestic level, some of it refers to international commitments and targets transnational relationships. Some of that litigation follows directly from the shift to environmental rights discourse as described above, though establishing notions of causality has proven difficult (see Setzer and Vanhala 2019, 10–11). This emerging terrain of action is complex and evolving – with multiple targets of litigation, wide-ranging sources of legal action and remedies sought, and most of the targets being private sector actors (e.g., fossil fuel producers, energy companies, financial institutions, etc.). While a full review is beyond the scope here (but see Setzer and Vanhala 2019), at least two observations are worth noting. First, many actors (governments, NGOs, and even some actors who wish to undermine climate regulation) at many scales and in reference to a variety of time frames are turning to the courts to clarify or enforce responsibilities, especially when enforcement is lacking or liability and accountability regimes are weak or ambiguous. Second, some cases are using the courts to leverage transnational responsibilities (Ganguly, Setzer, and Heyvaert 2018). One case receiving significant attention involves a Peruvian farmer (supported by the NGO Germanwatch) taking on RWE, Germany's largest energy company, with the argument that the farmer's community in the Peruvian Andes experiences the effects of climate change caused by the worldwide effects of RWE's emissions. As Setzer and Vanhala (2019, 8–9) describe such cases, "framing processes in these lawsuits localize[s] the global effects of climate change to specific communities [and attempt to put] responsibility on to global corporations who produced oil and gas in the first place."

Downloading and diffusing responsibility?

Whereas notions such as an environmental R2P suggest the possibility of the environment looking more like other systemically important international issue areas such as peace and security or global financial stability that support special responsibilities for great powers (Bernstein 2020), and the spate of litigation can be read as an attempt to formalize obligations, liability, and compensation by emphasizing causal responsibility, trends in global environmental and sustainability governance appear headed in the opposite direction: the dilution of, and diffusion from, direct assignments of responsibility to states for the global environment.

For example, a shift is underway from external to internal responsibility, often in the form of country ownership, where states are increasingly responsible for their own environmental and development outcomes. This turn is not without irony. Scholars traditionally pointed to international environmental law as central to the development of external responsibility. It has invoked notions such as common and collective responsibility for joint or cooperative action, enshrined state responsibility to individually and collectively contribute to addressing "common concerns" such as climate change or other global environmental problems that transcend borders or with planetary consequences, and to protect and share benefits of resources located in global commons under principles like the "common heritage" of humankind (Brunnée 2008). Whereas recognizing that state responsibility has an internal aspect is not new if defined by norms like "sovereignty over resources", this notion is usually interpreted as enshrining rights of control or limiting external interference on the development or exploitation of resources or domestic jurisdiction (including in the environment) except by consent. The new trend shifts the emphasis to a state's positive responsibility to ensure their own development, as opposed to protection from external interference. It could be read to suggest a diminution of cooperative or common responsibility to redistribute (in reference to development) or assist, transfer, or provide significant resources or increased capacities to address environmental problems, even those that have transnational or global consequences. This trend coincides with a shift from formal rules and treaties based on state responsibility to reliance on softer modes of governance like best practices, standards, benchmarks, or goal-based strategies like the SDGs (Best 2014; Bernstein and van der Ven 2017b; Kanie and Biermann 2017). The combination of these trends implies a more horizontal assignment of responsibility, not only away from differentiation to country ownership but also to other actors such as partnerships and corporations.

As Karp [this volume] discusses in some detail, the implications of this shift can be multifaceted. On the one hand, it can mean expanding the explicit moral responsibility to a wider range of actors and specifying those responsibilities in greater detail. For example, in the case of social and environmental certification systems – that create standards for companies that sign onto them in areas such as forests, fisheries, coffee, and apparel – it can include specific obligations to adhere to standards and include auditing or other accountability mechanisms in order to participate in and be recognized through a label or to maintain membership or certification. On the other hand, most such systems remain voluntary to join. Moreover, more general guidelines or best practices promoted by global institutions like the UN or OECD often do not include specific obligations for nonstate actors, although they might be expected to respect the relevant laws of the states in which they operate. As Karp points out in the related case of the UN Guiding Principles on Business and Human Rights, "the state duty to protect [human rights] and the corporate responsibility to respect" can work in tandem. But when they push beyond where some states are willing to go, responsibility to adhere to international standards generally lack enforcement mechanisms. The problem of lax standards or weak enforcement in host states or, conversely, the problem of limited ability or desire to enforce standards on corporations when operating outside of home states, also remain largely intact. In such circumstances, instruments like the guiding principles can shift responsibility to corporate actors to adhere to global standards, which opens up the possibility of such actors gaining political authority by being ascribed responsibility, as Shadmy (this volume) argues (see also Bernstein 2014). While certification standards, best practices, and guidelines can be useful in this regard to put pressure directly on corporate actors, there is still widespread debate on whether more legally binding rules are needed – or whether the result will be a watering down of those guidelines or standards, or have undemocratic consequences in shifting authority to less accountable actors (Karp, this volume; Kuyper, Linnér, and Schroeder 2018; Terán 2019 Zelli 2018).

These trends tap into a more general debate in global governance that has played out over the last two decades. Pouliot and Thérien (2018, 64), for example, have observed a similar tension playing out in development governance between what they label "global solidarity" and "national duty" positions. The tension originally became visible leading up to the 2000 Millennium Development Goals (MDGs):

> The main value conflict in the MDG debate revolved around… who should be responsible for development policymaking…. [Advocates of global solidarity] maintained that the rich have a moral responsibility toward the poor, and sought to link the MDGs with human rights obligations. While conceding that international support for development can sometimes be justified, [advocates for national duty] basically argued that the responsibility of development rests primarily with each individual state.

This debate arose in the context of rising inequalities and a growing sense of winners and losers from globalization, as well as the failures of IMF and World Bank structural adjustment programs and legitimacy crises of major international security and economic institutions (Best 2014). One consequence of attempts to manage such "failures" has been to push responsibility down to countries themselves, while supporting soft governing modes (Best 2014, 16).

In the environment and sustainability area, the 2015 SDGs take a similar approach, where accountability mechanisms focus on country-level reporting on progress as opposed to fulfillment of external responsibilities and commitments. While there are many possible benefits to this shift – including avoiding one-size-fits all policies, sensitivity to domestic contexts and encouraging accountability to a country's own citizens – such practices and mechanisms are notoriously uneven. Similarly, the shift from developing-country focused MDGs to universally applicable SDGs has many virtues, including generating a greater sense of collective responsibility. However, it can have the unintended effect of undermining differentiated responsibilities for addressing global problems based even in capabilities[7] or obligations to address global inequalities, distributive justice, or structural and institutional impediments to these goals. For example, SDG 17 has the official aim to "strengthen the means of implementation and revitalize the global partnership for sustainable development" (United Nations 2015, 26). However, in practice, it focuses almost exclusively on multi-stakeholder partnerships, voluntary commitments, and national responsibility for domestic mobilization of resources as means of implementation. This orientation marks a significant move away from "global solidarity" understandings of "partnership," which focused much more on responsibility of major economic powers and pressures for structural and institutional change in areas like development finance and trade.

Similar trends can be seen in the Paris Agreement. It too exhibits a shift to accountability for *nationally* determined commitments, that is, voluntary pledges as opposed to a negotiated distribution of commitments and obligations to meet the overall goal. While a global stocktake every five years will assess collective progress, its specific purpose is to use monitoring and review of each parties' performance to lead to "updating and enhancing" of their pledges, again leaving the focus on countries' national responsibility. The agreement and other decisions made in Paris also emphasize greater responsibility for action from nonstate and substate actors (Falkner 2016).

There are potentially advantages to organizing global responses to climate change along polycentric lines. For example, "orchestration" platforms like NAZCA[8] – the Global Climate Action portal which gathers and publicizes information on voluntary emission reduction commitments – may create a greater sense of responsibility among the myriad stakeholders, substate, and nonstate actors who must be mobilized at multiple scales and levels to address global climate change (Abbott, Bernstein, and Janzwood 2020; Jordan et al. 2018). However, who exactly is responsible for ensuring these actors follow through on their commitments is often unclear and soft steering through orchestration makes accountability difficult (Kuyper, Linnér, and Schroeder 2018). These concerns are not only over such platforms' ability to create a sense of obligation and directionality for actions that contribute to the desired result but also their ability to accurately account for the "value" of these initiatives or ensure they are contributing to the goals of the Paris Agreement or decarbonization more broadly (van der Ven, Bernstein, and Hoffmann 2017; Hsu et al. 2019).

In sum, the trends discussed above not only indicate a steady drift toward the "national duty" end of the responsibility spectrum but also to a horizontal and nondifferentiated diffusion of responsibility more broadly. In tandem with shirking and irresponsible behavior in evidence among as least some of the major powers (Bernstein 2020), which these trends may threaten to reinforce, these are grounds for concern.

Conclusions

While the decline of responsibility is worrisome for addressing global environmental problems, the diffusion of responsibility has more ambiguous implications. While it is obviously desirable in general that states – especially major powers and other states who contribute most to international environmental problems – take on greater responsibility (Bernstein 2020), the idea that many of the most serious environmental problems are best addressed by top-down collective action may be misplaced. Some environmental problems do fit this bill, such as those that have clear characteristics of common pool resources like high seas fisheries, protection of the ozone layer, or protection of frontier or (ostensibly) common spaces like Antarctica or outer space. However, many of the most serious environmental and sustainability problems require societal transformation where other actors and scales are equally important (Bernstein and Hoffmann 2018, 2019; Kanie and Biermann 2017). Climate change is a paradigmatic example. As I have argued elsewhere (Bernstein and Hoffmann 2019), climate change is more productively thought of as a challenge of decarbonizing societies rather than international cooperation:

> Changing perspective to consider the challenge of climate change as decarbonization means focusing attention on disrupting carbon lock-in [as opposed to a primary focus on international cooperation]... Global carbon lock-in is not a single coherent global system but rather arises because multiple, interdependent systems at local, regional, and national levels, as well as the economic activity within and among them, are locked into the use of fossil energy. In other words, carbon lock-in is a multilevel and multisectoral challenge of similar, overlapping and interdependent political, economic, technological, and cultural forces that reinforce dependence on fossil fuels in many places simultaneously.

When the problem is understood in this way, it is not surprising that climate change action in practice has been largely driven by more diffuse and de-centralized practices at multiple scales than by top-down collective management and a reliance on the latter misunderstands the structure of the problem. There may also be benefits of directing attention to improving a broader sense of responsibility and improved accountability as ways to pressure and support greater and more widespread transformative action that might also eventually bring states, especially the major polluters, along.

As noted earlier, there are many signs of moving beyond static notions of state responsibility, particularly in terms of corporations being asked to take on greater responsibilities for the global environment and their supply and consumption chains (as well as other transnational concerns such as human rights, labor standards, and other social goals). So far, however, at least internationally, these responsibilities are largely in the realm of soft law and best practices. While some forms of environmental and social standard setting through certification systems have relatively robust accountability mechanisms, monitoring, and consequences for noncompliance, which arguably gives them a quasi-legal status, even they are still voluntary to join and their coverage of targeted sectors is limited and variable. The trend toward "best practices" (Bernstein and van der Ven 2017b; Best 2014; Ruggie 2014) has an even more ambiguous relationship to responsibility. Even when included in standards that create clearer obligations, best practices criteria are treated less formally than other parts of the standard that generate more specific expectations. For example, ISO 26000, a "guideline" standard on Corporate Social Responsibility, differentiates between "minimum steps all organizations should take to be considered socially responsible and additional best practices which organizations may choose or be encouraged to adopt" (Wood 2011, 10). On the other hand, as I have argued elsewhere (Bernstein and van der Ven 2017b, 545):

> ...the universalizing tendency of best practices [especially when written into "codes" of organizations like ISEAL that sets best practices for social and environmental certification systems or widely endorsed principles like the UN Guiding Principles on Business and Human Rights] creates normative pressures for broader public legitimation... and hold the potential to transform actors previously defined as private by defining them as actors with public responsibilities in an explicit way that subjects them collectively to new forms of regulation, though this transformation through best practices is likely to be far from complete.

As in older formal doctrines of state responsibility, operationalizing and ensuring responsibilities are both accepted and have consequences will still require accompanying accountability mechanisms and often other institutional innovations. Other values have also complicated the question of responsibility, creating tension between an ethic of, or responsibility to, the environment and one that also incorporates equity within and between societies (Okereke and Coventry 2016). Meanwhile, more general shifts in, and challenges to, global order suggest new thinking may also be needed to buttress responsibility – especially among established and rising powers – given growing demands on resources, planetary boundaries, and complex legitimacy challenges confronting global governance more broadly (Bernstein 2020; Flockhart 2016; Hochstetler and Milkoreit 2015; Hurrell 2018; Zürn 2018). These concerns suggest significant challenges ahead.

Notes

1 This chapter contains some previously published material in revised form that appeared originally in: Bernstein, S. (2020). "The Absence of Great Power Responsibility in Global Environmental Politics." *European Journal of International Relations*, 26 (1): 8-32. It is reproduced here with permission from Sage. The author would also like to acknowledge helpful comments from Hannes Hansen-Magnusson and Antje Vetterlein, Susan Park, and other participants in the workshop help at the University of Münster on 27–29 May 2019.
2 The Agreement Relating to the Implementation of Part XI of the United Nations Convention on of the Law of the Sea of '10 December 1982' adopted at New York, July 28, 1994 (UNGA A/RES/48/263), passed by a vote of 121-0 with 7 abstentions, contains legally binding changes to Part XI and is to be applied and interpreted together with the Convention as a single instrument.
3 Chinese President Xi Jingpin has promoted an alternative idea – originally proposed in a 2011 white paper for the 18th Chinese Communist Party's national conference – of a 'Community of Shared Fate' or 'Common Destiny' as a central plank of Chinese foreign policy. Despite similar language to common heritage, and much ambiguity over its meaning and implications (Zhang 2018; Xiaochun 2018), it does not promote ideas of shared ownership or prioritize protection of global commons. Some pronouncements suggest it supports China taking on more responsibility as a great power, but I could find no reference to specific or special environmental responsibilities apart from those consistent with the CBDR norm and China's longstanding position that Western states have additional historical responsibilities. It arguably refers more generally to framing China's foreign policy goals to support cooperation, development goals and building markets, like the Belt and Road Initiative, for 'shared' benefit.
4 In addition, the preamble, para. 7, states that achieving environmental goals will 'demand the acceptance of responsibility by citizens and communities and by enterprises and institutions at every level, all sharing equitably in common efforts'. While it notes that governments bear responsibility for policy, domestic and international, it makes no mention of specific or differential responsibilities.
5 Paris Agreement, FCCC/CP/2015/L.9/Rev.1, https://unfccc.int/resource/docs/2015/cop21/eng/l09r01.pdf.
6 For a detailed discussion of how human rights bodies and tribunals have interpreted or inferred such rights for vulnerable individuals and groups, see Knox and Pejan (2018), particularly chapters by Magraw and Winhöfer and Atapattu. See also Duyck, Jodoin, and Johl (2018).
7 That is, even if one accepts a minimalist reading of CBDR and accepts that historical responsibility is essentially off the table.
8 https://climateaction.unfccc.int/

References

Abbott, K.W., Bernstein, S., and Janzwood, A. (2020). "Orchestration and Earth Systems Governance." In Biermann, F., and Rakhyun, E.K., eds., *Global Governance for the Earth: Transforming Institutional Architectures in the Anthropocene*, 233–253. Boston: MIT Press.

Allen, J., Roger, C., Hale, T., Bernstein, S., Balme, R., and Tiberghien, Y. (n.d.). *The Paris Agreement: How the Global Deal Was Done*. Under review.

Bernstein, S. (2014). "The Publicness of Private Global Environmental and Social Governance." In Best, J., and Gheciu, A., eds., *The Return of the Public in Global Governance*: 120–148. Cambridge and New York: Cambridge University Press.

Bernstein, S. (2020). "The Absence of Great Power Responsibility in Global Environmental Politics." *European Journal of International Relations*, 26(1): 8–32.

Bernstein, S., and Hoffmann, M. (2018). "The Politics of Decarbonization and the Catalytic Impact of Subnational Climate Experiments." *Policy Sciences*, 51(2): 189–211.

Bernstein, S., and Hoffmann, M. (2019). "Climate Politics, Metaphors and Fractal Carbon Trap." *Nature Climate Chang*, 9 (December): 919–925.

Bernstein, S., and van der Ven, H. (2017a). "Continuity and Change in Global Environmental Politics." In Fioretos, O., ed., *International Politics and Institutions in Time*: 293–317. Oxford and New York: Oxford University Press.

Bernstein, S., and van der Ven, H. (2017b). "Best Practices in Global Governance." *Review of International Studies*, 43(3): 534–556.

Best, J. (2014). *Governing Failure: Provisional Expertise and the Transformation of Global Finance*. Cambridge: Cambridge University Press.

Bodansky, D. (1994). "Prologue to the Climate Change Convention." In Mintzing, I.M., and Leonard, J.A., eds., *Negotiating Climate Change: The Inside Story of the Rio Convention*. Cambridge: Cambridge University Press.

Brunnée, J. (2005). "International Legal Accountability through the Lens of the Law of State Responsibility." *Netherlands Yearbook of International Law*, 36(1): 3–38.

Brunnée, J. (2008). "Common Areas, Common Heritage, and Common Concern." In Bodansky, D., Brunnée, J., and Hey, E., eds., *The Oxford Handbook of International Environmental Law*: 550–566. Oxford: Oxford University Press.

Brunnée, J. (2011). "An Agreement in Principle? The Copenhagen Accord and the Post-2012 Climate Regime." In Hestermeyer, H., et al., eds., *Law of the Sea in Dialogue*: 47–72. Heidelberg: Springer.

Conca, K. (2015). *An Unfinished Foundation: The United Nations and Global Environmental Governance*. Oxford University Press.

Duyck, S., Jodoin, S., and Johl, A. (eds.) (2018). *Routledge Handbook of Human Rights and Climate Governance*. Abingdon-on-Thames: Routledge.

Falkner, R. (2016). "The Paris Agreement and the New Logic of International Climate Politics." *International Affairs*, 92(5): 1107–1125.

Flockhart, T. (2016). "The Coming Multi-Order World." *Contemporary Security Policy*, 37(1): 3–30.

Ganguly, G. Setzer, J., and Heyvaert, V. (2018). "If at First You Don't Succeed: Suing Corporations for Climate Change." *Oxford Journal of Legal Studies*, 38: 1–28.

Hochstetler, K., and Milkoreit, M. (2015). "Responsibilities in Transition: Emerging Powers in the Climate Negotiations." *Global Governance*, 21(2): 205–226.

Hsu, A., Höhne, N., Kuramochi, T., Roelfsema, M., Weinfurter, A., Xie, Y., Lütkehermöller, K. et al. (2019). "A Research Roadmap for Quantifying Nonstate and Subnational Climate Mitigation Action." *Nature Climate Change*, 9(1): 11–17.

Hurrell, A. (2018). "Beyond the BRICS: Power, Pluralism, and the Future of Global Order." *Ethics and International Affairs*, 32(2): 89–101.

Jordan, A. et al., (eds.). (2018). *Governing Climate Change: Polycentricity in Action?* Cambridge: Cambridge University Press.

Kanie, N., and Biermann, F. (eds.). (2017). *Governance through Goals: New Strategies for Global Sustainability*. Cambridge, MA: MIT Press.

Klinsky, S. (2017). "Transitional Justice for Climate Change? An Initial Scoping." *Climate Policy*, 18(6): 752–765.

Klinsky, S., and Brankovic, J. (2018). *The Global Climate Regime and Transitional Justice*. New York: Routledge.

Knox, J., and Pejan, R. (eds.) (2018). *The Human Right to a Healthy Environment*. Cambridge: Cambridge University Press.

Kuyper, J.W., Linnér, B., and Schroeder, H. (2018). "Nonstate Actors in Hybrid Global Climate Governance: Justice, Legitimacy, and Effectiveness in a Post-Paris Era: Nonstate Actors in Hybrid Global Climate Governance." *WIREs Climate Change*, 9(1): 497.

Okereke, C., and Coventry, P. (2016). "Climate Justice and the International Regime: Before, During, and after Paris." *WIREs Climate Change*, 7(6): 834–851.

Pauwelyn, J. (2013). "The End of Differential Treatment for Developing Countries? Lessons from the Trade and Climate Change Regimes." *Review of European Community & International Environmental Law*, 22(1): 29–41.

Payoyo, P. B. (1997). *Cries of the Sea: World Inequality, Sustainable Development and the Common Heritage of Humanity*. The Hague: Martinus Nijhoff.

Pouliot, V., and Thérien, J.-P. (2018). "Global Governance: A Struggle over Universal Values." *International Studies Review*, 20(1): 55–73.

Ruggie, J. G. (2014). "Global Governance and 'New Governance Theory': Lessons from Business and Human Rights." *Global Governance*, 20(1): 5–17.

Setzer, J., and Vanhala, L. C. (2019). "Climate Change Litigation: A Review of Research on Courts and Litigants in Climate Governance." *WIREs Climate Change*, 580, Advanced Review. https://doi.org/0.1002/wcc.580.

Terán, D. U. (2019). "The Core Elements of a Legally Binding Instrument: Highlights of the Revised Draft of the Legally Binding Instrument on Business and Human Rights." *South Centre Policy Brief*. No. 68.

United Nations. (1972). "*Declaration of the United Nations Conference on the Human Environment.*" Stockholm. http://www.unep.org/Documents.Multilingual/Default.asp?documentid=97&articleid=1503.

United Nations. (1992). "*Rio Declaration on Environment and Development. Rio de Janeiro.*" http://www.unep.org/Documents.Multilingual/Default.asp?documentid=78&articleid=1163

United Nations. (1993). "*Report of the United Nations Conference on Environment and Development. Rio de Janeiro, 3–14 June 1992 Volume II Proceedings of the Conference.*" A/CONF.151/26/Rev.1 (Vol. II).

United Nations. (2015). "*Transforming Our World: The 2030 Agenda for Sustainable Development.*" Resolution adopted by the General Assembly on September 25, 2015. A/RES/70/1.

United Nations. (2018). Report of the Special Rapporteur on Human Rights Obligations Relating to the Enjoyment of a Safe, Clean, Healthy and Sustainable Environment. A/73/188.

United Nations Framework Convention on Climate Change. (1992). A/AC.237/18 (Part II)/Add.1.

van der Ven, H., Bernstein, S., and Hoffmann, M. (2017). "Valuing the Contributions of Non-State and Subnational Actors to Climate Governance." *Global Environmental Politics*, 17(1): 1–20.

Wilkinson, R., Hannah, E., and Scott, J. (2016). "The WTO in Nairobi: The Demise of the Doha Development Agenda and the Future of the Multilateral Trading System." *Global Policy*, 7(2): 247–255.

Wood, S. (2011). "Four Varieties of Social Responsibility: Making Sense of the 'Sphere of Influence' and 'Leverage' Debate via the Case of ISO 26000." *Osgood Hall Law School, Comparative Research in Law & Political Economy Research Paper* 2011(14): 1–27.

World Commission on Environment and Development. (1987). *Our Common Future*. Oxford: Oxford University Press.

Xiaochun, Z. (2018). "In Pursuit of a Community of Shared Future: China's Global Activism in Perspective." *China Quarterly of International Strategic Studies*, 4(1): 23–37.

Zelli, F. (2018). "Effects of Legitimacy Crises in Complex Global Governance." In Bäckstrand, K., Scholte, J.A., and Tallberg, J., eds., *Legitimacy in Global Governance: Sources, Processes, and Consequences*: 169–186. New York: Oxford University Press.

Zhang, D. (2018). "The Concept of 'Community of Common Destiny' in China's Diplomacy: Meaning, Motives and Implications." *Asia & the Pacific Policy Studies*, 5(2): 196–207.

Zürn, M. (2018). *A Theory of Global Governance*. Cambridge: Cambridge University Press.

11
MORAL GEOGRAPHIES OF RESPONSIBILITY IN THE GLOBAL AGRIFOOD SYSTEM

Tobias Gumbert and Doris Fuchs

Introduction

In the politics of governing food on the global level as well as in national contexts, notions of responsibility have become highly visible: the safe handling of food products is subject to extended producer responsibility (EPR) schemes, retailers and other actors of the food and drink industry are expected to develop corporate social responsibility (CSR) plans, and many policy strategies try to enhance consumer responsibility in food markets. Policy and governance strategies to steer responsible behaviours and practices in food-related matters include private standards, voluntary agreements, and best practices, as well as a range of informational tools, such as awareness-raising campaigns, and fair trade and organic food labels. These instruments aim to mitigate the negative external effects of global food production in social (e.g. labour relations) and ecological (e.g. greenhouse gas emissions) terms. Taking up responsible attitudes and actions appears, especially in the context of climate change and global hunger and malnutrition, as a self-evident and universal practice, and political debates suggest that solving these challenges is simply a question of whether business actors and consumers become responsible moral agents, or not.

This chapter questions this seeming existence of a universal notion of responsibility in global food governance by drawing on the concept of moral geographies of responsibility (see Cresswell 2005; Massey 2004). The concept postulates that actors' practices of responsibility actually tend to change according to the objects in question, which in turn are tied to geographic space. Studying responsibility in global food governance from the perspective of moral geographies of responsibility, we identify spatially structured practices of irresponsibility hidden behind the universal responsibility discourse. We posit that without this attention to space, influential and potentially dangerous forms of structural injustice (Young 2011) are removed from sight, limiting the range of possible governance responses.

In the global agrifood system, characteristics of space seem to play a natural role, and at the same time they may appear to be a negligible factor. The significance of the spatial dimension adheres for instance to the importance of climate and soil characteristics in production processes, of culture and traditions on the consumption side, and to the sheer distance food regularly travels from field to fork, connecting places and identities across space. Here, responsibility appears to derive from 'those relations through which identity is constructed' (Massey 2004, 10) and can therefore take multiple forms and meanings in practice. Looked at from a different perspective, however, the dominance and ubiquity of global supply chains provide the very reason why one may think that space, especially in the sense of distance, does not appear to be a novel frame for analyzing contemporary developments in the global agrifood system. After all, supply chains are increasingly controlled, if not owned, by transnational retail corporations (Clapp 2016; Fuchs et al. 2009). This form of global control exercised by certain actors in the agrifood system, in turn, gives rise to the assumption that responsibility can be enacted, attributed, and measured without attention to space, because its forms would be similar across the globe.

The concept of moral geographies of responsibility draws our attention to how different attributions of responsibility are always mediated by moral agency, normative discourses, and competing material interests. Norms of food safety, food security, food sovereignty, fair trade, agricultural productivity and efficiency, regionalism, or organic farming may pursue a universal ambition. And yet, they rely on different values and knowledge claims, and on negotiating (at least partly) competing interests, which adds to the variance of how responsibility is understood and how it functions in a given context. The concept of moral geographies helps to uncover to whom and how actors in the food system behave responsible and how such meanings can be differentiated and analyzed according to geographic space. By doing so, it allows to unveil how actors can at the same time further responsible and irresponsible practices, for instance by simultaneously voicing concerns for the work and living conditions of a particular group and deflecting (or actively ignoring) the work and living conditions of others.

The chapter proceeds by outlining a theoretical approach to studying the moral geographies of responsibility in global food governance. The subsequent section details the governance issue of food waste and explores the role and responsibilities of transnationally operating retail companies within this particular field. We argue that the scrutiny of retailers' practices of responsibility reveals their spatial differentiation: sharing responsibility for the generation of food waste downstream on the distribution and consumption stage in European countries, while continuing to shift responsibilities for waste upstream to weaker actors along food supply chains, predominantly in relation to Non-European producers and suppliers. Finally, the chapter concludes by suggesting that in studying responsibility in global food governance, a relational ontology as well as close attention to power differentials in the food system may help to generate a clearer picture of varying responsibility attributions.

Moral geographies of responsibility

As an analytical perspective, the concept of moral geographies 'help[s] us to analyse the taken-for-granted relationship between the geographical ordering of the world and ideas about what is good, right and true' (Cresswell 2005, 132). Generally, two specific foci can be distinguished: the relation of moral duties and geographic distance and the relation of moral agency and geographic space. The first focus describes moral geography as being centrally concerned with the relationship between morality and distance, and more specifically with 'our' relation to 'distant strangers' (Clarke 2011). This focus appears to run counter to Singer's (1972) claim that one's duty to help others is independent of geographical distance. His argument that '[…] if it is in our power to prevent something very bad from happening, without thereby sacrificing anything of comparable moral importance, we ought, morally, to do it' (ibid., 231) reveals the indirect importance of space, however, as well. What is conceived of 'comparable moral importance' directly relates to knowledge, emotions, and other factors in a given context and is influenced by our perceived distance to others, as is the ability to provide help (Binder and Heilmann 2017).

In the second line of inquiry, the notion of moral geography comprises 'the idea that certain people, things and practices belong in certain spaces, places and landscapes and not in others'

(Cresswell 2005, 128). Particular geographical imaginations establish people and things as 'in place' and 'out of place' through culturally coded sets of expectations, practices of moral ordering, or normative mappings. By making use of the notion of moral geographies, aspects of space or place are analyzed in their interdependence with sociological and cultural objects (such as class, race, and gender), and researchers adopting this perspective are interested in how geographical categories become laden with moral narratives (ibid., 130). The ability to 'create' moral geographies is here, by extension, a function of the discursive power of particular actors to frame and/or construct spatially differentiated objects of moral consideration. We use the concept of moral geographies according to this second understanding, to explore how practices in global food governance create differentiated objects of responsibility by linking moral obligations to act to geographic space.

Arguing for the importance of spatial differentiation within responsibility attributions rests on the underlying premise that understandings of responsibility are contingent upon particular socio-cultural contexts and their histories, specific social relations, and ethical principles. In order to grasp this difference analytically, we suggest to think of responsibility and corresponding judgments as the product of three interrelated elements: a subject of responsibility (an agent), an object of responsibility (e.g. human or nonhuman entities, including abstractions such as 'nature'), and the action of responsibility itself (practices of 'ought' and 'should' that establish a relation between subject and object) (see Gumbert 2019; Ulbert 2018). Since these three elements form a consistent triangle, responsibility can be expected to change if the composition of the triangle is altered (compare Sienknecht, this volume). In order to study the variance of responsibility attributions and practices, it is further important to distinguish particular notions along different dimensions. A first dominant differentiation concerns causality versus morality in attributing responsibility (e.g. Erskine 2008). Whereas the former stipulates that responsibility can only be assigned if an action can be linked to the cause of an effect, the latter involves imagining self and other as acting responsible on moral grounds, defining general duties and obligations (see also Chandler 2018). A second differentiation can be made concerning the ability of autonomous and rational actors to freely choose their actions and have control over the outcome of an event, and circumstances of chance (due to the complexities and unintended consequences of an event) that severely limit the power of individual actors to do something about specific outcomes (e.g. Sondermann et al. 2018). Lastly, a third line of inquiry into understandings of responsibility distinguishes between individual (or personal) and collective responsibilities, which contrasts ideas of singling out blameworthy acts and the constitution of shared responsibilities regarding responsible relations with human or nonhuman others. While certainly other differentiations could be made (for example, by referring to legal or political conceptions, see also Vincent 2011 and van de Poel 2011 for alternative taxonomies of responsibility), the analysis of responsibility within particular policy and governance contexts often draws on a variation of the three dimensions above.

Contemporary approaches to responsibility in the political realm typically attempt to assign responsibility on the grounds of causality and intentionality. They follow a notion that hinges on accountability for one's actions and thus focus largely on the individual responsibilities of actors, what they have done in the past, and how they can be held accountable to mitigate future harm (Mounk 2017; Pellizzoni 2020; Raffoul 2010). In fact, these approaches are so dominant that one may easily forget that other approaches, entailing notions of care and precaution and thus a so-called forward-looking orientation, for instance, are possible (Gumbert 2019). In contrast, the concept of moral geographies is especially interested in how moral obligations towards objects of responsibility are formed and enacted and how this differs according to their 'location'. Thereby, it allows us to show that a focus on behaving or acting responsible in one space may go hand in hand with the neglect of objects of responsibility elsewhere, objects which may not be directly tied to a given actor through causal connection (given the complexities of global supply chains), but whose wellbeing is nevertheless dependent on moral considerations and corresponding obligations.

We believe that such a research agenda is especially relevant today, where the notion of responsibility is broadly represented in food politics, and yet it is not clear how it may contribute to addressing current ecological and social challenges in the global agrifood system beyond calls for more information and transparency in global value chains. We therefore feel the need to substantiate the relevance of a 'moral geographies of responsibility' lens by drawing on the work of Iris Marion Young, who has, arguably, concerned herself in much of her writing on responsibility for justice and its focus on structural injustices in the world economy with moral geographies (Young 2006; 2011). Young argues that, if harm has occurred, concentrating on built-in chains of causation may help establish identifiable victims and wrong-doers, but fails to address structural injustices caused by the combined acts of literally billions of individuals and organizations. Understanding responsibility solely in causal, intentional, and individual terms 'works actively to obscure the structural character of injustices in ways that make it hard to achieve collective action' (Eckersley 2016, 349). To address these injustices, Young suggests that – because we participate in the institutional processes that produce them – a particular kind of solidarity is required which rests on the idea of political responsibility:

> The social connection model of responsibility says that individuals bear responsibility for structural injustice because they contribute by their actions to the processes that produce unjust outcomes. Our responsibility derives from belonging together with others in a system of interdependent processes of cooperation and competition through which we seek benefits and aim to realize projects…All who dwell within the structures must take responsibility for remedying injustices they cause, though none is specifically liable for the harm in a legal sense.
>
> *(Young 2011, 105; ct. in Eckersley 2016, 350)*

Through what Young calls the social connection model, she provides a framework to distinguish between blameworthy and non-blameworthy acts in order to make the structural nature of injustices visible. Even though we may not be able to directly establish a causal link between certain actors and unjust outcomes in the context of complex global value chains, the conditions of production and consumption that cause harm allow us to assign (more or less) responsibility to certain actors. For Young, considering an agent's power (position and influence), an agent's privilege (position without influence), an agent's interest (maintaining or improving position and influence), and/or collective ability (use of group resources) (Nussbaum 2011, xvii) provides a basis for determining moral obligation and assigning responsibility on the basis of what agents could potentially contribute to altering unjust outcomes, even in cases without direct cause or explicit intent.

Young's notion of responsibility ties in with the moral geographies of responsibility lens, because it aims to remedy effects of structural background conditions that cause harm in distant spaces of the global economy and asks the question of who we should extend care to across spatial divides. And Young provides a justification for adopting such a perspective, because it allows us to show how an actor's failure to accept responsibility and contribute to the solving of challenges in one location may add to the perpetuation and proliferation of structural injustices, even if that same actor may feel morally obligated towards contributing to the overcoming of challenges in other locations. In this manner, analyses of global commodity chains have drawn attention to the relation of geographical knowledge and moral choices (consumption choices and the role of individual consumers, as well as choice of production location and the role of transnationally operating businesses), for example in the global textile industry (Scheper 2018; Young 2004).

In sum, the concept of moral geographies of responsibility suggests the necessity to adopt 'a relational view of geographical scale and temporal connection, contrasting the attribution of individual blame with a politics of collective responsibility' (Jackson et al. 2009, 12). While the heuristic of the triangle of responsibility (subject, object, and norms of responsible behaviour) tells us what to look for, the three dimensions we discussed very briefly (causality-morality, intentional-unintentional, individual-collective) help to explain variations in responsible attitudes and attributions of the same agent. Thereby, the concept of moral geographies of responsibility aims to draw out specific practices of moral ordering which tend to escape notice in the omnipresent discourses on responsibility. By doing so, we hope to contribute to a better understanding of the circumstances in which actors feel and attribute responsibility differently across spatial contexts and resulting implications for the present and future developments within the global agrifood system.

Corporate actors and food waste reduction

The necessity to relate subjects, objects, and certain actions to each other in order to evaluate responsibility attributions calls for in-depth case study observations. In other words, we concentrate on a specific group of actors (or subject of responsibility) and analyze with the help of the concept of moral geographies how moral obligations and corresponding practices of an agent change in relation to the spatial differentiation of its objects – and what this implies. To advance this argument, we focus on the role of private actors in global food governance, and more specifically on transnationally operating retailers and their responsibility in reducing global food waste.

Research has documented the increasing power of private actors, especially corporations, in the agrifood system, for a while (Clapp 2016; Clapp and Fuchs 2009; McKeon 2015). In this context, scholars have pursued questions of the transparency, accountability, and legitimacy of private actors vis-à-vis the governance of public goods, analyzing for instance private forms of regulation, discursive influences in the public debate or lobbying of governmental actors (Fuchs and Hennings 2017; Williams 2009). Supermarkets, specifically, have become a nodal point in the food system over the course of the 20th century, exerting power over what is produced, how, and in which quantities, and simultaneously shaping societal food consumption norms on aesthetics, freshness, or year-round availability of certain products (Fuchs et al. 2009; Gumbert and Fuchs 2018). The rising number of global consumers, the lack of natural constraints (the ability to source their supplies globally), the level of control established over commodity chains (through technological innovations), and capital concentration, which led to highly oligopolistic regional market structures, have underpinned retailers' position of power vis-à-vis other actors (Burch and Lawrence 2005; Fuchs and Kalfagianni 2010; Morgan et al. 2006). However, along with the power and privilege global retailers have gained, calls for them to take on more responsibility for the socio-ecological characteristics of the food system have also increased. This is especially the case with respect to food waste reduction.

Studies estimate that approximately one-third of the food produced globally goes to waste (Gustavsson et al. 2011). In ecological terms, this constitutes not only a loss of edible material on a gigantic scale but also the waste of resources needed to produce such quantities of food, such as water, energy and arable land, as well as the production of greenhouse gas emissions. Food waste on a global scale coincides with the fact that, according to calculations by the Food and Agricultural Organization (FAO), 821 million people are still suffering from hunger and malnutrition (FAO et al. 2018). For these reasons, food waste has climbed rapidly on international governance agendas. For example, the UN Food and Agricultural Organization (FAO) has organized and steered a range of different forums on global food loss and food waste reduction, such as the SAVE FOOD multi-stakeholder initiative (Gustavsson et al. 2011), and collaborated with others to launch a global waste accounting and reporting standard in 2013 (released in 2016). These and other international developments were widely recognized when the issue of food loss and waste was included as a specific target under goal 12 'Responsible Production and Consumption' within the Sustainable Development Goals in 2015. Since then, partnerships have been established as the core of the global governance architecture: the responsibility of states is to stimulate more 'sustainable' investments in reducing food waste along food supply chains, to encourage more business actors to join voluntary agreements, to enhance transparency on food waste in their supply chains, and to engage in practices of self-accounting (Gumbert 2019).

These accountability strategies, however, largely omit the relations that businesses have established with other actors in the food system. Voluntary agreements that encourage responsible self-accounting still protect retailers from risks associated with perishability and hygiene and shift responsibility and the costs for food waste to the supplier by rejecting produce or terminating contracts unilaterally (Gille 2013; Gumbert and Fuchs 2018). Scholars have also argued that food waste results mainly from processes that lead to a massive oversupply of food on a global scale, such as market concentration (e.g. in the agricultural and biotech sectors), the commercial intensification of food production, or contractual obligations (which prevents food from being sold in alternative markets) (Alexander et al. 2013; Cloke 2013; Stuart 2009). We argue in the following that the concept of moral geographies of responsibility helps to explain that, while business actors increasingly adopt responsible practices to reduce food waste 'at home', they are at the same time deeply implicated in the structural background conditions of food waste generation that continue to produce ecological harm and social injustices for Southern producers and smallholders.

Spatially differentiated notions of responsibility in the food system

When food waste climbed as a regulatory issue and object of responsibility on international governance agendas in the years from 2007 to 2013, the initial response was to attribute most of the responsibility for its causes to the consumption stage, blaming predominantly consumers (Evans 2011;Evans et al. 2017; Meah 2014). Consumers where described as exhibiting irrational character traits due to a general lack of knowledge about the negative consequences of food wastage, and lacking the calculative skills to contribute to its reduction. Campaigns by public and private authorities focused, therefore, on 'rationalizing' consumer conduct, and articulated individual reduction efforts as an ethical obligation, motivating personal responsibility.

Specific discursive strategies helped to legitimize this focus on the consumer. Specifically, actors started to distinguish between 'food loss' and 'food waste'. The dominant discourse today describes the causes for food 'dropping out' of supply chains in the harvesting, storage, transport, processing, and packaging stages as 'food loss', whereas food disposed in the retail and consumption stages is considered to constitute 'food waste' (Lipinski et al. 2013; see also Parfitt et al. 2010). Food loss is seen as an unintended occurrence, and is therefore best addressed by technological solutions to increase efficiency, such as improved refrigeration and packaging, but also better marketing and management through producing 'value added' products. Food loss additionally is viewed as a problem primary related to the Global South (Gustavsson et al. 2011, v). Food waste, on the other hand, is depicted as 'the result of negligence or a conscious decision to throw food away' (Lipinski et al. 2013, 4). Food waste, thus, is seen as a consumer and retailer issue that occurs either because actors fail to pay attention or because they do not care. Prescriptions aiming to reduce consumption stage food waste thus include more transparent information (date labels on products) to reduce consumer confusion, as well as public awareness raising campaigns and other educational measures, primarily for consumers in European countries.

In interviews with retailers in the UK, Evans et al. (2017) have found a marked shift and changing dynamics in responsibility attributions since 2013, suggesting that a sense of distributed or shared responsibility has developed. They report that retailers increasingly acknowledge that responsibilities are distributed across more complex and extensive networks of actors and recognize that food waste is a systemic issue (ibid., 1404). Simultaneously, the notion of 'shared responsibility' springs up in the debate on the international level, where it is claimed that '[r]educing food loss and waste is everyone's responsibility' (Lipinski et al. 2017, 2). As a consequence, retailers in the UK became more active and visible in food waste reductions and responded with promotional strategies on the shopping floor (educating and incentivizing consumers to waste less) and innovations in packaging and labelling (Evans et al. 2017, 1405). The retailers who participated in the study explained their 'responsible' behaviour by invoking the figure of 'the consumer' for whom they would take action in light of perceived customer expectations that reducing food waste would equal a moral imperative. Supermarkets see their reduction efforts also as an investment in customer loyalty and work towards becoming 'cultural and lifestyle authorities who can help people solve problems in their everyday lives' (ibid., 1407; see also Dixon 2007). These findings suggest that retailers in the UK have started to see food waste and consumers as objects of responsibility, and their duties in terms of moral agency are directed towards improving the perceived problems and cultivating positive relationships. Simultaneously, these statements seem to indicate hints of a forward-oriented responsibility, defined by moral obligations and collective actions and solutions, rather than causality.

On the side of 'food loss', however, we hardly observe practices of shared and forward-looking responsibility. Retailers claim that they are orchestrating changes to cut waste in supply chains by working closely with their producers and suppliers, e.g. by improving forecasting, or helping them to find secondary markets for unwanted produce (Evans et al. 2017, 1405). However, civil society organizations strongly question the validity of these claims. The UK-based organization Feedback is one of the most visible non-governmental actors that demands more responsible business practices from retailers in relation to their suppliers and has published its own research on the causes of supply chain waste (Feedback 2015; 2018). For example, farmers and exporters from Kenya working with European retailers reported that, on average, 30 per cent of food is being rejected at farm level, and 50 per cent before export (Feedback 2015, 5). The reasons for the rejection tend to be cosmetic specifications and, also, include frequent order cancellations as a function of last minute forecast adjustments, which result in financial loss and increased debt on the part of farmers due to a lack of compensation. Feedback has uncovered similar business practices in Senegal, Peru, and South Africa. In other words, retailers shift financial risks down supply chains to the weakest actors and thereby accept if not foster 'normalized overproduction' (Feedback 2018, 13) and food waste.

Against the background of such findings and in part due to the pressure exerted by civil society campaigns, public authorities have slowly begun to address these business practices. For example, the UK Grocery Code Adjudicator (GCA), an independent regulator tasked with ensuring lawful and fair treatment of suppliers by regulated retailers, has investigated the business practices of Tesco and the Co-operative group (Groceries Code Adjudicator 2016; 2019). Both of them were found in violation of the Groceries Supply Code of Practice for extensive delays in payments to their direct suppliers (Tesco), and in relation to de-listing without reasonable notice

(Co-op). Overall, however, investigations and evidence of unfair business-to-business trading practices (UTPs) in food supply chains, such as these instances, are almost non-existent. Be it because of the political status and power of retailers and/or the dependence of suppliers on market access, most of these practices still go unnoticed.

Thus, while there is evidence that retailers have adopted responsible attitudes and practices in relation to European consumers, and their rhetoric claims that they are aware of problems upstream, they are hardly addressing how their conduct contributes to food waste in the nations of Southern producers. We find a considerable gap between moral obligations of retailers across geographic space. While it may be impossible to argue and prove a direct causal link between food waste at the production stage and retailers' (in)actions, the dynamics described above provide a basis for presuming that these dependencies are an important source for structural injustices – knowingly tolerated by TNCs.

Of course, efforts to reduce food waste in the Global South tend to be far less visible to consumers in the North and therefore have not as strong an impact on a company's image as 'responsible actor'. In consequence, it produces considerably fewer financial benefits. But this is certainly only part of the explanation. The logic of seeing the food system as a vast collection of linear food value chains is predominant among most private stakeholders. The notion of 'linearity' suggests that responsibility can be individualized and compartmentalized by singling out specific sectors (production, transportation, manufacturing, processing, retail, etc.) and defining the range of appropriate reduction efforts for each sector. Additionally, since internal elements of food chains are causally related, it is possible to focus on end points (consumption), thereby affecting the entire food chain. These food chain logics give rise to the belief that the system can be transformed by the sum of many individual, causally effective, and calculable acts of responsible conduct, leading almost automatically to system-wide outcomes. In other words, every actor has to contribute their 'fair share' according to their place within particular food value chains, but what is understood as 'fair' is precisely an indication of how 'the moral' operates in 'space, place, and politics' (Olson 2017, 937). Whereas retailers in the UK are increasingly interested in projecting a responsible image to consumers by doing 'more than they would have to', their business practices contribute to environmental and social harm production in selected countries without being directly liable for negative outcomes. That means they do not have to demonstrate any commitments to care, justice, or dignity – they do not understand political problems as moral problems (Olson 2017, 940).

This refers us back to the fundamental questions of 'how far should an organization's responsibilities extent and whether an organization should take responsibility for impacts across the entire supply chain' (Devin and Richards 2018, 207). Following Young's argument that powerful and resourceful actors have a greater responsibility to reduce harm, even if a direct causal relation between their actions and the negative outcomes cannot be established, retailers would seem to hold a position of power from which clear capacities and abilities to alter systemic conditions can be derived, and therefore the obligation to adopt more responsible attitudes and actions, especially considering how their business practices affect the livelihoods of farmers and suppliers. A concept of responsibility that emphasizes the characteristics of moral obligation, attention for unintended consequences, and collective action implies extension, which means that it is not restricted to the immediate or the local (Massey 2004, 9). It seems important to strengthen these dimensions in current negotiations and debates within food waste governance in order to question and rethink how actors forge relations at a distance, and to ask what their political and economic relation with those wider geographies should be (Massey 2004, 11).

In sum, analyzing responsibility practices in the global agrifood system from a perspective of moral geographies allows the identification of systemic irresponsibility hidden behind claims of universal responsibility. The social and economic conditions of food producers and suppliers in 'distant spaces' hardly appear as objects of moral consideration, whereas the figure of 'the consumer' is able to increasingly encourage forms of moral agency on the side of retailers. It is only due to the unveiling of these differentiated patterns of responsibility that the full range of necessary, possible, and appropriate governance interventions and specifically the need for initiatives that contribute to the institutionalization of more collective forms of responsibility and moral agency, become visible.

Conclusion

How responsibility is understood and enacted by various actors in the food system, from transnationally operating corporations (TNCs) and smallholder organizations to individual citizens, will have a profound effect on the future characteristics of the agrifood system. Given multiple opposing, large-scale tendencies, such as increasing market concentration and a growing influence of corporate interests, on the one side, and attempts to decentralize, regionalize, and democratize the food system, on the other, particular notions and forms of responsibility may contribute to or hinder the building of more just, fair, and sustainable food relations (Carolan 2012; Clapp 2016; Gumbert and Fuchs 2018).

This chapter has argued that the concept of moral geographies of responsibility can help to distinguish different notions of responsibility that are present in a particular policy field, even if enacted by a single agent. Discursive practices of moral ordering, tied in turn to particular spaces and subjectivities, legitimize specific interventions in relation to objects of responsibility. Specifically, notions of moral, forward-looking, anticipatory, and 'shared' responsibility are being practiced in spaces where their visibility is positively linked to the identity images of the relevant actors and can be translated into economic and political leverage vis-à-vis other stakeholders (legislators, consumers, competitors, etc.). This suggests that responsible business behaviour in terms of an engagement with social and ecological aspects is more likely where it improves profits. Where visibility is low, i.e. where business conduct is largely concealed from public observation due to the inherent complexities of global commodity chains, business practices are governed by backward-looking, narrowly prescribed causal responsibility, and ideas of strict liability, which shift the risks associated with food production to farmers and growers, predominantly in the Global South. Here, responsibility can be likened to an individualized and 'compartmentalized' notion, which is influenced by financial interests and universal value chain logics. The wider structural background conditions are rarely addressed and have a tendency to be removed from sight altogether.

In order to encourage agents to act more responsibly in light of the contemporary challenges in the global food system, it is important to foster collective and forward-looking notions of responsibility along the supply chain. Relevant governance initiatives need to entail a notion of ecological and social care or precaution, and can be furthered through transparent and participatory institutions. More specifically, they can strengthen the ability of enforcers to initiate broad investigations into abuses by retailers, for instance, or set up anonymous complaints procedures, thereby helping to address structural injustices in the system overlooked if not strengthened by spatially differentiated responsibility practices.

References

Alexander, C., Gregson, N., and Gille, Z. (2013). "Food Waste." In Murcott, A., Belasco, W., and Jackson, P., eds., *The Handbook of Food Research*: 471–485. London: Bloomsbury.

Binder, C., and Heilmann, C. (2017). "Duty and Distance." *The Journal of Value Inquiry*, 51(3): 547–561.

Burch, D., and Lawrence, G. (2005). "Supermarket Own Brands, Supply Chains and the Transformation of the Agri-Food System." *International Journal of Sociology of Agriculture and Food*, 13(1): 1–28.

Carolan, M. (2012). *The Sociology of Food and Agriculture*. London and New York: Routledge.

Chandler, D. (2018). "Distributed Responsibility: Moral Agency in a Non-linear World." In Ulbert, C., Finkenbusch, P., Sondermann, E., and Debiel, T., eds., *Moral Agency and the Politics of Responsibility*: 182–195. Abingdon: Routledge.

Clapp, J. (2016). *Food*. Cambridge, MA: Polity Press.

Clapp, J., and Fuchs, D. (2009). *Corporate Power in Global Agrifood Governance*. Cambridge, MA: MIT Press.

Clarke, N. (2011). "Moral Geography." In Southerton, D., ed., *Encyclopedia of Consumer Culture*: 998. Thousand Oaks: SAGE.

Cloke, J. (2013). "Empires of Waste and the Food Security Meme." *Geography Compass*, 7(9): 622–636.

Cresswell, T. (2005). "Moral Geographies." In Sibley, D., Jackson, P., Atkinson, D., and Washbourne, N., eds., *Cultural Geography. A Critical Dictionary of Key Concepts*: 128–134. London: I.B. Tauris.

Devin, B., and Richards, C. (2018). "Food Waste, Power, and Corporate Social Responsibility in the Australian Food Supply Chain." *Journal of Business Ethics*, 150(1): 199–210.

Dixon, J. (2007). "Supermarkets as new food authorities." In Burch, D., and Lawrence, G., eds., *Supermarkets and Agrifood Supply Chains*: 29–50. Cheltenham: Edward Elgar.

Eckersley, R. (2016). "Responsibility for Climate Change as a Structural Injustice." In Gabrielson, T., Hall, C., Meyer, J.M., and Schlosberg, D., eds., *The Oxford Handbook of Environmental Political Theory*: 346–361. Oxford: Oxford University Press.

Erskine, T. (2008). "Locating Responsibility: The Problem of Moral Agency in International Relations." In Reus-Smit, C., and Snidal, D., eds., *The Oxford Handbook of International Relations*: 699–707. Oxford: Oxford University Press.

Evans, D. (2011). "Blaming the Consumer – Once Again: the Social and Material Contexts of Everyday Food Waste Practices in Some English Households." *Critical Public Health*, 21(4): 429–440.

Evans, D., Welch, D., and Swaffield, J. (2017). "Constructing and Mobilizing 'the Consumer': Responsibility, Consumption and the Politics of Sustainability." *Environment and Planning A*, 49(6): 1396–1412.

FAO, IFAD, UNICEF, WFP, and WHO (2018). *The State of Food Security and Nutrition in the World 2018. Building Climate Resilience for Food Security and Nutrition*. Rome: FAO.

Feedback (2015). *Food Waste in Kenya. Uncovering Food Waste in the Horticultural Export Supply Chain*. London: Feedback.

Feedback (2018). *Causes of Food Waste in International Supply Chains*. A report by Feedback Funded by the Rockefeller Foundation. London.

Fuchs, D., and Kalfagianni, A. (2010). "The Causes and Consequences of Private Food Governance." *Business and Politics*, 12(3): 1–34.

Fuchs, D., Kalfagianni, A., and Arentsen, M. (2009). "Retail Power, Private Standards, and Sustainability in the Global Food System." In Clapp, J., and Fuchs, D., eds., *Corporate Power in Global Agrifood Governance. Challenges and Strategies*: 29–60. Boston: MIT Press.

Fuchs, D., and Hennings, A. (2017). "Governance by Contract from a Perspective of Power: The Case of Landgrabbing." In Cutler, C., and Dietz, T., eds., *The Politics of Private Transnational Governance by Contract*: 57–75. New York: Routledge.

Gille, Z. (2013). "From Risk to Waste: Global Food Waste Regimes." *The Sociological Review*, 60(S2): 27–46.

Groceries Code Adjudicator (2016). *Investigation into Tesco plc*. Online. https://www.gov.uk/government/publications/gca-investigation-report-into-co-operative-group-limited (retrieved: 01/05/2019).

Groceries Code Adjudicator (2019). Investigation into Co-operative Group Unlimited. Online. https://www.gov.uk/government/publications/gca-investigation-report-into-co-operative-group-limited (retrieved: 01/05/2019).

Gumbert, T. (2019). "*Unwrapping Responsibility in Global Environmental Governance. The Political Rationalities and Techniques of Governing Food Waste Reductions in the Anthropocene.*" Unpublished Dissertation. Münster.

Gumbert, T., and Fuchs, D. (2018). "The Power of Corporations in Global Food Sector Governance." In Nölke, A., and May, C., eds., *Handbook of the International Political Economy of the Corporation*: 435–447. Cheltenham, UK/Northampton, US: Edward Elgar.

Gustavsson, J., Cederberg, C., Sonesson, U., van Otterdijk, R., and Meybeck, A. (2011). *Global Food Losses and Food Waste. Extent, Causes and Prevention*. Rome: FAO.

Jackson, P., Ward, N., and Russell, P. (2009). "Moral Economies of Food and Geographies of Responsibility." *Transactions of the Institute of British Geographers*, 34: 12–24.

Lipinski, B. et al. (2013). "*Reducing Food Loss and Waste.*" Working Paper, Installment 2 of Creating a Sustainable Food Future. Washington, DC: World Resources Institute.

Lipinski, B. et al. (2017). "*SDG Target 12.3.*" On Food Loss and Waste: 2017 Progress Report. An annual update on behalf of Champions 12.3.

Massey, D. (2004). "Geographies of Responsibility." *Geografiska Annaler*, 86B(1): 5–18.

McKeon, N. (2015). *Food Security Governance. Empowering Communities, Regulating Corporations.* London: Routledge.

Meah, A. (2014). "Still Blaming the Consumer? Geographies of Responsibility in Domestic Food Safety Practices." *Critical Public Health*, 24(1): 88–103.

Morgan, K., Marsden, T., and Murdoch, J. (2006). *Worlds of Food.* Oxford: Oxford University Press.

Mounk, Y. (2017). *The Age of Responsibility. Luck, Choice, and the Welfare State.* Cambridge, MA: Harvard University Press.

Nussbaum, M. (2011). "Foreword." In Young, I.M., ed. *Responsibility for Justice*: iv–xxv. Oxford: Oxford University Press.

Olson, E. (2017). "Geography and Ethics III: Whither the Next Moral Turn?" *Progress in Human Geography*, 42(6): 937–948.

Parfitt, J., Barthel, M., and Macnaughton, S. (2010). "Food Waste Within Food Supply Chains: Quantification and Potential for Change to 2050." *Philosophical Transactions of the Royal Society*, 365(1554): 3065–3081.

Pellizzoni, L. (2020). "Responsibility." In Kalfagianni, A., Fuchs, D., and Hayden, A., eds., *Routledge Handbook of Global Sustainability Governance*: 129–140. London: Routledge.

van de Poel, I. (2011). "The Relation between Forward-Looking and Backward-Looking Responsibility." In Vincent, N.A., van de Poel, I., and van de Hove, I., eds., *Moral Responsibility: Beyond Free Will and Determinism*: 37–52. Dordrecht: Springer.

Raffoul, F. (2010). *The Origins of Responsibility.* Bloomington & Indianapolis: Indiana University Press.

Scheper, C. (2018). "The Business of Responsibility: Supply Chain Practice and the Construction of the Moral Lead Firm." In Ulbert, C., Finkenbusch, P., Sondermann, E., and Debiel, T., eds., *Moral Agency and the Politics of Responsibility*: 122–134. Abingdon: Routledge.

Singer, P. (1972). "Famine, Affluence, and Morality." *Philosophy & Public Affairs*, 1(3): 229–243.

Sondermann, E., Ulbert, C., and Finkenbusch, P. (2018). "Introduction: Moral Agency and the Politics of Responsibility." In Ulbert, C., Finkenbusch, P., Sondermann, E., and Debiel, T., eds., *Moral Agency and the Politics of Responsibility*: 1–18. Abingdon: Routledge.

Stuart, T. (2009). *Waste: Uncovering the Global Food Scandal.* New York: W.W. Norton.

Ulbert, C. (2018). "In Search of Equity: Practices of Differentiation and the Evolution of a Geography of Responsibility." In Ulbert, C., Finkenbusch, P., Sondermann, E., and Debiel, T., eds., *Moral Agency and the Politics of Responsibility*: 105–121. Abingdon: Routledge.

Williams, M. (2009). "Feeding the World? Transnational Corporations and the Promotion of Genetically Modified Foods." In Clapp, J., and Fuchs, D., eds., *Corporate Power in Global Agrifood Governance. Challenges and Strategies.* Boston: MIT Press.

Vincent, N.A. 2011. "A Structured Taxonomy of Responsibility Concepts." In Vincent, N.A., van de Poel, I., and van de Hove, I., eds., *Moral Responsibility: Beyond Free Will and Determinism*: 15–35. Dordrecht: Springer.

Young, I. M. (2004). "Responsibility and Global Labor Justice." *The Journal of Political Philosophy*, 12(4): 365–388.

Young, I. M. (2006). "Responsibility and Global Justice: A Social Connection Model." *Social Philosophy & Policy*, 23(1): 102–130.

Young, I. M. (2011). *Responsibility for Justice.* New York: Oxford University Press.

12
STATE RESPONSIBILITIES AND INTERNATIONAL NUCLEAR POLITICS

Laura Considine and James Souter

Introduction

Since the development of nuclear weapons during the Second World War, notions of nuclear responsibility have emerged, developed, been contested, and have come to play a central role in international nuclear politics. Such notions have, either implicitly or explicitly, taken centre stage in political rhetoric and action, international legal instruments, and theoretical debates concerning nuclear weapons. They have also been drawn on for diverse ends by a wide range of actors, whether as part of attempts to contain or eliminate the immensely destructive power of these weapons, or alternatively to legitimise their continued possession by certain states, while delegitimising them for others. Given this immensely destructive power, and the fact that their maintenance, use or non-use fundamentally depends on the often unchecked discretion of state leaders, the stakes surrounding these notions and practices are exceptionally high. One recent example of the shifting and contested nature of claims surrounding nuclear responsibility is the challenge posed to the nuclear status quo by the 2017 Treaty on the Prohibition of Nuclear Weapons (TPNW). Previous notions of nuclear responsibility have often been driven by the nuclear-armed states and typically framed as questions of non-proliferation and nuclear restraint. These dominant conceptions of responsibility have been legitimised through the institutions of global nuclear order, most notably the 1968 Treaty on the Non-Proliferation of Nuclear Weapons (the Non-Proliferation Treaty or NPT), which for five decades has been a touchstone for what is understood as responsible state nuclear behaviour. In contrast, the movement behind the TPNW seeks to stigmatise nuclear weapons as unequivocally irresponsible exercises of state sovereignty and to undermine the very idea of a 'responsible' nuclear-armed state.

In this chapter, we begin by outlining some prominent policy discourses surrounding nuclear responsibility since the development of nuclear weapons, identifying the international framework set forth by the NPT, academic debates surrounding the special responsibilities of nuclear powers, as well as some claims to nuclear responsibility made by states themselves. In the second half of the chapter, we canvass some of the main critiques of these dominant conceptions of nuclear responsibility which, taken together, might be thought to cast doubt on whether nuclear weapons can truly be exercised responsibly and to suggest that, by their very nature, they defy our conventional understandings of responsibility in international relations (IR) and political theory. We point to the ways in which critics have viewed nuclear deterrence as undermining liberal-democratic norms and as involving the issuing of immoral threats against civilian populations. We also introduce an emerging avenue of thought, inspired by republican political theory, which suggests that practices of nuclear deterrence curtail the freedom of the world's population at large, even if they are never used. Lastly, we look at ways in which nuclear weapons can be said to create dilemmas and conflicts of responsibilities for states.

Nuclear weapons and state responsibilities

There is a longstanding idea that the immense destructiveness of nuclear weapons creates particular forms of responsibility in the international domain. For instance, when the development of nuclear technology was in its infancy in 1945, the US Secretary of War, Henry Stimson, warned President Truman that US leadership in the development of the atomic bomb 'placed a certain moral responsibility upon us, which we cannot shirk without very serious responsibility for any disaster to civilization which it would further' (in Stimson 1947, np). In this account, the extreme destructiveness of these weapons and the disastrous consequences of their use place exceptional responsibilities on their possessors. This is a common reading of responsibility and nuclear weapons, in which states are the key holders of responsibility, and in which these state responsibilities are differentiated between both nuclear-armed and non-nuclear-armed states, as well as between states of greater and lesser power in the international system.

Institutionalized state nuclear responsibilities

The most notable example of formalised and differentiated state nuclear responsibilities is the NPT, which introduced a regime of nuclear non-proliferation and disarmament responsibilities that have, in practice, resulted in an understanding of difference depending on whether the state signatory is a nuclear weapons state (NWS) or a non-nuclear weapons state (NNWS). For example, Article VI, the most contested part of the Treaty, refers to the obligations of each state party 'to pursue negotiations in good faith on effective measures relating to cessation of the nuclear arms race at an early date and to nuclear disarmament'. However, in practice this is seen as a particular responsibility of the NWS, and one which many NNWS claim that they are failing to uphold (Tannenwald 2013; Müller 2010).

Frustration with this apparently inequitable division of international nuclear responsibilities was one starting point for the emergence of the Treaty on the Prohibition of Nuclear Weapons. Rejecting the unfulfilled promises of gradual disarmament made within the NPT framework, over the past decade a group of states and civil society actors have joined together as part of the Humanitarian Initiative on Nuclear Weapons (HINW) to highlight the catastrophic humanitarian effects of any use of nuclear weapons.[1] The campaign culminated in the TPNW, a prohibition treaty that aims to stigmatise the possession of nuclear weapons by casting them as an unavoidably irresponsible exercise of state sovereignty. This has led to heightened contestation over the meaning of nuclear responsibility. For instance, after 122 states at the United Nations voted to adopt the treaty, the United States, United Kingdom and France released a joint statement in response. These states had boycotted the negotiations and publicly denounced the nuclear ban as undermining international security. In their statement, the three nuclear-armed states cited the 'common responsibility to protect and strengthen our collective security system' (United States et al. 2017) that they claimed would be undermined by the ban as a reason for their boycott, thereby placing themselves as actors whose responsible practices of nuclear deterrence provide international security and stability, while labelling the nuclear ban advocates as irresponsible.

Nuclear weapons, 'special' and 'common' responsibilities

That certain states have larger responsibilities in the realm of nuclear weapons than others fits with the idea of the special responsibilities of great powers discussed in the work of theorists such as Hedley Bull. Bull (1980) gives an account of the special rights, duties and responsibilities of great powers and their role in maintaining global order, claiming that great powers should take the interests of other states into account when making policy and include within their own interests the preservation of international order. For Bull (1980, 446), the role of great powers as 'responsible managers' in the international system should always be open to challenge if these powers do not fulfil their special responsibilities. This approach has been developed in a recent study by a group of prominent IR scholars (Bukovansky et al. 2012), who argue that the assignment of special responsibilities in international politics can be a way of mediating the tension between the principle of sovereign equality and the reality of vastly differential material power between states, and use nuclear weapons as one of their examples. These scholars assert that, while special responsibilities can maintain structures of power and endow certain nuclear states with particular responsibilities for maintaining international order, they are not just reflective of existing power structures but also can attribute special responsibilities to other actors outside of the state and reshape existing power (Bukovansky et al. 2012, 49–50). An example of the assumption that great powers bear a special nuclear responsibility in political discourse can be seen in former US President Barack Obama's speech in Prague in 2009, in which he set out a special responsibility, stating that the United States, 'as the only nuclear power to have used a nuclear weapon … has a moral responsibility to act' towards disarmament (Obama 2009).[2]

Further academic work has engaged with the idea that the destructiveness of nuclear weapon technology places special responsibilities on nuclear-armed states and has attempted to determine what form such responsibilities might take. William Walker (2010) introduced the term 'responsible nuclear sovereignty' as a framework for understanding the responsibilities of nuclear-armed states. The notion of responsible nuclear sovereignty draws on the existing framework of 'responsible sovereignty' (see Feinstein and Slaughter 2004) – which treats sovereignty not as absolute but as conditional on certain fundamental standards and functions that a state must meet and perform – and applies it to the domain of nuclear weapons (Walker 2010, 449). Walker identifies a 'spectrum of views on the responsibility of "nuclear sovereigns"', ranging from the realist position that 'the prime responsibility of a state is to use nuclear deterrence for the protection of itself and its citizens', to the cosmopolitan idea that 'all states have a paramount responsibility to abolish nuclear weapons for ethical and prudential reasons' (Walker 2010, 449). Walker also identifies an 'intermediate position', which asserts that:

> …although 'nuclear sovereigns' have a responsibility to protect themselves and their citizens from attack or intimidation, nuclear weapons must be used politically and militarily with the utmost restraint, and nuclear-armed states have an exceptional duty of care over the capabilities that they have acquired. Furthermore, they have a responsibility to move themselves and others towards nuclear disarmament – to create the conditions in which it can happen safely, verifiably, and without unduly endangering international order.
>
> *(Walker 2010, 449–450)*

Later work by Walker and Nicholas J. Wheeler developed this concept of 'responsible nuclear sovereignty' and suggested it can act as a helpful means of articulating the responsibilities of nuclear-armed states (Walker and Wheeler 2013). Walker and Wheeler (2013, 412) linked the notion of responsible nuclear sovereignty to the 'internal "fitness" of states to engage with nuclear technology', stressing reliability and state capability as key criteria for responsible sovereignty in this domain. The authors suggest that weak states, which are unable to safeguard their nuclear arsenals effectively, will not meet these criteria of responsibility. They therefore claim that 'strong internal governance…must become a *universal* criterion of responsible sovereignty if states and peoples are to be protected from the vicissitudes of state weakness in the nuclear context' (Walker and Wheeler 2013, 428, emphasis in origin The concepts of 'special responsibilities' and 'responsible nuclear sovereignty' both focus, to a large extent, on the nuclear-armed state and its moral and legal obligations. Other work, however, has developed approaches to nuclear responsibility based more on conceptions of shared or common responsibilities. For example, Scott Sagan (2009, 158) has proposed an alternative notion of responsibility for nuclear disarmament that moves away from disarmament as a realm of decision-making solely reserved for the leaders of the nuclear-armed states and towards a 'coordinated global effort of shared responsibilities between NWS and NNWS'. He argues for a rethinking of the responsibilities within the NPT, reminding us that the NNWS states also have responsibilities under Article VI (to deal with disarmament) and that NWS can share the obligations under Article IV (to accept safeguards) that are most associated with the NNWS. In practice, this would mean NWS reaffirming that their nuclear facilities would someday be under safeguard, and perhaps accepting symbolic safeguards on a few sites. The effort would also include an increased shared financial contribution to safeguards inspections by the International Atomic Energy Agency (IAEA), as well as shared funding from all parties in order to develop the necessary technology towards verification that will eventually be needed to ensure disarmament, and a duty on the part of NNWS to go further in ensuring constraints are placed on fuel cycle facilities to reassure NWS about fears of latent weapons programmes that might prevent them from making deep reductions. This approach does well to expand the idea of nuclear responsibility, but it also comes with the assumption that progress towards disarmament is inhibited by mainly technological rather than political issues, and it asks the NNWS to assume further responsibilities in a political environment in which many of these states are already frustrated with what they see as the NWS' non-fulfilment of their basic responsibilities.[3]

Asserting nuclear responsibility

Whether concentrating on the responsibilities of nuclear-armed states or proposing a vision of shared responsibilities across both nuclear and non-nuclear armed states, the 'dominant norms and practices of nuclear responsibility generally centre on varying conceptions of nuclear restraint' (Leveringhaus and Sullivan de Estrada 2018, 486). What form this nuclear restraint takes can vary, and different state actors have often selectively chosen to emphasise different forms of nuclear responsibility. Nuclear-armed states have all described and justified their continuing nuclear weapons activities in terms of their responsible nature and practices. For instance, the United Kingdom has asserted its pivotal role in a 'rules-based order' (Ritchie 2013; Duncanson and Eschle 2008), its practice of minimum deterrence and the fact that it has the smallest arsenal of any NPT nuclear weapon state and only one nuclear weapon system. China stresses the policy of No First Use (Horsburgh 2015; Leveringhaus and Sullivan de Estrada 2018). India highlights its record on non-proliferation (Sasikumar 2007) and the United States has used the language of nuclear stewardship (Taylor 2010) and nuclear security to emphasise the management of fissile materials as a core nuclear responsibility.

These examples all illustrate the deeply political nature of nuclear responsibility. 'Responsibility talk'[4] in the nuclear context, therefore, not only involves recognition of additional duties borne by nuclear-armed states, but 'responsibility' also acts as a label through which states claim their fitness to possess nuclear weapons and through which this fitness can be affirmed or denied by other international actors. For example, at the signing of the US-Indian Civil Nuclear Agreement in 2005, former US President George W. Bush affirmed the United States' acceptance of India into the club of self-proclaimed legitimate nuclear states (if not into the NPT as a nuclear weapon state), declaring India to be a responsible nuclear state (Bush and Singh 2005). Indian Prime Minister Manmohan Singh in turn asserted India's willingness to abide by the practices and assume the responsibilities of states with advanced nuclear technologies. It was thus through the language of responsibility that India staked its claim to the status of legitimate nuclear-armed state (Chacko and Davis 2018; Narlikar 2011; Sasikumar 2007).

As Jan Ruzicka (2018, 381–382) has pointed out, differences in how responsibility is conceived in the nuclear realm – either in terms of the special responsibilities of great power nuclear states to maintain stability through deterrence or as the responsible nature of states that have abandoned or do not seek nuclear weapons – leads to a situation where almost any state can make claims towards responsible behaviour. The political and contested nature of claims to responsible status has been acknowledged by those who have developed the concept of responsible nuclear sovereignty. Several recent writings on this notion, for example, have recognised the possibility that the concept may reinforce, rather than challenge, the nuclear status quo. Walker himself (2010, 451) highlights the 'disconcerting' possibility that states' adherence to norms of responsible nuclear sovereignty 'might become (in part) a pretext for not crossing the threshold into disarmament—rather as alcoholics try to avoid demands to give up drinking by asserting that they are controlling it and generally observing the social graces'. Similarly, a roundtable report published by BASIC acknowledges that:

> the framing of responsible nuclear sovereignty alone does not necessarily imply obligations to disarm and therefore might be used to underpin the status quo. It is conceivable that states could coopt the phrase to justify their continued possession of nuclear weapons in well-managed stockpiles.
>
> *(Brixey-Williams and Ingram 2017, 12)*

As such, those who advocate the promotion of ideas of responsibility within the realm of nuclear weapons are often also aware that this term can be used in many different ways, both as a means of developing understanding and cooperation across both nuclear armed and non-nuclear-armed states, as well as a status and as a justification for the continuance of nuclear arsenals.

This section has provided an overview of some of the various ways in which responsibility has been a means through which global nuclear politics has been theorised and conducted. Nuclear armed states have increasingly used assertions of their responsibility as a means to legitimise their nuclear arsenals, through either promoting specific 'responsible' policies such as no first use, or by emphasising their role as responsible stewards of international security through practices of deterrence. International treaty regimes such as the NPT have ascribed and formalised responsibilities for state parties with regard to the peaceful use of nuclear technology, non-proliferation and disarmament. Yet these responsibilities, particularly regarding the responsibility for disarmament, remain a subject of great contestation and new actors such as the HINW have reasserted the responsibilities and rights of civil society and non-nuclear-armed states to lead on nuclear disarmament. Academic work that has theorised nuclear responsibility is at an earlier stage than research in other issue areas in international politics, but this emerging field has already gained traction in policy discussions at international forums such as the NPT review process. The following sections will turn to literature that has challenged and critiqued the idea of responsibility as a means through which to understand the politics of nuclear weapons.

Critiques of nuclear responsibility

In addition to more specific objections to the distribution of international nuclear responsibilities within global nuclear institutions, several authors have critiqued the use of the concept and the notion that states could be more or less 'responsible' nuclear actors. This section sets out three different challenges to the nuclear responsibility project. The first is based on a postcolonial critique of the idea of responsibility as a form of colonial governance, the second provides a structural realist rejoinder to the idea of differentiated types of nuclear state, and the third sets out empirical material that contests the idea of a responsible acceptance of nuclear risks and dangers.

Literature across IR, postcolonial studies and anthropology has critiqued the power structures and imbalances at play in the use of responsibility in the realm of nuclear weapons and its link to western ideas of 'standards of civilisation'. Work such as that of Hugh Gusterson (1999) and Shampa Biswas (2014) questions the orientalist assumptions of a feminised 'third world' which is portrayed as comprising of potentially less responsible nuclear actors in contrast to more 'reasonable' and 'responsible' nuclear states. The use of ideas of rationality and reasonability within the literature on responsibility can smuggle in ethnocentric assumptions. For example, Walker and Wheeler (2013, 415) link responsible nuclear sovereignty to what they term 'reasonable behaviour'. Himadeep Muppidi (2005, 281) critiques the idea of reasonable behaviour by arguing that what he terms 'colonial governance' assumes the inherent reasonableness of some actors while questioning that of others. He argues that the United States' acceptance of India as a 'responsible' nuclear state in 2005 amounted to the welcoming of India into a colonial order that it had previously challenged (see also Chacko and Davis 2018). Responsibility is also an example of what Ritu Mathur (2016, 59) has identified as the practice of 'sly civility', which for Mathur contributes to the maintenance of the 'nuclear order with its practices of inclusion and exclusion and the West's efforts to control the narrative of nuclear arms control and disarmament'.

From a different perspective, Kenneth Waltz has also challenged the idea of more or less responsible nuclear armed states. For Waltz (in Sagan and Waltz 2013), the distribution of responsibility within the international system rests with the distribution of power and the nature of polarity. Within Waltz's self-help model of international politics, war becomes less likely as its costs increase and, as nuclear weapons threaten the ultimate cost of complete destruction, the likelihood of war decreases with the spread of nuclear weapons. This is independent of the nature of the nuclear state as the 'effect of having nuclear weapons overwhelms the character of the states that possess them' (Sagan and Waltz 2013, 224) so that states of any sort that have nuclear weapons are highly incentivised to use them in a responsible way. Waltz instead dismisses the notion of more or less responsible new nuclear weapons states as exhibiting an 'imperialistic manner' and challenges the speculation that 'takes the place of evidence' in 'ethnocentric views' about non-western states and nuclear weapons (Sagan and Waltz 2013, 14).

A final challenge to the notion of responsible nuclear statehood comes from literature that argues that nuclear weapons carry inherent dangers that no amount of responsible behaviour can mitigate (Borrie and Caughley 2014). This literature points to the grave risk of global devastation and the potential for 'omnicide' (Craig 2003, xvii) that thermonuclear weapons have introduced to international politics, as well as the history of nuclear near-misses (Lewis et al. 2014), the danger of accidents and miscalculation, and the underappreciated role of luck in past nuclear crises (Pelopidas 2017). The catastrophic consequences of any nuclear explosion have been a focus of the HINW. At three international conferences between 2013 and 2014 on the 'Humanitarian Impact of Nuclear Weapons' in Norway, Mexico and Austria civil society and state representatives were presented with expert testimony on the effects of nuclear weapons on health, the environment, food security, migration and the economy. The findings of these conferences led to the adoption of the TPNW in 2017, which entered into force on 22 January 2021 and states that 'the catastrophic consequences of nuclear weapons cannot be adequately addressed, transcend national borders, pose grave implications for human survival, the environment, socioeconomic development, the global economy, food security and the health of current and future generations' (Treaty on the Prohibition of Nuclear Weapons 2017). These harms are not confined to the use of a nuclear weapon in conflict, given that nuclear testing and the maintenance of nuclear arsenals has caused environmental despoliation and damaging health effects, often with disproportionate effects on indigenous and colonised peoples (Unal et al. 2017; Ruff 2015). While nuclear risk reduction and responsible practices concerning the management and security of fissionable materials can significantly lower the risks posed by nuclear arsenals (see Morgan and Williams 2018), it is also important to recognise that these risks cannot be eliminated by even the most responsible nuclear sovereign.

The *ir*responsibilities of nuclear sovereignty

While both scholars and political actors have stressed the need for practices of responsibility in the nuclear domain, in ways which have been subjected to critique, other work poses a more radical challenge to notions of nuclear responsibility, by either implicitly or explicitly suggesting that the possession of nuclear weapons entails some inherent further *ir*responsibilities, however responsibly they may be managed in other ways. Whereas it is uncontroversial that the effects of an actual detonation of nuclear weapons would be an act of extreme irresponsibility, given the large-scale violation of the right to life that such an act would entail and the inability of such weapons to discriminate between combatants and civilians (Thakur 2016, 290), there are arguments suggesting that the mere presence of nuclear weapons in the international system involves some serious irresponsibility. As this section explains, arguments have been made which suggest that states' bare possession of nuclear weapons for deterrent purposes subvert their liberal-democratic character, irresponsibly involve an immoral posture towards other states, and curtail the freedom of the world's population even if they are never in fact used. Each line of thought will be outlined in turn.

Undermining liberal democracy

One argument which suggests an inherent irresponsibility associated with practices of nuclear deterrence is that such practices are incompatible with liberal-democratic governance and weaken states' ability to secure freedom for their citizens. Daniel Deudney, for instance, has suggested that 'nuclear weapons generate a profound *legitimacy deficit*' for states in general, but particularly for liberal states (Deudney 1995, 91–92; 102, emphasis in original). Deudney suggests that, if state legitimacy depends on its ability to offer security to its citizens, then this is 'fundamentally challenged' by the presence of nuclear weapons in the international system. If physical security (as a lack of physical interference) is understood as a precondition for individual freedom, then the advent of the nuclear age has stripped states of the capacity to secure their citizens' freedom. This then has an effect on the legitimacy of state institutions that the state manages through '*nuclear reclusion*' (Deudney 1995, 102) (i.e. practices obscuring the implications of nuclear weapons from society by keeping them from public view)[5] and '*declaratory anti-nuclearism*', which consists of publicly espousing anti-nuclear and disarmament rhetoric.

In addition to undermining the legitimacy of the state, nuclear weapons can also be said to undermine democratic governance in particular. While certain liberal authors such as Rawls (1999, 9) have claimed that nuclear weapons can be compatible with the norms of liberal democracy, Henry Shue (2004, 140) has argued that there is a deep tension between the commitment to the individual human being as 'the unit of ultimate value' within liberalism and the possession of nuclear weapons. Others, such as Deudney, claim that they are 'inherently despotic' for three reasons: 'the speed of nuclear use decisions, the concentration of the nuclear use decision into the hands of one individual, and the lack of accountability stemming from the inability of affected groups to have their interests represented at the moment of nuclear use' (Deudney 2007, 255; see also Taylor 2007, 671–672).

Relatedly, Elaine Scarry claims that nuclear weapons are irreconcilable not just with democracy but also with a wider and older idea of public consent. Populations cannot be consulted on the choice to use nuclear weapons and this lack of consent, combined with the pain it inflicts, associates nuclear conflict more with a 'mode of torture' than a mode of war (Scarry 1985, 151). She therefore claims that consent in nuclear war is 'a structural impossibility' (Scarry 1985, 152), and in later work points to a situation of 'thermonuclear monarchy' (Scarry 2014). Overall, then, to the extent that states have a responsibility to maintain or create liberal-democratic institutions which respect their citizens' freedom, the operation of nuclear deterrents can be said to undermine this goal.

Hostage-holding and immoral threats

An earlier wave of philosophical work in nuclear ethics centred around the 1980s identified and debated ways in which practices of nuclear deterrence may involve irresponsibly making immoral threats.[6] As Thomas Doyle (2010, 290) has summarised, when using nuclear deterrence 'officials must regard targeted peoples as mere pawns in the strategic chess game and hostages to state security policy rather than individuals with human rights and dignity'. In this vein, Paul Ramsey (1968, 171) famously compared nuclear deterrence to a policy of strapping babies to the bumpers of cars in order to reduce traffic accidents, given that it involves exposing innocent parties to great risk, while others have debated the moral significance of the fact that nuclear deterrence requires states to form an intention to act wrongfully (see e.g. Kavka 1978). More specifically, Steven Lee has argued that nuclear deterrence involves a form of unjustified hostage-holding. For Lee (1985, 553), if hostages are understood as 'persons threatened with harm without their consent in order to control the behaviour of some other person or group', and the act of holding hostages is wrong given their innocence and the risk of harm imposed on them without their consent, then nuclear deterrence involves this form of hostage-holding, for such deterrence wrongfully aims to control the behaviour of another state's leaders by threatening the wider population. Insofar as states bear a responsibility not to form immoral intentions and to engage in immoral behaviour, this line of thought runs, they have a responsibility to avoid engaging in practices of nuclear deterrence.

Subjection to arbitrary power

Arguments against nuclear deterrence that involve analogies with hostages and babies on car bumpers can be questioned because, unlike in the case of babies strapped to the front of cars, those 'held hostage' by nuclear weapons do not seem to have their liberty directly curtailed, at least not as commonly understood (see Lee 1985, 555), but are instead able to continue to lead their personal lives even under the shadow of this deterrence. However, one emerging line of argument draws on republican political theory developed by theorists such as Philip Pettit (1997) to suggest that there is a meaningful sense in which the liberty of the world's population is constrained by practices of nuclear deterrence, even in the absence of any physical interference akin to that suffered by the babies on the bumpers (Considine and Souter 2018). While *some* aspects of nuclear weapons *can* be seen as interfering in the lives and interests of some of the world's population – such as those communities harmed by the environmental effects of nuclear weapons programmes – there is also a case to be made that nuclear weapons irresponsibly violate the freedom of the world's population, whether or not they and their interests are tangibly affected by nuclear weapons, or those weapons cause them any felt harm.

Briefly, republican political theory aims to offer a conception of freedom that is distinct from a liberal conception. Whereas liberal theorists often conceive of freedom in terms of non-interference, republicans instead view it in terms of freedom from *domination*, which is defined as subjection to the arbitrary will of others. A frequent example used to explain the difference between the liberal and republican conceptions is the situation of a slave whose master refrains from interference in the slave's life (Lovett 2018). On the liberal conception of freedom, the slave does not seem to be unfree, as long as no interference takes place. But on the republican conception of freedom, even in the absence of any interference by the slave-owner, the slave is still fundamentally unfree by virtue of being subjected to his arbitrary will; she is dominated even if she is not interfered with.

A republican-inspired critique of nuclear deterrence applies this idea to nuclear weapons. Nuclear weapons may not interfere in the lives of many of the world's population at all and, as such, cannot be considered to violate freedom understood in liberal terms unless the weapons are used or their maintenance causes harm to certain individuals, for instance, through environmental despoliation. In contrast, a case can be made that the very existence of nuclear weapons means that the world's population remains dominated – that is, subjected to the arbitrary will of others – on an indefinite basis. As critics such as Deudney point out, decision-making power over nuclear arsenals is concentrated in state executives with little or no democratic oversight, allowing for potentially arbitrary and democratically unconstrained nuclear policy. Much like the slave in the example in at least one respect, for as long as nuclear weapons are not used, the world's population does not suffer interference, but is still dominated nevertheless. For republican theorists at least, and anyone convinced by the republican conception of freedom, this kind of domination constitutes an irresponsible action.

Conflicting nuclear responsibilities

If some or all of the above arguments are accepted, it may nevertheless be thought that, while nuclear deterrence involves some forms of inherent irresponsibility, there are some opposing responsibilities held by states, which may lead them to *maintain* their nuclear arsenals, namely the responsibility to secure their population against external attack. For instance, Rawls (1999, 9) has, in passing, claimed that 'so long as there are outlaw states…some nuclear weapons need to be retained to keep those states at bay and to make sure they do not obtain and use those weapons against liberal or decent peoples'. For those willing to accept that the state has a responsibility to secure itself through nuclear deterrence, a situation of conflicting responsibilities and moral dilemmas may seem to follow. In particular, Thomas Doyle (2013) has elaborated on particular dilemmas that nuclear deterrence can be said to engender. For example, returning to the arguments put forward by Deudney and Scarry concerning the subversive effect of nuclear deterrence on the liberal-democratic character of the state, and the ability of the state to secure its population's freedom on which its legitimacy depends, Doyle (2013, 160) observes a dilemma, insofar as:

> the requirement to secure liberal democracy from external nuclear threats obliges two incompatible courses of action. One is to deter nuclear aggression effectively *via* nuclear deterrence and the despotism with which it comes. The other is to preserve liberal constitutionalism from the threat of outlaw states.

In other words, for Doyle (2013, 160), 'the rule of securing constitutional democracy requires the subversion of the very devices that comprise it'. More generally, Doyle (2015, 20) points to a moral tension involving nuclear weapons, whereby 'cosmopolitan or universal moral principle obliges states to always choose nuclear avoidance while the "morality of states" or the morality of nationalism can oblige states to do whatever is necessary to realize national security or grandeur'. While the existence of these conflicts of responsibility depends on the belief that nuclear weapons are genuinely necessary to ensure the security of states' citizens, and that states have a responsibility to pursue national 'grandeur', such work highlights the ways in which notions of nuclear responsibility fit within larger understandings of international responsibility, potentially creating conflicts and dilemmas with them.

Conclusion

In this chapter, we have outlined some of the contemporary discourse surrounding nuclear responsibility in political rhetoric, international law and academic debate, and have introduced some critiques of this discourse. Overall, nuclear weapons might be seen as posing a deep challenge to conventional understandings of responsibility in world politics, given the unprecedented threat they pose to both state and human security. If, as Hans Jonas (1984) has argued, technological change in the modern world in general necessitates a rethinking of the nature of ethics and responsibility, it would be unsurprising if the presence of nuclear weapons on the world stage also required this kind of radical reconsideration of concepts of responsibility which originated in the pre-nuclear age (compare chapter by Baron in this volume). Given the threat they pose, we might also question whether the term 'nuclear responsibility' should ultimately be seen as oxymoronic, for some of the reasons outlined in the last sections of this chapter. This survey of notions and practices of nuclear responsibility raises questions pertinent to our understanding of responsibility in international politics more broadly: can notions of responsibility regulate state power in a domain where there is a lack of direct enforcement of international norms? Even if we accept theoretical arguments around responsibility in this context, how will these notions fare in the hands of states in the course of real-life international politics? In the specific case of nuclear responsibility, the ultimate question might be how far notions of responsibility can prevent global catastrophe.

Notes

1 Prominent actors involved in the process have included states such as Austria, Brazil, Ireland, Mexico, New Zealand and South Africa, and civil society organisations such as the International Committee of the Red Cross and the International Campaign to Abolish Nuclear Weapons (ICAN).
2 Obama's presidency saw an intensification of the discourse of responsibility relating to nuclear weapons in the United States (Chacko and Davis 2018). This was linked in particular to the administration's focus on issues of nuclear security and the conception of nuclear responsibility as secure management of nuclear materials and preventing nuclear terrorism. The focus on nuclear security and on responsibility diminished under the Trump administration.
3 Within the nuclear policy world, moreover, the idea of shared nuclear responsibilities has been proposed recently as a framework through which to promote dialogue and cooperation in an era of increasing tensions and division. For example, the 2019 NPT Preparatory Committee held a side event hosted by the British American Security Information Council (BASIC) on 'Foregrounding Nuclear Responsibilities for Nuclear Risk Reduction and Disarmament', with representatives from Malaysia, Japan, Australia and the United Kingdom. For further information on BASIC's 'nuclear responsibilities' project see https://www.basicint.org/portfolio/nuclear-responsibilities/
4 For analysis of 'responsibility talk' in world politics, see Bukovansky et al. (2012).

5 Indeed, much has been written about nuclear secrecy (Kinsella 2005), the prevalence of 'nukespeak' (Chilton 1982, 1985; Schiappa 1989) and use of acronyms, technical jargon and arcane language (Cohn 1987) which has discouraged public participation to obscure the terms of debate and discourage public participation in broader issues of maintaining and developing nuclear arsenals.

6 For a more recent overview of these debates, see Doyle (2010).

References

Biswas, S. (2014) *Nuclear Desire: Power and the Postcolonial Nuclear Order*. Minneapolis: University of Minnesota Press.

Borrie, J., and Caughley, T. (2014). *An Illusion of Safety: Challenges of Nuclear Weapon Detonations for United Nations Humanitarian Coordination and Response*. Geneva: United Nations Institute for Disarmament Research.

Brixey-Williams, S., and Ingram, P. (2017). *Responsible Nuclear Sovereignty and the Future of the Global Nuclear Order*. London: British American Security Information Council (BASIC) and the Institute for Conflict, Cooperation and Security, University of Birmingham.

Bukovansky, M. Clark, I. Eckersley, R. Price, R. Reus-Smit, C., and Wheeler, N. (2012). *Special Responsibilities: Global Problems and American Power*. Cambridge: Cambridge University Press.

Bull, H. (1980). "The Great Irresponsibles? The United States, the Soviet Union, and World Order." *International Journal*, 35(3): 437–447.

Bush, G., and Singh, M. (2005). "Joint Statement by President George W. Bush and Prime Minister Manmohan Singh of India, July 18, 2005." https://2001-2009.state.gov/p/sca/rls/pr/2005/49763.htm

Chacko, P., and Davis, A. E. (2018). "Resignifying 'Responsibility': India, Exceptionalism and Nuclear Non-proliferation." *Asian Journal of Political Science*, 26(3): 352–370.

Chilton, P. (1982). *Nukespeak: The Media and the Bomb*. London: Comedia.

Chilton, P. (1985). *Language and the Nuclear Arms Debate: Nukespeak Today*. London: Frances Pinter.

Cohn, C. (1987). "Sex and Death in the Rational World of Defense Intellectuals." *Signs: Journal of Women in Culture and Society*, 12(4): 687–718.

Considine, L., and Souter, J. (2018). "The Irresponsibility of Nuclear Sovereignty." Presentation at the Annual British International Studies Association Conference, Bath, June.

Craig, C. (2003). *Glimmer of a New Leviathan: Total War in the Realism of Niebuhr, Morgenthau and Waltz*. New York, Chichester: Columbia University Press.

Deudney, D. (1995). "Political Fission: State Structure, Civil Society and Nuclear Weapons in the United States." In Lipschutz, R., ed., *On Security*: 87–124. New York, Chichester: Columbia University Press.

Deudney, D. (2007). *Bounding Power: Republican Security Theory from the Polis to the Global Village*. Princeton, NJ: Princeton University Press.

Doyle, T. E. (2010). "Reviving Nuclear Ethics: A Renewed Research Agenda for the Twenty-First Century." *Ethics & International Affairs*, 24(3): 287–308.

Doyle, T. E. (2013). "Liberal Democracy and Nuclear Despotism: Two Ethical Foreign Policy Dilemmas." *Ethics and Global Politics*, 6(3): 155–174.

Doyle, T. E. (2015). *The Ethics of Nuclear Weapons Dissemination: Moral Dilemmas of Aspiration, Avoidance and Prevention*. London and New York: Routledge.

Duncanson, C., and Eschle, C. (2008). "Gender and the Nuclear Weapons State: A Feminist Critique of the UK Government's White Paper on Trident." *New Political Science*, 30(4): 545–563.

Feinstein, L., and Slaughter, A.-E. (2004). "A Duty to Prevent." *Foreign Affairs*, 83: 136–151.

Gusterson, H. (1999). "Nuclear Weapons and the Other in the Western Imagination." *Cultural Anthropology*, 14(1): 111–143.

Horsburgh, N. (2015). *China and Global Nuclear Order: From Estrangement to Active Engagement*. Oxford: Oxford University Press.

Jonas, H. (1984). *The Imperative of Responsibility: In Search of an Ethics for the Technological Age*. Chicago and London: The University of Chicago Press.

Kavka, G. (1978). "Some Paradoxes of Deterrence." *Journal of Philosophy*, 75(6): 285–302.

Kinsella, W. J. (2005). "One Hundred Years of Nuclear Discourse: Four Master Themes and their Implications for Environmental Communication." In Senecah, S., ed., *Environmental Communication Yearbook Volume 2*. Mahwah, NJ: Erlbaum.

Lee, S. (1985). "The Morality of Nuclear Deterrence: Hostage Holding and Consequences." *Ethics*, 95(3): 549–566.
Leveringhaus, N., and Sullivan De Estrada, K. (2018). "Between Conformity and Innovation: China's and India's Quest for Status as Responsible Nuclear Powers." *Review of International Studies*, 44(3): 482–503.
Lewis, P., Williams, H., Pelopidas, B., and Aghlani, S. (2014). *Too Close for Comfort: Cases of Near Nuclear Use and Options for Policy.* Chatham House Report. https://www.chathamhouse.org/sites/files/chathamhouse/field/field_document/20140428TooCloseforComfortNuclearUseLewisWilliamsPelopidasAghlani.pdf
Lovett, F. (2018). "Republicanism." *The Stanford Encyclopedia of Philosophy* https://plato.stanford.edu/archives/sum2018/entries/republicanism/ (accessed August 22, 2018).
Mathur, R. (2016). "Sly civility and the paradox of equality/inequality in the nuclear order: a post-colonial critique." *Critical Studies on Security*, 4(1): 57–72.
Morgan, A., and Williams, H. (2018). *A New Framework to Assess U.S. and Russian Behaviour Euro-Atlantic Policy Brief*, The European Leadership Network June 2018. https://www.europeanleadershipnetwork.org/wp-content/uploads/2018/06/ELN-Policy-Brief-Nuclear-Responsibility-A-New-Framework-to-Assess-US-and-Russian-Behavior.pdf
Müller, H. (2010). "Between Power and Justice: Current Problems and Perspectives of the NPT Regime." *Strategic Analysis*, 34(2): 189–201.
Muppidi, H. (2005). "Colonial and Postcolonial Global Governance." In Barnett, M., and Duvall, R., eds., *Power in Global Governance*. Cambridge: Cambridge University Press.
Narlikar, A. (2011). "Is India a responsible great power?" *Third World Quarterly*, 32(9): 1607–1621.
Obama, B. (2009). *Remarks by President Obama in Prague As Delivered, April 5th 2009.* obamawhitehouse.archives.gov/the-press-office/remarks-president-barack-obama-prague-delivered
Pelopidas, B. (2017). "The Unbearable Lightness of Luck. Three Sources of Overconfidence in the Manageability of Nuclear Crises." *European Journal of International Security*, 2(2): 240–262.
Pettit, P. (1997). *Republicanism: A Theory of Freedom and Government*. Oxford: Clarendon Press.
Ramsey, P. (1968). *The Just War: Force and Political Responsibility*. Lanham, MD and Oxford: Rowman and Littlefield.
Rawls, J. (1999). *The Law of Peoples, with "The Idea of Public Reason Revisited"*. Cambridge, Massachusetts and London: Harvard University Press.
Ritchie, N. (2013). "Valuing and Devaluing Nuclear Weapons." *Contemporary Security Policy*, 34(1): 146–173.
Ruff, T. A. (2015). "The Humanitarian Impact and Implications of Nuclear Test Explosions in the Pacific Region." *International Review of the Red Cross*, 97(899): 775–813.
Ruzicka, J. (2018). "Behind the Veil of Good Intentions: Power Analysis of the Nuclear Non-Proliferation Regime." *International Politics*, 55(3–4): 369–385.
Scarry, E. (1985). *The Body in Pain: The Making and Unmaking of the World*. Oxford: Oxford University Press.
Scarry, E. (2014). *Thermonuclear Monarchy: Choosing Between Democracy and Doom*. New York and London: W.W. Norton & Company.
Sagan, S. D. (2009). "Shared Responsibilities for Nuclear Disarmament." *Daedalus*, 138(4): 157–168.
Sagan, S. D., and Waltz, K. (2013). *The Spread of Nuclear Weapons: An Enduring Debate*. New York: W.W. Norton & Company.
Sasikumar, K. (2007). "India's Emergence as a 'Responsible' Nuclear Power." *International Journal*, 62(4): 825–844.
Schiappa, E. (1989). "The Rhetoric of Nukespeak." *Communication Monographs*, 56(3): 253–272.
Shue, H. (2004). "Liberalism: The Impossibility of Justifying Weapons of Mass Destruction." In Sohail, H. H., and Lee, S. P., eds., *Ethics and Weapons of Mass Destruction: Religious and Secular Perspectives*: 139–162. Cambridge: Cambridge University Press.
Stimson, H. (1947). "The Decision to Use the Atomic Bomb", *Harper's Magazine*, 194(1161).
Tannenwald, N. (2013). "Justice and Fairness in the Nuclear Nonproliferation Regime." *Ethics & International Affairs*, 27(3): 299–317.
Taylor, B. C. (2007). "'The Means to Match their Hatred': Nuclear Weapons, Rhetorical Democracy, and Presidential Discourse." *Presidential Studies Quarterly*, 37(4): 667–692.
Taylor, B. C. (2010). "A Hedge Against the Future: The Post-Cold War Rhetoric of Nuclear Weapons Modernization." *Quarterly Journal of Speech*, 96(1): 1–24.
Thakur, R. (2016). "The Ethical Imperatives and Means to Nuclear Peace." *Peace Review*, 28(3): 288–295.
Treaty on the Prohibition of Nuclear Weapons (2017). Full text available at https://www.un.org/disarmament/wmd/nuclear/tpnw/

Unal, B., Lewis, P., and Aghlani, S. (2017). "The Humanitarian Impacts of Nuclear Testing Regional Responses and Mitigation Measures", Chatham House Research Paper. https://www.chathamhouse.org/sites/files/chathamhouse/publications/research/2017-05-08-HINT.pdf.

United States, United Kingdom, France (2017). *Joint Press Statement from the Permanent Representatives to the United Nations of the United States, United Kingdom, and France Following the Adoption of a Treaty Banning Nuclear Weapons, July 7, 2017* https://onu.delegfrance.org/Adoption-of-a-treaty-banning-nuclear-weapons

Walker, W. (2010). "The UK, Threshold Status and Responsible Nuclear Sovereignty." *International Affairs*, 86(2): 447–464.

Walker, W., and Wheeler, N. J. (2013). "The Problem of Weak Nuclear States." *The Nonproliferation Review*, 20(3): 411–431.

13
DELEGATING MORAL RESPONSIBILITY IN WAR

Lethal autonomous weapons systems and the responsibility gap

Elke Schwarz

Introduction

> If we use, to achieve our purposes, a mechanical agency with whose operation we cannot efficiently interfere once we have started it, because the action is so fast and so irrevocable that we have not the data to intervene before the action is complete, then we better be quite sure that the purpose put into the machine is the purpose which we really desire and not merely a colourful imitation of it.
>
> *Norbert Wiener (1960)*

In 1960, one of the pioneers of cybernetics and a crucial figure in the advent of Artificial Intelligence (AI), Norbert Wiener, articulated a concern which would become one of the key points for debate on Lethal Autonomous Weapons Systems (LAWS) more than half a century later: What happens to our ability to control the actions and outcomes of technologies which we endow with an agency of their own? As militaries around the globe place increased importance on investing in greater levels of technological autonomy and military-grade AI, the prospect of being able to outsource the process of identifying, selecting, and attacking a target to an intricate autonomous weapon system is, at the time of writing, on the near horizon. The United States Department of Defense (DoD), for example, is investing heavily in technologies that increasingly harness new advances in AI technologies for military purposes. The 2019 Budget Request indicates an increase in spending for autonomy and AI related projects by 81%, suggesting that the relevance of AI-enabled weapons system is likely to grow exponentially in the near future (Gettinger 2018). In February 2019, the US Army released a solicitation for sources that would provide support for the Advanced Targeting and Lethality Automated System (ATLAS) program. The aim for this call for input is to "leverage recent advances in computer vision and Artificial Intelligence/Machine Learning (AI/ML) to develop autonomous targeting acquisition technology that will be integrated with fire control technology" with the aim to equip ground vehicles with the capacity to "acquire, identify, and engage targets" at three times the speed of present processes (Department of the Army, 2019). The US are not the only ones investing heavily in AI – China, Russia, France, and the UK are all prioritizing AI enabled warfare strategies (Beck et al. 2019). Where increasing levels of control are attributed to algorithmic systems and related technologies – today's equivalent of Wiener's above referenced mechanical agency – there are justified concerns about whether this might affect the possibility for taking moral and legal responsibility for acts of violence in future warfare.

Moral and legal frameworks for legitimate and appropriate conduct in war (*jus in bello*) are constituted through the Just War Tradition more broadly and are encapsulated in the stipulations of international law, in particular International Humanitarian Law (IHL). Both the moral foundations and the legal frameworks have as a rationale and core aim the limitation of the atrocities of war and the protection of the innocent. For this, the principles of proportionality and distinction are paramount. The principle of proportionality requires that the damage inflicted through an act of violence be in proportion to the military aim. Excessive use of force, excessive harm, or damage to civilians and civilian objects are not permitted under this principle, and a military commander or operator must be judicious in evaluating whether an action is proportional to the potential military advantages gained. Proportionality is widely understood "to involve distinctively human judgment" of common sense and reasonable military standards (Heyns 2013, 14). The principle of distinction stipulates that civilians and other nonlegitimate targets of war and combatants must clearly be differentiated. Civilians and non-combatants must not be targeted as such and combatants who have surrendered their weapons of war are no longer legitimate targets of war. The principle of distinction also extends to civilian objects and institutions. In asymmetric warfare differentiating between civilian and combatant targets often becomes a difficult task, which, like proportionality, requires a conscientious and knowledgeable commander or operative to avoid violations. These are the fundamental rules to govern the conduct of war and ensure restraint in the use of force. When violations occur, "individual and state responsibility is fundamental to ensure accountability for violations of international human rights and international humanitarian law" (Ibid.). Without attributable responsibility and accountability, Heyns, notes, "deterrence and prevention are reduced, resulting in lower protection of civilians and potential victims of war crimes" (Ibid.). In other words, having clear lines of responsibility is crucial to limiting war, protecting the innocent, and providing a basis for the possibility of justice and peace. Without responsibility, restraint in war is made less likely. Where new technologies render these lines of responsibility diffuse, blurry, or irrelevant, the worry is that a more extensive use of force becomes the norm and restraint in war is shifted to the margins. A decade of drone warfare has given grounds for such worries; weapon systems with increasing autonomy are the next iteration in the technological advancement of war.

This chapter engages with the complexities of assigning and taking responsibility in war when autonomous weapons systems are involved that have the capacity to make morally relevant decisions in the conduct of conflict. At stake in the debates on autonomous weapons systems, especially those that have lethal capacities, is whether the human can exert adequate levels of control over weapon systems that are capable of selecting and engaging targets autonomously, in line with traditional theories of responsibility. The advent of new complex and distributed technologies of autonomy, especially those that employ advanced modes of machine learning and deep neural networks, challenges conceptions of the human as knowledgeable and free moral agent, acting with intent in the conduct of warfare. This challenge to human agency and control has consequences not only for legal responsibility and accountability in war but also changes parameters for taking moral responsibility for lethal acts in warfare. This chapter begins with a brief overview of the technological capacities in question and some of the key positions in the debates on LAWS. It then addresses the potential for responsibility gaps in the use of autonomous intelligent weapons systems and examines where viable loci for legal responsibility might reside, whether that is with the programmer, commander, operator, or indeed the machine itself and argues that the characteristics of the technology itself pose a considerable challenge to our conventional understanding of lines of responsibility. The chapter closes with a brief discussion on how the concept of "meaningful human control," as put forward by civil society groups, might work to ensure that the use of lethal technologies "will not slip from human control" (Jasanoff 2016, 29) in legal terms, but may not adequately help foster moral competencies in the conduct of war.

The "Killer Robots" debate

As militaries around the globe are seeking to harness the benefits of new developments in artificial intelligence, debates about so-called Killer Robots and how to restrict their development and use gain in urgency and intensity. These discussions are often marred by technological complexities, contested definitions and hardened speculative positions on either side of the dialogue. The arguments put forward in many ways echo the drone debates, with proponents pointing toward the ostensibly more humane and efficient effects of new technological means, while critics raise questions about a lowered threshold for violence and the transfer of risk to targeted civilian populations. Unlike with drone warfare, however, with LAWS the levels of autonomous action by the machine in relation to any human operator in-, on-, or out of the loop are considerably amplified.

Autonomy in military weapons systems is not a new development, but it has made significant strides in the past decade. At the time of writing, seven countries, including the US, the UK, France, Israel, China, Russia, and South Korea, are in the process of developing autonomous weapon systems with lethal capacities (Beck et al., 2019). (Lethal) autonomous weapons systems are broadly defined as weapons systems "with autonomy in [their] *critical function* – that is, a weapon system that can select (search for, detect, identify, track or select) and attack (use force against, neutralize, damage or destroy) targets without human intervention" (International Committee of the Red Cross 2016).[1] This focus on the autonomous decision for the release of force – the so-called *critical function* – is at the heart of discussions. It is not autonomy in functions such as take-off and landing, navigation, or other non-targeting processes that is of primary concern to critics, but it is first and foremost autonomy in the "determination about the release of force" that stands at the center of the controversies (Heyns, 2016, 4).

Autonomy in technology is, in simple terms, "the ability of a machine to execute a task, or tasks, without human input, using interactions of computer programming with the environment" (Boulain and Verbruggen 2017, 5).[2] Paul Scharre distinguishes between different degrees of autonomy in military systems: a semi-autonomous operation where the human remains embedded in the action loop; a supervised autonomous operation, where the machine "can sense, decide and act on its own, but the human user can observe the machine's behavior and intervene to stop it, if desired" (Scharre 2018, 29). A system operates fully autonomously when no human is involved in the steps from sensing to taking action, here, the human is out of the loop. Whichever the relation of the human to the respective machine, technological autonomy is always constituted "by the integration of the same three fundamental capabilities: sense, decide and act" (Boulain and Verbruggen 2017, 7).

Unlike an automated system, which follows a set of simple if/then/else rules, an autonomous system works on the basis of probabilistic reason – it makes "guesses about best possible courses of action given sensor data input." (Cummings 2017, 3) This requires the system to gather sensory data input about the environment from which the system learns and within which, or upon which, the system operates, to form a "world model," so that incoming information can be processed through optimization and verification algorithms toward a decision and a subsequent action. This means that autonomous weapons, including LAWS, are always already of a systemic nature: they require an alliance of weapons capabilities in terms of material hardware and its necessary material correlates, and the computational capability in terms of software systems and networks to make sense of and act upon their environment.

The more complex the real-world environment, the more computational capability, volumes of data, sophistication of algorithms, and sheer processing power are required for the system to map out a world model with adequate fidelity and make a probabilistic evaluation for what might be the best course of action. The intricate and dynamic relationship between pre-set analytical structures, conditional assumptions and training data, and perpetually new input data from complex external environments by which a system "learns," means that "the system will on occasion follow pathways that are unpredictable due to the constant slippage between data and the context" (Jain 2016, 307).

This is particularly pertinent in the context of recent advancements in neural networks and machine learning algorithms, which operate beyond the capacity of the engineer to conceptualize the computational process of the neural network technology. As David Gunkel notes: "we now have [AI systems] that are deliberately designed to exceed our control and our ability to respond or answer for them" (Gunkel 2019, 60). Consider, for example, the self-learning capacity of the AlphaGo AI System[3]. Programmers and engineers for AlphaGo are willing (and able) to take responsibility for the system's actions only up to a certain point, as one of the programmers explains: "We just create the data sets and the training algorithms. But the moves it then comes up with are out of our hands" (Metz 2016). The system is, deliberately, designed to "do things that their programmers cannot anticipate or completely control" (Gunkel 2019, 58). Embedded in a technological system of AI decisions and virtualized interfaces, the human operator is no longer fully able to simply operate the machine in accordance with the manufacturer's specifications and directions, nor may the commanding officer have sufficient knowledge of the system's cognitive operations. In other words, the human programmer, commander, or operator might stipulate a particular goal for an autonomous system, but the computational basis on which the system decides on how to achieve the goal – "the internal cognitive processes" – is not always intelligible to the user (Scharre 2018, 31).

As with most technological advances, greater autonomy in weapons systems holds the promise of substantial advantages in warfare, on the one hand, while it also poses considerable challenges, on the other. Advocates of greater autonomy in military weapons systems stress that such systems offer substantial benefits for militaries in taking soldiers out of harm's way, lowering the cost of combat and holding the promise of significant advantages over enemies through efficiency and speed. The moral case advanced for LAWS often includes the argument that their superior capabilities might result not only in fewer deaths of military personnel but might also minimize civilian causalities and reduce friendly fire (Scharre 2018, 274). What is more, it is argued, LAWS take the sometimes erratic and unpredictable human element out of the equation: machines don't suffer from emotional unpredictability or psychological instability and are therefore able to make more clear-headed decisions in the fog of war (Arkin 2009, 7; 2010, 333–4). Other arguments put forth suggest that LAWS could more reliably be programmed to uphold the laws of war and thus reduce wars' dependence on human beings, whose "virtues" are always offset by "moral frailties" (Anderson and Waxman 2013, 15). Consequently, these capacities, if developed adequately and reliably, might make LAWS a more humane instrument in the messy conduct of warfare, so much so, that the use of such weapons systems might even become ethically mandated (Ackerman 2015; Umbrello et al. 2020).

Critics of LAWS and proponents of an international ban for the development and use of lethal autonomous military technology raise a number of contrasting concerns about technological, ethical, and legal challenges implicit in LAWS. A fundamental issue opponents of LAWS raise is that the benefits LAWS might yield in terms of low cost (financial as well as to military lives), efficiency, effectiveness, and expendability may make the decision to use force considerably easier, thereby transferring the risk and burden of war to civilian populations in targeted areas (Wareham 2014). This argument is also frequently raised in the context of drone warfare, where the increased distance and lower costs and risks to militaries might lower the threshold to use lethal force over other means of warfare. The further expanded psychological and physical distance between the human and the act of violence – implicit with LAWS – may exacerbate this condition further (Leveringhaus 2017).

More specifically to contemporary fully autonomous systems, many commentators question the capacity of a technological system to be programmed to select and engage target selection ethically. AI and Robotics expert Noel Sharkey, for example, convincingly outlines why lethal armed robots cannot comply with International Humanitarian Law on the account that they lack the capabilities necessary to ensure both discrimination between civilians and combatants, and proportionality in the appropriate use of force (Sharkey 2012, 787–99; see also Asaro 2012, 691–2). The concern here is that computational systems simply lack the technological components, appropriate data and overall capacity to draw an adequately sophisticated distinction between legitimate and illegitimate targets of war in an environment of high uncertainty (Christen et al. 2017, 57). Despite rapid advancements in technological refinements, including facial recognition and other pattern recognition and identification technologies, the risk that an autonomous system might hit the wrong target, especially in highly complex combat scenarios remains high (Heyns 2016, 9). Moreover, the level or scope of force applied by an autonomous system in a specific situation might exceed what is necessary for a given engagement scenario. Recall that the requirements of proportionality under IHL stipulate that incidental damage inflicted on civilians must not exceed any military advantage gained. This requires a finely balanced assessment and at this stage, it is unlikely that an autonomous system would be sophisticated enough to judge appropriately how much damage, injury or death might be inflicted on civilians for any given act of violence. Decisions like these are often grounded in complex human value systems which exceed those of a purely computational system (Ibid.) In other words, critics note that LAWS do not have adequate technological capacities to distinguish friend from foe; nor are they able to proportionately limit the level or scope of force used once activated, and that this is not likely to change in the near future.

LAWS also challenge the principle of human dignity as a parameter of warfare – the idea that a human life has incommensurable value and each life should be treated as such, not be reduced to a killable or non-killable data point. To do so and to leave the decision over life and death to a computational device serves as the ultimate indignity (Heyns 2016, 11). As Heyns summarizes: "A machine which is bloodless and without morality or mortality, cannot do justice to the gravity of the decision whether to use force in a particular case, even if it may be more accurate than humans" (Ibid). Given these considerations, a key challenge to LAWS critics raise centers directly on the question of responsibility for the act of killing in war: *should* we ever delegate the act of killing to a machine? Can, and should, the human moral agency for the decision to take a human life "be transferred to inanimate machines, or computer algorithms" (International Committee of the Red Cross 2018, 2). Specifically, where technologies are purposefully designed to display levels of independence and unpredictability, as it is the case with AI systems, the logic that humans can and will utilize this type of technology at will and with adequate knowledge is called into question where epistemic uncertainty prevails (Jain 2016, 324).

Robert Sparrow's (2007) article "Killer Robots" has become a widely referenced text tracing the challenges LAWS pose for attributing and taking responsibility in war. In it, he asks: "who should be held responsible if a[n] [L]AWS was involved in a wartime atrocity of the sort that would normally be described as a war crime?" (Sparrow 2007, 66). He notes that "the more autonomous systems become, the less it will be possible to properly hold those who designed them or ordered their use responsible for their actions" (Sparrow 2007, 74). As innovations in machine learning and neural networks advance at speed, exploring the question Sparrow posed over a decade ago remains pivotal: who *can* be held responsible for unlawful harm as a result of artificially *intelligent* LAWS and on what grounds? The worry is that as autonomy in lethal weapons systems increasingly displaces human agency in the decision to kill or damage a target, the locus of who is responsible for unpredictable behavior of the technology, errors, misuse, or indeed accidents becomes vague and dispersed to the point that perhaps nobody is seen to be, or can be, held responsible.

Risk and responsibility gaps

Engaging with the issue of the consequences of the use of LAWS in war relates to the broader question in the responsibility debate about the subject, or addressee of responsibility and the conditions of moral agency. If, following Fischer and Ravizza (1998), to assign responsibility to a moral agent, they must have control over their behavior and their consequences and must make a decision *freely* and *knowingly*, then the involvement of highly complex and intelligent autonomously functioning machines in decisions of moral relevance "makes it difficult to determine who can be held responsible with reason" (Olsthoorn and Royakkers, 2014, 2; 2019, 108).

Moral agency

Fischer and Ravizza's conception of responsibility begins with the premise that humans are unique in that only they can be held responsible for their actions, unlike other creatures or entities (Fischer and Ravizza 1998, 1). For an individual to take responsibility, he or she must see themselves as an agent and must accept that they are a "fair target of the reactive attitudes" in response to their actions, based on the condition of being able to act freely (i.e. not under duress or forced) and within reasonable assumptions of knowledge (which guides foreseeability of outcomes) (Ibid. 227). For conceptions of responsibility in a legal sense, the human is treated as the final agent in a chain of causation and here accountability is "premised on his or her capacity to act as moral agent who possesses the volition and intent to pursue his or her desires or goals" (Jain 2016, 306). This includes the assumption of intent, a certain level of control, and sufficient knowledge to be able to foresee consequences for certain acts. Such traditional theories of responsibility, which seek the locus of accountability for an action in one or more human moral agents are complicated with LAWS in at least two significant ways. It raises questions about the epistemic conditions of the human who programs, orders the use of, or operates the technology – what can they know about the specific conditions, environment, or context in which the technology is set to act? It also calls to question what it means to possess moral agency more broadly. The burgeoning literature that posits machines as moral agents in their own right is indicative here.

Discussions that consider the autonomy of intelligent machines not only in the engineering or technological sense but also in a moral sense – the machine as autonomous moral agent – are gaining ground. Arguments advanced in favor of machine moral agency (and possible responsibility) are underpinned in part by the aspiration that in some (distant) future it may be possible to achieve levels of artificial intelligence that approximate human level intelligence – and with it the possibility to make nuanced judgments – in a more general and comprehensive fashion (Dennett 1997). Sophisticated philosophical arguments about whether we should consider autonomous technological artefacts as full or partial moral agents (and what duties and responsibilities might arise from such moral status) abound, and covering the scope and complexities of the discussion far exceeds the scope of this chapter.[4] These examinations frequently hinge on very nuanced interpretations of the concepts of agency and responsibility, of free-will, intent, and consciousness, and these are indeed crucial parameters for the attribution of moral agency. Often, however, discussions about machine agency and responsibility simply reflect a tendency toward anthropomorphizing the decision capacity of an autonomous system (Sullins 2006, 24; Hellstroem 2013, 103). Where the moral responsibility of a gun is likely to be seen as quite thin (the truism "guns don't kill people, people kill people" comes to mind), this changes with increased perceived autonomy of a system, particularly learning systems. Thomas Hellstroem frames this in terms of degrees of autonomous power and suggests that "[o]ur tendency to assign moral responsibility to a robot increases with its degree of autonomous power" (Hellstroem 2013, 103).[5] A recent study among Dutch military and Ministry of Defence personnel confirms this extended perceived autonomy, whereby results indicate that participants in the study "attribute more agency to an Autonomous Weapon than to a Human Operated drone" (Verdiesen 2017, 4).

However, regardless of how autonomous intelligent weapons might be perceived as responsible moral agents, the question is, how, if at all, can they be held to account? As Neha Jain notes, "[a]ttribution of responsibility to the AWS itself will be difficult, not only because it has 'no soul to be damned and no body to be kicked' but arguably also because it lacks capacity to act in a manner deserving of criminal liability" (Jain 2016, 303). Sparrow explores these concerns in more detail and suggests that to hold someone (or something) responsible is "to hold that they are the appropriate locus of blame or praise, and consequently punishment or reward" (Sparrow 2007, 71). Following from this would be the requirement that a machine not only has a certain level of intent and autonomous agency but also the capacity to suffer or experience pleasure. In other words, the autonomous system would not only need to be intelligent but also to a certain degree, sentient, in order for punishment or reward for certain actions to be morally meaningful (Ibid., 72). Such machine capacities are not on the horizon for the foreseeable future and may not ever materialize and any notion that a machine should have to answer, autonomously, for its wrongful actions, is intuitively, practically, and also theoretically a dead end at this point. This leaves the question open as to who can, in reason, be held to account when something goes wrong.

Accidents, errors, mistakes, and unintended outcomes are a feature of warfare as the proverbial "fog of war" in unpredictable and highly dynamic environments persists, despite increased technological capabilities of modern militaries. With traditional lines of military responsibility the attribution of responsibility for misdeeds are relatively clear. The individual soldier and/or military commander are typically accountable for unintended harm and outcomes in warfare. This chain of accountability becomes much more diffuse for LAWS, where unintended consequences might mean that "harm occurs without apparent intention, precisely because [...] no single actor is ever in charge of the entire big picture and the order of risks is potentially considerably higher (Jasanoff 2016, 41). Adding to the challenging complexity of adaptive intelligent autonomy in war is the fact that the more complex the system and its components, the more can go wrong.

Technological risks

For all new and emerging technologies, there is always a risk involved as they come to interact with social environments. "Technological risk," as Jasanoff notes, "is the product of humans and nonhumans acting together" (Jasanoff 2016, 36). This is the case for technological system in civilian as well as military spheres and it applies to all military technologies, not just LAWS. But specifically with complex technological systems, responsibility is "distributed in ways that limit accountability" (Ibid. 40). The use of intelligent LAWS offers a wider spectrum of potential risks. Of concern here is not the often heralded Terminator-style robot going rogue, but rather a range of potential errors, accidents, misuses, and other risks which might result in harm.

Such risks of unpredictability can arise through unforeseen or unforeseeable environmental factors for which the system did not have an appropriate model. Examples from the field of autonomous driving are instructive here. Consider, for example, the fatal Tesla crash in central Florida in 2016, where the Model S Tesla in autopilot mode crashed into a tractor trailer, resulting in the death of the driver in the car. The sensors for the Model S could not recognize the tractor and its trailer on account of very bright light conditions and other unforeseen factors led to the fatal crash (Golson 2016). Similarly, in 2018 Elaine Herzberg was struck and killed by a self-driving Uber car as she attempted to cross a street with her bike in Tempe, Arizona. The car's autonomous system had not taken into account that pedestrians may cross streets anywhere other than a crosswalk and consequently the system misidentified Elaine Herzberg entirely. Moreover, the system was designed to avoid excessive false alarms and included a one-second delay between crash detection and action – a design feature that proved fatal for Ms Herzberg (Marshall 2019). In both instances, the manufacturers (Tesla and Uber, respectively) put the onus on the driver, who, as per instruction manual, is tasked with keeping an eye on the road and both hands on the wheel at all times, which proved to be challenging. And in both cases, the manufacturer did not face criminal liability for the accidents.

In the complex and dynamic context of warfare, it is easy to imagine that LAWS may run into similar and possibly more complex problems. If a system, for example, is designed to target combatants in a specific area, unless they use a particular symbol for their surrender – a white flag, for example – and the light conditions are such that the system cannot interpret the white flag appropriately and subsequently takes out the surrendering individuals, who might we be able to hold responsible for this oversight? Sparrow poses a related possible scenario in which the unpredictability of the autonomous intelligent system is a crucial factor. In that scenario, an AWS, guided by an intelligent software system, purposefully discharges its payload onto a group of enemy soldiers who have laid down their weapons in surrender, as before. But in this scenario, the bombing of the surrendering soldiers was not a mistake, but rather a deliberate choice enacted by the system, whereby the system made a calculation and decided this to be the optimal way forward (Sparrow 2007, 66). In this case the system's cognitive reasoning is not intelligible to the operator, commander, or perhaps even the programmer. Assessing what made the system decide this wrongful course of action as an optimal outcome can only take place *post hoc*, and even then, the system's actions may not be coherent to human reasoning. The same responsibility gap emerges as with the previous scenario when it comes to allocating who can be held responsible in reason for such actions.

Other risks that the use of LAWS might yield an unlawful or unjust outcome are of systemic and structural nature, whereby certain shortcomings are already implicit within the algorithmic and computational structure of the LAWS through poor data processing, focus, or other biases.[6] AI systems "are taught what they 'know' from training data" (Campolo et al. 2017, 14). Training data is a selected set of data that is deemed relevant to the problem at hand; however, this data can be incomplete (i.e. not sufficiently extensive to build an appropriate world model), inappropriate (i.e. not of the correct source to build an appropriate world model), skewed or otherwise biased (prioritizing factors that might influence certain selection over others). These biases are not always easy to identify and are often not intended. Just like human bias in society, these biases usually find their way into systems through already instituted practices.

When such opaque biased data sets find their way into autonomous weapons systems, the consequences might be unjust, if not unlawful. Consider, for example, the UK's use of NeoFace Watch, a face recognition system designed by NEC, to identify the faces of criminals in a crowd. A 2018 report published by the NGO Big Brother Watch found that by using the data made available to the UK police force only 5% of persons were identified correctly. This means "the average false face recognition was 95%" (Sharkey 2018b; Big Brother Watch 2018, 3). As Sharkey comments on this example: "Just imagine the humanitarian consequences if that had been an AWS selecting targets" (Sharkey 2018b). Other incidents might be less dramatic, but nonetheless impactful: improper or biased training data and fragile algorithmic systems might misidentify a school bus for a tank, or an umbrella for a rifle and make a lethal targeting decision based on flawed processing of the incoming data. This, as General Shanahan points out, is a problem for militaries: "you have certain challenges of data quality, data provenance and data fidelity, and every one of those throws a curve ball" (Shanahan quotes in Freedberg Jr 2019).

The unique features of LAWS pose thus unique risks and implicate a wide ranging set of agents as potential bearers of responsibility: "software programmers, those who sell and build hardware, military commanders, subordinates who deploy these systems and political leaders" (Heyns 2013, 14), and simultaneously make the possibility for fairly identifying a responsible agent extremely challenging. Where the chain of possible responsibility holders is highly diffuse and where conditions of adequate freedom, knowledge, and control over a particular action for each individual in the chain is limited or weakened, traditional responsibility theories are called into question (Jain 2016, 324).

The designer and programmer

If we consider the risk scenarios above, would it be fair and appropriate to hold the programmer to account? Andreas Matthias explores this question in light of the adaptive nature of autonomous intelligent systems and finds that the programmer's ability to know, control, and understand the actions of such systems would make them an inappropriate locus of responsibility. He argues that the character of autonomous intelligent systems is such that "the designer of a machine increasingly loses control over it, and transfers control to the machine itself." The role of the programmer shifts from being a coder to becoming a creator of a "software organism," over which they have little control or capacity to predict future behavior (Matthias 2004, 182). With nonadaptive, nonlearning machines (for example, an artillery weapon or a hand grenade), lines of responsibility are reasonably clear: the consequences of operating a machine is ascribed "to the operator of the machine, as long as the machine operates as specified by the manufacturer. The operator, by putting the machine into operation, according to the manufacturer's specification, signals her acceptance of this responsibility" (Matthias 2004, 175). If the nonadaptive machine has a flaw and does not work as it should and causes harm, it is the manufacturer's responsibility. If the machine is used in ways that exceed the manufacturer's specification, and causes harm, it is the operator's responsibility (Ibid.).

With autonomous intelligent systems, this line of responsibility is radically obscured. Recall that intelligent LAWS learn from their environment to better adapt their world model. In the progression from "coder to creator of a software organism," the programmer essentially "transfers part of his control over the product to the environment," thereby losing both control over the operating environment, and knowledge of the potential outcomes (Matthias 2004, 182). This, for Sparrow, reflects an autonomy (in the philosophical sense) for which the programmer cannot be held responsible: "if the [system] has sufficient autonomy that it learns from its experience and surrounding then it makes decisions which reflect these as much or more than its initial programming" (Sparrow 2007, 70). The relationship between the designer and the outcomes of the system which would "ground the attribution of responsibility" is disconnected by the system's autonomy (Ibid.). Moreover, the multicomponent dimension of LAWS as *systems* of multiple parts and nodes means that they are not designed as a single, and finite unit but rather, they "emerge or grow out of dispersed technological material and organizational human developments," making it exceptionally challenging to attribute responsibility to the original authorship of the machine (Coeckelbergh 2011, 267). Moreover, if the programmer or designer may have fulfilled their role as designers with utmost prudence, care and in accordance with organizational and design guidelines, he or she may not see themselves as viably responsible for adverse actions by a system once it is no longer under their control. He or she will have fulfilled their role responsibility and thereby have discharged any further lines of accountability. As Hin-Yan Liu notes: "accountability for the outcome remains elusive because individuals are only accountable for their failures within their roles, rather than for directly bringing about the consequences" (Liu 2016, 340).

Commanding officers and military users

We might instead be inclined to attribute responsibility within the area of use for LAWS. Here, some suggest, the responsibility might best reside with "the commanders and political leaders that chose to deploy the system" (Christen et al. 2017, 75). It is not authorship or design of the system itself within which responsibility should reside, but within the authorship of the "target signature" given to the system (Ibid.). Just as a commander may bear responsibility for the wrongful actions of their troops, so they might also be responsible for the actions of a LAWS by virtue of their rank, position, and responsibility for battle actions and their probable outcomes – this is considered command responsibility (Himmelreich 2019). A commander might, for example, be held responsible for deploying a LAWS with "unjust or inadequately formulated ROE [Rules of Engagement], for failing to ensure that the weapons can be used safely" (Schulzke 2013) or for deploying a lethal autonomous system for unethical reasons. In other words, a commander should make sure that the system is completely safe, that the commander can use it in a way that complies with all rules and that its actions are predictable for this reason.

But here too, the lines of responsibility are not as clear as one might think or desire when we take into account the emergent and unpredictable properties of a system, as outlined above. For Sparrow, the lack of control over, and understanding of, the lethal intelligent system, and the system's own, increased autonomy means that if the weapons system independently chooses its own targets, at some point it may "no longer be fair to hold the Commanding Officer responsible for the actions of the machine" (Sparrow 2007, 71). In other words, the system's causal responsibility for attacking a target may take place at such a distance from the initial command input control, and with such high levels of self-organization, that a commander may not viably be able to predict the action of the LAWS. In other words, the lack of epistemic certainty might be too great for the commanding officer to be able have enough knowledge to foresee any adverse consequences with LAWS, making it challenging to assign responsibility along the military chain of command, especially if the behavior of the system is only explainable *post hoc* (Christen et al. 2017, 57). As Heyns points out, traditional command responsibility stipulates that the commander "knew or should have known" that an actor under their command planned to commit a crime and failed to prevent it and/or punish the wrongdoing actor. With emerging autonomous intelligent technology it is not clear "whether military commanders will be in a position to understand the complex programming" of LAWS to warrant being held to account (Heyns 2013, 15). Recall that the logic, and speed of intelligent weapons systems exceeds human cognition – it is considerably faster and more comprehensive in the ability to analyze data and find patterns. This disproportionality between humans and machine requires that the commander and operator must place considerable trust into the machine capability, which means, as Feldman et al. point out, that "most, if not all lethal and sub-lethal interactions will only be analyzable in hindsight" (Feldman et al. 2019, 5), if it can be assessed at all.

If we consider that a commander should bear the burden for being able to foresee the likely or probable outcomes of actions under their command, a system that is designed to exceed the rational and intellectual capacities of the human complicates command responsibility considerably. It remains unclear whether any human commander or operator could have adequate cognitive abilities, an appropriate mental model for how the system behaves in various contexts, the relevant situational awareness, or simply the time to understand how a particular system makes its decisions and assess the validity and thereof (Schwarz 2018). With a growing control distance over targeting decisions and an increased hand-over of such decisions to sensors and algorithms, as is the nature of LAWS, there may well be a point that the distance between human knowledge and agency and life-and-death decisions is too great for either a commander or operator to be held, or feel, responsible for the taking of a life. A way forward might be to assign responsibility to the commander, on account of the tradition of command responsibility. This, for Liu, amounts to an unviable "over-extending [of responsibility] beyond the limits of individual role responsibility to cover the gap in accountability for consequences" which amounts to little more than scapegoating (Liu 2016, 341). And, as Olsthoorn and Royakkers rightly point out: "Whether one would want to have that responsibility is a different question altogether" (Olsthoorn and Royakkers 2019, 111).

For any society built on the principles of law and the values of human life and dignity, the act of taking a human life – even in war – requires that someone can be held responsible for such an act. This, as Heyns explains, is a crucial feature of "the protection of a particular right. A lack of accountability for the violation of the right to life is, […] in itself a violation of that right" (Heyns 2016, 12). Attempts to assign responsibility to the machine itself are, for reasons indicated above, a misguided equation of technological autonomy with moral agency, which complicates matters as it invites "people to offload responsibility onto [the machine], muddying the waters when it comes to assigning responsibility" (Parthemore and Whitby 2014, 157). In the absence of a viable theory of responsibility that establishes an autonomous system as a legal and moral agent in its own right, we are faced with a dilemma. And without control over autonomous weapons, there can be no accountability and we are faced with a vacuum because "[t]here is clearly no point in putting a robot in jail" (Heyns 2016, 12). It may not make a practical difference to the loved ones of a person killed in war whether the killing was decided by a machine or by a human, but it does make a difference for the moral fabric of a society. As Joanna Bryson rightly notes: "whether the machines are capable of learning while they are acting has little impact on the consequences for human society if we allow each other to displace our responsibility to our creations" (Bryson 2011, 18). Here perhaps the much debated concept of "meaningful human control" may refocus lines of responsibility, as a possible emergent norm, in the discussions about LAWS.

In lieu of a conclusion: "meaningful human control"

LAWS have been on the agenda of the UN Convention on Conventional Weapons (CCW) meetings since 2013, with regular meetings of the Group of Governmental Experts (GGE) to discuss the topic since 2017. A growing number of states are explicitly advocating for an outright ban[7], and while legislation on a prohibition is not yet on the horizon, there is a growing convergence around the idea that somewhere in the loop a human must retain relevant control.

Civil society groups have put forth the concept of "meaningful human control" as a fundamental requirement for lethal autonomous weapons, to draw limits to the autonomy of a system and indicate a line of responsibility for actions conducted with LAWS.

Although there is no clear consensus on what constitutes meaningful, or appropriate, human control for LAWS precisely, most of the participants in the CCW talks agree that somewhere in the operations of LAWS there should be a human decision maker to ensure that "humans, not computers and their algorithms should ultimately remain in control of and thus morally responsible for relevant decisions about (lethal) military decisions" (Article 36 quoted in Santoni de Sio and van den Hoven 2018, 3). Specifically, the critical functions should remain within human control to be able to determine when, where and how lethal force is use, against whom and to what effect (Human Rights Watch 2016). Two crucial and related questions emerge from this: (1) do the characteristics of autonomous intelligent weapons allow for meaningful human control in the use of force against human targets? and (2) what does, or could, meaningful human control mean, not just as a vague norm, but as a legal principle or a regulatory guide? (Santoni de Sio and van Hoven 2018, 3). To date, there is no clear answer to either question.

For proponents of a ban, the requirement entails that a human operator or commander has "sufficient opportunity […] to perform moral reasoning and deliberation prior to 'each and every use of violent force' (Saxon 2016, 202)." This requires not just that a human has the finger on the trigger point, but that those involved in a lethal decision have full contextual awareness, that they can identify and react to changes in the context of the attack quickly, that they have enough time and cognitive capacity to assess the necessity and appropriateness of the attack and abort it, if necessary (Sharkey 2018a, 3). This means that such meaningful controls must be given even in combat scenarios "where in the future – in light of the speed of events and the sheer amount of data that needs to be processed in real-world combat scenarios – there will be an increasingly stronger pull to leave decisions to autonomous systems" (Bhuta et al. 2016, 383). How, or indeed whether this is at all possible, is doubtful. Moreover, it casts a shadow over the role and importance of moral deliberation for lethal decisions and we should be mindful that technological structures might serve as moral architectures in ways that take us further away from a humanist framework of warfare, and toward a technological-administrative logic in which "responsibility" might become a formality without meaning.

Notes

1 While the definition for autonomous weapons system is far from settled, I am using the ICRC definition, as it is consistently drawn in debates on LAWS (ICRC 2016). The US Department of Defense issued a 2012 directive in which it defined autonomous systems as: "a weapon system that once activated can select and engage targets without further intervention by a human operator. This includes human-supervised autonomous weapons systems that are designed to allow human operators to override operations of the weapons system, but can select and engage targets without further human input after activation." (US Department of Defense 2017) The UK Ministry of Defence, in contrast, has to date defined autonomous systems as those "capable of understanding higher level intent and direction," thereby setting the standards for what they consider to be fully autonomous weapons considerably higher, focusing on a system's cognitive capacity to understand intent and directives given (UK Ministry of Defence 2017, 13) This matters insofar as the definition can facilitate or delimit discussions about systems with autonomy already on the near future horizon.
2 There are numerous definitions and explanations of autonomy circulating in the discussions on LAWS, perhaps too many to mention. I settle here for one that has a direct relation to autonomous system that learns from their environment to best reflect the autonomous intelligent systems I focus on here.
3 AlphaGo is an AI program designed by DeepMind to win at the highly complex game of Go. In 2016, the system beat the hitherto undefeated grandmaster of Go, Lee Sedol, with a set of innovative and

surprising moves. Unlike other systems, the AlphaGo system utilized reinforcement learning, whereby it refined its game by playing against itself. This led to a series of unexpected but very effective moves with which the system was able to beat Sedol.

4 See for example Daniel Dennett (1997), Luciano Floridi and J.W. Sanders (2004), John Sullins (2006), and Jaap Hage (2017).
5 For an insightful discussion on the human tendency to ascribe intelligence and intent to a machine, see Lucy Suchman (2007).
6 For a comprehensive discussion on LAWS and algorithmic biases, see the United Nations Institute for Disarmament Research (UNIDIR) Report: 'Algorithmic Bias and the Weaponization of Increasingly Autonomous Technologies: A Primer', 2018 (United Nations Institute for Disarmament Research 2018).
7 At the time of writing 30 states seek the prohibition of fully autonomous weapons systems (Campaign against Killer Robots 2019).

References

Ackerman, E. (2015). "We Should Not Ban "Killer Robots" and Here's Why'." *IEEE Spectrum*, 29 July. http://spectrum.ieee.org/automaton/robotics/artificial-intelligence/we-should-not-ban-killer-robots.

Anderson, K., and Waxman M. (2013). *Law and ethics for Autonomous weapon Systems Why a Ban Won't Work and How the Laws of War Can*. A National Security and Law Essay, 17 March. Hoover Institution. http://media.hoover.org/sites/default/files/documents/Anderson-Waxman_LawAndEthics_r2_FINAL.pdf.

Arkin, R. C. (2009). *Governing Lethal Behavior in Autonomous Robots*. Boca Raton: CRC Press.

Arkin, R. C. (2010). "The Case for Ethical Autonomy in Unmanned Systems." *Journal of Military Ethics*, 9(4): 332–341.

Asaro, P. (2012). "On banning autonomous weapon systems: human rights, automation, and the dehumanization of lethal decision-making". *International Review of the Red Cross - Humanitarian debate: Law, policy, action*, 94(886). http://www.icrc.org/eng/resources/international-review/review-886-new-technologies-warfare/review-886-all.pdf.

Beck, A., Kayser, D., and Slijper, F. (2019). "State of AI: Artificial Intelligence, the Military and Increasingly Autonomous Weapon Systems." *PAX NL Report* April 2019.

Bhuta, N., Beck, S., and Geiss, R. (2016). "Present Futures: Concluding Reflections and Open Questions on Autonomous Weapons Systems." In Bhuta, N., Beck, S., and Geiss, R., eds. *Autonomous Weapons Systems: Law, Ethics, Policy*. Cambridge: Cambridge University Press.

Big Brother Watch (2018). "Face Off: The lawless growth of facial recognition in UK policing." May. Big Brother Watch, available at: https://bigbrotherwatch.org.uk/wp-content/uploads/2018/05/Face-Off-final-digital-1.pdf.

Boulain, V., and Verbruggen, M. (2017). *Mapping the Development of Autonomy in Weapons Systems*. November. SIPRI.

Bryson, J. J. (2011). "A Role for Consciousness in Action Selection." In Clowes, R., Torrance, S., and Chrisley, R., eds., *Machine Consciousness 2011: Self, Integration and Explanation, Proc. Symp. AISB'11 Convention*: 15–19. The Society for the Study of Artificial Intelligence and Simulation of Behaviour (AISB), April 4–7, 2011, York, UK.

Campaign against Killer Robots (2019). "All Action and Achievement", October 24, 2019. https://www.stopkillerrobots.org/action-and-achievements/

Campolo, A., Crawford, K., Sanfilippo, M., et al. (2017). *AI Now 2017 Report*. New York: AI Now Institute. https://ainowinstitute.org/AI_Now_2017_Report.pdf.

Christen, M., Burri, T., Chapa, J., et al. (2017). *An Evaluation Schema for the Ethical Use of Autonomous Robotic Systems in Security Applications*. UZH Digital Society Initiative, October. University of Zurich. https://ssrn.com/abstract=3063617.

Coeckelbergh, M. (2011). "From Killer Machines to Doctrines and Swarms, or Why Ethics of Military Robotics is not (Necessarily) About Robots." *Philosophy & Technology*, 24(3): 269–278.

Cummings, M. (2017). *Artificial Intelligence and the Future of Warfare*. Chatham House Research Paper, January. Chatham House.

Dennett, D. (1997). "When Hal Kills, Who's to Blame? Computer Ethics". In Stork, D., ed., *Hal's Legacy: 2001's Computer as Dream and Reality*. Cambridge, MA: MIT Press.

Department of the Army (2019). *Industry Day for the Advanced Targeting and Lethality Automated System (ATLAS) Program*. W909MY-19-R-C004, 22 February. Army Contracting Command. https://www.fbo.gov/index.php?s=opportunity&mode=form&tab=core&id=6b5d5aeb584c667d4e6f5103bf6acac6&_cview=0.

Feldman, P., Dant, A., and Massey, A. (2019). *Integrating Artificial Intelligence into Weapon Systems*. arXiv.org arXiv:1905.03899v1, 10 May. https://arxiv.org/pdf/1905.03899.pdf.

Fischer, J., and Ravizza, M. (1998). *Responsibility and Control: A Theory of Moral Responsibility*. Cambridge: Cambridge University Press.

Floridi, L., and Sanders. J.W. (2004). "On the Morality of Artificial Agents." *Minds and Machines*, 14(3): 349–379.

Freedberg Jr, S.J. (2019). "Pentagon's Problem is 'Dirty' Data: Lt Gen Shanahan". Breaking Defense. November 13, 2019. https://breakingdefense.com/2019/11/exclusive-pentagons-ai-problem-is-dirty-data-lt-gen-shanahan/

Gettinger, D. (2018). *Summary of Drone Spending in the FY 2019 Defense Budget Request*. April. Centre for the Study of the Drone. https://dronecenter.bard.edu/drones-in-the-fy19-defense-budget/.

Golson, J. (2016). "Tesla driver killed in crash with Autopilot active, NHTSA investigating". *The Verge*, 30 June. https://www.theverge.com/2016/6/30/12072408/tesla-autopilot-car-crash-death-autonomous-model-s.

Gunkel, D. (2019). "Other Things: AI, Robots and Society." In Papacharissi, Z., ed., *A Networked Self and Human Augmentics, Artificial Intelligence, Sentience*. New York: Routledge.

Hage, J. (2017). "Theoretical Foundations for the Responsibility of Autonomous Agents." *Artificial Intelligence and Law*, 25(3): 255–271.

Hellstroem, T. (2013). "On the Moral Responsibility of Military Robots." *Ethics and Information Technology*, 15(2): 99–107.

Heyns, C. (2013). *Report of the Special Rapporteur on extrajudicial, summary or arbitrary executions, Christof Heyns*. A/HRC/23/47, 3 April. New York: United Nations Human Rights Council.

Heyns, C. (2016). "Autonomous Weapons Systems: Living a Dignified Life and Dying a Dignified Death". In Bhuta, N., Beck, S., Geiss, R., et al., eds., *Autonomous Weapons Systems: Law, Ethics, Policy*. Cambridge: Cambridge University Press.

Himmelreich, J. (2019). "Responsibility for Killer Robots." *Ethical Theory and Moral Practice*, 22(3): 731–747.

Human Rights Watch (2016). *Killer Robots and the Concept of Meaningful Human Control*. Human Rights Watch, April 11, 2016. https://www.hrw.org/news/2016/04/11/killer-robots-and-concept-meaningful-human-control

International Committee of the Red Cross (2016). *Views of the International Committee of the Red Cross (ICRC) on autonomous weapon system*. 11 April. Geneva: Convention on Certain Conventional Weapons, Meeting of Experts on Lethal Autonomous Weapons. https://www.icrc.org/en/document/views-icrc-autonomous-weapon-system.

International Committee of the Red Cross (2018). *Ethics and Autonomous Weapon Systems: An Ethical Basis for Human Control?* 3 April. Geneva: International Committee of the Red Cross (ICRC). https://www.icrc.org/en/document/ethics-and-autonomous-weapon-systems-ethical-basis-human-control.

Jain, N. (2016). "Autonomous Weapons Systems: New Frameworks for Individual Responsibility." In Bhuta, N., Beck, S., Geiss, R., et al., eds., *Autonomous Weapons Systems: Law, Ethics Politics*. Cambridge: Cambridge University Press.

Jasanoff, S. (2016). *The Ethics of Invention: Technology and the Human Future*. New York: W.W. Norton.

Leveringhaus, A. (2017). "Distance, Weapons Technology and Humanity in Armed Conflict." In *ICRC Humanitarian Law & Policy Blog*. https://blogs.icrc.org/law-and-policy/2017/10/06/distance-weapons-technology-and-humanity-in-armed-conflict/.

Liu, H.Y. (2016). "Refining Responsibility: differentiating two types of responsibility issues raised by autonomous weapons systems". In Bhuta, N., Beck, S., Geiss, R., et al., eds., *Autonomous Weapons Systems: Law, Ethics, Policy*. Cambridge: Cambridge University Press.

Marshall, A. (2019). "Uber's Self-Driving Car Didn't Know Pedestrians Could Jaywalk". Wired 05 November 2019. https://www.wired.com/story/ubers-self-driving-car-didnt-know-pedestrians-could-jaywalk/.

Matthias, A. (2004). "The responsibility gap: Ascribing responsibility for the actions of learning automata". *Ethics and Information Technology*, 6(3): 175–183.

Metz, C. (2016). "Google's AI Wins Pivotal Second Game in Match With Go Grandmaster." *WIRED*, 3 October. https://www.wired.com/2016/03/googles-ai-wins-pivotal-game-two-match-go-grandmaster/.

Olsthoorn, P., and Royakkers, L. (2014). "Military Robots and the Question of Responsibility." *Journal of Technoethics*, 5(1): 1–14.

Olsthoorn, P., and Royakkers, L. (2019). "Lethal Military Robots: Who Is Responsible When Things Go Wrong?" In *Unmanned Aerial Vehicles: Breakthroughs in Research and Practice*. Engineering Science Reference. Hershey, PA: IGI Global Publishing.

Parthemore, J., and Whitby, B. (2014). "Moral Responsibility, and Artifacts: What Existing Artifacts Fail to Achieve (and Why) and Why They Can (and Do!) Make Moral Claims upon Us." *International Journal of Machine Consciousness*, 6(2): 141–161.

Santoni de Sio, F., and Van den Hoven, J. (2018). "Meaningful Human Control over Autonomous Systems: A Philosophical Account". *Frontiers in Robotics and AI*, 5(15): 1–14.

Saxon, D. (2016). "A Human Touch: Autonomous Weapons, DoD Directive 3000.09 and the Interpretation of 'Appropriate Levels of Human Judgment Over the Use of Force." In Bhuta, N., Beck, S., Geiss, R. eds., *Autonomous Weapons Systems: Law, Ethics, Policy*. Cambridge: Cambridge University Press.

Scharre, P. (2018). *Army of None: Autonomous Weapons and the Future of War*. New York: W.W. Norton & Co.

Schulzke, M. (2013). "Autonomous Weapons and Distributed Responsibility." *Philosophy & Technology*, 26(2): 203–219.

Schwarz, E. (2018). "The (im)possibility of meaningful human control for lethal autonomous weapon systems". *ICRC Humanitarian Law & Policy Blog*. August 29, 2018. https://blogs.icrc.org/law-and-policy/2018/08/29/im-possibility-meaningful-human-control-lethal-autonomous-weapon-systems/.

Sharkey, N. (2012). "The Evitability of Autonomous Robot Warfare." *International Review of the Red Cross*, 94(886): 787–799.

Sharkey, N. (2018a). "Guidelines for the Human Control of Weapons Systems." In *ICRAC Briefing Paper*, Geneva, April 2018. https://www.icrac.net/wp-content/uploads/2018/04/Sharkey_Guideline-for-the-human-control-of-weapons-systems_ICRAC-WP3_GGE-April-2018.pdf.

Sharkey, N. (2018b). "The impact of gender and race bias in AI." In *ICRC Humanitarian Law & Policy Blog*, available at: https://blogs.icrc.org/law-and-policy/2018/08/28/impact-gender-race-bias-ai/.

Sparrow, R. (2007). "Killer Robots." *Journal of Applied Philosophy*, 24(1): 62–77.

Suchman, L. (2007). *Human-Machine Reconfigurations: Plans and Situated Actions*. Cambridge: Cambridge University Press.

Sullins, J. P. (2006). "When Is a Robot a Moral Agent?" *International Review of Information Ethics*, 6(12): 24–29.

UK Ministry of Defence (2017). *Joint Doctrine Publication: Unmanned Aircraft Systems*. JDP 0-30.2, August. UK Ministry of Defence.

Umbrello, S., Torres, P., and De Bellis, A. F. (2020). "The future of war: could lethal autonomous weapons make conflict more ethical?" *AI & Society*, 35(1): 273–282.

United Nations Institute for Disarmament Research (2018). *Algorithmic Bias and the Weaponization of Increasingly Autonomous Technologies A PRIMER*. No. 9, UNIDIR Resources. United Nations Institute for Disarmament Research (UNIDIR). http://www.unidir.ch/files/publications/pdfs/algorithmic-bias-and-the-weaponization-of-increasingly-autonomous-technologies-en-720.pdf.

US Department of Defense (2017). *DoD Directive 3000.09*. US Department of Defense.

Verdiesen, I. (2017). *Agency perception and moral values related to Autonomous Weapons: An empirical study using the Value-Sensitive Design approach*. Delft University of Technology, The Netherlands. https://pdfs.semanticscholar.org/d6b0/81733a0e12c4f1ac4efe0bbb524a222520b9.pdf.

Wareham, M. (2014). "Killer Robots: Keeping Control of Autonomous Weapons." *Fair Observer*, August 21. https://www.fairobserver.com/region/north_america/killer-robots-keeping-control-autonomous-weapons-99462/.

Wiener, N. (1960). "Some Moral and Technical Consequences of Automation." *Science*, 131: 1355–1358.

14
NEGOTIATING PROTECTION THROUGH RESPONSIBILITY

Erna Burai

Introduction

The Responsibility to Protect is a policy framework that member states of the United Nations (UN) endorsed at their 2005 World Summit. At the Summit, states accepted that they have a responsibility to protect their populations from war crimes, genocide, crimes against humanity and ethnic cleansing, and a responsibility to assist each other in fulfilling their responsibility to protect. Furthermore, they accepted that the international community bears responsibility to act collectively in accordance with the Charter of the United Nations, if national authorities are unwilling to take action or manifestly fail to do so. UN Secretary-General Ban Ki-moon later integrated these related responsibilities into one framework as the "three pillars" of R2P (Ban 2009). R2P built on the consensus that atrocities constitute threats to international peace and security and therefore warrant international action (Bellamy and Williams 2011). It provided a politically more salient way of debating international action than alternatives such as the "right to intervene". However, certain issues remain a subject of persistent disagreement, including the utility of the use of force in achieving protection or the Security Council's "code of conduct" in R2P situations.

Despite facilitating a discussion on a wide range of intervention measures, its ambiguities led R2P to being criticized as a working doctrine (Focarelli 2008). These ambiguities, however, can "cater towards governance problems that require a flexible set of norms and regulations that interact with their context and are experimentalist and polycentric" (Vetterlein 2018, 546). As we will see, protecting populations from R2P crimes is the kind of governance problem that requires such a flexible set of norms. In this chapter, I ask how the introduction of responsibility facilitated maneuvering among various viewpoints, by presenting the normative conundrums raised by protective action, and four levels on which responsibility addressed them. On the level of discourse, R2P provided less controversial terms of debate than its alternatives, creating more space for consensus. On the level of institutionalization, R2P inspired the creation of new positions and new institutional knowledge that also infused existing practices. On the level of collective expectations, R2P spurred debates on what the responsibility to protect is and to whom it should be allocated, thereby redefining the "web of relationships" (Hansen-Magnusson 2019) pertaining to protection. Finally, it provided a vocabulary for states to publicly justify their actions. Evaluating these claims in public debate in turn generated new understandings of responsibility and protection.

The normative conundrums of protection

Responsibility as a mechanism of negotiated governance often emerges as a response to normative conundrums, where strongly held values clash or existing regulations reach a stalemate (compare with the Introduction to this volume). The field of protection reflects this logic particularly well. From the early 1990s atrocities in internal conflicts were increasingly seen as an international concern. The UN and other organizations recognized the need to address such internal conflicts. Although they traditionally held different mandates, the North Atlantic Treaty Organization (NATO) intervened in the Yugoslav wars of dissolution, and the Economic Community of West African States (ECOWAS) sent military troops to settle the wars in Liberia and Sierra Leone. Intervention in these conflicts, however, challenged the existing interpretations of sovereignty and noninterference in internal affairs. Is it legal to intervene? Is it permissible, and if yes, under what conditions? Does sovereignty have supremacy over human rights, or the other way around? The international community first grappled with the question of the right to intervene, reviving the prudential principles of just war theory. The right to intervene, however, was a controversial formulation. It suggested the right of some over others to decide whether a situation demands intervention, and ignited fears that humanitarian motives might be hijacked to legitimize the unilateral use of force.

The practice of protection raised further dilemmas. In the Rwandan case, the absence of institutional knowledge within the UN, and the controversies of previous UN experience in Somalia, led to downplaying the gravity of genocidal violence in 1994. Combined with the lack of political will from member states, it ultimately resulted in inaction (Barnett and Finnemore 2004). At the other end of the spectrum, NATO intervened in Kosovo after circumventing the UN Security Council. Both cases pointed to the need for some framework within which to discuss international action in response to atrocities. Rwanda and Kosovo showed that, in the absence of such a framework, international order might erode either because its principles are violated with impunity or because certain states might choose to protect these principles by breaching the existing regulations (Annan 1999a).

Although protection increasingly emerged as an international duty, how to allocate this duty raised further questions. What the responsibility to protect is in specific situations and who should bear it marked a further normative stalemate. The emerging duty of protection, in other words, remained "imperfect," i.e. not allocated to any actor in particular (Tan 2006). This opened conceptual and practical debates on what the "remedial responsibility" to rectify the wrongs circumscribed by R2P is (Miller 2001).

Existing regulations reached a stalemate as both supporters and opponents of intervention were able to muster legal and moral arguments to justify their positions (Holzgrefe and Keohane 2003; Hurd 2011). Despite a growing consensus that atrocities require an international response, many doubted that military intervention is useful in achieving protection (Welsh 2006). Practical experience with protection only deepened normatively infused disagreements. Therefore, reinterpreting existing regulation did not in itself solve the problem. The normative conundrums around protection called for a new conceptual framework to discuss intervention. Sponsored by the Canadian government and enjoying the tacit support of then UN Secretary-General Kofi Annan, the International Commission on Intervention and State Sovereignty (ICISS) provided this conceptual framework in 2001, based on the concept of responsibility.

Responding to the normative conundrums: introducing responsibility on four levels

On the levels of discourse, institutionalization, collective expectations, and public justifications of state action, responsibility facilitated debates on how to act to protect populations from the crimes specified as falling within R2P's scope. It might not have resolved the normative stalemates around protection, some of them inherent to the structure of the undertaking (Paris 2014), but it led to a better specification of who should do what to rectify these wrongs, and strengthened collective expectations of holding actors accountable for their conduct in light of these specifications.

The discourse level

On the level of discourse, responsibility first became part of adapting the norm of sovereignty to post-Cold-War circumstances. The ICISS report adopted Francis Deng's concept of "sovereignty as responsibility" to formulate the responsibility to protect. The notion of sovereignty as responsibility, later endorsed by Annan (Annan 1999b), suggested that the strict notion of nonintervention needs to be replaced by a positive concept of sovereignty, whereby sovereigns perform for their people and remain answerable to their peers.

The ICISS also replaced the controversial notion of the right to intervene with that of the responsibility to protect, foregrounding the needs of the victims of atrocities. It refocused the debate on what can be done for the people caught up in atrocities, rather than on whether there is a right to intervene and whose right it is. Even if this formulation did not specify what exactly could be done for the victims, it at least made it "more difficult to do nothing" (Chesterman 2011, 279), since it was more challenging to deny the distress of victims than the existence of a right to intervene. R2P strengthened the notion that protection is an obligation rather than something states can choose to evade (Arbour 2008; Bellamy 2009b; Evans 2008).

Third, R2P dissociated protection from the notion of military intervention and placed it within a range of non-coercive measures. By emphasizing prevention (Sharma and Welsh 2015), reaction, and rebuilding (Bellamy 2009a; International Commission on Intervention and State Sovereignty 2001), R2P facilitated action from a broader toolkit, avoiding the deadlock around the use of force. By pointing to a plethora of noncoercive measures, R2P guided the international community toward less costly and less controversial actions to prevent, rather than to react to atrocities already underway.

The institutionalization level

The second important way in which responsibility impacted the contested field of protection is institutionalization. In addition to UN documents, R2P language and perspective was incorporated in the discussion of other issue areas such as the protection of civilians. Since 2011, the Security Council routinely referred to R2P in its resolutions (Bellamy 2015). The Secretary-General appointed a Special Adviser on the Prevention of Genocide (2004) and a Special Adviser on the Responsibility to Protect (2008). Responsible for prioritizing early warning within the UN system and monitoring conflicts, the Special Advisers regularly brief the Council on conflict situations. Putting distinctive R2P lenses on conflict prevention and management contributed to institutionalizing mass atrocity prevention "as a field in its own right" (Bellamy 2014, 99). Since 2008, states appoint national R2P focal points to help incorporate R2P into national legislation and to share best practices among themselves. Groups undertook the role of promoting R2P in international fora, expanding the reach of the R2P framework both nationally and internationally. Under the leadership of the Netherlands and Rwanda, the Group of Friends of the Responsibility to Protect comprise states, whereas the International Coalition for the Responsibility to Protect unites nongovernmental organizations in this effort.

These institutional developments have been part of broader mainstreaming efforts within the UN system (Bellamy 2013), including a range of diplomatic, humanitarian and peaceful measures such as disseminating human rights reports, encouraging states to ratify and implement human rights provisions, incorporating R2P into national legislation, and issuing public statements on situations of concern. Mainstreaming also ensued in the practice of peacekeeping, the protection of civilians becoming increasingly a part of peacekeeping mandates. Peacekeepers would work toward realizing R2P goals through capacity-building, assisting the work of the civilian components of peacekeeping missions, and through direct action if necessary (Hunt and Bellamy 2011). In both cases, mainstreaming aligns the work of existing institutions with the R2P objectives by adding "R2P lenses," i.e. by generating and consolidating institutional knowledge in accordance with R2P.

The level of collective expectations

Beyond institutionalizing new positions and practices, R2P also altered existing ones. Having reinforced the understanding that protection is a duty, the introduction of responsibility ignited specific debates on what R2P actually means in practice and how to allocate the task of protection. In its earliest formulation, the responsibility of the state meant providing basic means of living and basic security for the population (Deng et al. 1996). In terms of the ICISS report, the responsibility of state authorities was defined as protecting the safety and lives of citizens and promoting their welfare. In addition, state officials were responsible to both their citizens and the international community for their actions and omissions (International Commission on Intervention and State Sovereignty 2001, 13). The 2005 World Summit Outcome Document (WSOD) narrowed the scope of the responsibility to protect to the four specific crimes of war crimes, crimes against humanity, genocide, and ethnic cleansing. It emphasized, however, that responsibility includes prevention just as well as taking collective action. Early warning systems developed at the United Nations or the African Union are institutional manifestations of this understanding of responsibility.

The 2009 report of the Secretary-General, *Implementing the Responsibility to Protect*, restarted the conversation by specifying what R2P means. The report describes the range of possible actions to comply with the responsibility to protect, from dialogue through diplomatic and economic sanctions to military means (Ban 2009, 15–28). The annual General Assembly debates, each dedicated to a particular aspect of R2P, further shaped its meaning and content. They covered the role of early warning (2010, 2018), that of regional and sub-regional organizations (2011), accountability for prevention (2017), and mobilizing collective action (2016), among others. One idea that carried much weight at the GA debates was the notion that the responsibility to protect implies a responsibility "while" protecting (RwP). Inspired by the discontent with NATO's 2011 intervention in Libya, Brazil proposed that those carrying out Security Council mandates should be held accountable for the use of force (Viotti 2011; Tourinho, Stuenkel, and Brockmeier 2016). The core of RwP was the proposal that the Council should retain oversight over its mandates, including the right to stop military interventions.

Concerning the responsibility of the international community, there is a growing consensus that the international responsibility to protect stands for a duty of conduct (Welsh 2013) or a "responsibility to try" (Bellamy 2014, 72) to do "what one can" (Pattison 2015, 196). For Louise Arbour, such duty of conduct translates into the "duty of care," i.e. exercising "due diligence" and doing one's best to prevent genocide (Arbour 2008, 452). In terms of concrete action, the duty of conduct might be fulfilled by taking direct action to protect or supporting others in doing so, by authorizing action from the relevant institutional positions, advancing R2P as the best framework for protection to date, reforming existing institutions and, in certain cases, also by not acting (Pattison 2015, 206). A specific example of this latter case is the responsibility not to veto, or refraining from vetoing resolutions pertaining to R2P crimes (Blatter and Williams 2011;

Reinold 2014). This proposal has been on the table since 2001 but has so far failed to materialize as a principle of conduct.

Others questioned whether there is one definition of the R2P for everyone. Glanville argues that protection was a sovereign responsibility well before R2P, albeit with a historically changing, socially constructed content (Glanville 2013). Rao concurs by saying that the obligation of the state to protect its own population is traditionally involved in the "social contract," and it is qualitatively different from that of the international community where protection remains a matter of choice (Rao 2013).

The meaning of R2P also displays regional specificities. The African continent institutionalized its understanding of responsible sovereignty in the Constitutive Act of the African Union (AU) and in the African Peace and Security Architecture (Aning and Edu-Afful 2016; Geldenhuys 2014; Landsberg 2010; Williams 2009). The Constitutive Act grants the right to AU member states to intervene in a member state in cases of grave violation of human rights, i.e. war crimes, genocide and crimes against humanity, consistently with R2P (African Union 2000). However, the African position is distinctive in the sense that it also allows for intervention in cases of unconstitutional changes in government and in showing a preference for reconciliation and inclusive peace agreements in conflict resolution (de Waal 2012). The African preference for inclusive solutions potentially creates tensions with the Western emphasis on criminal accountability as a means of conflict management, especially with respect to prosecuting African heads of states at the International Criminal Court (Arcudi 2019; Birdsall 2015; Bower 2019; García Iommi 2019).

Other regions are more reluctant to depart from traditional notions of sovereignty, yet display particular understandings of the responsibility to protect. Southeast Asian countries in particular are often portrayed as very cautious toward R2P. They might, however, endorse a "responsibility to provide," the duty of the state to provide its population with minimum welfare, and the duty to allow in regional aid the case of natural catastrophes (Tan 2011). Although nominally upholding the norm of non-interference, countries in the region might be recalibrating regional politics to accommodate some aspects of R2P (Bellamy and Drummond 2011). China shares a state-centric interpretation of R2P, i.e. that the prevention of R2P crimes is best secured through long-term economic and infrastructural capacity-building (Foot 2016). China's position on R2P follows both from its support for traditional sovereignty and from its aspiration to assume its role as a great power, one attribute of which is being a "responsible power" (Friedmann 2015; Garwood-Gowers 2016; see also Plagemann and Narlikar in this volume).

In addition to the question of what responsibility is, it is equally pertinent who bears responsibility. One trend in the literature examines which actors could in principle be held responsible, while the other looks at how responsibility might be allocated among them. The WSOD talks about the responsibility of states to protect and to assist each other in protection, and that of the international community to protect in accordance with the UN Charter and its relevant mechanisms. This relatively straightforward formulation raises complicated questions. The first is, what, in practice, is the equivalent of the international community? The WSOD reaffirmed that the Security Council makes decisions on behalf of the international community to define R2P cases and authorize international action, although both the ICISS report and Ban outlined alternative ways of addressing atrocities. Such an alternative is the "Uniting for Peace" mechanism of the General Assembly, which allows for discussing matters of international peace and security if the Council is blocked (A/RES/377 1950). Allocating responsibility to different organs of the UN reflects the understanding that institutions might bear moral responsibility for their actions. This is the case, argues Toni Erskine, if they have the capacity to deliberate and to choose between different courses of action, and therefore the consequences of that action can be assigned to them (Erskine 2002; 2004). Based on such criteria, not only institutions but more ephemeral coalitions of the willing can also bear responsibility (Erskine 2014; 2019).

Although practice reaffirms the role of the Security Council in exercising the responsibility to protect on behalf of the international community, the ICISS report implicated the international community more widely. Echoing Kofi Annan that all of us should ask what we could do to alleviate suffering, it was straightforward in its conclusion that "ultimately, everyone" is responsible (Weiss and Hubert 2001, 147). Pattison also points to the importance of individuals, especially that of journalists and activists, acting on their responsibility to protect to raise awareness and push atrocity cases on the agenda (Pattison 2015). Serrano concurs by arguing that a transnational activist network was crucial to R2P's rise to prominence (Serrano 2011). Humanitarian actors might also be implicated in the responsibility to protect, especially if both states and the Security Council "manifestly fail" in their responsibility. Although what counts as manifest failure is contested in itself (Gallagher 2014), Labonte proposes that humanitarian actors should exercise their responsibility with due attention to the context of the conflict, by remaining pragmatic in terms of what they can achieve, and by cultivating accountability (Labonte 2012). As for nonstate actors as de facto rulers on sovereign territory, Francis Deng, in his work on sovereignty as responsibility, considered them equally responsible for providing the population with basic security and means of living (Deng 1995), although this aspect remain less examined in the literature.

The drafters of R2P, however, thought primarily of state actors and international organizations when allocating the international responsibility to protect. The 2001 R2P report considered three possibilities: that responsibility falls unevenly on those actors that have more capacity to protect, that it falls evenly on everyone, and that special relationships should define the portion of responsibility allocated to an actor (Weiss and Hubert 2001, 148). R2P shifted collective expectations of protective action toward actors in relevant positions, such as that of the Security Council, and those with sufficient capacity (Glanville 2011). These actors also negotiated the expectations among themselves. Analyzing Security Council debates between 2011 and 2016, Gaskarth shows in detail that contestation on applying R2P can be read as a proxy for negotiating responsibility among the great powers as an institution of international society (Gaskarth 2017). For Pattison, the two relevant principles in allocating the responsibility to protect are, first, who is in the institutional position to effectuate protection, and second, given its special ties, which actor has the highest chance of successfully exerting influence on parties to the conflict (Pattison 2010). Others, instead of specifying which particular actors should bear responsibility, think rather about its collective distribution within the international community (Peltonen 2013) or define what responsibility requires based on a pragmatic logic (Ralph 2018). In the latter case, relevant actors and action are defined by the specific circumstances at hand.

The level of justifications for state action

Finally, the introduction of R2P facilitated negotiating the duty of protection by providing a vocabulary for states and policy-makers to justify their actions. These justifications were a matter of public debate, generating new understandings of what protection is and what it is not. At particular critical junctures, the ensuing debates shifted R2P's trajectory (Kurtz and Rotmann 2016), partly as a function of states' historical and social predisposition. In others, contestation around R2P aimed at discrediting or weakening particular readings of norms (Burai 2016), sometimes as part of a broader normative undertaking of challenging the perceived Western dominance of international order (Kurowska 2014).

The initial expectation, in line with theories of norm development, was that contestation would clarify the remits of what R2P is and what it is not (see also Wiener in this volume). In time, certain normative proposals were indeed confidently discarded. This was the case of the

Russian proposal of protecting its citizens abroad in the context of the August 2008 war with Georgia, or the applicability of R2P's third pillar to the mismanagement of natural catastrophes, such as the aftermath of Cyclone Nargis in Myanmar in 2008 (Bellamy 2010; Badescu and Weiss 2010; Junk 2016). Other questions, however, remain the subject of persistent contestation, such as the utility of the use of force or the meaning of last resort in responding to R2P crimes.

Irresponsibility to protect?

Through the changes in discourse, institutionalization, collective expectations, and justifications for state action, R2P has contributed to negotiating protection in the face of value pluralism. On these levels, introducing responsibility meant being able to better identify who should do what to rectify wrongs specified by the R2P framework and to make actors answerable for their conduct. Some, however, argue that R2P had exactly the opposite effect and fostered irresponsibility in protection. Hehir points to the inconsequentiality of endorsing R2P in words but violating it in deeds and argues that R2P has become a "hollow norm" (Hehir 2018). For David Chandler, irresponsibility is manifest in the way political problems are redefined as administrative ones, placing non-Western states under international administration and turning them into objects of governance (Chandler 2011). On the other hand, turning political problems into matters of administration allows Western powers not to engage politically or militarily in conflict resolution. In consequence, R2P generates irresponsibility by making non-Western governments more accountable to international good governance standards than to their electorates at home. In other words, R2P mutes domestic accountability in favor of international accountability (Branch 2011; Cunliffe 2015).

Another way in which R2P might funnel irresponsibility instead of responsibility is in setting unattainable protection goals at the expense of attainable compromise solutions. For de Waal, this was the case in Darfur, where the focus on criminal accountability as part of the R2P discourse antagonized the Sudanese leadership and may have contributed to worsening the conditions on the ground (de Waal 2007a). De Waal also points to the reliance on R2P language as a double-edged sword. Although defining Darfur events as a genocide was meant to be a "rallying cry" to garner political will to act (Evans 2008; Stamnes 2009), it also created adverse effects on the ground (de Waal 2007b).

The R2P discourse might also inadvertently create hierarchies. International protection remains patchy and inadequate in most cases; yet, the discourse on R2P has the impact of emphasizing international protection over local protection efforts. The result is that the international community fails to take into consideration, let alone support, these local efforts (Baines and Paddon 2012; Mégret 2009; 2014). Furthermore, in its effort to emphasize the need of victims to receive support and their dependence on international protection, R2P language might downplay the agency of people caught up in conflict to protect themselves. The "victim" is created as a helpless subject, entirely dependent on international assistance (Conley-Zilkic 2014).

Conclusion

What can we learn from responsibility's functioning in the context of R2P for the broader study of responsibility in world politics? In the case of R2P, responsibility reinforced the understanding that protection is a duty, and it stimulated debates specifying what this duty means and how it should be allocated to particular actors. On the level of discourse, it provided politically acceptable terms for debating the international response to atrocities. On the level of institutionalization, it facilitated generating and consolidating institutional knowledge in accordance with

R2P lenses. On the level of collective expectations, it ignited debates on remedial responsibility and shifted expectations of protective action toward actors in particular institutional positions or with particular capabilities, toward institutions with moral agency, as well as to individuals who might contribute to the responsibility to protect through their professional involvement as journalists or humanitarians. Finally, R2P-related public justifications for state action kindled public debates that clarified new understandings of protection and responsibility. As part of R2P, a field particularly resistant to regulation due to genuine and persistent disagreements, responsibility moved debates forward on these four levels. In this sense, R2P is a prominent example of turning to responsibility to find transient consensus among divergent values and normative commitments.

References

African Union (2000). *The Constitutive Act of the African Union.* http://www.au.int/en/about/constitutive_act.
Aning, K., and Edu-Afful, F. (2016). "African Agency in R2P: Interventions by African Union and ECOWAS in Mali, Côte d'Ivoire, and Libya." *International Studies Review*, 18(1): 120–133.
Annan, K. (1999a). "Secretary General Presents His Annual Report to General Assembly." United Nations. http://www.un.org/News/Press/docs/1999/19990920.sgsm7136.html.
Annan, K. (1999b). "By Invitation: Two Concepts of Sovereignty." *The Economist*, September 26, 1999. http://www.economist.com/node/324795.
Arbour, L. (2008). "The Responsibility to Protect as a Duty of Care in International Law and Practice." *Review of International Studies*, 34(3): 445–458.
Arcudi, A. (2019). "The Absence of Norm Modification and the Intensification of Norm Contestation: Africa and the Responsibility to Prosecute." *Global Responsibility to Protect*, 11(2): 172–197.
A/RES/377 (1950). "A/RES/377: Uniting for Peace." United Nations. https://www.refworld.org/docid/3b00f08d78.html.
Badescu, C. G., and Weiss, T. G. (2010). "Misrepresenting R2P and Advancing Norms: An Alternative Spiral? Misrepresenting R2P and Advancing Norms." *International Studies Perspectives*, 11(4): 354–374.
Baines, E., and Paddon, E. (2012). "'This Is How We Survived': Civilian Agency and Humanitarian Protection." *Security Dialogue*, 43(3): 231–247.
Ban, Ki-moon (2009). "Implementing the Responsibility to Protect: Report of the Secretary-General. A/63/677." http://responsibilitytoprotect.org/SGRtoPEng%20%284%29.pdf.
Barnett, M., and Finnemore, M. (2004). "Genocide and the Peacekeeping Culture at the United Nations." In Barnett, M. and Finnemore, M., eds., *Rules for the World: International Organizations in Global Politics*: 121–155. Ithaca: Cornell University Press.
Bellamy, A. J. (2009a). *Responsibility to Protect*. Cambridge: Polity Press.
Bellamy, A. J. (2009b). "The 2005 World Summit." In Bellamy, A.J., ed., *Responsibility to Protect*: 66–97. Cambridge: Polity Press.
Bellamy, A. J. (2010). "The Responsibility to Protect—Five Years On." *Ethics & International Affairs*, 24(2): 143–169.
Bellamy, A. J. (2013). "Mainstreaming the Responsibility to Protect in the United Nations System: Dilemmas, Challenges and Opportunities." *Global Responsibility to Protect*, 5(2): 154–191.
Bellamy, A. J. (2014). *The Responsibility to Protect: A Defense*. Oxford: Oxford University Press.
Bellamy, A. J. (2015). "The Responsibility to Protect Turns Ten." *Ethics & International Affairs*, 29(2): 161–185.
Bellamy, A. J., and Drummond, C. (2011). "The Responsibility to Protect in Southeast Asia: Between Non-Interference and Sovereignty as Responsibility." *Pacific Review*, 24(2): 179–200.
Bellamy, A. J., and Williams, P. D. (2011). "The New Politics of Protection? Côte d'Ivoire, Libya and the Responsibility to Protect." *International Affairs*, 87(4): 825–850.
Birdsall, A. 2015. "The Responsibility to Prosecute and the ICC: A Problematic Relationship?" *Criminal Law Forum*, 26(1): 51–72.
Blatter, A., and Williams, P. D. (2011). "The Responsibility Not to Veto Civil Society Perspectives." *Global Responsibility to Protect*, 3(2): 301–322.
Bower, A. (2019). "Contesting the International Criminal Court: Bashir, Kenyatta, and the Status of the Nonimpunity Norm in World Politics." *Journal of Global Security Studies*, 4(1): 88–104.

Branch, A. (2011). "The Irresponsibility of the Responsibility to Protect in Africa." In Cunliffe, P., ed. *Critical Perspectives on the Responsibility to Protect: Interrogating Theory and Practice*: 103–124. New York: Routledge.

Burai, E. (2016). "Parody as Norm Contestation: Russian Normative Justifications in Georgia and Ukraine and Their Implications for Global Norms." *Global Society*, 30(1): 67–77.

Chandler, D. (2011). "Understanding the Gap between the Promise and Reality of the Responsibility to Protect." In Cunliffe, P., ed., *Critical Perspectives on the Responsibility to Protect: Interrogating Theory and Practice*: 19–34. New York: Routledge.

Chesterman, S. (2011). "'Leading from Behind': The Responsibility to Protect, the Obama Doctrine, and Humanitarian Intervention After Libya." *Ethics & International Affairs*, 25(3): 279–285.

Conley-Zilkic, B. (2014). "Who Is the Subject of Atrocities Prevention?" *Global Responsibility to Protect*, 6(4): 430–452.

Cunliffe, P. (2015). "From ISIS to ICISS: A Critical Return to the Responsibility to Protect Report." *Cooperation and Conflict*, 51(2): 233–247.

Deng, F. M. (1995). *Sovereignty, Responsibility and Accountability: A Framework of Protection, Assistance and Development for the Internally Displaced*. Washington, DC: Brookings Institution.

Deng, F. M., Kimaro, S., Lyons, T., Rothchild, D. S., and Zartman, I. W. (1996). *Sovereignty as Responsibility: Conflict Management in Africa*. Washington, DC: Brookings Institution.

de Waal, A. (2007a). "Darfur and the Failure of the Responsibility to Protect." *International Affairs*, 83(6): 1039–1054.

de Waal, A. (2007b). "Reflections on the Difficulties of Defining Darfur's Crisis as Genocide." *Harvard Human Rights Journal*, 20: 25–34.

de Waal, A. (2012). "Contesting Visions of Peace in Africa: Darfur, Ivory Coast, Libya." http://sites.tufts.edu/reinventingpeace/2012/05/11/contesting-visions-of-peace-in-africa-darfur-ivory-coast-libya/.

Erskine, T. (2002). *Can Institutions Have Duties?: Collective Moral Agency and International Relations*. Basingstoke: Palgrave Macmillan.

Erskine, T. (2004). "'Blood on the UN's Hands'? Assigning Duties and Apportioning Blame to an Intergovernmental Organisation." *Global Society*, 18(1): 21–42.

Erskine, T. (2014). "Coalitions of the Willing and Responsibilities to Protect: Informal Associations, Enhanced Capacities, and Shared Moral Burdens." *Ethics & International Affairs*, 28(1): 115–145.

Erskine, T. (2019). *Coalitions of the Willing and the Shared Responsibility to Protect*. Oxford: Oxford University Press.

Evans, G. (2008). "The Responsibility to Protect: An Idea Whose Time Has Come … and Gone?" *International Relations*, 22(3): 283–298.

Focarelli, C. (2008). "The Responsibility to Protect Doctrine and Humanitarian Intervention: Too Many Ambiguities for a Working Doctrine." *Journal of Conflict and Security Law*, 13(2): 191–213.

Foot, R. (2016). "The State, Development and Humanitarianism: China's Shaping the Trajectory of R2P." In Bellamy, A. J., and Dunne, T., eds., *The Oxford Handbook of the Responsibility to Protect*: 932–947. Oxford: Oxford University Press.

Friedmann, V. (2015). "Towards a Genealogy of Great Powers and Responsibility: China in Western Conceptions of Governing the World." Budapest: Central European University. www.etd.ceu.edu/2015/friedmann_viktor.pdf.

Gallagher, A. (2014). "What Constitutes a 'Manifest Failing'? Ambiguous and Inconsistent Terminology and the Responsibility to Protect." *International Relations*, 28(4): 428–444.

García Iommi, L. (2019). "Whose Justice? The ICC 'Africa Problem.'" *International Relations*, Online first. https://doi.org/10.1177/0047117819842294.

Garwood-Gowers, A. (2016). "China's 'Responsible Protection' Concept: Reinterpreting the Responsibility to Protect (R2P) and Military Intervention for Humanitarian Purposes." *Asian Journal of International Law*, 6(1): 89–118.

Gaskarth, J. (2017). "Rising Powers, Responsibility, and International Society." *Ethics & International Affairs*, 31(3): 287–311.

Geldenhuys, D. (2014). "The African Union, Responsible Sovereignty and Contested States." *Global Responsibility to Protect*, 6(3): 350–374.

Glanville, L. (2011). "On the Meaning of 'Responsibility' in the 'Responsibility to Protect.'" *Griffith Law Review*, 20(2): 482–504.

Glanville, L. (2013). *Sovereignty and the Responsibility to Protect: A New History*. Chicago: University of Chicago Press.

Hansen-Magnusson, H. (2019). "The Web of Responsibility in and for the Arctic." *Cambridge Review of International Affairs*, 32(2): 132–158.

Hehir, A. (2018). *Hollow Norms and the Responsibility to Protect.* New York: Palgrave Macmillan.
Holzgrefe, J. L., and Keohane, R. O., eds. (2003). *Humanitarian Intervention: Ethical, Legal and Political Dilemmas.* Cambridge University Press.
Hunt, C. T., and Bellamy, A. J. (2011). "Mainstreaming the Responsibility to Protect in Peace Operations." *Civil Wars,* 13(1): 1–20.
Hurd, I. (2011). "Is Humanitarian Intervention Legal? The Rule of Law in an Incoherent World." *Ethics & International Affairs,* 25(3): 293–313.
International Commission on Intervention and State Sovereignty (2001). "The Responsibility to Protect: Report of the International Commission on Intervention and State Sovereignty." http://responsibilitytoprotect.org/ICISS%20Report.pdf.
Junk, J. (2016). "Testing Boundaries: Cyclone Nargis in Myanmar and the Scope of R2P." *Global Society,* 30(1): 78–93.
Kurowska, X. (2014). "Multipolarity as Resistance to Liberal Norms: Russia's Position on Responsibility to Protect." *Conflict, Security & Development,* 14(4): 489–508.
Kurtz, G., and Rotmann, P. (2016). "The Evolution of Norms of Protection: Major Powers Debate the Responsibility to Protect." *Global Society,* 30(1): 3–20.
Labonte, M. T. (2012). "Whose Responsibility to Protect? The Implications of Double Manifest Failure for Civilian Protection." *The International Journal of Human Rights,* 16(7): 982–1002.
Landsberg, C. (2010). "Pax South Africana and the Responsibility to Protect." *Global Responsibility to Protect,* 2(4): 436–457.
Mégret, F. (2009). "Beyond the 'Salvation' Paradigm: Responsibility to Protect (Others) vs the Power of Protecting Oneself." *Security Dialogue,* 40(6): 575–595.
Mégret, F. (2014). "Helping the Syrians Help Themselves? The Ambiguities of International Assistance to the Rebellion." *Stability: International Journal of Security and Development,* 3(1): 1–12.
Miller, D. (2001). "Distributing Responsibilities." *Journal of Political Philosophy,* 9(4): 453–471.
Paris, R. (2014). "The 'Responsibility to Protect' and the Structural Problems of Preventive Humanitarian Intervention." *International Peacekeeping,* 21(5): 569–603.
Pattison, J. (2010). *Humanitarian Intervention and the Responsibility To Protect: Who Should Intervene?* Oxford: Oxford University Press.
Pattison, J. (2015). "Mapping the Responsibilities to Protect: A Typology of International Duties." *Global Responsibility to Protect,* 7(2): 190–210.
Peltonen, H. (2013). *International Responsibility and Grave Humanitarian Crises : Collective Provision for Human Security.* London: Routledge.
Ralph, J. (2018). "What Should Be Done? Pragmatic Constructivist Ethics and the Responsibility to Protect." *International Organization,* 72(1): 173–203.
Rao, N. (2013). "The Choice to Protect: Rethinking Responsibility for Humanitarian Intervention." *Columbia Human Rights Law Review,* 44(3): 697–751.
Reinold, T. (2014). "The Responsibility Not to Veto, Secondary Rules, and the Rule of Law." *Global Responsibility to Protect,* 6(3): 269–294.
Serrano, M. (2011). "The Responsibility to Protect and Its Critics: Explaining the Consensus." *Global Responsibility to Protect,* 3(4): 425–437.
Sharma, S. K., and Welsh, J. M., eds. (2015). *The Responsibility to Prevent: Overcoming the Challenges of Atrocity Prevention.* Oxford and New York: Oxford University Press.
Stamnes, E. (2009). "Speaking R2P and the Prevention of Mass Atrocities." *Global Responsibility to Protect,* 1(1): 70–89.
Tan, K.-C. (2006). "The Duty to Protect." *Nomos,* 47: 84–116.
Tan, S. S. (2011). "Providers Not Protectors: Institutionalizing Responsible Sovereignty in Southeast Asia." *Asian Security,* 7(3): 201–217.
Tourinho, M., Stuenkel, O., and Brockmeier, S. (2016). "'Responsibility While Protecting': Reforming R2P Implementation." *Global Society,* 30(1): 134–150.
Vetterlein, A. (2018). "Responsibility Is More than Accountability: From Regulatory towards Negotiated Governance." *Contemporary Politics,* 24(5): 545–567.
Viotti, M. L. R. (2011). "A/66/551–S/2011/701: Letter Dated 9 November 2011 from the Permanent Representative of Brazil to the United Nations Addressed to the Secretary-General: Responsibility While Protecting: Elements for the Development and Promotion of a Concept." http://www.securitycouncilreport.org/atf/cf/%7B65BFCF9B-6D27-4E9C-8CD3-CF6E4FF96FF9%7D/POC%20S2011%20701.pdf.

Weiss, T. G., and Hubert, D. (2001). *The Responsibility to Protect: Research, Bibliography, Background : Supplemental Volume to the Report of the International Commission on Intervention and State Sovereignty*. Ottawa: International Development Research Centre.

Welsh, J. M. (2006). "Taking Consequences Seriously: Objections to Humanitarian Intervention." In Welsh, J. M., ed., *Humanitarian Intervention and International Relations*: 52–68. New York: Oxford University Press.

Welsh, J. M. (2013). "Norm Contestation and the Responsibility to Protect." *Global Responsibility to Protect*, 5(4): 365–396.

Williams, P. D. (2009). "The 'Responsibility to Protect', Norm Localisation, and African International Society." *Global Responsibility to Protect*, 1(3): 392–416.

15
FROM LISBON TO SENDAI
Responsibilities in international disaster management
Marco Krüger and Friedrich Gabel

Introduction

In the morning of 1 November 1755, an earthquake, the cascading tsunami and the subsequent fire destroyed large parts of Lisbon and killed an estimated 100,000 people (Dynes 2000; Tierney 2014, 26). Although the Lisbon earthquake was neither the first nor the most devastating natural event in human history, it represents a landmark as "the first modern disaster" (Dynes 2000, 97). Occurring amidst the Enlightenment in a major European city, the Lisbon earthquake sparked a debate about responsibility and the impact of human decision-making. The idea that disasters are a divine punishment or inescapable fate was challenged by thinkers of the Enlightenment. In his correspondence with Voltaire, Jean-Jacques Rousseau gives the probably first sociological interpretation of a disaster, by stating that the building structure of the city, the height of the houses and the slow evacuation, and therewith contingent societal factors, contributed to the catastrophic consequences of the earthquake (Dynes 2000, 106). Moreover, the Lisbon earthquake was the first incidence of a state taking responsibility for a disaster by appointing Marquis de Pombal for leading the reconstruction of the city and installing a new building practice, which was more earthquake-resistant than the previous architecture (Dynes 2000, 112–13; Tierney 2014, 26). From 1755 to today, questions of responsibility in disaster management have changed significantly. The latest international treaty on disaster risk reduction from 2015, the United Nations Sendai Framework for Disaster Risk Reduction (SFDRR), still considers the state as the primarily responsible actor, but unfolds a significantly more nuanced understanding of responsibilities (UNISDR 2015, 5).

This chapter is based on an understanding of responsibility, as the legitimate entitlement to expect a conscious justification from another entity for (non-)actions (Sombetzki 2014, 33–42). Similar to Hansen-Magnusson's and Vetterlein's operationalisation of responsibility in the introduction of this volume, we distinguish the subject, object and the normative basis as dimensions of responsibility. In addition to this theoretical framework and following Loh, we treat Hansen-Magnusson's and Vetterlein's "how"-question as a dimension in its own in this contribution. We discuss the question of "How responsibility is enacted?" as the quality (or scope) of responsibility (Sombetzki 2014, 65).[1] This helps us to assess the changes in responsibility for international

Table 15.1 Dimensions of responsibility

Dimension of responsibility	Core question	Example in disaster management
Subject	Who?	An actor is responsible
Quality	How?	For a specific kind and extent of action
Object	For whom?	Towards an affected entity
Normative basis	What for?	Due to a specific understanding of disasters.

disaster management more precisely. Accordingly, in Table 15.1 we distinguish the following dimensions of responsibility:

Following Iris Marion Young (2013, 5, 92), (political) responsibility is the legitimately ascribed task to change a current or upcoming unjust situation according to one's societal capabilities and thus focuses on the interdependencies between individual living situations and social structures. In this vein, she speaks of a shared responsibility that understands social structures as the result of individual actors that nevertheless cannot be blamed individually (Young 2013, xiv, 70–71). Similarly, this shared responsibility requires collective actions to overcome structural injustice (Young 2013, 111–13). This understanding is attractive for modern disaster management, as it is well compatible with the idea of "disaster risk reduction". Furthermore, it emphasises the continuous reflection on existing societal structures. The latter goes hand in hand with the insight of modern disaster management, suggesting that disasters amplify everyday issues such as privileges and discrimination (Kelman and Stough 2015, 8; Young 2013, 45).

Against this theoretical backdrop, we argue that international disaster management policies have undergone significant changes that entail implications for how and to whom responsibility is negotiated and ascribed. More concretely, a four-fold change of the subject, the object, the normative basis as well as the quality of responsibility in international disaster management has taken place. First of all, the subject of responsibility – the (non-)acting entity in charge – has become fuzzier. Although reaffirming the prime responsibility of the nation-state, the role of the international community in engaging with disasters has been increasingly acknowledged (UN 1994, 4; UNISDR 2015). Furthermore, as the Hyogo Framework for Action and its successor, the SFDRR, both request the involvement of all stakeholders into disaster risk reduction processes, the subnational and particularly the local sphere have become increasingly responsibilised (UNISDR 2005). Additionally, non-state actors like inter- and transnational aid organisations, such as the International Red Cross and Red Crescent Movement, and other non-governmental organisations have constantly been playing an active role as disaster relief actor as well as a political authority since the early days of international disaster management (see, for example, UNECOSOC 1963, 1964).

Second, the object of responsibility has changed from the affected state, which had been the dominant recipient in the 1960s, to the individual (UN 1962, 28; 1994; UNISDR 2015). In this vein, the Yokohama Strategy from 1994 stated a "shared responsibility to save human lives, since natural disasters do not respect borders" (UN 1994, 4). This change from the state to the individual goes hand in hand with the emergence of human security in International Relations and thus echoes a broader development in academia (Peoples and Vaughan-Williams 2010, 121). Although the primary responsibility for disaster risk reduction is ascribed to the single state, the international community has increasingly taken over responsibility during the subsequent decades (UN 1962; 1994; UNISDR 2015). The emergence of resilience-thinking in several national disaster management policies, in turn, resulted in the transfer of subjectivity (e.g. responsibility and agency) to the local and the individual level (Grove 2014; Joseph 2018).

Third, the normative basis of responsibility – the way disasters are understood – has changed in two ways. On the one hand, the kind of responsibility changed from a reactive one, to set up financial assistance for rebuilding, to a proactive reduction of the risk for the occurrence of disasters. Thus, the responsibility of disaster management is expanded to actively mitigate the risks posed by both natural and man-made disasters, as stated in the preamble of the SFDRR (UNISDR 2015, 9). On the other hand, the normative basis of disaster management shifted from a narrative of protection to a resilience approach. While the first implies the "promise of security" (Aradau 2014, 75), i.e. the possibility to protect people by preventing a threat, the latter presumes the inevitability of natural hazards and seeks to reduce catastrophic events by improving coping abilities (Aradau 2014, 2017).

Fourth, the quality of responsibility – the scope of responsibility – broadened, according to a shift from the responsibility to protect vulnerable groups to the responsibility to mitigate vulnerability by reducing vulnerable situations (McEntire 2005; UNISDR 2015; Wisner et al. 2004). The shift from ontologically defined vulnerable groups to a dynamic and socially determined grasp on vulnerability is crucial, since it implies the scrutiny of discriminating societal conditions as a root cause of vulnerability.

The last part of this chapter points to the ethical implications this changing responsibility entails for disaster management. A comprehensive analysis of the questions of who can legitimately claim whose responsibility and how could a legitimate distribution of responsibility for disaster management look like is beyond the scope of this article. Nevertheless, we argue that deploying a situational understanding of vulnerability and the availability of adequate socio-economic resources are minimum requirements for an ethically justifiable distribution of responsibility for international disaster management (Gabel 2019; Krüger 2019a).

Who is responsible? The diffusion of responsibility in disaster management

Prior to the Lisbon earthquake, disasters had been mainly perceived as a divine punishment for committed sins. The debate about the causes for the horrific damage caused by the quake and its cascading consequences is the first incident of an altered understanding of disasters (Dynes 2000). The appointed Marquis de Pombal was tasked not only to rebuild the city but also to develop a more seismic-resistant type of houses, the Pombaline architecture (Tierney 2014, 26). Therewith, the state of Portugal took responsibility for the process of rebuilding the devastated city and therefore for mitigating the city's vulnerability against future earthquakes. Thus, it was this modern nation-state that first bore a collective responsibility for the restructuring process and became the subject of responsibility for disaster management. Since then, the state has remained the principal subject of responsibility for disaster management, as stated in the first guiding principle of the SFDRR (UNISDR 2015, 13). As a matter of state politics, disasters might even foster international cooperation despite tensed diplomatic relations, e.g. as between Turkey and Greece in 1999, when both countries were struck by several earthquakes within less than a month (Ganapati, Kelman, and Koukis 2010). Another example is Hurricane Katrina in 2005, when countries such as Cuba or Iran provided medical aid or crude oil to the US (Kelman 2007, 295–96). In these instances, disaster management is reproduced as a task of the nation-state, which is the sole subject of responsibility for disaster management. Other actors provided financial, personnel or material resources for the reconstruction of the damages witnessed, though on a voluntary basis.

What at first glance looks like a constant and clear-cut distribution of responsibility becomes increasingly fuzzy when looking at the developments in detail. Since 1962, the UN General Assembly (UN1962; 1963b; 1968a) has repeatedly passed resolutions on disasters for granting assistance to the affected countries. While these early resolutions and the establishment of a relief fund were reactions to particular disasters, the UN institutionalised their efforts in 1971 by creating the United Nations Disaster Relief Office (UNDRO) (UN 1971). However, the appointment of an UN Disaster Relief Co-ordinator did not mean that the international community took direct responsibility for disaster management. The General Assembly rather acknowledged the need for a coordinated knowledge generation on disasters and aims at contributing to mitigate "suffering caused by natural disasters and the serious economic and social consequences for all, especially the developing countries" (UN 1971, 85). Despite the strengthening of the UNDRO during the 1970s, the respective nation-state remains the sole subject of responsibility, while the UN serves as facilitator to ensure that states can live up to their responsibility (UN 1974, 46).

In 1987, the UN made a significant shift in the distribution of responsibility for international disaster management with Resolution 42/169 of the General Assembly, in which it recognises:

> the responsibility of the United Nations system for promoting international co-operation in the study of natural disasters of geophysical origin and in the development of techniques to mitigate risks arising therefrom, as well as for co-ordinating disaster relief, preparedness and prevention, including prediction and early warning.
> (UN 1987)

Although restricted to knowledge generation and early warning, Resolution 42/169 as the first one explicitly shifted responsibility for disaster management to the UN. Additionally, it declared the 1990s the "decade for natural disaster reduction" (UN 1987). Earlier resolutions only acknowledged that there are international organisations, like the International Red Cross and Red Crescent Movement, bearing responsibility for disaster relief due to their mission statements (see for example: International Committee of the Red Cross 1969; UN 1981; UNECOSOC 1963; 1964).

Several years later, the "Yokohama Strategy and Plan of Action for a Safer World" (UN 1994), which was adopted at the World Conference on National Disaster Reduction in May 1994 by the UN member states, went even further by declaring that: "All countries shall act in a new spirit of partnership to build a safer world based on common interests and shared responsibility to save human lives, since natural disasters do not respect borders" (UN 1994, 4). While the strategy insists on the primary responsibility of the affected state, it acknowledges the transnational character of disasters and thus argumentatively paved the way for an increasing shift of responsibility to the international community. In fact, the United Nations International Strategy on Disaster Reduction (UNISDR), adopted in the General Assembly resolution 54/219 in 2000, continued these efforts in order to provide an international framework for facilitating disaster management (UN 2000).

However, the most recent two UN strategies for international disaster management did not significantly expand the responsibility of the United Nations system. Both, the "Hyogo Framework for Action 2005-2015" (UNISDR 2005) and the "Sendai Framework for Disaster Risk Reduction 2015-2030" (UNISDR 2015) reaffirm the prime responsibility of the state while pointing to the facilitating role of the international system. Thereby, the UN institutions are called to "assist disaster-prone developing countries in disaster risk reduction through appropriate means and coordination" (UNISDR 2005, 16) and "by providing adequate resources through various funding mechanisms, including increased, timely, stable and predictable contributions to the United Nations Trust Fund for Disaster Reduction" (UNISDR 2015, 26).

This upscaling of responsibility is paralleled by the tendency to decentralise disaster management. For instance, the Yokohama Strategy repeatedly emphasised the importance of the local and therewith traditional knowledge and community engagement (UN 1994, 4–5). It also called for the "participation of all levels, from the local community through the national government to the regional and international level" (UN 1994, 8) to make disaster prevention most effective. The Hyogo Framework went even further and expanded the call to engage with local contexts to a delegation of responsibility to "subnational and local responsibility" (UNISDR 2005, 6). Although less explicit, the successor of the Hyogo Framework, the SFDRR, perpetuated this principle of broadening and devolving responsibility by emphasising the importance and the role of local authorities in disaster management (UNISDR 2015, 17–18). This tendency of attributing responsibility for disaster management to the local sphere, hence responsibilising it, coincides with the call to engage the private sector (UN 1994, 17; UNISDR 2005, 11; 2015, 20) as well as with an increasing emphasis of resilience in the international frameworks. This development is reproduced on the national level in several disaster management strategies that increasingly emphasise the role of the private and the individual sphere while delegating responsibility to a varying degree to the sub-national and local sphere (Joseph 2016, 2018; Kaufmann 2013).

From the 1960s to today, the nation-state has remained the main subject of responsibility for disaster management. This section demonstrated, however, that the previous sole responsibility became increasingly fuzzy and was distributed to various other levels, from the international community to the individual. Consequently, the broadening of attributing responsibility occurred in two directions, whereby the imposed delegation of responsibility to the local and the individual sphere entails particular problems, such as the de-politicisation of disaster management through the individualisation of responsibility, the potential withdrawal of the state, or the imposition of prescribed behavioural routines in case of a disaster (Evans and Reid 2014; Joseph 2018; Krüger 2019a).

Whom to protect? From the state to the individual

Another change in the characterisation of responsibility occurred with regard to the object of the responsibility in disaster management. While the state was long considered the entity to be protected, international disaster management policies have increasingly centred around the protection of human beings. Particularly the Hyogo and the Sendai Framework call for a stronger consideration of vulnerable groups, thus acknowledging societal diversity and potentially differing demands for help (UNISDR 2005; 2015). The latter reflects what international aid organisations, like the International Federation of Red Cross and Red Crescent, have claimed, due to their mission statements, for decades. Already in 1969, the International Red Cross stated in its International Review "that in the present century the international community has accepted increased responsibility for relief of human suffering in any form" (International Committee of the Red Cross 1969, 632).

When analysing the object of responsibility in disaster management it is telling how the Lisbon earthquake became the "first modern disaster" (Dynes 2000, 97). Indeed, half a century prior to the destruction of Lisbon, in 1693, two earthquakes hit Catania, Sicily, as well as Port Royal, Jamaica. However, both earthquakes occurred at the periphery and, thus, received far less attention than the one in Lisbon, a cultural centre in Europe (Dynes 2000, 98). Moreover, the royal palace and the houses of a good share of the nobles were located in the centre of the city, which was particularly exposed to floods and subsequently, to a large part destroyed, either by the earthquake, the tsunami induced flood or by the fire. Such hazard-exposed areas are usually inhabited by people of lower social status (Dynes 2000, 111). The general status of Lisbon as well as the social status of the victims of the earthquake, thus, the status of the object of responsibility, strongly contributed to Portugal taking responsibility for the reconstruction process of the city in the aftermath of the earthquake (Dynes 2000, 112; Tierney 2014, 26). In that, the Lisbon earthquake pointed out the central role of the object of responsibility that needs to be deemed sufficiently important to take responsibility for its protection and rebuilding (see also: International Federation of Red Cross and Red Crescent Societies 2006). Determining an object of responsibility is thus linked to a value judgement, since "[o]bjects of no value cannot be threatened in the same sense as those that do have value" (Burgess 2011, 13–14). The definition of the object of responsibility in disaster management thus allows an outlook on the normative priorities of the subject of responsibility.

In its early phase during the 1960s and 1970s, the object of responsibility in international disaster management was the affected state. In its resolution on assistance in cases of natural disasters in 1970, the UN General assembly (UN 1971, 85) stated "that throughout history natural disasters and emergency situations have inflicted heavy loss of life and property, affecting every people and every country". In this understanding, the country and the people as a unitary entity, not the single individual, is affected by disasters. The aid of the international community is then meant to remedy the losses from which the affected state suffers (UN 1970, 83). Consequently, it is the Westphalian sovereign state that was the object of responsibility for international disaster management during that time.

In the subsequent decades, the object of responsibility has continuously shifted from the international community's perspective. UN strategies have increasingly considered the protection of individuals as central aim of disaster management. The Yokohama Strategy (UN 1994), as the key document of the "International Decade for Natural Disaster Reduction", is one prominent example of this change. It opens the black box of the state as a unitary entity in international disaster management and differentiates between varying societal groups. It acknowledged that "the poor and socially disadvantaged groups in developing countries" (UN 1994, 4) are most affected by disasters. While this broke up the exclusively state-centric focus of previous UN resolutions, it still embraced particularly poor states and regions with a high exposure to natural hazards as particularly vulnerable and thus, as object of responsibility (UN 1994, 9). The 2005 Hyogo Framework for Action put the "survival, dignity and livelihood of individuals" (UNISDR 2005, 1) in the preamble of the text centrepiece. Just like the Yokohama Strategy, the Hyogo Framework portrayed the protection of people as a prime responsibility of states and (to a lesser degree) of the international community (UN 1994, 5; UNISDR 2005, 4). Finally, the SFDRR is the most explicit treaty in this regard by stating that disaster management "is aimed at protecting persons and their property, health, livelihoods and productive assets, as well as cultural and environmental assets, while promoting and protecting all human rights, including the right to development" (UNISDR 2015, 13).

The paramount importance of the individual as object of responsibility in international disaster management parallels the development in other policy fields, like the UN'S Responsibility to Protect (UN 2005, 30). The rise of human security as a general concept in the UN during the 1990s is mirrored in international disaster management, a policy field that links questions of security and development. From the Yokohama Strategy to the Hyogo Framework and the SFDRR, all recent international disaster management concepts reflect the "*people-centred*" (UNDP 1994, 23) human security approach claiming "freedom from fear and freedom from want" (UN 2005, 31), particularly for the most vulnerable people. Thereby, the state level's role in international disaster management has become a means to the end of human security. It is thus limited to granting protection to individuals and societal groups (UNISDR 2015, 13–14). The changed object of responsibility has led to a significant change of the normative basis of responsibility from a reactive responsibility to rebuild to a proactive responsibility to prevent or adapt.

What for? Rebuilding, risk reduction and resilience

Returning to the 1755 Lisbon earthquake, the rebuilding efforts in the aftermath of the destruction of vast parts of the city embraced both a proactive and a reactive element. The reactive element was the reconstruction process as such. In the process, the Marques de Pombal was charged with the long-term restructuring work of the city as well as with the immediate emergency responses (Dynes 2000, 112). Moreover, Pombal developed what was to be called Pombaline architecture, a style that was more earthquake-resistant than the previous architecture of the city, which had contributed to the large-scale losses. The creation of this new, more resistant architectural style complemented the reactive responsibility to rebuild with a proactive responsibility to reduce future losses. It was the materialisation of the idea that societal conditions, not divine judgements, determine vulnerability or, as Kathleen Tierney (2014, 26) puts it: "Pombaline architecture is the physical embodiment of the idea that both vulnerability and safety are the consequence of decisions about the design of urban forms." Nevertheless, it took another 200 years until the 1970s until the idea of vulnerability became the central concept of disaster studies that it is today. The change from perceiving disasters as divine punishment to scrutinising societal conditions with regard to their influence on vulnerability, exposure and eventually, affectedness, determines the issues, for which the respective subject of responsibility can take responsibility. Drawing from how the Enlightenment paved the way for taking proactive responsibility after the Lisbon earthquake, this section deals with how the normative basis of responsibility in international disaster management has changed from the passive and retrospective rebuilding of infrastructure to the proactive reduction of disaster risks.

During the 1960s the international community's efforts to disaster management focused on mobilising the UN structures and member states for helping countries hit by a natural disaster, such as Iran (UN 1962, 1968a), Yugoslavia (UN 1963a) and the Caribbean (UN 1963b). UN Resolution 1753 on the earthquake in Iran in 1962 mentioned the need to enhance prognostic means in seismological research for preventing disaster induced human suffering (UN 1962, 28). This reflects the primacy of the retrospective responsibility to help affected states to rebuild their infrastructure. A prospective responsibility to gather knowledge on disaster mitigation played only a subordinated role during this first decade of international crisis management under the umbrella of the UN.

Starting from the establishment of the UNDRO in 1971, this situation changed towards a more balanced emphasis of retrospective and prospective responsibility. Both resolutions on "Assistance in cases of natural disaster" (UN 1970) and on the establishment of the UNDRO dedicated only three paragraphs explicitly to general preparedness measures and knowledge-gathering about early warning mechanisms. Shortcomings in its ability to effectively coordinate disaster relief operations on a worldwide scale caused a further strengthening of the UNDRO in 1974. This resolution emphasised the importance of pre-disaster planning and disaster prevention for both, the national and the international political sphere (UN 1974, 46). Disaster preparedness increasingly gained importance in the subsequent years and led to the proclamation of the "International Decade for Natural Disaster Reduction" (UN 1987) in the 1990s. The UN's work in disaster management in this decade was explicitly dedicated to reducing the death toll of disasters by increasing preparedness, improving prediction, fostering scientific knowledge, implementing standards and building capacity vis-à-vis natural hazards (UN 1987). The Yokohama Strategy, as the key document of the UN decade, illustrates this shift by affirming that:

> Disaster prevention, mitigation and preparedness are better than disaster response in achieving the goals and objectives of the Decade. Disaster response alone is not sufficient, as it yields only temporary results at a very high cost. We have followed this limited approach for too long.
>
> *(UN 1994, 4)*

The emphasis on relief assistance in international disaster management represents a predominantly reactive attitude towards disasters prior to the "International Decade for Natural Disaster Reduction". While prevention and preparedness were mentioned, relief operations and restructuring processes had been at the core of international disaster management. The UN Decade and particularly the Yokohama Strategy changed this modus operandi to a proactive approach of reducing disaster risks and preventing harm. For the latter point, knowledge about how and why natural hazards inflict disastrous effects on societies are described to be key in disaster management (UN 1994, 4). This rather modernist approach assumes knowledge to be key for reducing the impact of disasters. It is an incidence of what David Chandler (2014, 27) calls "simple complexity", "an epistemological problem of knowledge of emergent causality". However, in contrast to the ideal of the Enlightenment to identify general laws (Chandler 2014, 20–21), the Yokohama Strategy calls for the acknowledgement of the specific "cultural and organizational characteristics of each society" (UN 1994, 4–5). Knowledge generation and the implementation of sustainable development policies were to increase capacities and decrease vulnerabilities (UN 1994, 8). The reduction of disaster risks for society was accompanied by the aim to prevent the likelihood of disasters through environmental protection (UN 1994, 8). In sum, the Yokohama Strategy in its claim for a better world revealed a proactive disaster management that aimed at mitigating both: the probability of occurrence and the negative consequences of hazards.

Although particularly the capacity building approach, linked to ideas of sustainable development, is remarkably compatible with resilience thinking, the term resilience was used only once in the Yokohama Strategy (UN 1994, 11). However, the document repeatedly emphasised the need to include local authorities and actors from the civil society into the national capacity building efforts.

Roughly 20 years later, in the 2005 Hyogo Framework for Action, the international community regarded a stronger involvement of individuals in disaster management in their local communities as the most crucial lesson learned (UNISDR 2005, 2). Although the overall objectives were in line with the Yokohama Strategy and the term "disaster reduction" keeps a central position, "disaster risk reduction" appears to be the most commonly used goal in the Hyogo Framework (UNISDR 2005). The difference is that disaster risk reduction aims at mitigating the adverse risks of a disaster rather than at minimising the likelihood of an event as such. In this vein, the Hyogo Framework (UNISDR 2005, 6) states that:

> Countries that develop policy, legislative and institutional frameworks for disaster risk reduction and that are able to develop and track progress through specific and measurable indicators have greater capacity to manage risks and to achieve widespread consensus for engagement in and compliance with disaster risk reduction measures across all sectors of society.

The emphasis of the local level links to the devolution of responsibility. Moreover, the focus on risk reduction through capacity building is in line with resilience thinking. In fact, the term resilience appeared more than 20 times in the Hyogo Framework; far more often than in the Yokohama Strategy. Thereby, resilience is linked to David Chandler's (2014, 28) "general complexity" emphasising the contextuality of knowledge. This requires to "[r]ecognize the importance and specificity of local risk patterns and trends, decentralize responsibilities and resources for disaster risk reduction to relevant sub-national or local authorities" (UNISDR 2005, 6), as the Hyogo Framework concluded. The increasingly fuzzy attribution of responsibility to a multitude of levels ranging from the global to the local and eventually to the individual as the entrepreneur of her own protection (Chandler 2016, 14; Evans and Reid 2014, 42). Moreover, the reference to different levels of responsibility reflects the idea of panarchy, which is rooted in the ecological understanding of resilience (Holling and Gunderson 2002; Holling, Gunderson, and Peterson 2002). Panarchy refers to the interconnectedness of different (societal) levels. Due to their interconnections, changes on one level of the system, so the argument goes, may result in changes on other systemic levels (Holling, Gunderson, and Peterson 2002). Accordingly, resilience towards disasters can only be achieved through granting resilience on all interconnected societal levels, from the individual to the global. Spreading responsibilities over all societal levels is thus the consequence of resilience thinking (Krüger 2019b, 63–64). This shared agency, however, relies on knowledge generation on the local level and thus responsibilises the individual and subnational levels (Kaufmann 2013).

The SFDRR echoes the very approach of the Hyogo Framework and goes even further by calling for "a broader and a more people-centred preventive approach to disaster risk" (UNISDR 2015, 10). The Sendai Framework sketches out a capacity-oriented approach that seeks to mitigate vulnerability by empowering the local sphere in general and marginalised societal groups in particular (UNISDR 2015). In fact, the devastating effects of natural hazards hit different societal groups to a different extent (Tierney 2019, 120). The SFDRR thus seeks to tackle the underlying social dynamics leading to a stratified vulnerability in society (UNISDR 2015, 10). The development of different understandings of vulnerability is closely linked to the quality of responsibility in international disaster management and thus subject to the subsequent section.

How? From vulnerable entities to vulnerable situations

Finally, a qualitative shift of responsibility in disaster management may be illustrated along the concept of vulnerability. Broadly speaking, vulnerability describes the social side of disaster risk (Hilhorst and Bankoff 2004; Wisner et al. 2004) besides a hazardous event. Although vulnerability has been a core term of UN disaster politics right from the beginning, its understanding and the resulting implications for state disaster politics has changed from improving building standards, similar to the case of Lisbon, over protecting specific social groups understood as especially vulnerable, to an approach focusing on the reduction of situations that make people vulnerable.

In the early years of UN disaster politics, vulnerability was mainly attributed to poor building conditions of areas and places (UN 1968b). This changed in the 1970s, when e.g. the "Guidelines for Disaster Prevention I" issued that vulnerability cannot be understood solely by technical or economic conditions, but had to involve socio-political arrangements as well (Office of the United Nations Disaster Relief Co-ordinator 1976, 30–41). Therefore, and in line with the lessons learned from Lisbon, a broader attention was put on the social history of bad building quality and densely populated areas as to be found disproportionally often in low-income quarters. Vulnerability was further defined as a characteristic of populations, buildings and civil engineering works, economic activities, public services, utilities and infrastructure that describes the degree of loss resulting from a natural phenomenon (Office of the United Nations Disaster Relief Co-ordinator 1980, 5).

In the course of the "International Decade for Natural Disaster Reduction" in the 1990s, the Yokohama Strategy marks another important step, as it puts emphasis on the vulnerability of communities and claims a need of community involvement, empowerment of disadvantaged groups and capacity building (UN 1994, 9). Furthermore, the "United Nations International Strategy for Disaster Reduction" (UNISDR) described a transition from a reaction to a reduction of vulnerability (UN 2000, 3). Acknowledging this, the UNISDR publication on "Countering Disasters, Targeting Vulnerability" defined disasters as the result of the impact of a hazard on a socio-economic system, promoting the fact that natural hazards themselves do not necessarily lead to disasters (UNISDR 2001, 1). Therefore, vulnerability should be part of development planning processes that recognise why some social groups are more vulnerable than others. This understanding of vulnerability, which takes into account physical/technical and infrastructural as well as social (economic) and cultural aspects, can also be found in the 2005 Hyogo Framework. Vulnerability is in this document defined as "the conditions determined by physical, social, economic, and environmental factors or processes, which increase the susceptibility of a community to the impact of hazards" (UNISDR 2005, 1). The reduction of vulnerability is therefore linked to taking cultural diversity, age, and vulnerable groups into account when planning for disaster risk reduction (UNISDR 2005, 1–5).

The SFDRR, as the latest agreement, finally calls for an inclusive strategy in dealing with disasters and vulnerability. Although it describes, e.g. women, children or people with disabilities, as particularly vulnerable (UNISDR 2015, 10), it adopts a different perspective on vulnerability. Instead of using the previous "vulnerable groups" narrative, the alternative approach of "vulnerable situations" refers to the complexity of factors for vulnerability and its potentiality. Therefore, a shift from integrating (predefined) vulnerable groups into disaster planning to identifying situations in which persons become vulnerable can be observed (Wisner et al. 2004).[2] A continuous academic debate on the factors and operationalization of vulnerability accompanies these political changes (Gallopín 2006; Mechanic and Tanner 2007; McEntire 2005; Oliver-Smith 2004; Sparf 2016; Wisner et al. 2004). The case of Lisbon itself serves, again, as an example. The rich and well-situated inhabitants were the most vulnerable, as their housings were right at the city centre, next to the palace, where the fires struck the most (Dynes 2000, 99).

In terms of responsibility, this broadening of the conditions and subjects of vulnerability refers to a change of quality. Instead of a purely technical standardization, responsibility for vulnerability needs to be understood as responsibility for the social conditions that lead to these situations. Therefore, attention needs to be paid especially to those groups and persons who are potentially affected the most by the consequences of an extreme event (UNISDR 2015, 10). In this vein, responsibility for vulnerability is not just encompassing a change of the "symptom" of, for instance, built environments, but the transformation of the "reasons" of inequality and discrimination in social structures and politics (Hartman and Squires 2006; Human Rights Council 2015; Parthasarathy 2018). In the word of the SFDRR:

> Prevent new and reduce existing disaster risk through the implementation of integrated and inclusive economic, structural, legal, social, health, cultural, educational, environmental, technological, political and institutional measures that prevent and reduce hazard exposure and vulnerability to disaster.
>
> *(UNISDR 2015, 12)*

To achieve this, not only the state authorities but also public and private stakeholders at all levels are responsible for adding their perspectives on gender, culture and disability living conditions and resulting needs (UNISDR 2015, 13). On a state level, this change of responsibility for vulnerability goes in line with the above-mentioned diffusion of responsibility. Rather than expecting the state to be the sole responsible instance for protection, citizens are considered stakeholders and requested to take self-protection efforts. Therefore, state responsibility broadens to ensuring capabilities for individual protection (Krüger 2019b). However, how this responsibility is to be implemented is an ongoing discussion that very much depends on the local conditions (Begg 2018, 393; Box et al. 2016; Christie et al. 2016, 244–45).

Conclusion

From Lisbon in 1755 to Sendai in 2015, the attribution of responsibility in international disaster management has shifted significantly in many regards. The reconstruction efforts after the destruction of Lisbon remarkably resembled the early years of international disaster management in the 1960s, with a strong focus on reactive disaster relief and the exclusive responsibility of the nation-sate. Although the primacy of state responsibility for disaster management has remained a constant until the Sendai Framework (UNISDR 2015, 13), the subject of responsibility (who?) has broadened, ranging from the individual to the global level. In another dimension, the object of responsibility (whom to protect?) has changed over time. While in the 1960s, states were expected to assist other states in disasters relief, the object of responsibility has shifted from the state to the individual. This change echoes the broader discourse in International Relations with the emergence of human security.

Moreover, the normative basis of responsibility (what for?) has changed and international disaster management has become increasingly proactive. In this vein, disaster relief, albeit always mentioned as a necessary part of disaster management, was replaced by prevention, mitigation and preparedness as top priority. The emergence of resilience politics has spurred a further change from mitigation and prevention to disaster risk reduction through capacity building, which became the leitmotif of the Sendai Framework (UNISDR 2015). These changes in the quality of responsibility (how?) are reflected in the altered treatment of vulnerability in international disaster management, which changed from an ontological characteristic of an individual to a situational understanding. The varying likelihood to be in a vulnerable situation results from processes of intersectional societal marginalisation and discrimination (Tierney 2019, 136).

The increased attention for the well-being of the individual as well as for processes of societal marginalisation and the production of vulnerability are ethically desirable developments in international disaster management. Both contribute to scrutinising current modes of disaster management instead of reinforcing a fatalistic acceptance of disasters or vulnerability as unchangeable givens. Granting agency to all societal levels, which comes with the multiplicity of subjects of responsibility, is therefore an improvement to previous understandings of disaster management, as it gives a voice to those who suffer from injustice and marginalisation. Iris Marion Young (2013, 146) argues in this context that "[i]t is they who know the most about the harms they suffer, and thus it is up to them, though not them alone, to broadcast their situation and call it injustice".

Although the Hyogo Framework primarily speaks about responsibility, it was the Sendai Framework that prominently emphasised the empowerment of the most vulnerable as a political goal (UNISDR 2015, 19). However, while responsibility is shifted very explicitly to the local sphere, it remains opaque how the promised empowerment will come into being. In order to be substantial, empowerment requires the proliferation of capacities and power as well as the reconsideration of so far unquestioned societal normalities (Gabel 2019; Krüger 2019a). Substantial empowerment "is fundamentally about changing power relations" (Cornwall and Rivas 2015, 405). It is a process that goes beyond the proliferation of coping capacities and needs to enable to scrutinise the status quo (Cornwall and Rivas 2015, 405). The mere declaration of intent, however, runs the risk of responsibilising the individual without following up on the required proliferation of capacities and reconsideration of constraining imaginations of normalities. Just as Jonathan Joseph (2018, 117) concluded for the UK disaster management policies, international disaster management also runs the risk of devolving responsibility while keeping the power to define necessary capacities and standards of resilience, as well as to enforce their enactment. In fact, the SFDRR is shaped by the neoliberal idea of an efficient and cost-effective disaster management. However, by addressing poverty, inequality, discrimination and exclusion as underlying drivers for vulnerability and thus as a disaster risk (UNISDR 2015, 10), the Sendai Framework might also be a vantage point for a substantial empowerment and a just distribution of responsibility in international disaster management.

Notes

1 Sombetzki discusses different relational outlines of responsibility that can be found throughout the literature. She distinguishes five dimensions and further subcategories of responsibility (Sombetzki 2014, 65–132). Particularly interesting for us is her differentiation between the *object* of responsibility (Sombetzki calls this *addressee*), the benefiting entity, and the *normative basis* (Sombetzki calls this *object*), which describes what responsibility is about (e.g. the protection from suffering due to extreme events). Further, we consider it necessary to introduce the *quality* of responsibility (Sombetzki calls this normative criteria) as this allows a clearer distinction between an act, in our case the disaster management practice, a certain distribution of responsibility and the addressee suffering from the disaster, the object. Additionally, Sombetzki brings up the *authority* of responsibility, i.e. the (normative) instance before which the *subject* is responsible for the *object*. Since this dimension is closely related to the object and the normative basis of responsibility, we included this category into the dimensions *object* and *normative basis*.
2 Similar ideas can also be found in the 1998 UN-Economic Council report on *Promoting social integration and participation of all people, including disadvantaged and vulnerable groups*, which although issuing vulnerability with regard to certain social groups, defining it as a human condition of every person that becomes significant depending on the specific situation (UNECOSOC 1998).

References

Aradau, C. (2014). "The Promise of Security: Resilience, Surprise and Epistemic Politics." Resilience, 2(2): 73–87.
Aradau, C. (2017). "The Promise of Security: Resilience, Surprise and Epistemic Politics." In Chandler, D., and Coaffe, J., eds., *The Routledge Handbook of International Resilience*: 79–91. London and New York: Routledge.
Begg, C. (2018). "Power, Responsibility and Justice: A Review of Local Stakeholder Participation in European Flood Risk Management." *Local Environment*, 23(4): 383–397.
Box, P., Bird, D., Haynes, K., and King, D. (2016). "Shared Responsibility and Social Vulnerability in the 2011 Brisbane Flood." *Natural Hazards*, 81(3): 1549–1568.
Burgess, J.P. (2011). *The Ethical Subject of Security: Geopolitical Reason and the Threat against Europe*. London and New York: Routledge.
Chandler, D. (2014). *Resilience: The Governance of Complexity*. London and New York: Routledge.
Chandler, D. (2016). "Debating Neoliberalism: The Exhaustion of the Liberal Problematic." In Chandler, D., and Reid, J., eds., *The Neoliberal Subject: Resilience, Adaptation and Vulnerability*: 9–16. London and New York: Rowman & Littlefield International.
Christie, N., Griffin, L., Chan, N., Twigg, J., and Titheridge, H. (2016). "Private Needs, Public Responses: Vulnerable People's Flood-disrupted Mobility." *Disaster Prevention and Management*, 25(2): 244–260.
Cornwall, A., and Rivas, A.-M. (2015). "From 'Gender Equality' and 'Women's Empowerment' to Global Justice: Reclaiming a Transformative Agenda for Gender and Development." *Third World Quarterly*, 36(2): 396–415.
Dynes, R.R. (2000). "The Dialogue Between Voltaire and Rousseau on the Lisbon Earthquake: The Emergence of a Social Science View." *International Journal of Mass Emergencies and Disasters*, 18(1): 97–115.
Evans, B., and Reid, J. (2014). *Resilient Life: The Art of Living Dangerously*. Cambridge: Polity Press.
Gabel, F. (2019). "Chancen dynamischer Konzeptionen von Vulnerabilität für den Katastrophenschutz." In Krüger, M. and Max, M., eds., *Resilienz im Katastrophenfall. Konzepte zur Stärkung von Pflege- und Hilfsbedürftigen*: 77–96. Bielefeld: transcript.
Gallopín, G.C. (2006). "Linkages Between Vulnerability, Resilience, and Adaptive Capacity." *Global Environmental Change*, 16(3): 293–303.
Ganapati, N.E., Kelman, I., and Koukis, T. (2010). "Analysing Greek–Turkish Disaster-Related Cooperation: A Disaster Diplomacy Perspective." *Conflict and Cooperation*, 45(2): 162–185.

Grove, K. (2014). "Agency, Affect, and the Immunological Politics of Disaster Resilience." *Environment and Planning D: Society and Space*, 32(2): 240–256.

Hartman, C., and Squires, G.D., eds. (2006). *There Is No Such Thing as a Natural Disaster: Race, Class, and Hurricane Katrina*. New York, NY: Routledge.

Hilhorst, D., and Bankoff, G. (2004). "Introduction: Mapping Vulnerability." In Bankoff, G., Frerks, G., and Hilhorst, D., eds., *Mapping Vulnerability: Disasters, Development and People*: 1–9. London, Sterling & VA: Earthscan.

Holling, C.S., and Gunderson, L.H. (2002). "Resilience and Adaptive Cycles." In Holling, C.S., and Gunderson, L.H., eds., *Panarchy: Understanding Transformations in Human and Natural Systems*: 25–62. Washington, Covelo, London: Island Press.

Holling, C.S., Gunderson, L.H., and Peterson, G.D. (2002). "Sustainability and Panarchies." In Holling, C.S., and Gunderson, L.H., eds., *Panarchy: Understanding Transformations in Human and Natural Systems*: 63–102. Washington, Covelo, London: Island Press.

Human Rights Council (2015). "Thematic Study on the rights of persons with disabilities under article 11 of the Convention on the Rights of Persons with Disabilities, on situations of risk and humanitarian emergencies: Report of the Office of the United Nations High Commissioner for Human Rights." http://ap.ohchr.org/documents/dpage_e.aspx?si=A/HRC/31/30. UN Doc. A/HRC/31/30.

International Committee of the Red Cross (1969). *International Review of the Red Cross*, (104)9. Geneva. https://www.loc.gov/rr/frd/Military_Law/pdf/RC_Nov-1969.pdf

International Federation of Red Cross and Red Crescent Societies (2006). *World Disaster Report 2006: Focus on neglected crisis*. Satigny/Vernier, Switzerland: ATAR Roto Presse. https://www.ifrc.org/Global/Publications/disasters/WDR/WDR2006-English-LR.pdf

Joseph, J. (2016). "Governing Through Failure and Denial: The New Resilience Agenda." *Millennium Journal of International Studies*, 44(3): 370–390.

Joseph, J. (2018). *Varieties of Resilience: Studies in Governmentality*. Cambridge: Cambridge University Press.

Kaufmann, M. (2013). "Emergent Self-organisation in Emergencies: Resilience Rationales in Interconnected Societies." *Resilience*, 1(1): 53–68.

Kelman, I. (2007). "Hurricane Katrina Disaster Diplomacy." *Disasters*, 31(3): 288–309.

Kelman, I., and Stough, L.M. (2015). "(Dis)Ability and (Dis)Aster." In Kelman, I., and Stough, L.M., eds., *Disability and Disaster: Explorations and Exchanges*: 3–14. New York, NY: Palgrave Macmillan.

Krüger, M. (2019a). "Building Instead of Imposing Resilience: Revisiting the Relationship Between Resilience and the State." *International Political Sociology*, 13(1): 53–67.

Krüger, M. (2019b). "Resilienz: Zwischen staatlicher Forderung und gesellschaftlicher Förderung." In Krüger, M., and Max, M., eds., *Resilienz im Katastrophenfall: Konzepte zur Stärkung von Pflege- und Hilfsbedürftigen im Bevölkerungsschutz*: 57–75. Bielefeld: transcript.

McEntire, D.A. (2005). "Why Vulnerability Matters." *Disaster Prevention and Management*, 14(2): 206–222.

Mechanic, D., and Tanner, J. (2007). "Vulnerable People, Groups, and Populations: Societal View." *Health affairs (Project Hope)*, 26(5): 1220–1230.

Office of the United Nations Disaster Relief Co-ordinator (1976). "Guidelines for disaster prevention: Volume I - Pre-Disaster Physical Planning of Human Settlement." Guidelines for disaster prevention I. UNDRO/10/76/Vol. I.

Office of the United Nations Disaster Relief Co-ordinator (1980). "Natural Disasters and Vulnerability Analysis: Report of Expert Group Meeting (9.-12.07.1979)".

Oliver-Smith, A. (2004). "Theorizing Vulnerability in a Globalized World: A Political Ecological Perspective." In Bankoff, G., Frerks, G., and Hilhorst, D., eds., *Mapping Vulnerability: Disasters, Development and People*: 10–24. London, Sterling & VA: Earthscan.

Parthasarathy, D. (2018). "Inequality, Uncertainty, and Vulnerability: Rethinking Governance from a Disaster Justice Perspective." *Environment and Planning E: Nature and Space*, 1(3): 422–442.

Peoples, C., and Vaughan-Williams, N. (2010). *Critical Security Studies: An Introduction*. London/New York: Routledge.

Sombetzki, J. (2014). *Verantwortung als Begriff, Fähigkeit, Aufgabe: Eine Drei-Ebenen-Analyse*. Research. Wiesbaden: Springer VS.

Sparf, J. (2016). "Disability and Vulnerability: Interpretations of Risk in Everyday Life." *Contingencies Crisis Management*, 24(4): 244–252.

Tierney, K.J. (2014). "The Social Roots of Risk: Producing Disasters, Promoting Resilience." *High Reliability and Crisis Management*. Stanford, California: Stanford University Press.

Tierney, K.J. (2019). *Disasters: A Sociological Approach*. Cambridge, Medford: Polity Press.

UN (1962). "General Assembly Resolution 1753 (XVII): Measures to be adopted in connexion with the earthquake in Iran." http://www.worldlii.org/int/other/UNGA/1962/12.pdf
UN (1963a). "General Assembly Resolution 1882 (XVIII). Measures in connexion with the earthquake at Skopje, Yugoslavia." http://www.worldlii.org/int/other/UNGA/1963/4.pdf
UN (1963b). "General Assembly Resolution 1888 (XVIII). Measures in connexion with the hurricane which has just struck the territories of Cuba, the Dominican Republic, Haiti, Jamaica and Trinidad and Tobago." http://www.worldlii.org/int/other/UNGA/1963/7.pdf
UN (1968a). "General Assembly Resolution 2378 (XXIII): Assistance to Iran in connexion with the earthquake of August 1968." http://www.worldlii.org/int/other/UNGA/1968/3.pdf
UN (1968b). "General Assembly Resolution A/Res/2435(XXIII): Assistance in cases of natural disaster." http://www.worldlii.org/int/other/UNGA/1968/67.pdf
UN (1970). "General Assembly Resolution 2717 (XXV). Assistance in cases of natural disaster." http://www.worldlii.org/int/other/UNGA/1970/106.pdf
UN (1971). "General Assembly Resolution 2816 (XXVI). Assistance in cases of natural disaster and other disaster situations." http://www.worldlii.org/int/other/UNGA/1971/50.pdf
UN (1974). "General Assembly Resolution 3243 (XXIX). Strengthening of the Office of the United Nations Disaster Relief Co-ordinator." http://www.worldlii.org/int/other/UNGA/1974/41.pdf
UN (1981). "General Assembly Resolution A/Res/36/225: Strengthening the capacity of the United Nations system to respond to natural disasters and other disaster situations." http://www.worldlii.org/int/other/UNGA/1981/181.pdf
UN (1987). "General Assembly Resolution A/RES/42/169: International decade for natural disaster reduction." http://www.worldlii.org/int/other/UNGA/1987/298.pdf
UN (1994). "Yokohama Strategy and Plan of Action for a Safer World: Guidelines for Natural Disaster Prevention, Preparedness and Mitigation." https://www.unisdr.org/files/8241_doc6841contenido1.pdf
UN (2000). "General Assembly Resolution A/Res/54/219: International Decade for Natural Disaster Reduction: successor arrangements." http://www.worldlii.org/int/other/UNGA/1999/279.pdf
UN (2005). "General Assembly Resolution A/Res/60/1. 2005 Word Summit Outcome." http://www.worldlii.org/int/other/UNGA/2005/47.pdf
UNDP (1994). Human Development Report. Oxford. http://hdr.undp.org/sites/default/files/reports/255/hdr_1994_en_complete_nostats.pdf
UNECOSOC (1963). "Economic and Social Council Resolution 970XXXVI: Measures to be adopted in connexion with the earthquake at Skopje, Yugoslavia." https://digitallibrary.un.org/record/213824/files/E_RES_970%28XXXVI%29-EN.pdf
UNECOSOC (1964). "Economic and Social Council Resolution 1049XXXVII: Assistance in cases of natural disaster." https://digitallibrary.un.org/record/213997/files/E_RES_1049%28XXXVII%29-EN.pdf
UNECOSOC (1998). "Report of the Secretary General E/CN.5/1998/2: Promoting social integration and participation of all people, including disadvantaged and vulnerable groups and persons." https://digitallibrary.un.org/record/249225/files/E_CN.5_1998_2-EN.pdf
UNISDR (2001). "Countering Disasters, Targeting Vulnerability and the Role of Science and Technology in Disaster Reduction." http://www.unisdr.org/files/4033_kit2001english1.pdf
UNISDR (2005). "Hyogo Framework for Action: Building the Resilience of Nations and Communities to Disaster." Extract from the final report of the World Conference on Disaster Reduction. https://www.unisdr.org/2005/wcdr/intergover/official-doc/L-docs/Hyogo-framework-for-action-english.pdf
UNISDR (2015). "Sendai Framework for Disaster Risk Reduction 2015-2030." http://www.unisdr.org/files/43291_sendaiframeworkfordrren.pdf
Wisner, B., Blaikie, P., Cannon, T., and Davis, I. (2004). *At risk: Natural Hazards, People's Vulnerability and Disasters*. London and New York: Routledge.
Young, I.M. (2013). *Responsibility for Justice*. Oxford and New York: Oxford University Press.

PART III

Responsibility relations: Subjects, objects and speakers of responsibility

16
RESPONSIBLE DIPLOMACY
Judgments, wider national interests and diplomatic peace

Markus Kornprobst

Introduction

In the 1980s, a number of important diplomatic documents sought to prescribe a responsible diplomacy. The 1980 Brandt Report called for the responsibility of the international community to re-make North-South relations (North-South: A Programme for Survival 1980). The 1982 Palme Report postulated a responsibility of states to exercise restraint in their relations with one another (Common Security: A Programme for Disarmament 1982). The 1987 Brundtland Report appealed to the responsibility of states to arrive at 'co-ordinated political action' (Our Common Future 1987, 1). Since then, there has been more and more mentioning of responsibility in international relations. This takes place within certain policy fields and references to responsibility become increasingly specified (albeit they remain at times highly contested). The responsibility to protect, for instance, is supposed to be a principle to regulate intervention in the domestic affairs of a state. Common but differentiated responsibilities structure negotiations on climate change. Other chapters in this *Handbook* address these and other specific notions of responsibility in detail.

For diplomacy as such, however, there are no such explicit principles. References to responsibility, if made at all, remain vague. This is why this chapter addresses the following normative questions: Should responsibility actually be a yardstick for diplomacy? If so, what is responsible diplomacy ought to be? These questions are well worth asking. Diplomacy, after all, is something akin to a meta-field of international order that lays down fundamental rules of the international game that structure the communication of representatives of state and non-state actors. In this chapter, I confine myself to state representatives. Non-state actors are covered elsewhere in this book.

Elaborating on Bjola and Kornprobst (2018, 124–127), I contend that the nexus of diplomacy and responsibility is an important issue for normative inquiries into world politics. I conceptualize this responsibility as judgments that balance concerns for the well-being of the nation to be represented by a diplomat and peaceful relations among nations adequately.[1] Diplomats ought to serve their countries. They are to pursue the wider national interests. At the same time, they also ought to work towards a diplomatic peace, i.e. restraint, compromise and polylogue.

This chapter is organized into six sections. First, I review the literature on diplomacy, inquiring what this literature tells us about the nexus of diplomacy and responsibility. Second, I examine to what extent international law prescribes responsibility to diplomacy. Third, I elaborate on the concept of wider national interests. Fourth, I conceptualize diplomatic peace. Fifth, I discuss responsible diplomatic judgments that balance pursuing wider national interests and diplomatic peace. Finally, the conclusion summarizes my main points and situates them in today's world politics.

Literature on diplomacy

How does literature on diplomacy contribute to grasping the link between responsibility and diplomacy? Although this literature is reluctant to use the term responsibility, it is possible to extrapolate a number of important insights from it. Many authors emphasize standing up for the national interest in the midst of international power politics. Yet, very few of them omit responsibilities beyond the confines of the nation altogether. In the conceptual language coined by Watson (1982), there is not only the *raison d'État* but also the *raison de système*. Many authors upon which Watson builds as well as those developing his thoughts further seek more of a *via media* between the two.

The commonsense view on diplomacy as being exclusively dedicated to serve the national interest is, of course, expressed in the literature on diplomacy. This applies, for instance, to authors who write about statecraft and diplomacy. Statecraft, at times, is equated with furthering the national interest (McKercher 2012; Ross 2007). Some former diplomats, reflecting on their trade, concur (Meyer 2013). There is a national interest, which these authors take as a given, and the job of the diplomat is to pursue this national interest vigorously and skillfully without much regard for other considerations.

This common sense understanding, however, is qualified to various degrees in classical writings on diplomacy. For the sake of simplicity two degrees of qualification may be distinguished. There is the argument that pursuing the interests of states represented by diplomats entails, among other things, to build some kind of a rudimentary order and, with it, stability, among these states. There is also a more far-reaching contention that emphasizes the order-building and maintaining potential of diplomacy much more strongly.

When it comes to pursuing interests vigorously and skillfully – even ruthlessly – two authors writing about diplomacy stand out, i.e. Machiavelli (2008) and Kautilya (1992). They reify interests and define them very much in terms of augmenting power. They write about deception, torture and even murder as means to pursue interests. At the same time, however, even they write about ordering interests. The overall purpose underpinning Machiavelli's Prince is to abolish disorder among Italian principalities at the time and move towards a new hierarchical order (Russell 2005).[2] Kautilya, in modern day language, understands diplomacy as an institution to be guarded. This thought, at times explicitly argued for and at times merely assumed, is a common thread in most influential 18th and 19th century writings on diplomacy. Rules about tact and subtleties of language usage are vehicles for guarding the institution of diplomacy (Callières 1917; Richelieu 1947; Murray 1855).

In his highly influential *Politics among Nations*, Morgenthau (1947) argues for defining the national interest in terms of power and being on guard against moralizing pursuits in international politics. This is not to say, however, that this book has nothing to say about order and diplomacy. The only kind of stability attainable in inter-state politics is the balance of power. This balance does not come about automatically. It has to be brought into being through the means of diplomacy. This entails the need to compromise.[3] Morgenthau even goes beyond the ordering device of a balance of power. He postulates that diplomatic compromises ought to take nuclear weapons out of the hands of sovereign states and transfer them to an international body

(Morgenthau 1960, 308–310). He does not even shy away from writing that "there can be no permanent peace without a world state" (Morgenthau 1947, 534). Diplomacy would be again the key to moving beyond inter-state relations and bringing such a world state about.

It appears that Morgenthau was, despite interpretations to the contrary (Speer 1968), rather skeptical about whether such a world state could be attained. This far-reaching goal is difficult to square with his pessimistic views on human nature as well as his heavy statist assumptions. But the ambivalence between *Realpolitik* on the one hand and a peaceful order on the other is certainly noteworthy. It is the recurring theme in his work. Kissinger, similarly to Morgenthau often labeled a Classical Realist, echoes some of this ambivalence. For decades, Kissinger (1964; 1994) contended that bringing about a balance of power is the key task of diplomacy. Such a balance, which oftentimes proves to be rather elusive, makes for some kind of stability in the international system.[4] After decades of practicing and writing about diplomacy, he (2015) came to add to this view, emphasizing the ordering responsibilities even more strongly. Building and maintaining order, in his view, is not only about balancing power but also about legitimizing rule. Without this legitimacy of an inadvertently hierarchical rule, an international order is bound to collapse. Producing and reproducing legitimacy, too, is a crucial task of diplomacy. With time, he also became increasingly outspoken about the need of nuclear disarmament. Teaming up with George Shultz, William Perry and Sam Nunn (Nunn et al. 2007; 2013), not necessarily all known for their dovish political practices when they wielded power in Washington, he wrote two op-ed pieces arguing strongly for a diplomacy of abolishing nuclear weapons.

There are quite a few historically minded scholars who take *Realpolitik* seriously but dismiss key tenets of Realism. Perhaps most notably, debates between Schroeder and Realist scholars (Elman, Elman, and Schroeder 1995; Schroeder 1994; Walt 1997) notwithstanding, Schroeder connected *Realpolitik* via diplomacy to creating and maintaining a balance of power. The latter is to bring "states together in a way that makes it difficult for any of them to undertake unilateral adventures" (Wetzel, Jervis, and Levy 2004, 7). Again, therefore, diplomacy is seen as the key force for establishing a kind of order that is achievable in a world that is ultimately governed by *Realpolitik*. Some authors emphasize the ordering task of diplomacy in the midst of *Realpolitik* even more. In his liberal account of statecraft, Baldwin (1985) takes the need of diplomats to pursue the national interest as a given but does not juxtapose that to building order. On the very contrary, if it suits the national interest, statecraft (especially economic statecraft) is about entering co-operative agreements. It is about building and maintaining order.

In short, even authors studying diplomacy whose assumptions come down heavily on *Realpolitik* rarely postulate that power politics is all there is to international politics. Looking at international relations through different theoretical lenses, a number of students converge around the view that diplomacy has the potential to create and maintain order. Authors who put somewhat less emphasis on *Realpolitik* tend to link diplomacy to more demanding forms of order.

Watson, coining the distinction between *raison d'État* and *raison de système*, defines the latter in terms of fostering international society. The international, according to him – and the English School more generally –, is not a mechanistic system but an international society. This society is to be nurtured by diplomacy (Watson 1982, 203). Great powers, according to Watson, play a particularly important role in this endeavor. They ought to contribute to the making and re-making of international society for selfish and moral reasons. Since they, being great powers, benefit disproportionately from the society, they pursue their interests in supporting international society. But they also have a moral obligation to do so. Great power status, to put this differently, comes with privileges and obligations (Watson 1982, 208).[5] It is no coincidence that Watson's often-quoted book is entitled *Diplomacy: The Dialogue Between States*. Diplomacy, broadly defined as dialogue between states, is what keeps international societies alive. Diplomats should always keep communication flows going (Watson 1982, 225–226). This is to provide international society with norms on restraint and compromise (Watson 1982, 212–214).

Bull refines some of the categories that Watson uses, perhaps most notably international society. He identifies foundational institutions – nowadays often referred to as primary institutions (Spandler 2015) – that constitute international society (Bull 1995/1997, 95–222). Diplomacy is one of these primary institutions. The task of diplomacy is to uphold these institutions. Thus, there is a feedback loop from diplomatic practices to the institution of diplomacy. Diplomacy is also heavily involved in producing secondary institutions, which are something akin to the institutional designs that regime theory focuses on (Krasner 1983). Bull, too, conceives of diplomacy mainly as communication. Somewhat reminiscent of de Callières, he writes about the nuances of diplomatic language and, similarly to Watson, he stresses the importance of keeping diplomatic communication going. In order to underline this point, he, too, uses the term "dialogue". Taken together, this makes it possible for diplomacy to work towards the "minimisation of the effects of friction in international relations" (Bull 1995/1997, 165).

Watson and Bull clarify that international society is not always the same. It changes over time. Vincent (1986) elaborates on the system-transforming potential of diplomacy even more than Watson and Bull do. Being interested in the relationship between state sovereignty and human rights, he is rather optimistic that diplomacy, over time, will make the pendulum swing more towards the latter. Sharp (2009, 291) appears to be more skeptical. To him, the *raison de système is,* first and foremost, about restraint among states. Challenges to this *raison de système* come from outside traditional diplomacy such as "rogue state diplomacy", "greedy company diplomacy", "crazy religion diplomacy" and "dumb public diplomacy" (Sharp 2009, 193–292).

To sum up, literature on diplomacy reminds us that responsible diplomacy cannot be reduced to pursuing the national interest. It is about a balancing act between this pursuit on the one hand and the generation of international stability on the other. But a number of open questions remain. What actually ought to be this national interest and what does doing diplomacy have to do with forming and representing this interest? By the same token, how is international stability ought to look like and what exactly ought diplomacy do to bring it about and maintain it? Finally, the balancing act requires specifying the pursuits of national interests and international stability.

International law

International law, itself produced by diplomacy, is the formal foundation upon which diplomacy is based. Thus, it is worth taking a look at international law – especially key principles of public international law – and examine how it helps us answer the three sets of questions identified in the previous section. Since the formation of the national interest is within the realm of sovereign politics, it provides only very few general guidelines about the *raison d'État*. But there is actually quite a bit on the *raison de système*. The latter is about peace. Peace is, among other things, restraint. But it is also about much more than restraint. In international law, too, we find something about compromise and "dialogue".

International law does not prescribe a certain national interest. On the very contrary, its most fundamental principle, state sovereignty, privileges domestic politics in forming the national interest. Self-determination further underlines the agency of nations to decide upon what is important for them. Domestic politics can play out very differently. The Vienna Convention on Diplomatic Relations is explicit about the heterogeneity of domestic "constitutional and social systems" (United Nations 1961, Preamble). Thus, there is not only one way – say a liberal democratic one – through which a national interest should be formed. But certain ways, nevertheless, are out. The national interest is not equivalent to the interests of those who govern. States have agreed to uphold certain rights of individuals and groups within their own boundaries. At times, they have done so in declarations, most importantly the Universal Declaration of Human Rights, and, at times, they concluded legally binding instruments (oftentimes built on his declaration), such as the International Covenant on Civil and Political Rights, the International Covenant on Economic, Social and Cultural Rights, the Convention on the Elimination of All Forms of Racial Discrimination, the Convention on the Elimination of All Forms of Discrimination Against Women, the Convention on the Rights of the Child and the Convention on the Rights of Persons with Disabilities. Taken together, this body of law protects individuals and groups as well as gives citizens a voice in domestic politics. Both has repercussions for how national interests are to be formed.

International law provides many more clues when it comes to the *raison de système*. The United Nations Charter specifies what many scholars of diplomacy refer to as stability as peace (United Nations 1945a, 1945b). Peace is the overall goal of the Charter (Simma et al. 1995, 50). When the Preamble and Chapter I define the purposes and principles of the United Nations, this overall goal is mentioned frequently. Peace appears twice in the Preamble and nine times in Section I. Security is mentioned only once and thrice, respectively, and always in conjunction with peace. Two interpretations of peace compete in the Charter. On the one hand, there is peace as the absence of war. This interpretation prevails in the critical Art 2(4). In the Preamble and in Art 1, by contrast, peace is more than the absence of war. Here, it encompasses developing "friendly relations" (Art 1(2)), achieving "international co-operation" (Art 1(3)) and even "harmonizing the actions of nations in the attainment of these common ends" (Art. 1(4)).

These two interpretations of peace echo what the scholarly literature on diplomacy refers to as restraint and compromise. The absence of war is to be achieved through a system of collective security. Restraint is to be underwritten by the expectation that a state that violates Art 2(4) will be confronted by all other United Nations member states. The passages on friendly relations, co-operation and common ends presuppose compromise-seeking behavior and, arguably, even more far-reaching modes of diplomatic communication.

The Constitution of the United Nations Educational, Scientific and Cultural Organization (UNESCO), elaborates quite a bit on the latter. Peace is again the overall goal. It is mentioned seven times in the Constitution. Security is mentioned only once and again only in conjunction with peace. The Constitution, especially the Preamble and Chapter 1, formulates important causal understandings of peace. According to the Preamble, the causes of peace are in the mind and not, say, constituted by an equal distribution of military capabilities: "[S]ince wars begin in the minds of men, it is in the minds of men that the defences of peace must be constructed". Ignorance is identified as major threat: "[I]gnorance of each other's ways and lives has been a common cause, throughout the history of mankind, of that suspicion and mistrust between the peoples of the world through which their differences have all too often broken into war". This ignorance is to be overcome through ongoing communication across nations. UNESCO vows to "increase the means of communication between their peoples and to employ these means for the purposes of mutual understanding and a truer and more perfect knowledge of each other's lives".

The Vienna Convention on Diplomatic Relations explicitly links the broader understanding of peace found in the UN Charter, and implicitly connects the even more far-reaching one found in the UNESCO Constitution to the institution of diplomacy. Diplomacy, by keeping communication across states going, is supposed to help bring about peaceful relations among states. The provisions found in the Convention, such as diplomatic immunity, inviolability of mission premises, protection of communication lines etc., are supposed to make diplomacy functional. They are supposed to serve the overall goal of peace (Denza 2008, 13).

We have now moved closer towards understanding what the *raison d'État* and the *raison de système* are. Drawing from political theory, conflict theory and communications theory, the following sections sharpen these categories further. Mirroring the previous sections on diplomatic studies and international law, the primary focus is on the *raison de système*. Diplomats, after all, act on the international stage. But they are carrying domestic baggage when they do so. Some elaborations on the *raison d'État*, therefore, are warranted, too.

Wider national interests

This section endorses the diplomat's pursuit of national interests. But it qualifies this endorsement in three important ways, arguing for pursuing the wider good, infusing domestic debates on national interests with an international perspective and translating them, when necessary, in the daily work of the diplomat.

The *raison d'État* is an important category for diplomats. The diplomat owes it to the nation to pursue its interests (Beardsworth 2015). Yet, this responsibility is linked to the nature of national interests, the participation of diplomats in forming it, and their role in specifying them when necessary. When it comes to the nature of national interests, the diplomat is to pursue the "wider good" (Jervis 1994, 856) of the nation. This wider good is not to be equated with the interests of a monarch, dictator, oligarchy or a ruling clique. It is not equivalent with the sectarian interests of religious groups, class interests or the priorities of specific ethnic groups within a state either. Instead, it is an interest that emerges out of the contestation among the different groupings of actors within a nation (Morgenthau 1952)[6] and does not violate 'the needs of the governed' (Beardsworth 2015, 76).

Diplomats ought to infuse pluralistic[7] domestic debates about national interests with their international perspectives on these interests. The perspectives they embrace tend to be more international than domestic in nature. This provides very important input in contestations through which nations come to define interests. It usually comes more natural to diplomats to think of how things hang together internationally than it does to local actors. Morgenthau (1952; 1960) has it exactly right when he postulates that national interests ought not be formed against the vital interests of other nations. Following two world wars and the advent of nuclear weapons, he contends that survival requires such an internationalist twist on the formation of interests. This twist makes sure that national interests, once formed, allow for some co-operation. Diplomats have a responsibility to uphold this international twist. Finnemore's work on international norms and the constitution of the national interest, albeit considerably more ideationalist than Morgenthau's, can be read this way, too (Finnemore 1996). Diplomats, being experts on these norms, play an important role in making sure that the national interest bears the imprints of these norms.

Diplomats ought to translate the national interest when they have to fill in blanks left by their instructions in a fashion that makes sure that the needs of the governed are represented. Capitals write instructions to their diplomats posted abroad. But these instructions only go thus far. If diplomats come together to negotiate the intricacies of, say, a new legal instrument to counter climate change, instructions may leave much room for interpretation and specification. The negotiators then have to translate the more abstract national interest into more concrete interests and preferences applicable to this bargaining situation. Adding up these three points on national interests, one could speak about wider national interests.

Diplomatic peace

This section specifies the *raison de système* further. I contend that it revolves around pursuing a diplomatic peace, i.e. work towards restraint, compromise and polylogue in international affairs.

Elaborating on the *raison de système* is facilitated by engaging with conflict theory. Anatol Rapoport (1960), a founding figure of conflict theory, may very well have coined the most comprehensive conceptualization of conflict. Any conflict, in his view, consists of three dimensions: fights, games and debates. Fights are about the urge to lash out against an enemy. In extreme cases, the enemy is to disappear from the face of the earth. Retaliation, for example, is a form of fight thus understood. Games are about trying to outwit an opponent, for example on the negotiation table. Actors are self-interested. They want to get the best for them. If this involves going to war, they will opt for what Clausewitz (1966 [1832]: chap. I, 1, 24) referred to as the "continuation of politics by other means". Debates are about trying to convert someone else; to try to make others believe what they believe themselves. This can be quite a severe conflict dimension. If the converting does not work – and it usually does not – the one actor is likely to confront the other. The crusades, for instance, were fueled by a religious debate. So is jihad.

Diplomacy can make a major difference about how these modes of conflict play out on the international stage. There are the three dimensions of diplomatic peace: restraint, compromise and polylogue: Restraint includes working towards deterrence, collective security and/ or disarmament. Its potential to deter is the rationale behind the endorsement of the balance of power by many scholars of diplomacy. Since military capabilities are distributed equally, the attacked party has capacities to inflict heavy costs on the aggressor. Although the military balance itself is within the material realm, the making of balanced alliance systems has a lot to do with diplomacy. Collective security arrangements, such as the one by the United Nations, is a more far-reaching system of restraint. Needless to say, it, too, was brought into being by diplomatic negotiations. By the same token, the lack of implementation of some crucial articles in Chapter 7 – Article 45 comes to mind immediately – have also been, among other things, due to diplomatic manoeuvers. Disarmament is a very demanding form of restraint. Unless it happens unilaterally, which is very rare, disarmament involves negotiating weapons and at times entire weapons categories away. The current pattern of disarmament agreements is, on the one hand, quite promising. There are, for example, bans on landmines and cluster munition, biological and chemical weapons, and even nuclear weapons. But great powers oftentimes do not participate. This is the great drawback of the bans on landmines, cluster bombs and nuclear weapons.

Compromise is about bargaining parties meeting in the middle. Actors make concessions, but the underlying controversy stays on (Bellamy, Kornprobst, and Reh 2012). Concessions are mutual albeit the degree to which they are varies. In diplomatic encounters, some compromises happen on an ad-hoc basis, for instance when stalled negotiations are resuscitated by problem-solving techniques (Hopmann 1995). A chairperson may re-package a deal to be negotiated, halt the clock, and appeal to the common good to be served by the negotiations. In the course of this re-configuration of the bargaining encounter, parties meet in the middle. Yet compromising can also become diplomatic practice. In the 1990s, for instance, diplomatic negotiations in the European Union approximated this practice to a considerable extent. Meeting over and over to bargain about multiple issues, compromising had become the seemingly natural way of doing things (Reh 2012).

Polylogue is quite close to what Watson and Bull mean when they write about "dialogue" (compare the chapter by Friedman in this volume). Dialogue, in usual scholarly parlance, however, is such a demanding form of communication that even its key proponents tend to use it as a counterfactual (Habermas 1995) to criticize modern democracies rather than as an analytical form of communication that is easily attainable in diplomatic affairs.[8] Dialogue is what Bächtiger et al. (2010) refer to as deliberation type I. Polylogue, by contrast, is deliberation type II. Actors communicate, to some extent, strategically.[9] Not only do they enter a communicative encounter with certain interpretations of what is to be communicated about and how this communication is to play out but also with certain interests on their minds. At the same time, actors commit to keeping the communication going and, in principle, are open to revisit these interpretations and interests to varying degrees. Actors, to put this differently, allow communication to reach its productive and transformative potentials. On the one hand, this potential is not easily reached because there is plenty of heterogeneity in polylogical encounters (Kristeva 1986). Actors proceed from different priors and they may end up speaking past one another. On the other hand, heterogeneity makes innovation possible. Being exposed to novelty at times ends up prompting actors to re-visit their own cherished ideas and embark on new journeys.

Polylogues are elusive in diplomatic relations and even if they happen they do not always yield tangible outcomes. Yet they are of vital importance for diplomacy in general and diplomatic peace in particular. Polylogues are something akin to the master-mode of diplomatic peace. It re-shuffles existing institutions and enables new ones to arise. Take disarmament, for example. When actors successfully bargain away entire weapons categories and stick to their promises to do away with them, be they landmines or cluster munition, or even weapons of mass destruction, they exercise a demanding form of restraint. But this restraint only becomes possible because prior to this polylogues paved the way for making sense of these weapons categories in radically different ways. In the 1990s, human security became an important reference object of arms control, competing more and more with what was largely taken for granted before, i.e. that security is all about national security. Seen through the human security lens, landmines, cluster munition and chemical weapons are an inherent threat (Kornprobst and Senn 2016; Price 2003). The re-making of the lens – debates about the nuclear prohibition treaty show that debates about this lens are by no means completed yet – happened in communicative encounters among a large number of diverse actors, including traditional and non-traditional diplomats (many of them representing NGOs) from the global south and global north.

Making responsible judgments: wider national interests and diplomatic peace

Diplomacy is not a science; it is an art (Leguey-Feilleux 2009, 9–11). At the core of this art is making judgments (Kornprobst 2019). Responsible diplomatic judgments balance the wider national interests and diplomatic peace in international affairs.

Making judgments is drawing from repertoires of taken-for-granted ideas, and putting these to use as universals in light of which actors come to see the particulars of a given situation. Judging, put more concisely, is subsuming particulars under universals (Arendt 1958; Beiner 1983; Kant 1974; Kornprobst 2019). This provides a threefold orientation to diplomats: make sense of the world, make decisions, and make meaning that they diffuse to others.[10]

Sense-making matters in many ways. Diplomats interpret instructions emanating from the capital, existing legal provisions upon which new legal instruments are to be built, scientific findings on at times highly specific and technical subjects, messages emanating from other diplomats, and so on. Decision-making is not to be under-estimated either. It is hardly contentious that a Foreign Minister makes important decisions and he or she is a diplomat. But it is worth keeping in mind that career diplomats located underneath the top level, too, regularly make decisions that have repercussions for the relations among states. Furthermore, they advise key members of the executive – presidents, prime ministers, chancellors, foreign ministers – when it comes to making critical political decisions. Given that the diplomat is a messenger, meaning-making is very important, too. Diplomatic cables are, among other things, supposed to make meaning for the capital. Practices of public diplomacy are geared towards making meaning in the host state.

Diplomatic responsibility is about responsible diplomatic judgments. Such judgments do two things: First, they violate neither the *raison d'État* (wider national interests) nor the *raison de système* (diplomatic peace). This means that they are grounded in the universal of the wider good of the nation, work towards upholding an international perspective in making and re-making the interest, and translate them adequately. When, for example, Ibrahim Dabbashi, Libya's deputy permanent representative to the United Nations in New York, refused to follow Gaddafi's instructions after the latter had announced that he would crush the opposition in Bengazi, the diplomat acted responsibly. Instructions to diplomatically defend targeting the own population cannot be an expression of wider national interests. Furthermore, this means that diplomats, as long as other nations allow for this, work towards restraint, compromise and polylogue with these other nations. This applies to restraint even more than to compromise and polylogue because it is the most fundamental element of a diplomatic peace. To come back to the Libyan example, when the intervening coalition, having secured UNSC 1973 in March 2016, violated the scope of the intervention mandate by working towards regime change instead of merely protecting the civilian population from being targeted by Gaddafi's forces, their diplomacy violated the *raison de système* (United Nations Security Council 2011). Their diplomacy to prepare and justify regime change does not qualify as having been responsible.

Second, responsible judgments balance the *raison d'État* and the *raison de système* thus defined. Judgments should not be one-sided in the sense that they only employ universals that pertain to wider national interests or only those relating to the diplomatic peace. At times, this is not all that difficult to do. Enlightened wider national interests, for example, tend to favor co-operation over conflict in world politics. It is, therefore, not that difficult to reconcile such a *raison d'État* with the compromise and even polylogue aspects of diplomatic peace. Yet at least some balancing between the two is often required. Wider national interests tend to come down more heavily on short-term goals than on long-term ones. This points away from enlightened interests.

Note that balanced judgments do not necessarily exclude *Realpolitik* or *Idealpolitik*. But there are five important qualifiers. First, *Realpolitik* is to serve the wider good of the nation. This is how von Rochau (1972) coined the term in the mid-19th century.[11] Second, pure *Realpolitik* is out, unless forced upon by a nation by the hostility of other nations. Diplomats ought to have an eye for the compatibility of interests across nations. Third, *Idealpolitik*, too, has to be an expression of the wider good of the nation. Fourth, pure *Idealpolitik* is out unless the wider good of the nation is in perfect harmony with the wider goods of other nations. This is rarely ever the case. Fifth, the rather unholy alliance of *Realpolitik* and *Idealpolitik* is out that pretends that pursuing the former is in the interest of all nations involved, including those at the receiving end of power politics.

Conclusion

This chapter contended that diplomatic responsibility ought to be about judgments that balance wider national interests and the pursuit of diplomatic peace. Instead of coming down heavily on either side of *Idealpolitik* or *Realpolitik*, this conceptualization steers a middle course that is anchored in key principles of international law, i.e. long-standing promises that diplomats have made themselves. My elaborations on the scholarly categories of *raison d'État* and *raison de système* are rooted in compartments of the toolbox that diplomats get taught before they enter the profession and put to use in their daily work once they have done so (compare the respective chapters by Wiener, Jackson, Busser and Baron in this volume).

Thus, my argument is not utopian. It does not deny that power politics exists and it does not deny either that there are different regime types in international relations. But it does postulate that diplomacy, despite all of this, ought to take key principles upon which it rests (and which it has produced in the first place) seriously.

This postulate may be even more important in our times than, say, two decades ago. On the one hand, we live in an era that requires co-managing international affairs more than ever before. This ranges from economic to health issues, from development to migration challenges, and from environmental to security concerns. On the other hand, restraint, compromise and polylogue appear to be in decline. Great powers, massively investing into a new generation of nuclear weapons, undermine arms control. Less and less international treaties are deposited with the United Nations, suggesting that states find it increasingly difficult to compromise. Strategic communication, often squarely directed towards the domestic grand standing of leaders, brushes polylogical encounters on pressing issues such as the ones listed above aside. Even commitments to pursuing wider national interests seem to become eclipsed by oligarchic, clientilistic and/or populist strategies to secure domestic power in a rising number of states in the global north and south.

Still, I would submit that it is precisely because of this worrisome development that it is important to remind diplomats – including the politically appointed ones – to stand up for key principles that constitute their profession and to encourage students of diplomacy to develop notions of diplomatic responsibility further.

Notes

1 This conceptualization of responsibility follows Warner (1991): responsibility to do something and for someone.
2 Determining the purpose as well as the means for how to achieve this purpose has a lot to do with value judgments (Wolfers 1962, 62).
3 This is a normative statement. Morgenthau maintains that diplomacy has plenty of potential to stabilize international politics although it can be put to use for very different endeavours, such as bringing about the most opportune moment to initiate war, too (Morgenthau 1947, 549).
4 For a similar point, see also Kennan (1984). Discussing historical cases, he contends that managing an existing balance of power at times requires accommodating a rising power. It would, for example, have been better to accommodate pre-WWI Germany than to fight it in two world wars.
5 See also power transition theory (Organski 1958) and hegemonic stability theory (Kindleberger 1973) for a similar line of reasoning on a constellation in which there is only a single great power (hegemon).
6 For Morgenthau, on-going contestation is actually good news. He cautions against being self-absorbed with patriotism and a nation's beliefs in its own greatness (Williams 2005, 326).
7 On the plurality of these debates, see Oeter (2019).
8 It sometimes is (Risse 2000) but this does not happen often.
9 Some writers on polylogues emphasize strategy more (Kerbrat-Orecchioni 2004) than others (Wimmer 2013).
10 On these categories, see Boin et al. (2016).
11 For a useful overview of the genesis of the concept of *Realpolitik* and its delineation to *Idealpolitik*, see Bew (2016).

References

Arendt, H. (1958). *The Human Condition*. Chicago: University of Chicago Press.
Baldwin, D.A. (1985). *Economic Statecraft*. Princeton: Princeton University Press.

Bächtiger, A., Niemeyer, S., Neblo, M., Steenbergen, M.R., and Steiner, J. (2010). "Disentangling Diversity in Deliberative Democracy: Competing Theories, Their Blind Spots and Complementarities." *Journal of Political Philosophy*, 18(1): 32–63.

Beardsworth, R. (2015). "From Moral to Political Responsibility in a Globalized Age." *Ethics & International Affairs*, 29(1): 71–92.

Beiner, R. (1983). *Political Judgment*. Chicago: University of Chicago Press.

Bellamy, R. Kornprobst, M., and Reh, C. (2012). "Introduction: Meeting in the Middle." *Government and Opposition*, 47(3): 275–295.

Bew, J. (2016). *Realpolitik: A History*. Oxford: Oxford University Press.

Bjola, C., and Kornprobst, M. (2018). *Understanding International Diplomacy: Theory, Practice and Ethics*. London: Routledge.

Boin, A., Stern, E., Sundelius, B., and Hart, P. (2016). *The Politics of Crisis Management: Public Leadership Under Pressure*. Cambridge: Cambridge University Press.

Bull, H. (1995/1977). *The Anarchical Society: A Study of Order in World Politics*. New York: Columbia University Press.

Callières, F.D. (1917). *De la Manière de Negocier avec les Souverains, de lutilité des Negotiations, du choix des Ambassadeurs & des Envoyez, & des Qualités Necessaires pour Reussir dans ces Employs*. Paris: Nouveau Monde Editions.

Clausewitz, C.V. (1966). *Vom Kriege*. Frankfurt am Main: Suhrkamp.

Common Security: A Programme for Disarmament (1982). *The Report of the Independent Commission on Disarmament and Security Issues under the Chairmanship of Olof Palme*. London: Pan Books.

Denza, E. (2008). *Diplomatic Law: Commentary on the Vienna Convention on Diplomatic Relations*. Oxford: Oxford University Press.

Elman, C., Elman, M.F., and Schroeder, P.W. (1995). "History vs. Neo-realism: A Second Look." *International Security*, 20(1): 182–195.

Finnemore, M. (1996). *National Interests in International Society*. Ithaca: Cornell University Press.

Habermas, J. (1995). *Theorie des kommunikativen Handelns I: Handlungsrationalität und gesellschaftliche Rationalisierung*. Frankfurt am Main: Suhrkamp.

Hopmann, P.T. (1995). "Two paradigms of negotiation: Bargaining and Problem Solving." *Annals of the American Academy of Political and Social Science*, 542(1): 24–47.

Jervis, R. (1994). "Hans Morgenthau, Realism, and the Scientific Study of International Politics." *Social Research*, 61(4): 853–876.

Kant, I. (1974). *Kritik der Urteilskraft*. Frankfurt am Main: Suhrkamp.

Kautilya (1992). *The Arthashastra*. New York: Penguin Books.

Kennan, G.F. (1984). *American Diplomacy*. Chicago: University of Chicago Press.

Kerbrat-Orecchioni, C. (2004). "Introducing Polylogue." *Journal of Pragmatics*, 36(1): 1–24.

Kindleberger, C. (1973). *The World in Depression: 1929–1939*. Berkeley, CA: University of California Press.

Kissinger, H. (1964). *A World Restored*. New York: Grosset & Dunlap.

Kissinger, H. (1994). *Diplomacy*. New York: Simon and Schuster.

Kissinger, H. (2015). *World Order*. New York: Penguin.

Kornprobst, M. (2019). *Co-managing International Crises: Judgments and Justifications*. Cambridge: Cambridge University Press.

Kornprobst, M., and Senn, M. (2016). "A Rhetorical Field Theory: Background, Communication, and Change." *British Journal of Politics and International Relations*, 18(2): 300–317.

Krasner, S.D., ed. (1983). *International Regimes*. Cornell University Press.

Kristeva, J. (1986). *The Kristeva Reader*. New York: Columbia University Press.

Leguey-Feilleux, J-R. (2009). *The Dynamics of Diplomacy*. Boulder, CO: Lynne Rienner Publishers.

Machiavelli, N. (2008). *The Prince*. Indianapolis, IN: Hackett.

McKercher, B.J.C. (2012). "Prologue: The International Order and the New Century." In McKercher, B.J.C., ed., *Routledge Handbook of Diplomacy and Statecraft*: xv–xxxiv. Oxford: Oxford University Press.

Meyer, C. (2013). *Getting Our Way*. London: Hachette.

Morgenthau, H. (1947). *Politics among Nations*. Chicago: Chicago University Press.

Morgenthau, H. (1952). "Another 'Great Debate': The National Interest of the United States." *American Political Science Review*, 46(4): 961–988.

Morgenthau, H. (1960). *The Purpose of American Politics*. New York: Knopf.

Murray, E.C.G. (1855). *Embassies and Foreign Courts: A History of Diplomacy*. London: G. Routledge & Company.

North-South: A Programme for Survival (1980). *The Report of the Independent Commission on International Development Issues under the Chairmanship of Willy Brandt*. London: Pan Books.
Nunn, S., Schultz, G., Kissinger, H., and Perry, W. (2007). "A World Free of Nuclear Weapons." *Wall Street Journal*, January 4. https://www.wsj.com/articles/SB116787515251566636 (accessed May 2, 2019).
Nunn, S., Schultz, G., Kissinger, H., and Perry, W. (2013). "Next Steps in Reducing Nuclear Risks: The Pace of Nonproliferation Work Today Doesn't Match the Urgency of the Threat." *Wall Street Journal*, March 5. https://www.wsj.com/articles/SB10001424127887324338604578325912939001772 (accessed May 2, 2019).
Oeter, S. (2019). "Conflicting Norms, Values, and Interests: A Perspective from Legal Academia." *Ethics & International Affairs*, 33(1): 57–66.
Organski, AFK. (1958). *World Politics*. New York: Knopf.
Our Common Future. (1987). *Report of the World Commission on Environment and Development under the Chairpersonship of Gro Harlem Brundtland*. Oxford: Oxford University Press.
Price, R. (2003). "Transnational Civil Society and Advocacy in World Politics." *World Politics*, 55(4): 579–606.
Rapoport, A. (1960). *Fights, Games and Debates*. The University of Michigan Press.
Reh, C. (2012). "European Integration as Compromise: Recognition, Concessions and the Limits of Cooperation." *Government and Opposition*, 47(3): 414–440.
Richelieu, Cardinal-Duc de, A.J.D.P. (1947). *Lettres, instructions diplomatiques et papiers d'état du cardinal de Richelieu*. Edited by Georges d'Avenal. *Collection de documents inédit sur l'histoire de France*, 8, 1653–1677.
Risse, T. (2000). "'Let's Argue!': Communicative Action in World Politics." *International Organization*, 54(1): 1–39.
von Rochau, L.A. (1972). "Grundsätze der Realpolitik." In Wehler, H.U., ed. *Angewendet auf die staatlichen Zustände Deutschlands*. Frankfurt am Main: Ullstein.
Ross, D. (2007). *Statecraft: and How to Restore America's Standing in the World*. New York: Farrar, Straus and Giroux.
Russell, G. (2005). "Machiavelli's Science of Statecraft: The Diplomacy and Politics of Disorder." *Diplomacy and Statecraft*, 16(2): 227–250.
Schroeder, P. (1994). "Historical Reality vs. Neo-realist Theory." *International Security*, 19(1): 108–148.
Sharp, P. (2009). *Diplomatic Theory of International Relations*. Cambridge: Cambridge University Press.
Simma, B., Khan, D.E., Nolte, G., and Paulus, A. (1995). *The United Nations Charter: A Commentary*. Oxford: Oxford University Press.
Spandler, K. (2015). "The Political International Society: Change in Primary and Secondary Institutions." *Review of International Studies*, 41(3): 601–622.
Speer, J.P. (1968). "Hans Morgenthau and the World State." *World Politics*, 20(2): 207–227.
United Nations (1945a). *Charter of the United Nations*. October 24. https://www.refworld.org/docid/3ae6b3930.html (accessed May 2, 2019).
United Nations (1945b). *Constitution of the United Nations Educational, Scientific and Cultural Organization*. 16 November. http://www.unesco.org/education/pdf/UNESCO_E.PDF (accessed May 2, 2019).
United Nations (1961). *Vienna Convention on Diplomatic Relations*. April 18. http://legal.un.org/ilc/texts/instruments/english/conventions/9_1_1961.pdf (accessed May 2, 2019).
United Nations Security Council (2011). *S/RES/1973 (2011)*. March 17. https://www.un.org/en/ga/search/view_doc.asp?symbol=S/RES/1973%282011%29 (accessed May 2, 2019).
Vincent, R.J. (1986). *Human Rights and International Relations*. Cambridge: Cambridge University Press.
Walt, S.M. (1997). "The Progressive Power of Realism." *American Political Science Review*, 91(4): 931–935.
Warner, D. (1991). *An Ethic of Responsibility in International Relations*. Boulder, CO: Lynne Rienner.
Watson, A. (1982). *Diplomacy: The Dialogue Between States*. London: Eyre Methuen.
Wetzel, D., Jervis, R., and Levy, J.S. (2004). "Introduction." In Schroeder, P., ed., *Systems, Stability, and Statecraft: Essays on the International History of Modern Europe*: 1–19. Basingstoke: Palgrave.
Williams, M.C. (2005). "What is the National Interest? The Neoconservative Challenge in IR Theory." *European Journal of International Relations*, 11(3): 307–337.
Wimmer, F.M. (2013). *Anlass, Begriff und Aufgabe interkultureller Philosophie*. Wien: Ontos.
Wolfers, A. (1962). "National Security as an Ambiguous Symbol." *Political Science Quarterly*, 67 (4): 481–502.

17
RISING POWERS AND RESPONSIBILITY

Johannes Plagemann and Amrita Narlikar

Introduction: growing expectations

Whereas a debate about all other contenders for global power persists,[1] accepting multipolarity as a key characteristic of world affairs necessarily includes the world's two most populous countries, China and India, as co-determinants of global governance in the 21st century. Foreign policy elites from both countries frequently welcome the advent of a "polycentric" (India) or "multipolar" order (China). As rising powers they compete for influence, tend to engage their regional neighbourhood proactively in pursuit of followers, and habitually claim to represent either the wider developing world or, as regional powers, their immediate neighbourhood in international negotiations (Narlikar 2010a; Wade 2011, 356 and 362). Both countries are globally active, continental in size, and are committed to a long-standing self-understanding as individual civilizations (rather than mere nation-states) and global (rather than merely regional) powers. Likewise, both are eager to undergird their foreign policy outreach with cultural diplomacy – from Narendra Modi's embrace of religion and tradition as foreign policy tool (Narlikar 2017; on Buddhism in Indian foreign policy, e.g. see Mohan 2014) to Xi Jinping's rhetoric around a "community of common destiny" in Asia (Chang-Liao 2016; Kai 2013). As it is the case in China, India's foreign policy establishment has shown an increasing interest in its history of political thought, ostensibly as a by-product of rising power status.

Multipolarity as a structural characteristic of global order is debated extensively in International Relations (IR) theory. Scholarship and public commentary broadly concurs that the rise to power by countries such as China and India, and a concomitant relative decline of US power, has fundamental implications for global order in the 21st century (Acharya 2014; Kupchan 2012).[2] Whereas abstract structural theories around the effects various types of polarity have on global order (see, in particular, Waltz 1979) dominated debates during the Cold War, the demise of the Soviet Union and, more so, the end of the "unipolar moment" (Wohlforth 1999) challenged western IR theorists' expectations: Neither has Neorealists' prediction of a return to anarchy and interstate war under conditions of multipolarity in Europe or elsewhere (Mearsheimer 1990) come true. Nor has Liberalists' belief in the eventual accommodation of new powers into a "liberal international order" composed of powerful global rules and backed by multilateralism as modus operandi (Ikenberry 2011) been realized so far.

Instead, the demise of Western hegemony heralds a new era of complexity in international affairs, described in a variety of concepts from Acharya's "multiplex" world to Womack's "multi-nodality" (2015). Seen through the lens of global governance, the two defining features of complex multipolarity are a parallelism of competition and cooperation between major powers – including both rising and established ones – as well as institutional fragmentation. Rather than contending oneself with a stronger voice in existing global institutions, rising powers partake in or establish new and alternative ones – from the Asian Infrastructure Investment Bank (AIIB) to the yearly BRICS and G20 summits. Meanwhile, entrenched rivalries amongst rising powers (India and China) and between rising and established powers (China and the US) promote competition over the support of minor powers. As a result, their room for negotiation has improved in some cases contributing to a greater willingness to global and regional public good provision on behalf of both established and rising powers. On the other hand, major power rivalries favour forms of public good provision that are at the least partially exclusive towards other rising powers. Moreover, both the legitimacy and effectiveness of global governance are under stress as multipolarity favours *exclusive* regional and global great power clubs, rather than *inclusive* global institutions with strong rules. The result is a multipolar "order" characterized by a paradox combination of institutional fragmentation, global cooperation, and regional competition.

Moreover, we maintain that complexity also entails a greater role for individual rising powers' specific strategic cultures and world views than acknowledged by conventional IR structuralists. In fact, rising powers' history as "dependent" parts of the developing world continue to provide important elements to their foreign policy discourses, including a pronounced suspicion vis-à-vis established powers' interests. The relevance of diverging worldviews is illustrated by the observation that repeated and intensifying interactions between rising and established powers in forums such as the G20 and elsewhere have "not been sufficient to generate convergences in their understanding of the root causes of global imbalances or complementarity in their policy responses" (Wade 2011, 3679). Clearly, globalisation's increasing interconnectedness notwithstanding, rising powers have maintained and nurture their own distinctive strategic cultures and foreign policy worldviews (Tellis, Szalwinski, and Wills 2016). And despite the fact that regional and rising powers coalesce, in principle, around the desire to counter the hegemony of established powers in international affairs (Acharya 2014, 74–75), they are by no means undivided on specific issues of global governance themselves (e.g. military intervention or currency policy). Complex multipolarity therefore not only implies the differentiation between rising and established powers but also "issue-specific divergences, multiple potential coalition partners, and the absence of a hegemon" (Schirm 2013, 22; cf. Schweller 2011, 290). Indeed, opposition to Western hegemony has not translated into a truly alternative vision of order beyond the call for a greater say in global affairs. As Ikenberry notes (2018), whereas established and rising powers alike embrace a variety of established global rules and reject others, some of the core elements of the international order created under American hegemony – Westphalian norms of state sovereignty and multilateral procedures of inter-state cooperation – continue to be in their best interest.

As a country gains in material power and diplomatic recognition, its capacity to act as a "veto-player" in international negotiations rises. Rising powers from India to Brazil and China have repeatedly illustrated this throughout the 2000s (Narlikar 2010a; cf. Tsebelis 1995). However, the ability to say "No" does not necessarily come along with the power for agenda-setting. For this to happen, leadership is required. And the power to lead in global politics hinges at least in part on contributing to public good provision; in other words, on the acceptance of responsibility for matters beyond a state's immediate domestic and foreign interests (Burns 1978; Kindleberger 1981).

This is so because global politics largely lack the dense formal regulatory framework characterizing most states domestically. The rise of new powers – multipolarity – has further undermined the hierarchy of states widely accepted (albeit often resented) throughout the "unipolar moment" of the 1990s. Thus, leadership in global politics today cannot rely exclusively on either the sheer superiority in material power or pre-established rules or convention. Instead, the power to lead requires the legitimacy derived from a commitment to a common interest shared by other states (cf. Beetham 2013, 59). To what extent then do rising powers accept the responsibility to provide for leadership in global affairs?

Although often criticized for their indifference to the preservation of the global commons, rising powers have in fact experimented with the provision of regional and global public goods. And furthermore, they have adapted their behaviour to the critique, and tried to consciously frame some of their endeavours as exercises in regional or global leadership. China, for example, in spite of the severe backlash it has come to attract in the first half of 2019, has repeatedly framed its Belt and Road Initiative (BRI) as an investment in the provision of connectivity as a regional and global public good (Narlikar 2019). Brazil's eventually unsuccessful "Responsibility while Protecting" (RWP) initiative in the UN has been debated as an attempt in reforming international rules to the benefit of all nations (Kenkel and Stefan 2016).

On the larger global issues, rising powers became important players too. China, India, Brazil and South Africa have become powerful voices in global climate change negotiations. India had always been an active member of the General Agreement on Tariffs and Trade (GATT) and the World Trade Organization (WTO). Both India and China (sometimes along with Brazil) have acquired greater prominence in decision-making in the WTO during the Doha negotiations, and have come to constitute the "New Quad" (comprising US, EU, China, and India, which replaces the "Old Quad" that had dominated the GATT with the US, EU, Canada and Japan at the helm of decision-making) (Narlikar 2010b, 719). Although they work in coalitions with smaller developing countries, it also appears that they are increasingly reluctant to act on behalf of smaller, less developed, and/or neighbouring countries.

This chapter proceeds with a closer look into the Indian case as a rising and regional power with an entrenched self-understanding as a "responsible" actor in international affairs. Outlining recent changes to its regional and global policies demonstrates both a growing commitment to its responsibilities in international affairs along its rise as well as remaining limitations and uncertainties. A subsequent section adds observations from other cases in order to substantiate the core argument of this chapter: Rather than uncritically accepting external ascriptions of responsibility rising powers turn to their own, historically evolved imaginaries of world politics and a concomitant understanding of responsibility; they tend to provide leadership and public goods in closely circumscribed issue areas but do not do so collectively; they cannot always be expected to act on behalf of smaller or least-developed countries, despite their frequent pronouncements to the contrary; and they show critical points of difference among themselves rather than a coherent agenda-setting vision.

The Indian case

Although the Nehruvian tradition of "idealism" has accompanied Indian foreign policy since independence (cf. Ganguly and Pardesi 2009), New Delhi's contributions to global and regional public goods have been limited. For years, in fact, Indian peacekeepers in UN missions were the notable exception. In all other policy fields receiving major publicity as public goods, such as trade or climate change mitigation, India has proven to be a tough negotiator unwilling to bend to Western appeals for (and definitions of) protecting the global commons (Malone 2011;

Narlikar and Narlikar 2014).³ India's record in the provision of public goods can be explained by three factors pertaining to the realm of economics, culture, and regional politics, respectively.

First, in a country with 176 million people, or 13.4 percent of the population, below the international poverty line (World Bank 2019), material constraints alone make a proactive and costly foreign policy difficult to realize. Indeed, even minor concessions for the greater global good (for example in trade and the environment) will be difficult to sell in India's democratic polity.

Second, frustrations over its own marginal role in global institutions, the UN in particular, New Delhi's leadership role in the Non Alignment Movement and a deeply entrenched identity as a developing country (Pant and Super 2015) have curbed India's willingness to cooperate with major western powers. Insistence on the principles of non-intervention and national sovereignty, a major concern for the Ministry of External Affairs (MEA), further limited the room for consensus in numerous policy fields from trade to humanitarian interventions. Closely related to this is India's negotiating culture. Several scholars have argued that India's negotiation behaviour is dominated by a proclivity to use a strictly distributive bargaining strategy and resort to excessive moralization (R. Cohen 1997; Narlikar and Narlikar 2014). This negotiation culture acts as a deterrent against reaching agreements, and also translates into a readiness to go against the flow on matters that include global and regional public good provision.

Third, an exceptionally belligerent regional environment has left little space for cooperation and the provision of public goods that regional powers elsewhere provide. Nowhere is this more apparent than in the dismal record of South Asia's regional grouping, the South Asian Association for Regional Cooperation (SAARC). Despite India's central position and political dominance, none of the great potentials for common gains, in trade and elsewhere, has been realized so far (Destradi 2011).

To differing degrees, all three factors above have been undergoing changes throughout the past decade, widely regarded as the ascendance of a multipolar world.

First and most obviously, material constraints continue to hamper India's foreign policies; yet, three decades of economic growth since India began liberalizing its economy have improved the MEA's as well as other foreign policy actors' room for manoeuver. Prime Minister Narendra Modi's commitment to economic development promised to reinforce this trend (Narlikar 2017). Improving growth rates and reducing poverty levels create the necessary (albeit not sufficient in themselves) enabling conditions for India to show more international leadership.

Second, an understanding that some public goods matter to India has become more widespread following a new dynamic in domestic debates, including a redefinition of Indian interests. Climate change today is seen as a threat to Indian security in a regional environment susceptible to droughts, floods, and rising sea levels. Already a hot topic, migration from Bangladesh may increase as a result of rising sea levels. And a growing domestic constituency is demanding clean water and air given the blatant pollution in Delhi and elsewhere. Arguably, India's large and diverse diaspora has internationalized domestic political debates further. Transnational interdependencies have become particularly visible in economics (IDSA 2012). In fact, given India's geographical location and trade pattern, the vast majority of its increasing trade is shipped through the sea. As a result, New Delhi's very concept of neighbourhood has expanded from a land-based understanding to a wider, maritime one encompassing the entire Indian Ocean region. And despite New Delhi verbally upholding long-held foreign policy principles, including the prioritization of domestic development over foreign commitments, references to India's responsibility in protecting the global commons and acting as a security provider regionally from within India's strategic community have become increasingly frequent (Bhaskar 2012, 50).

Third, although regional cooperation continues to be burdened by persistent historical grievances with almost all South Asian neighbours, a changing strategic environment has made

New Delhi more amenable to acting upon its decades-old commitment to non-reciprocal cooperation within its wider neighbourhood. On the one hand, Indian fears of Chinese intrusion into South Asia have made New Delhi more attentive to its immediate neighbours' demands from Sri Lanka to Bangladesh. On the other, fear of Chinese expansionism in East and South East Asia have provided for a new impetus in closer relations with India in countries from Vietnam to Japan. Indian state-owned Oil and Natural Gas Corporation's (ONGC Videsh) investments in off-shore resource extraction in Vietnamese waters add another dimension of interests in maritime security. None of this automatically results in India emerging as a provider of regional public goods or "responsible regional hegemon". Yet, cooperation in areas seen as particularly suitable for "building bridges of friendship", such as maritime security or disaster relief, and engagements in all kinds of fora – regional, minilateral or sub-regional – have become more likely under conditions of great power rivalry (Womack 2015).

The three factors outlined above suggest more space to allow India to carve out its own role as a "responsible" global power. Consider that India for long has claimed a leadership role within South Asia. As a regional power it aggressively, albeit unsuccessfully, sought to limit external powers' influence in South Asia. Since the 1990s, a verbal commitment to "asymmetric responsibility" and non-reciprocity in the region illustrated India's willingness to provide for regional public goods in principle. Throughout the past decade, maritime security and disaster relief, two regional public goods, have significantly added substance to the rhetoric. Key to this development has been a combination of several facilitating dynamics. Growing capabilities on behalf of the Indian Navy in particular allowed for forceful humanitarian interventions, anti-piracy missions, and military assistance to littoral states that had hitherto been beyond Indian capacities. Several crises – the Tsunami 2004 stands out – provided the opportunity to showcase Indian goodwill through major disaster relief operations and alerted the political class to the diplomatic benefits attached. Moreover, an increasingly expansionist China in the maritime domain not only reminded New Delhi's strategic community of the importance of its Navy but also contributed to a growing demand for naval cooperation on behalf of Indian Ocean littorals. Such cooperation, not least for diplomatic reasons, tends to begin in non-traditional security areas such as fighting piracy, securing sea lanes, or disaster responses.

Efforts in naval cooperation are visible both in terms of bilateral exercises and multilateral initiatives. Whereas the former corresponds with India's tradition of prioritizing bilateralism with smaller powers in its neighbourhood, engaging with major powers (US, Japan) militarily is a novelty, when compared to "India's military isolationism" (Mohan 2010) and opposition to external powers' presence in the Indian Ocean Region in previous times. Indeed, India's recent initiatives have made observers identify a "multilateral turn" in India's naval policies (Pant 2012, 12). For instance, India's national security advisors have met their counterparts from both Indian Ocean island countries and more recently BIMSTEC[4] member states – a novelty in light of India's traditional bilateral approach to regional affairs and security matters in particular.

The Indian Ocean Naval Symposium (IONS) exemplifies this approach. The IONS is held biannually since 2008 with India immediately exerting "a degree of unofficial pre-eminence" (Scott 2015, 469). Representatives from today 35 members' navies participate in what Indian Naval Chief, Admiral DK Joshi calls a "seminar-oriented [...] meeting of minds for benign tasks like humanitarian assistance and disaster relief" (Anandan 2014). Naval sources refer to the IONS as a unique initiative illustrating both Indian goodwill and its growing role as a regional hub in matters related to maritime security.

Albeit less pronounced, on the global level too, India has turned into a more constructive negotiator, which may reflect a certain sense of international responsibility on behalf of the political leadership. In climate change negotiations, Prime Minister Modi took ownership of the mitigation and sustainability agenda as natural elements of Hindu culture (Narlikar 2017). As a result, India reframed its traditionally recalcitrant negotiating position and emerged as a forceful supporter and facilitator of the Paris Agreement including new initiatives such as the Solar Alliance with France. In international trade negotiations, India's traditional role as "nay-sayer" has become somewhat more moderated. Especially at a time when the system of multilateral trade rules faces challenge from the US and China, India has been playing an important role to uphold and reform the system (e.g. Ministry of Commerce and Industry 2019). All of these developments suggest a rising India that may be more inclined to participate in the provision of public goods than ever before and thus contrasts with the existing literature depicting India as a self-contained, inward looking power unwilling to partake and contribute to safeguarding the global commons (Narlikar 2017).

Yet, the evidence provided above is only part of the story. Changes in foreign policy elites' frameworks of thought occur tentatively and are subject to contingent domestic developments, including, among other things, a continuingly strong growth trajectory. Thus, concessions in trade or climate talks may become more difficult to make if economic growth stumbles, or indeed if the trade wars launched by President Trump heat up further. Moreover, India's history as a regional power is full of disappointments on behalf of its neighbours. Events in the aftermath of the 2015 earthquake in Nepal are illustrative. The Modi government's public handling of the crisis, combined with New Delhi's heavy hand in Nepalese domestic politics in its aftermath, is widely regarded as a PR fiasco – despite India's substantial and immediate material help. India's claim to serve as a "net security provider" for the Indian Ocean may be perceived as an expression of hegemonic ambitions rather than of burden-sharing in the interest of littorals states. And whereas competition with China has made India more susceptible to smaller countries' needs, it may also lead to tension with countries in which China expands its footprint militarily, politically, or economically. Given Beijing's massive superiority in resources, such cases are likely to proliferate. Resorting to the entrenched foreign policy template of "strategic autonomy" – although in fact leaving ample space for interpretation – may be read as an argument against alliance building and compromise in global governance in the future thereby undermining India's role as a provider of regional and global public goods. Invoking culture, as in the climate case (Narlikar 2017), can be helpful in overcoming such contestations. However, it may also have opposite effects. In the past, significant factions within the ruling BJP equated national strength – Hindu nationalism – with self-reliance, not independence. And there is a risk that the appeal to traditions may be hijacked by extreme right-wing nationalism, which in turn would seriously undermine the agenda for economic reform that Modi has espoused.

Rising powers and responsibility in world affairs

India's words and actions exhibit elements of ideational change transforming the national interest from one focused on autonomy and self-reliance to one that appreciates the gains derived from international collaboration and interdependence. Influential former Foreign Secretary Subrahmanyam Jaishankar (and appointed Minister for External Affairs in Modi's new cabinet in June 2019) stated that "an aspiring leading power, at a minimum, needs to expand its global footprint" (Jaishankar 2016, paragraph 9). He also mentioned Indian contributions to disaster relief and humanitarian assistance, which "have had a resonance that is difficult to quantify" and have "increased respect for India as a global citizen" (Jaishankar 2016, paragraph 13). Growing means in terms of resources and political capital as well as a changing regional dynamic have contributed to such cognitive changes – and made them more meaningful. The result is an understanding of the national interest that is to a considerable degree reliant on certain public goods – such as limitation to climate change. Today, for instance, Modi's emphasis on diaspora politics suggest that the national interest includes the protection of India's growing diaspora – which in turn makes India a potential leader in evacuation operations and provides for the opportunity to showcase Indian capacity and goodwill.

Indian embrace of globalization as well as its growing reliance on overseas energy imports has made secure sea lanes a key security issue. Likewise, anti-piracy operations and the desire to forge more cooperative relations with littoral states, a vital part of India's Look East initiative, contributed to India's self-ascribed role as "net security provider" regionally. Faced with an increasingly assertive China, India's maritime neighbours have developed a growing appetite for naval cooperation at the same time as India has become more willing to engage the region multilaterally, rather than bilaterally only. Thus, a changing regional dynamic infused a hitherto lacking political interest into Indian naval diplomacy and its concomitant aims of providing maritime security, technical assistance and other benign tasks as regional public goods. Clearly, New Delhi now is in a situation in which its own maritime interests and those of important external – the US in particular – as well as most littoral states converge (Mohan, 2010, 144). Cooperation in disaster relief and humanitarian assistance emerged as particularly salient means for the expression of goodwill within a traditionally India-sceptic regional environment. Providing the platform for cooperation and dialogue on benign maritime tasks, it seems, helps in portraying India as a benevolent, responsible power and contrasts with the Chinese image across the region.

Thus, the Indian case suggests that rising powers do accept the popular link between power and responsibility in international affairs but they do so on their own terms. Also, consider Brazilian foreign policy under President Luiz Inácio Lula da Silva (2003-2011), which confirms some of the findings from the Indian case. As a regional power, Brasília invested political energy in a web of multilateral regional fora (Plagemann 2015, 76–94). Lula's commitment to an understanding of sovereignty "without adjectives" notwithstanding, his government proved more willing than his predecessors to shoulder costs of regional leadership, which came to be regarded as a prerequisite for global status (Saraiva 2010, 7). Examples include the establishment of a regional development fund, FOCEM, Brazilian funding for regional infrastructure projects, or, perhaps most visibly, leadership in the UN peace mission MINUSTAH in Haiti from 2004 to 2017. Some line ministries, health and education in particular, also became increasingly active in their regional engagements. Moreover, on the back of a discourse of a pro-poor policy commitment and the promotion of the Brazilian development model, Lula also intensified Brazilian relations with African nations. Although partially motivated by commercial interests, Lula's Africa policy came with significant costs his successors in the presidency were unwilling to shoulder once the domestic economic climate worsened. Whereas Brazil lost ground in comparison to other rising powers with the outbreak of severe economic and political crises after the Lula presidency, the preceding years nonetheless exhibit some of the trends identified in the Indian case, particularly a focus on the region and its instrumental understanding as a tool for gaining global status; limited investments in the provision of *global* public goods and an attempt in redefining responsibility on the basis of one's own political history and imaginary, rather than based on Western expectations.

Likewise, although there is a tendency to conveniently lump rising powers together, we see a considerable variation in the strategies they employ to signal global and regional responsibility. On the one hand, the BRI is an important case in point to illustrate difference and divergence between China and India. The BRI, under President Xi Jinping, began as a regional strategy and later developed into a global one by incorporating all kinds of investments and diplomatic Chinese activities abroad. Notwithstanding the BRI's promotion as a designated contribution to global public good provision by Chinese authorities, it can also be understood as a collection of various pre-existing, often sub-regionally initiated, infrastructure development projects under a new all-encompassing label (including, for instance the Bangladesh, China, India, Myanmar Economic Corridor, BCIM, or the North South Economic Corridor from Kunming in Yunnan province to Bangkok and Hanoi). Rather than operating through existing multilateral arrangements, the BRI remains unilaterally driven, includes the establishment of new institutions (the AIIB in particular), and strongly reflects Chinese domestic specificities, be it excess capacity in the construction sector or claims to civilizational uniqueness (Nymalm and Plagemann 2019). Partly also for these reasons, it is inviting considerable backlash from within the region and globally, from recipient countries as well third parties (most explicitly by the US under President Trump, but also some members of the European Union) (Benner et al. 2018; Narlikar 2019). India does not have a clear counter-strategy to the BRI, not least because it lacks the resources to launch a geoeconomic drive of this scale. But it is joining forces with other countries, for example, via the Quad initiative (along with Australia, Japan, and the US) in the Indo-Pacific, and developing what seems to be a strategy of soft balancing. On the other hand, we also see some similarities in the approaches of the two giants. For example, while turning into major sources of foreign aid themselves, not only China but India too have been fairly consistent in their refusal to abide by the rules and norms for development assistant developed by the Organisation for Economic Co-operation and Development (OECD).

Finally, the BRICS summit process itself provides for another set of interesting observations. Since its establishment as a leader-level forum in 2009 it developed into a constant of diplomatic summitry with consistent and outspoken support for the process from all members states (Brazil, Russia, India, China, and South Africa). BRICS summits expanded in terms of issue areas and fora, now including a variety of political representatives from Heads of State and Governments to subnational governors, and from media fora to meetings of National Security Advisors. The BRICS process, like the BRI, includes the establishment of new institutions (the New Development Bank, NDB) and within member states effectively functions as an emblem of a new and multipolar world order devoid of Western dominance. Although discussing global affairs and adopting declarations with reference to global issues from environmental affairs to fighting terrorism, BRICS summitry has not emerged as a major voice in either trade, climate change, or any of the major security related issues of the past decade, including non-proliferation. Coordination of its members in the UN, initially amongst the main objectives of the grouping, remains limited due to diverging interests and political rivalries. The NDB, moreover, with its limited capitalization of equal shares primarily funds projects within its five members states. And despite some attempts in outreaching to India's neighbours at the New Delhi Summit in 2016, least developed countries remain out of the process. Hence, the BRICS understood as an accumulated representation of rising powers' global role primarily displays their interest in closer bi- and mini-lateral ties as well as opposition to the Western dominated world order within established institutions, rather than a commitment to specific global responsibilities in global affairs.[5]

Conclusion

The rise of China, India, and other non-western powers in world politics has been paralleled by a declining influence of international organizations – as exhibited in the recent WTO negotiations. Strategic partnerships, leader-level summits and minilateral groupings, issue-specific alliances, and (sub-)regional arrangements have become the skeleton of global governance in a multipolar world. India's foreign policy – as a BRICS member, supporter of the Chinese-led Asian Infrastructure Investment Bank, and with recent attempts in developing BIMSTEC into a meaningful regional organization – is emblematic of this trend.

In such a context, responsibility for matters beyond individual rising powers' immediate domestic and foreign policy concerns is essential for the resolution of global collective action problems. Complex multipolarity's structural characteristics alone – institutional fragmentation, a simultaneity of cooperation and competition amongst the world's major powers, and important yet diverging worldviews – do not provide for the necessary incentives to resolve global collective action problems. Instead, the willingness to engage in public good provision depends on a highly contingent understanding of the national interest that incorporates – in one way or the other – significant investments in global cooperation. For rising powers to accept such responsibility does not come naturally. Entrenched grievances vis-à-vis the western powers have resulted in a history of foreign policy thinking that prioritizes national autonomy over international interdependence. Material constraints, although less severe than hitherto the case, demand for convincing arguments in favour of financial and political investments attached to foreign policy initiatives, particular so in a democratic polity such as India.

Rather than uncritically following external ascriptions of responsibility, rising powers develop their own priorities reflecting domestic political narratives and related global responsibilities, while still limited in their actual material and diplomatic capacities, they are willing to provide leadership in closely circumscribed issue areas rather than across the board, all the more so if such investments entail status gains globally.[6] Yet, at least so far, they do not do so collectively. In fact, within global fora and despite their regional predominance, rising powers rarely, if ever, act on behalf of smaller or less developed states. As a consequence, expect global politics to further fragment into a plethora of multilateral fora and issue-specific alliances including rising and established powers. Moreover, expect a variety of visions of order informing rising powers' foreign policy behaviour, where some key differences may be spotted between China and India.

Notes

1 Although Japan and Russia are sometimes described as regional and global powers respectively, they are not "new" or rising powers. Indonesia, despite its large population, so far has not been a prominent player on the world stage. Nigeria, although acting as a regional power in Western Africa, has remained insignificant on the global stage so far. Although South Africa is Africa's diplomatically most visible country and part of the BRICS alliance, it lacks the resources for global power projection. Brazil's status as a global power has been called into question following years of domestic turmoil and its continuing dependency on primary goods. Nevertheless, we included some observations from the early 2000s – that is when Brazil was widely regarded as a rising power both externally and internally – in the third section of this chapter.
2 Also see the special issues devoted to rising and regional powers in *Third World Quarterly* 34:6 (2013), *International Affairs* 89:3 (2013), *Global Society* 26:3 (2012, and *International Affairs* 82:1 (2006).
3 The field of nuclear non-proliferation is one other interesting exception. Here, India managed to stick to its rejection of the Non Proliferation Treaty (NPT), while at the same time ultimately contributing to the stability of the regime through its desire for the status of a constructive and responsible global player (Sullivan de Estrada forthcoming).
4 The Bay of Bengal Initiative for Multi-Sectoral Technical and Economic Cooperation includes Bangladesh, Bhutan, India, Myanmar, Nepal, Sri Lanka, and Thailand.
5 Also see Brosig (2019).
6 See Plagemann and Prys-Hansen (2018) for a more detailed discussion of this particular point with reference to India. On varying leadership provision across issue areas, also see Wæver (2017).

References

Acharya, A. (2014). *The End of American World Order*. Oxford: Oxford University Press.
Kupchan, C. (2012). *No One's World. The West, The Rising Rest, and the Coming Global Turn*. Oxford: Oxford University Press.

Anandan, S. (2014). "Indian Ocean Naval Forum to Take in More Members." *The Hindu*, February 5, 2014. http://www.thehindu.com/news/national/indian-ocean-naval-forum-to-take-in-more-members/article5656853.ece (accessed November 11, 2016).

Beetham, D. (2013). *The Legitimation of Power*. Basingstoke: Palgrave Macmillan.

Benner, T., Gaspers, J., Ohlberg, M., Poggetti, L., and Shi-Kupfer, K. (2018). *Authoritarian Advance: Responding to China's Growing Political Influence in Europe*. Berlin: GPPI and MERICS. Available at: https://www.merics.org/sites/default/files/2018-02/GPPi_MERICS_Authoritarian_Advance_2018_0.pdf (accessed 1 July 2019).

Bhaskar, C. U. (2012). "The Navy as an Instrument of Foreign Policy: The Indian Experience." In Pant, H.V., ed., *The Rise of the Indian Navy*. Farnham: Ashgate.

Brosig, M. (2019). *The Role of BRICS in Large-Scale Armed Conflict*. Basingstoke: Palgrave Macmillan.

Burns, J. M. (1978). *Leadership*. New York: Harper Perennial.

Chang-Liao, N. (2016). "China's New Foreign Policy under Xi Jinping." *Asian Security*, 12(2): 82–91.

Cohen, R. (1997). *Negotiating Across Cultures: International Communication in an Interdependent World*. Washington: United States Institute of Peace.

Destradi, S. (2011). *Indian Foreign and Security Policy in South Asia: Regional Power Strategies*. London: Routledge.

Ganguly, S., and Pardesi, M. S. (2009). "Explaining Sixty Years of India's Foreign Policy." *India Review*, 8(1): 4–19.

IDSA (2012). *Net Security Provider: India's Out-of-Area Contingency Operations*. New Delhi: Institute for Defence Studies and Analyses.

Ikenberry, J. G. (2011). "The Future of the Liberal World Order." *Foreign Affairs*, 90(3): 56–68.

Ikenberry, J. G. (2018). "Why the Liberal World Order Will Survive." *Ethics & International Affairs*, 32(1): 17–29.

Jaishankar, S. (2016). "Indian Foreign Secretary Subrahmanyam Jaishankar's Remarks." http://carnegieindia.org/2016/04/06/indian-foreign-secretary-subrahmanyam-jaishankar-s-remarks/iwq8 (accessed November 5, 2016).

Kai, J. (2013). "Can China build a Community of Common Destiny?" *The Diplomat*, November 28, 2013. http://thediplomat.com/2013/11/can-china-build-a-community-of-common-destiny/ (accessed 10 March 2017).

Kenkel, K. M., and Stefan, C. G. (2016). "Brazil and the Responsibility While Protecting Initiative: Norms and the Timing of Diplomatic Support." *Global Governance: A Review of Multilateralism and International Organizations*, 22(1): 41–58.

Kindleberger, C. (1981). "Dominance and Leadership in the International Economy: Exploitation, Public Goods, and Free Rides." *International Studies Quarterly*, 85(2): 242–254.

Malone, D. (2011). *Does the Elephant dance? Contemporary Indian Foreign Policy*. Oxford: Oxford University Press.

Mearsheimer, J. (1990). "Back to the Future: Instability in Europe after the Cold War." *International Security*, 15(1): 5–56.

Ministry of Commerce and Industry (2019). "Outcome of the WTO Ministerial Meeting of Developing Countries: Working collectively to strengthening the WTO to promote development and inclusivity." Delhi: 13–14 May. Press Information Bureau. http://pib.nic.in/newsite/PrintRelease.aspx?relid=190000 (accessed 1 July 2019).

Mohan, C. R. (2010). "Rising India: Partner in Shaping the Global Commons?" *The Washington Quarterly*, 33(3): 133–148.

Mohan, C. R. (2014). *Modi's World*. Noida: Harper Collins.

Narlikar, A. (2010a). "Introduction." In Narlikar, A., ed., *Deadlocks in Multilateral Negotiations*. Cambridge: Cambridge University Press.

Narlikar, A. (2010b). "New Powers in the Club: The Challenges of Global Trade Governance." *International Affairs*, 86(3): 717–728.

Narlikar, A., and Narlikar, A. (2014). *Bargaining with a Rising Power*. Oxford: Oxford University Press.

Narlikar, A. (2017). "India's Role in Global Governance: A Modi-fication?" *International Affairs*, 93(1): 93–111.

Narlikar, A. (2019). "Regional Powers' Rise and Impact on International Conflict and Negotiation: China and India as Global and Regional Players." *Global Policy*. Online first. https://doi.org/10.1111/1758-5899.12673.

Nymalm, N., and Plagemann, J. (2019). "Comparative Exceptionalism: Universality and Particularity in Foreign Policy Discourses." *International Studies Review*, 21(1): 12–37.

Pant, H.V. (2012). "Introduction." In Pant, H.V., ed., *The Rise of the Indian Navy - Internal Vulnerabilities, External Challenges*. New York: Routledge.

Pant, H.V., and Super, J.M. (2015). "India's 'nonalignment' Conundrum: A Twentieth Century Policy in a Changing World." *International Affairs*, 91(4): 747–764.

Plagemann, J., and Prys-Hansen, M. (2018). "'Responsibility', Change, and Rising Powers' Role Conceptions: Comparing Indian Foreign Policy Roles in Global Climate Change Negotiations and Maritime Security." *International Relations of the Asia-Pacific*. Online first. https://doi.org/10.1093/irap/lcy028.

Plagemann, J. (2015). *Cosmopolitanism in a Multipolar World*. Basingstoke: Palgrave Macmillan.

Saraiva, M. G. (2010). "A diplomacia brasileira e as visões sobre a inserção externa do Brasil: institucionalism pragmático x autonomistas" (ARI No. 46/2010). Madrid: Real Instituto Elcano.

Schirm, S. (2013). "Global Politics Are Domestic Politics: A Societal Approach to Divergence in the G20." *Review of International Studies*, 39(3): 685–706.

Schweller, R. (2011). "Emerging Powers in an Age of Disorder." *Global Governance*, 17(3): 285–297.

Scott, D. (2015). "The Indian Ocean as India's Ocean." In Malone, D., Mohan, C. R., and Raghavan, S., eds., *The Oxford Handbook of Indian Foreign Policy*. Oxford: Oxford University Press.

Sullivan de Estrad, K. (2020). "Understanding India's Exceptional Engagement with the Nuclear Non-proliferation Regime." In: Plagemann, J., Destradi, S. and Narlikar, A., eds., *India Rising: Ideas, Interests, and Institutions in Foreign Policy*. New Delhi: Oxford University Press.

Tellis, A., Szalwinski, A., and Wills, M. (2016). *Understanding Strategic Cultures in the Asia-Pacific*. Seattle and Washington, DC: The National Bureau of Asian Research.

Tsebelis, G. (1995). "Decision Making in Political Systems: Veto Players in Presidentialism, Parliamentarism, Multicameralism and Multipartyism." *British Journal of Political Science*, 23(3): 289–325.

Wade, R. H. (2011). "Emerging World Order? From Multipolarity to Multilateralism in the G20, the World Bank, and the IMF." *Politics & Society*, 39(3): 347–378.

Wæver, O. (2017). "International Leadership after the Demise of the Last Superpower: System Structure and Stewardship." *Chinese Political Science Review*, 2(4): 452–476.

Waltz, K. (1979). *Theory of International Politics*. Reading: Addison-Wesley.

Wohlforth, W. C. (1999). "The Stability of a Unipolar World." *International Security*, 24(1): 5–41.

Womack, B. (2015). *Asymmetry and International Relationships*. Cambridge: Cambridge University Press.

World Bank (2019). *Country Poverty Brief: India*. http://databank.worldbank.org/data/download/poverty/33EF03BB-9722-4AE2-ABC7-AA2972D68AFE/Global_POVEQ_IND.pdf (accessed 29 June 2019).

18
RESPONSIBILITY AS AN OPPORTUNITY

China's water governance in the Mekong region

Yung-Yung Chang

Introduction

When it comes to water governance, a considerable amount of literature centers on the issues of hegemony and cooperation. In general, Dolsak and Ostrom (2003) point out that upstream–downstream situations present the most challenging geographic contexts in dealing with international waters. The core concern lies in asking whether a hegemonic upstream state would cooperate with downstream states. Scholars like Lowi (1993), Waterbury (1994), and Zeitoun and Allan (2008) advocate the hegemonic stability theory and stress the impact of "power asymmetry." Focusing on political-military power and the enormous influence the hegemon possesses over international affairs, they argue that hegemonic upstream states have little interest and incentive to cooperate on managing transboundary waters. Rather different from believing in the hegemonic stability theory or stressing the dominant role played by the hegemon, other scholars look at another set of aspects like the role of third-party intervention (Weinthal 2002) and issue-linkage or the spill-over effects of non-water cooperation (Onishi 2011; Sadoff and Grey 2002) to explain interstate water cooperation between upstream and downstream states.

Building on such contributions, the chapter takes a joint perspective to understand water conflicts through the lens of "power asymmetry," while also considering the possibility of cooperation. It argues that an important role is played by the hegemon to bring upstream–downstream states together via soft measures like institution-building and issue-linkage to realize cooperation. The intended contribution of this chapter is to argue that being dominant or unilateral is not the only choice for the hegemony to govern transboundary watercourse; instead, a constructive approach in which responsibility is shared and thereby fosters cooperation among riparian states is a better alternative for the hegemon (see also the respective chapters by Friedman, Plagemann and Narlikar in this volume).

The article is divided into three major parts. First of all, it fundamentally reviews water as an important object of governance. It then provides a historical account to point out that transboundary water management involves varying intensities of conflicts and power relations. Before going into the next part, the article addresses the emergence of responsibility in the context of water governance. This brings out the idea of the hydro-hegemon, who possesses the ability to create a regime of shared responsibility.

Secondly, the article focuses on the Mekong River region, providing some historical background to the institutional development. Accordingly, in the third part, the chapter focuses on China as a hydro-hegemon and responsible actor to engage in multilateral cooperation and promote cooperation mechanisms. The Lancang-Mekong Cooperation (LMC), led by China, will be highlighted to see how this mechanism was established to become a key node to link China's "Belt and Road Initiative" (BRI). Lastly, the chapter concludes with a reflection that assesses China's responsibility arrangement in the Mekong Region. It particularly considers whether the cooperation mechanism is sustainable or whether it is just another platform for China to use responsibility as an opportunity to exert influences for realizing its strategic purposes.

Transboundary water management: water as a vital object of governance

Natural resources like water play a pivotal role in sustainable development. Water shortage or quality degradation can have tremendous impacts not only on economic and social development but also on political stability and ecosystem integrity (UNDP 2006). How to make good use of the water resources[1] is an increasingly critical issue. As the UNDP report (2004) points out, the water crisis (such as the access to safe and clean water for human health and survival) "has resulted chiefly not from the natural limitations of the water supply or the lack of financing and appropriate technologies, but rather from profound failures in water governance, i.e., the ways in which individuals and societies have assigned value to, made decisions about, and managed the water resources available to them" (Ibid. 2). The governance of water resources is thus of great importance to tackling water crises for poverty alleviation, human, and ecosystem health (Hope 2007). Managing water resources involves politically charged questions like, who gets how much of the water, how and why (Zeitoun and Warner 2006). It requires a set of systems, which include political, economic, social and administrative ones, controlling decision-making for water resource development and management (Batchelor 2007; Rogers and Hall 2003). Accordingly, governing or managing water resources lies much in "the way in which decisions are made than the decisions themselves" (Moench 2003, cited in Batchelor 2007, 5). Regarding this decision-making, a profoundly political element to water governance is then expected, as systems of water governance often reflect the political realities at various levels (Batchelor 2007).

Managing transboundary water resources, which are shared between two or more states, is even more complicated and difficult, as it introduces an international political dimension into the process (Earle and Neal 2017). Decisions over the management, use and conservation of the transboundary water are mainly assigned to different nation-states with their various national interests. Yet, how should one assign responsibility when it comes to utilizing a transboundary river? Should the country with the largest share of the transboundary river take the initiative, or should the country who positions in the uppermost location have a larger say, or should the external stakeholder who shares great interests take the lead? Such cross-national issues are at the heart of "hydro-politics." As Elhance (1999) defines it, hydro-politics is about conflict and cooperation between states taking place in shared water resources like transboundary rivers.[2] According to the United Nations, there are 286 transboundary river basins covering 151 countries and 2.8 billion people (UNEP 2016).[3] About two-thirds of the transboundary rivers lack cooperative management frameworks, which could easily cause transboundary disputes (Feng et al. 2019). Therefore, the need for governing transboundary water resources is urgent and required.

Yet, there is no one uniform mechanism or convention that is agreed in the international community (Rahaman 2009; Salman 2007). As early as in 1966, the Helsinki Rules on the Uses of the Waters of International Rivers were adopted and since then have been acknowledged as the groundwork for negotiating over shared waters among riparian states (Eckstein 2002; Rahaman 2009). In 1997 the *United Nations Convention on the Law of the Non-navigational Uses of International Watercourses* (commonly known as UN Watercourses Convention), was adopted in order to govern shared water resources for universal applicability. Nevertheless, this Watercourses Convention is of limited application (Paisley et al. 2016). Yet, for all that underdeveloped nature, principles of equitable and reasonable utilization, appropriate measures without causing significant harm, principles of cooperation, information exchange, notification and consultation, peaceful settlement of disputes, and protection of the ecosystems are widely recognized by international treaties and agreements concerning transboundary water management (Paisley et al. 2016; Rahaman 2009).

All in all, when it comes to transboundary water resources, three major themes are concerned: water scarcity, political implications and involvement due to the scarcity, and the management of these water resources moving between countries. Accessing safe, clean, and reliable water is demanded and is deemed a fundamental right by the riparian countries along a shared river. Yet, questions like how to define property rights, who would benefit from these rights and how are they enforced are all central issues (Batchelor 2007). As a matter of fact, ownership or the right to use a water resource or water supply infrastructure implies power and control (Batchelor 2007; UNDP 2007). In the case of a shared transboundary river, upstream states are assumed to enjoy inherent power and leverage over the downstream states in terms of governing and managing water resources (Lufkin 2017). Therefore, various roles and responsibilities among riparian countries are at stake when governing shared water resources.

This chapter argues that responsibility is derived not only from power-asymmetry but also from the realization of the interdependent essence of water governance. Responsibility is therefore defined as the *prominent capability* to take the initiative and use an interactive as well as cooperative approach to agree on action strategies for tackling the common problem concerning water resource management and finding the common ground for a solution (compare Introduction to this volume). One might take over responsibility for organizing a water governance regime when one's capability allows for this to happen, and when there is a critical juncture such as a power vacuum left by the international structure or the deterioration of one common problem. In considering how to ensure good governance in managing a shared transboundary river to meet the local needs and comply with the international principles, the chapter claims that the key point might lie in the role of the countries possessing more power and leverage to take more responsibility in bringing relevant parties together for more cooperation in water management. In contrast to hydro-politics, hydro-diplomacy stresses that communication and consultation deserve more attention to accelerate cooperation: although managing a transboundary river presents a potential conflict, it could also enhance regional as well as global cooperation (Lufkin 2017).

In fact, conflicts over transboundary water resources can be visualized in a conflict-cooperation continuum, where "water wars" reside on one side of the spectrum and "harmonious cooperation"[4] on the other. As Zeitoun and Warner (2006) claim, many water conflicts lie somewhere between the "water wars" and "harmonious cooperation." Although agreeing with Zeitoun and Warner (2006) that the imbalance of power between riparian countries is decisive for determining the extent that each riparian control over water resources, this chapter wants to make clear that transboundary contestation coexists with cooperation. Accordingly, power-relations or power asymmetry can define not only the intensity of conflicts but also the intensity of cooperation. That is, the more asymmetrical the power-relations are, the more possible that the conflict will be avoided, and the cooperation will be promoted. What truly matters is the role played and the responsibility taken by the actor who holds more power and leverage.

From hegemonic power to responsible leadership and cooperation

This chapter adopts the framework of hydro-hegemony to discuss China's responsibility in the Mekong region to govern the transboundary river.[5] As mentioned, to address responsibility in the context of capability and power, responsibility in this chapter is closely related to the idea of leadership in that it mainly refers to "managing water as a scarce resource in more efficient, equitable, and sustainable ways" (Hirsch 2006, 186). Leadership is loosely defined as an influence, an advantageous guiding role as well as a founder or defender of one regional mechanism. While admitting that every riparian state along the Mekong River has mutual responsibility to take to manage water resources in a sustainable way, it is important to have a leader who is able to bring relevant interested parties together for cooperation and for realizing the common good (compare chapter by Friedman in this volume). That is, the issue concerning the accountability of managing transboundary river is substantial to clarify the roles of riparian states and to overcome the free rider as well as commitment problem[6] (Onishi 2011). In this context, responsibility for water governance involves not only the willingness to do so, but mostly also the capabilities for setting up the inclusive institutions and mechanism to encourage participation and realizing cooperation. This highlights the role of the hegemon in managing transboundary river issues.

According to Zeitoun and Warner's hydro-hegemony framework (2006), the hegemon has a decisive role to play in transboundary water governance. Operating from a position of relative power, the hydro-hegemon has the capability to ensure a positive outcome when it comes to water resources competition. Such capability can be enforced into negative form of stressing dominance or into positive form of taking over the leadership to realize "benefit for all." This means that the hegemon can either take leadership supported by legitimacy and authority or it occupies the dominant position supported by coercion.

By adopting this framework and focusing on China as the hegemon, the chapter argues that China's hegemony is characterized by responsible and enlightened leadership rather than pressure. Different from brute force, legitimate leadership is based on the "intersubjective internalization of ideas, norms and identities" (Nabers 2008, 11). This also suggests the importance of the ideational resources to exercise leadership. Under the "ideological hegemony," subordinate actors are convinced to "accept not just the hegemon's authority, but to adopt and internalize its values and norms intended to impose one solution over others," and that "compliance with the 'way things are' is only a common sense (Zeitoun and Warner 2006, 438)."

Only via an interactive and cooperative approach can the hegemon's leadership be sustainable to take its responsibility to realize common goals in managing transboundary river. The chapter focuses on China's role as a *responsible* leader to stimulate the actions of the non-hegemon and prompt the cooperation between China and the other riparian countries to facilitate transboundary river management. Therefore, the leadership does not imply the absolute domination from the hegemonic leader; instead, it is the locomotive to initiate the process and realize the common goal.

The Mekong region

The Mekong River Basin is an economically and politically diverse region. The power asymmetry, plus the geographical proximity, cultural affinity and economic complementarity between China and the other riparian countries in the Mekong area makes the Mekong River Basin a good example to address how an upstream hegemon can be a responsible leader to cooperate with the downstream states and encourage cooperation for managing water resources. The following will provide some details concerning the economic and political situation along the Mekong River.

The Mekong River

The Mekong River is the longest watercourse in Southeast Asia (Grumbine et al. 2012) and has a length of about 4,350 km.[7] The river possesses considerable biodiversity and a unique ecosystem. Most importantly, it provides great opportunities for hydropower development. The basic feature of hydrology along the Mekong River is the dominance of the single wet-season flow peak (Adamson et al. 2009). The distinct wet and dry seasons underscore the value and importance of hydropower dams, which are able to control flows in the wet season and raise river flows during the dry season downstream (Paisley et al. 2016). Nevertheless, due to various reasons such as longstanding regional conflict (Indochina wars) and several geopolitical barriers, the Mekong region has a low density of large dams in comparison to other parts of the world (Molle et al. 2009).

Gradually, developmental progress has been made since the early 1990s. In Middleton and Allouche's (2016, 100) words, "the Mekong River has been transformed from a free-flowing river to one that is increasingly engineered by large hydropower dams." In fact, as Grumbine et al. (2012, 91) point out, "the Mekong River is under intense development pressure" that there are now manifold upstream dams under construction and different proposals are set about for developing the downstream dams. While the projects concerning constructing dams in the Lower Mekong are still at the proposal stage, plenty of hydropower projects led by China have been underway to build dams along the upper Mekong River. All in all, water resources management in the Mekong has progressed; yet, there are still gaps in both physical and institutional developments.

Historical account: development of cooperation in the Mekong region

As Dinar et al. (2007) suggest, the potential of the Mekong has not yet been fully realized due to past colonial experience and the intense historical hostility among riparian states. Nevertheless, various endeavors have been made to pursue cooperation. Since the 1940s, the Mekong River has been recognized to have hydropower potential (Matthews and Geheb 2014). As early as in 1946, the United Nations Economic Commission for Asia and the Far East (ECAFE) was founded, and in 1949 the Bureau of Flood Control for the Basin was established in order to deal with flood control and water resources management (Dinar et al. 2007; Molle et al. 2009). The ECAFE report "provided for a conceptual framework to develop the Mekong River Basin as an integrated system through close collaboration of the riparian countries" (InternationalWatersGovernance 2019). In 1952, the Mekong received recognition as an international waterway by the Lower Mekong states (Genugten 2015). In 1957, the Statute of the Committee for the Coordination of Investigations of the Lower Mekong Basin (the "1957 Statute") was adopted by the Lower Mekong states (Thailand, Cambodia, Vietnam, and Laos). The 1957 Statute "represent[ed] the first constitutional document for the Mekong Regime" (InternationalWatersGovernance 2019). In 1975, the Joint Declaration of Principles for Utilization of the Waters of the Lower Mekong Basin (the "Joint Declaration") was signed and it declared the Mekong to be "a resource of common interest not subject to major unilateral appropriation by any riparian State without prior approval by the other Basin States through the Committee" (TheJointDeclaration 1975), emphasizing the equal standing of riparian states. It was not until 1995 that the "Agreement on the Cooperation for the Sustainable Development of the Mekong River Basin" (the 1995 Mekong Agreement), a treaty among Cambodia, Lao PDR, Thailand and Vietnam, was negotiated and signed. This treaty provides the framework for cooperation to realize the utilization, management, and sustainable development of the Mekong

River. The 1995 Mekong Agreement is seen as the positive outcome of dozens of years of efforts from the regional and supra-regional level to cooperatively manage the Mekong River (Paisley et al. 2016).

In addition to all of the above, the institutionalized cooperation between upper- and lower-stream states was gradually developed. The following will provide some more details concerning the major institutional mechanisms that were, have been and are responsible for water governance in the Mekong River. The examination helps to understand not only the institutional development but also the shift of the responsibility for managing the Mekong River (from external contributions like US and Japan's financial supports to internal endeavors of Mekong River states). Most importantly, it paves the way to disclose China's evolving role and involvement in the process.

Institutional development for managing water resources of the Mekong River

The institutional history for managing the Mekong River reaches back to the 1950s. Yet its development was marked by a row of failed initiatives because of a dominance of foreign involvement and a simultaneous lack of Chinese engagement. The so-called Mekong Committee was established 1957 by Laos, Thailand, Cambodia, Vietnam and an observer from the United Nations Development Program with a mandate to "promote, coordinate, supervise and control planning and investigations of water resources development projects in the lower Mekong Basin" (Molle et al. 2009, 5). In this Mekong Committee, the USA were the largest non-riparian aid donor in the first ten years of its existence (Friesen 1999; Molle et al. 2009), mostly for the reason of suppressing communist influence in the region. Following the withdrawal of Cambodia and the USA's withdrawal from Southeast Asia the Mekong Committee was transformed into the "Interim Committee for Coordination of Investigations of the Lower Mekong Basin" containing three members, Lao PDR, Thailand and Vietnam (Hirsch and Jensen 2006; Molle et al. 2009). Upon Cambodia's reengagement in 1991, the Lower Mekong states began to work on a cooperative plan, which after a long negotiation reached the 1995 Mekong Agreement that has paved the road for establishing the Mekong River Commission (MRC) (Paisley et al. 2016). The MRC was established in 1995 and became the main regional management body to replace the previous two mechanisms (the Mekong and Interim Committee). Yet, it was funded and thus dominated by Japan and Western countries, not the Mekong countries themselves. Without China's active participation, the MRC has long faced difficulties to coordinate and realize its mandate for facilitating transboundary water governance and is therefore gradually marginalized (Hirsch and Jensen 2006).

Although in 1992 the *Greater Mekong Subregion* Economic Cooperation Program *(GMS)* was formed, sponsored by the Asian Development Bank (ADB), to boost market and regional integration of its members, which include China (the Yunnan Province), Myanmar, Laos, Thailand, Cambodia and Vietnam, it was not until the *Lancang-Mekong Cooperation (LMC)* that governance of the Mekong improved significantly. The first LMC Leaders Meeting was held in China in 2016. It is the most recent major transboundary initiative with three cooperation pillars: political and security issues; economic and sustainable development; and social, cultural and people-to-people exchanges (Middleton and Allouche 2016). Unlike the GMS stressing regional economic integration, the LMC has put both economic integration and water resource management in its priority areas. Besides, unlike the previous existing mechanisms relying largely on assistance from external actors like the USA, Japan or the ADB, the LMC was founded without external involvement and centers exclusively around countries along the Lancang-Mekong River.

The establishment of the LMC is significant in the following sense. First, the existing institutions for transboundary water governance are in a state of flux (Middleton and Allouche 2016). According to Hirsch and Jensen (2006), there is a significant disconnection as well as long-standing divide between the GMS and the MRC that the coordination between the two is weak and fragmented (Middleton and Dore 2015). Thus, the establishment of the LMC offers the opportunity to bridge and update the existing institutions. Secondly, the LMC brings China as the major Lancang-Mekong state back to the central stage. Rather than being excluded (as in the case of the Mekong Committee and the Interim Committee) or acting relatively passively (as in the MRC and GMS), China has proactively participated and been situated at the center of the regional planning in the LMC mechanism. Under the title "Shared River, Shared Future," the LMC's first Summit suggests to naturalize the relationship between China and the downstream countries (Hirsch 2016; Middleton and Allouche 2016). To demonstrate its commitment and earnestness, China released water in aid of the downstream countries (Bunyavejchewin 2016; Xinhua 2016). The establishment of the LMC can be understood as the *watershed* that manifested China's more active and responsible leadership of water governance in the Mekong.

China's evolving involvements in Mekong institutions

China was not part of the Mekong Committee in the 1950s due to the non-membership of the United Nations (UN) and due to international politics aiming at containing the spread of communism after Mao's takeover of China in 1949 (Molle et al. 2009). In the case of the MRC, although China is a dialogue partner, and has shown its growing commitment by signing an agreement with the MRC to share information and data about daily river flow and rainfall (MRC 2015), China has refrained from fully engaging in the MRC. The main reason for this is that China never fully identified with the features of the MRC as a Western donor-funded and rule-based organization. Without China's deep engagement and support the MRC could not realize its water governance effectively (Rein 2014). Quite different from the case of the MRC, China has shown more interests in being involved in the GMS program. Through contributing to infrastructure and hydropower development projects, China's role in the Mekong region evolved from being an initial beneficiary to a major benefactor ever since it got involved in the GMS (Bunyavejchewin 2016). China's increasing participation in the GMS is significant as it encouraged China to play a more active role not only in managing transboundary water but also in developing many infrastructural ties with the GMS to realize connectivity and promote integration. In turn, China realized the importance of water governance as it could be the springboard for broader developmental plans.

It was not until the foundation of the LMC, however, that China finally developed its own regional initiative (Middleton and Allouche 2016). The LMC was strongly supported and promoted as the new initiative to counterbalance the existing ones championed by other major powers (Middleton and Allouche 2016). During the LMC Summit in 2016, a center for technical cooperation and information sharing was proposed to be established in China (Middleton and Allouche 2016). Progressively, China has taken control of the framework-building process (Bunyavejchewin 2016). With no intention to develop into a rule-based organization, the LMC is designed to pursue a "soft path cooperation" and to be a "project-based" initiative providing a broader platform for cooperation (Middleton and Allouche 2016). Through all the efforts and commitment to the LMC, China has gradually consolidated its central position and extended its influences in managing the Mekong Region. In brief, the concept of the LMC symbolizes China's artful efforts to establish its own rules and institutions to encourage cooperation (Pongsudhirak 2016).

China's role: a responsible actor to encourage more cooperation than contestation

From the above-mentioned discussion, the role of China was gradually strengthened in managing the Mekong River. It is noteworthy that almost half of the Mekong River's length passes through China. As an upper Mekong state, China has a decisive role to play as its management would have tremendous impacts on the downstream countries. China's responsibility as a leader is defined and expected here as bringing more incentives for cooperation and reducing conflicts when dealing with transboundary water resources under the condition of asymmetrical power. That is to say, to take responsibility as a leader, China needs to build trust, confidence and the comfortable atmosphere for cooperation in water management. China's leadership entails not only the *structural one* which expresses "power based on the possession of material resources" but also the *entrepreneurial one* which implies skillful diplomacy to fulfill common interests or unify interests of stakeholders, and the *intellectual one* which refers to educating other actors and orienting their thinking (Young 1991, 288). In this way, China has utilized its material power to set up the LMC; its diplomatic skills to bring all willing parties together for "building a community of shared future of peace and prosperity among Lancang-Mekong Countries and establishing the LMC as an example of a new form of international relations featuring win-win cooperation" (LMC 2017); and its normative influences to set up rules and norms to build the trust and cooperative atmosphere among participants in order to manage Mekong river issues for a sustainable development of the Lancang-Mekong Sub-region. In short, by setting up the institution, rules and norms, China provided the middle ground for the Mekong countries to engage with each other. Importantly, it is crucial to point out that such responsibility and leadership are not unilateralism as the LMC follows a multiple-participation model and is structured as a multi-layered and multi-domain framework to include a Leaders' Meeting, Foreign Ministers' Meeting, Senior Officials' Meeting and Working Groups Meeting, so that cooperation can be planned according to the actual situation and needs (Ministry of Foreign Affairs 2016). From respecting and taking others' demands into consideration, the LMC has also followed the early harvest approach with a list of the Early Harvest Project, through which China has given special favorable economic treatments to the smaller ASEAN countries to build its reputation as a responsible great power promoting co-development and co-prosperity (Ye 2010).

In addition to China's prominent capability, it is the power vacuum left by international structure and the inability of other riparian countries that further encouraged China to take over responsibility. As mentioned, there were the Mekong Committee, the Interim Committee, and the MRC responsible for managing the Mekong River. Nevertheless, due to the growing tensions in the region, lack of financial resources, withdrawals of major powers (USA and Japan), and the change of some national governments, most of the proposed projects in managing the Mekong have not been successfully realized or implemented so that those mechanisms have become gradually marginalized (Biggs 2006, Hirsch and Jensen 2006; Molle et al. 2009).

The following will discuss China's responsibility for facilitating cooperation and turning the essentially zero-sum water-competition into a positive sum that could be of benefit for all. There will be mainly two aspects to observe: First, China's changing attitudes to be more willing to cooperate; and second, China's utilization of water resources to boost cooperation and development.

Hydropower development, from selfish concerns to more responsible actions

For China, the Mekong River is of significant strategic and economic interests. Among others, hydropower is a key component, as it allows the electricity produced to be imported into China's fast-growing urban centers and ensures energy security (Matthews and Motta 2013; Urban et al. 2009). Ever since China completed the first dam, the Manwan Dam, on the river in 1992, China's hydro-power development along the Upper Mekong has moved forward rapidly (Matthews and Motta 2013). It is noteworthy that China has gradually transformed its role in managing the Mekong. It did so by shifting its attitudes toward managing the Mekong River from passive and unilateral to active and cooperative. Such changing attitudes and increasing involvement determine the operation and performance of managing the Mekong River.

China's initial unilateral actions can be traced back to the early 1960s, when China began to develop the Upper Mekong and hydropower projects for its domestic uses (Onishi 2011). Solely for internal concerns, China followed a policy of noninterference and limited engagement with others as the country had no interest in cooperating with Lower Mekong states (Matthews and Motta 2013; Onishi 2011). In particular, hydrological information was widely identified as "classified state secrets" that involve national sovereignty and security (Elhance 1999; Onishi 2011). Thus, when managing water resources and planning hydropower projects along the Mekong River, China was not aware of and also not interested in either increasing transparency to share data with downstream countries or making a consultation with those Lower Mekong states beforehand.

China's hydropower development in the Mekong Basin has been viewed with ambiguity by downstream states. On the one hand, China's economic strength is welcomed by the Lower Mekong states who seek investment in their water resources and the associated economic development; on the other hand, China's unilateral actions without taking the interests of the neighboring countries into consideration (e.g. the lack of environmental and social safeguards) have urged protests from downstream countries (Hirsch 2010; Matthews and Motta 2013; Vu 2014).

However, since the 2000s, after becoming aware of the geography and geopolitical importance of the Lower Mekong States for its domestic economic development, especially for eliminating poverty in Yunnan and for its external security because of better access to the South China Sea, China has gradually changed its position to take a more constructive approach toward the Lower Mekong states, especially after 2010 when the protest from the downstream countries reached its climax (Matthews and Motta 2013). As Onishi (2007, 530) puts it, "China is [slowly] tending away from unilateralism, and is gradually getting involved in negotiation mechanism and process with the downstream states." In terms of information sharing, already in 2002, although only being a dialogue partner, China signed the "Agreement on the Provision of Hydrological Information of Lancang-Mekong River in Flood Season" with the MRC to offer more information about river flow and water levels for the Upper Mekong River; in 2009, China further expressed its willingness to share more information concerning the hydropower plans that are still in progress and its future constructions plans in the upstream area (Onishi 2007; Vu 2014). China's gesture to share data has significant implications. First, it helps to push basin-wide flood management and control ahead; second, it acts as a stepping-stone to foster further negotiations; third, it produces a sense of mutual-trust for basin-wide cooperation (Onishi 2007). As Onishi (2007) states, it is normally difficult to form a consensus about the validity of water-related data among riparian states due to the vested interests and the expectation of a particular outcome. Yet, hydrological data provided by China have been accepted as reliable as they enhance the accuracy of flood forecasts for stations in Laos and Thailand (MRC 2002; Onishi 2011). All in all, it shows China's efforts to initiate and encourage cooperation with downstream states.

Moreover, being increasingly aware of the reputational risk and the potential social and environmental impacts linked with water infrastructure, China has increasingly engaged in dialogues with downstream countries through various frameworks and forums like the Challenge Program on Water and Food's (CPWF) or the Mekong Forum on Water, Food and Energy (Matthews and

Motta 2013). Some solutions have also been released by China in order not to change the flow in the downstream area; as well as the commitment to take part in the environmental assessment on scheduled hydropower plants in the Lower Mekong Basin that were under operation by the MRC (Vu 2014). Through all of these involvements, China realized the importance to frame its "hydropower development as a win-win for both itself and the Lower Mekong Basin countries" (Matthews and Motta 2013, 3). Above all, drawing support from the newly established LMC, China has further switched its development focus and transformed its interests in the Mekong Basin from solely self-regarding to be more region-oriented. That is, China's national interests have been integrated into the wider regional and international interests, just as the "Five Features of Lancang-Mekong River Cooperation" displays:

> A shared River is the origin of Lancang-Mekong River cooperation, therefore water resource cooperation will be proactively carried out. We will develop hydroelectric resources of Lancang-Mekong River in a scientific manner, establish Lancang-Mekong water resource cooperation center, share information and data of the River, and jointly protect the ecological resources along the River, to provide better life for the residents living by the River.
>
> *(Ministry of Foreign Affairs 2016)*

China's responsibility as opportunity: connection with its own BRI

For a long time, the Mekong region has been seen as a springboard for China to get access to the broader Southeast Asian region. Cooperation in the Mekong Basin is increasingly treated as "part of China's larger picture to develop relations" with Southeast Asian countries (Summers 2008, 73), particularly, cooperation in the fields of economics and security. Through cooperation in managing the Mekong River, China has had the chance to get access to the broader cooperation beyond the scale of water governance and beyond the geographical scope of Mekong countries. This is an example of China taking a holistic approach to responsibility and becoming more influential at a global level. The LMC is a noticeable mechanism to observe how China promoted the broader cooperation and "engrafted" the cooperation onto its ambitious plan, the BRI.

A first aspect thereof is the wide range of priority areas for cooperation. From the LMC Concept Paper, the objectives of the LMC is clearly stated as promoting practical and value-added cooperation in facilitating sustainable development, narrowing developmental disparity, and supporting the creation of the ASEAN community as well as the overall development of regional integration (Ministry of Foreign Affairs 2015). Interestingly, the LMC specifies three priority areas of cooperation in line with the three pillars of the ASEAN Community: (1) political and security issues; (2) economic and sustainable development; and (3) social, cultural, and people-to-people exchanges (Ministry of Foreign Affairs 2015). For the initial stage of the LMC, the Foreign Ministers' Meeting agreed to focus on five issues: (1) regional connectivity, (2) industrial cooperation, (3) cross-border economic cooperation, (4) water resource management, and (5) agricultural cooperation and poverty reduction, which would serve as an important example of South-South cooperation (Ministry of Foreign Affairs 2015). All of them indicate that the LMC acts like a bridge to cover various cooperation area and expanded geographical scale: the Mekong Region, Southeast Asia and even East Asia.

A second aspects concerns China's huge investment. At the first LMC Summit in 2016, as a responsible leader, China promised a combined loan and credit package of US$1.6 billion and US$10 billion, respectively, for Mekong development projects such as railways or industrial parks (Giang 2018; Pongsudhirak 2016). A further US$200 million will be funded by China to alleviate poverty and another US $300 million will be provided for regional cooperation over the coming five years as well as for the establishment of a water resource center (Middleton and Allouche 2016; Pongsudhirak 2016).

Given a huge investment from China and the wide range of priority areas for cooperation in an expanded geographical space, it is rather obvious that the LMC is seen by China not only as a mechanism to manage water resource or settle conflicts over transboundary water. Instead, it is a serious channel for China to forge the Mekong sub-region as the key component to facilitate broader cooperation. As Foreign Minister Wang Yi stated, "we should strive to build Lancang-Mekong River cooperation into a new model for South-South cooperation" (Ministry of Foreign Affairs 2015a). It is planned as a bottom-up process to spill over the influence and weave the intertwined network to stimulate cooperation and boost integration. Utilizing the LMC framework will help to build a common destiny community among Lancang-Mekong River countries[8], which can contribute to the process of ASEAN integration, positive China-ASEAN relations and further to regional cooperation in East Asia. All of them in the end help to realize the grand BRI plan at the global scale.

From regional to global

Beginning with the Mekong, via ASEAN and East Asia, and finally to the global level, just as China admitted, the Mekong River countries are important cooperative partners in "building a Asian community of common destiny and constructing the Belt and Road" (Ministry of Foreign Affairs 2015b).

Realizing this opportunity to turn regional cooperation into a global one and taking the advantage of its position (both in terms of military-economic power and uppermost position in the Mekong), China has seized the chance to promote the ideas and take its responsibility as opportunity to promote the LMC by developing projects and plans that are connected to the BRI. The official document, the Sanya Declaration, explicitly expresses to take measures to "encourage synergy between China's Belt and Road initiative and LMC activities and projects, as well as relevant development programs of the Mekong countries, including the Master Plan on ASEAN Connectivity (MPAC)" (Ministry of Foreign Affairs 2016b). Chinese Premier Li Keqiang also requested for deeper trust-building between China and the Lower Mekong countries as it is clear that cooperation covered in the LMC is part of China's own development strategy centering around the BRI (Pongsudhirak 2016). To be more precise, the so-called signature projects of the LMC, such as the China–Laos railway, the Kunming–Bangkok road, the China-Myanmar land-water transportation facility and the Long Jiang Industrial Park in Vietnam, are enclosed in the BRI (Giang 2018). Moreover, as mentioned by the Premier Li Keqiang at the first LMC Summit in 2016, the Asian Infrastructure Investment Bank (AIIB) and the Silk Road Fund, which work closely with the BRI, will also be the major financial resources for the LMC projects (Giang 2018; Ministry of Foreign Affairs 2016a). All in all, China has skillfully utilized its responsibility as opportunity to engraft the regional water governance onto its sophisticated plan of global governance, the BRI.

Conclusion: sustainable management

Theoretically speaking, basin-wide cooperation is hard to picture in the Mekong River. Given the poorer economic situations and rather weak institutions, plus the number of riparian states and the presence of Chinas as a hegemonic upstream country, the Mekong Region is expected to have bigger difficulties when it comes to overcoming the collective action problem with successful side payments and reaching basin-wide cooperation (Dinar 2006; Falkenmark 1986; Onishi 2011). Yet, against the theoretical expectations, without denying the existence of the conflicts, this chapter tried to stress the role of China as a leader to take responsibility for managing water in a cooperative way.

In terms of water governance, China has cleverly utilized its hegemonic position to lead the establishment of the institutional mechanism for cooperation (the LMC) and applied its economic strength to motivate and attract other riparian states along the Mekong to join the cooperative frameworks for the common good. It is without doubt that China has its own strategic concerns (domestic and geopolitical interests) while promoting the cooperation and that Mekong countries are not with no worry to join the proposed frameworks. Yet, cooperation has been ongoing in a sustainable manner for several years. Cooperation under the LMC is enlarged, and water resources governance has even become a major issue in the noticeable BRI.

To briefly sum up, China's increasing capabilities of managing water resources in the Mekong region have created opportunities for China to be the privilege taker (Vu 2014), as the LMC and the BRI indicate. Nevertheless, without inciting conflicts but taking more responsibility as a cooperative actor, China has used both hard and soft methods to exercise its leadership to increase cooperative incentives and bring the organizational capacity into full play so that other downstream countries are prompted to voluntarily adapt their policies to the Chinese one. Mainly through issue-linkage and an integrated diplomacy approach with its neighbors, China managed to graft the transboundary water governance onto the broader perspective, stressing the common goal of regional development (Biba 2012). By doing so, the interaction and cooperation could be stirred to avoid conflicts in the Mekong Basin, and every actor could be encouraged to take its own responsibility for realizing a *common* sustainable and prosperous region, which further makes the region central to the governance at the global level.

In return, for the LMC per se and water governance in general, embedding instead of isolating water governance in a broader network that includes economic, political, and strategic practices, plus connecting the Mekong sub-region with Southeast and East Asia, the LMC has been assigned the role as a complementary and fundamental mechanism that is legitimized and irreplaceable to govern water issues, positioning it as a central node in the network of various cooperative mechanisms. In such position, the LMC is well placed to get access to resources and information from dense institutional networks, which allow it to function as a broker and bridge to prioritize and manage transboundary water issues.

Being committed to South-South water cooperation that is closely connected to the ambitious BRI project for realizing common interest and attaining to a harmonious world, China has made a sophisticated construction of ideational narrative for water governance (Renwick, 2016). Namely, water management has been evolved into the kind of governance in which national interests are subsumed to the interests of the wider regional and international community. This is the value and significance of considering China's responsibility in water governance as an opportunity in a broader sense.

Notes

1 The utilization of the water resources includes, navigation, hydropower generation, irrigation, and other related water uses (Molle et al. 2009).
2 Turton (2002, 16) defines hydro-politics more generally as "the authoritative allocation of values in society with respect to water."
3 According to McCracken and Wolf (2019), there are currently 310 register of transboundary river basins.
4 Here the harmonious cooperation is defined as the cooperation without disputes or controversies that decisions are reached fairly as well as peacefully and allocations are achieved grossly equitable.

5 Governing water resources like transboundary river, in practical term, refers to dam construction, flood control, irrigation schemes design, inter-basin transfers, and so on. The discussion in this chapter centers mainly on dam construction.
6 The problem occurs when some riparian states along the transboundary river fail to contribute or take the fair share of responsibility to consume the shared water resources.
7 Geographically, the Mekong River origins from China and is called the Lancang River in Chinese.
8 As President Xi put it, "when the big river is full of water, the smaller ones will never run dry" (Cited in Ha 2018, 11).

References

Adamson, P.T., Rutherfurd, I.D., Peel, M.C., and Conlan, I.A. (2009). "The Hydrology of the Mekong Rive." In Campbell, I.C., ed., *The Mekong (Biophysical Environment of an International River Basin)*. New York, USA: Elsevier.

Batchelor, C. (2007). "Water Governance Literature Assessment." https://pubs.iied.org/G02523/

Biba, S. (2012). "China's Continuous Dam-building on the Mekong River." *Journal of Contemporary Asia*, 42(4): 603–628.

Biggs, D.A. (2006). "Reclamation Nations: The US Bureau of Reclamation's Role in Water Management and Nation Building in the Mekong Valley, 1945–1975." *Comparative Technology Transfer and Society*, 4(3): 225–246.

Bunyavejchewin, P. (2016). "The Lancang-Mekong Cooperation (LMC) Viewed in Light of the Potential Regional Leader Theory." *Journal of Mekong Societies*, 12(3): 49–64.

Dinar, A., Dinar, S., McCaffrey, S.C., and McKinney, D. (2007). *Bridges over Water: Understanding Transboundary Water Conflict, Negotiation and Cooperation*. Singapore: World Scientific Publishing.

Dinar, S. (2006). "Assessing Side-Payment and Cost-Sharing patterns: The Geographic and Economic Connection." *Political Geography*, 25(4): 412–437.

Dolsak, N., and Ostrom, E. (2003). *The Commons in the New Millennium: Challenges and Adaptation*. Cambridge, MA: The MIT Press.

Earle, A., and Neal, M.J. (2017). "Inclusive Transboundary Water Governance." In E. Karar, ed., *Freshwater Governance for the 21st Century*: 145–158. Cham: Springer.

Eckstein, G. (2002). "Development of International Water Law and the UN Watercourse Convention." In Turton, A., and Henwood, R., eds., *Hydropolitics in the Developing World: A Southern African Perspective*: 81–96. Pretoria: University of Pretoria, African Water Issues Research Unit.

Elhance, A.P. (1999). *Hydropolitics in the 3rd world: Conflict and Cooperation in International River Basins*. Washington, DC: United States Institute of Peace Press.

Falkenmark, M. (1986). "Fresh Water as a Factor in Strategic Policy and Action." In Westing, A.H., ed., *Global Resources and International Conflict: Environmental Factors in Strategic Policy and Action*: 85–113. Oxford: Oxford University Press.

Feng, Y., Wang, W., Suman, D., Yu, S., and He, D. (2019). "Water Cooperation Priorities in the Lancang-Mekong River Basin Based on Cooperative Events Since the Mekong River Commission Establishment." *Chinese Geographical Science*, 29(1): 58–69.

Friesen, K.M. (1999). *Damming the Mekong: Plans and Paradigms for Developing the River Basin from 1951 to 1995*. PhD dissertation, American University, Washington, DC.

Genugten, B.V. (2015). *Power and Hydropower Development in the Lower Mekong Basin*. Radboud Universiteit Nijmegen, Netherlands.

Giang, N.K. (2018). "China is making Mekong friends." *East Asia Forum. Economics, Politics and Public Policy in East Asia and the Pacific*. https://www.eastasiaforum.org/2018/05/19/china-is-making-mekong-friends/ (accessed: 2019/04/12).

Grumbine, R.E., Dore, J., and Xu, J. (2012). "Mekong Hydropower: Drivers of Change and Governance Challenges." *Frontier in Ecology and the Environment*, 10(2): 91–98.

Ha, H.T. (2018). "ASEAN's Ambivalence Towards a 'Common Destiny' with China." In *ASEAN Focus*, ASEAN Studies Centre, ISEAS-Yusof Ishak Institute: 10–11.

Hirsch, P. (2006). "Water Governance Reform and Catchment Management in the Mekong Region." *The Journal of Environment & Development*, 15(2): 184–201.

Hirsch, P. (2010). "The Changing Political Dynamics of Dam Building on the Mekong." *Water Alternatives*, 3(2): 312–323.

Hirsch, P. (2016). "The Shifting Regional Geopolitics of Mekong Dams." *Political Geography*, 51(3): 63–74.
Hirsch, P., and Jensen, K.M. (2006). *National Interest and Transboundary Water Governance in the Mekong*. Sydney: Australian Mekong Resource Center, University of Sydney.
Hope, R.A. (2007). "Evaluating Social Impacts of Watershed Development in India." *World Development*, 35(8): 1436–1449.
InternationalWatersGovernance (2019). *Mekong*. http://www.internationalwatersgovernance.com/mekong.html
LMC (2017). A Brief Introduction of Lancang-Mekong Cooperation. http://www.lmcchina.org/eng/gylmhz_1/jj/t1519110.htm
Lowi, M. (1993). "Bridging the Divide: trans-boundary water resource disputes and the Case of West Bank Water." *International Security*, 18(1): 113–138.
Lufkin, B. (2017). "Why 'hydro-politics' will shape the 21st Century?" *BBC*. http://www.bbc.com/future/story/20170615-why-hydro-politics-will-shape-the-21st-century
Matthews, N., and Geheb, K. (2014). "On Dams, Demons and Development: The Political Intrigues of Hydropower Development in the Mekong." In Matthews, N., and Geheb, K., eds., *Hydropower Development in the Mekong Region. Political, Socio-economic and Environmental Perspectives*. London: Routledge.
Matthews, N., and Motta, S. (2013). "China's Influence on Hydropower Development in the Lancang River and Lower Mekong River Basin." *State of Knowledge, Series 4* (Challenge Program on Water and Food).
McCracken, M., and Wolf, A.T. (2019). "Updating the register of international river basins of the world." *International Journal of Water Resources Development*, 35(5): 732–782.
Middleton, C., and Allouche, J. (2016). "Watershed or Powershed? Critical Hydropolitics, China and the 'Lancang-Mekong Cooperation Framework'." *The International Spectator*, 51(3): 100–117.
Middleton, C., and Dore, J. (2015). "Transboundary Water and Electricity Governance in Mainland South East Asia: Linkages, Disjunctures and Implications." *International Journal of Water Governance*, 3(1): 93–120.
Ministry of Foreign Affairs (2015). *Minister of Foreign Affairs attends the 1st Mekong-Lancang Cooperation Foreign Ministers' Meeting*. Thailand. http://www.mfa.go.th/main/en/media-center/28/62146-Minister-of-Foreign-Affairs-attends-the-1st-Mekong.html
Ministry of Foreign Affairs (2015a). *Wang Yi Talks about Multiple Great Significances of Lancang- Mekong River Cooperation Mechanism*. China. https://www.fmprc.gov.cn/mfa_eng/zxxx_662805/t1315487.shtml
Ministry of Foreign Affairs (2015b). *Wang Yi: Together Build a Common Destiny Community among Lancang-Mekong River Countries*. China. https://www.fmprc.gov.cn/mfa_eng/zxxx_662805/t1252944.shtml
Ministry of Foreign Affairs (2016a). *Address by H.E. Li Keqiang Premier of the State Council of the People's Republic of China At the First Lancang-Mekong Cooperation Leaders' Meeting*. Sanya, China. https://www.fmprc.gov.cn/mfa_eng/topics_665678/lkqcxboaoyzlt2016nnh/t1350422.shtml
Ministry of Foreign Affairs (2016b). *Sanya Declaration of the First Lancang-Mekong Cooperation (LMC) Leaders' Meeting–For a Community of Shared Future of Peace and Prosperity among Lancang-Mekong Countries*. China. https://www.fmprc.gov.cn/mfa_eng/zxxx_662805/t1350039.shtml
Ministry of Foreign Affairs (2016). *Five Features of Lancang-Mekong River Cooperation*. Beijing. https://www.fmprc.gov.cn/mfa_eng/zxxx_662805/t1349239.shtml
Moench, M. (2003). *The Fluid Mosaic: Water Governance in the Context of Variability, Uncertainty and Change, A Synthesis Paper*. Institute for Social and Environmental Transition (ISET).
Molle, F., Foran, T., and Flach, P. (2009). "Introduction: Changing Waterscapes in the Mekong Region – Historical Background and Context." In Molle, F., Foran, T., and Kakaonen, M., eds., *Contested Waterscapes in the Mekong Region – Hydropower, Livelihoods and Governance*. London: Earthscan.
MRC (2002). *Annual Report*. Phnom Penh: Mekong River Commission Secretariat.
MRC (2015). *Annual Report 2014 Mekong River Commission*. http://www.mrcmekong.org/assets/Publications/governance/MRC-Annual-Report-2014.pdf
Nabers, D. (2008). "China, Japan and the Quest for Leadership in East Asia." In Zorob, Anja, ed., (English editor Nelson Melissa), *GIGA Working Paper. Violence, Power and Security*. Hamburg: German Institute of Global and Area Studies.
Onishi, K. (2007). "Interstate Negotiation Mechanisms for Cooperation in the Mekong River Basin." *Water International*, 32(4): 524–537.
Onishi, K. (2011). "Reassessing Water Security in the Mekong: The Chinese Rapprochement with Southeast Asia." *Journal of Natural Resources Policy Research*, 3(4): 393–412.

Paisley, R.K., Weiler, P., and Henshaw, T. (2016). "Trans-boundary Water Governance Through the Prism of the Mekong River Basin." In Gray, J., Holley, C., and Rayfuse, R., eds., *Trans-jurisdictional Water Law and Governance*. London: Routledge.

Pongsudhirak, T. (2016). "China's Water Grab and its Consequences." *Bangkok Post*. https://www.bangkokpost.com/opinion/opinion/910004/chinas-water-grab-and-its-consequences.

Rahaman, M.M. (2009). "Principles of international water law: creating effective transboundary water resources management." *International Journal of Sustainable Society*, 1(3): 207–223.

Rein, M. (2014). *Power Asymmetry in the Mekong River Basin: The Impact of Hydro- Hegemony on Sharing Transboundary Water*. Universität Wien, Vienna. http://othes.univie.ac.at/33852/1/2014-06-23_1209093.pdf.

Renwick, N. (2016). "China as a Development Actor in Southeast Asia." *IDS Evidence Report, 187*.

Rogers, P., and Hall, A.W. (2003). *Effective Water Governance*. Technical Committee Backgroundpapers No. 7, Global Water Partnership. Stockholm.

Sadoff, C., and Grey, D. (2002). "Beyond the River: the Benefits of Cooperation on International Rivers", *Water Policy*, 4(5): 389–403.

Salman, M.A.S. (2007). "The Helsinki rules, the UN watercourses convention and the berlin rules: perspectives on international water law." *Water Resources Development*, 23(4): 625–640.

Summers, T. (2008). "China and the Mekong Region." *China Perspectives*, 3(Special Issue): 68–77.

TheJointDeclaration (1975). *The Joint Declaration of Principles for Utilization of the Waters of the Lower Mekong Basin*. Vientiane. http://gis.nacse.org/tfdd/tfdddocs/374ENG.pdf

Turton, A. (2002). "Hydropolitics: The Concept and Its Limitations." In Turton, A., and Henwood, R., eds., *Hydropolitics in the Developing World: A Southern African Perspective*: 13–22. Pretoria: African Water Issues Research Unit Centre for International Political Studies (CIPS), University of Pretoria.

UNDP (2004). *Water Governance for Poverty Reduction: Key Issues and the UNDP Response to Millenium Development Goals*. https://www.undp.org/content/dam/aplaws/publication/en/publications/environment-energy/www-ee-library/water-governance/water-governance-for-poverty-reduction/UNDP_Water%20Governance%20for%20Poverty%20Reduction.pdf

UNDP (2006). *Beyond Scarcity: Power, Poverty, and the Global Water Crisis*. New York: UNDP.

UNDP (2007). *Water Governance Facility*. Retrieved from http://www.watergovernance.org/

UNEP (2016). *Transboundary River Basins: Status and Trends*. Nairobi: United Nations Environment Programme (UNEP). http://twap-rivers.org/assets/GEF_TWAPRB_SPM.pdf

Urban, F., Benders, R.M.J., and Moll, H.C. (2009). "Renewable and Low-carbon Energy as Mitigation Options of Climate Change for China." *Climatic Change*, 94(1-2): 169–188.

Vu, T.-M. (2014). "Between System Maker and Privileges Taker: The Role of China in the Greater Mekong Sub-region." *Revista Brasileira de Política International*, 57(Special Issue): 157–173.

Waterbury, J. (1994). "Transboundary Water and the Challenge of International Cooperation in the Middle East." In Lydon, P.R.P., ed., *Water in the Arab world: Perspectives and prognoses*. Cambridge: Division of Applied Sciences, Harvard University.

Weinthal, E. (2002). *State Making and Environmental Cooperation: Linking Domestic and International Politics in Central Asia*. Cambridge, MA: The MIT Press.

Xinhua (2016). "China eyes cooperation plan for Lancang-Mekong countries." *Xinhua*. http://news.xinhuanet.com/english/2016-03/23/c_135213554.htm

Ye, S. (2010). "China's Regional Policy in East Asia and Its Characteristics." *China Policy Institute Discussion Paper*, 66: 1–31.

Young, O.R. (1991). "Political Leadership and Regime Formation: On the Development of Institutions in International Society." *International Organization*, 45(3): 281–308.

Zeitoun, M., and Allan, J.A. (2008). "Applying Hegemony and Power Theory to Transboundary Water Analysis", *Water Policy*, 10(Supplement 2): 3–12.

Zeitoun, M., and Warner, J. (2006). "Hydro-hegemony—A Framework for Analysis of Trans-boundary Water Conflicts." *Water Policy*, 8(5): 435–460.

19
RESPONSIBILITY AS PRACTICE
Implications of UN Security Council responsibilization
Holger Niemann

Introduction

The purpose of the United Nations (UN) is to maintain international peace and security. To that end, its members credit the UN Security Council with having primary responsibility. Notable failures by the UN in carrying out this responsibility in the late 1990s have been the subject of much discussion (Buchanan and Keohane 2011; Erskine 2004). In the aftermath, the Council gradually started considering an increasing list of transnational and cross-cutting issues, such as the protection of children or climate change, as falling under its responsibility. As I argue, these acts of claiming or attributing responsibility for an increasing range of issues represent an ongoing "responsibilization" of the Security Council. Although many Council activities are still state-centered, the fact that currently almost one-third of all Council meetings are devoted to thematic issues (United Nations 2019) underlines the relevance of responsibilizing the Council. Furthermore, the changing meaning of Security Council responsibility has also been mainstreamed into traditional state-centered fields of Council activity – as the use of protection language in country-specific resolutions demonstrates (Gifkins 2016). The process of shifting the meaning of the Council's primary responsibility marks a significant development, changing for whom the Council bears responsibility and what form this responsibility takes. This chapter discusses the emergence of these practices as well as their implications for the Security Council. In doing so, it contributes to ongoing debates about the moral agency of international organizations (Dobson 2008; Erskine 2003a) and the role of responsibility as an element of global governance (Ainley 2011; Vetterlein 2018).

It matters that we achieve a better understanding about the implications of such responsibilization, because the Council's power ultimately depends on "others seeing it as legitimate" (Hurd 2007, 174). Given that identifying new objects of responsibility broadens the scope of Security Council responsibility, responsibilization thus serves to expand the Council's power. At the same time, responsibilization also creates new entanglements and expectations that limit Council powers. As I argue, taking a practice theory perspective (Adler and Pouliot 2011; Bueger and Gadinger 2018) allows us to focus on both the changes of Security Council responsibility and how this affects the Council's role as an actor performing responsibility. For the purpose of this chapter, practice theory's approach of zooming in and out seems especially helpful. Zooming in allows us to better understand the actual accomplishment of practices, whereas zooming out embeds these practices in their broader contexts and allows us to identify processes of ordering (Nicolini 2012). Consequently, the chapter first discusses the Council's moral agency from a practice theory perspective. Second, it illustrates the changing meaning of Security Council responsibility by zooming in on a number of empirical shifts observable in Council practice since the late 1990s. The chapter then zooms out by discussing the implications of such responsibilization for conceptualizing Security Council responsibility. It concludes by depicting the effects of the Council's responsibilization and how traditional and novel understandings of Security Council responsibility coexist.

Responsibility as moral practice

The UN Charter credits the Security Council with a primary responsibility, creating a "position of trust" (Peters 2012, 766) given to the Council by UN members. Their relationship, however, is better understood in terms of moral rather than strictly legal obligations. As Charter provisions are vague, UN members cannot foresee if and how the Council is willing to exercise its responsibility. Although the Council relies on the material resources of UN members for implementing its decisions, this puts the Council in the "privileged position" an actor obtains by being responsible for specific objects (compare with the chapter by Hansen-Magnusson and Vetterlein in this volume). This is especially true of the five permanent Security Council members (P5). While their privileges have been the subject of much criticism, they also constitute special responsibilities, pointing to the intertwined relationship between power and responsibility nested within the framework of Security Council responsibility (Bukovansky et al. 2012, 31). However, responsibility is not a process of compliance but of a community's morals (Erskine 2003b, 7; Pillinger, Hurd, and Barnett 2016, 79). The simultaneity of extraordinary powers and only vaguely defined obligations vis-à-vis UN members underline that Security Council responsibility is first and foremost a matter of practice.

Such a concept of responsibility relies on moral agents being capable of determining their own obligations (Hoover 2012, 238). It understands moral agency as "being answerable for a particular act or outcome in accordance with what are understood to be moral imperatives" (Erskine 2008, 700). Responsibility also points to questions as to who obtains the necessary capacities to act in a particular situation (Erskine 2003b, 2; Harbour 2004, 62). At the same time moral agency is not a given, but results from social processes in a concrete context. Responsibility is a relational social construct (Vetterlein 2018, 553). Referring to social norms and specific understandings of appropriateness in a given situation, makes responsibility also subject to change (Kutz 2004, 555). Responsibilization defines the practices of realizing these changes. In this chapter, I thus understand "responsibilization" as a set of practices of deliberately claiming or attributing responsibility with a "background set of social, moral, and political relations and ideas" (Kutz 2004, 587). Responsibilization questions the idea of clearly identifiable causal or legal relations of responsibility. Instead, it emphasizes that responsibility is often negotiated in ambiguous social contexts and affected by power, normative expectations, and institutional settings.

Whether international organizations can obtain moral agency has been the subject of much debate (Crawford 2007; Erskine 2003a; Harbour 2004). Toni Erskine (2001, 72) argues that they can be considered moral agents as long as they meet a number of criteria, such as having a genuine identity as well as specific concepts of membership and decision-making processes. The Security Council has not only clearly defined decision-making processes, but Council membership also comes with a strong identity in being part of a community of peers (Johnstone 2011). Nevertheless, the Council's existence demonstrates the difficulties of crediting international organizations with moral agency: The UN Charter gives the Council, not its members, a primary responsibility to act on their behalf. However the Council is no monolithic bloc, but an assemblage of member states with competing interests. Therefore, Council decisions are often a result of their "calculations of interests" (Brown 2001, 92). Hence neither external attributions alone nor claims by the Council itself constitutes Security Council responsibility, rather its moral agency is a relational social construction. A practice theory perspective emphasizes that its moral agency is in constant flux, and inextricably linked to contextualized meanings of responsibility.

Responsibilizing the Security Council[1]

The meaning of Security Council responsibility has always been the subject of interpretation. Notable instances during the 1990s, including the cases of Rwanda, Srebrenica, and Kosovo were widely understood however as unparalleled evidence for the Council's inability to fulfill its responsibility. As a response to such criticism, the Council itself – as well as actors from inside the UN and outside actors from civil society – started to reinterpret the meaning of Security Council responsibility. "Never again" became the leitmotif of the UN in the late 1990s (Erskine 2008, 704), which initiated a process of responsibilization by defining new objects of Security Council responsibility.

Sovereignty as responsibility

The most important dimension of the Council's responsibilization stems from the reinterpretation of state sovereignty. The concept of *responsibility to protect* (R2P) reframed "sovereignty" from a notion of control and authority to one of protection (Peltonen 2013, 15; Thakur and Weiss 2009, 38). It also implied a changing role for the Security Council. The International Commission on Intervention and State Sovereignty whose report introduced R2P argued that the Security Council bears a particular responsibility when states do not live up to their primary responsibility as "there is no better or more appropriate body […] to deal with military intervention issues for human protection purposes" (International Commission on Intervention and State Sovereignty 2001, 49). Given that "nonintervention" and "state sovereignty" are core principles of the UN Charter, reinterpreting the Council's role from protecting state sovereignty to eventually protecting people against state sovereignty marks a fundamental shift.

Crediting the Security Council with such a key role was not an organic development though. In fact, identifying alternatives to a Security Council unwilling or unable to invoke its responsibility was actually the motivation behind R2P's genesis. However, the Council's leading role was reinforced by the 2005 World Summit Outcome Document stating that the UN takes collective action "in a timely and decisive manner, through the Security Council" (UN document A/RES/60/1, 30).[2] Although praised as an important step toward implementing R2P at the UN level, the document was thought to water down the spirit of R2P because of its strong emphasis on the leading role of the Security Council (Bellamy 2008, 616; Thakur and Weiss 2009, 38). Most notably, the document lacks clear criteria and thresholds for action giving the Council considerable leeway to interpret its responsibility (Bellamy 2008, 623).

Security Council practices in the aftermath demonstrated the challenge of "turning words into deeds" (Welsh 2010). Especially the Council's indifference regarding gross human rights violations in Darfur in 2003 emphasized the gap between formal attribution of responsibility and its actual application by the Security Council. Preventing the spread of violence during the 2007 Kenyan elections, as well as the humanitarian crisis in the aftermath of Cyclone Nargis in 2008, spurred controversies around what precisely would constitute a case of R2P (Badescu and

Bergholm 2009, 289; Haacke 2009, 182; Sharma 2012, 31). Also in 2008, the Russian government attempted to legitimize military action against Georgia as a case of protecting its people abroad. However, this has been widely considered a "misrepresentation" of R2P (Badescu and Weiss 2010, 364; Evans 2008, 53). It was only with Resolutions 1970 and 1973 on Libya in early 2011, that the Council finally explicitly referred to R2P to authorize the use of force (Bellamy and Williams 2011). The lack of a similar reaction to the situation in Syria, however, underlines the contingency of these developments (Ralph and Gifkins 2017).

Security Council practice has shown mixed results in reifying the Council's responsibility to protect people. Irrespective of broad support from UN members and a clear trend toward R2P (Bellamy 2016, 263), the P5 in particular were keen to uphold their special privileges (Morris 2015). Therefore, R2P demonstrates the complex processes of attributing responsibility to the Council. However, the constant use of R2P terminology in an increasing number of resolutions has helped to define "agreed language" (Gifkins 2016) regarding the Council's responsibility. While this has not secured the immediate implementation of R2P, it has been important for establishing a novel understanding of the Council's responsibility.

New subjects of responsibility

Since 1999 the Security Council has also increasingly discussed the necessity of protecting groups particularly affected by violent conflict, such as civilians, children, and women representing a "people-centered" shift (Chandler 2001) in its responsibility. The Council has claimed first and foremost responsibility for the protection of civilians in armed conflict. Herewith the Council has expanded its responsibility towards humanitarian issues in UN peacekeeping. Formally there is a division of labor between the Security Council and humanitarian agencies, such as the Office for the Coordination of Humanitarian Affairs, the UN Development Program, or the High Commissioner for Refugees, with them reporting to the UN General Assembly or to the Economic and Social Council. In actual UN peace operations, however, this division of labor often does not hold firm. In September 1999, therefore, the Council adopted Resolution 1265, its first thematic resolution on the issue. It stated that, while bearing in mind that its primary responsibility was for the maintenance of international peace and security, the Council now expressed "its willingness to respond to situations of armed conflict where civilians are being targeted or humanitarian assistance to civilians is being deliberately obstructed" (UN document S/RES/1265, 3).

Subsequent resolutions and presidential statements furthered the Council's responsibility for the protection of civilians in armed conflict. An informal Council working group was established in 1999 and, most importantly, the Council initiated an open-ended process of engaging on the issue with UN members through biannual open debates. While the Council's responsibility for the protection of civilians now seems widely recognized, the ambiguity of the language used in actual Council decision-making has been criticized (Lie and de Carvalho 2013, 51). The Council, for example, has considered the effects of hunger (UN document S/RES/2417) as well as attacks on healthcare workers (UN document S/RES/2286) as a threat to the protection of civilians. There is also confusion as to where to draw the boundaries between civilians and other groups in need of protection. While separate agendas have emerged for the protection of children and women, "civilians" currently include humanitarian personnel (UN document S/RES/1502), journalists (UN document S/RES/1738), victims of trafficking (UN document S/RES/2331), and persons with disabilities (UN document S/RES/2475).

Children as a group in need of protection in armed conflict have been on the Council's agenda since Resolution 1261 was unanimously adopted in 1999. The resolution expressed for the first time the Council's concerns regarding the situation of children as internally displaced persons and victims of sexual abuse. Special consideration has also been given to the exploitation of children as soldiers. Since 1999 the Council has adopted 18 resolutions and 14 presidential statements on the issue.[3] Resolution 1612, adopted in 2006, marked a ground-breaking development in the protection of children in armed conflict by establishing a Monitoring and Reporting Mechanism (MRM) as well as country-level task forces for its implementation (UN document S/RES/1612). The Council thereby claimed responsibility for the reporting of grave violations committed against children in armed conflict. Resolution 1612 also established a Working Group on Children and Armed Conflict as a subsidiary body to the Council "empowered to take concrete actions towards halting violations and holding perpetrators accountable, and also to make recommendations for concrete actions to the Security Council" (Watchlist on Children and Armed Conflict 2009). While this established a compliance and reporting mechanism, it emphasizes largely non-legalistic measures. Critics therefore argue such a politically induced "non-compliance mechanism" (Happold 2010, 375) lacks effective enforcement measures. Furthermore, the lack of recognition of the relatively substantial legal framework intended to improve the rights of children in violent conflict in actual Council practice amounts to little more than "paper protection" (Francis 2007, 208). Another potential controversy about differentiating subjects of Security Council responsibility has emerged since the Council initiated an agenda on youth, peace, and security in 2015 (UN document S/RES/2250).

By adopting Resolution 1325 on women, peace, and security (WPS) in 2000, the Council began to acknowledge its responsibility for protecting women in violent conflict. The WPS agenda also calls for their inclusion at all levels of peacebuilding processes and stresses the importance of their equal participation in the maintenance and promotion of peace and security. Resolution 1325 is remarkable, because it not only identifies women as especially vulnerable subjects of violent conflict but simultaneously emphasizes also their agency and crucial role in peace processes (Binder, Lukas, and Schweiger 2008, 25). It has also fostered discussions among academics and practitioners about the complex relationship between gender and conflict as well as regarding the agency of women in peace processes (Davies and True 2019; Pratt and Richter-Devroe 2011; Shepherd 2008). By identifying women as falling under its responsibility, the Council expanded its moral agency in two ways: it now claimed responsibility both for their protection as well as for including gender mainstreaming as a principle of UN peace operations.

However it took the Council until 2008 to effectively invoke the WPS agenda. Since then the Council has furthered the latter by identifying a number of responsibilities related to the role of women in conflict, such as the prevention of sexual violence (UN document S/RES/1820; UN document S/RES/1888) and the role of women in post-conflict peacebuilding processes (UN document S/RES/1889). With Resolution 1960, the Council also established a MRM on sexual violence in order to further the WPS agenda and to help elaborate its normative framework. These steps were strengthened by Resolution 2106, on accountability for perpetrators of sexual abuse, and by Resolution 2122, on gaps in implementing the women, peace, and security agenda, as well as by further resolutions on sexual exploitation in peace operations (UN document S/RES/2272) and on sexual and reproductive health (UN document S/RES/2467). There is, however, no consensus on whether implementing the WPS agenda has actually ensured these ambitious aims are met in reality (Basu, Kirby, and Shepherd 2020; Tryggestad 2009). Nevertheless, Resolution 1325 and its successors have significantly changed the meaning of Security Council responsibility. The WPS agenda shows how Security

Council responsibilization leads to a diverse set of commitments to considering the role of women as both victims of violence and as agents in peace processes as part of the Council's moral agency.

Responsibility for transnational security threats

Security Council responsibilization is also apparent in the consideration of a diverse range of transnational security threats, including terrorism, the utilization of natural resources, climate change, and the spread of infectious diseases. These topics have altered the Council's moral agency. That is so, because they indicate an increasing responsibility for non-state security threats beyond and below national boundaries, thus representing a more complex and holistic understanding of Security Council responsibility.

The Council's reaction to terrorism since September 11, 2001, is the most significant turn to transnational security threats. While terrorism was on the Council's agenda beforehand (Gehring and Dörfler 2013, 574), the attacks initiated a decision-making process in which the Council broadened its authority and established a comprehensive approach with far-reaching competences. By adopting Resolution 1373 on September 28, 2001, the Council established a Counter-Terrorism Committee and decided that all states should prevent and suppress the funding of terrorism by freezing funds and financial assets. In 2004 the Council adopted Resolution 1540 to prevent the proliferation of weapons of mass destruction, especially with regard to non-state actors. It requires all states to make information about potentially suspicious activities available to the Council's 1540-Committee. As these requirements were imposed on "all states" without reference to specific cases and fall under Chapter VII of the UN Charter, both resolutions demonstrate that Security Council responsibilization has tangible implications for UN members. Critics described the Council as a "world legislature" (Talmon 2005), and its interference in national jurisdictions as a violation of its legal authority (Happold 2003; Joyner 2007). Despite or perhaps due to the overwhelming support of UN member states for the Council's counter-terrorism activities (Johnstone 2008, 308), the need for legal safeguards has been discussed (Tzanakopoulos 2011, 154). While the Council is often criticized for not living up to its responsibility, in this case a "too active" Council became the greater concern (Gray 2008, 90). Counter-terrorism also demonstrates that responsibilization has material effects too, as it comes with an unusual authoritative bureaucratic apparatus in the form of the related committees.

The Council also pays attention to an increasing number of other transnational security issues. These include the proliferation of small arms and light weapons (UN document S/RES/2117), piracy (UN document S/PRST/2013/13), as well as drug trafficking and organized crime (UN document S/PRST/2009/32). Besides this focus on transnational flows of goods, the Council has also turned to the utilization of natural resources by conflict parties (UN document S/PV.6982). Illicit trading of resources such as oil, timber and diamonds was prohibited in resolutions on Angola, Cote d'Ivoire, Liberia and Sierra Leone for example. In resolutions on the Central African Republic (UN document S/RES/2134) and the Democratic Republic of the Congo (UN document S/RES/2136) of 2014, the Council considered poaching a transnational security threat. So far, however, the Council has seemed reluctant to adopt thematic resolutions on the impact of natural resources on conflicts (Peters 2014). Instead, it has continued to promote respective action on the state level demonstrating that responsibilization is a gradual and non-linear process. The Council has also discussed climate change as a potential threat to international peace and security at various times (Conca, Thwaites, and Lee 2017; Scott and Ku

2018). The United Kingdom was a strong advocate for the issue in the beginning initiating the first open debate on climate change in April 2007 (UN document S/PV.5663). Most importantly, the Council adopted a presidential statement in June 2011 expressing its concerns "that possible adverse effects of climate change may, in the long run, aggravate certain existing threats to international peace and security" (UN document S/PRST/2011/15, 1). After a hiatus of several years, Germany in collaboration with Nauru established a Group of Friends on climate and security in 2018, advocating the topic during its term as elected member in 2019-2020. The Council has also held a number of meetings on the issue over the years, the latest in February 2021 (UN document S/2021/198).

The Council's flexibility in defining new objects of its responsibility has also been demonstrated by its response to the COVID-19 pandemic. Following a plea by UN Secretary-General António Guterres for a global ceasefire, the Council responded to the unparalleled situation in July 2020 by stating that "the unprecedented extent of the COVID-19 pandemic is likely to endanger the maintenance of international peace and security" and calling for "the cessation of hostilities in all situations on its agenda" (UN document S/RES/2532, 1-2). In February 2021 the Council adopted Resolution 2565 demanding conflict parties pause hostilities to allow vaccination in areas of armed conflict. While the Council herewith clearly interpreted a global pandemic as falling under its responsibility, it did so only reluctantly and under great criticism. It took the Council more than three months to adopt Resolution 2532, with negotiations being significantly hampered by competing views among the P5 on how to address the pandemic in the most appropriate manner.

However the pandemic was not the first time the Council addressed issues of global health. Resolution 2177, adopted in September 2014 to address the Ebola crisis, is considered a landmark for introducing new objects of responsibility on the Council's agenda. It states that "the unprecedented extent of the Ebola outbreak in Africa constitutes a threat to international peace and security" (UN document S/RES/2177, 1). Furthermore, the Council has previously touched on health issues with regard to HIV/AIDS and their impact on conflict too (Security Council Report 2014).

The expansion of the Council's responsibility to transnational security threats such as climate change or global health crises represents a significant enhancement of its moral agency. It also demonstrates that Security Council responsibilization is often the result of deliberate action by nongovernmental organizations or non-Council members who succeed in agenda-setting, such as on children in armed conflict. At the same time, this is a non-linear process yielding mixed results. Especially politicized topics such as climate change and the COVIDs-19 pandemic demonstrate the challenges of developing coherent responses and consensus among Council members. While the Council has addressed some of these topics quite thoroughly, others have been discussed only infrequently and reluctantly – underlining the prevalent effects of the institutional framework constituting the context of responsibilization.

Implications of Security Council responsibilization

What are the implications, then, of these empirical developments for understanding Security Council responsibilization? By zooming out, this section highlights how responsibilization affects the relationship between the "who" and the "how" of responsibility: that is, the various ways in which the Council's moral agency is tied to objects and practices of its responsibility. It emphasizes that the objects of Council responsibility have been segmented, responsibility routinized, and accountability measures established – that all occurring alongside the rise of anticipatory practices within the Security Council too.

Segmenting objects of responsibility

The Council's traditional understanding of responsibility would employ a state-centered concept of security. Within these boundaries the Council's understanding of its responsibility remained quite broad and holistic though. Developments since the late 1990s, however, have emphasized the existence of multiple yet distinctive objects of responsibility instead. Responsibilization, thus, demonstrates a composite approach to Security Council responsibility, whereby the hitherto holistic understanding of (state-centered) security is now disaggregated into respective parts. Instead of being responsible for peace and security, broadly defined, the Council has become responsible for particular types of security issues (such as climate change) and for specific groups of people in need of protection (such as children).

While this might be beneficial in tailoring effective responses, it also holds the potential for contestation and political deadlock due to disagreements regarding whether and how an issue can even be interpreted as an object of Council responsibility. The cases of poaching or the protection of LGBTI people, both addressed by the Council reluctantly, demonstrate this. By segmenting objects of Security Council responsibility, they also become essentialized. The protection agendas give ample evidence hereof in the accompanying necessity to define particular groups in need of protection. Stable and binary distinctions, such as "women" or "journalists", do not leave much room for ambiguity or multiple identities. Critics also see a tendency for the Council to particularize protection in a way that favors groups relevant for the conduct of UN peace operations rather than to approach the needs of local populations broadly and holistically (Shesterinina and Job 2015). This can lead to unintended consequences. For example, the purpose of the WPS agenda is to strengthen the agency of women in peace processes, but actual rhetoric often frames them as victims and vulnerable subjects in need of special measures of protection instead (Pratt 2013; Shepherd 2008). Not only are women defined herewith as target groups of Security Council responsibility in a very particular way but their role is also essentialized without leaving much room for multiple identities.

Segmentation also partly explains incoherent and selective Council decision-making. Responsibilization is shaped by an ever-growing list of items falling under Security Council responsibility. Many of these topics result from agenda-setting by non-permanent Council members. Once they leave the Council, their "pet projects" become less important for the body itself, causing incoherence and selectivity. The Council has frequently been criticized for its selective approach (Binder 2015), even though the Charter provides the Council with the sole authority to set its agenda. Responsibilization, however, complicates such a selective decision-making process in two ways: A growing list of items on the agenda makes consistent consideration by the Council simply more difficult and enhances the risk of double standards. Furthermore, while segmenting objects of Council responsibility broadens the scope thereof it also has the potential to undermine the Council's legitimacy.

Routinizing responsibility

As Security Council responsibility is no longer a matter of deciding on a case-by-case basis alone, but also one of moral commitment to a growing list of transnational security issues, routinized practices have become more important. Given that the Council was established as an ad hoc decision-making body with the leverage to table agenda items more or less based upon the political will of its member states (Hurd 2002, 40), this marks a significant change. Responsibility for transnational security threats, as well as for groups of people in particular need of protection, creates entanglements. While the Council has discretion in tabling country-specific agenda items, its responsibility to protect children in armed conflict cannot just be invoked in one case and then simply be negated in another. Responsibilization, thus, implies that coherent Council action assumes greater importance. As a result, routinized practices become paramount. The various protection agendas in particular provide evidence for this view: over the years, they have not only become more complex through the differentiation and expansion of their scope and content but have also been mainstreamed into actual country-level crisis management.

Routines are also evident in actual Council practices. Open debates on the protection of civilians are a case in point. Held biannually, they are attended by a large number of participants from UN member states – and occasionally representatives from other international and civil society organizations. These meetings serve as a forum for the exchange of views, rather than for adopting actual decisions about specific crises as the Charter intends the Council to do. For two decades now, these meetings have contributed to mainstreaming a specific understanding of the Council's responsibilities into the UN's normative framework (Bellamy 2013). An increasingly dense web of references to these principles, with almost no resolution adopted under Chapter VII nowadays lacking such attributions (Gifkins 2016), has turned the Council's responsibility for civilians into a routinized point of reference in its decision-making. This not only underlines a shift in understanding regarding who becomes an addressee of the Council's responsibility but also has an effect on the ways in which the Council fulfills its obligations. Even if it does not translate into actual implementation practices on the ground, a set of moral commitments has been established – spanning from open debates to country-level resolutions, becoming agreed language and ultimately a staple in the Council's repertoire of action. As a result, this agreed language creates entanglements and expectations –thus requiring the Council to engage in routinized practices to uphold its responsibility.

Establishing accountability mechanisms

Routinized practices also point to the establishment of accountability mechanisms, such as deliberation and dialogue with external stakeholders. Given that the Council was founded primarily as a venue for an exchange of views among the P5 (Keating 2016), this marks an important shift in how the Council understands its responsibility. Herewith the Council has followed the recent trend of international organizations opening up and increasingly engaging with non-state actors (Tallberg et al. 2013). Nevertheless, the Council is frequently criticized for being shuttered, for the rifts between permanent and elected members, as well as for its inaccessibility to external actors. Responsibilization changes that, because it raises questions regarding how and toward whom the Council fulfills its responsibility exactly.

Open debates in particular underline the growing importance of accountability in these processes. They usually do not include an actual decision by the Council, but serve as a forum for the exchange of views between the Council and stakeholders. The Council tends to hold open debates on a monthly basis and on a diverse set of topics. On those of great relevance, speaking lists often include more than 50 individuals with debates sometimes scheduled for consecutive days. In addition the Council has established a number of meeting formats for enhancing dialogue with stakeholders, such as Arria-meetings for informal interactions with nongovernmental organizations, or the consultations held with troop-contributing countries. These developments point to a change of the Council from being only a site of decision-making by a select few to a forum for communicative action among a broader set of stakeholders (Johnstone 2003, 452). However, this shift is a gradual one and civil society interaction in particular remains scarce. The Council's accountability mechanisms are also "soft" representing only cautious challenges to the established institutional setting and legal notions of "accountability" (Murphy 2020).

Nevertheless responsibilization demonstrates the importance of such accountability mechanisms, of which a number have been established in the Council. Their informality and limited scope, however, emphasizes the moral rather than legal obligations stemming from responsibilization.

Anticipatory practices

Responsibilization also points to anticipatory practices, such as prevention and forecasting, as new ways of invoking Security Council responsibility. The Council carries out its responsibility primarily retrospectively, as its mandate is to authorize measures only once a situation has been defined as a threat to international peace and security. The developments discussed above, however, are often focused on the potentially preventive effects of Council decision-making. If it does not simply react to a situation of mass atrocities but anticipates the need to protect vulnerable groups of people in the first place, Council responsibility become proactive instead of retrospective.

Counter-terrorism is a case in point, exemplifying anxieties and uncertainties caused by the omnipresence of the 'next terrorist attack' (Aradau and van Munster 2012). Asset freezing and the listing of suspicious persons can be interpreted as specific examples of such Council practices (Gehring and Dörfler 2013, 572). Prevention itself is not a novel practice for the Council. In fact, much of the criticism of the UN in the 1990s directly stemmed from the Council's inability to act preventively in situations of mass atrocities (Erskine 2004). The implications of Security Council responsibilization are, however, different. As the WPS agenda demonstrates, responsibilizing the Council implies not only a responsibility to protect women in conflict but also to foster their active promotion in peace processes (Basu and Shepherd 2017). Consequently, the Council needs to anticipate the different roles women could play in peace processes and what measures are required to actively support these roles.

Anticipatory practices require knowledge. Especially transnational security threats are knowledge-intensive, because they cut across policy fields and are often shaped by complex constellations of actors, interests and authorities. For example, competing interpretations of the links between climate and security have had a considerable effect on the Council's consideration of the issue (Conca, Thwaites, and Lee 2017). Hence, access to knowledge about the causes of climate-induced security risks is an important constraint on the Council's ability to engage in anticipatory practices vis-à-vis related security risks. As such, responsibilization points not only to anticipatory practices but also to the production and consumption of knowledge. The growing significance of activities such as Security Council visiting missions to conflict regions, or technological developments for improving interaction with field offices such as video-teleconferencing, demonstrate the importance of knowledge production as an anticipatory practice. Institutionalized structures such as the Counter-Terrorism Committee and the MRM have a similar purpose, as their role is to collect and evaluate relevant information. They demonstrate that Security Council responsibilization not only implies to engage in anticipatory practices but also underlines the extent to which Council decision-making then becomes knowledge-dependent.

Conclusion

Security Council responsibility has always been the subject of contextual interpretations, being accompanied by related discourses and practices. Developments since the late 1990s, however, have a different quality to them. My approach of zooming in and out has revealed a shift in meaning vis-à-vis Security Council responsibility, as well as the implications hereof: namely segmenting objects of Council responsibility, the growing importance of routines, the establishment of accountability mechanisms, and the rise of anticipatory practices. Responsibilization changes not only the meaning of Security Council responsibility but also how and toward whom it is applied.

One conclusion that can be drawn from this analysis is that the question of potential Council "mission creep" (Clark and Reus-Smit 2013) might become more important going forward. Responsibilization comes with entanglements and expectations. It gives the Council's moral agency a new quality, addressing some of the concerns raised about its inability to live up to its premier role in global politics. However, it also enhances the possibility of institutional overstretch, for example, with regard to the division of labor between the Council and the UN Secretariat. The responsibilization of the Security Council also underlines the need to study the agents thereof. This chapter focused primarily on responsibility claims by the Council itself. The developments discussed, however, occurred in close interaction with other actors, namely civil society organizations. Therefore, the relationship between claiming and attributing responsibility in the institutional setting of the Council deserves closer observation henceforth.

The role of formal versus informal elements seems especially important here. As many of the effects of Security Council responsibilization occur via informal practices, their relationship to the underlying formal framework demands greater attention. How other UN agencies deal with responsibilization and how that affects the moral agency of the Council seem also to be important factors when it comes to gaining a better understanding of the implications of Security Council responsibilization. Examining these would also provide a more complex view on responsibility as practice of the entire UN.

Furthermore, cautious evaluation of the effects of responsibilization seems advisable. Despite significant shifts in the meaning of Security Council responsibility, many established conditions still prevail. While responsibilization has also affected country-level decision-making, it has not replaced the often state-centered, case-based traditional understanding of Council obligations. Rather, the former complements the latter, pointing to the concurrence of diverse understandings of responsibility within the Council. Then again, this chapter has demonstrated the astonishing flexibility of the Council in interpreting the meaning of its responsibility. Security Council responsibility is in flux; so are the implications regarding the effectiveness, legitimacy and ultimately authority of the Security Council as the bearer of primary responsibility for international peace and security.

Notes

1 This section partly builds on Niemann (2019, 23–32).
2 UN documents are quoted in this chapter by using their official UN code. All quoted documents can be found online at https://documents.un.org (last accessed 18 October 2019).
3 Presidential statements are statements made by the acting president of the Council on behalf of the entire Council. Unlike resolutions, they require consensus among Council members as there is no vote about the adoption of a presidential statement. Therefore, these statements are an important device for the normative positioning of the Council. See Niemann (2019, 33).

References

Adler, E., and Pouliot, V., eds. (2011). *International Practices*. Cambridge: Cambridge University Press.
Ainley, K. (2011). "Excesses of Responsibility: The Limits of Law and the Possibilities of Politics." *Ethics & International Affairs*, 25(4): 407–431.
Aradau, C., and van Munster, R. (2012). "The Time/Space of Preparedness: Anticipating the 'Next Terrorist Attack'." *Space and Culture*, 15(2): 98–109.

Badescu, C.G., and Bergholm, L. (2009). "The Responsibility to Protect and the Conflict in Darfur: The Big Let-down." *Security Dialogue*, 40(3): 287–309.
Badescu, C.G., and Weiss, T.G. (2010). "Misrepresenting R2P and Advancing Norms: An Alternative Spiral?" *International Studies Perspectives*, 11(4): 354–374.
Basu, S., and Shepherd, L.J. (2017). "Prevention in Pieces: Representing Conflict in the Women, Peace and Security Agenda." *Global Affairs*, 3(4-5): 441–453.
Basu, S., Kirby, P. and Shepherd, L.J. (2020). "Women, Peace and Security: A Critical Cartography." In Basu, S., Kirby, P. and Shepherd, L.J., eds., *New Directions in Women, Peace, and Security*: 1–25. Bristol: Bristol University Press.
Bellamy, A. (2008). "The Responsibility to Protect and the Problem of Military Intervention." *International Affairs*, 84(4): 615–639.
Bellamy, A. (2013). "Mainstreaming the Responsibility to Protect in the United Nations System: Dilemmas, Challenges and Opportunities." *Global Responsibility to Protect*, 5(2): 154–191.
Bellamy, A. (2016). "UN Security Council." In Bellamy, A.J., and Dunne, T., eds., *The Oxford Handbook of the Responsibility to Protect*: 249–268. Oxford: Oxford University Press.
Bellamy, A., and Williams, P.D. (2011). "The New Politics of Protection? Côte D'ivoire, Libya and the Responsibility to Protect." *International Affairs*, 87(4): 825–850.
Binder, C., Lukas, L., and Schweiger, R. (2008). "Empty Words or Real Achievement? The Impact of Security Council Resolution 1325 on Women in Armed Conflicts." *Radical History Review*, 101(Spring): 22–41.
Binder, M. (2015). "Paths to Intervention: What Explains the UN's Selective Response to Humanitarian Crises?" *Journal of Peace Research*, 52(6): 712–726.
Brown, C. (2001). "Moral Agency and International Society." *Ethics & International Affairs*, 15(2): 87–98.
Buchanan, A., and Keohane, R.O. (2011). "Precommitment Regimes for Intervention: Supplementing the Security Council." *Ethics & International Affairs*, 25(1): 41–63.
Bueger, C., and Gadinger, F. (2018). *International Practice Theory: New Perspectives*. Basingstoke: Palgrave Macmillan.
Bukovansky, M., Clark, I., Eckersley, R., Price, R., Reus-Smit, C., and Wheeler, N.J. (2012). *Special Responsibilities: Global Problems and American Power*. Cambridge and New York: Cambridge University Press.
Chandler, D. (2001). "The People-centred Approach to Peace Operations: The New UN Agenda." *International Peacekeeping*, 8(1): 1–19.
Clark, I., and Reus-Smit, C. (2013). "Liberal Internationalism, the Practice of Special Responsibilities and Evolving Politics of the Security Council." *International Politics*, 50(1): 38–56.
Conca, K., Thwaites, J., and Lee, G. (2017). "Climate Change and the UN Security Council: Bully Pulpit or Bull in a China Shop?" *Global Environmental Politics*, 17(2): 1–20.
Crawford, N.C. (2007). "Individual and Collective Moral Responsibility for Systemic Military Atrocity." *Journal of Political Philosophy*, 15(2): 187–212.
Davies, E. and True, J., eds. (2019). *The Oxford Handbook of Women, Peace and Security*. New York: Oxford University Press.
Dobson, L. (2008). "Plural Views, Common Purpose: On How to Address Moral Failure by International Political Organisations." *Journal of International Political Theory*, 4(1): 34–54.
Erskine, T. (2001). "Assigning Responsibilities to Institutional Moral Agents: The Case of States and Quasi-States." *Ethics & International Affairs*, 15(2): 67–85.
Erskine, T., ed. (2003a). "Can Institutions Have Responsibilities?" *Collective Moral Agency and International Relations*. Houndmills, Basingstoke: Palgrave Macmillan.
Erskine, T. (2003b). "Making Sense of 'Responsibility' in International Relations: Key Questions and Concepts." In Erskine, T., ed., *Can Institutions Have Responsibilities? Collective Moral Agency and International Relations*: 1–18. Houndmills, Basingstoke: Palgrave Macmillan.
Erskine, T. (2004). "'Blood on the UN's Hands'? Assigning Duties and Apportioning Blame to an Intergovernmental Organisation." *Global Society*, 18(1): 21–42.
Erskine, T. (2008). "Locating Responsibility: The Problem of Moral Agency in International Relations." In Reus-Smit, C., and Snidal, D., eds., *The Oxford Handbook of International Relations*: 699–707. Oxford and New York: Oxford University Press.
Evans, G.J. (2008). "Russia in Georgia: Not a Case of the 'Responsibility to Protect'." *New Perspectives Quarterly*, 25(4): 53–55.
Francis, D.J. (2007). "'Paper Protection' Mechanisms: Child Soldiers and the International Protection of Children in Africa's Conflict Zones." *The Journal of Modern African Studies*, 45(2): 207–231.

Gehring, T., and Dörfler, T. (2013). "Division of Labor and Rule-Based Decisionmaking Within the UN Security Council: The Al-Qaeda/Taliban Sanctions Regime." *Global Governance: A Review of Multilateralism and International Organizations*, 19(4): 567–587.

Gifkins, J. (2016). "R2P in the UN Security Council: Darfur, Libya and Beyond." *Cooperation and Conflict*, 51(2): 148–165.

Gray, C. (2008). "The Charter Limitations on the Use of Force: Theory and Practice." In Lowe, R.A., Welsh, J., and Zaum, D., eds., *The United Nations Security Council and War: The Evolution of Thought and Practice Since 1945*: 86–98. Oxford: Oxford University Press.

Haacke, J. (2009). "Myanmar, the Responsibility to Protect, and the Need for Practical Assistance." *Global Responsibility to Protect*, 1(2): 156–184.

Happold, M. (2003). "Security Council Resolution 1373 and the Constitution of the United Nations." *Leiden Journal of International Law*, 16(3): 593–610.

Happold, M. (2010). "Protecting Children in Armed Conflict: Harnessing the Security Council's 'Soft Power'." *Israel Law Review*, 43(2): 360–380.

Harbour, F. (2004). "Moral Agency and Moral Responsibility in Humanitarian Intervention." *Global Society*, 18(1): 61–75.

Hoover, J. (2012). "Reconstructing Responsibility and Moral Agency in World Politics." *International Theory*, 4(2): 233–268.

Hurd, I. (2002). "Legitimacy, Power, and the Symbolic Life of the UN Security Council." *Global Governance*, 8(1): 35–51.

Hurd, I. (2007). *After Anarchy: Legitimacy and Power in the United Nations Security Council*. Princeton: Princeton University Press.

International Commission on Intervention and State Sovereignty (2001). *The Responsibility to Protect: Report of the International Commission on Intervention and State Sovereignty*. Ottawa.

Johnstone, I. (2003). "Security Council Deliberations: The Power of the Better Argument." *European Journal of International Law*, 14(3): 437–480.

Johnstone, I. (2008). "Legislation and Adjudication in the UN Security Council: Bringing down the Deliberative Deficit." *American Journal of International Law*, 102(2): 275–308.

Johnstone, I. (2011). *The Power of Deliberation: International Law, Politics and Organizations*. Oxford: Oxford University Press.

Joyner, D. (2007). "Non-Proliferation Law and the United Nations System: Resolution 1540 and the Limits of the Power of the Security Council." *Leiden Journal of International Law*, 20(2): 489–518.

Keating, C. (2016). "Power Dynamics between Permanent and Elected Members." In von Einsiedel, S., Malone, D., and Ugarte, B.S., eds., *The UN Security Council in the Twenty-First Century*: 139–155. Boulder: Lynne Rienner.

Kutz, C. (2004). "Responsibility." In Coleman, J.L., Shapiro, S., and Himma, K.E., eds., *The Oxford Handbook of Jurisprudence and Philosophy of Law*: 548–587. Oxford and New York: Oxford University Press.

Lie, J.H.S., and de Carvalho, B. (2013). "Conceptual Unclarity and Competition: The Protection of Civilians and the Responsibility to Protect" In de Carvalho, B., and Sending, O.J., eds., *The Protection of Civilians in UN Peacekeeping: Concept, Implementation and Practice*: 47–61. Baden-Baden: Nomos.

Morris, J. (2015). "The Responsibility to Protect and the Great Powers: The Tensions of Dual Responsibility." *Global Responsibility to Protect*, 7(3–4): 398–421.

Murphy, B.L. (2020). "Situating the Accountability of the UN Security Council: Between Liberal-Legal and Political 'Styles' of Global Constitutionalism?" *Global Constitutionalism*, online first: 1–35.

Nicolini, D. (2012). *Practice Theory, Work, and Organization: An Introduction*. Oxford: Oxford University Press.

Niemann, H. (2019). *The Justification of Responsibility in the UN Security Council: Practices of Normative Ordering in International Relations*. London: Routledge.

Peltonen, H. (2013). *International Responsibility and Grave Humanitarian Crises: Collective Provision for Human Security*. Abingdon: Routledge.

Peters, A. (2012). "Article 24." In Simma, B., Khan, D., Nolte, G., and Paulus, A., eds., *The Charter of the United Nations: A Commentary*: 761–788. Oxford: Oxford University Press.

Peters, A. (2014). "Novel Practice of the Security Council: Wildlife Poaching and Trafficking as a Threat to the Peace." http://www.ejiltalk.org/novel-practice-of-the-security-council-wildlife-poaching-and-trafficking-as-a-threat-to-the-peace/ (accessed March 21, 2015).

Pillinger, M., Hurd, I., and Barnett, M. (2016). "How to Get Away with Cholera: The UN, Haiti, and International Law." *Perspectives on Politics*, 14(1): 70–86.

Pratt, N. (2013). "Reconceptualizing Gender, Reinscribing Racial-Sexual Boundaries in International Security: The Case of UN Security Council Resolution 1325 on 'Women, Peace and Security'." *International Studies Quarterly*, 57(4): 772–783.

Pratt, N., and Richter-Devroe, S. (2011). "Critically Examining UNSCR 1325 on Women, Peace and Security." *International Feminist Journal of Politics*, 13(4): 489–503.

Ralph, J., and Gifkins, J. (2017). "The Purpose of United Nations Security Council Practice: Contesting Competence Claims in the Normative Context Created by the Responsibility to Protect." *European Journal of International Relations*, 23(3): 630–653.

Scott, S.V., and Ku, C., eds. (2018). *Climate Change and the UN Security Council*. Cheltenham: Edward Elgar Publishing.

Security Council Report (2014). "In Hindsight: The Security Council and Health Crises." http://www.securitycouncilreport.org/monthly-forecast/2014-10/in_hindsight_the_security_council_and_health_crises.php.

Sharma, S. (2012). "The 2007-08 Post-Election Crisis in Kenya: A Success Story for the Responsibility to Protect?" In Hoffmann, J., Nollkaemper, A., and Swerissen, I., eds., *Responsibility to Protect: From Principle to Practice*: 27–35. Amsterdam: Pallas Publications.

Shepherd, L.J. (2008). "Power and Authority in the Production of UN Security Council Resolution 1325." *International Studies Quarterly*, 52(2): 383–404.

Shesterinina, A., and Job, B.L. (2015). "Particularized Protection: UNSC Mandates and the Protection of Civilians in Armed Conflict." *International Peacekeeping*, 23(2): 240–273.

Tallberg, J., Sommerer, T., Squatrito, T., and Jönsson, C. (2013). *The Opening Up of International Organizations: Transnational Access in Global Governance*. Cambridge: Cambridge University Press.

Talmon, S. (2005). "The Security Council as World Legislature." *American Journal of International Law*, 99(1): 175–193.

Thakur, R., and Weiss, T.G. (2009). "R2P: From Idea to Norm-and Action?" *Global Responsibility to Protect*, 1(1): 22–53.

Tryggestad, T. (2009). "Trick or Treat? The UN and Implementation of Security Council Resolution 1325 on Women, Peace, and Security." *Global Governance*, 15(4): 539–557.

Tzanakopoulos, A. (2011). *Disobeying the Security Council: Countermeasures Against Wrongful Sanctions*. Oxford: Oxford University Press.

United Nations (2019). *Highlights of Security Council Practices 2018*. New York: United Nations.

Vetterlein, A. (2018). "Responsibility Is More Than Accountability: From Regulatory Towards Negotiated Governance." *Contemporary Politics*, 24(5): 545–567.

Watchlist on Children and Armed Conflict (2009). *UN Security Council Resolution 1612 and Beyond: Strengthening Protection for Children in Armed Conflict*. New York.

Welsh, J. (2010). "Turning Words into Deeds? The Implementation of the 'Responsibility to Protect'." *Global Responsibility to Protect*, 2(1): 149–154.

20
REBEL WITH A CAUSE
Rebel responsibility in intrastate conflict situations
Mitja Sienknecht

Introduction[1]

Responsibility describes a relation between a subject and an object based on norms. In the realm of international politics, responsibility is a central principle of the modern world political order. For example, it provides the most normative link between governments and their national constituencies. A (democratic) government is expected to assume responsibility for the security of its citizens, and the citizens demand transparency and justification from their government when its ethics of responsibility are called into question. However, these fairly clear-cut relations have diffused due to a variety of globalization processes and a normative integration of the world political system (Albert 2016). In the field of security politics, new actors – such as international or regional institutions – are assuming responsibility for a broadened scope of objects, such as the protection of the individual against atrocities of states. In this regard, the Responsibility to Protect (R2P) norm is indicative for the diffusion and de-bordering of responsibility structures. Where governments do not comply with their duties toward their populations, the responsibility to protect individuals is thus transferred to the international community (Gholiagha 2015; United Nations 2005). With the dawn of the normative integration of world politics via human rights norms, new subjects and objects of responsibility have emerged. Many studies have analyzed and problematized the diffusion and de-bordering of responsibility relations in current world politics (Chandler 2018; Crawford 2018; Daase et al. 2017a; Neyer, Sienknecht, and Martin-Russu 2017; Vetterlein 2018). While this complexity can lead to unclear responsibility attributions (Daase et al. 2017b), these studies tend to overlook that the diffusion of responsibility also entails windows of opportunities for political actors, who are not naturally associated with moral and political responsibility: rebel groups. In case of intrastate conflicts, nonstate armed groups[2] gain in relevance as they often seek to take responsibility for a certain (ethnic or religious) group of people, therefore challenging the state as natural bearer of responsibility. This chapter focuses on the rebel groups' claims of responsibility in intrastate conflicts and discusses the embeddedness of these relations in world political structures. Therefore, the chapter contributes to a nuanced understanding of the interplay between different subjects of responsibility [international organizations (IOs), states, rebel groups] and puts special emphasis on overlapping responsibility relations in intrastate conflict situations.

Intrastate conflicts between a government and a nongovernmental party represent the most common conflict type around the globe (Petterson and Öberg 2020). In most of the conflicts, both conflict parties are responsible for severe human rights violations against civilians or combatants. Being a huge source of human suffering, questions about responsibility are inherent in the analysis of these conflicts. In conflict situations, rebel groups claim – both violently and nonviolently – responsibility for different actions. They take responsibility for violent acts – such as bombings, attacks, kidnappings, etc. – but they also claim a moral responsibility for an ethnic, political, or religious group, and fight governments that are perceived to have acted irresponsibly toward the group. They often develop a form of governance and thereby assume a de facto responsibility for the respective group across a limited territory – parallel to the state structures. This political responsibility claimed by rebel groups forms the core of the present chapter. It seeks to answer the following questions: How is responsibility constituted and contested in intrastate conflict situations, and how are these responsibility structures influenced by the world political system? By answering these questions, the chapter discusses an important aspect of responsibility relations in highly securitized contexts. While several studies analyze the behavior of states and rebel groups in conflict situations regarding war crimes, so far no research has dealt with conceptualizing rebel groups as responsible actors who claim responsibility for a group of people, challenge given responsibility relations and, as a consequence, are set in relation with international political actors.

To answer the research questions, this contribution conceptualizes world politics as a set of responsibility triangles, which can be complementary or conflictual. These triangles compose of a subject that takes responsibility for things or people (objects) on grounds of a normative reference framework. They will help to set different subjects in relation to each other and illustrate how conflicts emerge, develop, and change in relation to developments on the international level. Thus, the chapter develops an analytical lens that helps to distinguish between different levels and dimensions of responsibility and demonstrates the interrelations between different political actors. Furthermore, it introduces the differentiation between the *internal claim* of responsibility and the *external recognition* of responsibility, which helps to analyze possible tensions between different responsibility triangles in world politics.

The *internal claim of responsibility* establishes a relation between a rebel group and the respective population. Rebel groups such as the Liberation Tigers of Tamil Eelam (LTTE) in Sri Lanka, the Kosovo Liberation Army (KLA) in Serbia, or the Somali National Movement (SNM) in North Somalia, claim to represent a certain part of the population, often accompanied by a demand for greater autonomy or independence. In light of globalization processes, responsibility relations do not, generally speaking, emerge in a political vacuum; they are observed, supported, condemned, or even enabled by the decisions of the international community, and especially the United Nations (UN). In light of global norms that span from something as complex as R2P (Welsh 2013) to the UN Security Council's responsibility for the maintenance of international peace and security (Art. 39 UN Charta), the international community positions itself in intrastate conflicts and frequently either supports or condemns any claimed "rebel responsibility". In case of a supportive international community, the established internal claim of the rebel group is complemented with an *external recognition*. This usually means a boost of legitimacy for the rebel's cause. Against this backdrop, the present study analyzes how rebel groups claim and take responsibility in conflict situations, and how these structures are influenced by responsibility relations in world politics.

In the next section, I will briefly introduce the chapter's concept of responsibility and specify it with regard to intrastate conflict situations. I argue that different, competing and contradicting responsibility relations characterize the world political system. I develop a conceptual perspective based on a triangular understanding of responsibility (Chapter 3) and discuss tensions that might arise between the internal claim and the external recognition of responsibility. Therefore, the present chapter puts special emphasis on the embeddedness of intrastate conflicts in the net of responsibility relations in world politics. The case of the Kurdish population in Iraq and their struggle for autonomy over the past decades serves as a case in point (Chapter 4). I will focus on retracing the dynamics in the responsibility relationship between Kurdish organizations, the Iraqi government, and the international community (namely the UN). The analysis is framed by a brief historical review of the international dimension of the conflict and a summary of the current situation of the Kurds in Iraq after the international nonrecognition of the Kurdish referendum for independence in 2017. In the conclusion, I will discuss the findings drawing broader conclusions about rebel responsibility in conflict situations.

Responsibility relations and its contestation in world politics

The concept of responsibility in world politics can be described as a triangle that comprises (1) a subject that takes responsibility for (2) things or people (objects) on the ground of (3) a normative reference framework (Zimmerli and Aßländer 1996). Responsibility refers to the duty to act or to abstain from acting (Klein 2005), and it means to be answerable for a social act – both prospective and retrospective (Erskine 2003). Responsibility basically describes the "blameworthiness" and the "praiseworthiness" of the actions of moral agents (Isaacs 2011, 13). The assessment of social actions arises from moral duties, qualified in normative reference frameworks. Examples reach from religious guidelines to universally accepted norms, such as codified or customary human rights law.[3]

But who counts as a responsible actor? And what are the common characteristics of responsible actors in world politics? Today, it is out of the question that besides individuals and states, collective actors such as international institutions can also be responsible and be regarded as subjects of moral responsibility (Crawford 2018; Erskine 2003). According to Erskine, a collectivity is a candidate for moral agency, if it has "an identity that is more than the sum of the identities of its constitutive parts and, therefore, does not rely on a determinate membership; a decision-making structure; an identity over time; and a conception of itself as a unit" (Erskine 2003, 24). She refers to collectivities with these characteristics as "institutional moral agents" who do not automatically behave morally, but are vulnerable to assignments of duty and blame. This chapter understands responsibility as the agency and the autonomy to act intentionally. Only when this "double autonomy in agency" is given, can actors be praised or blamed for their actions (Sondermann, Ulbert, and Finkenbusch 2017, 3). Because agency is a relational concept, it is important to consider the position and role of the respective actor within the respective field. From this perspective, political responsibility is not a task assigned only to governments but to all those who are capable of taking collectively binding decisions (Beardsworth 2015; Young 2004).

World politics can be understood as consisting of multiple responsibility triangles, which establish relations between a subject (left angle) that takes responsibility for an object (right angle) based on specific norms (top angle) (see Figure 20.1). The classical triangle between a political actor and its object is realized within the nation-state (triangle A). The government takes responsibility for its population on the grounds of a national legal framework. With the emergence and integration of the world political system, additional triangles have entered the picture and changed the traditional framework of responsibility in international politics. To address

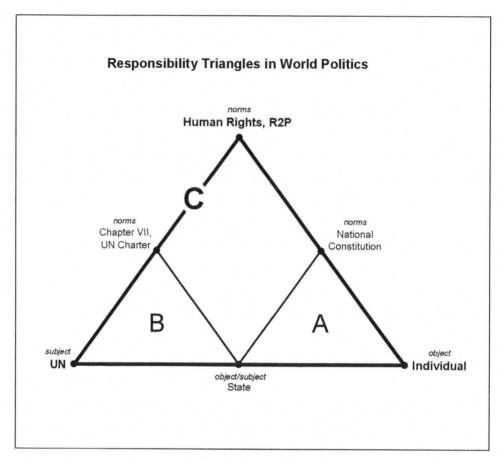

Figure 20.1 Responsibility triangles

international problems, governments established international institutions and vested them with responsibility for certain groups or issues via international treaties. The UN, and more specifically the Security Council, became paramount for questions of peace and security. According to the UN Charter, agreed upon by the member states, the Security Council has the exclusive responsibility to maintain peace and security worldwide (triangle B). The atrocities in the 1990s in Rwanda, the Balkans, and especially Kosovo, as well as the overall shift from international to intrastate conflicts, led to the emergence of the R2P norm (Bellamy 2006). This norm, while not uncontested, established the international community as a fail-safe that assumes responsibility for groups of individuals if their home states fail to do so in the face of atrocities. Together with *ius cogens* human rights norms, this sets the UN Security Council and the individual in direct relation to each other (triangle C). These three triangles are depicted in Figure 20.1, leaving out multiple other triangles that are also relevant in the security field but not so much for the present study.

The figure demonstrates how, depending on the social situation, subjects of responsibility such as states (triangle A) can simultaneously be objects of responsibility in a different setting (triangle B), based on different normative reference frameworks. This refers to the fact that the triangles are interwoven, connected and interrelated. The artificial split merely serves to deconstruct and analyze responsibility structures in world politics.

(Ir)responsibility in intrastate conflict situations

In intrastate conflict situations, responsibility relations are contested in multiple ways. Intrastate conflicts take place between a government and a nonstate armed actor. Among intrastate conflicts, ethnic conflicts are the most common form (Denny and Walter 2014), representing 64% of all intrastate conflicts worldwide. In ethnic conflicts, at least one conflict party defines itself as a distinct ethnic group and mobilizes supporters based on this distinction (Walter 2004). Such conflicts are often characterized by a history of exclusion of an ethnic group from a political system (Wimmer, Cederman, and Min 2009; Vogt et al. 2015). For example, people of Kurdish origin in Turkey have faced multiple policies of repression, ranging from the prohibition to speak Kurdish to the political exclusion as punishment for referring to the Kurdish ethnicity and identity (Bezwan 2008; Somer 2004; Strohmeier and Yalçın-Heckmann 2003).

In many cases, the (political) exclusion is a consequence of the *active rejection of responsibility* for a specific group by the government. While bearing responsibility for the rest of the national population, in ethnic conflicts, the exclusion of one group is constantly reproduced by governmental decisions, cementing the group's disadvantaged social status. The justification for such exclusion might even be drawn from the national constitution or other national laws, which allows a government to frame such policies as a proper and even legitimate way of governing.[4] In doing so, the government does not take responsibility for the group or its well-being, but actively excludes the corresponding group from the national responsibility triangle. This opens up room for subnational actors to claim moral and political responsibility for the oppressed or not-adequately-represented part of the population, which has led to several violent conflicts. But conflicts over responsibility are not always the result of an active rejection by the government; they can also occur in reaction to a minority group's self-exclusion from national responsibility relations. In such cases, the minority group is not pushed out of the triangle, but it tries to pull itself out and attempts to secede from the nation-state by setting up responsibility relations between the minority organization and the minority group. Examples are the Catalonians in Spain or the secession from South Sudan from Sudan.

In both cases, the responsibility relations between the state and its population are contested. However, while governments enjoy a kind of "natural" agency in responsibility relations, armed nonstate actors must achieve the transition from mere objects to subjects of responsibility – both within a state territory and on the international floor of diplomacy.

Internal claim of responsibility by rebel groups

In conflict situations with a political struggle about *who* is able and allowed to make collectively binding decisions, responsibility is negotiated, delegated, and contested. These negotiation processes underline that responsibility always goes along with questions about agency – who bears responsibility, who claims it, but also who grants recognition of responsibility claims? In the framework of nation states, the government is the original bearer of responsibility but might be challenged by an armed nonstate group that claims responsibility for (a part of) the respective population and fights against the government to achieve it. In such situations, the responsibility of the state is (violently) contested, and the rebel group attempts to elevate itself into the position of a responsible actor. But can rebel groups be understood as institutional moral agents in line with the proposed definition by Erskine? While a thorough examination of each nonstate actor is necessary to give a decisive answer, one can generally state that many rebel groups fulfil the criteria of an institutional moral agent. Many groups spend a lot of time and resources on the ideological training of their fighters with the aim to develop a shared and unitary identity over time. They develop an organizational – often hierarchical – structure and to be able to reach decisions in the name of the group (Gurr 1993, 128). In their effort to become recognized actors in world politics, some rebel groups develop a political arm to coordinate and professionalize their political behavior.

In many intrastate conflicts, a nonstate group claims *responsibility* for an (ethnic) group. Rebel groups frequently seek to infiltrate the disrupted national responsibility triangle and establish new responsibility relations between themselves and the ethnic group they claim to represent. To succeed in such an endeavor, rebel groups do not only fight the government, but some also try to transfer their responsibility claim into political practice. They build up state-like governance structures, which has also been referred to as "rebel governance" (Arjona, Kasfir, and Mampilly 2015, 3). While not every rebel group decides to govern a group of civilians, "a surprisingly large number of rebel groups engage in some sort of governance, ranging from creating minimal regulation and informal taxation to forming popular assemblies, elaborate bureaucracies, schools, courts, and health clinics" (Arjona, Kasfir, and Mampilly 2015, 1).

For researching questions of responsibility, it does not matter whether a rebel group espouses a specific religious, ideological, economic or ethnic agenda, or whether it follows a profit-motivated path. Intrastate conflicts become political because they involve "parties that disagree over some fundamentally *political* aspect of the state" (Arjona, Kasfir, and Mampilly 2015, 2). By establishing governance structures, such as decision-making mechanisms, courts and social services, rebel groups can increase their acceptance by the civilian population and improve their positioning and social status in the world political system.[5] This can even result in the founding of a de facto state as in the case of Somaliland. Here, the rebel group SNM in North Somalia fought against the Somali government and unilaterally declared its independence in 1991, setting up a state with functioning institutions. Like the SNM, many rebel groups provide services usually deemed the responsibility of the state (Kassimir 2001). Such service provisions are central as they connect the civilian population with the provider of the social services.

External recognition of responsibility by the international community

For the longest time, intrastate conflicts have been regarded as the internal affairs of the respective states. With the normative and institutional integration of the world political system and the weakening of the sovereignty norm for the benefit of individual norms, however, such developments became an object of international concern. The international community condemns or supports certain actors of intrastate conflict situations based on political interests but also international norms such as human rights, self-determination or state sovereignty. In effect, by supporting or rejecting claims of responsibility, IOs, such as the UN Security Council, elevate intrastate conflicts from the national to the world political stage. This is a profoundly political process, because "defining what is right and wrong, making someone "answer to," and blaming her for an action entails an element of power that does not necessarily rest on causal accountability" (Ulbert and Sondermann 2017, 197). In other words, with state sovereignty increasingly perforated by competing international norms such as human security, the international community can exercise power by assigning blame and (re-)attributing responsibility. By bestowing or denying responsibility, a process of inclusion and exclusion is implemented on the international level, underlining the asymmetric power relationships and power imbalances of the world political system (Ulbert and Sondermann 2017, 198).

While responsibility describes a mutual relationship between a subject and an object, external recognition of responsibility refers to a rather unbalanced relation in which one actor, usually the more powerful one, recognizes another one as legitimate. Biene and Daase (2015) conceptualize recognition and nonrecognition as a gradual process on a continuum with two poles. "This continuum runs from highly formalized to extremely informal modes of recognition, and from the recognition of nonstate actors and other political collectives as legitimate negotiating partners to the recognition of entities as sovereign states and as states with specific entitlements" (Geis et al. 2015, 16). Exposed to such power relations, rebel groups are dependent on the recognition of their claim by the international community if they want to become a legitimate actor of the international system. While being politically excluded on the national level, the world political level offers a way to become an accepted and responsible political actor (Sienknecht 2018a, 103ff). In order to attract attention and recognition by the international community, rebel groups have to espouse the most fundamental norms of the international system (Sienknecht 2018b, 15f.).

Figure 20.2 shows how a new responsibility triangle can emerge within triangle A, which symbolizes a governance structure in the making between a rebel group and a part of the population (triangle D). The overlap between the two triangles marks the intrastate conflict between the government and the rebel group. The responsibility triangle in the making challenges the authority, integrity, and sovereignty of the state and is therefore often violently contested by the government. For many rebel groups, a tempting way forward is to circumvent the national channels of political communication and address the world political level,

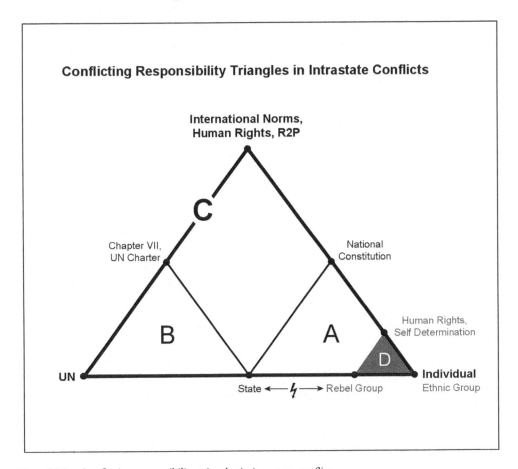

Figure 20.2 Conflicting responsibility triangles in intrastate conflict

which promises the power to recognize the group and transform it into a legitimate, responsible representative of a specific population. In doing so, rebel groups attempt to transfer their responsibility relation with their constituency out of the national framework and establish a new and politically self-sufficient responsibility system, which might result in the foundation of a new state.

Complementarity and tensions in security politics

When we assume that the concept of responsibility triangles helps us to understand world politics as a multi-relational process, then we need to clarify how these four triangles (A, B, C, D) are interrelated. In an ideal and peaceful world, the responsibility triangles are complementary to each other: States take responsibility for their entire population (A); the UN takes responsibility for international peace and security between states (B) and for the protection of the individual (C). Most of the current relations between different actors in world politics are peaceful, but tensions arise in certain situations where two subjects of responsibility clash. These tensions concern questions about who is responsible (subject dimension) for whom or what (object dimension) and on which normative ground.[6]

In case of (ethnic) intrastate conflicts, tensions arise between a state and a rebel group around the responsibility for a certain part of a population. Either both the government and the rebel group claim responsibility for a respective group or the government disregards its responsibility for a certain group, leaving room for a nonstate conflict party to claim responsibility on their behalf. The tension between a state and a nonstate conflict party characterizes the social situations that are of interest in this paper. While these conflicts are often violent, the tensions that might arise between the state and the UN, or between the rebel group and the UN, are seldom violent. They rather reveal points of significant disagreement.

If we want to set the international, national, and subnational triangles in relation to each other, three scenarios in the relation between the triangles are theoretically conceivable: First, the state and the nonstate actors agree upon the division of the territory and the division of responsibility. This leads to the separation from the state territory and the foundation of a new state (triangle D), as in case of South Sudan. The international community recognizes this responsibility attribution by recognizing the new state. All responsibility triangles are complementary to each other and interlinked, leading to the foundation of a new state.

Second, the state and the nonstate actor conflict about the responsibility toward a part of the population. The internal claim of responsibility by the rebel group is contradicted by the government (tension in triangle A). Furthermore, the internal claim by the rebel group is not supported by the international community – either because the latter does not recognize the responsibility of the former or because it does not position itself on either side in the conflict. This might lead to tensions between the rebel group and the UN (triangle C). An empirical example is the conflict between the LTTE and the government of Sri Lanka. The international community did not support their secessionist agenda, which created tensions between the LTTE and the UN. The internal claim of responsibility was not complemented by an external recognition. At the same time, the UN condemned the behavior of the government (tensions in triangle B), but without directly intervening in the conflict. Therefore, each subject (UN, rebel group, government) is in conflict with each other.

Third, the state and the nonstate actor conflict about the responsibility toward a part of the population. The internal claim of responsibility by the rebel group is contradicted by the government (tension in triangle A). Other than the second scenario described above, this situation is characterized by the perceived necessity of the international community to take responsibility in order to protect civilians from atrocities by the state. Should the UN intervene in such a conflict situation, it is to reattribute responsibility for a population that has been failed by its government (R2P). The UN can take over responsibility for a certain period and then transfer it to representatives of the respective group. This was the case in East Timor, where the UN ran a transition government. The UN can also empower the nonstate conflict party from the very beginning, granting external recognition of the responsibility claim. This might lead to the foundation of a new state without the consent of the government, as happened in the case of Kosovo. Thus, the claimed responsibility of the rebel group is recognized by the international community, while the government is in conflict with both the international community and the rebel group.

These three scenarios broadly describe the interrelation of triangles in the field of security politics and in cases of intrastate conflict situations. It is apparent that the scenarios only mirror one moment in time, and do not cover a development over time. The case of Sudan was characterized by a civil war between the government of Sudan and the rebel group Sudan People's Liberation Army (SPLA) before they agreed upon the separation of South Sudan in 2011, which was accompanied by the recognition from the international community. Despite their time invariance, the triangles help to understand the development within a conflict and its respective conflict outcome, and are therefore helpful to describe changes in the triangle relations over time.

In the following empirical study, I validate the plausibility of the assumed analytical concept.

Empirical illustration: the case of the Kurds in Iraq

The modern history of the Kurdish people was largely determined by the dissolution of the Ottoman Empire and the formation of nation-states in the Middle East – the colonial decreeing of a responsibility relation between a government and a (randomly constituted) population by European powers. While the Treaty of Sevres in 1920 promised the right to self-determination to all groups of the former empire (including the Kurds), the Treaty of Lausanne revised this provision in 1923. Since then, the fourth-largest ethnic group in the Middle East with around 40 million people is scattered across four states: Iraq, Turkey, Syria, and Iran. In all of their host countries, the Kurds faced and mostly still face a policy of subjugation and repression out of fear of Kurdish uprisings and separatist movements (Jongerden 2019). This chapter focuses on the Kurds in Iraq who have relations to other Kurdish organizations in the different countries, but are mainly independent.

In Iraq, with its 4 to 4.5 million people, the Kurds represent roughly 20% of the population. Since the dawn of Iraqi statehood, the Kurds faced suppression by the central government. The political exclusion and constant repression led to a series of uprisings (McDowall 2004). Since World War II, the Kurdish uprisings against the Iraqi state have been led by the Barzani clan. Mustafa Barzani founded the Kurdistan Democratic Party (KDP) in 1946 and became president of the political organization. The KDP was the first broad Kurdish organization in Iraq that was able to recruit many supporters. Besides its political arm, the organization has a military arm – the so-called Peshmerga[7]. Regarding the definition of an institutional moral agent by Erskine (2003), the KDP can confidently be considered to fall into this category: It developed an own identity over time and has a conception of itself as a unit. The KDP is hierarchically organized and therefore has a decision-making structure, which grants the organization the capacity for moral deliberation and moral action (Erskine 2001, 2003). Solely the freedom to act – meaning to have a certain degree of independence from other agents – is difficult to achieve for a nonstate conflict party within any intrastate conflict situation. Several constraints and exceptional circumstances influence the behavior of such organizations. Therefore, this chapter focuses on the interplay of responsibility between the subnational, national, and international level.

The declared goal of the KDP changed over its time of existence. When Barzani returned to Iraq in 1958 from his exile in the Soviet Union, the KDP fought for independence against the government in Baghdad. These conflict episodes were alternated by some phases of cooperation between the KDP and the government that even resulted in a peace agreement and a recognized autonomy for the Kurds in Northern Iraq (1970), negotiated with the Ba'ath Party, which came into power in 1968. This fragile peace, however, lasted only until 1974 when the agreements and the conceded autonomy collapsed, leading to a war between the Kurds and the Iraqi government.[8] After the death of Mustafa Barzani in 1979, the presidency of the KDP was passed on to his son Masoud Barzani. In the 1960s and 1970s, a second group claiming to represent the Kurds emerged under the leadership of Jalal Talabani, the so-called Patriotic Union of Kurdistan (PUK). Until today, the KDP and the PUK remain the dominant groups among Iraqi Kurds, both claiming responsibility for the entire ethnic group of the Kurds. Though many tensions marred the relationship between the KDP and the PUK, they decided to form a united front against the Iraqi government in 1987. The KDP's strongholds were in the North, where it controlled the entire border with Turkey from Syria to Iran. The PUK recruited members and fighters from Rawanduz, a border region to Iran in the north east (Marr 2012). In the Iran–Iraq war (1980–1988), the Kurds supported Iran, which further intensified the animosities with the Iraqi government.

The Al-Anfal campaign against the Kurds (1987–1988) – Iraq actively rejects responsibility toward the Kurds

In light of the Iran–Iraq war and Kurdish support of Iran, the Ba'ath regime, which had vehemently opposed the Kurds since the dissolution of their autonomy status in 1974, decided to take the most drastic measures against its Kurdish population. After the war ended in 1988, the tensions between the Iraqi government and the Kurds culminated in the Halabja chemical attack against the Kurdish population. This attack was part of the Al-Anfal Campaign that contained eight stages and targeted both PUK- and KPD-controlled areas with the extensive use of poisonous gas against the civilian population. Exactly how many Kurds perished during the Al-Anfal Campaign is not certain, but numbers vary between 50,000 and 100,000. Over 4,000 villages were destroyed, with around 1.5 million people forcibly displaced or resettled.

By August 1988, 60,000–150,000 Kurds had fled over the border to Turkey, while up to 200,000 crossed the border to Iran (Marr 2012). The attacks against the Kurds ended in an effective defeat of the Peshmerga (Jongerden 2019). Part of this Al-Anfal Campaign was also the "Arabization" strategy, which aimed to destroy the Kurdish majority in the northern areas, notably the oil-rich cities like Kirkuk.

While the historical relations between the Iraqi government and the Kurdish population had always been conflictual, being characterized by a certain degree of political exclusion, with the Al-Anfal Campaign it became more than apparent that not only the organizational unit of the Kurds but the Kurdish population as a whole was regarded as a threat by the Iraqi government. Saddam Hussein relinquished the responsibility relationship between the Iraqi state and the Kurdish people by using the most extreme form of rejection: the violent persecution of a part of its own population by the state. This corresponds to the intrastate conflict situation in triangle A, with the Kurdish organizations challenging the Iraqi government and claiming responsibility for the Kurdish population.

The implementation of the "no-fly zone" (1991) – the international community assumes responsibility

The deepening of Kurdish alienation and Kurdish aspirations to step out of the Iraqi governor structure was one result of the Al-Anfal Campaign (Marr 2012). The invasion and annexation of Kuwait by Iraq in 1990 were followed by a military intervention by the UN-authorized coalition of forces led by the United States (US). The so-called "Operation Desert Storm" led to international involvement in Iraq. After the allied forces had retreated from the country, secessionist movements of the Kurds in Northern Iraq and the Shiites in Southern Iraq erupted. The Iraqi military, still strong, reacted without mercy (Rudd 2004). The fear of another poisonous gas attack caused the flight of about half of the Kurdish population to the Turkish and Iranian borders. Within some weeks, more than a million Kurds fled to these mountainous regions (Benard 2004). From today's perspective, not taking responsibility and actively persecuting the Kurdish population is grounds to transfer responsibility to the international community – but back then, the R2P norm was still 15 years away.

To guarantee the return of the refugees to their hometowns, the US and its coalition forces took responsibility for the Kurdish population by implementing a no-fly zone. The no-fly zone prohibited all Iraqi military aircraft north of the 36th parallel (Schmitt 1998). The operation "Provide Comfort" facilitated the safe return of the Kurdish refugees to their hometowns and was transformed into the Operation "Provide Comfort II," which was essentially an air patrol to guarantee the safety of the Kurdish population centers. The main goal of the coalition was to prevent further atrocities against the Kurdish minorities. In some ways, this was an early precedent for the R2P norm; it restricted the sovereignty of the Iraqi government on grounds (at least the US interpretation) of different Security Council resolutions (UNSC 1991/687; 1991/688; 1991/707). In this regard, the coalition took responsibility for the Kurdish population and paved the way for the Kurdish autonomous region in Northern Iraq (Gunter 2008; Jongerden 2019).

The international coalition replaced the Iraqi government as the first instance of responsibility, effectively establishing a new triangle of responsibility. Thus, the Iraqi government was in conflict with both Kurdish organizations and the international community. Under the cover of the international coalition, a Kurdish de facto autonomy was established, which set the cornerstones for a new triangle of responsibility between the KDP/PUK and the Kurdish population. The withdrawal of Iraqi troops from the Kurdish areas helped to advance the new Kurdish autonomy, which was referred to as "Kurdistan region in Iraq" or "Kurdistan autonomous region," and comprised the governorates of Sulaymaniyya, Erbil and Duhok (Bengio 2012). At the same time, it guaranteed a responsibility transfer to the Kurdish organizations. Therefore, the triangles A and D were complementary to each other.

Rebel responsibility – from morality to politics: establishment of governance structures

Under the protection of the coalition, the Kurdish parties (the KDP and the PUK) were able to build governance structures within the Kurdistan autonomous region. After years of repression, the Kurds were eager to fill the administrative vacuum left by the Iraqi government (Bengio 2012, 202). As before, the two parties claimed responsibility for the Kurdish population but were now able to materialize their claims into governance structures. Since 1991, both parties had favored a federal approach to the question of self-administration (Jongerden 2019, 65). In 1991, Kurdish leaders joined the Iraqi National Congress (INC), a US-backed opposition group, and organized elections. They set up an administration in their enclave and held elections for a provisional parliament in 1992. The KDP and the PUK together gained 50 seats, and five seats went to Christian groups. Lacking a clear winner in the presidential election, the KDP and the PUK decided to jointly govern the region. In 1992, the Kurdish parliament called for the creation of a Federated State of Kurdistan within a democratic parliamentary Iraq, thereby committing to Iraq's territorial integrity. The Iraqi regime declared the elections "illegitimate" and "unconstitutional," referring to its national sovereignty and integrity (Bengio 2012, 202f.).

The Kurdish elections were relevant in two ways: First, they conferred legitimacy on the Kurdish leadership and the two parties, thereby cancelling out smaller Kurdish organizations and setting the stage for a Kurdish administration. Second, they served as a sign for the international community that the majority of the Kurdish population supported the internal claim of responsibility by the Kurdish organizations. The Kurdistan National Assembly formed a Kurdish cabinet, which became the government of the region. It included fifteen ministries and marked the transition of the Kurdish rebel group into a (legitimate) political actor in the region. Furthermore, the Kurdish administration promoted the development of the legal and educational system. By the end of 1992, in 1,100 schools, Kurdish was the language of instruction, as well as in three universities and a military college (Bengio 2012, 203).

These developments demonstrate that the elected Kurdish government filled the responsibility gap that was opened by the Iraqi government. The international community and especially the US-led coalition played an important role for the transition from a rebel group to a legitimate political representation because, by taking responsibility for the Kurdish population and by safeguarding the region for several years, they enabled the de facto autonomy of the Kurds in the first place. In effect, the coalition recognized the responsibility of the Kurdish organizations on the basis of international norms – a novelty in the Kurdish history.[9]

These rebel governance structures were formalized through the Iraqi federal constitution of 2005, which constituted Iraq as a federation with Kurdistan as a federal part. In the aftermath of the US-led invasion of Iraq in 2003 and the fall of Saddam Hussein, in which the Kurds played an important role, the Kurds were substantially involved in the writing of the new Iraqi constitution, which enshrined the Kurdish federal status within the borders of the state. While tensions between the two Kurdish parties remained but were somewhat stabilized, the tensions with the Iraqi government increased over time.

From cooperation to tension – international rejection of an independent Kurdish responsibility triangle

After the joint fight with the US-led coalition against the so-called Islamic State of Iraq and Syria (ISIS), the Kurds held a referendum on the question of secession from the Iraqi state in 2017. This referendum was an attempt to implement an independent responsibility triangle at last, which would emancipate them from the borders of the Iraqi state. Already in 2016, Barzani had stated that the "world owes responsibility for a real resolution in Iraq" (Moradi 2016), setting the international community in relation with the Kurds. The international reactions to the referendum were almost unanimously adverse, rejecting the decision of a vast majority of the Kurdish people. The international community thus directly influenced the remaining of Iraqi Kurdistan under the jurisdiction of the Iraqi government. This illustrates the fact that the degree to which a nonstate actor can assume responsibility is dependent on the position of the respective actor within the international system and on the recognition of the respective actor by international powerful actors. Responsibility is a relational concept, strongly tied to agency. Even when the international community granted the Kurdish Regional Government (KRG) responsibility and

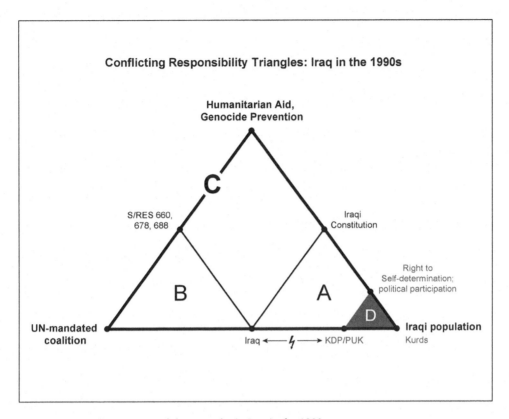

Figure 20.3 Conflicting responsibility triangles in Iraq in the 1990s

some agency, the full freedom of action and independent statehood did not find support on the world political stage. These developments underline that responsibility does not automatically translate into authority. Furthermore, it becomes apparent that it is not only the norms that are relevant but also (geo-political) interests of powerful players within the international community. The territorial integrity of Iraq was perceived as more important than the support of the Kurdish secessionist ambitions. This refers to the fact that there are "degrees" of recognition: The group and its claim for autonomy are recognized by the international community, while their claim to statehood is not. Consequently, the recognition of the group does not automatically mean the rejection of state authority.

Therefore, the relationship between the triangles B and D was not complementary but conflictual, and the Kurds felt betrayed by the international community (compare Figure 20.3). In the aftermath, the Kurds tried to find a peaceful agreement with the current Iraqi government concerning their autonomy status within the borders of Iraq. They also sought to normalize their relations with the international community and especially the US.

Conclusion

With this analysis of the case of the Iraqi Kurds in mind, how can we answer the research questions at hand? How is responsibility constituted and contested in intrastate conflicts and how are these responsibility structures influenced by the world political system? Most intrastate conflicts seem to have one aspect in common: a crisis of the responsibility structure between the government and its population. In one way or another, the relationship is challenged either by the government, leading to a certain form of exclusion of an identifiable group, or by a rebel group that rejects its constituency's affiliation to the state or claims responsibility in light of irresponsible behavior of the state. In both situations, a disturbed relationship is the consequence, and tension ensues between the responsibility triangle of the state and the claimed responsibility triangle of the rebel group. In the case of Iraq, the constant suppression of the Kurds led to the emergence of two Kurdish organizations (the KDP and the PUK), who both claimed to represent the Kurds and to take responsibility for the Kurdish population. In this regard, the Kurdish groups tried to constitute a responsibility triangle – at first within the broader framework of the Iraqi state, and later detached from it, which became manifest in the referendum in 2017 (triangle D).

In the case of Iraq, actors of the world political system entered the picture at two points, first being at the time the UN Security Council conflicted with the Iraqi government over the invasion of Kuwait and the atrocities toward the Kurds and the Shiites in 1990. With the resolution 687 of the Security Council and its successors concerning Iraq, a conflict system between the Iraqi government and the Council emerged with the consequence of an intervention into Iraq and the implementation of a no-fly zone. Through this process, the international community took responsibility for international peace and security (triangle B) and for the protection of the Kurdish population (triangle C). When the US-led coalition entered the picture, the Kurdish organizations had the chance to set up governance structures and materialize their claim of responsibility. By setting up political, legal, military, health and education systems, they built up rebel governance structures, which created an alternative responsibility relation within the borders of Iraq. For setting up the de facto autonomy of Kurdistan, the endorsement from the world political system in form of the no-fly zone was an indispensable precondition. In this way, the rebel group was set in relation with actors of the world political system. That these relations are not uncontested became obvious in the aftermath of the referendum in 2017. The referendum can be interpreted as an attempt by the KRG to finally and fully detach from the Iraqi state. As it was not supported by the international community, tensions between the KRG and the international community arose.

What does the discussion of responsibility add to the analysis of the conflict? The concept of responsibility and my specification of it enable distinguishing between different layers, subjects, objects, and norms of responsibility in world politics, making it possible to analyze how these different layers interact. The analysis has shown that responsibility in intrastate conflict situations is not a monolithic structure, but a pattern of parallel, overlapping, and contradicting triangular relations that bear the potential for conflict – not only between the two conflict parties. The differentiation between the forfeiting of responsibility by a state, the internal claim of responsibility by a rebel group and the external recognition of responsibility by the international community helped to analyze the manifold responsibility relations and to consider the international dimension of intrastate conflicts. It is not only about how a certain group becomes a recognized political actor but also about how the group claims responsibility and possibly receives international recognition. It became apparent that a group can claim responsibility, but needs a certain degree of autonomy and authority (either self-accomplished or guaranteed/granted from the outside) to be able to deploy its responsibility/agency over the respective group.

The empirical analysis of the situation in Iraq is without any claim to comprehensiveness, as it highlights only some of the main developments and omits much of the delicate branching of the conflict. But what became visible is the embeddedness of intrastate conflicts in the broader political system of world society and the multilayered system of responsibility triangles. Intrastate conflicts do not occur in a political vacuum but are influenced by decisions in the world political system. In the case of the conflicts in Iraq, we were able to observe both the compliance between the internal claim of responsibility by the Kurdish organizations and the external responsibility takeover from the international community in form of the US-led coalition. This external responsibility went along with a recognition of the agency of the Kurdish organizations and thus reflected the international power structures. Furthermore, it demonstrates that a window of opportunity can emerge from the compliance, resulting in the installation of a de facto state with functioning governance structures as the Kurdish example has shown. At the same time, the case of Kurdistan has demonstrated that tensions between the subnational and the global level restrict the freedom of development and the breakout of the Kurds from the Iraqi state. In general, the study has demonstrated that responsibility relations are interwoven and diverse, forming a net of triangles that are either complementary or conflictual. The complexity and diffusion of responsibility relations do not only cause problems of attribution but they also offer opportunities for different actors to take political responsibility.

Notes

1 I would like to thank Barçın Uluışık for her careful proofreading (all remaining errors are my responsibility), Johanna Gottschalk for her assistance in creating the figures in this chapter, and Lukas Lambert for his valuable comments. Special thanks to Antje Vetterlein and Hannes Hansen-Magnusson for putting together this handbook and their valuable comments on earlier drafts of this paper.
2 "Non-state armed groups are defined as distinctive organizations that are (1) willing and capable to use violence for pursuing their objectives and (2) not integrated into formalized state institutions such as regular armies, presidential guards, police, or special forces. They, therefore, (3) possess a certain degree of autonomy with regard to politics, military operations, resources, and infrastructure" (Hofmann and Schneckener 2011, 2). Rebel groups and nonstate armed actors are used interchangeably in the present chapter.
3 The international relations (IR) literature dealing with responsibility broadly differentiates between moral, legal and political responsibility (Erskine 2003; Isaacs 2011, 13–14). While I explicitly refer to moral and political responsibility in this paper, legal responsibility is rather left out of the picture. "Legal responsibility" is normatively based on and upheld by a legal system that recognizes, creates and enforces obligations (Isaacs 2011, 14). Legal responsibility implies less an understanding of responsibility based on moral values than an understanding linked to tasks and duties. Nevertheless, international law does not refer only to states, but also to individuals, as the criminal prosecution of individuals such as Slobodan Milošević of Serbia or Joseph Kony of Uganda's Lord's Resistance Army (LRA) reveals. War crimes of rebel groups remain not unpunished, which might explain the tendency of nonstate actors to comply with international standards of conduct in warfare (Jo 2015).
4 In the case of Turkey, the Treaty of Lausanne (1923) specifies who is defined as Turk and who is allowed special minority rights; the Kurds were defined as Turks and were therefore subject to a comprehensive policy of assimilation. The Turkish government in the early 20th century denied all claims that it had relinquished the responsibility over this part of its population because Kurds were allowed to vote and to participate in Turkish politics. Yet this only held true as long as they never referred to their Kurdish identity.
5 The response of the civilian population is of course not always supportive of the rebel group; this depends inter alia on the quality of the local institutions in place prior to the claim of the armed group and the moral behavior towards the population.
6 For a discussion about the contestation of norms and its effect on the normative order, see Wiener (2017).
7 The military forces of the Kurds are called Peshmerga – "before death" or "those who face the death" – and its history is dated back to the end of the 19th century. Only since the self-declared Republic of Mahabad (1946–1947), the Peshmerga have become a well-trained and disciplined guerilla force.
8 Already during this time, the Kurds approached the United States (US) and called them to assist in the nearing conflict with the Ba'ath regime (Bengio 2012).
9 Due to space limitations, I am not discussing the internal conflicts between the PUK and the KDP, which flared up in 1994 and led to different spheres of influence. The KDP controlled the northern area along the Turkish border, and the PUK controlled the urban areas and the eastern province of Sulaymaniyya and Erbil (Bengio 2012, 213). Furthermore, during the internal conflict, Barzani called on the Iraqi government for military support against the rival Kurdish Party, the PUK.

References

Albert, M. (2016). *A Theory of World Politics*. Cambridge: Cambridge University Press.
Arjona, A., Kasfir, N, and Mampilly, Z. C., eds. (2015). *Rebel Governance in Civil War*. Cambridge: Cambridge University Press.
Beardsworth, R. (2015). "From Moral to Political Responsibility in a Globalized Age." *Ethics & International Affairs*, 29(1): 71–92.
Bellamy, A. J. (2006). "Whither the Responsibility to Protect? Humanitarian Intervention and the 2005 World Summit." *Ethics & International Affairs*, 20(2): 143–169.
Benard, A. (2004). "Lessons from Iraq and Bosnia on the Theory and Practice of No-Fly Zones." *Journal of Strategic Studies*, 27(3): 454–178.
Bengio, O. (2012). *The Kurds of Iraq: Building a State Within a State*. Boulder, Colorado: Lynne Rienner Publishers.
Bezwan, N. (2008). *Türkei und Europa: Die Staatsdoktrin der Türkischen Republik, ihre Aufnahme in die EU und die kurdische Nationalfrage*. Baden-Baden: Nomos.
Biene, J., and Daase, C. (2015). "Gradual Recognition: Curbing Non-State Violence in Asymmetric Conflicts." In Geis, A., Fehl, C., Daase, C., and Kolliarakis, G., eds., *Recognition in International Relations. Rethinking a Political Concept in a Global Context*: 220–236. London: Palgrave Macmillan.
Chandler, D. (2018). "Distributed Responsbility: Moral Agency in a Non-Linear World." In Ulbert, C. Finkenbusch, P., Sondermann, E., and Debiel, T., eds., *Moral Agency and the Politics of Responsibility*: 182–195. London: Routledge.
Crawford, N.C. (2018). "Promoting Responsible Moral Agency: Enhancing Institutional and Individual Capacities." In Ulbert, C. Finkenbusch, P., Sondermann, E., and Debiel, T., eds., *Moral Agency and the Politics of Responsibility*: 36–50. London: Routledge.
Daase, C., Junk, J., Kroll, S. and Rauer, V., eds. (2017a). *Politik und Verantwortung: Analysen zum Wandel politischer Entscheidungs-und Rechtfertigungspraktiken*. 1st ed. Sonderheft PVS. Baden-Baden: Nomos.
Daase, C., Junk, J., Kroll, S. and Rauer, V., eds. (2017b). "Verantwortung in der Politik und Politik der Verantwortung: Eine Einleitung zum Sonderheft." In Daase, C., Junk, J., Kroll, S. and Rauer, V., eds. (2017a). *Politik und Verantwortung: Analysen zum Wandel politischer Entscheidungs-und Rechtfertigungspraktiken*: 3–11. Baden-Baden: Nomos.
Denny, E. K., and Walter, B. F. (2014). "Ethnicity and Civil War." *Journal of Peace Research*, 51(2): 199–212.
Erskine, T. (2001). "Assigning Responsibilities to Institutional Moral Agents: The Case of States and Quasi-States." *Ethics & International Affairs*, 15(2): 67–85.
Erskine, T., ed. (2003). *Can Institutions Have Responsibilities? Collective Moral Agency and International Relations*. Houndmills, Basingstoke, Hampshire: Palgrave Macmillan.
Geis, A., Fehl, C., Daase, C. and Kolliarakis, G., eds. (2015). *Recognition in International Relations. Rethinking a Political Concept in a Global Context*. London: Palgrave Macmillan.
Gholiagha, S. (2015). "To Prevent 'Future Kosovos and Future Rwandas': A Critical Constructivist View on the Responsibility to Protect." *International Journal of Human Rights*, 19(8): 1074–1097.
Gunter, M. M. (2008). *The Kurds Ascending: The Evolving Solution to the Kurdish Problem in Iraq and Turkey*. New York, NY: Palgrave Macmillan.
Gurr, T. R. (1993). *Minorities at Risk: A Global View of Ethnopolitical Conflicts*. Washington, DC: United States Institute of Peace Press.
Hofmann, C., and Schneckener, U. (2011). "Engaging non-state armed actors in state- and peace-building: options and strategies." *International Review of the Red Cross*, 93(883): 1–19. https://www.icrc.org/en/doc/assets/files/review/2011/irrc-883-schneckener.pdf (accessed October 17, 2019).
Isaacs, T. L. (2011). *Moral Responsibility in Collective Contexts*. Oxford: Oxford University Press.
Jo, H. (2015). *Compliant Rebels: Rebel Groups and International Law in World Politics*. Cambridge: Cambridge University Press.
Jongerden, J. (2019). "Governing Kurdistan: Self-Administration in the Kurdistan Regional Government in Iraq and the Democratic Federation of Northern Syria." *Ethnopolitics*, 18(1): 61–75.
Kassimir, R. (2001). "Producing Local Politics: Governance, Representation, and Non-State Organizations in Africa." In Callaghy, T., Kassimir, R., and Latham, R., eds., *Intervention and Transnationalism in Africa: Global-Local Networks of Power*: 93–114. Cambridge: Cambridge University Press.
Klein, M. (2005). "Responsibility." In Honderich, T., ed., *The Oxford Companion to Philosophy*: 815–816. Oxford: Oxford University Press.
Marr, P. (2012). *The Modern History of Iraq*. Boulder, Colorado: Westview Press.

McDowall, D. (2004). *A Modern History of the Kurds*. London: I.B. Tauris.

Moradi, A. (2016). "Barzani: World owes 'responsibility' for a resolution in Iraq." https://www.rudaw.net/english/kurdistan/160520164 (accessed August 22, 2019).

Neyer, J., Sienknecht, M., and Martin-Russu, L. (2017). "Kosmopolitische Verantwortung: Zwischen normativem Anspruch und politischer Praxis." In Daase, C., Junk, J., Kroll, S. and Rauer, V., eds. (2017a). *Politik und Verantwortung: Analysen zum Wandel politischer Entscheidungs- und Rechtfertigungspraktiken*: 311–333. Baden-Baden: Nomos.

Petterson, T., and Öberg, M. (2020). "Organized violence, 1989-2019." *Journal of Peace Research*, 57(4): 597–613.

Rudd, G. W. (2004). *Humanitarian Intervention: Assisting the Iraqi Kurds in Operation Provide Comfort, 1991*. Washington, DC: Diane Pub Co.

Schmitt, M.N. (1998). "Clipped Wings: Effective and Legal No-Fly Zone Rules of Engagement." *Loyola of Los Angeles International and Comparative Law Review*, 20(4): 727–789.

Sienknecht, M. (2018a). *Entgrenzte Konflikte in der Weltgesellschaft. Zur Inklusion internationaler Organisationen in innerstaatliche Konfliktsysteme*. Wiesbaden: Springer VS.

Sienknecht, M. (2018b). "Entgrenzte Konfliktkommunikation. Zum Aufbau von Kommunikationsstrukturen von nichtstaatlichen Konfliktparteien in das weltpolitische System." *Zeitschrift für Internationale Beziehungen*, 25(1): 5–35.

Somer, M. (2004). "Turkey's Kurdish Conflict: Changing Context, and Domestic and Regional Implications." *Middle East Journal*, 58(2): 235–253.

Sondermann, E., Ulbert, C., and Finkenbusch, P. (2017). "Moral Agency and the Politics of Responsibility." In Ulbert, C., Finkenbusch, P., Sondermann, E. and Debiel, T., eds., *Moral Agency and the Politics of Responsibility*: 105–121. London: Routledge.

Strohmeier, M., and Yalçın-Heckmann, L. (2003). *Die Kurden: Geschichte, Politik, Kultur*. München: Beck.

Ulbert, C. (2018). "In Search of Equity: Practices of Differentiation and the Evolution of Geography of Responsibility." In Ulbert, C., Finkenbusch, P., Sondermann, E. and Debiel, T., eds., *Moral Agency and the Politics of Responsibility*: 1–18. London: Routledge.

Ulbert, C., and Sondermann, E. (2017). "Conclusion: Practising the Politics of Responsibility." In Ulbert, C., Finkenbusch, P., Sondermann, E. and Debiel, T., eds., *Moral Agency and the Politics of Responsibility*: 135–150. London: Routledge.

United Nations (2005). "2005 World Summit Outcome: A/RES/60/1." https://www.un.org/en/development/desa/population/migration/generalassembly/docs/globalcompact/A_RES_60_1.pdf (accessed August 27, 2019).

Vetterlein, A. (2018). "Responsibility is More than Accountability: from Regulatory towards Negotiated Governance." *Contemporary Politics*, 24(5): 545–567.

Vogt, Manuel, Bormann, Nils-Christian, Rüegger, Seraina, Cederman, Lars-Erik, Hunziker, Philipp, and Girardin, Luc. 2015. "Integrating Data on Ethnicity, Geography, and Conflict: The Ethnic Power Relations Data Set Family." *Journal of Conflict Resolution* 59(7): 1327–1342.

Walter, B.F. (2004). "Does Conflict Beget Conflict? Explaining Recurring Civil War." *Journal of Peace Research*, 41(3): 371–388.

Welsh, J.M. (2013). "Norm Contestation and the Responsibility to Protect." *Global Responsibility to Protect*, 5(4): 365–396.

Wiener, A. 2017. "Responsibility Contestations: A Challenge to the Moral Authority of the UN Security Council." In Ulbert, Finkenbusch, Sondermann, and Debiel, eds., *Moral Agency and the Politics of Responsibility*: 85–102. London: Routledge.

Wimmer, A., Cederman, L.E., and Min, B. (2009). "Ethnic Politics and Armed Conflict: A Configurational Analysis of a New Global Data Set." *American Sociological Review*, 74(2): 316–337.

Young, I.M. (2004). "Responsibility and Global Labor Justice." *The Journal of Political Philosophy*, 12(4): 365–388.

Zimmerli, W.C., and Aßländer, M. (1996). "Wirtschaftsethik." In Nida-Rümelin, J., eds, *Angewandte Ethik: Die Bereichsethiken und ihre theoretische Fundierung*: 290–345. Stuttgart: Alfred Kröner Verlag.

21
WHAT RESPONSIBILITY FOR INTERNATIONAL ORGANISATIONS?

The independent accountability mechanisms of the multilateral development banks

Susan Park

Introduction

On 27 February 2019, the United States Supreme Court ruled that the International Finance Corporation (IFC), the private sector lender and investor arm of the World Bank Group, has only limited immunity in the Jam V International Finance Corporation case.[1] Hitherto, international organizations (IO) like the IFC were unable to be prosecuted for their actions because they were immune under international law. The basis for the immunity was to protect IOs from the interference of member states in their operations, leaving them unencumbered in meeting their mandates (Bradlow 2019). The Supreme Court ruled that there were limits to IFC's immunity, in the same way that states are limited (US Supreme Court 2019). This ruling was made in light of the human rights protections now afforded to individuals that check states', and now IOs', prerogatives. This is important because over the past 70 years interactions between IOs and member states have changed considerably. The activities of IOs are increasingly recognised for affecting domestic political processes in ways not previously acknowledged (Park 2017a). In the Jam V IFC case, local farmers and fishers in Gujarat India challenged IFC's immunity through the US courts given the air, water, and land pollution stemming from the power plant financed by the IFC. IFC's actions are not isolated: projects like this are financed by the Multilateral Development Banks (MDBs) including the World Bank, the Asian (ADB), African (AfDB), and Inter-American Development Banks (IDB), the European Bank for Reconstruction and Development (EBRD), sub-regional development banks (see Zappile 2016), as well as bilateral and export credit agencies (Hunter 2008), and private sector development project financiers (Wright 2012).

The ruling is important for our understanding of the responsibility of IOs, and the World Bank Group in particular, in international relations. Over the last two decades, IOs have taken on "democratic" norms including representation, participation, transparency and accountability mechanisms (Grigorescu 2016; Tallberg et al. 2013). Accountability mechanisms have been used to hold IOs responsible and answerable for their actions, including the establishment of post-facto independent accountability mechanisms (IAMs) that assess whether the MDBs have contributed to environmental and social harm (Heldt 2018). In this way, IOs can be held to account by their member states for meeting their mandates through acceptable standards of behaviour or face sanctions. This can be understood as meeting public renderings of accountability (Park and Kramarz 2019). In this chapter, I argue that the IAM process is delinked from positive understandings of responsibility as a guide to avoid unwanted outcomes (Vetterlein 2018, 547), because IOs operate as bureaucracies that view responsibility as an obligation with which they must comply. In other words, member states can request that IOs are responsive to their concerns and answerable for their actions, but this does not mean that they have a positive "responsibility to do good, which also captures the acts of responsibility-taking even if one is not directly responsible" compared with negative responsibility which "has to do with the avoidance of harm" (Vetterlein 2018, 553).

Section 1 distinguishes responsibility from accountability, where the former is understood to be part of accountability but in the context of IOs has been understood only in a negative compliance sense. Demands for IO accountability have been met through public accountability systems of representation and delegation. This is exemplified in Section 2, which analyses how states demanded vertical and horizontal accountability processes for the World Bank Group, including establishing the IAMs to hold them answerable for negatively affecting communities and ecosystems through financing international development projects. Section 3 argues that the IAMs can identify whether the World Bank Group is responsible and answerable, but that as bureaucracies the World Bank and IFC prioritise lending and efficiency over taking responsibility for contributing to environmental and social harm. It provides an example of how a typical "mega-loan for a mega-project," the IFC financed Pangue Dam in Chile, led protestors to make a claim to the World Bank Inspection Panel to demand accountability. Given the Inspection Panel had no remit over the IFC, this in turn led to the creation of the Compliance Advisor/Ombudsman for the World Bank Group. Throughout, the IFC's stance was reactive; it did not take responsibility for the harm caused by the dam. The case is intriguing, however, because over a decade after the first claim demanding accountability, the IFC's Compliance Advisor Ombudsman went beyond its mandate to take responsibility to provide redress for the people negatively affected by the project. The chapter concludes by arguing that the case demonstrates that IAMs can hold the World Bank Group to account but that taking responsibility requires positive actions that go beyond bureaucratic incentives and contractual obligations.

Responsibility and accountability

There is general agreement in the literature on global governance as to what constitutes accountability (Dowdle 2006; Ebrahim and Weisband 2007; Held and Koenig-Archibugi 2005). Fundamentally, it is the notion of being responsible and answerable for one's actions that affect others and are undertaken on their behalf (Byrne 1990, xi cited in Jones 1992, 73). Grant and Keohane provide an explicit definition for international relations where accountability is when "some actors have the right to hold other actors to a set of standards, to judge whether they have filled their responsibilities in light of those standards, and to impose sanctions if they determine that those responsibilities have not been met" (2005, 29; cf. Schedler 1999). Most scholars therefore recognise that giving an account is for someone, and that this is based on a social exchange that implies rights and authority, where "those calling for an account are asserting rights of superior authority over those who are accountable, including the rights to demand answers and to impose sanctions" (Mulgan 2000, 555).

These definitions highlight the relationship of who is giving account to whom, that there are standards for doing so, and that there are consequences of not meeting them. While responsibility appears in many of these definitions, the focus of responsibility is outwardly conceived in the sense that actors can be responsible for an action without necessarily accepting moral culpability (Vetterlein 2018, 547). However, responsibility is implicit in the definitions above, where those who are being held accountable accept being held to account for their actions. Often this is because they accept being responsible and answerable as part of their legitimate claim to hold authority. Being accountable, therefore, is to have legitimised power and to accept being both answerable and responsible for wielding that power. If one does not accept moral or legal culpability for one's actions in wielding authority, then legitimacy may be lost as those who previously accepted those in authority reject them.

In democratic settings from which accountability for governing legitimately is central (Dowdle 2006), the government may lose support if it does not accept moral or legal culpability for its actions, leading it to be ousted at the ballot box. Arguably, such public renderings of accountability have been transposed from primarily domestic democratic setting to international organisations. This means that we conceive of the accountability of IOs in the same way as domestic level public accountability. Public accountability is "to express a belief in that persons with public responsibilities should be answerable to 'the people' for the performance of their duties" (Dowdle 2006, 3). Thus, we hold public institutions to account through democratic elections or through bureaucratic procedures. The focus on bureaucracy has been taken up in analysing IOs (Grigorescu 2008; Woods and Narlikar 2001). For example, IOs like the World Bank are nominally held to account for the activities they have been delegated to undertake by their member states to their member states (Koenig-Archibugi 2004, 236; Grant and Keohane 2005). This system of representation is widely perceived to be the legitimate basis for IOs to undertake their duties, even though many states themselves are not democratic and are not directly answerable to their peoples. The bureaucratic basis for IO accountability is discussed further in the section below, where I argue that the moral and legal culpability of IOs is absent in bureaucratic processes and contractual delegation.

Public renderings of accountability compare with market or social accountability (Chan and Pattberg 2008; Park and Kramarz 2019), which have very different normative priors, standards, processes, and sanctions. Arguably, for market (corporations) and voluntary (non-government organisations, NGOs) accountability the normative prior is based on the fact that corporations and NGOs can wield legitimate authority in global governance, but they are guided by different goals that they seek to achieve. This determines to whom and for what they can be held to account (and by whom), including how accountability is measured according to different standards, processes, and sanctions (Mashaw 2006, 118).

Park and Kramarz (2019) argue that public institutions prioritize their responsiveness to constituencies, private institutions prefer economic benefit and profit, and voluntary institutions rank moral value foremost. These goals influence the design and execution of global governance by these wielders of authority, as well as shaping their accountability mechanisms. Following this logic, while there is a moral and legal component to legitimately wielding authority in democratic settings, for corporations legitimately wielding authority stems from market share (Fuchs 2007) and market and structural power (Guzzini and Neumann 2012); while legitimately wielding authority for NGOs stems from moral conduct that is "informed by judgments of appropriateness" (Chan and Pattberg 2008, 105). Precisely because the normative goal for corporations is economic benefit and profit, their focus is not to do what is right so much as rationally choosing to meet legal and accountability requirements to avoid incurring costs. Responsibility for corporations, and as argued next for IOs, becomes understood in a negative and backwards sense (after the event) for attributing blame, rather than viewing responsibility as a positive obligation that shapes decision-making (Vetterlein 2018, 546–7). How IOs incorporate the public understandings of accountability that limit responsibility to a negative conception is detailed next.

The public accountability of IOs

Member states confer authority and therefore obligations on MDBs as a result of member states' financial and political support (Grant and Keohane 2005). They do so through establishing the Banks' Articles of Agreement which details the organizations' mandate, structure, and function that binds the Banks to their constitutions (Woods and Narlikar 2001, 573). The system of representation is based on member states ensuring the Banks do as mandated in their Articles of Agreement and are guided by member states deliberations as Governors of the Banks. Each member state appoints a Governor (usually the state Treasurer or Minister for Finance) who meet at least annually to oversee their operations and provide policy direction for the Banks' operations. Much of the work on IOs is situated within the 'delegated' model with the aim of increasing representation to all member states given their weighting voting systems (Nye 2001; Woods 2001), or 'participatory' models of accountability that seek to hold the Banks responsible or answerable to the public given their domestic level impacts (Held and Keonig-Archibugi 2005).

The MDBs are similarly structured, modelled on the World Bank. Member states control the MDBs through the Board of Governors, who in turn delegate authority to smaller Executive Boards that oversee MDBs operations year-round. Large states appoint their own Executive Director; the rest share Executive Directors according to their capital subscriptions to the Bank in mixed constituencies. Membership dues determine states' voting shares in the Banks, creating weighted voting systems (otherwise known as the one-dollar, one-vote model). The Board of Directors is usually chaired by the President of the Bank who leads the organisation's management and staff and provides policy and project information to the Board for deliberation. The organisational structure of the MDBs allows for substantial autonomy with the Banks' management designing programs and projects for member state approval. The weighted representative voting system means that "member governments (with the obvious exception of the United States) are too far removed from the workings of the representative body (the Executive Board), which in turn exerts too little control over the staff and management of the institutions" (Lombardi 2008; Woods 2001, 84). Thus, even when member states direct the Banks to establish new policies, it may be difficult for member states to oversee implementation (Hawkins et al. 2006; Lombardi 2008).

Within democratic states, public accountability is not only for elected representatives but also for the civil service. The bureaucratic or administrative forms of accountability are also evident in IOs (Rubin 2006, 54). IOs are bureaucracies that have been delegated tasks by their member states whose authority and accountability in turn rests on state sovereignty (with an increasing presumption that this in turn rests on popular sovereignty). A bureaucratic accountability is based on a hierarchy where a superior imposes substantive or procedural standards that the subordinate must meet (Rubin 2006, 75–6).

Scholars have examined the extent to which IOs as bureaucracies are accountable through vertical and horizontal processes (Grigorescu 2008; Lombardi 2008; Woods 2001). Both processes seek to hold staff to account for their actions by management. In terms of vertical accountability, the delegation chain is longer for IOs: it is not just from management to staff but a chain from member states to management to staff. IO scholars, particularly of the World Bank, have examined how the bureaucracy is held to account by management on behalf of member states through contracts, detailed management plans, and oversight procedures (Nielson and Tierney 2003). MDB performance is therefore "evaluated by those entrusting them with powers" (Grant and Keohane 2005, 30) with the ability to enforce accountability through punishments and sanctions (Grigorescu 2008, 292). However, there are limitations to being responsible and answerable through the delegation chain. For example:

> if the World Bank lends donor funds to borrower countries for environmentally damaging projects (such as coal-fired power plants), and both donors and borrowers are satisfied, then the World Bank is perfectly accountable to both. This contractual relationship which adheres to the Banks own standards omits being held to account by those outside the contract that who are nonetheless affected by the World Bank financing the project.
>
> *(Park and Kramarz 2019, 21).*[2]

This demonstrates the limits of bureaucratic accountability because it does not take responsibility for unwanted outcomes resulting from being accountable to those with whom one has a contractual relationship (the World Bank with donors and borrowers), to the exclusion of others that may be affected by the actions of the Bank, such as people in the project area. As discussed below, the MDBs have created standards to offset the broader impacts beyond those with whom they have an accountability relationship, and the World Bank Group has a post-hoc Independent Evaluation Group to evaluate the impact of its projects including on the environment. I argue below, however, that bureaucratic imperatives limit their use to negative rather than positive understandings of responsibility.

There are also horizontal accountability mechanisms within IOs that include "internal units that perform audits, inspections, evaluations, and investigations. These units are staffed by experts charged to find ways to avoid, identify, and solve the growing number of cases of mismanagement and fraud involving IO bureaucrats" (Grigorescu 2008, 286). The rise of ombudsman, ethical conduct and integrity departments and anti-fraud and corruption units all attest to the importance of holding IOs to account (Grigorescu 2008; Hoffman and Megret 2005). For example, the World Bank Group's Integrity Vice Presidency investigates allegations of fraud and corruption in World Bank Group-financed projects.

Both vertical and horizontal forms of holding bureaucracies such as IOs to account are internal to the organization (Heldt 2018). Thus, accountability may be measured according to internal goals of the actor. Although the Banks must adhere to their Articles of Agreement specifying their technical apolitical mandates and the member states retain oversight, IOs can insulate themselves from member state control (Johnson 2014). This means that the IO can limit what they will be responsible for by establishing their own internal standards and procedures to which they will be evaluated on (or face member state sanctions). What does this mean for international bureaucracies? This raises two questions: first, do these standards provide room for the IO to enact positive responsibility that allow for discretion in seeking to obtain broadly desirable outcomes rather than merely for attributing blame for unwanted outcomes? Second, what happens if IOs fail to meet these standards?

In response to the first question and focusing here on to the case of the MDBs and environmental and social impacts: the MDBs have created environmental and social safeguards for seeking to prevent harm from their activities in financing international development projects. While these are considered the gold standard (Hunter 2008) for mitigating the negative impacts of international development financing, the MDBs have been loath to respond as to how their activities do or do not meet international environmental and human rights law, arguing that it is the role of member states to meet their international treaty obligations (Darrow 2003). Outside whether or not these standards meet international law, or even constitute global administrative law themselves (Kingsbury 1999), the standards themselves do allow positive responsibility by enabling the environmental and social safeguard specialists within the Banks the means of identifying how best to meet the needs of communities and minimise the impact on the environment in evaluating the design of a development project.

However, and as has been well documented, the possibility of enacting such positive behavioural understandings of responsibility are traded-off within the administrative process for higher order goals such as efficiency and loan approvals. In response, internal incentive structures have become entrenched that reward staff for lending volumes rather than supervising project performance (Culpeper 1997; Weaver 2008). As Ben-Artzi notes, the:

> [The] trap multilateral financial institutions fall into is entirely counterproductive for achieving their goals: from the point of view of the Banks, loans were approved and disbursed after thorough investigation into their worthiness, expected value, and returns. The various country departments also compete for budgets and therefore must disburse their given budget during the year so as not to lose funds for the following year. Therefore, making the loan can sometimes be more important than the loan's substance. (2016, 106)

The lending imperative focuses on ensuring large loans that generate a revenue stream are made to borrowers within the Banks' budget cycle (Ben-Artzi 2016, 111). Larger loans are equated with prestige and career advancement. Even when loan conditions are not being met, staff in the country departments feel pressure to disburse the loan anyway. This is combined with a lack of staff incentives and resources allocated to mainstreaming environmental and social ideas (Park 2010). The bureaucratic incentives structures therefore limit the ability of using self-prescribed standards to enable positive responsibility. Instead they become limited to being understood as standards against which one can be assigned guilt for not meeting. In sum, IOs like the MDBs have understood their responsibility in an obligatory sense, in terms of complying with their own internal procedures and guidelines rather than in a positive sense of seeking to prevent unwanted outcomes.

What happens if the organisation does not meet its standards? Not meeting environmental and social standards raises questions of both being legally and morally responsible although as outlined at the beginning of the chapter, IOs are only now having their legal immunity proscribed. In terms of being held morally responsible: IOs like the UN have been held morally culpable for following internal understandings of their rules that inhibited a response to the Rwandan Genocide (Lipson 2007). Attributing moral responsibility is, however, to recognise IOs as moral agents, which in turn require the following conditions to be met: that the IO should have a collective identity beyond the individuals that comprise it, that it exists over time, and is self-perceived; that is has a deliberative capacity and established decision-making procedures of the group as a whole; and the means of enacting those decisions (Erskine 2015, 7). Assigning IOs moral agency is to recognise that they can exercise responsibility according to ethical standards in addition to legal ones. Here the focus has been on how responsibility for IOs has been circumscribed to negative obligations of compliance compared with positive behaviours to guide desired outcomes. Arguably, this is the result of bureaucratic preferences for prior normative goals such as efficiency and lending approvals. How this limits responsibility while being accountable to member states is detailed empirically next.

The limits of accountability: the World Bank group and the IAMs

Member states argued for greater accountability of the MDBs as they became aware of a disconnect between MDB actions and desired outcomes. States attention was drawn to the inefficacy of the MDBs in the 1990s after taskforces undertaken to assess their operations revealed their ineffectiveness (Babb 2009). Member states pushed the Banks to devise measures to monitor their operations. This included establishing monitoring and evaluation tools to be implemented by newly created evaluation departments as noted above (Park 2010; Weaver 2008). Member states can direct Bank behaviour through establishing incentives to align with member state preferences and overseeing Bank activities through implementing ongoing, costly and detailed management plans (Nielson and Tierney 2003).

The IAMs of the large MDBs were created between 1994 and 2004, with an increasing number of multilateral, bilateral and private lenders adopting the model thereafter (Park 2017b). The first MDB to do so was the World Bank in reacting to an internal report (the Wapenhans report) outlining the Bank's high level of project failures, as well as a wave of environmental and social campaigns against large-scale Bank projects in the late 1980s and early 1990s, which culminated with the Narmada dam project in India. The Narmada dam was in part funded by two World Bank loans, and activists demanded the Bank address the environmental and social fall-out of the project. This led the Bank to establish an independent investigation into the effects of the dam which upheld many of the activists' claims, facilitating US and other member state demands for the instantiation of the World Bank Inspection Panel in 1993. The Inspection Panel is a three-member body that investigates claims from two or more people in a project area who may be or have been materially and adversely affected by the project financed by the World Bank. The majority of the claims are on environmental and social issues including harm to Indigenous Peoples, involuntary resettlement, a lack of information about the project and not meeting the environmental impact assessment (Park 2018).

After the World Bank created its Inspection Panel the other Banks followed suit. All of the MDBs were perceived to be non-transparent, ineffective and unaccountable. Donors like the US made it clear that greater MDB accountability was needed. The World Bank's Inspection Panel created a 'ripple effect on the global decision-making process' because the MDBs had the same major shareholders. To that end, the IDB created its mechanism in 1994, the ADB 1995, the rest of the World Bank Group in 1999, the EBRD in 2003 and the AfDB in 2004. The IAMs instituted by the Banks are both vertical in responding to member states on the Banks' Boards and horizontal in that the IAMs are a separate unit that assesses if Bank policy non-compliance led to harm at the project site. This complicates the division within the literature into delegated versus participatory accountability because the IAMs report to their member states on the Banks' Boards while being responsive to project affected people. This is because the IAMs are 'citizen-driven': the people adversely affected or likely to be can make a claim to the IAMs to hold the Banks to account (Lewis 2012).

The next section uses the case of the Pangue Dam in Chile as an example of the negative responsibility of the Banks in responding to a claim of their unaccountability in financing and investing in a project with harmful environmental and social impacts. The case is typical of a claim to the IAMs in terms of the types of harms documented although it was the largest project undertaken by the IFC at the time. It is also significant for triggering the creation of the Compliance Advisor/Ombudsman for the IFC, which pertinent to the discussion here because a decade after the first claim against IFC over Pangue, the CAO went beyond its mandate to take responsibility for the negative impacts of the IFC invested and funded project.

Holding IFC to account for the impacts of the Pangue Dam in Chile

IFC's first large-scale project, the Pangue Dam in Chile, remains controversial because of its negative environmental and social impacts. The fall-out from the project had widespread repercussions influencing IFC's projects, policies and institutions (Park 2010). Pangue also galvanised the US to demand accountability for the World Bank Group (IFC, a private sector investor and lender, and MIGA, a political risk insurer) leading to the creation of the Compliance Advisor/Ombudsman. The Bio Bio, one of Chile's largest rivers, was targeted by Empresa Nacional de Electricidad

S.A. (Endesa) a multinational corporation, to construct six hydroelectric dams, to meet Chile's increasing electricity demands. The first dam, Pangue, was designed to be the most efficient in the world 'generating 450 megawatts of power while flooding 1,250 acres, a much smaller amount than other large dams' and purportedly only requiring the resettlement of 53 non-indigenous individuals. Despite the US Executive Director's abstention from voting for the project, in April 1992 IFC authorised $170 million in loans and approved an equity investment of $4.9 million in Pangue S.A, the Endesa subsidiary undertaking the project (IFC 1992). The Pangue dam was constructed between 1993 and 1996 and began operating in 1997.[3]

As with the Narmada dam campaign against the World Bank, IFC was under intense pressure to respond to criticisms of environmental and social harm. IFC Management, like the World Bank before them, authorised an independent investigation of the impacts of the dam in 1995, by American anthropologist Dr Theodore Downing. The Downing report identified extensive deforestation, severe limitation of the Pehuenche indigenous people's land rights, and the general failure on the part of the Pehuen Foundation (established as part of its investment agreement with IFC) to meet its objectives. The projects along the Bio led to unchecked in-migration to a previously isolated area, land speculation and deforestation (Downing 1996, 5).

In response to the dam, on 17 November 1995, a local environmental and social network Grupo de Accion por el Bibio (GABB) and close to 400 Chileans, including members of the Chilean Congress, filed a complaint with the World Bank Inspection Panel. It was rejected because the Inspection Panel does not investigate IFC projects. This is despite the fact that, at that time, IFC had to meet the appropriate World Bank environmental guidelines and policies. GABB argued that because IFC shares the same President and member states as the World Bank, IFC should be investigated by the Inspection Panel (GABB 1995, 4–5). The incident provided impetus for World Bank Group President Wolfensohn to commission an internal autonomous review of Pangue's environmental and social impacts similar to the Morse report for Narmada. In 1996, Dr Jay Hair, the former head of the National Wildlife Federation and the World Conservation Union (IUCN), was appointed to undertake the evaluation.

The Pangue Inspection Panel claim triggered discussions over the need to extend the Inspection Panel to cover the World Bank Group or establish a separate mechanism (Udall 1997, 52). As with the large campaign against the World Bank's Narmada dam, the high-profile campaign against IFC highlighted the importance of an adequate response to claims of harm, and the need for an independent accountability mechanism for the World Bank Group.

Meanwhile, the Hair report investigating IFC's actions in relation to the Pangue project was completed in April 1997. It concluded that IFC was unable to enforce its own environmental and social guidelines. The report argued that there "was no evidence in the record that comprehensive and systematic monitoring of requirements to determine compliance with relevant World Bank Group requirements were either a) identified within IFC or to the project sponsor [Endesa] or b) subsequently monitored" (Hair 1997, 38). One of the institutional recommendations the Hair report made to the World Bank Group was that "IFC projects should be subjected to an Inspection Panel process such as the one currently in place at the World Bank Group's International Bank for Reconstruction and Development. Preferable, the IFC would be incorporated into the existing system" (Hair 1997, Section B, 6). While the outcomes of the investigations of the harmful impacts of the Pangue dam invested in and financed by the IFC were emerging, Endesa the company financing Pangue withdrew from IFC financing in 1998 (Park 2010). This meant that there was little that IFC could do in relation to the dam.

In response to the Hair report, on 30 September 1998 President Wolfensohn announced to the IFC and MIGA's Boards of Executive Directors that he had established the position of the CAO. Coming into effect in 1999 the CAO has vice presidential status within IFC and reports directly to the WBG President (not the IFC's Executive Vice president who manages the organisation). It has three functions: compliance, advisor, and ombudsman. The first entails the evaluation of IFC's and MIGA's compliance with their environmental and social policies through either an informal analysis or a compliance audit. Compliance audits may be triggered by the WBG president, IFC or MIGA management, the CAO, or from the ombudsman function (see below). The second role is as an advisor to IFC and MIGA staff, management and president on policies triggered by a CAO complaint, either informally or formally through regular reporting to the president and periodic reporting to the Boards. The final role is the ombudsman role, which was established to respond and mediate problems regarding people adversely affected by World Bank Group projects.

The ombudsman is significantly different than the quasi-judicial Inspection Panel processes established by the World Bank although they were both established to enact accountability. The CAO acts as an independent mediator compared to the World Bank's Inspection Panel, which determines whether people were adversely affected as a result of Bank non-compliance with its own policies. Like the other IAMs, the CAO becomes involved when it receives a complaint from peoples adversely or potentially affected but the CAO was the first of the IAMs to have a mediation function. Under its compliance function the CAO operates like the other IAMs, which may require a change in Bank behaviour if it has breached its own environmental and social safeguards.

The CAO was unique in directly attempting to influence IFC or MIGA project sponsors where they have breached IFC or MIGA policies, which the other mechanisms initially could only achieve indirectly through investigating the cause of Bank non-compliance. While all of the IAMs investigate Bank compliance, the CAO directly mediates between the affected community, IFC or MIGA, the project sponsor (corporation) and the host government. However, the ombudsman can only persuade parties to reconcile through conflict resolution and mediation. Consequently, the only leverage the CAO has is the cooperation of IFC or MIGA in investing in or guaranteeing the project. This depends on the percent IFC has invested or at what time the complaint occurs and how much IFC has invested or recouped; or whether the corporation retains political risk coverage with MIGA. Beginning with the ADB in 2003 the other IAMs would introduce "problem-solving" functions that sought to directly mediate with affected people to resolve the problem. Although the problem-solving practices of the other IAMs face bureaucratic pressures to limit this function and could be read as preferencing negative responsibility (Park unpublished). The World Bank Inspection Panel does not have a problem-solving function although the Bank created an internal Grievance Redress Service in 2015, and changes to the Panel are expected to be announced in October 2019.

The ombudsman function is crucial for providing recourse to affected people. It recommends "practical remedial action" while addressing "systemic issues that have contributed to the problems" (IFC 1999, Appendix). The process includes mediation, dialogue and conciliation leading to a report to the President, notification to the parties and, hopefully, a settlement agreement. The complaint is closed, subject to continued monitoring and follow-up. Possible outcomes include the successful settlement between the parties; an unsuccessful settlement of the parties with a report to the President outlining recommendations for a compliance investigation or unsuccessful efforts to reach settlement with a report to the President outlining that no CAO action could resolve the problem. From 2007, the second outcome automatically triggers the CAO's compliance function (Compliance Advisor/Ombudsman (CAO) 2007). A compliance audit may ascertain whether IFC and MIGA policies or a lack of monitoring failed to prevent environmental and social harm. The advisory function incorporates a learning feedback loop from the cases to the IFC and MIGA.

The creation of the CAO was not welcomed by the IFC or MIGA. The WBG was "a sometimes hostile, antagonistic, reluctant environment that has difficulty learning and changing in the newer areas of accountability, openness, and trust vis-à-vis environmental and social development results" (Dysart et al. 2003, 12). Indeed, it was not until 2009 that IFC and MIGA "made a concerted effort to institutionalise processes" for responding to the CAO's operations (Compliance Advisor/Ombudsman (CAO) 2009, 3). Moreover, IFC management responses to the CAO's compliance audits remain dismissive (Compliance Advisor/Ombudsman (CAO) 2013, 4). IFC investment officers fear the CAO and do not want to be investigated for compliance. IFC staff are overwhelmed in trying to ensure that the organisation is policy compliant with regards to monitoring and supervision. Although "interviews suggest that Management sees the Ombuds function as a net positive for IFC and wishes to support it, but the Risk Management Committee has not always ensured a constructive or usefully neutral IFC role in Ombuds cases" (Fairman et al. 2010, 27). Feedback during a review of CAO operations in 2010 revealed that the CAO was "cleaning up the mess" made by the IFC (Compliance Advisor/Ombudsman (CAO) 2012, 9).

Yet, there are limitations as to how the IAMs can clean up the mess made by the Banks. The CAO is dependent, as noted above, on the willingness of the project sponsor and the IFC. The people affected by the Pangue dam continued to be affected after Endesa withdrew its loan from the IFC in 1998. As IFC still held a 2.5% equity interest in the Pangue project, the CAO could still accept claims from affected people pertaining to the Pangue dam. In 2000, the CAO accepted a claim for mediation by a Pehuenche individual people resettled by the Panque Project on the basis that he had not been compensated sufficiently. The mediation was resolved with an agreement between the individual and the company in 2001.

Another subsequent claim was also accepted for mediation in July 2002 from a group of Pehuenche women on the basis of IFC's weak and inappropriate social and environmental mitigation measures in relation to the dam and inadequate compensation (Compliance Advisor/Ombudsman (CAO) 2019). Despite accepting the claim for mediation, it was put in jeopardy because IFC chose to exit the project, divesting from the project in the same month. They omitted telling the CAO of their decision to exit. The CAO then chose to take responsibility for addressing the claim, requesting to the World Bank Group president that she be allowed to continue with the mediation despite having no legal or contractual authority to do so. President Wolfensohn agreed to commit the CAO to respond to the claim even though IFC was no longer involved. In the CAO's assessment report on the case, they recommend the IFC publicly release the 1997 Hair report and other documents on the project's impacts, in other words, to publicly take responsibility for their actions. The CAO engaged in mediation until 2006 when an agreement was reached between the parties, and the CAO remained engaged in monitoring the agreement until 2008 (Compliance Advisor/Ombudsman (CAO) 2006).

Pangue remains an "open sore" for the IFC (Interview with IFC staff, 23 February 2009), triggering the need for accountability for publicly funded private sector investments. The case demonstrates how the private sector company chose to withdraw from an IFC loan rather than be subject to being responsible and answerable for its actions through the CAO. It also demonstrates how the IFC chose to exit from the Pangue dam in Chile in 2002 rather than address outstanding issues. It reveals the failure to take responsibility for the negative environmental and social impacts of lending and investing in a dam with harmful effects, and for not following their own environmental and social safeguards. Moreover, they failed to inform the CAO of their exit. What is striking, is the commitment of the CAO to take responsibility for the plight of the community and remaining engaged to alleviate problems despite not having the mandate or policy requirement to do so. This is unique in the case history of the IAMs (Park 2018). As a unique case, it reveals how the IAMs do incorporate responsibility but generally in a compliance sense rather than in a positive sense. Arguably, this is a result of the bureaucratic preference of the MDBs to preference lending over performance, despite having environmental and social safeguards that could be used by the Banks to take responsibility.

Conclusion

Examining if and how IOs are responsible is important given the wide reach of these actors in international relations. Over the last two decades, IOs have become much more open, taking on "democratic" norms including accountability in order to demonstrate that they are responsible and answerable for their actions. However, the basis for IOs responsiveness remains through the delegation process or systems of representation of their member states. Presumably, IOs can be held to account for meeting certain standards of behaviour or face sanctions. Yet IOs like the Multilateral Development Banks have discretion as to what those standards are and how they should be enacted. In other words, states can request answerability, but they may have little means to ensure the Banks take responsibility in a positive sense of enacted change they want to see rather than in a negative sense of duty and compliance. This chapter examined how the MDBs are responsive to their member states through public renderings of accountability, such as systems of representation and delegation to a bureaucracy. It identified the range of accountability procedures established by the Banks in response to member state demands. Section 3 analysed how the Independent Accountability Mechanisms enable member states to hold the Banks answerable for the negative environmental and social impacts of their actions, but this is prescribed by bureaucratic incentives and contractual obligations. The case study of IFC's actions in relation to the Pangue dam in Chile highlighted how accountability mechanisms could be devised to hold the World Bank Group to account through the creation of the Compliance Advisor/Ombudsman, but the case also reveals how taking responsibility goes beyond the bureaucratic incentives and contractual obligations of IOs.

Notes

1 The International Bank for Reconstruction and Development (IBRD) is popularly known as the World Bank, which also manages funds from the International Development Association (IDA). The World Bank Group (WBG) is composed of the IFC, the political risk insurer Multilateral Investment Guarantee Agency (MIGA) and the International Centre for Settlement of Investment Disputes (ICSID), which is not a lending body. IFC and MIGA have the same member states as the World Bank on their Boards but have different voting weights, and decisions for IFC and MIGA are made separately from the World Bank and from each other (i.e. by IFC and MIGA management under their Executive Vice Presidents). The President of the World Bank is also the President of the World Bank Group. Over the last decade, there has been a push to bring the separate entities closer together under the World Bank Group banner.
2 In 2013, the World Bank's Board approved a policy to only fund new coal-fired power plants in rare circumstances.
3 The following section, unless otherwise noted, is from Park (2010).

References

Babb, S. (2009). *Behind the Development Banks*. Chicago: Chicago University Press.
Ben-Artzi, R. (2016). *Regional Development Banks in Comparison: Banking Strategies Versus Development Goals*. Cambridge: Cambridge University Press.
Bradlow, D. (2019). "Multilaterals Must Earn the Right to Limited Immunity." *Financial Times*, March 28. https://www.ft.com/content/2512aa84-515d-11e9-9c76-bf4a0ce37d49 (accessed September 10, 2019).
Chan, S., and Pattberg, P. (2008). "Private Rule-Making and the Politics of Accountability: Analyzing Global Forest Governance." *Global Environmental Governance*, 8(3): 103–121.
Compliance Advisor/Ombudsman (CAO) (2006). *The Pangue Complaint Settlement Agreement between CAO and UNIMACH*, February 9, 2006. www.cao-ombudsman.org (accessed November 21 2006).
Compliance Advisor/Ombudsman (CAO) (2007). *CAO Operational Guidelines*. Washington, DC: IFC.
Compliance Advisor/Ombudsman (CAO) (2009). *Annual Report 2008–2009*. Washington, DC: IFC.

Compliance Advisor/Ombudsman (CAO) (2012). *Comments Submitted: CAO Operational Guidelines Consultation 2012.* Washington, DC: IFC.
Compliance Advisor/Ombudsman (CAO) (2013). *Annual Report 2013.* Washington, DC: IFC.
Compliance Advisor/Ombudsman (CAO) (2019). "Chile/Empresa Electrica Pangue S.A.-02/Upper Bio-Bio Watershed." CAO Cases. http://www.cao-ombudsman.org/cases/case_detail.aspx?id=93 (accessed September 13, 2019).
Culpeper, R. (1997). *Titans or Behemoths? Multilateral Development Banks.* London: Intermediate Technology Publications and Lynne Rienner.
Darrow, M. (2003). "Human Rights Accountability of the World Bank and IMF: Possibilities and Limits of Legal Analysis." *Social & Legal Studies*, 12(1): 133.
Dowdle, M. (2006). *Public Accountability: Designs, Dilemmas and Experiences.* Cambridge: Cambridge University Press.
Downing, T. (1996). "A Participatory Interim Evaluation of the Pehuen Foundation." International Finance Corporation 2067, AGRA Earth and Environment, Downing and Associates.
Dysart, B., Murphy, T., and Chayes, A. (2003). "Beyond Compliance? An External Review Team Report on the Compliance Advisor/Ombudsman Office of IFC/MIGA." *Prepared for Meg Taylor, IFC/MIGA Compliance Advisor Ombudsman*, July 24, 2003, Washington, DC: The World Bank Group.
Ebrahim, A., and Weisband, E. (2007). *Global Accountabilities: Participation, Pluralism and Public Ethics.* Cambridge: Cambridge University Press.
Erskine, T. (2015). 'Coalitions of the willing' and the shared responsibility to protect. Unpublished paper presented at an ISA Venture Research Workshop entitled "Responsibility in World Politics", 2015 in New Orleans.
Fairman, D., Joscelyne, G., and Udall, L. (2010) Internal Review of CAO Terms of Reference, Operational Guidance and Operational Practices, Final Report. Washington D.C. IFC and MIGA, CAO.
Fuchs, D. (2007). *Business Power in Global Governance.* Boulder Colorado: Lynne Rienner.
Grant, R., and Keohane, R. (2005). "Accountability and Abuses of Power in World Politics." *American Political Science Review*, 99(1): 29–43.
Grigorescu, A. (2008). "Horizontal Accountability in Intergovernmental Organisations." *Ethics & International Affairs*, 22(3): 285–308.
Grigorescu, A. (2016). *Democratic Intergovernmental Organisations? Normative Pressures and Decision-Making Rules.* Cambridge: Cambridge University Press.
Guzzini, S., and Neumann, I., eds. (2012). *The Diffusion of Power in Global Governance: International Political Economy Meets Foucault.* Basingstoke: Palgrave Macmillan.
Hair, J. (1997). *Pangue Hydroelectric Project (Chile): An Independent Review of the International Finance Corporation's Compliance with Applicable World Bank Group Environment and Social Requirement,'* IFC Internal Review. Washington, DC: IFC.
Hawkins, D., Lake, D., Nielson, D., and Tierney, M. (2006). *Delegation to International Organisations.* Cambridge: Cambridge University Press.
Held, D., and Koenig-Archibugi, M. (2005). *Global Governance and Public Accountability.* Malden, Oxford and Carlton, Blackwell.
Heldt, E. (2018). "Lost in Internal Evaluation? Accountability and Insulation at the World Bank." *Contemporary Politics*, 24(5): 568–587.
Hoffman, F., and Megret, F. (2005). "Fostering Human Rights Accountability: An Ombudsman for the United Nations." *Global Governance*, 11(1): 43–63.
Hunter, D. (2008). "Civil Society Networks and the Development of Environmental Standards at International Financial Institutions." *Chicago Journal of International Law*, 8(2): 437–477.
International Finance Corporation (1992). *IFC Board Approves Pangue Dam.* IFC Press Release No 92/32.
International Finance Corporation (1999). *IFC Annual Report 1999.* Washington, DC: IFC.
Johnson, T. (2014). *Organizational Progeny: Why Governments are Losing Control over the Proliferating Structures of Global Governance.* Oxford: Oxford University Press.
Jones, G.W. (1992). "The Search for Local Accountability." In Leach, S., ed., *Strengthening Local Government in the 1990s*: 49–78. London: Longman.
Kingsbury, B. (1999). "Operational Policies of International Institutions as Part of the Law-Making Process: The World Bank and Indigenous Peoples." In Goodwin-Gill, G., and Talmon, S., eds., *The Reality of International Law: Essays in Honour of Ian Brownlie.* Oxford: Clarendon Press.
Koenig-Archibugi, M. (2004) "Transnational Corporations and Public Accountability," Government and Opposition 39(2): 234–259.

Lewis, K. (2012). *Citizen-Driven Accountability for Sustainable Development: Giving Affected People a Voice 20 Years On*. A Paper by the Independent Accountability Mechanisms Network.http://siteresources.worldbank.org/EXTINSPECTIONPANEL/Resources/Rio20_IAMs_Contribution.pdf (accessed July 7, 2006).

Lipson, M. (2007). "Organized Hypocrisy? Peacekeeping in the United Nations." *European Journal of International Relations*, 13(1): 5–34.

Lombardi, D. (2008). "The Governance of the World Bank: Lessons from the Corporate Sector." *Review of International Organisations*, 3(3): 287–323.

Mashaw, J. (2006). "Accountability in Institutional Design: Some Thoughts on the Grammar of Governance." In Dowdle, M.D., ed., *Public Accountability: Designs, Dilemmas and Experiences*: 115–156. Cambridge: Cambridge University Press.

Mulgan, R. (2000). "Accountability: an Ever-expanding Concept?" *Public Administration*, 78(3): 555–573.

Nielson, D., and Tierney, M. (2003). "Delegation to International Organisations: Agency Theory and World Bank Environmental Reform." *International Organization*, 57(2): 241–276.

Nye, J. (2001) "Globalization's Democratic Deficit: How to Make International Institutions More Accountable." *Foreign Affairs*, 80(4): 2–6.

Park, S. (2010) *World Bank Group interactions with Environmentalists: Changing International Organisation Identities*. Manchester: Manchester University Press.

Park, S. (2018). "Claims Submitted to the Multilateral Development Bank Accountability Mechanisms 1994-2016." The Sydney eScholarship Repository, The University of Sydney. https://researchdata.ands.org.au/claims-submitted-multilateral-1994-2016/1356063.

Park, S. (2017a). "IOs in World Politics." In Baylis, J., Smith, S. and Owens, P., eds., *Globalization in World Politics*: 316–330. Oxford: Oxford University Press.

Park, S. (2017b). "Accountability as Justice for the Multilateral Development Banks? Borrower Opposition and Bank Avoidance to US Power and Influence." *Review of International Political Economy*, 24(5): 776–801.

Park, S. (unpublished). *The Good Hegemon: US Power, Accountability as Justice, and the Multilateral Development Banks*, manuscript.

Park, S., and Kramarz, T. (2019). *Global Environmental Governance and the Accountability Trap*. Cambridge, MA: MIT Press.

Rubin, E. (2006). "The Myth of Non-Bureaucratic Accountability and the Anti-Administrative Impulse." In Dowdle, M.D., ed., *Public Accountability: Designs, Dilemmas and Experiences*: 52–82. Cambridge: Cambridge University Press.

Schedler, A. (1999). "Conceptualising Accountability." In Schedler, A., Diamond, L., and Plattner, M., eds., *The Self-Restraining State: Power and Accountability in New Democracies*: 13–28. Boulder, Colorado: Lynne Rienner.

Tallberg, J., Sommerer, T., Squatrito, T., and Jönsson, C. (2013). *The Opening Up of International Organizations: Transnational Access in Global Governance*. New York: Cambridge University Press.

Udall, L. (1997). *The World Bank Inspection Panel: A Three Year Review*. Washington, DC: Bank Information Center.

US Supreme Court. (2019). "Jam et al. V International Finance Corporation: Certiorari to the United States Court of Appeals for the District of Columbia Circuit, No. 17–1011. Argued October 31, 2018—Decided February 27, 2019." https://www.supremecourt.gov/opinions/18pdf/17-1011_mkhn.pdf (accessed September 10, 2019).

Vetterlein, A. (2018). "Responsibility is More than Accountability: From Regulatory towards Negotiated Governance." *Contemporary Politics*, 24(5): 545–567.

Weaver, C. (2008). *The Hypocrisy Trap: The World Bank and the Poverty of Reform*. Princeton: Princeton University Press.

Woods, N. (2001). "Making the IMF and the World Bank More Accountable." *International Affairs*, 77(1): 83–100.

Woods, N., and Narlikar, A. (2001). "Governance and the Limits of Accountability: The WTO, the IMF and the World Bank." *International Social Science Journal*, 53(170): 569–583.

Wright, C. (2012). "From 'Safeguards' to 'Sustainability:' the Evolution of Environmental Discourse inside the International Finance Corporation." In Stone D., and Wright, C., eds., *The World Bank and Governance: A Decade of Reform and Reaction*: 67–87. London and New York: Routledge.

Zappile, T. (2016). "Sub-Regional Development Banks: Development as Usual?" In Park, S., and Strand, J.R., eds., *Global Economic Governance and the Development Practices of the Multilateral Development Banks*: 187–211. Abingdon, Routledge.

22
THE INTERNATIONAL LABOUR ORGANIZATION'S ROLE TO ENSURE DECENT WORK IN A GLOBALIZED ECONOMY

A contested responsibility?

Julia Drubel

Introduction

Sixteen million people are affected by forced labor within the private economy for the purpose of exploiting their labor power (ILO et al. 2017, 10). Forced labor constitutes a human rights violation. Responsibility to protect these rights is assigned within the International Labour Organization (ILO). In times of global markets, supply chains, production networks, and globally intertwined economies, this process has become an ever more complicated endeavor. Labor is increasingly organized within triangular employment relations[1] based on a growing and complex 'cascade system' (Barrientos 2011, 4) with a multiplicity of tiers (van der Linden 2008). These labor supply chains sometimes draw on coercion via restrictive migratory regimes, e.g., in the case of Brazilian and Indian seasonal migrant workers (Breman 2012, 4; Phillips 2013, 185), construction workers in the kafala system (Millward 2017, 756) or domestic workers under tied visa in the United Kingdom (Demetriou 2015, 5, 9). Hence, the question arises in how far actors within the ILO and the organization itself are able and willing to translate these changed contexts of global labor supply into new or adapted arrangements of responsibilities for forced labor in the private economy?

Forced labor is delineated in Convention C29 as 'all work or service which is exacted from any person under the menace of any penalty and for which the said person has not offered himself voluntarily' (ILO 1930b, Art. 2.1) and is complemented by Convention C105 regulating state-imposed labor. The ILO obliges signatory states to promote prescribed normative or legally mandated practices via conventions and recommendations and to participate in the respective procedure. It provides a two-level procedure to examine a state's compliance with normative standards. This mechanism includes the yearly review of state reports on ratified conventions by the Committee of Experts on the Application of Conventions and Recommendations (CEACR). The independent committee comprises 20 lawyers and examines the reports juridically. Cases of notable non-compliance are depicted as observations within the CEACR's report. Based on adopted observations, selected cases are further discussed within the Conference Committee on the Application of Standards (CAS). This tripartite committee meets within the confines of the annual International Labour Conference (ILC) and is a political forum in which states and social partners argue and deliberate about their compliance status. During these debates, states pass on responsibilities for forced labor on transnational corporations (TNCs) and vice versa, while the workers' representatives emphasize the shared responsibilities of states and TNCs.

Responsibility ascriptions can also be found in nonbinding instruments like recommendations and declarations (Maupin 2003; Stübig 2015, 68) or in guidelines like the core labor standards (CLS) based upon the Declaration on Fundamental Principles and Rights at Work from 1998 (Declaration on FPRW), the 2001 Decent Work Agenda (DWA), and the affirmative Declaration on Social Justice for a Fair Globalization from 2008. The ILO issues estimates under the DWA (ILO 2012, 2014a; ILO et al. 2017), and Global Reports as follow-ups of the Declaration on FPRW (ILO 2001, 2005). Moreover, 'InfoStories' (ILO 2016) as interactive online documents narrate fictitious individual life stories, i.e., how a person is trapped in forced labor (Drubel 2019). The compliance procedures, as well as the ILO's engagement with the CLS, are well documented. The chapter draws on this ILO documentation and applies a qualitative content-analysis in order to map out the ascription of responsibility within the ILO as well as by the ILO within global politics, e.g., vis-à-vis the World Bank. It further discusses possible political outcomes regarding the regulation of forced labor in the global economy.

The following section delineates the historical emergence of the prohibition of forced labor, from a regulatory approach of compulsory labor in the colonies (1929/30), to a problem mainly conceived as state-imposed (1956/57) and eventually as a problem embedded in processes of global production and consumption (late 1990s). These latter consultations and standard-based governance modes include the re-negotiation of responsibility of state actors as the primary subject of international law and the responsibility of companies and consumers. The section furthermore illustrates the ILO's conception of its responsibility in global politics. Next, the chapter reviews the ILO estimates of forced labor within the global economy to depict the phenomenon's embeddedness in global economic undertakings.

The final section maps out the responsibility assignments that are predominant within the contemporary labor law regime. These arrangements are portrayed as a specific topology of responsibility that is assigned either to different levels (global, national, local) or to a specific group of actors (states, corporations, organized crime). Moreover, the section elaborates on the topology's limits regarding conceptions of legal responsibility and mechanisms of individualizing the problem of forced labor. The chapter concludes with a discussion in how far these responsibility arrangements and the relationships that are established between actors fit the conditions under which forced labor is organized within a globalized economy.

The prohibition of forced labor in the ILO

The ILO regulates social-political issues via the adoption and promotion of normative standards.[2] It is one of the oldest international organizations and the only one with tripartite membership. The ILO has been established as a 'preventive buffer against communism, two years after the 1917 Russian Revolution' (Landau and Beigbeder 2008, 11; cf. Maupain 2009, 832) that shapes regulated national labor markets based on models of welfare capitalism. Hence, the ILO considered itself responsible for standard employees, namely 'male workers in stable full-time, unionized jobs' (Standing 2008, 358; Valticos 1996). Until today, these trajectories translate into a social protection model that is 'based on formal employment and a male breadwinner' (Standing 2008).

The ILO, a European institution in its beginnings, further assumed that the colonies would close the gap to the 'advanced economies' in terms of labor standards and issued regulations accordingly, like the prohibition of forced labor. The underlying definition of forced labor not only prescribes which measures are seen as sufficient to solve the problem (legal enforcement) but also ascribes responsibility by identifying specific actors as perpetrators, victims, or regulators. These ascriptions can be reconstructed by analyzing the 'double-discussion procedures' within the ILC in 1929/1930 and 1956/1957, including the negotiations of the Forced Labour Protocol in 2014. The section closes with the transcription of these responsibilities into modes of market-based governance during the negotiations of the Declaration on FPRW (1998).

The ILO's efforts to regulate forced labor in 1929 were influenced by the developments within the League of Nations that adopted the Slavery Convention in 1926. During the ILC, state delegates differentiated between forced labor in the colonies, including punishments, private forced labor, compulsory labor for public purposes (ILO 1929, 42), and the general obligation to work pertaining in 'all civilised States' (ILO 1929, 58). These differentiations were based on particularistic and racist ideas about 'civilizing' native labor as a moral obligation of the so-called more civilized nations (cf. Ollus 2015, 227 on patronizing language). Compulsory labor was seen as 'a regrettable necessity' to develop the colonies (Quirk 2011, 103; ILO 1929, 81).[3] Based on liberal conceptions of an autonomous individual that can sell its labor on its own terms at the market and a capitalistic development model, delegates argued that de jure freedom of choice was sufficient to end forced labor (ILO 1929, 56–57).

Thus, while the majority of delegates successfully reasoned for a regulation of compulsory labor within the colonies, workers' representatives as well as some government delegates, e.g., from Japan argued for the complete abolition of forced labor in all its forms based on considerations of 'justice and humanity' (ILO 1929, 46, 50, 56, 70, 75).[4] Forced labor was neither justifiable from an economic nor a moral point of view (cf. Ollus 2015, 227 on the humiliating and demoralizing effects of forced labor). Additionally, the universal prohibition of forced labor was not realizable via single legal provisions about the individual freedom of a person to enter or leave an employment relationship, which implicitly neglects de facto relationships of power. Instead, the broader legal-institutional framework needed adaptation, including vagrancy laws, land reservation, levying of poll taxes, and labor recruitment systems (ILO 1929, 46). One exception was the private use of forced labor that has been morally condemned within the discussions of C29 unless the company works under a public contract (ILO 1929, 72). The discussion was biased toward native forms of forced labor based on traditions of servitude, which were considered as inefficient (ILO 1929, 66). In conclusion, the idea of regulating forced labor also under consideration of competitive fairness gained acceptance. Thus, C29 has been designed to regulate forced labor in the colonial territories allowing for some exceptions.

During the negotiations of a complementary convention in the 1950s, the idea that capitalism excludes forced labor has been renegotiated. After the caesura of the Second World War, forced labor was mainly perceived as a state-imposed problem. The exposure of forced labor exacted in concentration camps under National Socialist rule in Germany and the developments within the USSR, especially during the Stalin administration, led to this dominant view.[5] Hence, in the 1950s, the UN General Assembly and the ECOSOC discussed state-imposed forms of forced labor. Based on the request by the ECOSOC (ECOSOC 1956, 7–8), the ILO Governing Body put the negotiation of Convention C105 on the agenda of the ILC. Accordingly, the 'double-discussion procedure' focused on the issue of state-imposed forced labor. The USSR which joined the ILO in 1954, suggested several adjustments, like extending C29 to the colonial territories and expanding the legal definition of forced labor to figure in other forms of coercion that are present within capitalism (ILO 1956, 517, 1957b, 355). The workers' group supported the amendments that included forced labor as a consequence of the method of payment to the worker or of debt bondage, among others.

This incorporation of the de facto affiliation between employer and employee, besides the de jure relationship, was sharply criticized as 'including even normal and incidental employer-worker-relationships' (ILO 1956, 504). Ultimately, the amendment failed due to the resistance by the governments and the employers' group, in particular (ILO 1956, 505, 508, 510; cf. Ollus 2015).[6] Correspondingly, the legal definition remained unchanged, and neither scope nor the geographic range of the definition was extended. Until today, C105 deals with state-imposed forced labor as delineated in Art. 1 (a-e) of C105 (ILO 1957a).[7]

Via the application of both conventions, the CEACR has been able to develop a detailed legal conception of forced labor. However, the ILO is not equipped to factor in significant changes in the geographic and temporal organization of work (Nußberger 2006, 59) and has been facing difficulties in defining its responsibilities within global politics. During the 1960s the ILO's membership became more heterogeneous with newly independent and less developed states joining it. The ILO framed its new responsibilities in terms of technical cooperation, basic needs, and the informal sector (ILO 1969, 279; Standing 2008). These paradigms prevailed during the 1980s and 1990s, even though by the mid-1990s pro-collective and protective regulations had been dismantled in favor of pro-market institutions, privatization, and labor flexibilization under the auspice of the World Bank which ultimately translated in devastating 'experiments' in the post-Soviet realm (Standing 2008, 364). The ILO has neither been willing nor capable of offering alternative policies, intellectual criticism of the World Bank's policies, or an argumentative strategy in reply to these developments. Turning to Standing (2008) one finds two reasons for this shortcoming, a feeling of inferiority vis-à-vis the World Bank concerning economic policies and dependency on funds from the World Bank.

The ILO instead dealt with these changing contexts of a globalized economy by promoting market-based governance forms like the CLS and developing an agenda for decent work worldwide (ILO 1999, 2017), knowing full well that it forfeited its ability to fulfill its mandate and that it runs the danger of being replaced by other agencies. Therefore, the Declaration on FPRW has been the ILC's attempt to 'establish the ILO as the primary multilateral organization on social issues in the twenty-first century [and to prevent it from] remaining on the sidelines while others, without its expertise and history, took its place.' (ILO 1998b, 9/14). The idea of fundamental rights and minimal standards regarding working conditions already existed (World Summit for Social Development 1995, §54b).

Three years later, the ILO adopted the Declaration on FPRW and established four CLS, namely freedom of association, non-discrimination, the prohibition of forced labor, and the worst forms of child labor (ILO 1998a, 2; cf. Senghaas-Knobloch 2010, 9). The CLS are based upon the obligations that are codified in the respective conventions. These standards are nonbinding but shall promote the conventions' ratification and substances regardless of ratification status (Thomann 2011; ILO 1998b, 20/4).

> The basis for evaluation under the follow-up procedures would not be legal rules as may be the case after a country had ratified a fundamental Convention; rather the issue would be whether there had been a policy failure which was so serious that the country's circumstances fell below a basic level to which no civilized nation should fall, regardless of whether or not it had ratified the fundamental Conventions.
>
> *(ILO 1998b, 4/20)*

The fear of trade protectionism and of potentially binding standards under customary law (ILO 1998b) played out into defining the CLS as minimum standards that promote negative rights of equity. They neither constitute a 'progressive agenda' nor endorse material equality and well-being (Standing 2008, 367). The ILO's approach hones in on the legal definition of forced labor as an interpersonal relationship that is understood as a criminal abbreviation from the otherwise well-functioning economy (Lerche 2007). It excludes the structural conditions under which forced labor flourishes. Even though the Declaration is equipped with follow-up mechanisms including the Global Reports that depict the stage of affairs regarding the realization of the CLS on a yearly basis,[8] it lacks pro-active policies. However, the CLS are acknowledged as universal standards whose realization is not dependent on political capacities but political will (ILO 1998b, 20/7).

Within the DWA, the ILO has identified private actors like firms and consumers as new norm addressees and has increased its responsiveness toward nontraditional representations of workers' interests (see Vosko 2002 on domestic work). However, this strengthened approachability has not been translated into new forms of representation within the ILO (Standing 2008). On the basis of successfully mainstreaming decent work into other specialized UN agencies and ultimately into the Sustainable Development Goals, it may be inferred that the ILO is reclaiming its position as advocate for social equality within global politics. Unfortunately, it does so with varying degrees of success. Given that SDG 8 relates the right to decent work with economic growth contradicts the ILO's and human rights approach (Di Ruggiero et al. 2014, 2015; Frey and MacNaughton 2016a, 2016b).

In the last decade, the ILO has increased the consideration of forced labor as embedded within the business and political-economic practices of a globalized economy (e.g., ILO 2019). Simultaneously, global value chains have not been included as an object of regulation within the Forced Labour Protocol (ILO 2014b). A significant weakness of the legal perspective is that market-dominating, leading companies have no legal liability for human rights violations of suppliers. Nonetheless, major transnational corporations (TNCs) shape the institutional settings that facilitate conditions under which abusive labor relations are reproduced. The ILO's labor law regime in comparison provides legally binding conventions that are subject to ratification and state implementation.[9] The DWA and the Declaration on FPRW provide nonbinding standards that emphasize voluntariness and address corporations as well as individuals. Nonetheless, the standard-based approach builds upon the legal enforcement approach, especially in terms of problem definitions. In conclusion, the above-depicted developments indicate a potential misfit between the de facto responsibility and its legal ascriptions.

Forced labor within the global economy

Forced labor exploitation within the private economy constitutes the most common type of forced labor (see Table 22.1). Sectors that are highly internationalized are mostly affected: domestic work, construction, production and manufacturing, agriculture and fishery, as well as mining (ILO 2014a, 5; ILO et al. 2017, 9–10).

Forced labor is exposed as a problem of globalization that has been dominantly shaped by

> a theory of political-economic practices that proposes that human well-being can best be advanced by liberating individual entrepreneurial freedoms and skills within an institutional framework characterized by strong private property rights, free markets, and free trade.
>
> *(Harvey 2011, 2)*

Table 22.1 People affected by forced labor in millions[10]

Period	Forced labor (Convention 29, Art. 2.1)		
	Private forced labor	State forced labor	Total
2005[1]	9.2	2.49	11.69
2012[2]	18.7	2.2	20.9
2017[3]	20.8	4.1	24.9
	Forced labor exploitation	Forced sexual exploitation		
2005	7.81	1.39	2.49	11.69
2012	14.2	4.5	2.2	20.9
2017	16	4.8	4.1	24.9

Sources: ILO 2005, 2012; ILO et al. 2017; drawn by the author.

[1] Date of publication of estimated minimum. Number is valid for any point in time for the period between 1995 and 2004 (ILO 2005, 12).
[2] Date of publication of estimated minimum. Number is valid for any point in time for the period between 2005 and 2011. The standard error is 7 per cent (1.4 million) and the confidence interval is 6 per cent (ILO 2012, 13).
[3] Date of publication of estimate that is based on data collected between 2012 and 2016. In sum, 89 million cases have been identified that had experiences with modern slavery, including forced marriage. The estimates for forced labor are valid for any point in time of the year 2016 (ILO et al. 2017, 5, 10, 21, 40).

Statutory regulations[11] have been gradually replaced by market-based regulations (Standing 1999, 40). Market regulation allows for higher rewards for risk-taking, fosters an atmosphere of entrepreneurship, and lowers transaction costs of economic activities. However, it also 'encourages short-termism' (Standing 1999, 42), it gives room for decision-makers to circumvent responsibilities for negative external effects including forms of social hardship (Crouch 2010). It tends to be anti-egalitarian and also permits opportunism as the monitoring capacity is rather low. Market regulation itself relies on restrictive or fiscal regulatory arrangements 'opposing protective, pro-collective regulations and institutions' (Standing 1999, 42).

Since the 1960s, TNCs use offshoring to transfer jobs to developing and industrializing economies by considerations of relative costs and the availability of suitable labor (Standing 1999, 64). 'The spatial disbursement of productive processes' (Taylor 2008, 18) into single, geographically separate units is a typical corporate strategy to maximize profits (Göbel 2010, 14; Helpman 2011, 127), to reduce risk and to enhance flexibility (Standing 1999). This approach does not only apply to the processes of production and sourcing but also the supply of labor (van der Linden 2008)[12], e.g., through employment agencies. The Malaysian government promotes this strategy of labor outsourcing to reduce labor costs, including placement fees, wage deductions, termination of contracts at the sole discretion of the outsourcing company and deportations of migrant workers (CAS 2014, 13 Part II/21). As a consequence, Malaysian-based companies can deny any obligations as an employer, reduce risks as well as costs and thereby enhance its attractiveness as a supplier for foreign lead companies. The Malaysian example illustrates how global supply chains might induce fragmented production networks in which forced labor appears beyond a lead company's direct control (Lund-Thomsen and Lindgreen 2014).[13]

The asymmetric mobility between capital and labor leads to a high elasticity in the demand of the latter since capital 'can respond to changes in the economic environment with greater ease (by moving offshore, for example)' (Rodrik 1997, 17). Thereby capital exercises control over labor in all its forms and appearances. Guaranteeing de jure freedom to choose, enter, and leave an employment relationship, hence, does not factor in these dependencies. People affected from poverty, lacking access to resources or wage labor often do not enjoy the de facto freedom to 'say no' (Widerquist 2013, 15).[14] In Qatar, for example, forced labor is common in construction work (ITUC 2017). By legally restricting the workers' mobility through the kafala system, i.e., an employer sponsorship system (cf. Babar et al. 2019), employers have disproportionate scrutiny about the worker who can be denied to change jobs or leave the country (Human Rights Watch 2019).[15]

Hence, capitalism does not preclude forced labor. It is instead necessary that states are capable and willing to enforce hard laws prohibiting forced labor, and that companies are able and willing to adhere to the law. These conditions may be lacking, especially concerning the global political economy, global supply chains, and local societal conditions. Commonly, states provide special provisions for foreign investors and export-oriented firms that create a 'dual economy of advanced production for global markets [that] coexists with the local economy, with often limited interaction between the two' (Kleibert 2015, 891). Both realms have differing effects on labor within the global value chain and the local environment. Thus, the competition for foreign direct investments, for example, might impede upon the successful eradication of forced labor. Under these conditions, the lax implementation of legal provisions might become part of a state's political economy. Alongside state strategies to attract foreign direct investments (LeBaron and Phillips 2019), local competitors might perceive forced labor as a rational business strategy[16] under conditions of price competition and refuse to follow the law (cf. Bofinger 2003 on the rationality trap; cf. Anner 2018 on price and sourcing squeeze). Even forms of state-imposed forced labor are embedded within global value chains. Cotton harvest in Turkmenistan, for example, is carried out via a state-imposed forced labor system (CEACR 2016; Evans and Gill 2017).[17] Turkmenistan's overall prominent position on the global market and the Turkmen apparel and textiles production pose a significant risk of cotton harvested by forced laborers to enter global supply chains (Anti-Slavery International 2019, 4).

Supply and demand of labor, employment relations, and ultimately, what is considered work, after all, change perpetually (Ruhs and Anderson 2012). In addition to that, as a matter of fact, 'labour is no longer politically organized within national labour markets' (Mezzadra and Neilson 2013, 97), but via different global configurations, e.g., global labor supply chains often based in migratory schemes. Transnational labor markets shape the demand and supply of labor also via migratory regimes which are not neutral frameworks.

> [T]hey are a means of *producing status*. When it comes to employment, immigration controls effectively subject workers to a high degree of regulation, giving employers mechanisms of control that they do not have over other citizens.
>
> *(Anderson 2013, 91 [original emphasis])*

Restrictive migration policies are another factor actively contributing to forced labor (cf. O'Connell Davidson 2015). Seventy-four percent of victims of forced sexual exploitation and 14 percent of victims of forced labor exploitation are located outside their country of permanent residence (ILO et al. 2017, 29–30). Coercive measures include confiscation of documents, the threat of denunciation, and limitations of freedom of movement. Processes of migration, labor outsourcing, and capital mobility manifest within different examples of cases of forced labor that have been discussed within the ILO compliance procedures in the last decade, including Eritrea, Malaysia, Paraguay, Poland, and Saudi Arabia.

The ILO's topology of responsibility and its limits

While the prohibition of forced labor is universally acknowledged, forced labor conditions remain a pervasive human rights violation around the world. In order to explain this discrepancy, the following section is going to map out how responsibility for forced labor on the one hand and its regulation, on the other hand, is ascribed. The emerging arrangements of responsibilities translate into political outcomes that are designated to abolish forced labor within the private economy. These fit the current requirements to give effect to the prohibition of forced labor to a variable extent. If key actors like states and TNCs pass responsibilities between them (see *Places of responsibility*, below) or if the responsibility ascriptions deviate from the actual state of the problem (see *Legal responsibility*, below), this has detrimental effects on the ILO's capacity to combat forced labor.

Since the ILO has been engaging in a legal liability or enforcement approach to realize its normative standards through legislative changes within ratifying states, it ascribes responsibility predominantly to the state as the primary subject of international law. While the instance of responsibility, namely C29 and the CEACR reports' conclusions, is most widely accepted, questions of who constitutes the subject or the object of responsibility remain disputatious.[18] Thus, the relationship between states as primary subjects of international law and corporations as de facto norm addressees is negotiated in terms of their responsibilities. Furthermore, the discrepancy between national regulation and transnational business activity is regularly emphasized by state and workers' delegates within the CAS discussions. Therefore, responsibility is not only located at different geographical levels and hence social contexts either at the national level or the transnational level but is also ascribed to different actors like the nation-state (labor inspection systems), corporations (labor outsourcing TNCs, labor service provider, labor agencies), or criminality (organized crime, human trafficker). This analytical differentiation is not distinct since naming a specific actor implies a reference to a specific (geographical) level.

Nonetheless, these complex arrangements can, in sum, be understood as a *topology of responsibility* considering cross-level (global, national, local) and inter-actor ascriptions. Interactor ascriptions refer to a two-dimensional or horizontal map, while the according cross-level ascriptions refer to a third, namely the vertical dimension. The metaphor of a topology helps to depict the status quo of responsibility ascriptions within the international labor law regime provided by the ILO.

In accordance, the following subsections deal with 'places of responsibility', hence, at which level responsibility is located as well as how responsibility is assigned to different individual actors. The strengths and weaknesses of this topological map of responsibility depend upon the underlying models of responsibility and the corresponding criteria to fixate responsibility applied within the ILO procedures. Thus, the concluding subsection assesses different models of responsibility, considers the problem of passing on responsibility between different actors, and identifies underlying processes of individualization in fixating (legal) responsibility. It elucidates impediments toward steering for meaningful political outcomes.

Places of responsibility

Within the CAS discussions states question their sole responsibility to regulate forced labor, and especially union members emphasize business responsibilities for forced labor. Furthermore, regarding the problem itself, criminal organizations are regularly made responsible for specific types of forced labor that are discussed within the committee. At least since 2014 discussions within the CAS explicitly consider corporations as jointly responsible for combatting forced labor. Even though states are responsible for giving effect to the prohibition of forced labor, the realization of the goals of this norm was only possible, if forced labor was no longer profitable and accessible for corporations and investors (CAS 2015, 14 Part II/10). In this regard, state delegates regularly refer to problems of nationally regulating the transnational actions of third parties, like TNCs but also networks of organized crime. The employers' group, however, emphasizes that it is not feasible to transfer responsibility to corporations since their operations depend on the legal-institutional frameworks provided by states.

States furthermore tend to argue that the causes of forced labor lie abroad in the country of origin of migrant workers who are specifically vulnerable to abusive labor relations.[19] Foreign labor service providers charge high recruiting fees and hence perpetuate systems of debt bondage. Unions from the United Arab Emirates, for example, argue that the prevalence of forced labor in Qatar is caused by foreign placement agencies that should be made responsible for it. Lack of transparency further impedes the regulation of these foreign actors (CAS 2015, 14 Part II/19-20). Thus, states and employers pass responsibility between them. As described above, both are key actors in giving effect to the legal prohibition of forced labor.

Generally, these difficulties regarding governance gaps between national regulation and transnational activity are taken seriously within the CAS committee. However, workers' delegates emphasize that corporations are obliged to respect international standards like the OECD principles and the Ruggie Principles as well as regional and national provisions, like the resolution of the European Parliament about the responsibility of European Corporations and the French Bill on extraterritorial responsibility. Unions further argue that corporate responsibility for human rights violations along the global value chain is shared among all actors, including subsidiaries, lead firms, intermediaries, retailers, suppliers, subcontractor, corporate partners, and financial institutions (CAS 2015, 14 Part II/21). Especially lead corporations had to examine if their operations are directly or indirectly involved in the violation of human rights (CAS 2016, 16 Part II/129). Thus, corporations that outsource labor via employment agencies are still responsible for observing labor law, including housing, wages, and social security contributions (CAS 2014, 13 Part II/21). The French workers' delegation emphasizes that those corporations obtaining workers from placement agencies are responsible for their employment. They cannot evade this responsibility by circumventing a formal employment relationship (CAS 2014, 13 Part II/21). Corporations should be induced by strategies of 'naming and shaming' to tackle forced labor within their value and supply chains, e.g., through measures of corporate social responsibility (CSR) (CAS2011, 18 Part II/12; 2014, 13 Part II/16).

In summary, the assigned responsibility is translated into voluntary self-regulation via corporate governance. Public actors, however, are called upon not to consider corporations that engage in forced labor in public procurements (CAS 2017, 15 Part II/28).[20]

> [R]esponsible enterprises and public entities needed to refrain from placing orders with companies associated with the violation of universal and fundamental human rights and should also abstain from participating in state-organized systems of forced labor […].
>
> *(CAS 2017, 15 Part II/28)*

Especially, receiving states are obliged to tailor corresponding measures to prevent cofinancing of state-imposed forced labor through public procurements. To realize this responsibility of corporations but also of public actors, the state delegation of Norway suggested measures to increase transparency in labor supply chains by publishing reports of labor inspections. The reports should then be subject to an ILO review (CAS 2017, 15 Part II/28).

States and corporations are passing responsibility for the realization of the prohibition of forced labor between them, while they make criminal networks and foreign labor placing agencies responsible for the problem itself. This shifting of responsibility not only creates a specific topology of legal responsibility but also includes processes of individualization. The fixation of legal responsibility with states translates into their obligation to regulate the conduct of individual (criminal) actors. Unions, however, try to fixate responsibility based on a broader model, including political and ethical considerations of power and obligation. They open up these ascriptions to more strongly consider the transnational realm as well as the topology's vertical dimension, including cross-level effects on forced labor. Unfortunately, these important additions are mainly translated into voluntary measures of corporate governance. Based on these different ways to establish responsibility, limits of the ILO's topology can be identified. Therefore, the following subsection introduces models of responsibility from a legal and ethical perspective.

(Legal) responsibility?

Responsibility in law is very often established by 'showing that a specific action or event or state of affairs has caused specific harm or loss to another' (Honoré 2010, n.p.). The criteria upon which these causal relations are described are not always 'properly attuned to the function of fixing responsibility' (Honoré 2010, n.p.). Opinion is divided upon which sort of condition must be fulfilled to call an action causal in a legal sense. It is disputed if it needs to be a necessary condition or just a necessary part of a constellation of conditions that is sufficient for the outcome. Further approaches consider 'substantial factors' and 'contributions' as conditions to fixate legal responsibility. All positions share the requirement of ensuring the 'law's commitment to vindicating rights and securing a fair distribution of risks.' (Honoré 2010, n.p.). This distribution of risks, opportunities, and responsibilities enshrined within the ILO's regulation of forced labor is not well-balanced. Certainly, employers and states cannot individually be made liable for all economic circumstances (ILO 2012), and it is neither feasible nor possible 'to trace how each person's actions produce specific effects on others because there are too many mediating actions and events' (Young 2006, 106).

Nonetheless, there is an obligation to consider how actions enable or restrict others' capacities to fulfill their potential. As described above, some people are more vulnerable to coercion than others, while other actors are more capable, due to their institutional and material situation, to affect these conditions of vulnerability. The latter, thus, have greater obligations to engage with these problems (O'Neill 1996). Unfortunately, the ILO enforcement approach did not succeed in including these obligations. A problem rendered visible not only by the exclusion of global value chains from the Forced Labour Protocol but also by the fact that if corporations are considered responsible, this responsibility is narrowed down to mechanisms of CSR. CSR, however, does not guarantee an expansion of standard obligations prescribed by market demands and legal-institutional frameworks.

Accordingly, means of any penalty within the forced labor definition only refer to direct either legal, political, or economic coercive means (ILO 2012). 'This means that, for example, working for low wages is not considered forced labor unless it results from coercion applied by the employer or recruiter.' (ILO 2014a, 4–5; CEACR 2007, 21). The interpersonal conception of forced labor neglects economic pressures or missing de facto exit options.[21] Coercion does not include 'situation[s] of people being forced into dangerous or difficult work by economic circumstances or other impersonal forces.' (Craig et al. 2007, 13).

These are factors that cannot easily be reduced to causal mechanisms or clearly responsible actors. Accordingly, the ILO states that

> the employer or the State are not accountable for all external constraints or indirect coercion existing in practice; for example, the need to work in order to earn one's living could become relevant only in conjunction with other factors for which they are answerable.
>
> *(ILO 2003, 37)*

While companies profit from specific societal conditions, they may not directly contribute to them. That is why it is problematic to hold corporations accountable for these broader circumstances. Furthermore, these issues relate to the misfit or 'the incongruence of the accountability [companies] are ascribed by society and the responsibility they are assuming themselves with their actual reach of power' (Gold et al. 2015, 488). Models of legal liability like the one the ILO is promoting do not consider all kinds of 'background conditions' and 'agents who contribute by their actions to the structural processes that produce injustice' (Young 2006, 103). Defining these processes would include a discussion of economic circumstances that delineate the 'freedom to say no' (Widerquist 2013, 15).[22]

Therefore, only state authority, in combination with individual misbehavior, leads to forced labor within a given socio-economic context (Steinfeld and Engermann 1997). However, the degree of coercion created by legal or political means utilized by an individual or corporate actor can even be less severe than the coercion created by economic circumstances.[23] In fact, from a legal perspective, it has been argued that it is the legal sanction for the nonperformance of labor which distinguishes forced or compulsory labor from voluntary labor (ILO 1930a, 136–137). Thus, if there is no legal sanction for the non-performance of the labor, either it is voluntary or it is exacted illegally under circumstances which would probably constitute an offense. This offense would be punishable in any case.

The ILO's DWA and CLS try to address this unfair distribution of 'risks and benefits for capital and labour' (ILO 1999, 3), yet, reproduce legal approaches that are solely equipped to delineate responsibility under due consideration of the actors' direct interpersonal relations. They draw exclusively on the legal text provided by C29. Even though structural conditions of forced labor, like the unequal distribution of social resources that are reinforced by economic policies, are mentioned within the broader discussions of the Global Reports and the CAS, these are not considered as a complementary part of a definition of forced labor (CEACR 2007, 20). These are instead addressed as individual vulnerabilities.

Accordingly, states and employers discuss individual misbehavior as causes of forced labor. Criminal individuals, greedy or complicit corporations, corrupt or complicit security officials that enable illegal migration, for instance, are individually responsible for deceiving or forcing individuals into abusive labor relations (CAS 2014, 13 Part II/20). Even though, the individual behavior is lastly permitted or even enforced by economic policies like the flexibilization of labor markets, restrictive migratory regimes, or resource allocation, states and employers discuss forced labor as an exclusive issue of criminal law. Via legal prosecution criminal organizations and corporations that are responsible for the problem in the first place can be identified and punished (CAS 2014, 13 Part II/17, 21). Accordingly, forced labor is discussed as a global problem, yet its roots are declared as being based on individual shortcomings (cf. LeBaron and Ayers 2013, 874).

Conclusion

The chapter asked the question in how far changed contexts of global labor supply have been translated into an adapted topology of responsibility for forced labor. It has been shown, first, that these assignments of responsibility are already laid out in the evolution of the norm against forced labor and the corresponding problem definitions; and second, that the historically grown topology of responsibility assignments is outdated due to the transnational organization of labor markets. It is based on models of legal responsibility that neglect defining cross-level effects on forced labor.

The global economy is characterized by an altered relationship between the state, labor, and business. Accordingly, market forces are being less and less mediated through national legislation, and international capital markets are disentangled from the real economy as well as from national labor markets. These conditions are constitutive of the prevalence of private forms of forced labor, and the entanglement of state-imposed forced labor. These processes become especially visible in cases that use restrictive migratory regimes to control highly flexible labor supply. Ultimately, the demand for low-cost labor and sourcing even utilizes systems of state-imposed forced labor. The pressure to realize low-cost orders placed by firms higher up the chain, e.g., in industries characterized by processes of price squeeze, increase for suppliers downwards the chain. Simultaneously, lead firms 'have no legal responsibility for the policies and operations of the firms below with which they contract' (Young 2006, 110). Similar processes are traceable in public procurements.

The legal definition that refers to direct and intentional actions is well equipped to identify and describe single cases of forced labor, yet, does not allow to consider these unintentional, indirect influences within the ascription of responsibility. Hence, it is not able to explain forced labor as a phenomenon embedded in the global economy. The chapter does not argue that the misbehavior of specific agents does not constitute a necessary condition of forced labor. However, since these legal understandings of responsibility are translated into policies like the CLS, the respective political outcomes are in danger of treating the interpersonal relationships as a sufficient condition of forced labor. Since forced labor results 'from the participation of thousands or millions of people in institutions and practices that produce unjust results' (Young 2006, 120), an interpersonal understanding of responsibility is deficient. Hence, the conforming topology of responsibility is not equipped to navigate through these relations and to pin down responsibilities of key actors effectively (see Mende and Drubel 2020 on models of business responsibility for modern slavery).

The ILO has furthermore not been very successful in establishing a forum to deal with migration. Its conventions on migration are either deficiently ratified (with 24 to 50 ratifications) or abrogated and withdrawn (ILO 2018). Interestingly, even though employment agencies are made answerable for situations of forced labor, especially if these operate illegally, they are again not understood as an object of regulation in terms of a broader policy strategy to combat forced labor. The conventions to regulate private employment agencies are also barely ratified and hence, unfold only limited effects within the classical labor law regime (ILO 2018, cf. Standing 2008 on the ILO's reluctance to acknowledge private intermediaries). Future discussions of the ILO's responsibility topology should include those issues that are not identified as important objects of regulation within the ILO's labor law regime. Migration, as well as economic policies of labor supply, constitute such white areas.

Ultimately, states and corporations relativize their responsibility by blaming individual, criminal actors – instead of acknowledging how migratory regimes, labor laws, the global political economy, including processes of price and sourcing squeeze and other legal-institutional settings of the internationalized economies enable and demand these forms of labor exploitation. Hence, processes of fixating responsibility remain inadequate in light of the global political economy of forced labor. The ILO's topology of legal responsibility no longer meets the conditions under which forced labor is reproduced.

Notes

1 Triangular employment relations entail not only the producer or service provider employing a worker (dyadic relation), but so-called intermediaries that legally employ the worker. Labor force is then leased to a company that is licensed to issue directives. Hence, even though legally there is one employer, namely the intermediary, in social reality triangular employments describe labor relations with more than one employer.
2 The ILO furthermore provides technical cooperation programmes that are nowadays aligned with the DWA, e.g., Decent Work Country Programmes.
3 This is comparable with views of poverty as a required motivation for work in mercantilist societies and the desideratum of consumption in today's advanced economies (Steinfeld and Engermann 1997, 109).
4 For the composition of the ILC and the underrepresentation of those affected see ILO (1929, 45).
5 Delegations from Denmark and Sweden delivered a suggestion to include 'concentration camps and deportation camps' in the preamble of the convention (ILO 1956, 508).

6 Within the historical context of the East-West-Conflict, some delegations accused the USSR to not work on content aspects but rather to use a variety of suggestions to stall the negotiations, ultimately leading to its failure. Its adjustments would denote 'a deliberate misinterpretation of the definition of "forced labour"' (ILO 1956, 504) to weaken the ILC's efforts to conclude a forced labor convention.
7 The article includes the following forms of state imposed forced labor: '(a) as a means of political coercion or education or as a punishment for holding or expressing political views or views ideologically opposed to the established political, social or economic system; (b) as a method of mobilising and using labour for purposes of economic development; (c) as a means of labour discipline; (d) as a punishment for having participated in strikes; (e) as a means of racial, social, national or religious discrimination'.
8 In 2001, 2005, 2009 the Global Reports dealt with forced labor. Follow-up mechanisms further allow for the ascription of complementary reporting duties by the Governing Body, see ILO (1919, Art. 19).
9 The ILO further provides follow-up mechanisms to improve ratification and application of the CLS and furthermore provides technical assistance to support states in realizing decent working conditions.
10 Numbers displayed within the table cannot be compared to each other due to different methodologies, with regard to data from 2005 and 2012 see ILO (2012, 17).
11 Including among others protective regulations (workers' protection, preventing abusive relations) and fiscal regulations (taxes, subsidies to encourage/ discourage certain activities).
12 In the beginning of outsourcing strategies states have been able to provide highly flexible, cheap and subversive labor. Developing states were able to 'mould disciplined (often largely female) and flexible labor forces [through] state imposed extensive regulatory and more direct controls on workers, often including restrictive legislation banning unions in Export Processing Zones (or everywhere) and freeing employers in export industries from limits on working time, wages or benefits' (Standing 1999, 64).
13 There is a lively debate about whether, and if so, how global supply chains influence labor standards. It has been argued that their effects on labor standards depend on the financial strategy of the lead firm. While foreign direct investments may raise labor standards, subcontracting schemes depress them (Mosley 2011).
14 Widerquist (2013, 15) defines freedom as 'the effective power to accept or refuse active cooperation with other willing people – in short – freedom as the power to say no'.
15 Until September 2018, labor migrants were legally prohibited from leaving the country without the permission of their employers. The Qatari Emir signed a decree that allowed about 1.5 million foreign workers to leave Qatar without permission of their employers (ITUC 2018). It excluded workers not covered by the Labor Law including those in the military, public sector, and domestic work, and allowing employers to further exclude some other workers (Human Rights Watch 2019).
16 Furthermore, corruption can constitute structural conditions in which forced labor can thrive, either on the side of state officials in preventing inspections, or on the side of labor inspectors. Finally, business is more likely to succeed in establishing forced labor relations, if based on socially accepted norms and structures, e.g. alongside racist, sexist or other axes of inequality justified by caste, tradition, religion or other beliefs.
17 Forced labor in Central Asia is also connected to migratory pressures, employment agencies and trafficking schemes. These forms of forced labor are in the case of Turkmenistan not discussed within the CEACR or the CAS. The effects of state enforced labor on employment loss and hence an increased pressure to migrate for work are also not considered within the ILO.
18 The instance of responsibility describes the norm or entity that delineates and evaluates an actor's responsibility and in how far it has been or should have been met. The subject of responsibility refers to the entity who is made responsible for something, who has to answer for something, while the object of responsibility refers to the issue an entity is responsible for.
19 States further tend to describe the global nature of forced labor and that every state is affected. This rhetoric is mainly aimed at discrediting the choice of CAS-cases. It implies that cases are not chosen due to their severeness but either randomly or politically.
20 The following citation refers to the case of shipbuilding in Poland. It is very common that shipbuilders outsource labor. In the Polish case some of these workers originated from state imposed forced labor schemes established by North Korea.
21 While the ILO indeed considers aspects of de jure exit options, it does not consider if the overall economic conditions impede leaving an abusive employment relationship.
22 Lerche (2007) emphasizes that the ILO's approach includes conceptions of forced labor as criminal abbreviation from an otherwise well-functioning global economy and renders these legal conceptions

problematic. Their basis in historical ideas has also been critically discussed by Ollus (2015). The current chapter additionally shows, how capitalistic models of economic development assume that market based economies preclude forced labor, since they provide individual de jure freedoms.

23 Steinfeld and Engermann (1997, 109) argue that job exit that is punishable by twelve days of jail is a less severe threat compared to a life of social exclusion and on public welfare.

References

Anderson, B.L. (2013). *Us and Them?: The Dangerous Politics of Immigration Control*. Oxford: Oxford University Press.
Anner, M. (2018). "CSR Participation Committees, Wildcat Strikes and the Sourcing Squeeze in Global Supply Chains." *British Journal of Industrial Relations*, 56(1): 75–98.
Anti-Slavery International (2019). *Turkmen Cotton and the Risk of Forced Labour in Global Supply Chains*. London: Anti-Slavery International.
Babar, Z., Ewers, M., and Khattab, N. (2019). "Im/mobile Highly Skilled Migrants in Qatar." *Journal of Ethnic and Migration Studies*, 45(9): 1553–1570.
Barrientos, S. (2011). *'Labour Chains': Analysing the Role of Labour Contractors in Global Production Networks*. Manchester: Brooks World Poverty Institute.
Bofinger, P. (2003.) *Grundzüge der Volkswirtschaftslehre: [eine Einführung in die Wissenschaft von Märkten]*. München: Pearson Studium.
Breman, J. (2012). *Outcast Labour in Asia: Circulation and Informalization of the Workforce at the Bottom of the Economy*. New Delhi: Oxford University Press.
CAS (2011). International Labour Conference, 100th session. Report of the Committee on the Application of Standards. Extracts from the Record of Proceedings, Geneva: International Labour Office.
CAS (2014). International Labour Conference, 103rd session. Report of the Committee on the Application of Standards. Extracts from the Record of Proceedings, Geneva: International Labour Office.
CAS (2015). International Labour Conference, 104th session. Report of the Committee on the Application of Standards. Extracts from the Record of Proceedings, Geneva: International Labour Office.
CAS (2016). International Labour Conference, 105th session. Report of the Committee on the Application of Standards. Extracts from the Record of Proceedings, Geneva: International Labour Office.
CAS (2017). International Labour Conference, 106th session. Report of the Committee on the Application of Standards. Extracts from the Record of Proceedings, Geneva: International Labour Office.
CEACR (2007). *Eradication of Forced Labour: Report III (Part 1B) General Survey*. 1st ed. International Labour Conference, 96th session. Geneva: International Labour Office.
CEACR (2016). *Report of the Committee of Experts on the Application of Conventions and Recommendations*. International Labour Conference, 105th session. Report III (Part 1A). Application of International Labour Standards 2016 (I). Geneva: International Labour Office.
Craig, G., Gaus, A., Wilkinson, M., Skrivankowa, K., and McQuade, A. (2007). *Contemporary Slavery in the UK: Overview and Key Issues*. York: Joseph Rowntree Foundation.
Crouch, C. (2010). "CSR and Changing Mode of Governance: Towards Corporate Noblesse Oblige?" In Utting, P., and Marques, J. C., eds., *Corporate Social Responsibility and Regulatory Governance: Towards Inclusive Development?* New York: Palgrave Macmillan.
Demetriou, D. (2015). "'Tied Visas' and Inadequate Labour Protections: A Formula for Abuse and Exploitation of Migrant Domestic Workers in the United Kingdom." *Anti-Trafficking Review*, (5): 69–88.
Di Ruggiero, E., Cohen, J. E., and Cole, D. C. (2014). "The Politics of Agenda Setting at the Global Level: Key Informant Interviews Regarding the International Labour Organization Decent Work Agenda." *Globalization and Health*, 10(56): 1–10.
Di Ruggiero, E., Cohen, J. E., Cole, D. C., and Forman, L. (2015). "Competing Conceptualizations of Decent Work at the Intersection of Health, Social and Economic Discourses." *Social Science & Medicine* (1982) 133: 120–127.
Drubel, J. (2019). "Regulation by Visibility: New Forms of Global Social Governance." *Global Social Policy* 40(2), online first.
ECOSOC (1956). Resolutions adopted by the Council during its twenty-first session.
Evans, J., and Gill, A. (2017). *"We Can't Refuse to Pick Cotton": Forced and Child Labor Linked to World Bank Group investments in Uzbekistan*. New York: Human Rights Watch.
Frey, D. F., and MacNaughton, G. (2016a). "A Human Rights Lens on Full Employment and Decent Work in the 2030 Sustainable Development Agenda." *SAGE Open* 6(2): 1–13.

Frey, D. F., and McNaughton, G. (2016b). "Full Employment and Decent Work in the Post-2015 Development Agenda." In N. Shawki, ed., *International Norms, Normative Change, and the UN Sustainable Development Goals*: 185–201. Lanham, Boulder, New York, London: Lexington Books.

Göbel, T. (2010). *Decent Work and Transnational Governance: Multi-stakeholder Initiatives' Impact on Labour Rights in Global Supply Chains*. Baden-Baden: Nomos.

Gold, S., Trautrims, A., and Trodd, Z. (2015). "Modern Slavery Challenges to Supply Chain Management." *Supply Chain Management: An International Journal*, 20(5): 485–494.

Harvey, D. (2011). *A Brief History of Neoliberalism, Reprinted*. Oxford: Oxford University Press.

Helpman, E. (2011). *Understanding Global Trade*. Cambridge, MA: The Belknap Press of Harvard University Press.

Honoré, A. (2010). "Causation in the Law." In Zalta, E. N., ed., *The Stanford Encyclopedia of Philosophy* (Winter 2010 edition): n.p. https://plato.stanford.edu/archives/win2010/entries/causation-law/ (accessed March 31, 2021).

Human Rights Watch (2019). *World Report 2019: Qatar – Events of 2018*, New York. https://www.hrw.org/world-report/2019/country-chapters/qatar#b94615 (accessed June 24, 2019).

ILO (1919). The Constitution of the International Labour Organization (as amended by 1974).

ILO (1929). International Labour Conference, 12th session in May–June. Record of Proceedings, Vol. I (Part 1–3; including the General Discussion on Forced Labour). Geneva: International Labour Office.

ILO (1930a). International Labour Conference, Item I on the Agenda of the 14th session in June. Second Discussion, Report I: Forced Labour. Geneva: International Labour Office.

ILO (1930b). Forced Labour Convention: C 29. Adopted June 28th at the International Labour Conference, 14th session, Geneva.

ILO (1956). International Labour Conference, 39th session in June. Record of Proceedings, (Part 1–3, including the General Discussion on Forced Labour, Item VI on the Agenda). Geneva: International Labour Office.

ILO (1957a). Abolition of Forced Labour Convention: C105. Adopted June 25th at the International Labour Conference, 40th session, Geneva.

ILO (1957b). International Labour Conference, 40th session in June. Record of Proceedings, (Part 1–3, including discussion and adoption of the Abolition of Forced Labour Convention). Geneva: International Labour Office.

ILO (1969). International Labour Conference, 53rd session in June. Record of Proceedings, (Part 1–3). Geneva: International Labour Office.

ILO (1998a). ILO Declaration on Fundamental Principles and Rights at Work and its Follow-up. Adopted at the International Labour Conference, 86th session in June. Record of Proceedings Vol. II (including Authentic Texts). Geneva: International Labour Office.

ILO (1998b). International Labour Conference, 86th session in June. Record of Proceedings Vol. I (including Provisional Record). Geneva: International Labour Office.

ILO (1999). *Decent Work: Report of the Director-General* to the International Labour Conference, 87th session in June. Geneva: International Labour Office.

ILO (2001). *Stopping forced labour: Report of the Director General – Global Report under the Follow-Up to the ILO Declaration on Fundamental Principles and Rights at Work*. Geneva: International Labour Office.

ILO (2003). *Fundamental Rights at Work and International Labour Standards*. Geneva: International Labour Office.

ILO (2005). *A Global Alliance against Forced Labour: Report of the Director General – Global Report under the Follow-Up to the ILO Declaration on Fundamental Principles and Rights at Work*. Geneva: International Labour Office.

ILO (2012). *ILO Global Estimate of Forced Labour: Results and Methodology*. Geneva: International Labour Office.

ILO (2014a). *Profits and Poverty: The Economics of Forced Labour*. Geneva: International Labour Office.

ILO (2014b). Protocol of 2014 to the Forced Labour Convention, 1930. Adopted June 11th at the International Labour Conference, 103rd session, Geneva.

ILO (2016). Forced labour: Deceptive recruitment and coercion. http://www.ilo.org/infostories/Stories/Forced-Labour/Deceptive-Recruitment-and-Coercion (accessed July 27, 2017).

ILO (2017). Report VI: Fundamental Principles and Rights at Work. From Challenges to Opportunities: A Recurrent Discussion on the Strategic Objective of Fundamental Principles and Rights at Work, Under the Follow-up to the ILO Declaration on Social Justice for a Fair Globalization, 2008. International Labour Conference, 106th session, Item VI on the Agenda, Geneva.

ILO (2018). NORMLEX Information System on International Labour Standards (ILO database). Ratification by Convention and Subject. https://www.ilo.org/dyn/normlex/en/f?p=NORMLEXPUB:1 (accessed March 31, 2021).

ILO (2019). Committee on Decent Work in Global Supply Chains. https://www.ilo.org/ilc/ILCSessions/previous-sessions/105/committees/supply-chains/lang--en/index.htm (accessed June 29, 2019).

ILO, Walk Free Foundation, and IOM (2017). *Global Estimates of Modern Slavery: Forced Labour and Forced Marriage*. Geneva: International Labour Office.

ITUC (2017). ILO Extends Probe into Forced Labour of Migrant Workers in Qatar. https://www.ituc-csi.org/ilo-extends-probe-into-forced?lang=en (accessed June 24, 2019).

ITUC (2018). ITUC, BWI and ITF Welcome End of Exit Permits for 1.5 Million Migrant Workers in Qatar. https://www.ituc-csi.org/ituc-bwi-and-itf-welcome-end-of?lang=en (accessed June 24, 2019).

Kleibert, J. M. (2015). "Islands of Globalisation: Offshore Services and the Changing Spatial Divisions of Labour." *Environment and Planning A*, 47(4): 884–902.

Landau, E. C., and Beigbeder, Y. (2008). *From ILO Standards to EU Law: The Case of Equality Between Men and Women at Work*. Leiden and Boston: Martinus Nijhoff Publishers.

LeBaron, G., and Ayers, A. J. (2013). "The Rise of a 'New Slavery'? Understanding African Unfree Labour through Neoliberalism." *Third World Quarterly*, 34(5): 873–892.

LeBaron, G., and Phillips, N. (2019). "States and the Political Economy of Unfree Labour." *New Political Economy*, 24(1): 1–21.

Lerche, J. (2007). "A Global Alliance against Forced Labour?: Unfree Labour, Neo-Liberal Globalization and the International Labour Organization." *Journal of Agrarian Change*, 7(4): 425–452.

Lund-Thomsen, P., and Lindgreen, A. (2014). "Corporate Social Responsibility in Global Value Chains: Where Are We Now and Where Are We Going?" *Journal of Business Ethics*, 123(1): 11–22.

Maupain, F. (2009). "New Foundation or New Facade?: The ILO and the 2008 Declaration on Social Justice for a Fair Globalization." *European Journal of International Law*, 20(3): 823–852.

Maupin, F. (2003). "International Labour Organization: Recommendations and Similar Instruments." In D. Shelton, ed., *Commitment and Compliance: The Role of Non-binding Norms in the International Legal System*: 372–392. Oxford: Oxford University Press.

Mende, J. and Drubel, J. (2020). "At the Junction: Two Models of Business Responsibility for Modern Slavery." *Human Rights Review*, 21: 313–335.

Mezzadra, S., and Neilson, B. (2013). *Border as Method, or, the Multiplication of Labor*. London: Duke University Press.

Millward, P. (2017). "World Cup 2022 and Qatar's Construction Projects: Relational Power in Networks and Relational Responsibilities to Migrant Workers." *Current Sociology*, 65(5): 756–776.

Mosley, L. (2011). *Labor Rights and Multinational Production*. Cambridge and New York: Cambridge University Press.

Nußberger, A. (2006). "Die Implementierung der sozialrechtlichen Konventionen der Internationalen Arbeitsorganisation und des Europarats." In Becker, U., von Maydell, B.B., and Nußberger, A., eds., *Die Implementierung internationaler Sozialstandards: Zur Durchsetzung und Herausbildung von Standards auf überstaatlicher Ebene*: 57–78. Baden-Baden: Nomos.

O'Connell Davidson, J. (2015). *Modern Slavery: The Margins of Freedom*. Basingstoke: Palgrave Macmillan.

Ollus, N. (2015). "Regulating Forced Labour and Combating Human Trafficking: The Relevance of Historical Definitions in a Contemporary Perspective." *Crime, Law and Social Change*, 63(5): 221–246.

O'Neill, O. (1996). *Tugend und Gerechtigkeit: Eine konstruktive Darstellung des praktischen Denkens*. Berlin: Akademie-Verlag.

Phillips, N. (2013). "Unfree Labour and Adverse Incorporation in the Global Economy: Comparative Perspectives on Brazil and India." *Economy and Society*, 42(2): 171–196.

Quirk, J. (2011). *The Anti-slavery Project: From the Slave Trade to Human Trafficking*. Philadelphia: University of Pennsylvania Press.

Rodrik, D. (1997). *Has Globalization Gone Too Far?* Washington: Institute for International Economics.

Ruhs, M., and Anderson, B., eds. (2012). *Who Needs Migrant Workers?: Labour Shortages, Immigration and Public Policy*. Oxford: Oxford University Press.

Senghaas-Knobloch, E. (2010). *Sisyphus at Work: On the Efforts to Achieve a Fair, Internationally Recognised Labour, and Social Order*, Bremen.

Standing, G. (1999). *Global Labour Flexibility: Seeking Distributive Justice*. Basingstoke: Macmillan.

Standing, G. (2008). "The ILO: An Agency for Globalization?" *Development and Change*, 39(3): 355–384.

Steinfeld, R. J., and Engermann, S. L. (1997). "Labor – Free or Coerced? A Historical Reassessment of Differences and Similarities." In Brass, T., and van der Linden, M., eds., *Free and Unfree Labour: The Debate Continues*: 107–126. Bern and New York: Peter Lang.

Stübig, S. (2015). *Flexibilität und Legitimität in der ILO: Ursachen der Akzeptanz von Kernarbeitsnormen*. Wiesbaden: Springer VS.

Taylor, M. (2008). "Power, Conflict and the Production of the Global Econ." In Taylor, M., ed., *Global Economy Contested: Power and Conflict Across the International Division of Labor*: 11–31. London & New York: Routledge.

Thomann, L. (2011). *Steps to Compliance with International Labour Standards: The International Labour Organization (ILO) and the Abolition of Forced Labour*. Wiesbaden: VS Verlag.

Valticos, N. (1996). "The ILO: A Retrospective and Future View." *International Labour Review*, 135(3-4): 473–480.

van der Linden, M. (2008). "The 'Globalization' of Labour and Working-class History and Its Consequences." In Lucassen, J., ed., *Global Labour History: A State of the Art*: 13–38. Bern and New York: Peter Lang.

Vosko, L.F. (2002). "'Decent Work': The Shifting Role of the ILO and the Struggle for Global Social Justice." *Global Social Policy*, 2(1): 19–46.

Widerquist, K. (2013). *Independence, Propertylessness, and Basic Income: A Theory of Freedom as the Power to Say No*. New York: Palgrave Macmillan.

World Summit for Social Development (1995). Programme of Action: WSSD. Chapter 3, Copenhagen.

Young, I. M. (2006). "Responsibility and Global Justice: A Social Connection Model." *Social Philosophy and Policy*, 23(1): 102–130.

23
BUSINESS AND RESPONSIBILITY FOR HUMAN RIGHTS IN GLOBAL GOVERNANCE

David Jason Karp

Introduction

The policy field of business and human rights can be viewed as one example of a broader trend of the 'rise of responsibility' in world politics today (Hansen-Magnusson and Vetterlein 2020). This chapter investigates this in three sections. The first section provides an overview of the way the idea of 'responsibility' has been conceptualized in the literature—as well as elsewhere in the current Handbook—in relation to other related concepts such as accountability and duty. The chapter goes against the grain of some of this literature by viewing 'responsibility' as an umbrella category that transcends easy placement on any one side of the binary dichotomies that might be drawn to define it, such as those between prospective and retrospective, negative and positive, moral and legal, or discretionary and non-discretionary obligations. The concept of responsibility helps to structure thought on the questions of why, for what and to whom agents are answerable for their conduct. This theorization enables the second part of the chapter to situate contemporary 'business and human rights' practices within a broader historical context going back to the colonial period. This section emphasizes continuity alongside change, thereby problematizing the question of what is truly new and/or 'rising' within this field of practice. The third section analyzes and evaluates the most significant recent policy initiative in this area, the UN Guiding Principles on Business and Human Rights (UNGPs). Together, these three sections generate an analysis of the forms of legal, moral, and political responsibilities for human rights that contemporary global governance initiatives are assigning/attributing (or not) to business actors. The UNGPs are consequentialist and assign responsibilities that are both legal and moral in nature, but they underemphasize political responsibility.

Theorizing responsibility in world politics

The existing literature, particularly in the area of the corporate social responsibility of businesses, often defines 'responsibility' in relation to a perceived opposite such as 'accountability' or 'duty'. For example, a rich and insightful article by Vetterlein (2018) contrasts responsibility and accountability. Accountability discourse in global governance has asked primarily empirical questions of how agents can be made to change and/or to answer for breaches of international rules and norms, outside of the context of bounded and legally/politically authoritative sovereign states (Grant and Keohane 2005). This has led to a retrospective focus on holding agents to account for breaches of negative obligations. Vetterlein (2018) tracks the rise of responsibility discourse as an alternative to this legacy of 'accountability', emphasizing that responsibility is used to invoke obligations that are prospective and positive, and contains relational, discretionary, and commitment-based aspects. Similarly, Shadmy's chapter in the current Handbook defines responsibility in the law prospectively, as involving spheres of care and relationships, which she aims to contrast with a traditional understanding of 'duty'. On the one hand, her chapter contains valuable insights for the sake of understanding the idea of responsibility in contemporary legal discourse. But on the other hand, it is important to note that her prospective conceptualization of the term 'responsibility' in legal theory *contrasts* with Hart's (1968, 210–230) seminal discussion, which defines it in a primarily retrospective mode (Karp 2015, 153): in a terms of a role that could or should have been performed better in the past, leading to the valid attribution of guilt.

My own research contributes to this theme by analyzing the nature of duties and responsibilities as prospective and retrospective (Karp 2015), negative and positive (Karp 2020b), discretionary and non-discretionary (Karp 2009), and as related to the capacities and authority of the agents who bear them (Karp 2014). However, this work differs from the ideas in the literature mentioned above because it views duties and responsibilities as involving *both* sides of each of these putatively binary distinctions, rather than being sharply separable into one side or another. Duties can be both prospective *and* retrospective (Miller 2001), justice-based (non-discretionary) *and* virtue-based (discretionary) (O'Neill 1996), negative *and* positive (Linklater 2006; Shue 1980). Responsibility, too, should be understood as *both at once* along each of these axes, rather than needing to be defined as on one side or the other. The concept of responsibility builds on this dual nature of duties, and simultaneously activates a further and broader set of questions about why agents are responsible for their conduct and to whom. This short chapter cannot possibly defend each of these points comprehensively while still analyzing its case. Therefore, it focuses on a few key areas which are seen to represent the 'broadening' of responsibility discourse beyond an exclusive focus on negative, retrospective and non-discretionary duties. Specifically, it aims to show what light can be shed on the policy field of business and human rights by conceptualizing responsibilities as discretionary/non-discretionary; as related to questions of authority; and as combining (interrelated) legal, political and moral dimensions.

The four major philosophical traditions that have structured the question of what constitutes responsible action are consequentialism, deontology, discourse ethics, and virtue ethics (for an excellent critical overview, see Hutchings 2018). Consequentialism holds that responsibility consists in achieving the right outcomes (see Table 23.1). Deontology holds that responsibility consists in taking the right action for the right reasons and/or in aligning one's beliefs and actions with the right rules. Discourse ethics holds that responsibility consists in doing whatever can achieve a consensus in an open and power-free discussion amongst all affected stakeholders. Virtue ethics holds that responsibility rests in the contextual judgment of a moral agent who has the requisite character and experience to take the best decisions.

An unresolved tension cuts across these approaches. This is the tension between discretionary and non-discretionary duties. Non-discretionary duties arise from a prescription that moral agents need to disregard their own subjective judgments about what to do, in favor of following an intersubjectively agreed or objectively determined (and often context-independent) set of moral rules and requirements. Discretionary duties, by contrast, permit agents to exercise discretion about when, how and in which way to act on moral principles and standards (Karp 2009; Meckled-Garcia 2008). This distinction has its roots in earlier discussions of 'perfect' and 'imperfect' duties (linked respectively to non-discretionary and discretionary duties), which has

Table 23.1 What constitutes responsibility approaches to global ethics?

Approach to global ethics	What constitutes responsible action?
Consequentialism	Responsibility consists in achieving the right outcomes.
Deontology	Responsibility consists in taking the right action for the right reasons and/or in aligning one's beliefs and actions with the right rules.
Discourse ethics	Responsibility consists in doing whatever can achieve a consensus in an open and power-free discussion among all affected stakeholders.
Virtue ethics	Responsibility rests in the contextual judgment of a moral agent who has the requisite character and experience to take the best decisions.

appeared political thought of Grotius, Hume and Kant, among others (Schneewind 1990). These can be understood as contested cluster concepts that explore how different kinds and categories of responsibility relate to one another within an overall ethical theory. For example, consequentialist ethics holds that responsible action consists in achieving the right outcomes. But how is this to be operationalized? The desired outcomes, whatever they are, could be achieved by crafting a set of specific rules and requirements that all agents need to follow. Say that social science research could establish that if everyone does A, B, C, in a way that is enforced/policed effectively by D, then this is likely to lead to outcome E. This makes E look like something that can be achieved by removing discretion from agents and requiring that everyone follows the rules. However, consequentialism is also compatible with requiring all agents to commit to a general outcome-based principle such as 'do no harm', and then permitting agents maximum discretion about how to achieve this end—with authoritative intervention only occurring retrospectively in instances of intentional and egregious violations. The former model is non-discretionary and the latter model is discretionary, but both stem from consequentialist ethics. Similarly, virtue ethics is often thought of as consisting entirely of discretionary responsibility: responsible action, on this view, consists in agents' properly executed judgments about the right thing to do in particular situations and contexts. However, this interpretation overlooks that Aristotle's (1996) original formulation of virtue ethics required most people to *defer* to the authority of what a virtuous agent would decide: on the assumption that most people lack the required skills, experience, or character to judge on their own. This alternative interpretation makes responsible action seem largely non-discretionary, even within a virtue-ethics approach. This is an illustration of how a distinction between discretionary and non-discretionary duties first relates to questions of authority; and second cuts across the main approaches to responsibility in moral/political philosophy rather than sitting neatly with any one of them. The next two sections apply these insights to the history and contemporary policy of businesses' responsibility for human rights, through which the chapter also develops its definitions of legal, political and moral responsibility.

Historical context: four models of businesses' responsibility for human rights in modern history

Private-sphere economic actors' ability to have detrimental effects on human lives is not unique to our era. What has changed over time are the strategies readily available to and/or employed by relevant governance actors in order to respond. This, in turn, connects with changes and continuities in the predominant structure of international organization within which such attempts to respond have occurred. This section identifies four different models, not with the intention of claiming that they are sharply separable in the real world, but rather, in order analytically to distil predominant features from each context that might bleed into and/or shape the others.

First, in the era of the existence of the East India Company (1600–1873), transnational economic entities were themselves engaged in an infamous form of governance over colonized parts of the world. The public and the private became blurred as they increasingly engaged in direct rule over colonized peoples. This intersected with a broader set of imperial and colonial global power relations. Large trading companies, in doing what they did, effectively acted as arms-length extensions of their imperial metropole's foreign and economic policies. As another more recent example within this model, Shell (then Shell D'Arcy) was granted a license in 1937 to explore the Nigerian territory for oil, and this license was granted by the *British* political authorities. Companies' only *legal* responsibilities in this model are to their imperial metropole. Imperial metropoles not only established the boundaries of the legal rights and duties for private economic actors in a way that would now (anachronistically) be viewed as extraterritorial. They also conferred legal existence itself upon what are now understood as the 'subsidiaries' of transnational companies. To the extent that companies understood themselves to have any *political* and/or *moral* responsibilities at all in the colonized environments in which they operated—which was not always the case—these were viewed through the racialized lens of the 'civilizing mission' or 'white man's burden' (Donnelly 1998; Easterly 2006): according to an ideology that colonized peoples needed outside help to live in a modern context. Call this the 'colonial' model.

Second and third, the twentieth century tried out two very different forms of response. The world's largest wave of decolonization occurred in between the end of World War II in 1945 and the 1970s. But in practice, at least at first, not very much changed in terms of colonial metropoles' influence over 'their' home-based transnationals, even in long-since decolonized states. For example, in 1954, the US-based United Fruit Company worked together with the Central Intelligence Agency in order to push for a US-backed coup that toppled the democratically elected left-wing populist government led by Colonel Arbenz. The Arbenz government's policy platform had included promises to improve the working conditions on banana plantations, which was perceived as a risk to profits in the company's American headquarters. The structure of world politics had supposedly changed from one that was predominantly imperial and colonial to one marked by the increasing ubiquity of separate, formally sovereign states. In practice, however, companies existing in more than one state at one time (such as the United Fruit Company in this example) continued to view their legal, political, and moral responsibilities in terms of a single transnational unit: typically one based in and responsible to the headquarters in the global North. In the face of subsidiaries behaving like the tentacles of an octopus—acting effectively as extensions of powerful home-states' foreign and economic policy priorities to the detriment of those of their host states in the global South—the prescription of progressively minded people working on business and human rights in this era was to *make real* the complete legal and political separation of subsidiaries from their parents. Companies' main *political* responsibility in this model is *not* to be political: not to interfere in domestic or international politics, whether by sponsoring coup attempts, or by engaging in any of the other myriad political activities that had explicitly characterized their role in the colonial model. Parents' *legal* responsibility is exclusively to the home state; subsidiaries' *legal* responsibility is exclusively to the host state; and *moral* responsibility becomes effectively subsumed under these political and legal prescriptions, rather than something to be considered on its own terms. Call this the 'sovereignty' model.

While perhaps being a well-intentioned idea in theory, this led to a race to the bottom in many parts of the world. Juridically-sovereign states used their newfound regulatory capabilities to compete with one another for the laxest regulations, to make themselves more attractive to foreign direct investors. More broadly, as history marched on during the second half of the twentieth century, it became replete with examples of the state and its sovereignty being the problem rather than the solution to the major human rights challenges facing the world. Apartheid South

Africa and the Jim Crow-era United States of America, both of which were systems of racial segregation, provide two clear examples of how a prescription that companies should follow all legal requirements laid down by states is not a panacea that leads to better human rights outcomes in all cases and contexts. This led to the third kind of response: 'politics beyond the state' (Wapner 1995), tied to voluntary corporate social responsibility in a context of neo-liberalism. Companies' perceived power combined with the inability of states to regulate led to an attempt to foster new accountability mechanisms, such as 'market', 'peer' and 'public-reputational' accountability, all of which are meant to operate in the absence of any meaningful authority above the actors themselves (Grant and Keohane 2005). For example, Nike had been accused since the 1970s of operating sweatshops and employing child labor in Southeast Asia to manufacture its products. The first step in the 'politics beyond the state' response was the creation of voluntary codes of conduct outlining *moral* responsibilities for those companies that wanted to follow best practice and be 'good', for example: at the Organization for Economic Cooperation and Development in 1976, and at the International Labour Organization in 1977 (Karp 2014, 30). The second step consisted of consumer campaigns in the 1990s to boycott bad practices and encourage these 'good' ones. This fit (better than their proponents would have been comfortable with) into the neo-liberal zeitgeist of their time. The idea behind consumer campaigns is that increasingly open global markets, combined with activist consumers, could be used to manipulate companies into respecting human rights voluntarily simply to improve their own profitability. Within this model, soft law becomes a replacement for the perceived inability of weak states to place *legal* responsibilities on powerful economic actors. The expected *political* responses from companies are to transnational consumers, and to a lesser extent, to transnational activist networks, rather than to territorially bounded communities. Call this the 'neo-liberal' model.

The fact that none of these three models truly worked either ethically or practically—combined with the fact that the twentieth-century responses were concerned mainly with labor standards rather than with the very broad range of civil, political, social, economic, and cultural rights that private-sphere actors' activities can affect—sets the backdrop for today's business and human rights initiatives, which began in the 1990s. These are intended as distinct from the third model in the following ways. First, they aim to re-establish political authority over companies rather than relying on markets or pure ethical voluntarism. This is intended to respond to weaknesses in the 'neo-liberal" model. Second, they do so beyond the level of home/host states. This is intended to respond to weaknesses in the 'sovereignty' model. Third, they are modelled as based on the principle of international consensus/consent. This is intended to respond to weaknesses in the 'colonial' model. To see this another way, consider how Ostrom (1990) analyzes the typical responses to collective-action problems, such as the 'tragedy of the commons', in terms of *either* a strategy of Leviathan (creating and submitting to a powerful central authority such as the state) *or* privatization and property rights (ownership without a higher authority, leading to incentive structures that channel self-regarding action into desirable public outcomes). These reflect the theoretical assumptions behind the second and third models, respectively. The fourth model aims to move beyond the weaknesses in each. Contemporary business and human rights practices are intended to be distinct from earlier discussions of 'corporate social responsibility': first because they relate to *all* human rights (civil, political, social, economic, and cultural) rather than just to a subcategory of human rights thought to be uniquely relevant for businesses (for example, labor rights in connection with supply chains); and second because they involve *limiting* the decision-making discretion of agents through the establishment of authoritative rules and principles, rather than *encouraging* the exercise of moral discretion (Karp 2009; Ramasastry 2015). To do all of this at once is a tall order—I would have considerable sympathy with readers whose initial reaction is to suspect that the order is *too* tall—and it can be characterized as a 'global governance' model. The

Table 23.2 Moral, political, and legal responsibility of businesses for human rights across four models

	Moral responsibility	Political responsibility	Legal responsibility	Overall characterization of the 'response' to businesses' impact on what we now call human rights
Colonial model	Civilizing mission / 'white man's burden'	Companies become *de facto* political authorities, as part of colonial politics and power relations. They self-identify as part of the metropole's political community.	Colonial metropoles establish legal rights and duties for companies	Universal humanitarian moral imperative to do good when/where one can
Sovereignty model	Subsumed under political and legal responsibility	Be apolitical	Follow all legal requirements of host states	Noninterference
Politics beyond the state model (neo-liberalism)	Maximize social benefit for stakeholders. Develop and follow codes of best practice.	Respond to the demands of international NGOs, transnational consumer groups, and intergovernmental organizations	'Realistic' assumption that law will fail to regulate. Soft law fills gaps.	Corporate social responsibility
Global governance	?	?	?	Re-establish political authority, do so beyond the level of states, based on international consensus/ consent

points that this section has made so far are summarized in Table 23.2. This table sets the context for the next section's analysis and evaluation of the specific contours of legal, moral, and political responsibility assigned to businesses and to states within contemporary policy initiatives.

Policy: legal, moral, and political responsibility in the UN guiding principles on business and human rights

The most significant recent business and human rights initiative is the United Nations Guiding Principles on Business and Human Rights, which were developed between 2005 and 2011 (Ruggie 2011, 2013). Their ubiquity within this policy field is the reason that they have been selected for analysis. Subsequent initiatives—such as states' national action plans on business and human rights (which already exist in 24 countries across both the global North and the global South), and the creation in 2014 of a UN intergovernmental working group, led by Ecuador, aimed at developing a future business and human rights treaty—are both direct reactions to the dominance of the UNGPs (Cassel 2018; Cantú Rivera 2019). The former constitute ways of directly embedding the UNGPs at the domestic level, and the second is a reaction to some of the UNGPs' perceived weaknesses. The antecedent UN Global Compact, first proposed in 1999, required companies to commit to best practices by literally signing up (Karp 2014, 31–32). The Global Compact can thus be viewed as an initiative on the tail end of the 'politics beyond the state' model, which draws on market, peer and public-reputational accountability mechanisms (Grant and Keohane 2005), inside of a framework that de-emphasizes the role of the state. The UNGPs, by contrast, attribute responsibilities to *all companies*, whether they want to be involved or not. Furthermore, it emphasizes that states—despite not being the only relevant actors—are still particularly important actors, both in terms of the development and implementation of global policy, and also in terms of the normative centrality of their role in human rights protection (Ruggie 2013, 2014). These are reasons to think of it as moving beyond the third model into something distinctive and (in some ways) new.

Underpinning the UNGPs are the three responsibility pillars of 'protect, respect and remedy' (Ruggie 2008). Within this, the policy framework draws a central separation between the state duty to protect human rights and the corporate responsibility to respect human rights. The state duty to protect human rights involves the need to act both internationally (in coordination with other global actors) to prevent and to react to harm to human rights occurring within one's sphere of sovereign authority. This includes the state duty to protect against harms to human rights for which business actors are causally responsible. The corporate responsibility to respect human rights involves the need not to cause or to contribute to that harm: whether through intentional action, through negligence, or through a failure to conduct due diligence. 'Due diligence' for this purpose is defined as the proactive investigation of the various kinds of harm to human rights to which a business's activities may be connected (McCorquodale et al. 2017). The distinction that the UNGPs draw between states' *duty* and companies' *responsibility* seems central to the themes of this Handbook, and also to deepening the analysis of the set of questions raised in the first section of this chapter. One might assume at first glance that 'duty' refers to legal responsibility, whereas 'responsibility' is intended to sit in the 'moral' domain, the implication of which—if this were an accurate interpretation—would be that businesses' responsibilities are exclusively moral, in contrast to the more solid and justiciable legal requirements that fall on states. In fact, this kind of interpretation is behind a commonly levelled critique of UNGPs: that they are inadequate because (like the 'colonial' and 'politics beyond the state' models) they are voluntarist about the nature of the responsibilities that are being assigned. This is thought to be true both at the level of states, because they only have the international-legal responsibilities to which they have consented, and also at the level of companies, because their responsibilities are thought to have a moral rather than legal character. However, this interpretation is overly simplistic, for reasons that the chapter will now explain.

In terms of businesses' potential legal responsibilities under the UNGPs, it is important to distinguish between really/already existing legal rules, on the one hand, and 'legal responsibility' as a category, on the other. Legal responsibility as a category can be used to refer to responsibilities that are permissible and/or obligatory *in principle* to legalize, even if those responsibilities do not already form part of the law (Raz 1986). Conversely, there can be really/already existing legal rules that, from a normative perspective, ought to be removed from the law, because they are unjustifiable as legal responsibilities in principle (Fuller 1969; Hart 1965).[1] The genocidal system of Nazi Germany provides a paradigmatic example of the latter (Fuller 1969). Retroactive laws provide another less extreme case of how so-called laws can lack a truly 'legal' character, thereby failing to generate legal responsibility (Waldron 2008). Courts should not enforce such requirements because they cannot be part of the law. Some responsibilities can be moral, political, and legal all at once. However, it is possible that some responsibilities—for example, a requirement to drive only on the left/right side of the road on a two-way street—have an exclusively legal character, without clear moral and/or political components. It is therefore inaccurate, or at least incomplete, to that the UNGPs are uninterested in the assignment or attribution of legal responsibilities to businesses, and to critique the framework primarily on this basis. Obligations are not assigned *directly* to companies under *international* law by the framework. However, the state duty to protect and the corporate responsibility to respect are meant to work in tandem. This means that the UNGPs provide standards that are clarified at the international level, which—through the state duty to protect—impose requirements on states to hold companies to account for failures to respect human rights in regional and domestic 'hard' law. This is a discussion of responsibility with a fundamentally legal character. Moreover, it is a discussion that has already produced direct legal effects at the intended governance levels, through: the creation of states' human rights national action plans; domestic legislation such as France's 2017 law on companies' 'duty of vigilance'; and regional instruments such as EU directives on financial reporting (Cantú Rivera 2019; Cossart et al. 2017; Neglia 2016; see also Karp 2020a, 629).

In terms of businesses' moral responsibilities, the UNGPs can be understood as overridingly consequentialist in their approach, while also incorporating, in a limited way, a few aspects from deontology and discourse ethics.[2] The definition of the responsibility to respect human rights is grounded in the need to 'do no harm'. Businesses violate their responsibilities if harm is caused, in breach of a 'due diligence' standard of liability. The due diligence standard enhances businesses' responsibility for any harm to human rights that occurs within a businesses' sphere of activities and operations, beyond the standard notion of fault (Karp 2020a). It can include the attribution of responsibility to a business even if a harm was unintended, and even if the company's causal link to the harm is remote rather than proximate. Despite this expansion of liability, the responsibility is *for* (avoiding and/or remedying) an outcome, and that outcome is human rights harm. For these reasons, businesses' moral responsibilities within the UNGPs have an overridingly consequentialist character. On the one hand, this lends itself well to quantitative metrics that enable the measurement of how well both businesses are meeting their responsibilities. If human rights outcomes are improving—if the amount of 'harm' to human rights declines in an empirically measurable way—then this suggests to observers that human rights are being 'respected' (Sikkink 2017). On the other hand, the translation of responsibility for human rights into metrics that are possible to quantify and measure is not without shortcomings (for an excellent overview of these shortcomings, see Goodale 2018). For better or for worse, this is the main mode of ethical reasoning within which the UNGPs operate when it comes to the question of what businesses are responsible to do.

Within this overarching consequentialism, the UNGPs also introduce limited/incomplete elements from deontological and discourse-ethics reasoning in interpreting what businesses need to do in order to meet a responsibility to respect human rights. For example, Principle 23 says: 'Where the domestic context renders it impossible to meet [the responsibility to respect human rights] fully, business enterprises are expected to respect the principles of internationally recognized human rights to the greatest extent possible in the circumstances, and to be able to demonstrate their efforts in this regard (Ruggie 2011, 21)'. This suggests a hierarchy of moral responsibility, where international human principles provide reasons that need to be taken so seriously that they have the potential to override other forms of domestic obligation (compare this to the structure of and normative problems with the 'colonial' governance model). Discussions of how to prioritize moral reasons or principles within an overall system of value, especially where competing principles have the potential to conflict, fit broadly into deontological approaches. However, the fact that 'internationally recognized human rights' are themselves interpreted in a consequentialist way mitigates the extent to which this can be fully considered as deontological mode of reasoning about moral responsibility for human rights.

Another example to consider is Principle 18, which says:

> In order to gauge human rights risks, business enterprises should identify and assess any actual or potential adverse human rights impacts with which they may be involved either through their own activities or as a result of their business relationships. This process should:
>
> a. Draw on internal and/or independent external human rights expertise;
> b. Involve meaningful consultation with potentially affected groups and other relevant stakeholders, as appropriate to the size of the business enterprise and the nature and context of the operation.
>
> *(Ruggie 2011, 17, see also Karp 2014, 84–85)*

The need to draw on both internal and external expertise, as well as to consult with 'potentially affected groups and other relevant stakeholders, are ideas that fit broadly into a discourse-ethics approach. However, the UNGPs largely sidestep a discussion of the social-structural changes that would be necessary for such consultation to be power-free and therefore 'meaningful'; these sidestepped elements are central to the discourse-ethics tradition. Finally, the virtue-ethics tradition, which focuses on the judgments of particularly constituted agents, acting/deciding in particular contexts and circumstances, is largely missing from the UNGPs. But it is missing in a way that sheds further light on how moral responsibility for human rights is being conceptualized within the policy. The UNGPs explicitly consider the question of corporate rather than collective responsibility (Erskine 2003; French 1984). This means that its analysis and guidance are at the level of the responsibility of a business itself, rather than at the level of the responsibilities borne by directors, employees, shareholders, and/or other stakeholders when a business fails to do what it should. However, this fails to address the question of whether businesses are the kinds of agents that have the requisite skills, experience, and character—the rich inner moral life, analogous to the human soul—that would render meaningful a consideration of whether their contextual judgments can form a valid basis for responsibility in a virtue-ethics framework (Karp 2014, 85-86; see also Sison 2018). If businesses, because of the kinds of corporate agents that they are, need their actions to be informed by judgments of a specific internal or external decision-maker other than 'the corporation' itself, then their responsibilities seem non-discretionary even in a virtue-ethics context. This raises the further question of whether one needs to look 'down' to the level of individual directors, managers, and employees in order to locate the capacity for virtue-based (as distinct from consequentialist) moral judgment; or alternatively, if the capacities rests 'upward' at the level of state political institutions, supra-state political institutions, and/or other nonstate actors.

The UNGPs emphasize that companies have a responsibility to follow the law of host states, as well as a responsibility to follow international human rights standards in cases where legal requirements may be absent and/or unclear. The due-diligence processes required under the responsibility to respect human rights need to be done in all cases. Subjective judgment is not permitted, at least on the macro-level question of whether and when due diligence is required. From this perspective, the point of governance initiatives such as the UNGPs seems to be to place 'red-line' limits on, rather than to enhance, the exercise of companies' discretion about how they can legitimately go about their business. In these ways, the moral responsibility assigned to companies under the UNGPs seems to be non-discretionary. However, even though the discretion might not rest with companies themselves, there is still a wide sphere of judgment that can be exercised by agents at other levels when assessing whether companies have met their required standard of care (Hazenberg 2016). This is for three reasons. First, the UNGPs leave open the possibility that different kinds and sizes of companies, in different circumstances, will need to do due diligence differently. There is no 'one-size-fits-all' approach to respecting human rights. Second, the due-diligence standard—despite requiring a greater degree of proactive action in its attribution of responsibility than a fault-based model—is not nearly as 'positive' as strict liability (Bonnitcha and McCorquodale 2017). In other words, companies are not automatically responsible for any harm that befalls someone just because that harm happens. A due diligence standard requires significant interpretation of the question of whether due diligence has been done sufficiently, and this requires the exercise of discretion. Third, the UNGPs also seem to be motivated by a belief that companies and their decision-making structures should be thinking *more* in moral, judgment-based terms, not less: as contrasted with blindly following profits, wherever they may lead. These suggest ways in which the kind of responsibility assigned to companies under the UNGPs can also be thought of as discretionary, even if the location of the exercise of that discretion does not always or necessarily rest with the company itself (i.e. at the corporate level of analysis).

Comparing all of this with the historical context of businesses' moral responsibility for what we now call human rights: The 'sovereignty' model suggests that following the law is an adequate account of companies' moral responsibility, due to the kinds of agents that companies are. This seems in retrospect to have swung the pendulum too far to the non-discretionary side, regardless of the ways in which that seemed, to campaigners at the time, to be a progressive corrective to excessive interference by companies in a decolonizing context. On the other hand, to the extent that moral responsibility featured at all in the 'colonial' model, it was understood according to a hubristic and racialized notions of the discretionary responsibilities of the powerful to weak and vulnerable others. This generates an uncomfortable continuity when compared to the UNGPs, whenever they seem to require companies to act benevolently and to exercise moral judgment, from a position of power, about how they act toward vulnerable others. This is compounded by the transnational context of both colonialism and contemporary neo-liberal globalization.

The UNGPs do not address the question of businesses' political responsibility very directly. This is unsurprising given the structural state-centrism of any United Nations initiative. But a few key points can still be inferred. First, whereas the colonial model and 'politics beyond the state' models seem to draw on a perceived positive correlation between responsibility, on the one hand, and power/capacity/authority on the other (see also Shadmy's chapter in this Handbook), the UNGPs present a strikingly different picture of these concepts and how they interrelate. States' *duty* to protect human rights stems from and relates to their political authority. By contrast, companies' *responsibilities* are conceptualized in the absence of a clearly prescribed authoritative role. For example, Principle 23 says that companies must '*comply with*' all applicable laws and respect internationally recognized human rights, wherever they operate', and also that they should '*seek ways to honour*' the principles of internationally recognized human rights when faced with conflicting requirements' (Ruggie 2011, 21, emphasis added). It will not go unnoticed that to 'comply with' is much stronger language than to 'seek ways to honour'. This addresses the question of what companies are permitted to do if the law is weak, absent, or unclear. However, often sovereign states' laws are quite strong and clear, and they explicitly require agents within a domestic context to *disrespect* human rights (Karp 2009). This was the core weakness of the 'sovereignty' model. The UNGPs dance around the edges of this issue by juxtaposing the obligation to follow the law with the responsibility to respect human rights, but then steer clear of resolving it in a way that could meaningfully guide action through this kind of dilemma. Second, should companies use their voice and their power to lobby for the law to be changed in a more human rights-friendly direction (for example, multinational companies in Apartheid South Africa) (Wettstein 2012)? Or is this kind of political engagement from this kind of actor *inherently* problematic, regardless of the *content* or *context* of that lobbying, either because it starts to look neo-colonial or because it undercuts the more legitimate (in principle) political authority of states? This is one of the key questions raised by comparing the historical models developed earlier this chapter. It remains unanswered. Third and finally, why does the 'duty to protect' fall only on states? Clearly, private economic actors have been and can still be *de facto* political authorities (Karp 2014). This question about political responsibility also goes largely unanswered by the policy framework. When questions of responsibility are connected to questions of authority, it becomes easy to conflate the empirical issue of *de facto* authority with the normative issue of who or what should have authority over whom and why. The view that companies *should not* have political authority or responsibility has ended up de-emphasizing the implications of the *de facto* political authority that companies still wield in many of the contexts in which they operate. States' 'duty to protect' comes from their political authority. But what happens to and for this duty when private sphere actors become political authorities too?

Conclusion

This chapter theorized responsibility in world politics by rejecting its decoupling from the concept of 'duty', and by focusing instead on a distinction between responsibilities that do and do not permit discretion. This links to questions of moral and political authority. It then situated business and human rights practices in a broader historical context, through which it analyzed the changing forms of legal, moral, and political responsibility that the international system has assigned and/or attributed to businesses over time. This enabled an analysis of the United Nations Guiding Principles on Business and Human Rights. The UNGPs are fundamentally consequentialist in character. They contain elements of the 'colonial', 'sovereignty', and 'neo-liberal' models, while also moving beyond these in other respects toward something new. Finally, they could benefit from further critical reflection on the relevance of a virtue ethics approach to business actors and on enriching the notion of political responsibility that they employ.

This analysis from a single policy field reflects a much broader trend of how questions of *legal* and *moral* responsibility—and their interrelationship—have come to dominate discussions of responsibility in world politics today. This can have the effect of underemphasizing perhaps more fundamental questions of *political* responsibility and authority. The four models of international organization laid out by this chapter emphasize both continuity and change, and they provide a broader context within which the renewed interest in 'responsibility' in world politics today can be analyzed and evaluated, beyond the specific field of business and human rights.

Notes

1 For one interpretation of the application of Fuller's ideas to international law, see Brunnée and Toope (2010).
2 Note that the point of this exercise is not to evaluate the UNGPs from a normative perspective using these approaches. Rather, it is to enable a mapping exercise to visibilize the responsibilities within the UNGPs that are thought of internally (within that policy framework) as having a genuinely 'moral' character.

References

Aristotle (1996). *The Nicomachean Ethics.* Translated by Harris Rackham. Ware, Hertfordshire: Wordsworth.
Bonnitcha, J., and McCorquodale, R. (2017). "The Concept of 'Due Diligence' in the UN Guiding Principles on Business and Human Rights." *European Journal of International Law*, 28(3): 899–919.
Brunnée, J., and Toope, S. J. (2010). *Legitimacy and Legality in International Law: An Interactional Account.* Cambridge: Cambridge University Press.
Cantú Rivera, H. (2019). "National Action Plans on Business and Human Rights: Progress or Mirage?" *Business and Human Rights Journal*, 4(2): 213–237.
Cassel, D. (2018). "The Third Session of the UN Intergovernmental Working Group on a Business and Human Rights Treaty." *Business and Human Rights Journal*, 3(2): 277–283.
Cossart, S., Chaplier, J., and Beau de Lomenie, T. (2017). "The French Law on Duty of Care: A Historic Step Towards Making Globalization Work for All." *Business and Human Rights Journal*, 2(2): 317–323.
Donnelly, J. (1998). "Human Rights: A New Standard of Civilization?" *International Affairs*, 74(1): 1–23.
Easterly, W. (2006). *The White Man's Burden: Why the West's Efforts to Aid the Rest Have Done So Little Good.* Oxford: Oxford University Press.
Erskine, T., ed. (2003). *Can Institutions Have Responsibilities? Collective Moral Agency and International Relations.* Basingstoke: Palgrave Macmillan.
French, P. (1984). *Collective and Corporate Responsibility.* New York: Columbia University Press.
Fuller, L.L. (1969). *The Morality of Law.* revised ed. New Haven: Yale University Press. Original edition, 1964.
Goodale, M. (2018). "What Are Human Rights Good For?" *Boston Review*, 19 July. http://bostonreview.net/global-justice/mark-goodale-what-are-human-rights-good (accessed May 16, 2019).
Grant, R.W., and Keohane, R. O. (2005). "Accountability and Abuses of Power in World Politics." *American Political Science Review*, 99(1): 29–43.
Hansen-Magnusson, H., and Vetterlein, A., eds. (2020). *The Rise of Responsibility in World Politics.* Cambridge: Cambridge University Press.
Hart, H. L. A. (1965). "The Morality of Law, Lon L. Fuller." *Harvard Law Review*, 78(6): 1281–1296.
Hart, H. L. A. (1968). *Punishment and Responsibility.* Oxford: Clarendon Press.
Hazenberg, J. L. J. (2016). "Transnational Corporations and Human Rights Duties: Perfect and Imperfect." *Human Rights Review*, 17(4): 479–500.
Hutchings, K. (2018). *Global Ethics: An Introduction.* 2nd ed. Cambridge: Polity Press.
Karp, D. J. (2009). "Transnational Corporations in 'Bad States': Human Rights Duties, Legitimate Authority and the Rule of Law in International Political Theory." *International Theory*, 1(1): 87–118.
Karp, D. J. (2014). *Responsibility for Human Rights: Transnational Corporations in Imperfect States.* Cambridge: Cambridge University Press.
Karp, D.J. (2015). "The Responsibility to Protect Human Rights and the RtoP: Prospective and Retrospective Responsibility." *Global Responsibility to Protect*, 7(2): 142–166.
Karp, D. J. (2020a). "Fixing Meanings in Global Governance? 'Respect' and 'Protect' in the UN Guiding Principles on Business and Human Rights." *Global Governance*, 26(4): 628–649.
Karp, D.J. (2020b). "What is the Responsibility to Respect Human Rights? Reconsidering the 'Respect, Protect, and Fulfill' Framework." *International Theory*, 12(1): 83–108.
Linklater, A. (2006). "The Harm Principle and Global Ethics." *Global Society*, 20(3): 329–343.
McCorquodale, R. Smit, L. Neely, S., and Brooks, R. (2017). "Human Rights Due Diligence in Law and Practice: Good Practices and Challenges for Business Enterprises." *Business and Human Rights Journal*, 2(2): 195–224.
Meckled-Garcia, S. (2008). "On the Very Idea of Cosmopolitan Justice: Constructivism and International Agency." *Journal of Political Philosophy*, 16(3): 245–271.
Miller, D. (2001). "Distributing Responsibilities." *Journal of Political Philosophy*, 9(4): 453–471.
Neglia, M. (2016). "The UNGPs - Five Years On: From Consensus to Divergence in Public Regulation on Business and Human Rights." *Netherlands Quarterly of Human Rights*, 34(4): 289–317.
O'Neill, O. (1996). *Towards Justice and Virtue: A Constructive Account of Practical Reasoning.* Cambridge: Cambridge University Press.
Ostrom, E. (1990). *Governing the Commons: The Evolution of Institutions for Collective Action.* Cambridge: Cambridge University Press.
Ramasastry, A. (2015). "Corporate Social Responsibility Versus Business and Human Rights: Bridging the Gap Between Responsibility and Accountability." *Journal of Human Rights*, 14(2): 237–259.
Raz, J. (1986). *The Morality of Freedom.* Oxford: Oxford University Press.

Ruggie, J. G. (2008). Protect, Respect and Remedy: A Framework for Business and Human Rights. A/HRC/8/5. Human Rights Council, UN General Assembly, 8th session. New York: United Nations. http://www.ohchr.org/EN/Issues/TransnationalCorporations/Pages/Reports.aspx (accessed August 7, 2015).

Ruggie, J. G. (2011). Guiding Principles on Business and Human Rights: Implementing the United Nations "Protect, Respect and Remedy" Framework. A/HRC/17/31. Human Rights Council, UN General Assembly, 17th session. New York: United Nations. http://www.ohchr.org/EN/Issues/TransnationalCorporations/Pages/Reports.aspx (accessed August 7, 2015).

Ruggie, J. G. (2013). *Just Business: Multinational Corporations and Human Rights*. New York: W.W. Norton.

Ruggie, J. G. (2014). "Global Governance and 'New Governance Theory': Lessons from Business and Human Rights." *Global Governance*, 20(1): 5–17.

Schneewind, J. B. (1990). "The Misfortunes of Virtue." *Ethics*, 101(1): 42–63.

Shue, H. (1980). *Basic Rights: Subsistence, Affluence, and U.S. Foreign Policy*. Princeton: Princeton University Press.

Sikkink, K. (2017). *Evidence for Hope: Making Human Rights Work in the 21st Century*. Princeton: Princeton University Press.

Sison, A. J. G. (2018). "Virtue Ethics and Natural Law Responses to Human Rights Quandries in Business." *Business and Human Rights Journal*, 3(2): 211–232.

Vetterlein, A. (2018). "Responsibility is More than Accountability: From Regulatory Towards Negogiated Governance." *Contemporary Politics*, 24(5): 545–567.

Waldron, J. (2008). "Hart and the Principles of Legality." In Kramer, M. H., Grant, C., Colburn, B. and Hatzistavrou, A., eds., *The Legacy of H.L.A. Hart: Legal, Political and Moral Philosophy*. Oxford: Oxford University Press.

Wapner, P. (1995). "Politics Beyond the State: Environmental Activism and World Civic Politics." *World Politics*, 47(3): 311–340.

Wettstein, F. (2012). "Silence as Complicity: Elements of a Corporate Duty to Speak Out Against the Violation of Human Rights." *Business Ethics Quarterly*, 22(1): 37–61.

24
SOCIAL MEDIA ACTORS
Shared responsibility 3.0?
Gabi Schlag

Introduction

Is Facebook responsible for hate speech, fake news, online extremism or images of child pornography shared on its platform? Is CEO Mark Zuckerberg, as he said in a public hearing before the US Senate in April 2018, 'responsible for what happens here'?[1]

How the Internet is regulated and governed has become a major issue of academic debate as well as public concern (Hofmann, Katzenbach, and Gollatz 2017; see also chapter by Calderaro in this volume). Given its rather short history, Internet regulation developed in four phases. From the 1960s to 2000, the Internet was an open space with no rules ('Open internet'). From 2000 to 2005, governments recognized that some activities and content on the World Wide Web should be blocked ('Access Denied'). The next years, from 2005 to 2010, filters and blocks were applied to regulate and control access ('Access Controlled'). Since then, the regulation of the infrastructure and content has become a contested political issue where different actors negotiate the right and appropriate degree and procedures of regulation ('Access Contested'). Today, governments demand Internet Communication Technology (ICT) companies, in particular intermediaries as Facebook, Google (with YouTube) and Twitter – the big three providers worldwide – to remove harmful and allegedly illegal content based on national law. However, national laws vary and an effective demand for removal only applies in the requesting jurisdiction. A company's terms of service, however, generally apply globally.[2] For reasons of clarity, this chapter focuses on one big social media platform provider – Facebook Inc. – and its responsibilities to remove content that is perceived as harmful and graphic. Although such content (and the actions it shows) is often illegal, it may not violate national laws in some countries. Hence, violations of community standards, as Facebook (2019a) calls their service terms, do not necessarily match illegal content, and vice versa.

This chapter contributes to the ongoing debate on the responsibility of public and private actors concerning common goods online. Policies of content moderation have to balance the freedom of expression on the one hand, and the safety of their users on the other hand. I argue that being responsible and acting responsibly in the field of social media is a shared enterprise. Shared responsibility implies that not one but many actors hold responsibility. Who should be responsible when and how is not a given fact but negotiated. It is relational and performative. The flipside of shared responsibility, however, is often diffused responsibility where nobody seems to be in charge. As the Facebook case illustrates, the dualism of shared and diffused responsibility is not a contradiction but shows the negotiated and contested character of acting responsibly in social media.

Since the livestreaming of the terror attack in Christchurch, New Zealand, in March 2019, public debates on social media responsibility and content regulation have increased globally. Theoretically and conceptually informed research, however, remains the exception. Therefore, this chapter has two main goals. First, I ask what it means to hold responsibility for the content uploaded and shared on social media platforms like Facebook. On the one hand, Corporate Social Responsibility (CSR) requires that the business models of companies respect human rights. Harmful, graphic and illegal content on Facebook often violates the rights of individuals and groups as hate speech and videos of sexual assaults. On the other hand, the freedom of expression marks a reference point for regulating online content at a global scale where state interests, business interests and user interests sometimes clash. Second, I discuss how Facebook addresses challenges of responsibility, accountability and liability as the policies and practices of reviewing, moderating and deleting harmful content often remain opaque. Finally, I show that Facebook's approach to content regulations is shaped both by shared responsibility and its diffusion.

Discourses of responsibility within the World Wide Web

The politics of online content moderation: responsibility, accountability and liability

As Hansen-Magnusson and Vetterlein write in the introduction to this handbook, responsibility has become a buzzword. Increasing references to responsibility, however, do not go hand in hand with a clear meaning of what it means 'to be responsible' or 'to hold responsibility' (Hoover 2012). While calls for more responsibility indicate the emergence of a 'new system of negotiated governance' (Vetterlein 2018), governance on a global scale has also become a fluid and multi-layered practice. It includes public and private actors, different sectors as well as modes and levels of decision-making. These transformations of governance towards a polycentric system, then, often imply that legitimacy, that is, who has the right and authority to govern, is negotiated and contested (Tallberg, Bäckstrand, and Scholte 2018).

Given these transformations, Internet governance is no exception. Governments and ICT companies are developing new approaches for content moderation as the joint venture of Facebook and French President Emmanuel Macron illustrates (Scott and Young 2018). As Zuckerberg acknowledged, 'I do not believe individual companies can or should be handling so many of these issues of free expression and public safety on their own' (Zuckerberg 2018). Therefore, he advocates enhanced cooperation between public and private actors leaving former policies of autonomy and non-interference behind. Although CEOs like Zuckerberg cooperate with governments, the 'new governors' of the Internet are private companies like Facebook, Google and Twitter (Klonick 2017). They are the leading actors who regulate what can be said and shown on their platforms. How ICT companies should respond to harms, offenses and wrongs poses a new challenge as concepts of responsibility, accountability and liability are only vaguely defined for social media.

Responsibility is based on ethical considerations whose right, duty and obligation it is to prevent harm and to respond to wrongs. Given its literal meaning, it refers to the requirement to respond to demands articulated by others. Moral responsibility 'involves *being answerable* for a particular act or outcome' (Erskine 2010, 700; italics added) and thereby constitutes a social relationship. As a discursive practice, responsibility is therefore defined by the obligation to respond to others. In the light of controversial decisions, actors hold responsibility and are held answerable by demanding justifications for actions (Forst 2011). At least, actors have to give a reason why no more response is necessary (Buddeberg 2018). Such situations where claims of responsibility evolve require situated knowledge as it defines the doings that are perceived as right or wrong. This knowledge, though, is inherently normative as it mobilizes and invokes more or less generalized moral principles, believes, and norms. Therefore, responsibility is not only a relational concept in the sense that it 'is always to someone and for something' (Hansen-Magnusson 2019, 4), but performative as the subjects and objects of responsible behaviour do not exist independently from the discourses of responsibility. Hence, '[t]he responsible agent is a socially constructed agent and the act of holding responsible is a coercive and creative political act' (Hoover 2012, 236). These creative acts constitute an invisible contract between the parties defining who has the duty to respond to whom. Emphasizing the relational and performative nature of responsibility, Iris Marion Young writes '(o)ur responsibility derives from belonging together with others in a system of interdependent processes of cooperation and competition through which we seek benefits and aim to realize projects' (Young 2011, 105). Forward-looking responsibility, then, requires joint and combined efforts of agents who acknowledge that they have a duty, obligation and to some extent the resources and power to alter the present situation and to prevent future wrongs (Erskine 2010, 701; Young 2011). For Facebook, drafting community rules and constantly revising content regulation through reviewers, moderators and algorithms is an attempt to act responsibly and to prevent future wrongs.

Accountability, though, defines subjects and objects of responsible behaviour often in terms of causal liability. It is rather backward than forward-looking as it focuses on past wrongdoings (Young 2011). Rules, norms and procedures laid down in formal and informal institutions shape these discourses of accountability. Facebook, for example, has only recently developed institutional arrangements of accountability based on its community standards where users can be held responsible for their posts and could be banned from the community when they violate these standards. Accordingly, users can flag problematic content, teams of reviewers and moderators constantly screen content and upload filters based on the technology of PhotoDNA (Zakrzewski 2019) automatically detect, remove and report illegal content like child pornography or terrorist propaganda.[3]

Liability, finally, is associated with causality and legality. Based on the interpretation of laws, a person may be liable for unjust, illegal or criminal behaviour. Causal liability requires that a causal connection between an action and its harmful outcome can be made and proofed. This implies to evaluate the intentions, motives and reasons of action (Young 2011, 97–8). Accordingly, only voluntary acts count as liable actions which presupposes that s/he has a (more or less free) choice. Finally, liability is directed at wrong-doings that are already committed but cannot account for future harmful and damaging behaviour. An example of legal liability in the field of Internet governance is the German Network Enforcement Act (NetzDG), introduced by the government in 2017. If content, which is illegal in Germany, for example, the denial of the Holocaust is not deleted within 24 hours, respectively, seven days, platform providers face serious penalties. For Germany, the NetzDG (and similar approaches by other governments) already enables legal prosecution of user-shared content and should be seen as an approach to strengthen accountability and liability. Cooperation between ICT companies and legal enforcement agencies is evolving to prosecute apparently illegal content (Zeit online 2019). National courts have also revised decisions to ban a user or to remove content as recent cases in Germany illustrate (Zeit online 2018). They have taken controversial decisions that extreme statements of insult have to stay online (Köver 2019). Another example is the initiative of a group of non-governmental agencies who formulated the Manila Principles on Intermediary Liability. They are calling for a judicial authority who approves the removal of content and demand that restrictions must comply with the criteria of necessity, proportionality, due process, transparency and accountability.[4]

Given these distinctions between responsibility, accountability and liability, it is necessary to understand how the invocation of responsibility for social media content is intertwined with discourses on CSR and the freedom of expression. These two discourses give meaning to claims by various actors (including ICT companies themselves) that social media providers hold responsible for what user share on their platforms. They constitute responsibility as a shared practice under negotiation.

Corporate social responsibility, human rights and online content moderation

Approaches to content regulation and moderation are linked to CSR where ICT companies are expected to respect human rights. The Guiding Principles on Business and Human Rights, established in 2011 by the United Nations, define global standards of behaviour (Carroll 2008; Ruggie 2011). This document declares that companies should 'avoid causing or contributing to adverse human rights impacts and seek to prevent or mitigate such impacts directly linked to their operations, products or services'. As CSR defines voluntary standards, governments leave it mostly to ICT companies whether and how they incorporate and apply a human rights approach in their business models. Human rights protection by ICT companies, though, is sometimes subverted by governments. States like Turkey, China and Thailand have pressured platform providers to limit the freedom of expression by referring to problematic national restrictions.[5]

How CSR works for ICT companies, in particular social media platform providers, therefore remains an ambiguous question. On the one hand, critics claim that standards and compliance mechanisms to protect human rights online are insufficient and should be improved (Laidlaw 2015; Taddeo and Floridi 2017). Facebook, for example, currently creates an independent oversight body for reviewing decisions where content was removed or users were banned from the community (Facebook 2019b; Klonick and Kadri 2018). One the other hand, platform providers face difficult decisions where they have to balance different rights. While companies are expected to respect human rights as well as national laws, conflicting normative expectations may create a situation where the freedom of expression clashes with human dignity and the freedom from discrimination. In these cases, should ICT companies respect the freedom of expression or should they protect users from misogyny, racism and other forms of harassment? How should they respond to a governments' request to put content offline that is a threat to national security or insulting a state leader?

As the UN special rapporteur David Kaye formulated in his report on content regulation to the UN Human Rights Council, state as well as company practices increasingly violate the freedom of expression, defined as a human right under Article 19 of The Universal Declaration of Human Rights: 'Everyone has the right to freedom of opinion and expression; this right includes freedom to hold opinions without interference and to seek, receive and impart information and ideas through any media and regardless of frontiers'. Any approach to regulate online content either by states or companies, he explains, should be guided by standards of legality,[6] necessity and proportionality,[7] as well as legitimacy.[8]

US legislation, freedom of expression and online content moderation

Internet governance is very much informed by US legislation as many big ICT companies have a US-based origin. In 1996, the US Congress introduced the Communications Decency Act to regulate sexually offensive and pornographic content on the internet.[9] Section 230 gives ICT companies who operate as an intermediary broad immunity for user generated content that is shared on their services. This section states that 'no provider or user of an interactive computer service shall be treated as the publisher or speaker of any information provided by another information content provider'. Platforms like Facebook or YouTube are not accountable and liable for content shared as they are not a publisher or the speaker. Accordingly, this exception allows them to regulate and control content due to their terms of service. Practically, intermediaries are free to choose whether they want to regulate content based on Section 230 or deny moderation by referring to norms like the freedom of expression and freedom of information. Critics, therefore, argue that US legislation puts decisions over free speech in the hands of private companies and their shady rules and procedures of monitoring user content. Hence, deleting a provocative video on YouTube, for example, would not necessarily be a violation of free speech protected by the First Amendment to the US Constitution as Google is not a 'publisher'. However, ICT companies can also refer to the First Amendment to deny the moderation of excitable speech declaring that it falls under the freedom of expression protection. In the US, hate speech, for example, is not by definition a violation of rights but often falls under the guarantees of the First Amendment. Only speech that calls for immanent violent action upon a person or group is prohibited (Butler 1997; Herz and Molnár 2012; Stone 1994). As Supreme Court decisions over time illustrate, what counts as hate speech is highly contested in the US (and elsewhere).[10]

Given the US based background of the big three ICT companies in this field (Facebook, Google and Twitter), Section 230 informs the discourses and practices of content moderation globally. Although the EU and some member states recently implemented a more forceful approach to regulate online content, ICT companies are mostly allowed to decide whether and how they control their platforms. Therefore, Klonick calls them the 'New Governors' who regulate and moderate content 'with an eye to American free speech norms, corporate responsibility, and the economic necessity of creating an environment that reflects the expectations of their users' (Klonick 2017, 1602). Different norms and rationales therefore motivate platform providers to regulate content by defining terms of service and implementing procedures of reporting, reviewing and, if necessary, blocking or removing content. UN special rapporteur David Kaye, however, reminds us that ICT companies 'remain enigmatic regulators, establishing a kind of 'platform law' in which clarity, consistency, accountability and remedy are elusive'. Kaye poses the same questions as most experts do: What responsibilities do companies have to ensure that their platforms do not interfere with rights guaranteed under international law? What standards should they apply to content moderation?

Debates on content regulation and moderation illustrate that different rights and norms can be in conflict with each other: freedom of expression versus safety from discrimination, harassment, violence and obscenity; freedom of information versus privacy rights and protection of intellectual property. But how do ICT companies like Facebook draw the line between 'free speech' and 'hate speech', safety from harmful content and the right to information? And, equally important, who is authorized and legitimized to formulate, implement, even enforce these decisions? Based on the Ranking Digital Rights[11] as well as the UN report on content moderation, ICT companies provide only limited information on the policies and procedures of self- and co-regulation. How they formulate and carry out their rules and standards remain ambiguous although many of these companies are publishing transparency reports nowadays.[12] As the following overview of Facebook's policies and practices of moderation illustrates, shared responsibility between Facebook's leadership, reviewers, moderators and the application of algorithms as well as its users is under negotiation.

Facebook's approach to content moderation: shared responsibility under negotiation

Given the contestedness of content regulation in social media, providers struggle with demands of responsibility, accountability and liability if and when harmful content is shared on their platforms. For clarity, I'll focus on Facebook's approach to content moderation as a key case. It shows that responsibility is not a given fact but it is negotiated, relational and performative.

Terms of service: the evolution of Facebook's community standards

Community rules, standards and codes of conducts define the does and don'ts of behaviour on social media. These standards are set by the platform providers which thereby respond to demands by others. As Facebook's evolution of community standards illustrates, they are not only revised in relation to events like Christchurch but were created as a response to complaints by users. Google has been publishing transparency reports since 2010[13] while YouTube was only added recently in 2018[14]; Facebook joined with the publication of a Community Standards Enforcement Report in May 2018 (Facebook 2018b), including two update blog posts in November 2018 (Rosen 2018) and in May 2019 (Rosen 2019). In general, the leadership of ICT companies defines and implements these policies and thereby holds responsibility.

By 2000, most social media platform providers had begun to develop terms of use. eBay banned Nazi and Ku Klux Klan memorabilia from its platform, governments and providers cooperated to detect, take down and prosecute child abuse worldwide (Buni and Chemaly 2016). Facebook introduced a proactive approach to content moderation in 2008 when Dave Willner joined the company. Until then, Facebook had no clearly defined terms of service or guidelines for appropriate behaviour. Complaints about inappropriate or illegal content were only reported by users and delivered to the customer service team. Willner developed an internal rule book starting with categorizing child abuse, animal abuse, and Hitler. 'We were told to take down anything that makes you feel bad, that makes you feel bad in your stomach', Willner explained in an often-cited statement (Buni and Chemaly 2016; van Zuylen-Wood 2019). As a way of responding to user complaints, Facebook took responsibility for preventing future wrongs.

In 2009, Facebook's first draft for 'abuse standards', which later became the community standards, encompassed 15,000 words. Over time, rules became more precise and Facebook created new jobs for reviewing content. The training of new staff members was often based on examples to understand the context, meaning and intension of expressions and images. In 2012, such a training manual was leaked which illustrates the hands-on character of Facebook's approach to moderate content.[15] Several cases, however, show that Facebook constantly struggles to assess the appropriateness and newsworthiness of graphic content.[16] Hence, responsibility is constantly negotiated between the leadership of Facebook, its user and third parties trying to find the right balance between freedom and regulation.

It was not until 2018, that Facebook clarified its community standards publicly. In May 2017, Facebook's 'internal rulebook on sex, terrorism and violence' as The Guardian titled was leaked (Hopkins 2017). According to Nick Hopkins who saw more than 100 internal training manuals, Facebook 'tries to navigate a minefield' where reviewers and moderators have to balance freedom of expression on the one hand, and the safety of its users on the other hand' (Hopkins 2017). While illegal content is easier to detect based on national laws, most reviewed content belongs to grey zones. The statement 'Someone shoot Trump', for example, has to be deleted, but the announcement 'Let's beat up fat kids' stays online. Facebook applies a concept of protected categories based on race, sex, gender identity, religious affiliation, national origin, ethnicity, sexual orientation and serious disability/disease. In practice, this meant that a statement 'All white people are racist' should be removed as it is an attack against a protected category. Sub-categories like 'black children' or 'female drivers', however, did not enjoy the same kind of protection (Angwin & Grassegger 2017). In response to these leaked manuals, Monika Bickert reminded the public that 'we feel responsible to our community to keep them safe and we feel very accountable. It's absolutely our responsibility to keep on top of it. It's a company commitment. We will continue to invest in proactively keeping the site safe, but we also want to empower people to report to us any content that breaches our standards (cited in Hopkins 2017).'

In December 2018, Mark Zuckerberg explicated Facebook's new approach to 'content governance and enforcement' as he writes in a rare note to users (Zuckerberg 2018). He explains that 'we have a responsibility to keep people safe on our services – whether from terrorism, bullying, or other threats. We also have a broader social responsibility to help bring people closer together – against polarization and extremism.' While asking the right questions – 'What should be the limits to what people can express? What content should be distributed and what should be blocked? Who should decide these policies and make enforcement decisions? Who should hold those people accountable?' – Zuckerberg reminds users that 'there isn't broad agreement on the right approach'.

In this note, Zuckerberg promises that Facebook will develop a content appeals process, including the creation of an oversight body – Facebook's so called 'Supreme Court' (Facebook 2019b; Klonick and Douek 2019; Klonick and Kadri 2018) – and will provide more transparency into their moderation policies. With the proposal of an independent oversight body, Facebook is introducing new mechanisms of accountability that will clearly move beyond the rhetoric of responsibility. Beside the establishment of this oversight body, Zuckerberg explains that quarterly transparency and enforcement reports as well as the support of academic research 'into how our systems are performing' (Zuckerberg 2018) will enhance accountability.

Facebook's leadership frames the community standards as a response to past wrongs in order to prevent future wrongs. While the transparency reports are rather backward looking, the explication and implementation of community standards looks forward. However, as the policies and practices described in the following section illustrate, Facebook's leadership shares responsibility with reviewers, moderators, algorithms and users.

Facebook's review and moderation policies

Today, approximately 15,000 to 30,000 people work for Facebook's safety and security business strand. Officially, about 7,500 people, including full-time employees, contractors and partner companies, review content around the clock, globally, and in over 50 languages (Silver 2018). The approximately 20 locations worldwide that are specialized in content review include offices in Facebook's headquarter in Menlo Park/California, Phoenix/Arizona, Austin/Texas and Tampa/Florida, which is operated by the professional services contractor Cognizant.[17] Major content review centres outside the US are in Berlin and Essen (Hoppenstedt and Stächelin 2018), Dublin (O'Connell 2019), Hyderabad and Manila (Chen 2014; Dwoskin, Whalen, and Cabato 2019; Roberts 2019), with most recent new offices in Barcelona (May 2018), Riga (December 2018) and Sofia (January 2019).

With major updates in March 2015 (Lapowsky 2015; Bickert 2015) and most importantly April 2018 (Haselton 2018), the community standards define what is allowed and forbidden on Facebook (Facebook 2018a, 2019c). Since former prosecutor and legal scholar Monica Bickert joined Facebook Inc. in 2013, content moderation is constantly evolving (Rosen 2013). The rules defining what is allowed and not allowed on Facebook are written and reviewed by the content policy team led by Bickert. Facebook's product team, then, develops tools to support these efforts, in particular artificial intelligence and machine learning to remove harmful and inappropriate content. But, as Ellen Silver, Vice President of Operations, explained in July 2018 'technology can't catch everything – including things where context is key like hate speech and bullying – so we also rely on another critical means of enforcement: the thousands of content reviewers we have all over the world' (Silver 2018).

The moderators and users

In the case of Facebook's moderation policies, users are perceived as an integral site of implementing these community standards. By flagging and reporting alleged violations, each individual user shares responsibility for what kind of content stays online or should be removed. User behaviour, though, remains unpredictable as the livestreaming of the terror attack in Christchurch reminds us. Nearly 200 users watched the shooting live before Facebook was informed by the police, and about 4,000 users viewed the video before it was removed. Facebook alone blocked 1.5 million attempts to upload the video again.

Those who actually make decisions about content removal, however, often remain invisible. Only a few reviewers and moderators have talked to journalists, often under the assurance of anonymity as Facebook enforces nondisclosure agreements with contractors and employees (Dwoskin 2019; Koebler and Cox 2018a; Newton 2019a, 2019b; O'Connell 2019). Silver justifies this invisibility with 'partly safety reasons'. Cultural competence and language proficiency are a job requirement beside resilience and a 'candidate's ability to deal with violent imagery for example' (Silver 2018). An open job advertisement for the position of a Community Operations Escalation Specialist in Singapore, one of the teams who respond to events like Christchurch, states about the preferred qualifications of candidates that a degree in International Relations, Political Science, Law, or related field is a plus; experience working with NGOs and/or government entities as well as experience in investigations, internet safety or equivalent environment is preferred; ability to use and learn tools like SQL and Excel to drive analytics and reporting required; and, finally, project management experience is highly desired.[18] To become a moderator, it is necessary to pass through the following three training steps (Koebler 2019): First, shadowing means that you observe how more experienced moderators do their job. Second, during the formal curriculum you learn how to apply the community rules based on practical exercises with on the job coaching and mentoring. Finally, during reinforcement, your moderation activities are supervised, mentored and counselled.

A former contractor based in Dublin/Ireland told reporters that he reviewed around 300 to 400 tickets on average per day, scaling up to 800 to 1,000 pieces on a busy night (O'Connell 2019). If reviewers and moderators were not able to take a decision, the report can escalate up the chain to subject matter experts in the Community Operations Escalations team or the content policy teams (Silver 2018). A sample of reviewer decisions is audited every week to evaluate the quality and accuracy – and even these auditors are audited on a regular basis, Silver writes. Given that journalists and former employees have accused Facebook (and its contractors) of quotas, Silver clarifies: 'content reviewers aren't required to evaluate any set number of posts – after all nudity is typically very easy to establish and can be reviewed within seconds, whereas something like impersonation could take much longer to confirm' (Silver 2018). Although Silver confirms that Facebook cares for their reviewers and provides medical and psychological care for them, former employees and contractors have criticized the company's reluctance leading some even to sue Facebook for PTSD (Koebler and Cox 2018b). Within the network of shared responsibility, content reviewers and moderators do not just exercise standards but have to actively interpret and assess the meaning of content.

The algorithms

Because we all make mistakes sometimes due to misleading interpretations, companies, experts and politicians proposed to use automated programmes to detect inappropriate, harmful and illegal content on the internet. Algorithms and so called 'upload filters' are controversially discussed, including more general questions regarding the development and implementation of Artificial Intelligence (AI). The already mentioned PhotoDNA is one way of screening the internet to find copies of an already deleted content. Scientists have created a variety of mathematical and linguistic models to detect hate speech on the internet more systematically (Johnson et al. 2019). However, the application of most algorithms does not help to prevent the streaming and circulation of newly created content.

Deployed for diverse aims as gathering intelligence, predictive policing and detection of online child pornography, Amoore and Raley (2017, 1) have recently called to pay more attention 'to the embodied actions of algorithms as they extend cognition, agency and responsibility beyond the conventional sites of the human'. Algorithms are designed and deployed by human agents, and share, when activated, responsibility with their creators and operators. Being aware of the empirical and normative questions at stake when automated systems are developed and applied, in 2013 Facebook started to recruit researchers specialized in neural networks, founded an Applied Machine Learning team (Metz and Isaac 2019) and invests 7.5 Million USD to set up an AI Ethics Institute at the Technical University in Munich (Quinonero Candela 2019).

Facebook's application of AI was first put to a test after the terror attacks in Paris in November 2015. The Applied Machine Learning team used a technology that was programmed by members of the new Facebook AI lab. The program identified terrorist propaganda on the social network by analyzing posts that mentioned the Islamic State or Al Qaeda. It flagged those posts that most likely violated the Facebook's community rules. Moderators then reviewed the posts (Metz and Isaac 2019).

Since the scandal of Cambridge Analytica and illegal data sharing, Facebook's investment in AI has become an issue of public debate. In a hearing before U.S. Senate Committees in April 2018, Zuckerberg testified that Facebook was developing machine-based systems to 'identify certain classes of bad activity' and declared that 'over a five- to 10-year period, we will have A.I. tools' that can detect and remove hate speech. Algorithms, however, are seen critical as they are often designed to detect patterns of behaviour for commercial interests and might be applied wrongfully.

The contested nature of AI and algorithms shows that non-human agents participate in the responsibility network that shapes internet governance. The application of AI, though, raises some tough questions where responsibility, accountability and liability can be located when finally algorithms decide whether to delete content or not. In a nutshell, it poses the question whether autonomous learning programs hold responsibility and should be held accountable for their decisions and the consequences their actions facilitate (Lin, Abney, and Jenkins 2017).

Conclusion

Discourses and practices of responsibility are changing for social media providers. As New Zealand's Prime Minister Jacinda Ardern made clear after the terror attack in Christchurch, '(w)e cannot simply sit back and accept that these platforms just exist and that what is said on them is not the responsibility of the place where they are published' (Ardern 2019). Governments are no longer willing to accept that social media platforms are intermediaries that hold no responsibility for user-generated and shared content, either live-streamed or posted on its platform. And companies like Facebook acknowledge that they have to respond pro-actively to removing and prohibiting the distribution of harmful and graphic content. This responsibility, though, is shared between a variety of actors and currently under negotiation. As the case of Facebook illustrates, policies and practices of content moderation are the outcome of a continuous exchange process between Facebook's leadership, its reviewers, moderators and users. Additionally, cooperation between governments, law enforcement agencies and Facebook are developing rapidly.

The flipside of such shared and negotiated responsibility, however, is diffusion. Lacking established procedures of liability, references to responsibility can disperse accountability and authority (Vogelmann 2017). As the case of Facebook illustrates, it can remain unclear who should respond to specific wrongs and who should prevent future wrongs. While a user can flag a harmful content, s/he is technically not able to remove it. Reviewers and moderations, then, have to carefully interpret posts and may fail to acknowledge the wrongs. While algorithms remove and delete content as instructed, the coding of the algorithm itself might be problematic. Finally, Facebook's leadership has to revise its community standards and moderation procedures in response to new events. Within this network, disruptions of responsibility can lead to a diffusion of who should be responsible. However, Facebook's proposal to establish an oversight body and attempts by several European governments to prosecute harmful and illegal content on social media may enhance accountability and liability in the future.

Understanding how ICT companies respond to wrongs on their platforms shows how a network of shared responsibility is evolving. It is of utterly importance to understand the discourses and practices that inform content regulation as these networks finally define what can and cannot be said and shown in the global digital public sphere. While CSR on the one hand and the freedom of expression on the other hand shape these discourses and practices of responsible behaviour, much is currently under negotiation.

Notes

1 The main theme of this hearing, however, was to discuss data protection and Russian disinformation on social media in the US Presidential elections. For the wording, see Transcript of Mark Zuckerberg's Senate Hearing, Washington Post, 10 April 2018 (https://www.washingtonpost.com/news/the-switch/wp/2018/04/10/transcript-of-mark-zuckerbergs-senate-hearing/).
2 Report of the Special Rapporteur on the promotion and protection of the right to freedom of opinion and expression, A/HRC/38/35. New York. (https://www.ohchr.org/EN/Issues/FreedomOpinion/Pages/ContentRegulation.aspx).
3 A unique set of pixels is contracted from a visual and a numerical identification tag or hash is created and placed in a database. Content that is uploaded can be automatically screened based on this database. For more information, see https://www.microsoft.com/en-us/photodna.
4 See https://www.manilaprinciples.org. See also the Global network Initiative, a network of internet and telecommunication companies including Facebook, Google and Twitter and its principles for freedom of expression, privacy and responsible company decision-making (https://globalnetworkinitiative.org/gni-principles/).
5 Turkey as well as Thailand requested to remove and delete content that was offending Atatürk, respectively, the King of Thailand based on prohibitions by national law. Technically, geo-blocking enables to make content unavailable for users in the host country while the content stays online.
6 Legality refers to restrictions by law securing a regular legal process of how and what kind of content is managed. It generally involves the oversight of an independent judicial authority as well as a mechanism for appealing decisions.
7 States or companies must demonstrate that the protection of rights and interests prevails the exercise of the right to free expression.
8 As legitimacy is a notoriously fuzzy concept, the UN report uses examples to define its meaning: 'Any restriction, to be lawful, must protect only those interests enumerated in article 19 (3): the rights or reputations of others, national security or public order, or public health or morals'.

9 For the EU, the most important legislation for the Internet is the e-commerce Directive adopted in 2000.
10 The EU has passed a law in 2008 that defines hate speech as 'the public incitement to violence or hatred directed to groups or individuals on the basis of certain characteristics, including race, color, religion, descent and national or ethnic origin'. EU Council (2008). Framework decision on combating certain forms and expressions of racism and xenophobia by means of criminal law, 2008/913/JHA. Brussels (https://eur-lex.europa.eu/legal-content/EN/TXT/HTML/?uri=LEGISSUM:l33178&from=EN). The Code of Conduct on countering illegal online hate speech carried out by NGOs and public bodies is regularly evaluated. For the latest report, see https://europa.eu/rapid/press-release_MEMO-18-262_en.htm.
11 See https://rankingdigitalrights.org/index2019/assets/static/download/RDRindex2019report.pdf
12 For Facebook, see https://transparency.facebook.com; For Google/YouTube, see https://transparencyreport.google.com/?hl=en; For Twitter, see https://transparency.twitter.com/en.html.
13 For an overview of Google Transparency reports, see https://transparencyreport.google.com/about?hl=en.
14 For an overview of removals on YouTube, see https://transparencyreport.google.com/youtube-policy/removals?hl=en.
15 For a variety of manuals, see https://www.theguardian.com/news/series/facebook-files. For the manual leaked in 2012, see https://publicintelligence.net/facebook-abuse-standards/.
16 While failing to remove a crime video that shows how Robert Godwin is killed in Cleveland/Ohio in April 2017 (Dreyfuss 2017; Isaac and Mele 2017), moderators removed the live-streamed documentation of Philando Castile's deadly police shooting in July 2016 before it was publicly released months later (Smith 2017). Facebook, though, also struggles with live-streamed suicides (Singer 2018).
17 This kind of outsourcing content moderation to the Global South and or private agencies is more and more criticized. The documentary 'The Cleaners' (2018), produced and directed by Block and Riesewieck, provides an excellent insider's view.
18 Retrieved from Facebook on 24 May 2019.

References

Amoore, L., and Raley, R. (2017). "Securing with algorithms: Knowledge, decision, sovereignty." *Security Dialogue*, 48(1): 3–10.

Angwin, J., and Grassegger, H. (2017). "Facebook's secret censorship rules protect white men from hate speech but not black children." *ProPublica*, 28 June (https://www.propublica.org/article/facebook-hate-speech-censorship-internal-documents-algorithms).

Ardern, J. (2019). "Statement delivered by Prime Minister Jacinda Ardern on Christchurch mosques terror attack on 19 March 2019" (https://www.mfat.govt.nz/en/media-and-resources/ministry-statements-and-speeches/prime-minister-jacinda-arderns-house-statement-on-christchurch-mosques-terror-attack/).

Bickert, M. (2015). "Explaining our community standards and approach to government requests." 15 March (https://newsroom.fb.com/news/2015/03/explaining-our-community-standards-and-approach-to-government-requests/).

Buddeberg, E. (2018). "Thinking the other, thinking otherwise: Levinas' conception of responsibility". *Interdisciplinary Science Reviews*, 43(2): 146–155.

Buni, C., and Chemaly, S. (2016). "The secret rules of the internet." *The Verge* (https://www.theverge.com/2016/4/13/11387934/internet-moderator-history-youtube-facebook-reddit-censorship-free-speech).

Butler, J. (1997). *Excitable speech: A Politics of the Performative*. New York and London: Routledge.

Carroll, A.B. (2008). "A History of Corporate Social Responsibility". In Crane, A., Matten, D., McWilliams, A., Moon, J., and Siegel, D.S., eds., *The Oxford Handbook of Corporate Social Responsibility*. Oxford: Oxford University Press.

Chen, A. (2014). "The laborers who keep dick pics and beheadings out of your Facebook feed". *The Wire*, 23 October (https://www.wired.com/2014/10/content-moderation/).

Dreyfuss, E. (2017). "Facebook streams a murder, an must now face itself". *Wired*, 16 April (https://www.wired.com/2017/04/facebook-live-murder-steve-stephens/).

Dwoskin, E. (2019). "Inside Facebook, the second-class workers who do the hardest job are waging a quiet battle." *The Washington Post*, 8 May (https://www.washingtonpost.com/technology/2019/05/08/inside-facebook-second-class-workers-who-do-hardest-job-are-waging-quiet-battle/?noredirect=on).

Dwoskin, E., Whalen, J., and Cabato, R. (2019). "Content moderators at YouTube, Facebook and Twitter see the worst of the web – and suffer silently." *The Washington Post*, 25 July (https://www.washingtonpost.com/technology/2019/07/25/social-media-companies-are-outsourcing-their-dirty-work-philippines-generation-workers-is-paying-price/).

Erskine, T. (2008). "Locating Responsibility: The Problem of Moral Agency in International Relations". In Reus-Smit, C, and Snidal, C., eds., *The Oxford Handbook of International Relations*: 699–707. Oxford: Oxford University Press.

Facebook (2018a). *Promoting Safety with Policy, Product and Operations*. 15 November (https://newsroom.fb.com/news/2018/11/inside-feed-community-integrity-keeping-people-safe/).

Facebook (2018b). *Understanding the Facebook Community Standards Enforcement Report* (https://fbnewsroomus.files.wordpress.com/2018/05/understanding_the_community_standards_enforcement_report.pdf).

Facebook (2019a). *Community Standards Enforcement Report* (https://transparency.facebook.com/community-standards-enforcement).

Facebook (2019b). "Global feedback and input on the Facebook oversight board for content decisions." *Facebook Newsroom* (https://fbnewsroomus.files.wordpress.com/2019/06/oversight-board-consultation-report-2.pdf).

Facebook (2019c). "Writing Facebook's rulebook." *Facebook Newsroom*, 10 April (https://newsroom.fb.com/news/2019/04/insidefeed-community-standards-development-process/).

Forst, R. (2011). *The Right to Justification: Elements of a Constructivist Theory of Justice*. New York: Columbia University Press.

Hansen-Magnusson, H. (2019). "The web of responsibility in and for the Arctic." *Cambridge Review of International Affairs*, 6(1): 1–26.

Haselton, T. (2018). "Here's Facebook's once-secret list of content that can get you banned." *CNBC online*, 24 April (https://www.cnbc.com/2018/04/24/facebook-content-that-gets-you-banned-according-to-community-standards.html).

Herz, M., and Molnár, P., eds. (2012). *The Content and Context of Hate Speech: Rethinking Regulation and Responses*. Cambridge: Cambridge University Press.

Hofmann, J., Katzenbach, C., and Gollatz, K. (2017). "Between coordination and regulation: Finding the governance in Internet governance." *New Media & Society*, 19(9): 1406–1423.

Hoover, J. (2012). "Reconstructing responsibility and moral agency in world politics." *International Theory*, 4(2): 233–268.

Hopkins, N. (2017). "Revealed: Facebook's internal rulebook on sex, terrorism and violence." *The Guardian*, 21 May (https://www.theguardian.com/news/2017/may/21/revealed-facebook-internal-rulebook-sex-terrorism-violence).

Hoppenstedt, M., and Stächelin, D. (2018). "A visit to Facebook's recently opened center for deleting content." *Vice*, 2 January (https://www.vice.com/en_us/article/qv37dv/facebook-content-moderation-center).

Isaac, M. and Mele, C. (2017). "A murder posted on Facebook prompts outrage and questions over responsibility." *The New York Times*, 17 April (https://www.nytimes.com/2017/04/17/technology/facebook-live-murder-broadcast.html).

Johnson, N.F., Leahy, R., Jonshon-Resrepo, N., Velasquez, N., Zheng, M., Manrique, P., Devkota, P., and Wuchty, S. (2019). "Hidden resilience and adaptive dynamics of the global online hate ecology." *Nature*, 573(7773): 261–265.

Klonick, K. (2017). "The new governors: The people, rules, and processes governing online speech." *Harvard Law Review*, 131(6): 1598–1670.

Klonick, K., and Douek, E. (2019). "Facebook's Federalist papers." *Slate*, 27 June (https://slate.com/technology/2019/06/facebook-oversight-board-community-standards-federalist-papers.html).

Klonick, K., and Kadri. T. (2018). "How to make Facebook's 'Supreme Court' work." *The New York Times*, 17 November (https://www.nytimes.com/2018/11/17/opinion/facebook-supreme-court-speech.html).

Koebler, J., and Cox, J. (2018a). "The impossible job: Inside Facebook's struggle to moderate two billion people." *Vice*, 23 August (https://www.vice.com/en_us/article/xwk9zd/how-facebook-content-moderation-works).

Koebler, J. (2019). "How Facebook trains content moderators." *Vice*, 26 January (https://www.vice.com/en_asia/article/43z7gj/facebook-content-moderators).

Koebler, J., and Cox, J. (2018b). "Content moderation sues Facebook, says job gave her PTSD." *Vice*, 24 September (https://www.vice.com/en_us/article/zm5mw5/facebook-content-moderation-lawsuit-ptsd).

Köver, C. (2019). "Urteil: Politikerin Künast darf auf Facebook beschimpft warden." *Netzpolitik.org*, 19 September (https://netzpolitik.org/2019/urteil-politikerin-kuenast-darf-auf-facebook-beschimpft-werden/).
Laidlaw, E.B. (2015). *Regulating Speech in Cyberspace: Gatekeepers, Human Rights and Corporate Responsibility*. Cambridge: Cambridge University Press.
Lapowsky, I. (2015). "New Facebook rules show how hard it is to police 1.4b users." *Wired*, May (https://www.wired.com/2015/03/facebook-guidelines/).
Lin, P., Abney, K., and Jenkins, R., eds. (2017). *Robot Ethics 2.0: From Autonomous Cars to Artificial Intelligence*. Oxford: Oxford University Press.
Metz, C., and Isaac, M. (2019). "Facebook's A.I. whiz now faces the task of pleasing up." *The New York Times*, 17 May (https://www.nytimes.com/2019/05/17/technology/facebook-ai-schroepfer.html).
Newton, C. (2019a). "Bodies in seats." *The Verge*, 19 June (https://www.theverge.com/2019/6/19/18681845/facebook-moderator-interviews-video-trauma-ptsd-cognizant-tampa).
Newton, C. (2019b). "The trauma floor." *The Verge*, 25 February (https://www.theverge.com/2019/2/25/18229714/cognizant-facebook-content-moderator-interviews-trauma-working-conditions-arizona).
O'Connell, J. (2019). "Facebook's dirty work in Ireland." *The Irish Times*, 30 March (https://www.irishtimes.com/culture/tv-radio-web/facebook-s-dirty-work-in-ireland-i-had-to-watch-footage-of-a-person-being-beaten-to-death-1.3841743).
Quinonero Candela, J. (2019). "Facebook and the Technical University of Munich announce new independent TUM Insitute for Ethics in Artifical Intelligence." *Facebook Newsroom*, 20 January (https://newsroom.fb.com/news/2019/01/tum-institute-for-ethics-in-ai/).
Roberts, S.T. (2019). *Behind the Screen: Content Moderation in the Shadows of Social Media*. New Haven and London: Yale University Books.
Rosen, G. (2018). "How are we doing at enforcing our community standards?" *Facebook Newsroom*, 15 November (https://newsroom.fb.com/news/2018/11/enforcing-our-community-standards-2/).
Rosen, G. (2019). "An update on how we are doing at enforcing our community standards." *Facebook Newsroom*, 23 May (https://newsroom.fb.com/news/2019/05/enforcing-our-community-standards-3/).
Rosen, J. (2013). "The delete squad." *The New Republic*, 29 April (https://newrepublic.com/article/113045/free-speech-internet-silicon-valley-making-rules).
Ruggie, J.G. (2011). "Guiding principles on business and human rights: Implementing the United Nations 'Protect, Respect and Remedy' framework." *Netherlands Quarterly of Human Rights*, 29(2): 224–252.
Scott, M., and Young, Z. (2018). "France and Facebook announce partnership against online hate speech." *Politico*, 12 November (https://www.politico.eu/article/emmanuel-macron-mark-zuckerberg-paris-hate-speech-igf/).
Silver, E. (2018). "Hard Questions: Who reviews objectable content on Facebook." *Facebook Newsroom*, 26 July (https://newsroom.fb.com/news/2018/07/hard-questions-content-reviewers/).
Singer, N. (2018). "In screening for suicide risk, Facebook takes on tricky public health role." *The New York Times*, 31 December (https://www.nytimes.com/2018/12/31/technology/facebook-suicide-screening-algorithm.html).
Smith, M. (2017). "Video of police killing of Philando Castile is publicly released." *The New York Times*, 20 June (https://www.nytimes.com/2017/06/20/us/police-shooting-castile-trial-video.html).
Stone, G.R. (1994). "Hate speech and the US constitution." *East European Constitutional Review*, 3(2): 78–82.
Taddeo, M., and Floridi, L. eds. (2017). *The Responsibility of Online Service Providers*. Cham: Springer Nature.
Tallberg, J., Bäckstrand, K., and Scholte, J.A., eds. (2018). *Legitimacy in Global Governance: Sources, Processes, and Consequences*. Oxford: Oxford University Press.
van Zuylen-Wood, S. (2019). "'Men are scum': Inside Facebook's war on hate speech." *Vanity Fair*, 26 February (https://www.vanityfair.com/news/2019/02/men-are-scum-inside-facebook-war-on-hate-speech).
Vetterlein, A. (2018). "Responsibility is more than accountability: from regulatory towards negotiated governance." *Contemporary Politics*, 24(5): 545–567.
Vogelmann, F. (2017). *The Spell of Responsibility: Labor, Criminality, Philosophy*. Lanham: Rowman & Littlefield International.
Young, I.M. (2011). *Responsibility for Justice*. Oxford: Oxford University Press.
Zakrzewski, C. (2019). "The technology 202." *The Washington Post*, 16 May (https://www.washingtonpost.com/news/powerpost/paloma/the-technology-202/2019/05/16/the-technology-202-a-researcher-is-still-surfacing-videos-of-the-christchurch-attacks-on-facebook-and-instagram-two-months-later/5cdcc65da7a0a435cff8c07f/?noredirect=on&utm_term=.76734ad7cdae).

Zeit online (2018). "Facebook darf Kommentare nicht nach Belieben entfernen." *Die Zeit*, 6 September (https://www.zeit.de/digital/internet/2018-09/oberlandesgericht-muenchen-facebook-kommentare-loeschen-meinungsfreiheit-urteil).

Zeit online (2019). "Sonderermittler bringt Internet-hetzer vor Gericht." *Die Zeit*, 21 July (https://www.zeit.de/news/2019-07/21/sonderermittler-bringt-internet-hetzer-vor-gericht).

Zuckerberg, M. (2018). "A blueprint for content governance and enforcement." 15 November (https://www.facebook.com/notes/mark-zuckerberg/a-blueprint-for-content-governance-and-enforcement/10156443129621634/).

PART IV

Global commons as responsibility objects

25
RESPONSIBILITY ON THE HIGH SEAS

J. Samuel Barkin and Elizabeth R. DeSombre

Introduction

The politics of the global commons are different from other areas of global politics in ways that have important implications for the issue of responsibility. To the extent that international relations presents states with collective action problems, issues of the global commons complicate that framework. With standard collective action problems, free-riding can be a tempting proposition. States rely on each other for collective defense, to which they may not all contribute equally. Some states provide stabilizing actions for the global economy that others benefit from without contributing to. Collective action problems can undermine global cooperation when states opt out of taking action that others would benefit from, or intend to benefit from, actions taken by others that no one steps up to take, because all would prefer that others act. These types of collective action problems may prevent states from achieving goals, such as security, that they would all benefit from.

But the types of environmental issues faced on the oceans are also common pool resource problems, which adds the characteristic of rivalness to the standard public goods problems of international relations: what one state does affects the condition of the resource for others (compare chapter by Bernstein in this volume). In standard collective action problems, one state that cares enough about addressing an issue may be able to provide a public good, such a security or monetary stability, on its own or by contributing more than its share. But in a rival issue, the states that do not participate in collective action may undermine the ability of those who do to provide the good in question. States that continue to allow overfishing, for instance, when others agree to limit their fishing behavior to protect the resource, may undermine the sustainability of the fishery altogether, thereby preventing those who practice restraint from succeeding in their efforts. To make matters worse, free-riders may even benefit from the protective action of others, initially finding more fish to catch because of the protective action of some states.

It is in this context of issue structure that questions of responsibility on the oceans arise (Barkin and DeSombre 2013). Because common pool resources can only be effectively managed collectively, responsibility in the context of such resources, including the high seas, necessarily has more collective overtones than is the case with other kinds of international goods. Both ethically and legally, a call to responsible use of the commons only makes sense in the context of coordinated collective action, because absent such coordination responsible management of common pool resources is not possible. Furthermore, since the condition of the commons changes over time, responsible coordination requires constant renegotiation of details such as catch or pollution limits; agreeing on a set of rules and sticking to them is insufficient.

Parts of the oceans (referred to as the high seas) are issues of the global commons, beyond the jurisdiction of any one state, and manageable only by collective action (compare the chapter by Tiller et al. in this volume). What that part is has been subject to collective re-negotiation over the history of ocean politics in ways that touch centrally on ideas about responsibility. These issues encompass both pollution and resource extraction. The pollution that affects the high seas is primarily pollution that is released from ships – either intentionally (as in disposing of waste) or unintentionally (as in accidents or pollution incidental to ship operations) – although there are some types of land-based pollution that find their ways into the ocean. Resource extraction involves either marine living resources (primarily fish) or minerals of various types (primarily from the seabed).

This chapter examines the development what responsibility (primarily, but not only, legal responsibility) means in the context of the oceans as a global commons. This discussion centers on the historical evolution of state responsibility in the management of that commons in the last century, in a context that worked to carve out sections of the formerly common areas of the ocean that states control, separating those from a newly evolving high norm of collective responsibility for resources on the high seas. We demonstrate how this norm has evolved in the context of management of marine living resources (e.g. fisheries), pollution, and minerals at the same time that a norm of responsibility for environmental effects of state behavior was developing more generally in international environmental law. The limitations of this developing norm of responsibility in the context of the commons characteristics of the high seas form a counterpoint to this evolution; norms require matching mechanisms for implementation to have the intended effect on commons resources. We therefore conclude both by lauding the shift from norms of open access to those of responsible management, and by calling for better mechanisms of implementation to back up those norms.

Responsibility and the commons

The international commons nature of the high seas makes the politics of responsibility different from the way responsibility has developed in other areas of international relations. The oceans are not, practically, excludable – anyone is permitted to access them and make use of their resources. Any excludability has to be created via a legal framework agreed to by all states and even then can be difficult to practically enforce. And the resources are rival. This aspect is easiest to see with extractable resources like fish or minerals, because when anyone takes them out of the system, less of them remain. But pollution has that characteristic as well, in that pollution put into the system diminishes the quality of the ocean, making a clean ecosystem less available to all others. This rivalness, in combination with nonexcludability, makes it difficult or even impossible for a small number of states to successfully protect ocean resources on their own. And the fact that this situation transpires internationally, where states cannot be forced to take on rules they do not choose to, increases the difficulty.

At the same time, most international politics involve issues that happen within or across state borders, where individual governments have clear jurisdiction. Global commons, on the other hand, can only be managed collectively, without a central authority to fall back on and without the possibility of one or a small group of governments taking it upon themselves to deal with the issue. This makes issues of implementation, and of the enforcement of norms of responsibility, more fraught than in other issue areas and settings. It also creates different kinds of responsibility with respect to different aspects of commons management. There is the collective responsibility of agreeing to legal mechanisms for commons management, the responsibility that all parties to the agreement bear for implementing it, and the responsibility that only some actors need undertake to enforce it.

This chapter looks at the high seas as a global commons. The high seas are defined here as areas outside of state-controlled waters. The extent of ocean areas that states control has changed over time. In the present, states have authority over the resources of areas in exclusive economic zones, extending 200 miles from the territorial seas (which at this point usually extend up to 12 nautical miles from shore), although that change has come about in a set of collective negotiations coinciding with the expansion of collective responsibility over the waters that states do not control. From a practical perspective, states have a responsibility to each other to participate in governance of the resources of the high seas, since the structure of the issue means that they are unable to manage these resources alone. They also have the responsibility not to cause harm, by their own action, to the environmental of other states or areas beyond national jurisdiction.

The evolution of responsibility on the high seas

Before the twentieth century, the high seas were considered to be open access, meaning that all who could access the ocean's resources were free to take as many of them as they could. Hugo Grotius, in *Mare Liberum* (1609), argued that the high seas in general were free to all and could not be legally claimed by any one state (or, for that matter, by any group of states). It followed that the resources of the sea were similarly free to all. This argument was disputed at the time, but over the course of the seventeenth century came to be accepted as the law of the sea, in no small part because its champions, England and Holland, were rising powers, and its opponents, Spain and Portugal, were waning. Grotius' idea of freedom of the sea included the freedom to fish, a logical extension given that the fishing technology of the time could not threaten stocks in the open ocean (Thornton 2004). States were responsible for ensuring that their nationals used the commons peacefully, but were not responsible (either ethically or legally) for what they took from it.

Over the following two centuries the idea of, and the details of, freedom of the high seas both in navigation and resource extraction were increasingly codified in international law and practice. Some ideas of responsibility were to be found in this codification, addressing questions of who was responsible in cases of maritime accidents, the responsibility of ships to each other in times of emergency, and so on. But these were all about the responsibility of ships, and based on nationality of the ships. The fact that ships themselves were seen as extensions of states – granted the nationality of the owner – suggested that this was seen as an aspect of state responsibility to other states, and a directly transactional responsibility at that. There was no sense of collective responsibility to the seas themselves, or to the resources that lay within them.

The resources that could be accessed in the high seas at that time were in any case seen as limitless (and no one imagined that waste deposited in a vast global ocean could have a meaningful effect), so the idea of responsible use meant little as a concept. As the limits of the oceans to provide food and absorb pollution became clearer over the course of the twentieth century, it became apparent that responsible use was becoming a practical prerequisite for continued use over the long term. In response, norms of collective responsibility for the oceans commons have been developed over the course of the last century, most notably between the 1970s and 1990s, with the norm developing in different ways and at a different pace with respect to different ocean resources.

This idea of collective responsibility developed concomitantly with a re-drawing of ocean borders. Even more so than on land, borders in the ocean are legal constructs that exist only by the collective understanding of states. In the modern era, states have always claimed some parts of the oceans as national jurisdiction, treated as part of a state's territory. For centuries the territorial sea was considered to be about three miles, the length (supposedly) that a cannon on shore could reach to defend that section of ocean. Some states began to claim ocean territory 12 miles or even more from their shore by the 1950s (and earlier iterations of international efforts to negotiate this limit collectively had failed), and by the early 1970s at least 40 states had claimed such an extension. At the same time, the United States had, under the Truman Proclamation of 1945, claimed jurisdiction over the natural resources of the continental shelf, which extends far beyond the territorial sea, and includes most of the fishery resources in this area. Other states took inspiration from this move and claimed control – or even territorial ownership – over ocean areas further and further from their coasts (Coquia 1979).

In other words, as it became clear that ocean resources were limited and vulnerable, one of the first reactions by states was try to claim these resources for their own use instead of looking for collective management. This was in part based on the economic logic of privatization of the commons, which suggests that actors will take more responsibility for resources they own individually than resources they own collectively. It was in this context that global negotiations worked to clarify where responsibility for ocean resources resided.

UNCLOS III

The 1982 United Nations Convention on the Law of the Sea (UNCLOS III) resolved this issue by enshrining a 12-mile territorial sea, and with it the creation of Exclusive Economic Zones (EEZs) that extend 200 miles beyond that but only allow states access to the resources of the area. This process put 35% of the oceans under some form of national jurisdiction (Sanger 1986, 67) One answer to the challenge of governing the global commons was thus to make that commons smaller – to essentially privatize state access to many of the resources of the ocean. At the same time, and also codified within UNCLOS, states were negotiating increasing norms and practices of collective responsibility for the remaining high seas that states did not individually control access to.

The biggest formal legal steps toward a norm of collective responsibility for the high seas commons were taken in conjunction with the UNCLOS process. The 1982 agreement had several effects on the collective governance of the commons. After making the commons significantly smaller by formalizing and regularizing the territorial seas and EEZs that some countries had been claiming for years, it identified the remaining area of the high seas as a "common heritage" (United Nations 1982, preamble) of humankind. In many ways, this identification reinforces Grotius' idea of *mare liberum*; it disallows any claims of sovereignty over the high seas, and guarantees rights of navigation, research, etc. At the same time, however, the idea of heritage undermines free access, because it implies that the resources of the high seas should be managed in a way that allow all people to benefit, not just those actors who can get to the resource first.

It is in the context of common heritage the UNCLOS explicitly introduced the idea of responsibility, the "responsibility to ensure that activities in the Area [the high seas], whether carried out by States Parties, or state enterprises or natural or juridical persons which possess the nationality of States Parties or are effectively controlled by them or their nationals, shall be carried out in conformity with this Part." (United Nations 1982, Part XI) UNCLOS serves as an important turning point in the development of norms and practices of responsibility with respect to the three types of issues we examine here – marine living resources, pollution, and mineral resources. Prior to UNCLOS efforts to develop this norm and put it into practice existed but these were codified, strengthened, and in some cases taken to a new level within

UNCLOS. Since the agreement the norms and practice of responsibility has continued to develop in all three of these areas.

Marine living resources

The origins of international cooperation in the management of marine living resources began with evidence that those resources were not, as previously believed, limitless. The earliest international agreements protecting ocean resources were actually about marine mammals; the earliest ones is generally considered to be the North Pacific Fur Seal Convention of 1911 (though it was negotiated in 1905), among Britain, the United States, Russia, and Japan. The treaty banned the hunting of seals in the open ocean, and enacted a managed on-shore hunt after what turned out to be an initial five-year moratorium. Its focus was specifically on conservation. (The earliest ocean resources agreement still in effect is the 1946 International Convention for the Regulation of Whaling (ICRW).) Both of these treaties were created with the acknowledgement of resource overuse. As the ICRW put it, "the history of whaling has seen over-fishing of one area after another and of one species of whale after another to such a degree that it is essential to protect all species of whales from further over-fishing" (IWC 1946, preamble).

Early fisheries agreements followed a similar model, focusing on the management of specific depleted resources, and involved only a few countries active in the fishery. Among the earliest ocean fisheries agreements was the 1882 Convention on North Sea Overfishing, which simply harmonized domestic fishing regulations in the area. Many of these early marine fisheries treaties concerned freedom from harm while fishing or the delimitation of fishing rights where territorial waters of different states joined (Daggett 1934). These early agreements were not couched in any broader norm of collective responsibility.

But they began a process of multilateral cooperation that led to the development of such a norm. Fisheries agreements explicitly about collective management began in the mid twentieth century, with measures like the Agreement for the Establishment of the Asia-Pacific Fishery Commission (1948) and the International Convention for the Northwest Atlantic Fisheries (1949). Over the course of the second half of the twentieth century a network of intergovernmental organizations, known collectively as Regional Fisheries Management Organizations (RFMOs) expanded the processes of multilateral cooperation on the high seas to cover most international fisheries. These RFMOs often were not particularly effective at the sustainably management of marine living resources, but had the effect of generating through practice a norm that these resources should be collectively managed rather than being free access. A key weakness in the RFMO system is the voluntary nature of international cooperation; states that did not choose to participate in particular RFMOs were not bound by the rules, or the limitations on resource extraction, agreed to within those organizations.

Before the negotiation of UNCLOS, RFMOs existed to manage many of the ocean's most valuable and threatened stocks, but not all relevant states belonged to them. In fact, fishing vessels began to intentionally register in states that remained outside of RFMOs to protect their legal rights to fish unencumbered by international rules, and these "flag of convenience" states chose not to participate in RFMOs to lure ship registration (DeSombre 2005).

UNCLOS reaffirms the right of the nationals of all states to fish on the high seas but also specifies a "duty" of all states to "to take, or to cooperate with other States in taking, such measures for their respective nationals as may be necessary for the conservation of the living resources of the high seas." It also specifies that states do so, when appropriate, through negotiation and the creation of RFMOs, and that they do so "on the best scientific evidence available" (United Nations 1982, Articles 117 and 119). "Duty" can be reasonably understood in this context as legal responsibility.

Since UNCLOS 1982 there have been further steps in institutionalizing the idea of collective responsibility of the ocean commons. The Agreement for the Implementation of the Provisions of the United Nations Convention on the Law of the Sea relating to the Conservation and Management of Straddling Fish Stocks and Highly Migratory Fish Stocks (1995) generally referred to as the Straddling Stocks Agreement, was negotiated in 1995 under the auspices of, and as an implementing agreement for, the fisheries sections of UNCLOS. This agreement does not discuss collective responsibility in those terms (it mentions responsibility only in the context of individual state liability for damages caused by its nationals and in the context of the relationship between the EU and its member states), although it does mention responsible conduct and responsible fisheries. But it does present as its general principle the duty of states to cooperate in the management of straddling and highly migratory fish stocks; it makes clear that states have an obligation to conduct their fishing in accordance with RFMO rules, to join them where they exist, and to negotiate them where they don't (United Nations, Article 118). The agreement legitimizes a norm of collective responsibility that can be seen as applying to all high seas fisheries.

This approach directly overrules the practice by vessels of registering in states that remain apart from RFMOs (and the choice by states to do so). In the wake of this agreement, and of concerted efforts by states within RFMOs to decrease access to markets of fish caught on the high seas outside of RFMO authority (DeSombre 2005), the practice of reflagging to avoid fisheries regulation has decreased significantly.

With fisheries many of the formal institutions involved in managing the resource preceded the development of the legal norm of collective responsibility. Fishing in the high seas has been a well-established activity for centuries, and there are strong vested interests, both commercial and national, in maintaining existing levels of extraction. Furthermore, cheating (what is called in the field illegal, unreported, and unregulated (IUU) fishing) can be difficult to identify in the first place, and to stop once identified. Nonetheless, the norm has enabled new ways of addressing IUU fishing, and of managing high seas fisheries more sustainably. Specifically, it has allowed individual states to police IUU fishing on the high seas, and to disallow IUU catch from ports and markets. Whereas such individual state policing and exclusion, previous to the new norm construct, would have been a violation of international law, it is now more acceptable under a variety of international rules ranging from freedom of the seas to World Trade Organization rules on free trade.

Ocean pollution

Ocean pollution followed a similar trajectory to fisheries. Initially, few considered the possibility that unwanted substances put into the vast ocean system could accumulate sufficiently to make a meaningful difference to the health of the ecosystem. The ocean was therefore used as a place to deposit ("dump") unwanted waste (including low-level nuclear waste) as well as operational pollution (slops and bilge or ballast water). As global shipping of oil increased (and more ships registered in low-standard states to escape domestic or international regulation), oil pollution from tanker accidents increased. This oil pollution – both from accidents and from operational discharges – became more visible by the 1960s as tar began washing up on beaches, coinciding with increased awareness of other effects of ocean pollution.

States began to negotiate, often with the assistance of the International Maritime Organization, restrictions on ocean pollution. Among the most important was the Convention on the Prevention of Marine Pollution by Dumping of Wastes and Other Matter (1972), referred to as the London Convention, which initially prohibited the dumping by ships of wastes specified on an appendix (and regulated the rest). This agreement was ultimately amended to prohibit all waste dumping form ships unless explicitly allowed by the agreement. Other agreements, like the International Convention for the Prevention of Pollution from Ships (1973/1978) addressed both operational and accidental oil pollution – and later other types of pollution – from ships. It is worth noting that the London Convention, even in 1972, included in the preamble the acknowledgement that "States have, in accordance with the Charter of the United Nations and the principles of international law, the sovereign right to exploit their own resources pursuant to their own environmental policies, and the responsibility to ensure that activities within their jurisdiction or control do not cause damage to the environment of other States or of areas beyond the limits of national jurisdiction" (Convention on the Prevention of Marine Pollution by Dumping of Wastes and Other Matter 1972, preamble).

At the same time, the polluter pays principle, which holds that states are responsible for damage caused by pollution generated within their borders was developing within international law. It was first articulated internationally in the context of the Organization for Economic Cooperation and Development (OECD) in 1972, and has been reiterated and refined in international declarations and agreements since then, most notably the Rio Declaration on Environment and Development in 1992. As originally envisioned within the OECD, this principle may have been intended to signal the need to "internalize" externalities; in other words, to work within a market system to account for the environmental costs. But once it moved from that origin to be taken up in the Rio Declaration and other contexts its interpretation became divorced from its origin, and has been interpreted more broadly. To some extent, the different ways of seeing it as pertaining to either good capitalist accounting (as OECD states may have) or actual moral or legal responsibility for the effects of one's actions (as developing states are more likely to) may account for the principle's widespread acceptance within international law. In either interpretation, this principle is not easy to apply to the high seas, where clearly tracing environmental damage in one state to sources in another is difficult at best, but it did set a precedent for the idea of environmental responsibility in international law.

In 1982, UNCLOS expanded the general obligations of states and the ships they are responsible for in terms of pollution, regardless of which international agreements they participate in. It requires that states take any necessary measures to "prevent, reduce and control pollution of the marine environment from any source;" they must also ensure that "activities under their jurisdiction or control are so conducted as not to cause damage by pollution to other states." (United Nations 1982, Articles 194(1–2) and 211). In addition, UNCLOS indicates that "States … shall be responsible and liable pursuant … for damage caused by pollution of the marine environment arising out of marine scientific research undertaken by them or on their behalf" (United Nations 1982, Article 263(3). Though less explicitly a norm of collective governance than is the one articulated for fisheries, it does suggest that states have a general obligation to reduce ocean pollution.

Mining

Extraction of mineral resources from the seabed has predominantly taken place within territorial seas, with drilling for oil as the most common type of extraction. Taking mineral resources from the ocean floor creates two potential problems: pollution (along with ecosystem disruption) from the extraction activities, and the actual removal of the resources, which leaves less available for others. From outside of territorial waters (and the later-created EEZs) the primary concern has been access to the mineral resources (such as manganese) found in nodules in the deep seabed. In this issue area, unlike the others discussed here, there was little if any actual extraction taking place before UNCLOS was negotiated.

Norms about access to these resources, however, were especially contested. Richer countries for the most part, the ones who actually could afford the technology to enable such extraction, were in favor of a principle that whoever could reach the resources had the right to take them. Developing countries argued in favor of an approach that would deem these resources "common heritage," and allow their extraction only for the benefit of all. In other words, richer countries favored an individual-responsibility model and poorer countries favored a collective responsibility model.

Although the resulting arrangements were a compromise between the two positions, UNCLOS institutionalized the idea of common heritage with respect to minerals to a much greater degree than with respect to either pollution or fishing. It created a new intergovernmental organization, the International Seabed Authority (ISA) to oversee mining of the deep seabed. Anyone wishing to mine the seabed is required to work through the ISA, which is tasked both with creating and enforcing environmental standards for mining under the high seas and with distributing the benefits of such mining. This latter task is accomplished through equitable distribution of mining permits when these are requested by actors from a variety of states, through technology transfer, and through actual redistribution of some of the wealth from minim operations. These provisions have been weakened over time, in an effort to lure the reluctant United States into the agreement, but the concept of the deep seabed as common heritage generally remains. At this point only limited deep seabed mining has occurred, most of it exploratory, but contracts have been granted and mining is taking place.

In this case, the development both of the norm and of the formal institution codifying collective responsibility preceded any actual mining activity. This makes it difficult for any prospective miners to act outside the ISA regime, particularly since mining the deep seabed is a sufficiently capital-intensive and intrusive activity that it would be difficult to undertake surreptitiously. It is not yet clear in what manner, or how well, the ISA will fulfill its role as overseer of collective responsibility on this issue; the answer to this question will likely become much clearer over the next half decade, as mining becomes commercialized.

Implementing responsibility on the high seas

Collectively, these legal developments have led to the replacement of the norm of open access with that of collective responsibility. The development of this ocean-specific norm coincided with increased acceptance of the general international environmental norm that states have the responsibility to ensure that their activities do not cause environmental damage in ways that affect other states, including in areas beyond national jurisdiction.

There are three key issues hindering the implementation of norms of responsibility on the high seas, as we will explain in more detail below. The first of these is the question of enforcement of rules created by RFMOs and international agreements on marine pollution. The norms make enforcement easier, but do not ensure that it is done sufficiently. A second and prior issue is the creation of those rules in the first place. Responsible management is supposed to be based on the best science available, but there is room for interpretation of, and sometimes there is outright denial of, that science. Furthermore, the decision-making structure of the relevant institutions is often biased toward those parties most skeptical about responsible management. A third and more politically fundamental issue is that the creation of norms of responsibility for the high seas and their incorporation into international law has generally been driven by the global north, and more specifically by those states with the most to gain in the short term from more sustainable use of the oceans. This can make for a contested norm.

With respect to the question of enforcement of rules, a norm of responsible use of a commons is only as strong as users' ability to find and deal with free riders. In other words, monitoring and enforcement are key. Technology is making monitoring of both fishing and pollution easier, through mechanisms like required transponders to locate vessels fishing on the high seas and satellite photography to spot pollution from ships. This is where a norm of responsibility comes in; it allows actors (state or otherwise) access to mechanisms that encourage or force recalcitrant state actors into agreements and enforce the terms of those agreements on IUU fishers and polluters where their flag states will not. Primary among these mechanisms with respect to fishing are policing action on the high seas, denial of IUU vessels access to ports, and denial of markets to fish not certified to be caught within RFMO rules.

With a norm of open access and no norm of collective responsibility many of these mechanisms would have (and were) deemed infringement on state sovereignty. With a norm of collective responsibility they are not. Nevertheless, even with the norm, monitoring and enforcement remain collective action problems. Actors have access to a broader range of mechanisms to enforce more sustainable management of the ocean commons if they choose to do so. But the difficulty of the commons remains intact: with enforcement being to some extent a voluntary activity, the specter of free riders undermining collective management of the commons is always present. In other words, responsibility as a constitutive or background norm is necessary but not sufficient. Effective collective management also requires an active concern among a group of actors collectively able to enforce the norm.

A prior difficulty with implementing a norm of collective responsibility with respect to the high seas commons is that collective management is built on a problematic institutional structure. The general norm, as stated in UNCLOS, is premised on "the best science available." This seems at first as if it should be non-problematic. But there is room for interpretation of what constitutes the best science and how precautionarily that science should be interpreted. And as is often seen in environmental politics, scientific uncertainty (which is usually present to some extent) can be used as an excuse to argue against active management when there is a political incentive to do so. The upshot is that the scientific advice offered, for example, by the scientific bodies within RFMOs, is often not accepted at face value by the rules-setting bodies. States that want to fish more sometimes do so through arguments over how to interpret the science, and the procedural gaps between the science and the rules.

In addition, the rules-making procedures of the relevant intergovernmental organizations, whether RFMOs or bodies such as the International Maritime Organization, either require unanimity or allow countries to recuse themselves from specific rules. For example, the Convention for the Conservation of Antarctic Marine Living Resources (CCAMLR) requires unanimity to generate specific annual quotas, giving the state(s) least interested in sustainable management effective veto power in the setting of the rules on which collective responsibility is based. On the other hand, individual members of the Northwest Atlantic Fisheries Organization (NAFO) can object to specific rules such as quota allocations and thereby not be bound by them, even as the general quota on which the allocation is based is adopted as a rule. The norm of responsibility is to general to give clear guidance on how to address either of these sorts of manipulations of exiting management institutions.

A final issue with the norm of collective responsibility in the management of the high seas commons is that not all states are equally enthusiastic about it. The norm was promoted by, and is in large measure enforced by, a small number of predominantly Western states. These are not necessarily the states one would normally think of as hegemonic; change in high seas norms was driven in part by Iceland in the cod wars with the UK, and Canada in the turbot war with the

EU (primarily Spain). The main nonstate supporters of the norms of responsibility are environmental NGOs that are, again, overwhelmingly Western. While few states will argue in principle against norms of responsible use of the high seas, different levels of enthusiasm in implementing these norms across countries (including across countries within the West, and for that matter within the EU) can make them brittle and difficult to implement. This difficulty underlies both the continuing issues with institutional design of the relevant intergovernmental organizations and some of the challenges of implementation and contributes to the politicization of the science and rule-making.

Finally, the state-centric nature of the governance of the oceans has implications for how norms of responsibility are created and enacted. In part because so much of what happens on the high seas takes place so far from land, and in part because the effects resource or pollution problems have on people are indirect or disconnected in time from the activities that create them, most of the discussions of responsibility focus on state collective action in ways that seem remote from more individual normative concerns. One exception is the context of marine mammal protection. The ICRW regime designed for conservation (and sustainable use) of whales has, for some states, become an effort to protect the well-being of whales as entities. This change is directly traceable to actions by nongovernmental organizations and citizen action, but, again, fits into the model of Northern and Western activists pushing a normative agenda with which other states disagree – so much so that Japan has just exited the ICRW in order to continue to pursue commercial whaling.

Conclusion

The good news is that a norm of collective responsibility for the resources of the high seas has developed over the past half-century or so and has become institutionalized in international law and practice. This norm is based on the principle that the high seas are part of the common heritage of humankind, that their resources should be used in a sustainable way, and that all users of those resources have a duty to do in a manner consistent with this responsibility. It is also based on the explicit idea that this responsibility should be implemented collectively, through formal institutions of international cooperation. This norm of collective responsibility is not a panacea. It ensures that all states recognize that they have a duty to preserve the resources in questions and to do so collectively, but it is left to politically processes to negotiate the specifics of what that means and how it will be done.

This norm has been institutionalized and implemented differently with respect to different categories of resources in the high seas. The norm is least institutionalized with respect to pollution and seems to have had a smaller impact on behavior there than with other resources; it has been most fully implemented in the normative pronouncements about the resource so the deep seabed, though in practice it is less clear how well these norms are implemented. With fishing the institutional structure for managing the resource for the most part preceded the norm. Partly as a result, the structure is designed in a way that can interfere with the implementation of responsible collective management. In the case of minerals, the norm preceded both the creation of the management institution and any extractive activities; it remains to be seen how this different institutional history will affect patterns of resource extraction. In all three cases, though, one can reasonably make the case that the norm has made sustainable management of the resources in question easier (if not easy).

Responsibility works differently with respect to international commons than elsewhere, because free riding can undo the effects of, rather than just hinder, cooperation. This creates a need for effective enforcement for meaningful norm implementation in a way that is not the case in many other issue areas in international relations. The dramatic shift from open access and a race for resources to the widespread acceptance of at least the principle of collective responsibility is a major change in how the world has approached ocean resources, but translating this shift into sustainable management of these resources in practice requires careful attention to, and political support for, implementation.

References

Barkin, J. S., and DeSombre, E. R. (2013). *Saving Global Fisheries: Reducing Fishing Capacity to Promote Sustainability*. Cambridge, MA: MIT Press.

Coquia, J. R. (1979). "Development and Significance of the 200-Mile Exclusive Economic Zone." *Phillipine Law Journal*, 54(4): 440–448.

Daggett, A. P. (1934). "The Regulation of Maritime Fisheries by Treaty." *American Journal of International Law*, 28(4): 693–717.

DeSombre, E. R. (2005). "Fishing Under Flags of Convenience: Using Market Power to Increase Participation in International Regulation." *Global Environmental Politics*, 5(4): 73–94.

Grotius, H. (1609 [2009]). *Mare Liberum*. Original Latin Text and English Translation by Robert Feenstra) Leiden: Brill.

IWC (1946). International Convention for the Regulation of Whaling. Cambridge: International Whaling Commission.

Sanger, C. (1986). *Ordering the Oceans: The Making of the Law of the Sea*. London: Zed Books.

Thornton, H. (2004). "Hugo Grotius and the Freedom of the Seas." *International Journal of Maritime History*, 16(2): 17–38.

United Nations (1982). *United Nations Convention on the Law of the Sea*. New York.

26
THE ROLE OF HUMANITY'S RESPONSIBILITY TOWARDS BIODIVERSITY

The BBNJ treaty

Rachel Tiller, Elizabeth Nyman, Elizabeth Mendenhall and Elizabeth De Santo

Introduction

In a tweet on 12 May 2019, Ambassador and Permanent Representative of Palau to the United Nations, Ngedikes Olai Uludong credits President of the Republic of Palau, Tommy E. Remengesau, Jr., with the following statement: 'Here in the Pacific, we know how central the ocean is to our economies, livelihoods and traditions. And we cannot, will not, address the climate crisis without turning to our greatest resource-the ocean'. The concept of human responsibility to confront climate change and ocean acidification relative to the role of the ocean therein is especially important when considering that the current concentration of carbon dioxide (CO_2) in the atmosphere has increased by 40% since the 277 parts per million (ppm) that was estimated in 1750 (Le Quéré et al. 2017). We have also seen that ocean pH is declining at an unprecedented rate compared to the last 300 Million years of the Earth's history (Hönisch et al. 2012; Pearson and Palmer 2000), corresponding with the post-industrial revolution increase in anthropogenic CO_2 emissions (Turley et al. 2010; Zeebe and Ridgwell 2011). As such, environmental challenges at global, regional and local levels require joint efforts of state and non-state actors and parties to responsibly manage and preserve the ocean.

However, more than half of the global ocean area is located in what is termed Areas Beyond National Jurisdiction (ABNJ), where only a patchwork of uncoordinated governance efforts actualizes this responsibility. In these areas, scientific discoveries have identified seamounts, hydrothermal vents and cold-water corals in rare and vulnerable ecosystems, as well as the potentials of marine genetic resources that could be used in biotechnology industries globally. None are governed, as they are not the possession or responsibility of any sole state. Concern over contradictions in terms of sustainable development and conservation efforts to preserve the biodiversity of these areas responsibly have therefore increasingly been vocalized by ocean users, potential users, and advocates. In light of this, the United Nations General Assembly (UNGA) called for an intergovernmental negotiation process towards a new multilateral treaty in Resolution 69/292, adopted in June 2015, on biodiversity in areas beyond national jurisdiction (BBNJ). The resultant treaty will act as a governance mechanism, meant to establish methods to conserve and protect marine biodiversity and provide guidelines to regulate its exploitation responsibly in the ABNJ.

In light of this, the current chapter will discuss the human interactions and explore different sources and manifestations of responsibility within the context of ocean biodiversity protection in areas with little or no governance, but where unknown potentials for resource exploitation exist. In doing so, we ask questions about *processes of regime formation*, the *design of effective regimes* and *interaction with other regimes* and analyse humanity's responsibility towards biodiversity, within the framework of *complex institutional dynamics*, in order to determine how the process of regime development could lead to adequate governance of our common heritage in this new frontier. We discuss this within the framework of the negotiations towards a new implementing agreement to the Law of the Sea, where the ambition is to develop a common regulatory framework to cover previously unmanaged areas outside national jurisdiction as a common responsibility of all states, sectors and individuals.

Human responsibility for ocean protection

In 1609, Hugo Grotius wrote Mare Liberum, or 'Freedom of the Seas', the most influential argument in favour of the freedom of navigation, trade and fishing at sea. This document declared that no country can enclose or possess the oceans, as the oceans cannot be placed under sovereign control of any one country (Grotius 2012). The principle that Grotius espoused is reflected in the contemporary ocean governance regime, which identifies a set of inalienable freedoms that are available to all on the high seas beyond national jurisdiction. The challenge with this concept lies in the fact that this principle, while ensuring freedoms for states, sectors and individuals, also removes all responsibility from any and all to ensure that these areas are protected. All actors have a right to use the high seas, while no actor has a specific duty to protect them (compare also the chapter by Barkin and DeSombre in this volume).

In this vein, more than two decades ago, Costanza et al. (1998) listed five anthropogenic challenges to the ocean that have largely persisted into the 21st century. These were (1) over-fishing, (2) ocean waste disposal and spills, (3) the destruction of coastal ecosystems, (4) land-based contamination and (5) climate change. Only minor changes are needed to 'age proof' this list for 2019, and mostly by way of expanding its categories. For example, if we rename (1) 'overfishing' to the more encompassing 'unsustainable resource exploitation', (2) 'Ocean disposal and spills' to include marine litter in general (including marine plastics) and add 'and ocean acidification' to (5) 'climate change', the list is largely brought up to date to the issues currently in vogue in global ocean governance as well as in the popular and scientific communication channels around the world. Costanza et al. also present six core principles named the 'Lisbon Principles', which they argue should be considered key for sustainable governance of the oceans to be achieved within the paradigm of adaptive governance '… whereby policy-making is an iterative experiment acknowledging uncertainty, rather than a static 'answer'. The first of these principles introduced is that of '*Responsibility*'[1]:

> Principle 1: Responsibility. Access to environmental resources carries attendant responsibilities to use them in an ecologically sustainable, economically efficient, and socially fair manner. Individual and corporate responsibilities and incentives should be aligned with each other and with broad social and ecological goals.
>
> *(Costanza et al. 1998)*

McKinley and Fletcher (2010) discuss responsibility further in assessing the evolution from '… top down, state directed regimes towards a more participatory, community-based governance framework.' In their study, they assessed sense of responsibility and attitudes towards what they call 'Marine Citizenship' by UK marine practitioners, and what factors they considered important in the development of this citizenship, as well as its implications for ocean governance in general.

One of the factors that interviewees considered important in the building of this citizenship, or stewardship as one might call it today, is that of marine education. This is considered important since it could raise awareness about the importance of the ocean which could ultimately lead to a higher degree of marine citizenship. However, though the interviewees in this study recognized that an inclusion into the curriculum could increase awareness, especially with children, and that this could then trickle to the parent generations, there would be a time lapse before this knowledge would filter into the consciousness of the adult population. Generally, though, the interviewees considered the government as having the ultimate responsibility, but that all levels of governance would have to be involved, including national and regional. One interviewee of McKinley and Fletcher (2010), stated what is more obvious though in asking '… perhaps the question should be who isn't responsible?'

The question of responsibility – who has it, what they are responsible for and how this should be reflected in governance – is an important one for the development of the law of the sea as well. For hundreds of years, the freedom of the seas, whereby none were responsible (Grotius 1916), was the principle institution for global ocean management, until the 1982 United Nations Convention on the Law of the Sea (United Nations 1982) established among others the 200 nm Exclusive Economic Zones (EEZ), effectively nationalizing large portions of the oceans. Various types of responsibility are now largely spelled out in in UNCLOS, which has since become the authoritative treaty for managing the resources of the ocean. UNCLOS extended state control over territorial waters to 12 nautical miles and created an Exclusive Economic Zone (EEZ) to allow for the state to take responsibility for the governance of the marine resources up to 200 nautical miles from shore. It also provided for state responsibility for continental shelf resources out to 200 nautical miles, with a potential extension to 350 nautical miles. In fact, the word 'Responsibility' is in the headings of different sections 9 times in the Law of the Sea (UNCLOS),[2] ranging from issues of damages caused by warships to the flag state responsibility of managing anadromous fish stocks in rivers to collisions at sea. Section 9 however is the most overarching one on Responsibility, where it is explicit that "States are responsible for the fulfilment of their international obligations concerning the protection and preservation of the marine environment'.

However, beyond these areas within national jurisdiction, the concept of state responsibility is more controversial. There were differing views during the UNCLOS negotiations on how best to handle the high seas and the deep seabed – those areas that were outside of the enclosures created by EEZs and continental shelves, and where the potential for future financial gains from extractive exploitation were uncertain at best (Hollick 2017). UNCLOS reaffirmed the principle of 'freedom of the seas', though, and kept the high seas open and free for all to use and the responsibility of none. States could use it both for transit and for resource gathering among others (Article 87), provided that they followed the then-new rules set down in the Convention for the Prevention of Pollution from Ships (MARPOL) (1973/78) and the Convention on the Prevention of Marine Pollution by Dumping of Wastes and Other Matter (International Maritime Organization (IMO) 1972). There is also a general 'duty to cooperate in the repression of piracy', which could be understood as a responsibility (Article 100). Assigning responsibility for protecting these marine commons was not of great concern for states at the time, and they were content with continuing with a regime of freedom of the seas, with the major exception of the deep seabed (Friedheim 1993).

Responsibility for areas where nobody responsible

UNCLOS provides as such the umbrella – both in terms of the legal framework, but also the international context – for the current negotiations which goal it is to address this known weakness, namely the lack of an encompassing legal regime that assigns responsibility for protecting the ocean that lies beyond national jurisdiction as well, including the sea surface, water column, and seabed. Tiller et al. (2019) present the background for these treaty negotiations, including the four main elements of the package of issues that the states are to negotiate during the conferences, which is anticipated to span four meetings over two years. The issues are (1) marine genetic resources, including questions on benefit sharing, (2) area-based management tools, including marine protected areas, (3) environmental impact assessments, and (4) capacity-building and the transfer of marine technology (United Nations General Assembly 2011) and the negotiations, and eventual agreement, are referred to as 'BBNJ', which stands for 'Biodiversity Beyond National Jurisdiction'.

The BBNJ negotiations intend to extend the goals of conservation and sustainable use to marine biodiversity in areas of the ocean beyond national jurisdiction. The BBNJ process is an example of what the literature calls *institutional layering* (van der Heijden 2011; Thelen 2003, 2004). This is a process whereby new elements are grafted onto an already stable institutional framework, in this case the BBNJ treaty on to UNCLOS. These are institutional frameworks that have a need of changes because of different circumstances and that potentially may alter the institutional trajectory of the given institution itself. The layering process is customarily gradual, and not a result of an exogenous shock to the system necessarily, such as for instance the hole in the ozone layer and the effect that had on the Montreal Protocol (Morrisette 1989) or the impact that the 11 September 2001 terrorist attacks had on generating the 2005 Protocol for the Convention of the Suppression of Unlawful Acts Against the Safety of Maritime Transport (Kraska 2017).

In the realm of the ocean, marine geoengineering activities (such as iron fertilization) are examples of issue areas that have already been layered onto existing agreements, filling in patches that were previously not managed. We can also see evidence of institutional layering in the amendments to the various International Maritime Organization treaties on shipping, such as the Safety of Life at Sea Treaty (SOLAS) or MARPOL. SOLAS was originally drafted after the Titanic disaster, to ensure that there were minimum standards for merchant and passenger ships. We are currently on the fifth version of the SOLAS treaty, effective as of 1974, due to the many updates that have been needed as both the shipping industry and technology have changed. The last version in 1974 introduced a smoother process for emendation to prevent the need for continual renegotiations in the face of changing needs. MARPOL, which came into force in 1983, was an answer to increasing marine pollution from the shipping industry, and attempted to strike a balance between the needs for marine protection as well as the need for economic efficiency of the shipping industry (Griffin 1994). This environmental agreement has since had six annexes to its original text, and ninety-four (94) amendments throughout the years until 2016, updating its original content with up to date information and new realities, and expanding its remit to include air pollution from ships (Mitchell 2017).

Though it is undecided whether the BBNJ agreement will ultimately fuse with UNCLOS, like the Part XI agreement on the area (in which case you would have to join both UNCLOS and the BBNJ treaty – or neither) or if it will be independent like the 1995 Fish Stock Agreement (FSA), the latter is more likely given the narratives of some of the delegates that are non-parties to UNCLOS, including El Salvador, Eritrea, Iran, Turkey and Colombia. This was stated very specifically by the EU in the first session of negotiations when they stated that the '… EU cannot accept the insertion of a reference to non-parties in a text … This inclusion is not necessary. Participation in the implementing agreement will not affect the status of non-parties to the convention. Some states are party to this agreement but not to UNCLOS and this has not affected their legal status to the LOS'. In the case of the FSA, when it became clear that the original UNCLOS agreement had not adequately addressed the issue of straddling – and highly migratory fish stocks, the global governance community negotiated a second major international agreement that together with the original now constitute the Law of the Sea regime (Asgeirsdottir 2009; Mendenhall 2019). While the Part XI agreement was functionally an amendment to UNCLOS, it was characterized as an 'implementing agreement' for political reasons, to avoid highlighting the divergence from the original settlement. In contrast, the FSA was designed to complete the 'unfinished business' of UNCLOS, and 'fill in the gaps' for fisheries management (Harrison 2011). The BBNJ treaty thereby, once implemented, will be the third implementing agreement to UNCLOS along with these two, attempting to ensure our responsibility to the ocean moves beyond EEZs.

Complex institutional dynamics and regime effectiveness

To explore to what degree the attempts to responsibly manage this area will be effective, however, it is important to explore the groundwork made during these negotiations towards the implementing agreement to the ocean regime. As such, for the purposes of this chapter, we consider the BBNJ instrument within the framework of regime theory. The concept of a 'regime' emerged in political science in the late 1970s and 1980s, during the time when UNCLOS was being negotiated. An international regime is customarily considered as being set up by a set of principles, norms, rules and procedures for making decisions about a specific issue of importance to several actors in the international arena (Krasner 1982), such as that of biodiversity protection in ABNJ. Regimes can include multiple governance institutions, which focus converging expectations, establish normative frameworks, and include behavioural injunctions. Regimes are aimed at a specific task: solving or ameliorating socio-economic, environmental and/or political issues that are or could become a challenge for stakeholders in the area (Hasenclever, Mayer, and Rittberger 2000; Krasner 1982; Stokke 2007).

While attempting to design a regime that is implemented by state parties and enters into force is a natural goal of a negotiation process, the post-negotiation time is critical in the life of a regime. Only when having been successfully negotiated through all three parts in the regime formation process, namely Agenda Formation, Negotiation and Operationalization, will a regime have the opportunity to be implemented and to effectively manage the behaviours and resources it was designed to govern (Young 1998). The most basic condition of operation is typically ratification by sovereign states, who thereby 'consent to be bound' by the dictates of a given treaty. But many regimes require other types of actions and institution-building to become fully operational. There are different political processes that characterize each of three stages identified by Young (1998). Table 26.1 identifies six sub-sections of each stage in the regime creation process and their expected differences.

For the purposes of the BBNJ instrument, the agenda formation stage has been completed and has been thoroughly discussed in the literature (e.g. Ardron et al. 2014; Ardron, Ruhl, and Jones 2018; Blasiak et al. 2017; Druel and Gjerde 2014; Druel, Gjerde, and Warner 2014; Gjerde and Rulska-Domino 2012; Lallier and Maes 2016; Marciniak 2017; Wright et al. 2018). This is a regime formation stage that takes place when a given issue, such as biodiversity protection in the ABNJ, finds its way onto the international political agenda with enough recognized importance that actors are able to justify both time and capital (political and real), so that the issue can be given a spark moving it in the direction of negotiations (Young 1998). At the negotiation stage, however, where the BBNJ instrument currently is, the issues should usually be well defined, and the majority of time during negotiation would be spent removing the areas of the text where there is disagreement between the groups involved. This can include boiling agreements down to the so-called lowest common denominator of consensus, but it can also include issue linkages, side payments, and other kinds of deals that actually build agreement around text and commitments.

Table 26.1 Stages and subsections in regime creation processes

Expected differences	Agenda formation	Negotiation	Operationalization
Driving Forces	Ideas	Interests	Material conditions
Players (individuals – not organizations)	Intellectual Leadership	Entrepreneurial Leadership	Structural Leadership
Collective Action Problems	Miscommunication	Stalemate or gridlock	Asymmetries in levels of effort
Context	Broad changes in the political environment	More specific exogenous events	Domestic constraints
Tactics	Efforts to influence the framing of the problem	Threats and promises	Tactics of administrative or bureaucratic politics
Design Perspective	Focusing on the big picture	Concern for language to be included in agreements	Focus on domestic concerns to the detriment of efforts to set up the relevant international machinery

Source: Authors.

It is at this stage that the path towards effectiveness during the operationalization stage is set, because the negotiation phase determines the requirements and outlines the mechanisms for behavioural change on the part of users and other actors.

Given that a regime is constituted under the premises of responsibly managing a given resource, or to solve a collective challenge that has arisen, such as overfishing or pollution or overexploitation of resources in general, an effective regime would for some naturally entail the regime solves these environmental issues within a designated timeframe. In other words, to assess its effectiveness, one would explore to what degree the environment has improved for the given issue area for which the regime was created (Helm and Sprinz 2000, 632; Keohane, Haas, and Levy 1993, 7; Zürn 1998, 637). Others though would evaluate regime effectiveness from a legal perspective, where the question to be answered would be whether the environmental challenges have been solved within the statutory framework of the given regime as well as international law, and whether member states have followed the rules and regulations they made a commitment to when signing the agreement. One can therefore argue, purely definition wise, that effectiveness can be explored from either an institutional or environmental perspective (Kütting 2000, 30; Zürn 1998, 637), both of which would affect the concept of responsibility differently.

Negotiating the BBNJ regime – paper tiger or teeth that bite?

For the purposes of argument in this chapter, we will consider the institutional perspective, making the assumption that these are developed to ensure the latter and apply the effectiveness calculation developed by Breitmeier, Young, and Zürn (2006). The elements needed for effectiveness according to this calculation, when measured as a sign of compliance with regulations produced by the instrument, or the institutional perspective, are: Horizontal enforcement + strong mechanisms for verification + legalization + participation by voluntary organizations + institutional development = high compliance with regime rules. Notably, this formula does not include strong penalties for violate of regime rules, nor does it explicitly require the creation of independent dispute settlement functions.

We therefore want to explore to what degree the delegates of the BBNJ negotiations for this new treaty discuss the elements of the effectiveness calculation when moving towards the stage of agreement to a final version of the treaty?

Table 26.1 shows that at the negotiation stage, the players are clearly identified as self-interested actors who naturally seek to craft agreements that are congenial to their own interest in the ABNJ; the *driving force* in this case. During the negotiations, as well as during the PrepComs, the role of national self-interest has been evident, especially when considering the differences between the narratives of the developing nations and those of OECD countries as well as Russia. The OECD countries and the developing states (the G77, SIDS, and African Group) have major areas of contention, particularly regarding the consideration of the water column of the high seas as the 'common heritage of mankind', the nature and extent of capacity building and technology transfers from developed to developing states, and the need or not for a special funding mechanism to aid those states who would be ill able to afford exploitation of BBNJ resources. This is also tied into the *collective action challenges* at this stage, which mostly are in terms of stalemate or gridlock in negotiations, over issues where the positions of different actors are largely irreconcilable. Similarly tied into this is the *tactics* of the actors at the negotiation stage, which centre on both threats and promises. For instance, Russia said during one of their interventions in the first intergovernmental conference in September 2018 that '… we wouldn't want to see a text that includes readymade decisions – this could lead to some delegations finding themselves in an uncomfortable position about whether they'd be able to adopt this, or would have to refuse to participate in this in the future – a "take it or leave it approach"'.

According to the literature, the *players* at this stage would be the entrepreneurial leadership. This group, however, is not heavily represented during the negotiations; at least not in terms of direct involvement in the process. However, when it implies business interests, the PSIDS have arguably been a bit entrepreneurial during the negotiations, really formulating and pushing versions of text that would benefit them, take their interests into consideration. Furthermore, the players at the negotiation stage are however those who can craft agreements, broker the deals needed to achieve a consensus, and facilitate in the bargaining process between the delegates and these will also need to take their national sector stakeholders and entrepreneurial interests into account. Prior to making it to the international negotiation table, a given country is likely to have been at a national negotiation table as well, where several of these players will have participated, giving their opinion on the different elements of the instrument up for negotiations. The *contextual settings* during the negotiation stage can furthermore either energize or impede the process of institutional bargaining, and we see examples of these discussions with the emphasis by the PSIDS on both ocean acidification, climate change and in some cases marine plastics.

The *design perspective* of the instrument is another important element of the negotiation process. This focuses on how to develop the instrument, and this discussion will at this stage centre on the actors' concern for language that they need to see included in the agreement. Evidence of this was present during the second round of negotiations already, where the delegates diligently assessed all aspects of sentence structures of the president's guide to discussions (ICG-2 2018). It is also worth noting that there is one major design restriction on the proposed treaty. Early on in the negotiations it also became clear that one of the previously agreed upon aspects of the agreement, that it not interfere with the currently existing regional mechanisms for ocean management, was going to be an issue as well. Regional fisheries management organizations and other ocean management organizations that touched on areas of the ABNJ have been around for decades, and when deciding a new treaty was necessary, the plan had been to not interfere with the work done by these groups. Ardron et al. (2014) discuss the existing legal framework in the ABNJ, and the extent to which these treaties and regulatory bodies have attempted to improve their position and apply themselves to the challenges of ABNJ. In fact, existing in the ABNJ today are a number of management regimes that can be divided into sectoral and conservation type agreements, and further subdivided into regional seas and global reach. The main focus of the first group is that of resource extraction such as fisheries and whaling, and the manage thereof, as well as maritime activities such as shipping and seabed mining for instance – all of which have the potential of having a large effect on the ecosystem in this area. The latter category consequently focuses on the conservation of nature and ecosystems, as a direct opposite of the former. However, exactly how these regimes were to be incorporated into this new treaty was not clear – it is not easily apparent how states can recognize the work done by these organizations without impinging on them in some way. There are many of these groups, and not all are alike in their ability to adequately manage their area of expertise. Furthermore, the existence of these organizations did not negate the need for a new treaty, at least in the eyes of the states that decided to move forward with this process. Unfortunately, the admonition to protect the role played by these organizations in the ABNJ and the difficulty of so doing may be used by some states as an excuse to weaken the overall treaty.

Conclusion: who is ultimately responsible for areas where none have responsibility?

Tying this into effectiveness calculation of Breitmeier, Young, and Zürn (2006), the final responsibility for biodiversity protection in ABNJ lies with the states themselves. Speculating on future effectiveness, though it is like considering whether Schrödinger's cat really is dead or not (Gribbin 1984), recall that the elements of the regime effectiveness calculation when measured as a sign of compliance with regulations produced by the instrument were (1) horizontal enforcement, (2) strong mechanisms for verification, (3) legalization, (4) participation by voluntary organizations and (5) institutional development. In the case of the BBNJ treaty and compliance with regulations produced for the high seas, (1) horizontal enforcement may be taken care of if each member state has inspectors who have the right to board all vessels of other signatories to the instrument and be treated as a national inspector when so happens. In fact, flag state jurisdiction on the high seas already divides up the responsibility for enforcement in a particular, unhelpful way, so that if the BBNJ agreement doesn't allow for this concept of horizontal enforcement, the conditions of effectiveness won't be achieved. This inspector can then give his or her report to the flag state under which the vessel sails, who in turn is responsible for criminal prosecution of the ship owner when necessary. Verification in turn (2) could be done by the same inspector, through picture documentation and reports that would be commented on and signed by the captain onboard the inspected vessel. These pictures and reports would be sent to the flag state, who in turn would be the final party responsible for transferring these to the regime secretariat. As such, the first two elements of the effectiveness equation would be handled.

However, there is a physical disconnect between all states that will be part of the BBNJ agreement in that the geographical area covered is located at far distances from the states themselves. There would therefore likely be a lack of physical presence of inspection vessels, and flags of convenience vessels would also pose a challenge. In terms of legalization (3), we refer here to the process by which rules and regulations of the instrument are considered clear, relevant, logical, adaptive and consistent by the members to the agreement both at a global level, but also in terms of being internalized within domestic politics and become part of the norms there (Breitmeier, Young, and Zürn 2006). This internalization may take place without any challenges so long as it does not involve the potential for economic loss for the member states in question. However, as evident from the negotiations so far, this is a fear that many of the developed nations hold, and why some of these consistently prefer the freedom of the seas to be continued. The participation of NGOs (4), however, is strong in the BBNJ process and they have been continuously involved in both the agenda formation and negotiation stages thus far, giving advice and input during the process. The final variable in the effectiveness calculation, institutional development (5) of the new instrument, has not yet been tested and the design is not clear at this time in terms of regime infrastructure. However, being layered onto UNCLOS like that of the FSA should provide it with the stability and the development that is required for effectiveness to be possible in this link.

As such, it is clear that the path towards regime effectiveness and actual taking of responsibility for ocean preservation in the ABNJ post implementation will be no easy task. This is true for global governance in general, but especially so in areas that are outside of all national jurisdiction and concrete feelings of responsibility. We expect from the literature that as the regime formation process moves from negotiations towards the operationalization of the instrument, and the path towards taking real responsibility for the protection of biodiversity in the areas that lie outside of national jurisdiction, the driving forces will centre on material conditions. The players at that stage will be part of the structural leadership of the instrument itself, and the collective action problems will be relative to the asymmetries in the levels of effort that the different players put into the process. The context will primarily be the constraints that come from the domestic sphere, which feeds into the design perspective as well, where this focus will challenge the efforts to set up the relevant international machinery critical for the infrastructure of the instrument. The tactics in turn will be centred on administrative or bureaucratic politics.

In Tiller et al.'s work called 'The Once and Future Treaty' (2019), the authors state that one of the aims of the instrument is to bolster ecosystem resilience, so that the Ocean has a better ability to adapt to stressors such as ocean acidification and marine pollution, including plastics. These issues are not specifically part of the negotiations, though, which could be an indication that *Rather than "Biodiversity", it is "Beyond National Jurisdiction" that determines what states are willing to commit to'.* (Tiller et al. 2019). We must acknowledge that though there is no overarching responsible entity for these ABNJ, resource exploitation in these areas do not operate in a complete void. There is a myriad of existing agreements that cover the high seas to some extent, though fragmented. These regimes will not become redundant upon a successful negotiation and ratification of a BBNJ treaty. In fact, coordination and cooperation between existing regimes will continue to have high priority, and the patching of governance gaps is one of the paths that could be the result of the BBNJ negotiations, should they fail.

Failure to produce a binding treaty would likely be considered a failure, but the production of a treaty that failed to address and solve the major issues of BBNJ should hardly be considered a rousing success either. Likewise, a treaty with flaws is not necessarily a failure – UNCLOS itself has many flaws, including the lack of attention to BBNJ being addressed in these negotiations, but has overall proven to be a valuable treatise successful in the creation of a new maritime regime. As the negotiations proceed, it will become evident what kind of success is likely. At best, we will see a useful adjunct to UNCLOS that preserves and protects BBNJ while still allowing for sustainable use and scientific research to better mankind. At worst, total failure. Most likely, the result will be somewhere in between – but where?

Notes

1 The other principles are 2: Scale-matching, 3: Precaution, 4: Adaptive management, 5: Full cost allocation, and 6: Participation. For more detailed information on these, see Costanza et al. (1998).
2 Article 31: Responsibility of the flag State for damage caused by a warship or other government ship operated for non-commercial purposes; Article 139: Responsibility to ensure compliance and liability for damage; Section 9 and Article 235: Responsibility and liability; Section 5 and Article 263: Responsibility and liability; Article 304: Responsibility and liability for damage; Annex 3, Article 22: Responsibility; Annex IX, Article 6: Responsibility and liability.

References

Ardron, J.A., Rayfuse, R., Gjerde, K., and Warner, R. (2014). "The sustainable use and conservation of biodiversity in ABNJ: What can be achieved using existing international agreements?" *Marine Policy*, 49(3): 98–108.

Ardron, J.A., Ruhl, H.A., and Jones, D.O.B. (2018). "Incorporating transparency into the governance of deep-seabed mining in the Area beyond national jurisdiction." *Marine Policy*, 89(2): 58–66.

Asgeirsdottir, A. (2009). *Who Gets What?: Domestic Influences on International Negotiations Allocating Shared Resources*. New York: SUNY Press.

Blasiak, R., Durussel, C., Pittman, J., Sénit, C., Petersson, M., and Yagi, N. (2017). "The role of NGOs in negotiating the use of biodiversity in marine areas beyond national jurisdiction." *Marine Policy*, 81(3): 1–8.

Breitmeier, H., Young, O., and Zürn, M. (2006). *Analyzing International Environmental Regimes: From Case Study to Database*. Cambridge, MA: MIT Press.

Costanza, R., Andrade, F., Antunes, P., Van Den Belt, M., Boersma, D., Boesch, D.F., Catarino, F., Hanna, S., Limburg, K., and Low, B. (1998). "Principles for sustainable governance of the oceans." *Science*, 281(5374): 198–199.

Druel, E., and Gjerde, K.M. (2014). "Sustaining marine life beyond boundaries: options for an implementing agreement for marine biodiversity beyond national jurisdiction under the United Nations Convention on the Law of the Sea." *Marine Policy*, 49(11): 90–97.

Druel, E., Gjerde, K.M., and Warner, R. (2014). "An International Instrument on Conservation and Sustainable Use of Biodiversity in Marine Areas beyond National Jurisdiction." The International Union for the Conservation of Nature. https://www.iucn.org/downloads/iucn_bbnj_matrix_december_2015.pdf.

Friedheim, R.L. (1993). *Negotiating the New Ocean Regime*. Columbia: University of South Carolina Press.

Gjerde, K.M., and Rulska-Domino, A. (2012). "Marine protected areas beyond national jurisdiction: some practical perspectives for moving ahead." *The International Journal of Marine and Coastal Law*, 27(2): 351–373.

Gribbin, J. (1984). *In Search of Schrödinger's Cat: Quantum Physics and Reality*. New York: Bantam Books.

Griffin, A. (1994). "MARPOL 73/78 and vessel pollution: A glass half full or half empty?" *Indiana Journal of Global Legal Studies*, 1(2): 489–513.

Grotius, H. (1916). *Mare Liberum*. New York: Oxford University Press.

Grotius, H. (2012). *The Free Sea*. Indianapolis, IN. https://muse.jhu.edu/book/17941, Liberty Fund.

Harrison, J. (2011). *Making the Law of the Sea: A study in the Development of International Law*. Cambridge: Cambridge University Press.

Hasenclever, A., Mayer, P., and Rittberger, V. (2000). "Integrating theories of international regimes." *Review of International Studies*, 26(1): 3–33.

van der Heijden, J. (2011). "Institutional layering: A review of the use of the concept." *Politics* 31(1): 9–18.

Helm, C., and Sprinz, D. (2000). "Measuring the effectiveness of international environmental regimes." *Journal of Conflict Resolution*, 44(5): 630–652.

Hollick, A.L. (2017). *US Foreign Policy and the Law of the Sea*. Princeton: Princeton University Press.

Hönisch, B., Ridgwell, A. Schmidt, D.N., Thomas, E., Gibbs, S.J., Sluijs, A., Zeebe, R., Kump, L., Martindale, R.C., and Greene, S.E. (2012). "The geological record of ocean acidification." *Science*, 335(6072): 1058–1063.

ICG-2 (2018). President's aid to discussions - Intergovernmental conference on an international legally binding instrument under the United Nations Convention on the Law of the Sea on the conservation and sustainable use of marine biological diversity of areas beyond national jurisdiction: Second session, New York, 25 March–5 April 2019. In *A/CONF.232/2019/1*, edited by United Nations General Assembly. https://undocs.org/A/CONF.232/2019/1.

International Maritime Organization (IMO) (1972), Convention on the Prevention of Marine Pollution by Dumping of Wastes and Other Matter (London Convention). https://www.imo.org/en/OurWork/Environment/Pages/London-Convention-Protocol.aspx (accessed 12.04 2021).

Keohane, R.O., Haas, P.M., and Levy, M.A. (1993). "The Effectiveness of International Environmental Institutions." In Keohane, R.O., Haas, P.M., and Levy, M.A., eds., *Institutions for the Earth: Sources of Effective International Environmental Protection*. Cambridge, MA: MIT Press.

Kraska, J. (2017). "Effective implementation of the 2005 convention for the suppression of unlawful acts against the safety of maritime navigation." *Naval War College Review*, 70(1): 10–23.

Krasner, S.D. (1982). "Structural causes and regime consequences: regimes as intervening variables." In Krasner, S.D., ed., *International Regimes*. Ithaca and London: Cornell University Press.

Kütting, G. (2000). *Environment, Society and International Relations: Towards More Effective International Environmental Agreements*. London: Routledge.

Lallier, L.E., and Maes, F. (2016). "Environmental impact assessment procedure for deep seabed mining in the area: independent expert review and public participation." *Marine Policy*, 70(8): 212–219.

Le Quéré, C., Andrew, R.M., Friedlingstein, P., Sitch, S., Pongratz, J., Manning, A.C., Korsbakken, J.I., Peters, G.P., Canadell, J.G., and Jackson, R.B. (2017). "Global carbon budget 2017." *Earth System Science Data Discussions*: 1–79. https://www.earth-syst-sci-data.net/10/405/2018.

Marciniak, K.J. (2017). "New implementing agreement under UNCLOS: A threat or an opportunity for fisheries governance?" *Marine Policy*, 84(10): 320–326.

McKinley, E., and Fletcher, S. (2010). "Individual responsibility for the oceans? An evaluation of marine citizenship by UK marine practitioners." *Ocean & Coastal Management*, 53(7): 379–384.

Mendenhall, E. (2019). "The Ocean Governance Regime: International Conventions and Institutions." In Harries, P.G., ed. *Climate Change and Ocean Governance: Politics and Policy for Threatened Seas*: 27–42. Cambridge: Cambridge University Press.

Mitchell, R.B. (2017). International Environmental Agreements (IEA) Database Project. edited by University of Oregon. https://iea.uoregon.edu/.

Morrisette, P.M. (1989). "The evolution of policy responses to stratospheric ozone depletion." *Natural Resources Journal*, 29(3): 793–820.

Pearson, P.N., and Palmer, M.R. (2000). "Atmospheric carbon dioxide concentrations over the past 60 million years." *Nature*, 406(6797): 695.

Stokke, O.S. (2007). "Examining the Consequences of Arctic Institutions." In Stokke, O.S., and Hønneland, G., eds., *International Cooperation and Arctic Governance: Regime effectiveness and Northern region building*. London: Routledge.

Thelen, K. (2003). "How Institutions Evolve: Insights from Comparative Historical Analysis." In Mahoney, J., and Rueschemeyer, D., eds., *Comparative Historical analysis in the Social Sciences*. Cambridge: Cambridge University Press.

Thelen, K. (2004). *How Institutions Evolve: The Political Economy of Skills in Germany, Britain, the United States, and Japan*. Cambridge: Cambridge University Press.

Tiller, R., De Santo, E., Mendenhall, E., and Nyman, E. (2019). "The once and future treaty: Towards a new regime for biodiversity in areas beyond national jurisdiction." *Marine Policy*, 99(1): 239–242.

Turley, C., Eby, M., Ridgwell, A.J., Schmidt, D.N., Findlay, H.S., Brownlee, C., Riebesell, U., Fabry, V.J., Feely, R.A., and Gattuso, J.P. (2010). "The societal challenge of ocean acidification." *Marine Pollution Bulletin* 60(6): 787–792.

UNCLOS (1982). United Nations Convention on the Law of the Sea of 10 December 1982. edited by Division for Ocean Affairs and the Law of the Sea. http://www.un.org/depts/los/convention_agreements/texts/unclos/unclos_e.pdf: United Nations.

United Nations General Assembly (2011). Resolution adopted by the General Assembly on 24 December 2011. In *66/231*. http://undocs.org/A/RES/66/231.

Wright, G., Rochette, J., Gjerde, K.M., and Seeger, I. (2018). The long and winding road: negotiating a treaty for the conservation and sustainable use of marine biodiversity in areas beyond national jurisdiction. https://www.iddri.org/sites/default/files/PDF/Publications/Catalogue%20Iddri/Etude/201808-Study_HauteMer-long%20and%20winding%20road.pdf: IDDRI.

Young, O.R. (1998). *Creating Regimes: Arctic Accords and International Governance*. Ithaca and London: Cornell University Press.

Zeebe, R.E., and Ridgwell, A. (2011). "Past Changes of Ocean Carbonate Chemistry." In Gattuso, J.P., and Hansson, L., eds., *Ocean Acidification*: 21–40. Oxford: Oxford University Press.

Zürn, M. (1998). "The rise of international environmental politics: A review of current research." *World Politics*, 50(4): 617–649.

27
A RESPONSIBILITY TO FREEZE?
The Arctic as a complex object of responsibility
Mathias Albert and Sebastian Knecht

Introduction

The Arctic is currently in high demand as a popular image of, and for, global climate change. Most documentaries, media stories and political campaigns addressing climate and environmental change lead with calving icebergs as an unmistakable sign of global warming, or with supposedly starving polar bears deprived of their natural habitat, in order to demonstrate the latent realities of climate change that would otherwise remain mostly invisible in terms of direct visual sensation. In doing so, most of these public representations of Arctic change engage in attributing responsibility to the world at large, and to each and every individual, in what often amounts to a critique of capitalist society, industrialization and consumerism in the Anthropocene epoch. The world needs to act on climate change, it needs to act now and it needs to act fast – or sensitive ecosystems like those in the polar regions might be gone forever. This message is nowadays widely understood by relevant audiences in the international community, and yet achieving global consensus on effective solutions to climate change continues to be very much out of reach (Abbott 2012; Keohane and Victor 2011). Only few countries currently meet the commitments made under the 2015 Paris Agreement to limit global warming to 1.5°C compared to pre-industrial levels. Too numerous and varied are states' national interests, energy systems and environmental policy planning that negotiations at the level of the United Nations (UN) all too regularly result in gridlock, delay or non-binding commitments.

Scientists think that the Arctic is close to a tipping point where change will become irreversible. Warming takes place at a rate much higher than the global average, and current models predict the Arctic to warm by 9°C by the end of the century compared to mean levels for the period from 1986 to 2005. The Arctic Ocean is likely to be ice-free in the summer by then, possibly even much earlier than that (AMAP 2017, 19-20). This fundamental state change will have, and partly already has, severe adverse impacts across the world. The Arctic performs a number of functions that cushion the processes of global climate change; it is a sink for chemicals, microplastics and climate pollutants transported north through ocean, river and wind currents; it is a refrigerator for the global ocean system, and it is a reflector of solar radiation. The region will only be able to continue to perform these functions as long as the fragile ecosystem proves resilient and relatively stable. In turn, a melting Arctic will amplify global warming through the additional release of large amounts of harmful climate pollutants like methane currently locked in the permafrost and the absorption of more sunlight by open waters and darker surfaces that follow the retreat of ice and permafrost in the region (see Serreze and Francis 2006). Deglaciation is further expected to contribute to the rise of the global sea-level, threatening low-lying islands and contributing to further coastal erosion. There is no disputing the fact that climate change has already had significant impacts on polar bear habitats and can be expected to reduce populations in the long run (Stirling and Derocher 2012; cf. Lone et al. 2018), and this presents a serious matter of concern for Arctic food chains and biodiversity. Although subject of an *Agreement on Conservation of Polar Bears* adopted between the five Arctic coastal states already in 1973 in order to prohibit any hunting, killing and capturing of polar bears on the territory of the signatory parties, today climate change poses a much more imminent threat to their survival.

These examples are meant to illustrate how much the Arctic is a 'globally embedded space' (Keil and Knecht 2017) deeply integrated in global climate and environmental systems. It should be stressed, however, that most of what affects the Arctic region today has its origins elsewhere and consequently the new buzzword of a 'global Arctic means dealing with the pollution of others' (Dodds and Nuttall 2019, 203). While this may again only indicate a special responsibility of the international community for the protection of the Arctic region, it also raises the question of who bears responsibility for managing the causes and consequences of Arctic change in the absence of effective and concerted action on climate change. There is no easy answer to the question of how to stop glacial melting, or even of how to reverse it, in order to preserve what is considered the natural state of the Arctic environment. In contrast to normative calls for global action, we acknowledge that there is a governance system in place for the Arctic region and that this can serve as the locus for responsibility with regard to Arctic affairs (cf. Hansen-Magnusson 2019), although it does not allow for all too simple solutions for complex issues like environmental protection and sustainable development. This is mostly due to the fact that political responsibility for the causes and consequences of Arctic change and effective responses to it cannot be easily attributed and enforced. This makes the Arctic a particularly interesting case for the study of responsibility in international relations, although it is certainly not one of the main subjects that usually first comes to mind when discussing international responsibility. In the present contribution, we argue that this may be not only due to the Arctic's peripherality – in both geographic terms as well as in terms of academic attention in the field of IR –, but particularly also because of the specific complexity of the Arctic as an object of governance and responsibility.

We do not claim the Arctic to be exceptional as on object of governance in terms of its complexity. However, we will demonstrate in the following that the Arctic is characterized by a specific combination of addressees of governance and responsibility, combining different kinds of actors, institutions and symbolisms across various levels, which in that combination are unique to the Arctic, yet that also allow us to raise a range of interesting questions on responsibility in international relations more generally. This particularly pertains to the issue of who can be responsible, and more generally the question of moral agency, in cases in which the 'object' of responsibility seems to elude easy or fixed ascriptions of agency or the identification of the relevant (structural) links to various levels. The issue raised in this context, however, is also one of whether, and to which degree, concepts about responsibility in international relations make sense at all in social contexts that are difficult to project onto the established cognitive maps of what constitutes 'international relations', even in the widest sense, in the first place.

We will pursue our argument in three steps: First, we provide a brief overview of the institutional context for Arctic governance in order to be able to discuss what (or who) could be, or in fact are, the 'subjects' and 'objects' of responsibility that play a role in the Arctic governance system and the various discourses on the present and future development of the region. In a second step, we scrutinize the difficulties associated with Arctic issues that stem from the fact that 'the Arctic' cannot but be seen as a highly complex regional representation of many interlocked social and natural systems. This leads us to the question of whether the 'bazaar governance' (Depledge and Dodds 2017), which has been identified as a peculiar feature of handling Arctic affairs, points to a somewhat 'deficient' mode of governance, or could not rather be seen as an appropriate form of governance under the conditions mentioned. This leads us, in a third step, to discuss whether responsibilities in and towards the Arctic could be regarded as holding lessons for thinking about the future of responsibility in IR more broadly.

The Arctic as a governance object

The Arctic is widely understood as a region covering the marine and terrestrial areas north of 66° 33′. As such, it exists less as a naturally given geographical space clearly defined by geomorphological or climatic criteria, but rather as a relational construct invented, used and reinvented by political actors to establish a social collective around which to form spaces of belonging, common principles and joint action (see also Albert forthcoming; Keskitalo 2004; Medby 2018). Most of the region consists of the world's smallest ocean, the Arctic Ocean, surrounded by the land territories of Canada, Finland, Norway, Russia, Sweden and the United States and with the islands of Greenland (Denmark) and Iceland. While this may make these eight states with territory above the Arctic Circle 'natural bearers' of responsibility and leadership in the region (see for instance Exner-Pirot 2011; Griffiths 1989; Nord 2019), Arctic governance is hardly a matter of domestic politics and circumpolar collaboration alone. Many sources of Arctic change originate elsewhere, but unfold their full effect most visibly within the region. Global warming causes the Arctic sea-ice to shrink, laying open vast amounts of newly available oil and gas resources whose extraction and burning would further contribute to the rise in global temperature – and ultimately accelerate Arctic melting. What scholars refer to as an 'Arctic paradox' (Palosaari 2019) entails a great deal of a responsibility trap in that potential gains from Arctic change are privatized by the eight Arctic states by virtue of their sovereign and jurisdictional rights, while the resulting costs and externalities of Arctic economic development are mostly globalized. Wherever transboundary pollution or environmental risks such as greenhouse gas emissions, ocean acidification or plastic pollution are concerned, responsibility neither rests nor can fully and causally be attributed to a single source, but is shared by a larger community of actors who contribute to a harmful outcome of material or non-material damage to other parties (Nollkaemper and Jacobs 2013).

For the case of the Arctic, shared responsibility may serve as a normative goal then, but is far from easy to enforce in practice because it provides a shelter for each individual actor. Exactly because 'transboundary air pollution is cumulative in nature, it is difficult to prove the precise time or place of damage attributable to a particular state or states' (Tanaka 2014, 239). States can more easily be held accountable where transformations of the Arctic environment can be traced directly to a pool of emitters causing the pollution, and where hence mitigation measures could show immediate effects. One such example is the emission of black carbon (BC), a short-lived climate pollutant that reaches the Arctic through air currents on shorter distances and darkens snow and ice, thereby reducing the reflection of solar radiation and accelerating the melting of these surfaces. A recent study found that the eight Arctic states, the European Union (EU), Belarus, Kazakhstan, Moldova, Ukraine and China account for almost all BC emissions found in the Arctic (Winiger et al. 2019, 4). The Arctic Council started to act on BC emissions in 2015 with a 'Framework for Action' on *Enhanced Black Carbon and Methane Emissions Reductions*, in which the Arctic states '*[c]ommit* to take leadership based on this Arctic Council Framework by further reducing the overall black carbon and methane emissions from our countries and by working with Arctic Council Observer States and others to also reduce emissions produced beyond the borders of Arctic States' (Arctic Council 2015, 1). Based on national reports to the Council, the Expert Group sets a collective goal for black carbon emission reductions, makes recommendations for adaptive measures, and shares policy experiences and best practices. Observer states[1] are invited to also submit national reports and implement the Framework. In 2017, the Expert Group recommended to cut black carbon emissions by another 25–33% until 2025 compared to 2013 levels (Arctic Council 2017, 5). This is a collective goal that avoids assigning individual responsibility for black carbon emissions and future burden-sharing. According to the latest progress review submitted to the Arctic Council Ministerial Meeting in May 2019, all eight Arctic states and ten Observer states have submitted black carbon inventories (Arctic Council 2019).

At the same time, there is no single actor or institution in the position to change fate and fortune of the region and its people to any substantial degree alone. Neither are the eight Arctic states willing to assume full responsibility for the entirety of past, current and potential future developments in the region nor is there any single regulatory authority to stimulate responsible management for the region as a whole. With no one institution in place to steer the course of regional governance, Corry notes that 'the Arctic climate has been rendered an object of governance without clarity about the subjects doing the governance or the directly affected parties such as Arctic populations and indigenous peoples. A technocratic global governance-object thus co-exists with a relative silence about the responsibility and rights to govern and be heard (Corry 2017, 72). As Arctic change denotes the object of responsibility, the problem of identifying relevant governance subjects to be held responsible and accountable for the change is to a large extent a result of the functionally differentiated and multi-faceted governance system in place for the Arctic. Although with the Arctic Council a regional forum had been established in 1996 with the intention to 'provide a means for cooperation, coordination and interaction among the Arctic states, with the involvement of the Arctic indigenous communities and other Arctic inhabitants on common Arctic issues' (Arctic Council 1996, Art. 1[a]), the body holds no political authority to establish, monitor or enforce common rules and regulations for regional governance. To a substantial degree regional cooperation has been made easier because the Arctic Council explicitly does not address certain policy issues, particularly not the many security issues pertaining to the Arctic. Instead, its mandate is limited to questions for environmental protection and sustainable development.

The Council, which describes itself as the 'preeminent international forum for addressing Arctic issues' (Arctic Council 2018, 2), is an integral part of a weakly integrated but nested and non-hierarchical regime complex spanning state and non-state actors as well as international institutions across multiple levels and geographical scales from the very local to the global (Stokke 2013; Stokke and Hønneland 2007; Young 2012). The role of the Council in this complex is best understood as a hub for Arctic issues, its acceptance in that role being underscored by the high number of inter-governmental and inter-parliamentary organizations (14) and non-governmental organizations (12) that have so far have been granted observer status in addition to thirteen non-Arctic states. The Council's main competence lies in the study of the sources and consequences of Arctic transformations, and disseminating its assessment reports and policy recommendations to raise awareness among international audiences and shape policy initiatives at the domestic and global level.

The regulatory anchor of the Arctic regime complex is the *UN Convention on the Law of the Sea* (UNCLOS). UNCLOS provides a legally binding governance framework for issues pertaining to the Arctic Ocean, maritime borders, and the sovereign rights and claims of Arctic coastal states. It is complemented on the international level by several agreements under the International Maritime Organization (IMO), including the 1973 *International Convention for the Protection of Marine Pollution from Ships* (MARPOL), the 1974 *International Convention for the Safety of Life at Sea* (SOLAS), and the 1972 *Convention on the Prevention of Marine Pollution by Dumping of Wastes and Other Matter* (London Convention) and its corresponding 1996 Protocol and the 1990

International Convention on Oil Pollution Preparedness, Response and Co-operation (OPRC). One more IMO agreement is specifically designed for Arctic and Antarctic waters. The *International Code for Ships operating in Polar Waters*, or short Polar Code, in effect since January 2017, contains a set of mandatory regulations and standards that shall enhance the safety of ships operating in polar waters and lower the impact of shipping on the Arctic marine environment. Besides the *Polar Code*, three other international institutions are particularly relevant for the protection of the Arctic: the *UN Framework Convention on Climate Change* (UNFCCC), the 2001 *Stockholm Convention on Persistent Organic Pollutants*, and the 2013 *Minamata Convention on Mercury*. Further applicable in the Arctic regime complex are regulations concerning fisheries under the Food and Agriculture Organization (FAO), specifically the 1993 *Agreement to Promote Compliance with International Conservation and Management Measures by Fishing Vessels on the High Seas*, the 1995 *Code of Conduct for Responsible Fisheries* and the *Agreement on Conservation and Management of Straddling Fish Stocks and Highly Migratory Fish Stocks* of the same year. While there is no specific regional fisheries management organization (RFMO) for the Arctic, the geographical coverage of several existing RFMOs also touch Arctic waters.

Past research on Arctic governance has focused on issues of responsibility and accountability mostly for single components of the regime complex or certain groups of actors (for one of the few exceptions taking a structural view on the relations between responsibility subjects and objects, see Hansen-Magnusson 2019). Most research points to the state as primary unit for responsible management of the Arctic, first and foremost with regard to the eight Arctic states (for instance, Johnstone 2014), but increasingly also with reference to non-Arctic states that articulate a distinct interest in the region and participate in its governance (Kopra 2019; Shibata et al. 2019). Scholarship also highlights the role of corporate social responsibility (CSR) held by business and industries who operate in the fragile Arctic environment and whose actions might have adverse effects on the local population and indigenous peoples (Henry et al. 2016; Hubbard 2013; Ulfbeck et al. 2016). Most studies see CSR as a complementary strategy to state responsibility that 'could fill the gap opened by the failure of the states and the state-centered international law instruments to impose direct responsibility on corporate actors' (Garipova 2016, 992). While the literature accounts for a variety of subjects of responsibility, the structural relationship between different subjects as well as governance objects they hold responsibility for has not been addressed so far.

We do not want to invest here in the debate about whether, or to what degree and by what measures, this governance system is purposeful, adequate and effective in order to steer international cooperation among a diverse set of responsibility holders towards common solutions. Although gaps remain in this governance system with regard to certain policy issues or areas of human activity (Koivurova 2013; Vinogradov and Azubuike 2018), it has proven resilient over the past three decades and is likely to remain the institutional context for the foreseeable future in which Arctic affairs are governed and in which responsibility will have to be sought and attributed. However, what we wish to emphasize is the various voices and diagnoses that have identified the Arctic as some kind of 'laboratory' for global governance, which in this sense has to 'give back' something to the international system at large (see Bertelsen 2019). We hold that this 'special' status of governance in and for the Arctic has some potentially wider implications for thinking about responsibility in IR, which we will outline in the next section below. Before doing so, however, it is worth exploring what constitutes this alleged 'specialty' of Arctic governance. This special characteristic does not pertain to the basic architecture of regimes in place, but more to the modes and processes that feed into their (re-)production. While specific to the Arctic, the architecture of governance described above is by no means special in its mix of global and regional regimes, with varying participation of interested actors and stakeholders. What we claim to be special is how these regimes come about or are reproduced and performed, namely through an extraordinary high degree of inter- and transnational knowledge-based exchange that goes along with a strong role for science diplomacy, able to at least cushion the impact of conflicting interests (cf. Bertelsen 2019). The visible representation of both the architecture of Arctic governance and its specific means of reproduction is the array of many fora in which, in varying but often repeating and overlapping constellations, various stakeholders from politics, business and industries, science and local communities meet and interact.

Regime complexity, responsibility and 'bazaar governance'

Highly fragmented regime complexes such as those in place for the Arctic pose a number of challenges for assuming and/or assigning responsibility for any concrete governance object. Who is responsible for what, and who can thus be held accountable or even liable for (in)action, is not entirely clear as mandates, memberships and modes of governance may overlap between different components of the complex and across scales. In a symposium on the politics of international regime complexity, Alter and Meunier (2009, 20) describe the pros and cons of regime complexes for international responsibility and holding political actors and institutions accountable for their actions: 'On the one hand, international regime complexity blurs which institution is authoritative, and thus makes it harder to assess which actors or institutions to hold accountable. On the other hand, international regime complexity can create access for more actors, and thereby be a force for greater political accountability'. This may generally be true, but it should not be overlooked that it is a central aspect of networked governance in regime complexes that political authority is distributed unequally across actors and institutions in the regime and thus its components, states and non-state actors alike, hold dissimilar positions and possibilities of access, participation and influence over policy outcomes. They may thus hold moral agency to different degrees and only for partial action in the regime complex. The resulting central question for a preliminary assessment of the Arctic responsibility regime is how 'responsibilities for tasks such as adopting rules and funding public goods are shared among multiple organizations that have diverse memberships and operate at different scales' (Abbott 2012, 571)? Each institution's responsibility is often limited because regime complexes tend to govern otherwise complex issues in a fragmented system where each part addresses a distinct policy-issue, often fairly in isolation from other governance objects.

Over the past years, the Arctic states have more and more assumed direct and concrete responsibility for several Arctic governance objects in an effort to substantiate political authority in the region. In the founding declaration of the Arctic Council, signed in Ottawa in September 1996, the eight states declare their 'commitment to the protection of the Arctic environment, including the health of Arctic ecosystems, maintenance of biodiversity in the Arctic region and conservation and sustainable use of natural resources' (Arctic Council 1996, 2). In 2008, the five Arctic Ocean Coastal states (Canada, Denmark, Norway, Russia and the USA) issued a joint declaration in response to a rising number of calls by non-Arctic states for deeper involvement in regional governance and 'to challenge the notion that the Arctic should be internationalized' (Dodds 2013, 49). In this *Ilulissat Declaration*, the five states declare that the 'Arctic Ocean is a unique ecosystem, which the five coastal states have a stewardship in protecting. […] We will take steps in accordance with international law both nationally and in cooperation among the five states and other interested parties to ensure the protection and preservation of the fragile marine environment of the Arctic Ocean' (Arctic Five 2008, 2). The five states justified their claim to a stewardship role for the governance of the Arctic Ocean with their sovereign rights and jurisdiction in the area that would put them 'in a unique position to address these possibilities and challenges' that result from Arctic change (Arctic Five 2008, 1). In 2017, the Arctic Council's *Task Force on*

Arctic Marine Cooperation (TFAMC) reiterated this special role of Arctic states for the marine environment, this time adding Finland, Iceland and Sweden, by concluding that the 'Arctic states, including the Permanent Participants and Arctic inhabitants, are uniquely placed to serve as stewards for Arctic marine ecosystems as a whole' (TFAMC 2017, 3),[2] yet without elaborating why Arctic non-coastal states without any sovereign rights over the Arctic Ocean should be in a privileged position to assume marine stewardship in the region vis-à-vis non-Arctic states. The concept of stewardship used in this context seems to rest not only on the normative assumption that the Arctic states ought to be responsible for issues pertaining to the Arctic Ocean but also ultimately that they should act on behalf of the international community to preserve and protect this marine area (for a discussion, see Henriksen 2016).

In addition to the need to negotiate new agreements in order to address emerging policy problems, recent circumpolar policy initiatives can also be regarded as an attempt to institutionalize sovereignty as responsibility. Over the past decade, the Arctic states have adopted several cooperative agreements through which they assume responsibility in various policy areas of Arctic governance and which, through the exercise of this same responsibility, can help to reinforce their national sovereignty over Arctic maritime governance (see Humrich 2018). To this end, the Arctic states have legally bound themselves in responsibility coalitions in different composition, and according to various functional requirements. Negotiated under the auspices of the Arctic Council, the eight Arctic states adopted in 2011 an *Agreement on Cooperation on Aeronautical and Maritime Search and Rescue in the Arctic*, followed by an *Agreement on Cooperation on Marine Oil Pollution Preparedness and Response in the Arctic* in 2013 and an *Agreement on Enhancing International Arctic Scientific Cooperation* in 2017. In 2018, the five Arctic Ocean coastal states together with China, the EU, Iceland, Japan and South Korea (so-called 'A5+5') signed an *Agreement to Prevent Unregulated High Seas Fisheries in the Central Arctic Ocean* (CAOF Agreement) which applies precautionary conservation and management measures in the high seas areas of the central Arctic Ocean in which no fishing has taken place to date. The fact that the CAOF Agreement has the EU and three Asian states, all of which are major fish exporting markets in close proximity to Arctic waters, as signatories indicates a greater role for multilateral cooperation in managing transboundary issues in the region (see Molenaar 2019). Through their participation as observers in the Arctic Council, many non-Arctic states have become accepted and legitimate players in the High North. These are states that recognize and claim a role in the governance of the region and increasingly assume responsibility for the Arctic environment and the consequences of their actions towards it.

These responsibility coalitions emerge and reconfigure rather spontaneously, strategically and voluntarily on the Arctic governance 'bazaar'. Depledge and Dodds (2017) have coined the term 'bazaar governance' for a situation in which, figuratively speaking, many stakeholders wander through the Arctic bazaar to gather at various shops in order to negotiate a new deal. This style of bazaar governance has come to be epitomized in the annual 'Arctic Circle' meetings that have been taking place in Reykjavik since 2013: a gathering well-attended by an eclectic, if high-profile mix of all kinds of stakeholders from science, shipping and mining companies, the military, indigenous communities, environmental NGOs, politics, etc.[3] This is visibly the place where the Arctic – or better: interests in relation to the Arctic – 'come together', often with high-level celebrity participation. While at its core a meeting of several days taking place in Reykjavik, the Arctic Circle (launched and further promoted by the former president of Iceland, Olafur Ragnar Grimsson) continues to spread in various regional fora across the globe, with notable Asian involvement.

While we agree that particularly the science/policy nexus plays a very prominent role in Arctic governance, we would probably not go so far as to proclaim a difference in kind to governance arrangements in other regions. The difference is one of degree, and we hold that for this reason the analysis of this specific case holds a lot of as yet unearthed potential for the study of governance arrangements in other areas. We mention the prominence of science as well as the 'bazaar'-style governance not because of its style as such, but because we suspect that this kind of organizing exchanges around a science/policy interface is strongly influenced by, and often operatively linked to, the 'role model' of the Antarctic case. While being a completely different governance arrangement (with the Antarctic Treaty at its core), the organization of exchanges at the science/policy interface in the Arctic cannot but remind of representing an evolution towards the more institutionalized interface that is the Scientific Committee of Antarctic Research (SCAR). This similarity certainly has its roots not only in simple institutional 'copying'. In fact, most countries have institutionalized Arctic and Antarctic research and policy under the rubric of 'polar' institutes and departments, and thus many specializations exist under common headings. What this 'stylistic' reference to the Antarctic does for the Arctic governance complex, however, is to create a lasting and strong reference to the Arctic as some common area of responsibility for the entirety of humankind.[4]

Conclusion: the Arctic and limits of IR responsibility

It would be straightforward to conclude from the above that the entire global community bears responsibility for the present and future of the Arctic region (see for instance Rey 1987). However, such a conclusion not only runs into normative and practical problems usually associated with cosmopolitan visions of 'humankind' as the ultimate and sole bearer of responsibility in global governance (Caney 2005; Held 2010). If all shall be responsible, the risk is high that no one will feel responsible. There are further political, institutional and legal limits to global responsibility for Arctic governance, first and foremost in the form of national sovereignty, the right of indigenous peoples to autonomy and self-determination and existing regulations and arrangements of the Arctic regime complex.

We argue that the diffuse governance arrangement for the Arctic results in a global responsibility complex for the region in which responsibility cannot easily be attributed to a particular governance subject. Though often praised for its flexibility and adaptive capacity, the regime complex establishes a barrier to responsibility attribution that may have negative consequences for Arctic governance in the long run. It is in this sense that the Arctic could be seen as a good case for the study of responsibility in international politics. One could even argue that the Arctic is an exemplary case for studying the ongoing negotiation and formation of the *relata* of responsibility (see Hansen-Magnusson 2019; Loh 2017). In this context, it would seem like making an almost too obvious point to argue that complexity of social situations as well as unclear attributions of specific rights and duties present an almost 'natural' barrier for assigning responsibility. In fact, one could argue that the dynamic here works in the opposite way as well: exactly because there are unclear attributions of specific rights and duties, the requirement of 'normative compensations' in the form of ascriptions of responsibility arises in the first place. Of course, both complexity and attribution do not refer to fixed measures, but cover a broad range of degrees. In relation to responsibilities, the main issue however does not seem to be one of degree, but one of the successful semantic condensation of these complexities and attribution to one point of reference: and it is here that there is a gap wide and huge between the polar bear population or the difficult dynamics of ocean currents on the one hand, and the mass killing of people in a war.

What unites both ends of the spectrum is that they lie in a zone at least implicitly covered by a claim to 'jurisdiction without territory' (cf. Orford 2018), that is, a universalist claim that law and some jurisdiction apply, yet without being covered fully or exclusively by national laws or international law. The concrete normative scope of that claim, as well as its empirical transformation into political and legal arrangements varies extremely widely, as attested by the vast range of subjects covered in this volume. What seems fair to say, however, is that in relation to the Arctic a crucial point is whether, and to which degree, it is possible to frame and semantically condense the Arctic as a global object of responsibility. On the pure level of political interest and involvement, this does not seem to happen: on the one hand, there persists a regionality of governance in and around the Arctic Council and its eight member states; on the other hand, the involvement of non-Arctic states, and particularly China, seems rather clearly to be dominated by concrete economic and political agendas. It is against this background that arguably the dense connections between science and politics provide for but one, yet promising opening for framing the Arctic as a global object of responsibility. As mentioned before, and despite all the differences and incomparability, the Antarctic and the ATS here often seem to lie in the background at least as a stylized model for how the Arctic should be addressed.

Needless to say, stylized representations often can overstretch as projections of some future 'good' not attainable elsewhere[5]. Nonetheless, they are necessary in the sense that configuring the Arctic as an object of global responsibility requires more than the articulation and harmonization of interests. It requires reaching at least partial agreement on the relevant parameters that characterize the object in question in the first place. In this sense, configuring here includes 'reconfiguring identity, space, and time' (so the subtitle of Pram Gad and Strandsbjerg 2019). The scale of this reconfiguration becomes clear when reflecting on the fact that the task at hand might not actually be a responsibility to preserve polar bear habitats, make arrangements for search and rescue, and provisions for dealing with oil spills, but that in the web of different Arctic futures envisioned and discussed in the Arctic bazaar (cf. Wormbs 2018), the main responsibility turns out to be nothing less than re-freezing it (King 2018).

By way of conclusion, it might be possible to say that underlying our depiction of responsibility in and for the Arctic remains a twofold use of the very concept of responsibility: on the one hand lies an analytical-descriptive account of how responsibility is attributed, and on what the relevant actors and subjects are in this context. In a sense, responsibility here is about the broad spectrum of responsibility discourses. On the other hand lies at least a normative subtext that could be described as one of 'meta-responsibility' in the sense of a responsibility to be responsible: given the maze, the specifics, and the complexities of organizing things in and for the Arctic described, one could here talk about a responsibility to make arrangements in the 'bazaar' of Arctic governance as effective and efficient as possible.

Notes

1 As of 2019, the Arctic Council has granted access to 13 non-Arctic states in an observer capacity. These include eight European states (France, Germany, Italy, the Netherlands, Poland, Spain, Switzerland and the United Kingdom) and five Asian states (China, India, Japan, Singapore and South Korea).
2 Permanent Participants is a special membership category of the Arctic Council held by six organizations representing Arctic indigenous populations. These are the Aleut International Association (AIA), the Arctic Athabaskan Council (AAC), the Gwich'in Council International (GCI), the Inuit Circumpolar Council (ICC), the Russian Association of Indigenous Peoples of the North (RAIPON) and the Saami Council (SC).
3 One could probably take 'bazaar governance' as an example for 'experimentalist governance' as described by de Burca, Keohane and Sabel (2014). The only caveat here would be that ultimately we do not think that this is a governance different in kind from other forms of governance, but different only in degree.
4 It should be noted that this reference has nothing to do with the question of whether similar governance regimes would be feasible for both polar regions – this remains questionable as the differences between an uninhabited continent under a treaty freezing all sovereignty claims and what is at its core an ocean surrounded by inhabited sovereign states with corresponding continental shelf claims simply seem to big in this respect.
5 See, for example, the chapter on 'Antarctica: democracy at the end of the world' in Kean (2018, 347–375).

References

Abbott, K.W. (2012). "The Transnational Regime Complex for Climate Change." *Environment and Planning C: Government and Policy*, 30(4): 571–590.

Albert, M. (forthcoming). "Regions in the System of World Politics." In Kohlenberg, P. J., and Godehardt, N., eds., *The Multidimensionality of Regions in World Politics*. Abingdon: Routledge.

Alter, K.J., and Meunier, S. (2009). "The Politics of International Regime Complexity." *Perspectives on Politics*, 7(1): 13–24.

AMAP (2017). *Snow, Water, Ice, Permafrost in the Arctic (SWIPA) – 2017*. https://www.amap.no/swipa2017.

Arctic Council (2015). Enhanced Black Carbon and Methane Emissions Reductions. An Arctic Council Framework for Action (Annex 4 to the Iqaluit 2015 SAO Report to Council of Ministers). https://oaarchive.arctic-council.org/bitstream/handle/11374/610/ACMMCA09_Iqaluit_2015_SAO_Report_Annex_4_TFBCM_Framework_Document.pdf?sequence=1&isAllowed=y.

Arctic Council (1996). *Declaration on the Establishment of the Arctic Council*. https://oaarchive.arctic-council.org/handle/11374/85.

Arctic Council (2017). *Expert Group on Black Carbon and Methane: Summary of Progress and Recommendations 2017*. https://oaarchive.arctic-council.org/handle/11374/1936.

Arctic Council (2018). *Arctic Council Communications Strategy 2018*. https://oaarchive.arctic-council.org/handle/11374/2242.

Arctic Council (2019). *Expert Group on Black Carbon and Methane: Summary of Progress and Recommendations 2019*. https://oaarchive.arctic-council.org/handle/11374/2411.

Arctic Five (2008). *The Ilulissat Declaration, Arctic Ocean Conference, Ilulissat, Greenland, 27–29 May 2008* (copy with the authors).

Bertelsen, R. G. (2019). "The Arctic as Laboratory of Global Governance: The Case of Knowledge-based Cooperation and Science Diplomacy." In Finger, M., and Heininen, L., eds., *The Global Arctic Handbook*: 251–267. Cham: Springer.

Caney, S. (2005). "Cosmopolitan Justice, Responsibility, and Global Climate Change." *Leiden Journal of International Law*, 18(4): 747–775.

Corry, O. (2017). "Globalising the Arctic Climate: Geoengineering and the Emerging Global Polity." In Keil, K., and Knecht, S., eds., *Governing Arctic Change. Global Perspectives*: 59–78. Basingstoke: Palgrave Macmillan.

De Búrca, G., Keohane, R. O., and Sabel, C. (2014). "Global Experimentalist Governance." *British Journal of Political Science*, 44(3): 477–486.

Depledge, D., and Dodds, K. (2017). "Bazaar Governance: Situating the Arctic Circle." In Keil, K. & Knecht, S., eds., *Governing Arctic Change. Global Perspectives*: 141–160. Basingstoke: Palgrave Macmillan.

Dodds, K. (2013). "The Ilulissat Declaration (2008): The Arctic States, 'Law of the Sea', and Arctic Ocean." *SAIS Review of International Affairs*, 33(2): 45–55.

Dodds, K., and Nuttall, M. (2019). *The Arctic: What everyone needs to know*. Oxford: Oxford University Press.

Exner-Pirot, H. (2011). "Canadian Leadership in the Circumpolar World: An Agenda for the Arctic Council Chairmanship 2013–2015." *Northern Review*, 33: 7–27.

Garipova, L. (2016). "Corporate Social Responsibility in the Arctic." *Georgetown Law Journal*, 104: 973–1000.

Griffiths, F. (1989). "Challenge and Leadership in the Arctic." In Dosman, E.J., ed., *Sovereignty and Security in the Arctic*: 211–227. London: Routledge.

Hansen-Magnusson, H. (2019). "The Web of Responsibility in and for the Arctic." *Cambridge Review of International Affairs*, 32(2): 132–158.

Held, D. (2010). *Cosmopolitanism: Ideals and Realities*. Cambridge: Polity Press.

Henriksen, T. (2016). "The Arctic Ocean, Environmental Stewardship, and the Law of the Sea." *UC Irvine Law Review*, 6(1): 61–82.

Henry, L. A., Nysten-Haarala, S., Tulaeva, S., and Tysiachniouk, M. (2016). "Corporate Social Responsibility and the Oil Industry in the Russian Arctic: Global Norms and Neo-Paternalism." *Europe-Asia Studies*, 68(8): 1340–1368.

Hubbard, R. (2013). "Risk, Rights and Responsibility: Navigating Corporate Responsibility and Indigenous Rights in Greenlandic Extractive Industry Development." *Michigan State International Law Review*, 22(1): 101–66.

Humrich, C. (2018). "Souveränitätsdenken und Seerecht: Regionalisierung von Meerespolitik in der Arktis als neue Staatsräson." In Albert, M., Deitelhoff, N. & Hellmann, G., eds., *Ordnung und Regiere in der Weltgesellschaft*: 211–241. Wiesbaden: Springer VS.

Johnstone, R. L. (2014). *Offshore Oil and Gas Development in the Arctic under International Law: Risk and Responsibility*. Leiden: Martinus Nijhoff.

Kean, J. (2018). *Power and Humility. The Future of Monitory Democracy.* Cambridge: Cambridge University Press.
Keil, K., and Knecht, S. (2017). "Introduction: The Arctic as a Globally Embedded Space." In Keil, K., and Knecht, S., eds., *Governing Arctic Change. Global Perspectives*: 1–18. Basingstoke: Palgrave Macmillan.
Keskitalo, E. C. H. (2004). *Negotiating the Arctic: The Construction of an International Region.* London: Routledge.
King, S. D. (2018). "Address at the 2018 Arctic Circle Assembly". https://vimeo.com/296187282 (accessed April 30, 2019.
Keohane, R. O., and Victor, D. G. (2011). "The Regime Complex for Climate Change." *Perspectives on Politics*, 9(1): 7–23.
Koivurova, T. (2013). "Gaps in International Regulatory Frameworks for the Arctic Ocean." In Berkman, P. A., and Vylegzhanin, A. N., (eds.), *Environmental Security in the Arctic Ocean*: 139–156. Dordrecht: Springer.
Kopra, S. (2019). "China, Great Power Responsibility and Arctic Security." In Heininen, L., and Exner-Pirot, H., eds., *Climate Change and Arctic Security: Searching for a Paradigm Shift*: 33–52. Cham: Palgrave.
Loh, J. (2017). "Strukturen und Relata der Verantwortung." In Heidbrink, L., Langbehn, C., and Loh, J., eds., *Handbuch Verantwortung*: 35–56. Wiesbaden: Springer VS.
Lone, K., Merkel, B., Lydersen, C., Kovacs, K. M., and Aars, J. (2018). "Sea Ice Resource Selection Models for Polar Bears in the Barents Sea Subpopulation." *Ecography*, 41(4): 567–578.
Medby, I. A. (2018). "Articulating State Identity: 'Peopling' the Arctic State." *Political Geography*, 62(1): 116–125.
Molenaar, E. J. (2019). "Participation in the Central Arctic Ocean Fisheries Agreement." In Shibata, A., Zou, L., Sellheim, N., and Scopelliti, M., eds., *Emerging Legal Orders in the Arctic: The Role of Non-Arctic Actors*: 132–170. London: Routledge.
Nollkaemper, A., and Jacobs, D. (2013). "Shared Responsibility in International Law: A Conceptual Framework." *Michigan Journal of International Law*, 34(2): 359–438.
Nord, D. C. (ed.) (2019). *Leadership for the North: The Influence and Impact of Arctic Council Chairs*, Cham: Springer.
Orford, A. (2018). "Jurisdiction without Territory: From the Holy Roman Empire to the Responsibility to Protect." *Michigan Journal of International Law*, 30(3): 981–1015.
Palosaari, T. (2019). "The Arctic Paradox (and How to Solve It): Oil, Gas and Climate Ethics in the Arctic." In Finger, M., and Heininen, L., eds., *The Global Arctic Handbook*: 141–152. Cham: Springer.
Pram Gad, U., and Strandsbjerg, J. (eds.) (2019). *The Politics of Sustainability in the Arctic. Reconfiguring Identity, Space, and Time.* London: Routledge.
Rey, L. (1987). "The Arctic: Mankind's unique Heritage and Common Responsibility." *Arctic and Alpine Research*, 19(4): 345–350.
Serreze, M. C., and Francis, J. A. (2006). "The Arctic Amplification Debate." *Climatic Change*, 76(3–4): 241–264.
Shibata, A., Zou, L., Sellheim, N., and Scopelliti, M. (eds.) (2019). *Emerging Legal Orders in the Arctic: The Role of Non-Arctic Actors.* London: Routledge.
Stirling, I., and Derocher, A. E. (2012). "Effects of Climate Warming on Polar Bears: A Review of the Evidence." *Global Change Biology*, 18(9): 2694–2706.
Stokke, O. S. (2013). "Political Stability and Multi-level Governance in the Arctic." In Berkman, P. A., and Vylegzhanin, A., eds., *Environmental Security in the Arctic Ocean*: 297–311. Dordrecht: Springer.
Stokke, O. S., and Hønneland, G. (eds.) (2007). *International Cooperation and Arctic Governance: Regime Effectiveness and Northern Region Building.* Abingdon: Routledge.
Tanaka, Y. (2014). "Reflections on Transboundary Air Pollution in the Arctic: Limits of Shared Responsibility." *Nordic Journal of International Law*, 83(3): 213–250.
TFAMC (2017). *Report to Ministers of the Task Force on Arctic Marine Cooperation.* https://oaarchive.arctic-council.org/handle/11374/1923.
Ulfbeck, V., Møllmann, A., and Gram Mortensen, B. O. (eds.) (2016). *Responsibilities and Liabilities for Commercial Activity in the Arctic: The Example of Greenland.* Abingdon: Routledge.
Vinogradov, S., and Azubuike, S. I. (2018). "Arctic Hydrocarbon Exploration & Production: Evaluating the Legal Regime for Offshore Accidental Pollution Liability." In Heininen, L., and Exner-Pirot, H., eds., *Arctic Yearbook 2018*: 307–327. Northern Research Forum, Akureyri.
Winiger, P. et al. (2019). "Source Apportionment of Circum-Arctic Atmospheric Black Carbon from Isotopes and Modeling." *Sciences Advances*, 5(2): 1–10.
Wormbs, N. (2018). "Introduction: Back to the Futures of an Uncertain Arctic." In Wormbs, N., ed., *Competing Arctic Futures. Historical and Contemporary Perspectives*: 1–18. London: Palgrave.
Young, O. R. (2012). "Building an International Regime Complex for the Arctic: Current Status and Next Steps." *The Polar Journal*, 2(2): 391–407.

28
SHAREHOLDERS, SUPERVISORS, AND STAKEHOLDERS
Practices of financial responsibility and their limits
Michael C. Sardo and Erin Lockwood

Introduction

Financial markets are systemically risky, crisis-prone, and a site of wealth valued many times in excess of world trade or production.[1] As such, finance has been historically and continues to be an important site for discussions about responsibility. What does it mean to manage wealth responsibly? To whom are financial actors responsible? Does corporate responsibility extend beyond shareholders to some broader public audience? Who should be held accountable when financial systems tip into crisis, impacting the real economy and the savings, job prospects, and retirement accounts of ordinary people?

Financial markets have stark distributional consequences, consolidating wealth in ways that many contend is unjust while increasingly permeating the everyday lives of subjects not conventionally seen as part of the world of high finance. The lightly regulated growth of financial capital and its high returns have fueled inequality, concentrating wealth in the top 1% of the global population (Milanovic 2016, 36–40; Piketty 2014). At the same time, and in spite of massive geographic and class-based variation in income and wealth, nearly everyone's life has become increasingly entangled with debt and credit, fueled by development-oriented projects of financial inclusion and the expansion of financial technology into new sectors of everyday life (see Gabor and Brooks 2017). While financial markets have been shaped and governed by doctrines of fiduciary and corporate social responsibility, so too have they developed in ways that exceed and elude conventional causal and individualistic theories of responsibility. As they have grown more complex and uncertain, financial markets have come to pose distinctive empirical and theoretical challenges to conventional theories of responsibility.

In this chapter, we first provide an overview of how responsibility has conventionally been conceived – and to varying degrees institutionally and legally encoded – in the context of finance before turning to a discussion of how responsibility was allocated for the 2008 financial crisis in popular and academic narratives. We then discuss how the crisis brought to light dynamics and characteristics of contemporary financial markets that fit poorly with traditional theories of responsibility. We conclude by discussing the challenges for theorizing and taking responsibility for global financial markets.

Relations of responsibility in global finance

Fiduciary responsibility and shareholder value

While finance's excesses and single-minded focus on profit maximization have been deemed irresponsible by some (Curran 2015; Herzig and Moon 2013), relationships of responsibility have played a constitutive role in the development of modern financial strategy, practice, and governance. Indeed, even finance's exclusive pursuit of profits has been legitimized and institutionalized in the doctrine of shareholder value which has at its core an explicit, albeit narrowly conceived, definition of responsibility (Lazonick and O'Sullivan 2000, 13–14). However, attempts to delimit and enforce financial responsibility beyond this paradigm in the guise of fraud prevention and corporate social responsibility have failed to reckon with the broader structural injustices perpetuated and funded by financial markets.

The principle of shareholder value, a cornerstone of contemporary corporate governance in the US, UK, and – increasingly – the OECD more broadly, assigns responsibility for maximizing shareholder value to corporate executives as agents of their shareholder principals, "in accordance with [shareholders'] desires, which generally will be to make as much money as possibly while conforming to the basic rules of society, both those embodied in law and those embodied in ethical custom" (Friedman 1970, 33). This conceptualization of responsibility, which became dominant in the Anglo-American financial sphere in the 1980s, represents a change from earlier corporate governance paradigms which figured corporate executives as responsible chiefly for retaining revenues on the books for purposes of reinvesting them in human and physical capital (Lazonick and O'Sullivan 2000).

Shareholder value theory is premised on the idea that the firm is little more than a bundle of private contracts which allocate claims on asset and cash flows and which therefore clearly delineate responsibility (Jensen and Meckling 1976, 311). Motivated by the massive growth in corporate size which exacerbated the risk of managers directing profits in self-serving (and inefficient) directions as well as by heightened external competition from Japan, the theory of shareholder value has its origins in principal-agent theory and 1980s United States financial economics.[2] Shareholder value theory specifies that corporate managers' responsibility is to their shareholders and can be measured directly through corporate stock performance (see Fama and Jensen 1983; Jensen and Meckling 1976). As such, the long stock market boom of the 1990s was interpreted by shareholder value proponents as evidence of the merits of this doctrine.

The idea that corporate managers' responsibility is primarily to their shareholders has been institutionalized in regulatory policy and corporate governance with material consequences that go beyond stock return data. During the 1980s, the shareholder value theory of responsibility was explicitly encouraged by regulatory changes in the United States which allowed insurance companies, pension funds, money-market funds, and banks to compete more effectively with mutual funds by freeing them from restrictions on investment activity, fueling investment in junk bonds and hostile takeovers through the 1980s and 1990s, as well as share buy-back schemes (Lazonick and O'Sullivan 2000, 17–18). The search for returns throughout subsequent decades fueled financialization, putting pressure on cross-shareholding models of corporate governance in Europe (Jürgens, Naumann, and Rupp 2000; Morin 2000).

In assigning corporate managers responsibility for maximizing shareholder value, the shareholder value theory of responsibility implicitly – and in some case explicitly (Friedman and Friedman 2002, 133) – relieves financial actors from broader responsibilities, legitimizing the massive labor force restructuring and downsizing that characterized corporate strategy in the

1980s and 1990s, and abjuring any responsibility to the significant percentage of workers who did not have significant savings invested in the stock market (Williams 2000, 2). For these reasons, shareholder value – and in particular its underlying conception of responsibility – has been critiqued. As David Ciepley (2013, 140) writes:

> The corporation became a pure creature of the market rather than a creature of government, exempting it from any duty to the public, or accountability to the public, or even publicity to the public, and rendering it eligible for a raft of constitutional rights, including electioneering rights […] In construing shareholders as the corporation's owners and principals, it also fixates corporations on short-term share price, sinking their productivity while upping their irresponsibility. […] Reducing corporations to private contracts is theoretically confused, economically deleterious, and normatively askew.

Financial fraud and the responsible corporate officer doctrine

While shareholder value theory defines responsibility to shareholders narrowly, it does, per Friedman's formulation, also require "conforming to the basic rules of society" (1970, 33). With executives held accountable to shareholders by stock market outcomes, financial regulation during the 1990s and early 2000s shifted primarily to identifying and preventing fraud and other illegal financial behavior. Although proponents of the efficient markets hypothesis and shareholder value theory like Eugene Fama (1990) held that those with residual claims on corporations' financial assets would have sufficient incentive to monitor firms for fraud themselves, empirical evidence suggests otherwise.[3] Even as financial markets were significantly deregulated in the 1980s and 1990s, financial regulators like the Securities and Exchange Commission and Commodity Futures Trading Commission retained a narrowed authority to oversee financial firms with the goal of preventing fraud. For example, regulators' interest in the wake of derivatives-related bankruptcies and collapses in the 1990s attributed these losses to fraud, rather than excessive risk-taking or the increasingly complex and interconnected financial system itself (Lockwood 2020).

This regulatory focus on fraud was intensified by a series of corporate and accounting scandals in the late 1990s, culminating in the 2002 Sarbanes-Oxley Act (the House of Representatives version of which was entitled "Corporate and Auditing Accountability, Responsibility, and Transparency Act") which was passed in the USA to improve securities regulation and auditing and incentivize whistle-blowing. The Sarbanes-Oxley Act's conception of responsibility is highly individualistic, specifying in Section 302 that the CEO and CFO take direct individual responsibility for internal controls and for the accuracy and completeness of financial reports. In defining responsibility in these terms, the Act drew on the responsible corporate officer (RCO) doctrine with respect to mandating the accuracy and validity of corporate financial reports.

Originating in the Supreme Court's decision in *United States v. Dotterweich* (320 U.S. 277, 1943), the RCO doctrine emerged in the context of public welfare misdemeanor law.[4] According to this doctrine, corporate officers can be held liable for corporate crimes committed, of which they had, or should have had knowledge, and had the authority and responsibility to prevent or stop (See, Block and Voisin 1992; Bragg et al. 2010; Hustis and Gotada 1994). While the doctrine remains controversial – Matrin Petrin (2012, 286) argues that it represents "an unwarranted augmentation of corporate agents' duties and runs contrary to established tort, criminal, and corporate law principles" – there have been both public and scholarly calls to expand the doctrine in the context of financial crime.[5] Christina M. Schuck (2010) calls for expanding the doctrine to include mortgage fraud in the name of public welfare. Similarly, Amy J. Sepinwall (2014, 377) argues that the doctrine "allows prosecutors to evade the purported systemic risks of going after entities that are 'too big to jail' or prompting dissolution of entities that are 'too big to nail,'" a necessity in the post-crisis context.

However, while Attorney-General, Eric Holder (2014) called for expanding the doctrine, because "we need not tolerate a system that permits top executives to enjoy all of the rewards of excessively-risky activity while bearing none of the responsibility," the value of the doctrine remains limited in financial contexts. Even its defenders note that it can only be applied to actual statutory violations and would thus be limited only to cases of financial fraud (Sepinwall 2014, 405–406). To apply it, as Holder suggested, to discourage risky but legal financial practices and would be an excessive expansion of prosecutorial authority contrary to criminal and corporate law. In the context of the "everyday injustices" of global finances, the RCO doctrine remains either toothless or excessive.

Corporate social responsibility and socially responsible investing

Shareholder value was a deliberate challenge to a different concept of responsibility which had emerged in the second half the twentieth century: corporate social responsibility (CSR), a discourse which has been reinvigorated in recent decades in response to the excesses of shareholder value maximization (Carroll 1999). A broad concept, with diverse and contested meanings (Garriga and Melé 2004), CSR refers to a firm's capacious set of responsibilities to and for society as a whole, beyond its responsibilities to its shareholders and legal obligations, by virtue of its reliance upon and effects on a broad set of societal stakeholders. According to its advocates, adopting CSR practices can simultaneously restrain the worst impulses of businesses while still maximizing shareholder value.

In the context of finance, much of the literature on CSR focuses on the concept of socially responsible investing (SRI). Here, investors negatively or positively screen firms' social behaviors for exclusion or inclusion in their portfolios, engage in practices of shareholder activism to pressure firm behavior, and invest in specially marketed socially responsible mutual funds (Kurtz 2008).[6] Finance serves as an intermediary institution through which socially conscious investors can act to hold corporations to higher ethical, social, and environmental standards than existing laws (Clark and Hebb 2005). However, theoretical and empirical studies of SRI have been mixed at best (Kurtz 2005). In a meta-analysis of such research, Revelli and Viviani (2015) find that SRI itself neither promotes nor hinders financial performance, suggesting that, at a minimum, SRI is no less profitable than traditional investment strategies. Others (Haigh and Hazelton 2004; Johnsen 2003; Scholtens 2006) have noted a number of limitations on the effectiveness of SRI including the limited share of global finance constituted by SRI and broader structural constraints.

CSR has also been adopted by investment banks and financial institutions themselves. Goldman Sachs, JP Morgan Chase, Barclays, Bank of America, Morgan Stanley, and Deutsche Bank all have webpages devoted to their CSR practices, suggesting that finance itself can and should be an object rather than only a tool of CSR. Noting the absence of a suitable framework for studying CSR in the banking industry itself, Bert Scholtens (2009) has generated a framework based on four dimensions – codes of CSR principles, environmental management, responsible financial products, and social conduct – to rank 32 banks in 15 countries. Chih, Chih, and Chen (2010), studying the determinants of CSR in the financial industry, find that a firm's size, competitive environment, and legal environment all contribute to adopting CSR, and that there is a negligible link between CSR adoption and financial performance. Surveying discourses of CSR and corporate social irresponsibility in the financial industry following the 2007–2008 financial crisis, Christian Herzig and Jeremy Moon (2013) show the diversity of purposes for which CSR practices and discourses are invoked, from rationalization and justifying the behavior of the financial industry to calls for a more fundamental restructuring of the industry as a whole. This research suggests that despite the growth of CSR in global finance, its ability to fulfill its promise of holding firms – both financial and otherwise – to higher standards of social and environmental responsibility remains limited at best.

If CSR neither enhances financial performance nor restraints financial excess, what, then, explains its embrace by global finance? More critical analysis places CSR within the context of neoliberal governmentality, in which social responsibility is transferred from public entities to private actors while moral behavior and social goals are commodified as means of market differentiation (Bannerjee 2008; Sharmir 2008). Rather than holding finance responsible for its effects on social welfare, CSR projects are pursued strategically (Windsor 2001). Contra Revilli and Viviani, Wu and Shen (2013) find a positive link between CSR and financial performance, suggesting that investment banks may pursue CSR for strategic and not altruistic ends. CSR practices provide a way of branding financial products and appeal to investors who are concerned with sustainability in a competitive environment (Ogrizek 2002). For example, in 2018, responding to shareholder activism – in particular by Robeco and the Church of England Pensions Board – Royal Dutch Shell announced a policy linking executive compensation to carbon emissions targets. Additional strategic uses of CSR include legitimizing the size and profits of the industry (Haigh and Hazelton, 2004), cultivating a sense of identity for investors (Markowitz 2007), or staving off formal regulation (Gentzoglanis 2019). CSR's ambiguity provides a strategic value for financial firms, as its rhetorical promise – for firms, shareholders, and social activists – far exceeds its empirical purchase. The mythology surrounding CSR, Markowitz (2007, 149) summarizes, "has not only allowed the growth of the SR mutual fund industry but has given it the freedom to avoid answering difficult questions about the product it is selling." Therefore, rather than holding the global financial system accountable for the social harms it engenders, CSR practices and discourse at best represent side payments to cover negative externalities and at worst work to legitimate business as usual.

Financial responsibility in crisis

If the social consequences of shareholder value maximization had strained conventional practices of responsibility during ordinary times, the 2008 financial crisis exposed the insufficiencies of their conceptual underpinnings. The collapse of the US housing market was magnified and transmitted well beyond defaulting homeowners and mortgage-issuing banks in the United States. Many people, from those with retirement funds invested in financial funds to workers laid off in the wake of crisis-induced corporate losses, suffered not solely because of fraud, failure to fulfill fiduciary responsibility, or socially irresponsible investments, but as a result of finance's deep imbrication in society. In the aftermath of the 2008 global financial crisis, the question of who was to blame for such large and systemic economic damage loomed large in both popular and academic circles.[7] Popular narratives tend to emphasize individual moral responsibility on the part of borrowers, investors, and bankers. Borrowers were blamed for having taken on irresponsible levels of debt and for being bad financial citizens. Investors and consumers were criticized for their poor understanding of market dynamics, leading OECD Secretary-General Angel Gurría to conclude that the appropriate solution lay in helping consumers and investors "make more informed decisions" (qtd. in Griffin 2012, 10). Perhaps less surprisingly, bankers were often identified as especially culpable. Timothy Hellwig and Eva Coffey's (2011, 417) survey data from Britain found that 65% of respondents identified "banks and investment companies" as "the most responsible for the recent problems facing world financial markets," with 25% choosing "governments and regulators."⁸ The latter attribution of responsibility is consistent with the trope of regulators "asleep at the wheel" in the lead-up to the financial crisis, emphasizing the close relationship between regulators and industry and the possibility that this proximity has captured or compromised regulatory actors.

In contrast with popular narratives, which tend to single out particular firms and people, scholarly accounts of the crisis focus less on individuals and more on actors' institutional position within the global financial system, their incentives, and their relations with other actors, with the goal of generating a causal account of the crisis. Eschewing the moralistic tone of popular accounts, scholarly accounts are more likely to provide an empirically substantiated *causal* account. Much of the academic literature on the financial crisis causally attributes responsibility to specific financial innovations, relationships among financial actors, and predictive models and accounting practices that make up the global financial ecosystem.

Frank Partnoy (2009, 431) locates financial innovation as being at the core of the 2008 financial crisis, citing its tendency to outpace investors' ability to process information and arguing that the subsequent information asymmetries exacerbated misunderstandings and crucial gaps in knowledge. Structured finance – products like securitized assets, credit derivatives, and collateralized debt obligations – has been singled out for the role it played in magnifying and transmitting the collapse of the US residential mortgage market (Benmelech and Dlugosz 2010, 161). Assembling new financial products out of assets like residential mortgages and selling them on to third parties allowed banks to make more and riskier loans to borrowers. At the same time, it eroded market incentives to accurately measure risk and hold appropriate amounts of capital as investment banks transferred the biggest risks associated with securitized loans off their balance sheets to special purpose vehicles while retaining on their books those tranches of the securitized loans rated highly enough to avoid capital charges (Acharya and Richardson 2009, 195; Benmelech and Dlugosz 2010, 165). According to Viryal Acharya and Matthew Richardson (2009, 196–197), the resulting concentration of risk in the unsupervised shadow banking sector and overleveraging in the regulated financial sector was the ultimate cause of the financial crisis.

Other scholars have focused on the role that private credit raters played in reassuring buy-side investors and in-house risk managers that securitized assets and the derivatives written on those structured products were safe investments (Blinder 2007; Partnoy 2009). The relationship between credit raters and banks has come under particular scrutiny; banks pay for credit rating services, creating an incentive for raters to use models that generate more favorable ratings.⁹ Partnoy (2009, 431), for example, has argued that credit raters should be understood less as providing accurate information to investors and more as providing "regulatory licenses" that allowed banks to carry out asset securitization and swap deals outside the scope of regulators' capital requirements. Benmelech and Dlugosz (2010, 162) cite the "overreliance on statistical models that failed to account for default correlation" as a "main cause of the credit rating disaster."

An overreliance on the methodology of predictive models and the subsequent over-confidence in risky financial transactions is also central to Patricia Arnold's (2009) account of accounting practices' contribution to the financial crisis. Major accounting firms in the US and Europe were directly involved in the process of asset securitization and directly advised their investment banking clients. Like credit raters, they relied on models that not only failed to predict the crisis, but may even have exacerbated it by requiring assets to be priced according to their market value (fair value accounting) which is highly volatile (and often very low) during crises (Arnold 2009, 803). Mary Barth and Wayne Landsman (2010, 399) dispute this conclusion, exonerating fair value accounting, and laying the blame instead at the feet of financial disclosures and reporting on asset securitization and derivatives which they contend was "insufficient for investors to assess properly the values and riskiness of bank assets and liabilities." They couch their conclusions explicitly in the language of responsibility arguing that, "it is the responsibility of bank regulators, not accounting standard setters, to determine how best to mitigate the effects of procyclicality on the stability of the banking system" (Barth and Landsman 2010, 407).

Exceptions to moralized and causal accounts have focused on the role that dominant ideas played in legitimating self-regulation of the financial sector. Alison Kemper and Roger Martin (2010) document the shift in the locus of responsibility for financial firms' social consequences from the state to the firm level, culminating in the paradigm of shareholder value discussed above. They contend that the crisis was an obvious failure of the idea that firms discharge their social responsibility by maximizing shareholder return, creating an opening for governments to resume their position as the actors responsible for regulating firm behavior (2010, 229). David Colander et al. (2009) push this critique a step further to implicate the role that the economics profession as a whole played in the financial crisis. Like other scholars, they cite unwarranted confidence in flawed risk models that, in failing to account for feedback loops and irrationality, led both regulators and market participants to overestimate the stability of the financial system and to underestimate – or even ignore – systemic risk (Colander et al. 2009, 254; King 2017, 120ff). They also call the profession to task for its post facto assessment of the crisis as an exogenous shock rather than the product of deeply flawed assumptions and models (Colander et al. 2009, 249–250).

At the core of Colander et al.'s critique is the disparity between the individualist assumptions of economic models versus the systemic risks produced by large number of market participants using the same models and identical micro strategies. This disparity is echoed in the sheer number and variety of scholarly analyses of the causes of the financial crisis, and it speaks to both the complexity of the financial system and the difficulty of matching causal explanations of the crisis with theories of responsibility. While there have been some moves toward more structural accounts of the financial crisis,[10] referencing broader macroeconomic factors (e.g., low interest rates fueling "irresponsible" borrowing, the global savings glut), even these tend to fall back on an individualized conception of responsibility, concluding, for example, that it was the Fed who was ultimately responsible for keeping interests rates too low.

Finance and the limits of personal responsibility

The dynamics of global finance undermine traditional conceptions of moral responsibility, in which "one is accountable as a subject who is the cause of his or her actions through the freedom of the will" (Raffoul 2010, 5). Ascriptions of moral and legal responsibility rely on a series of onto-political conditions – linear causality, calculable risk, unified agency, and rational control – that do not prevail in the context of financial markets.

Clear causal connection

The first condition, causal connection, is relatively straightforward: to be responsible for something, there must be a clear causal connection between the agent and some event or change in the world. As Iris Marion Young (2006, 116) summarizes, "one assigns responsibility to a particular agent (or agents) whose actions can be shown to be causally connected to the circumstances for which responsibility is sought." While this usually takes the form of some action, failing to take an action can also be grounds for ascriptions of responsibility, when such inaction directly leads to some harm, such as in cases of strict liability (Sankowski 1990).

The complexity of the financial system means that establishing clear causal connections between actions and harms is difficult. Each actor within the financial system has multiple counterparties, each of whom has many other counterparties, resulting in a dense network of relationships of debt and credit which have proven difficult to value, especially during times of crisis when the risk of nonpayment by one counterparty can set into motion a chain of knock-on downgrades to creditworthiness, forced sale of assets at very low prices, and thereby threats to the solvency of multiple firms in the system. As Andrew Haldane (2009, 5) of the Bank of England observed in early 2009:

> The financial system is […] a network, with nodes defined by the financial institutions and links defined by the financial interconnections between these institutions. Evaluating risk within these networks is a complex science; indeed, it is the science of complexity. When assessing nodal risk, it is not enough to know your counterparty; you need to know your counterparty's counterparty too. In other words, there are network externalities. In financial networks, these externalities are often referred to as contagion or spillovers.

Calculable risk

The second condition presupposes the existence of alternative possibilities arranged as calculable risks, which amounts to a claim that the agent could have known the consequences of their action. If it is fundamentally impossible for an agent to predict the consequences of their action, ascribing moral responsibility would be unfair. As Steve Vanderheiden (2004, 143) writes in the context of climate change, "agents are assumed to be morally responsible (as opposed to merely being causally responsible) for their acts (or omissions) insofar as they can reasonably anticipate the consequences of those actions (or inactions.)" While an agent may be causally responsible for some harm, they can only be held morally responsible if the risks of action, or inaction, could be determined in advance.

This is not always the case in finance. Financial networks are characterized not only by externalities but also by feedback loops and reflexive dynamics, whereby individual actions generate outcomes in excess of intentions, expectations, what the simple aggregation of individual decisions might lead one to expect. For example, the widespread use of a common methodology used to calculate risk led to correlated investment strategies that, rather than making the financial system less crisis-prone as intended, in fact rendered it more vulnerable to disruption and contagion (Lockwood 2015). As a result, the condition of known, calculable risks does not always obtain. While we may rightly hold a number of actors responsible for failing to anticipate the possibility – indeed, probability – of systemic contagion in the financial sector, it is considerably more difficult to contend that, at every juncture, each actor involved could have knowingly made crisis measurably less likely by acting differently. The financial crisis was not the sum of knowable, calculable risks. Instead, it was characterized at least in part by incalculable uncertainty (Nelson and Katzenstein 2014).

Unified individual agent

Ascribing responsibility also makes implicit claims about the nature of the agent themselves. The third condition, reflecting a broadly liberal conception of the self as a unified and sovereign actor, is that the responsible agent is relatively discrete. Whether a natural or corporate person, theories of moral responsibility point to a single, unified individual agent to be held accountable (Lavin 2008, 8–10; Young 2011, 101–104). This both reflects the insistence that someone must answer for some social harm and an individualist social ontology that understands social outcomes as the result of interactions between discrete individuals.

The emergent properties and reflexive dynamics of global finance mean that the global financial system is better conceptualized precisely *as a system* and not as an aggregation of individual traders, managers, and firms acting in isolation. Firms' investment strategies are not forged in a vacuum; they variously reflect, compete with, and amplify the strategies of their competitors. They are social phenomena, driven not just by rational calculation but also by market sentiment, irrational expectations and exuberance, and Keynes's animal spirits. Even individually purely rational calculation – like continuing to invest in what you know is likely a bubble as long as it has not yet burst – can produce collectively suboptimal results. The result of these interactions is Kindleberger's (2005) manias, panics, and crashes: outcomes that are greater than the sum of their parts and which are difficult or impossible to understand in a methodologically individualist paradigm.

Rational control

Finally, commonsense accounts of responsibility assume a fourth condition: that the agent has a level of rational control over their actions. Thomas Nagel (1993, 60–61) summarizes: "it seems irrational to take or dispense credit or blame for matters over which a person has no control, or for their influence on results over which he has partial control."[11] To hold an individual responsible is, therefore, to make an implicit claim that not only could the event have been otherwise, but that the responsible agent alone determined the course of events that happened. Despite voluminous philosophical debate in the metaphysics of agency, this intuition is widespread in contemporary political thought, underpinning both liberal (Berlin 2002; Dworkin 2000, 5–8; Hayek 1960, 72) and republican (Petit 2001, 8–11, 45–47) conceptions of responsibility.

While individual traders, risk managers, CEOs, and financial regulators were not powerless in the lead-up to the financial crisis, their agency was constrained by the systems and structures in which they were embedded. In the case of flawed market risk models that may have inadvertently rendered the financial system less stable, banks did not decide to use Value-at-Risk independently; the methodology (though not its specifics) was recommended by the Basel Accord and incorporated into national capital adequacy regulations. The reliance on flawed systems of risk-modeling continued after the crisis. In 2012, JPMorgan Chase sustained $6.2 billion in losses as a result of the so-called "London Whale" trades, which occurred far in excess of regulatory and internal risk limits.[12] While risk managers, traders, and executives at JPMorgan Chase bear responsibility for gaming and ignoring risk limits and capital requirements, the use of manipulable risk models in the first place, banks' ability to effectively set their own capital requirements, and lax regulatory oversight of the whole process has a much longer history, and one that surely bears some responsibility for the resulting losses. Similarly, although the AAA ratings that senior tranches of CDOs enjoyed almost certainly made investors overconfident in the soundness of these products, the use of private credit ratings is incorporated into U.S. law and regulation governing the valuation of bank assets and allowable purchases (Carruthers 2013).

Conclusion

Global finance represents a critical yet challenging case for scholars of responsibility. On the one hand, finance is conceptually and practically bound to responsibility, whether in the form of the fiduciary responsibility owed by fund managers, the legal liability for financial fraud, or the growing calls for socially responsible investing. On the other hand, as became painfully clear in the wake of the 2008 financial crisis, the dynamics of financial markets render traditional theories and practices of moral and legal responsibility inadequate. This "responsibility gap" (Buell 2018) is intensified by the distributive consequences of financial practices and crises and the corresponding calls for greater accountability in finance. Curran (2015, 405) contends that "the massive *mismatch* between those who gained from financial system risks and those who suffered damages from them" contribute to widening inequality as a privileged few are able to extract gains while many others suffer the losses.

More fundamentally, this responsibility gap should itself be understood as a structural feature of global finance, analogous to what Beck (1995, 63–65; 1998) has called "organized irresponsibility" – despite the highly organized and regulated nature of contemporary social and economic structures, their complexity render it increasingly difficult to hold any individual agent or node in such a network accountable for harms. In fact, "it is the application of prevalent norms that guarantees the non-attributability of systemic hazards [...] Whoever waves the banner of rigorous causal proof while demanding that the injured parties do the same, not only demands the unachievable," but also "holds aloft a shining shield to keep rising, collectively conditioned hazards out of the reach of politics or attribution to individuals" (Beck 1995, 64). The very ways in which finance organizes relationships of responsibility insulates both individual financial actors and the financial system itself from accountability, while also providing a legitimating narrative to the status quo. Because no one agent is responsible for the harm, it can be absolved away as a market failure or tragic misfortune.

The same individualistic and causal accounts of responsibility that continue to shape both financial practices and scholarship are ubiquitous in contemporary political life. Nevertheless, the 2008 financial crisis revealed their empirical and normative inadequacy and the need for more collective and political conceptions of responsibility. This tension between conventional accounts of responsibility and the structure of global finance can be found in a perhaps surprising source: the final report of the Financial Crisis Inquiry Commission (FCIC) in the United States.

The FCIC's mission was cast in explicitly causal terms (to "examine the causes of the current financial and economic crisis in the United States"[13]), and its report was "intended to provide a historical accounting of what brought out financial system and economy to a precipice and to help policy makers and the public better understand how this calamity came to be" (FCIC 2011, xi). *The Financial Crisis Inquiry Report* begins with a conventional recitation of how the financial crisis developed, and cited a familiar concatenation of factors as causally contributing to the crisis, among them failures in supervision and regulation, excessive borrowing and opaque risky investments, and an inconsistent government response (FCIC 2011, xvi–xxiii).

Nevertheless, the FCIC's (2011, xxii–xxiii) conclusions – and indeed, conception of responsibility – are more nuanced than their statutory instructions might lead one to anticipate, and are worth quoting at some length:

> [...A] crisis of this magnitude cannot be the work of a few bad actors, and such was not the case here. At the same time, the breadth of this crisis does not mean that 'everyone is at fault'; many firms and individuals did not participate in the excesses that spawned disaster. We do place special responsibility with the public leaders charged with protecting our financial system [...] These individuals sought and accepted positions of significant responsibility and obligation. Tone at the top does matter and, in this instance, we were let down. No one said 'no.' But as a nation we must also accept responsibility for what we permitted to occur. Collectively, but certainly not unanimously, we acquiesced to or embraced a set of policies and actions, that gave rise to our present predicament.

The *Report's* concludes with an explicit call for collective responsibility: "The greatest tragedy would be to accept the refrain that no one could have seen this coming and thus nothing could have been done. If we accept this notion, it will happen again. This report should not be viewed as the end of the nation's examination of this crisis. There is still much to learn, much to investigate, and much to fix. This is our collective responsibility. It falls to us to make different choices if we want different results." (FCIC 2011, xxviii). This outlines not only a political agenda, but also a scholarly one. Future scholarship on finance and responsibility should begin not doctrines of moral responsibility or liability, but with the structural dynamics of financial markets, which simultaneously unevenly distribute risk and loss while obscuring attributions of responsibility. The challenge of global finance calls for a more fundamental rethinking of the concepts and practices of responsibility to move beyond the reliance on individualistic causal attribution.

Notes

1 A 2014 Deutsche Bank study estimates the stock of global financial assets (stock market capitalization, outstanding public debt securities, financial institutions' bonds, nonfinancial corporate bonds, and securitized and nonsecuritized loans) at US$242 trillion, or 329% of global GDP (Sanyal 2014, 1–2). Notional amounts of outstanding derivatives dwarf these numbers, totaling over $700 trillion in 2013, according to the Bank of International Settlements (Sanyal 2014, 6).
2 Knafo and Dutta (2019) contend that the financialization of the firm, commonly understood as having its origin in the shareholder revolution of the 1980s, in fact should be understood as the result of changes in corporate governance beginning in the 1960s. They argue that shareholder value theory emerged from strategic choices by corporate managers rather than from shareholder demands. Whereas conventional narratives serve to shield corporate managers from responsibility by casting their actions as responding shareholders, Knafo and Dutta shift the locus of responsibility to corporate managers themselves.
3 In their analysis of 216 cases of alleged corporate fraud between 1996 and 2004, Alexander Dyck, Adair Morse, and Luigi Zingales (2010, 2214) find that debt holders are absent from those reporting and detecting fraud and equity holders account for just 3% of cases. These actors' agents (auditors and analysts) account for just 24% of fraud reports.
4 The Court clarified this concept in *United States v. Park*, 421 U.S. 658 (1975).
5 For a robust theoretical defense of expanding the doctrine on the basis of criminal omission, see: Aagaard (2006).
6 On SRI in the American context, see: Schueth (2003); for SRI globally, see: Hill et al. (2007).
7 TIME magazine's (2009) list of "25 people to blame for the financial crisis" is illustrative of this kind of popular post mortem. Their list was discussed and dissected by a number of other news outlets including *The Guardian, Huffington Post,* and *The New York Daily News.*
8 They also found that the likelihood of blaming governments and regulators was higher among respondents with low political sophistication and Conservative Party identifiers. Economic ideology played no role in determining individual assignment of responsibility.
9 Benmelech and Dlugosz (2010, 200; 162) note, however, than more than 80% of the tranches of asset-back securities derivatives were rated by two or three agencies which provided the same rating. Nonetheless, tranches with only one rater were more likely to be downgraded, providing some evidence for the idea that raters provided overly rosy scenarios in order to attract the business of banks. Prem Sikka (2009) argues that similar conflicts of interest also undergirded auditors' relationship with banks in the lead-up to the financial crisis.
10 James Crotty (2009), for example, attributes the financial crisis to the flawed institutions and practices of what he calls the New Financial Architecture, an amalgamation of rapid innovation and cycles of booms and crises accompanied by government bailouts, followed by further expansions. He enumerates a list of flaws in this architecture, including its weak theoretical foundation; the perverse incentives that created excessive risk; the complexity and opacity of financial products that prevented accurate pricing; self-regulation; channels of contagion created by relying on complex financial products in a tightly integrated financial system; and high system-wide leverage.
11 This assumption is taken to underpin ordinary feelings of regret, which turn on the belief that things could have been different (James 1919). Joel Feinberg's (1968) conception of contributory fault similarly emphasizes that causal connection alone in insufficient (compare chapter by Shadmy in this volume).

12 The United States Senate Permanent Subcommittee on Investigations (2013, 1) writes that JPMorgan Chase's "inadequate derivative valuation practices enabled traders to hide substantial losses for months at a time; lax hedging practices obscured whether derivatives were being used to offset risk or take risk; risk limit breaches were routinely disregarded; risk evaluation models were manipulated to downplay risk; inadequate regulatory oversight was too easily dodged or stonewalled; and derivative trading and financial results were misrepresented to investors, regulators, policymakers, and the taxpaying public who, when banks lose big, may be required to finance multi-billion-dollar bailouts."

13 The FCIC's mission was specified as part of the Fraud Enforcement and Recovery Act (Public Law 111–21) signed in May 2009.

References

'25 people to blame for the financial crisis.' (2009). *TIME Magazine Online*. http://content.time.com/time/specials/packages/article/0,28804,1877351_1877350,00.html

Aagaard, T.S. (2006). "A fresh look at the responsible corporate officer doctrine." *The Journal of Criminal Law & Criminology*, 96(4): 1245–1292.

Acharya, V.V., and Richardson, M. (2009). "Causes of the financial crisis." *Critical Review*, 21(2–3): 195–210.

Arnold, P. (2009). "Global financial crisis. The challenge to accounting research." *Accounting, Organization, and Society*, 34(6–7): 803–809.

Bannerjee, S.B. (2008). "Corporate social responsibility: the good, the bad and the ugly." *Critical Sociology*, 34(1): 51–79.

Barth, M.E., and Landsman, W.R. (2010). "How did financial reporting contribute to the financial crisis?" *European Accounting Review*, 19(3): 399–423.

Beck, U. (1995). *Ecological Politics in an Age of Risk*. Translated by A. Weisz. Cambridge: Polity Press.

Beck, U. (1998). "Politics of risk society." In Franklin, J., ed., *The Politics of Risk Society*. Cambridge: Polity Press.

Benmelech, E., and Dlugosz, J. (2010). "The credit rating crisis." In Acemoglu, D., Rogoff, K., and Woodford, M., eds., *NBER Macroeconomics Annual 2009*, 24: 161–208. Chicago: University of Chicago Press.

Berlin, I. (2002). "Historical inevitability." In Hardy, H., ed., *Liberty: Incorporating Four Essays on Liberty*: 115–131. Oxford: Oxford University Press.

Blinder, A.S. (2007). "Six fingers of blame in the mortgage mess." *The New York Times*. September 30, 2007.

Block, J.G., and Voisin, N.A. (1992). "The responsible corporate officer doctrine – can you go to jail for what you don't know?" *Environmental Law*, 22(4): 1347–1374.

Bragg, J., Bentivoglio, J., and Collins, A. (2010). "Onus of responsibility: the changing responsible corporate officer doctrine." *Food and Drug Law Journal*, 65(3): 252–238.

Buell, S.W. (2018). "The responsibility gap in corporate crime." *Criminal Law and Philosophy*, 12(3): 471–491.

Carroll, A.B. (1999). "Corporate social responsibility: evolution of a definitional construct." *Business and Society*, 38(3): 268–295.

Carruthers, B. (2013). "From uncertainty toward risk: the case of credit ratings." *Socio-Economic Review*, 11(3): 525–551.

Chih, H.-L., Chih, H.-H., & Chen, T.-Y. (2010). "On the determinants of corporate social responsibility: international evidence on the financial industry." *Journal of Business Ethics*, 93(1): 115–135.

Ciepley, D. (2013). "Beyond public and private: toward a political theory of the corporation." *American Political Science Review*, 107(1): 139–158.

Clark, G.L., and Hebb, T. (2005). "Why should they care? The role of institutional investors in the market for corporate global responsibility." *Environment and Planning A*, 37(11): 2015–2031.

Colander, D., Goldberg, M., Haas, A., Juselius, K., Kirman, A., Lux, T., and Sloth, B. (2009). "The financial crisis and the systemic failure of the economics profession." *Critical Review*, 21(2–3): 249–267.

Curran, D. (2015). "Risk illusion and organized irresponsibility in contemporary finance: rethinking class and risk society." *Economy and Society*, 44(3): 392–417.

Crotty, J. (2009). "Structural causes of the global financial crisis: a critical assessment of the 'new financial architecture'." *Cambridge Journal of Economics*, 33(4): 563–580.

Dworkin, R. (2000). *Sovereign Virtue*. Cambridge, MA: Harvard University Press.

Dyck, A., Morse, A., and Zingales, L. (2010). "Who blows the whistle on corporate fraud?" *The Journal of Finance*, 65(6): 2213–2253.

Fama, E.F. (1990). "Contract costs and financing decisions." *Journal of Business*, 63(1): 71–91.

Fama, E.F., and Jensen, M.C. (1983). "Separation of ownership and control." *Journal of Law and Economics*, 26(2): 301–325.

FCIC (2011). *The Financial Crisis Inquiry Report*. Washington DC: U.S. Government Printing Office.

Friedman, M. (1970). "The social responsibility of business is to increase its profits." *The New York Times Magazine*, September 13, 1970: 32–33, 122–126.

Friedman, M., and Friedman, R.D. (2002). *Capitalism and Freedom*. Chicago: University of Chicago Press.

Feinberg, J. (1968). "Collective responsibility." *The Journal of Philosophy*, 65(21): 674–688.

Gabor, D., and Brooks, S. (2017). "The digital revolution in financial inclusion: international development in the Fintech era." *New Political Economy*, 22(4): 423–436.

Garriga, E., and Melé, D. (2004). "Corporate social responsibility theories: mapping the territory." *Journal of Business Ethics*, 55(1–2): 51–71.

Gentzoglanis, A. (2019). "Corporate social responsibility and financial networks as a surrogate for regulation." *Journal of Sustainable Finance and Investment*, 9(3): 214–225.

Griffin, P. (2012). "Gendering global finance: crisis, masculinity, and responsibility." *Men and Masculinities*, 16(1): 9–34.

Haigh, M., and Hazelton, J. (2004). "Financial markets: a tool for social responsibility?" *Journal of Business Ethics*, 52(1): 59–71.

Haldane, A. (2009). Rethinking the financial network. Speech at the Financial Student Association, Amsterdam. April, 28, 2009.

Hayek, F.A. (1960). *The Constitution of Liberty*. Chicago: University of Chicago Press.

Hellwig, T., and Coffey, E. (2011). "Public opinion, party messages, and responsibility for the financial crisis in Britain." *Electoral Studies*, 30(3): 417–426.

Herzig, C., and Moon, J. (2013). "Discourses on corporate social ir/responsibility in the financial sector." *Journal of Business Research*, 66(10): 1870–1880.

Hill, R.P., Ainscough, T., Shank, T., and Manullang, D. (2007). "Corporate social responsibility and socially responsible investing: a global perspective." *Journal of Business Ethics*, 70(2): 165–174.

Holder, E. (2014). "Attorney General Holder remarks on financial fraud prosecutions at NYU School of Law", *The United States Department of Justice*, September 17, 2014. https://www.justice.gov/opa/speech/attorney-general-holder-remarks-financial-fraud-prosecutions-nyu-school-law

Hustis, B.S., and Gotada, J.Y. (1994). "The responsible corporate officer: designated felon or legal fiction?" *Loyola University of Chicago Law Journal*, 25(2):169–198.

James, W. (1919). "The dilemma of determinism." In James, W., *The Will to Believe and Other Essays on Popular Philosophy*: 145–183. London: Longmans, Green, and Co.

Jensen, M.C., and Meckling, W.H. (1976). "Theory of the firm: managerial behavior, agency costs and ownership structure." *Journal of Financial Economics*, 3(4): 305–360.

Johnsen, D.B. (2003). "Socially responsible investing: a critical appraisal." *Journal of Business Ethics*, 43(3): 219–222.

Jürgens, U., Naumann, K., and Rupp, J. (2000). "Shareholder value in an adverse environment: the German case." *Economy and Society*, 29(1): 54–79.

Kindleberger, C. (2005). *Manias, Panics, and Crashes: A History of Financial Crises*, 5th ed. New York: Wiley.

Kemper, A., and Martin, R. (2010). "After the fall: the global financial crisis as a test of corporate social responsibility theories." *European Management Review*, 7(4): 229–239.

King, M. (2017). *The End of Alchemy: Money, Banking, and the Future of the Global Economy*. New York: W.W. Norton.

Knafo, S. & Dutta, S.J. (2019). "The myth of the shareholder revolution and the financialization of the firm." *Review of International Political Economy*, OnlineFirst.

Kurtz, L. (2005). "Answers to four questions." *The Journal of Investing*, 14(3): 125–140.

Kurtz, L. (2008). "Socially responsible investment and shareholder activism." In Crane, A., Matten, D., McWilliams, A., Moon, J., and Sielge, D.S., eds., *The Oxford Handbook of Corporate Social Responsibility*: 249–280. Oxford: Oxford University Press.

Lavin, C. (2008). *The Politics of Responsibility*. Urbana, IL: The University of Illinois Press.

Lockwood, E. (2015). "Predicting the unpredictable: value-at-risk, performativity, and the politics of financial uncertainty." *Review of International Political Economy*, 22(4): 719–756.

Lockwood, E. (2020). "From bombs to boons: explaining the unchecked growth of OTC derivatives and systemic risk." *Theory and Society*, 49: 215–244.

Lazonick, W., and O'Sullivan, M. (2000). "Maximizing shareholder value, a new ideology for corporate governance." *Economy and Society*, 29(10): 13–35.

Markowitz, L. (2007). "Structural innovators and core-framing tasks: how socially responsible mutual fund companies build identity among investors." *Sociological Perspectives*, 50(1): 131–153.

Milanovic, B. (2016). *Global Inequality: A New Approach for the Age of Globalization*. Cambridge, MA: Harvard University Press.

Morin, F. (2000). "A transformation in the French model of shareholding and management." *Economy and Society*, 29(1): 36–53.

Nagel, T. (1993). "Moral luck." In Statman, D., ed., *Moral Luck*: 57–72. Albany: State University of New York Press.

Nelson, S.C., and Katzenstein, P. (2014). "Uncertainty, risk, and the financial crisis of 2008." *International Organization*, 68(2): 361–392.

Ogrizek, M. (2002). "The effect of corporate social responsibility on the branding of financial services." *Journal of Financial Services Marketing*, 6(3): 215–228.

Partnoy, F. (2009). "Historical perspectives on the financial crisis: Ivan Krueger, the credit-rating agencies, and two theories about the function, and dysfunction, of markets." *Yale Journal on Regulation*, 26(2): 431–443.

Petit, P. (2001). *A Theory of Freedom: From the Psychology to the Politics of Agency*. Cambridge: Polity Press.

Petrin, M. (2012). "Circumscribing the 'prosecutor's ticket to tag the elite' – a critique of the responsible corporate officer doctrine." *Temple Law Review*, 84(2): 283–324.

Piketty, T. (2014). *Capital in the Twenty-First Century*. Translated by A. Goldhammer. Cambridge, MA: The Belknap Press of Harvard University Press.

Raffoul, F. (2010). *The Origins of Responsibility*. Bloomington, IN: Indiana University Press.

Revelli, C., and Viviani, J-L. (2015). "Financial performance of socially responsible investing (SRI): what have we learned? A meta-analysis." *Business Ethics: A European Review*, 24(2): 158–185.

Sankowski, E. (1990). "Two forms of moral responsibility." *Philosophical Topics*, 18(1): 123–141.

Sanyal, S. (2014). "The random walk: mapping the world's financial markets 2014." *Deutsche Bank Research*. Hong Kong, April 1, 2014.

Scholtens, B. (2006). "Finance as a driver of corporate social responsibility." *Journal of Business Ethics*, 68(1): 19–33.

Scholtens, B. (2009). "Corporate social responsibility in the international banking industry." *Journal of Business Ethics*, 86(2): 159–175.

Schuck, C.M. (2010). "A new use for the responsible corporate officer doctrine: prosecuting industry insiders for mortgage fraud." *Lewis & Clark Law Review*, 14(1): 371–396.

Schueth, S. (2003). "Socially responsible investing in the United States." *Journal of Business Ethics*, 43(3): 189–194.

Sepinwall, A.J. (2014). "Responsible shares and shared responsibility: in defense of responsible corporate officer liability." *Columbia Business Law Review*, 2: 371–419.

Sharmir, R. (2008). "The age of responsibilization: on market-embedded morality." *Economy and Society*, 37(1): 1–19.

Sikka, P. (2009). "Financial crisis and the silence of the auditors." *Accounting, Organizations, and Society*, 34(6–7): 868–873.

United States Senate Permanent Subcommittee on Investigations (2013). *JPMorgan Chase Whale Trade: A Case History of Derivatives Risks and Abuses*. Majority and Minority Staff Report, Washington, DC. April 11, 2013.

Vanderheiden, S. (2004). "Knowledge, uncertainty, responsibility: responding to climate change." *Public Affairs Quarterly*, 18(2): 141–158.

Williams, K. (2000). "From shareholder value to present-day capitalism." *Economy and Society*, 29(1): 1–12.

Windsor, D. (2001). "Corporate citizenship: evolution and interpretation." In Andriof, J., and Shen, C.H., eds., *Perspectives on Corporate Citizenship*: 39–52. New York: Routledge.

Wu, M.-W., and Shen, C.H. (2013). "Corporate social responsibility in the banking industry: motives and financial performance." *Journal of Banking and Finance*, 37(9): 3529–3547.

Young, I.M. (2006). "Responsibility and global justice: a social connection model." *Social Philosophy and Policy*, 23(1): 102–130.

Young, I.M. (2011). *Responsibility for Justice*. Oxford: Oxford University Press.

29
DIPLOMACY AND RESPONSIBILITIES IN THE TRANSNATIONAL GOVERNANCE OF THE CYBER DOMAIN

Andrea Calderaro

Introduction

The internet has been designed as a decentralised structure consisting of multiple distributed networks working independently without a steering government. As a result of this, the functioning of the internet is ensured by evolving technical protocols, norms, international standards and transnational regulations, which are regularly at the centre of international negotiations between multiple actors including industry, transnational non-state actors, governments and civil society organisations (DeNardis 2013; Mueller 2010). Internet Governance is defined as negotiations around these issues, and in particular, the development and implementation of '[…]shared principles, norms, rules, decision-making procedures, and programmes that shape the evolution and use of the Internet' (Working Group on Internet Governance [WGIG] 2005). In other words, the governance of the internet consists of all transnational technical negotiations and policy discussions around the functioning of connectivity infrastructure and online services.

Given the impact that the internet has on critical aspects of our economy, politics and society, the debate concerning governance responsibility has emerged as one of the relevant challenges in the field. The governance of the internet has traditionally generated new spaces of contentious politics, driven by stakeholders involved in the governance, policy development and setting of technical standards of the internet (Calderaro and Kavada 2013). If, on the one hand, private actors are largely responsible for developing digital infrastructure and creation of services, on the other, state actors claim their role in designing the legal framework regulating citizens' online experience of these services. In this context, the concept of responsibility in the internet domain is characterised by the contention between actors engaged in negotiating priorities, competences and questions of accountability in governing this decentred issue area.

This chapter traces the evolution of the concept of responsibility in the transnational governance of the cyber domain, paying particular attention to how the various stages were affected by the tension between conflicting agendas over the core question: whose responsibility is the internet from a governance, legal and technical perspective? It shows that questions of legal accountability are embedded in normative debates over who is or should be in charge of the internet, including the physical infrastructure and technological standards. Institutional discussions are linked to organisational questions, such as whether a multistakeholder or a multilateral approach should be taken. The chapter also shows how, over time, we can witness a shift in power towards so-called internet giants and states, because they benefit from the increasingly fragmented multi-fora discussion and a shift in the agenda towards (national- and cyber-) security issues. Yet, whose responsibility the internet is, remains an evolving issue.

The early public–private partnership of the internet: the establishment of ICANN

Debates on how to combine responsibilities in internet governance have traditionally been characterised by the tension between a self-regulatory approach on the one hand, and state-control on the other (Eriksson and Giacomello 2009). Inspired by the anarchical spirit that motivated the original development of the internet, supporters of the former approach argue that the decentralised architecture of the internet goes beyond national state borders, so no single actor nor any centralised steering structure would have the full responsibility to govern it (Drezner 2008). Therefore, from a self-regulatory perspective, it is commonly held that no state or governmental institution is entitled to intervene in the functioning of the internet (Barlow 1996; Brown and Marsden 2013), which would mean that the public and the industry should have the opportunity to develop the internet freely. In this view, the governance of the internet is seen as ideally led by agreements between private companies and transnational non-state and non-profit actors, while states ought to play a rather limited role (Mueller 2010).

On the other hand, the state-control approach argues that despite its transnational, decentralised technical nature, the use of the internet takes place within legal frameworks applicable within national borders, and that national sovereignty over the internet is required (Drake 1993). This approach is particularly relevant when we refer to state actors aiming to exercise their control over the use of the internet among their citizens, monitoring the internet and filtering digital contents (Deibert and Crete-Nishihata 2012). More recently, a call for reinforcing a Digital Sovereignty is emerging across multiple state actors with the goal to gain more control over the telecom industry both from an infrastructural and service perspective. Relevant examples giving evidence to this point are the recent tensions between the US administration against Huawei's ambition to implement 5G infrastructure worldwide, while with the 'General Data Protection Regulation (GDPR)' adopted by the EU Parliament in 2016, the EU has set some limitations within which digital intermediaries can offer their services in respect of EU citizens. German Chancellor Angela Merkel (2019) also stressed the urgent need to reinforce Digital Sovereignty in her opening speech at the UN Internet Governance Forum held in Berlin in November 2019, and also by the EU Commissioner at the Directorate General (DG) Digital Market Thierry Breton (2019).

Although, these cases offer empirical evidence of the recent developments in the relationship between state and private actors, this tension emerged already during the early stages of internet governance. The establishment of the Internet Corporation for Assigned Names and Numbers (ICANN) in 1998 represented not only the institutionalisation of a leading body responsible for the technical management of the internet, but given the multiple political, economic and policy dimensions affected by decisions taken on the technical nature of the internet, this also represented the first relevant opportunity to push the debate on the administration of the internet beyond its technical dimension, and launching *de facto* an international debate questioning its governance dimension. This makes the scrutiny of the establishment of ICANN and the following stages of the debate relevant for developing our understanding of the distribution of responsibilities in this field.

ICANN is a private non-profit organisation legally based in Los Angeles with authority to administrate the internet Domain Names System (DNS), a key technical aspect of the internet that makes our access to digital content sustainable. Each website is identified by a unique number (Internet Protocol address – IP), with which its contents are made accessible to the public. Without the DNS, navigating the internet relying on the human capacity to remember the endless amounts of IPs allocated to websites available online would be ineffective, and it would limit our capacity to access information and experiences online. The DNS consists of the translation of these numbers referring to all internet websites, to more human-recognisable alphanumeric references. In simple terms, the DNS makes the public experience of surfing the internet as easy as it is nowadays. The management of the DNS goes beyond the technical dimension of the internet, however, and as detailed below, it has several political and economic implications. For this reason, ICANN is commonly perceived to be the most influential body concerning the functioning of the internet (Mueller 2010). As such, the debate on the responsibility of the management of the DNS and the functioning of ICANN has been a crucial aspect of transnational negotiations around the governance of the internet.

Before the establishment of ICANN, the DNS was managed in the personal capacity of John Postel, a faculty member of the University of Southern California. Being the author of the protocol that generated the DNS, Postel had the responsibility of managing the DNS while the number of websites was limited (Abbate 2000). However, following on from the launch of the World Wide Web in the 1990s, the requests for the allocation of internet addresses increased dramatically due to the expanding demand of online presence from industry, government and individuals, making the DNS unmanageable for one person (Yu 2003). It became evident that it was necessary to identify a more sustainable long-term solution. Given that in the early stages of the internet, internet domain names were very much related to copyrights and trademarks attracting particular attention from industry, the US Department of Commerce appeared as the natural institution taking the lead in finding a definitive solution for the management of the DNS. On February 1998, the US Department of Commerce agency National Telecommunications and Information Administration (NTIA) released the so-called Green Paper, titled 'A Proposal to Improve the Technical Management of Internet Names and Addresses' (National Telecommunications and Information Administration 1998a). The launch of this open consultation seeking a solution for the management of the DNS offered a first opportunity to open the debate on responsibilities over the governance of the internet.

In the late 1990s, access to the internet was still limited and only a small portion of international actors were aware of the real issue at stake, and prepared to negotiate possible internet governance models inclusive of all actors responsible for a sustainable functioning of the internet from technical and policy perspectives. Nonetheless, the debate around the institutionalisation of an authority with full responsibility for the functioning of the internet gradually saw international pressure to weaken US leadership. The proposal from the international community led by the European Union was to establish an intergovernmental body that would have diminished the influence of the USA. However, not surprisingly, this option was not in line with the ambition of the US Department of Commerce to support the growth of US industry in the telecom sector. In contrast, given that the internet was until then perceived as an industry-led sector in line with the US neo-liberal outlook, the intention was to protect the governance of the internet from any governmental influence and let the internet self-regulate.

Moreover, most of the private actors engaged in developing the internet were US-based companies, and US Department of Commerce's main interest was to protect them from a potential intergovernmental body.[1] The involvement of state actors, could have indeed limited the self-regulatory approach typically in line with the US call for a free market. As a consequence of these considerations, and following the period of debate initiated with the release of the Green Paper, with the publication of the 'Statement of Policy on the Management of Internet Names and

Addresses' (National Telecommunications and Information Administration 1998b) in June 1998, the US Government called for the establishment of an ad-hoc, private and non-profit organisation serving as manager of the DNS, but controlled by the US Department of Commerce through a so-termed Internet Assignment Number Authority (IANA) stewardship. In September 1998, ICANN was established. This solution ensured the US Department of Commerce that the governance of the internet would be self-regulated by the industry while maintaining its oversight capacity. While the establishment of ICANN can therefore be considered to represent the withdrawal of the state from the governance of the internet, with the consequent waive of governments from their responsibility over the internet, this is a limited interpretation of events. Indeed, international state actors had the opportunity to claim an influential role in controlling the functioning of the internet in the following stages of the establishment of ICANN (Mueller 1999).

Once ICANN was created, the second phase of international negotiations started in order to define how to govern it. Given the failure of international actors to move the responsibility to an intergovernmental body, international pressure grew to create a governance model where state actors would be influential in the functioning of the ICANN. Following this pressure, promoted in particular by the European Union (Christou and Simpson 2011), the Global Advisory Committee (GAC) was created in 1999 as an advisory board including representatives from governments, multinational governmental organisations and treaty organisations (Principle 14: GAC 2017). Specifically, the GAC was designed as and still is a multilateral body representing more than 100 governments and international organisations, especially on those issues where ICANN functioning might conflict with national regulatory and legal frameworks. As such, GAC represents the crucial, formalised involvement of state actors in the governance of the internet, through their influence in ICANN decision-making processes. Although the GAC is an external body, meeting three times per year in parallel with ICANN meetings, its oversight capacity over the functioning of ICANN has grown over time. In particular, the ICANN Bylaws from 2002 recognise that ICANN cannot ignore proposals coming from the GAC and its represented governments (Mueller 2008). As a result of this, the establishment of GAC represents a significant expression of the unique public–private governance model of the internet (Christou and Simpson 2011).

The establishment process of ICANN was a milestone of the short yet rich history of internet governance. The international narrative developed on this occasion and the relations between industry and state actors still characterises the governance of the internet to this day. However, this debate took place just at the very early stages of international negotiations, and although ICANN is still a significant actor in the field, the management of the DNS is now one of many governance components pertaining to the functioning of the internet (DeNardis and Raymond 2013). With the increasing influence that the internet has on our political, economic and social life, a general interest in how to govern the internet has increased, and new stakeholders have emerged, claiming their right to influence it.

Beyond a dichotomous approach to internet governance: multistakeholderism and the inclusion of civil society

Following the establishment of ICANN, new developments and new sets of actors revitalised the international debate and ignited new phases of internet governance. As the attention of most US and EU actors was focused on the establishment of ICANN and the formalisation of its functioning model, internet connectivity further expanded globally, increasing the number of international actors interested in having a say in how the internet should be governed. Despite the status as an independent body, ICANN was still a US-based non-profit organisation operating in accordance with California State legislation and functioning under contract with the United States Department of Commerce. Although the negotiations around the establishment of ICANN were already influenced by the growing concerns on the potential political and economic aspects of internet governance, its functioning mostly focused on the technical management of the internet. If ICANN had taken responsibility for the technical management of the internet, the discussion was still open on how to create a more comprehensive form of internet governance by moving the debate beyond its technical aspects. The United Nations, as an inter-governmental agency with the mandate to coordinate international cooperation on global challenges, was the actor that would take the lead in governing the internet under the responsibility of the International Telecommunication Union (ITU), i.e. the agency of the UN responsible for the governance of the telecommunications sector (Klein 2004).

The United Nations welcomed this emerging international demand to move the debate of the governance of the internet beyond its technical dimension with the launch of the first World Summit on the Information Society (WSIS). The WSIS was a two-phase event held in Geneva in 2003 and Tunis two years later in 2005, representing the first open international internet governance forum. This event offered the first opportunity to representatives of governments, together with civil society organisations and the private sector, to gather together in order to discuss governance issues beyond the technical dimension of the internet for which ICANN was responsible. In other words, the WSIS was the first attempt to launch cooperation for the transnational governance of the internet. However, despite the ambition, the initiative was premature: most countries were still slowly developing their connectivity infrastructure, and only a limited number of international actors had a clear agenda and were prepared to engage in the discussions.

Although the WSIS did not lead to any binding solutions, general principles were identified on how to share responsibilities in a transnational internet governance model (Radu 2019). In particular, one of the issues high on the WSIS agenda was the definition of a sustainable governance model inclusive of all stakeholders involved and affected by the functioning of the internet. This debate created the opportunity to formally recognise that state, industry and civil society actors do contribute to the functioning of the internet, making them all eligible to negotiate on equal terms. The outcome of this debate was the recognition of a multistakeholder approach as the preferred model of governance (Working Group on Internet Governance [WGIG] 2005). Accordingly, the term multistakeholderism refers to the distribution of responsibilities across the categories of actors involved in the governance of the internet, including state actors, industry and civil society. In contrast to other models of global governance that focus on states and the role of international organisations (Zürn 2018), a distinct feature of internet governance is that by fully adopting the multistakeholder approach the active role of civil society is formalised (Padovani 2005; Scholte 2005).

Once an inclusive model that represented shared responsibilities between stakeholders was adopted, it was necessary to identify the right platform for turning the multistakeholder approach into practice. The launch of the Internet Governance Forum (IGF) was the second key outcome of the WSIS. Launched as a natural follow-up of the two-phase WSIS summit, the IGF is a UN-sponsored event hosted annually by countries applying and open to all stakeholders interested in contributing to the internet governance debate, bringing together around 3000 representatives from industry, governments and civil society. The adoption of the multistakeholder model is significant in this context, as it evolves into providing new ideas and influences policies of governments that have not yet developed a clear agenda regarding the role of internet-related issues in their foreign policy (Brousseau and Marzouki 2013). The development of a multistakeholder approach in internet governance is commonly welcomed by the (civil society) internet community as an outstanding achievement of creating bottom-up forms of governance, and a best practice that could be exported in other fields of global governance (De La Chapelle 2009; Scholte 2004). Multistakeholderism has been welcomed as an innovative form of governance, and particularly lauded for its inclusion of civil society in emerging global challenges.

Fast-forward: multilateral versus multistakeholder and the return to the state

The constant expansion of connectivity infrastructure and the consequent narrowing of the digital divide has meant that the internet is increasingly used across political contexts, including in incomplete or non-democratic political systems (Calderaro 2014; Howard 2010; Livingston 2014). In this scenario, late internet adopter countries who had remained peripheral in the early stages of the internet governance debates are increasingly vocal and positioning themselves internationally by asserting state-control over the use of the internet infrastructure.

This new geopolitical scenario over the internet has pushed the diplomatic challenges over the governance of the internet into a new phase, in which the leading role played by Western liberal democracies has been challenged. Emerging state actors in the field of internet governance have become particularly vocal in challenging the lack of a steering authority over the internet beyond its technical functioning and processes. In particular, countries like Russia, China, and Iran advocate in favour of allocating the responsibility of leading the governance of the internet to the UN agency International Telecommunication Union. This idea reflects the preference of this bloc of countries to shift the internet governance processes from the *multistakeholder approach* to a *multilateral approach* typically adopted in the context of the United Nations. This preference is functional to the ambition of these state actors to gain control of the governance of the internet, by putting the state at the centre of decision-making processes.

This renewed phase of tensions between state-regulated and self-regulatory approaches was emphasised by the announcement of the World Conference on International Telecommunications in 2012 (WCIT 12). This event offered the opportunity to renegotiate the 1988 ITU Regulation (ITUR) in order to revise the treaty according to the latest developments in the global telecom sector. The original ITUR treaties said very little about the internet, which at the time of their adoption in 1988 was still an emerging technology. Although the drastically changed transnational telecom infrastructure justified an update of these treaties, the main goal of this new diplomatic challenge was to allocate primary steering responsibility for the governance of the internet to the ITU, which would effectively mean a shift from a multistakeholder approach, inclusive of industry and civil society in addition to governments, to a multilateral model more typical of UN institutions. This shift would have *de facto* offered the opportunity to state actors to impose an intergovernmental approach to the governance of the internet. However, countries traditionally in support of a multistakeholder approach, including the US and EU member states, together with most civil society organisations and private actors, opposed this solution during the eleven-day WCIT meeting held in Dubai from 3 to 14 December 2012 and attended by more than 1,600 delegates representing 151 ITU countries worldwide. Given the disagreement, it was not possible to reach a final agreement through consensus and the original idea to give the ITU full control over the governance of the internet was abandoned. The polarising nature of this debate was reflected in the final vote when most newly connected countries together with Russia, China and Arab states responded favourably to the revised version of the new ITUR treaties. In contrast, another group of countries including the US, the EU member states but also Canada, Australia, Japan and others, voted against the proposal.

Although the ITU was not successful in gaining full steering control over the governance of the internet, the treaties increased state actors' control over the functioning of the internet. This change was justified by the international pressure to empower states' capacity to manage national cybersecurity initiatives. However, given that initiatives taken in this direction have implications for the protection of human rights, Western liberal democracies voted against the proposed solutions included in revised versions of the ITU treaties. What is noteworthy from the point of view of new conflict lines in the debate about the internet and responsibility is how the WCIT 12 served as a venue where a more polarised debate over the governance of the internet surfaced and manifested deeper geopolitical tension (Radu 2019). The contention between a multilateral model and a multistakeholder approach came to represent the new frontline between a Western liberal view of the internet, and governments claiming a state-centric approach in the cyber governance domain.

Following the WCIT in 2012, a subsequent event reshuffled power relations between actors in internet governance platforms. Until the early 2010s, the US had sustained its influence in setting the internet governance agenda, not only because of its historical role played in creating and developing the internet as such, but because the US was also perceived to have successfully ensured the freedom of the internet and protected digital rights from the influence of those countries claiming state control over the internet, notably Russia, China and Arab countries (Deibert 2013). However, following the PRISM[2] scandal, in which whistle-blower Edward Snowden revealed the mass-surveillance strategy operated by the US, this narrative significantly lost credibility, and with it the US weakened its legitimacy as a defender of the internet, bringing renewed pressure in renegotiating its role in maintaining oversight of the functioning of the internet.

One of the most tangible effects of this process was the withdrawal of the US from the control of ICANN. Following years of debate calling for the internationalisation of ICANN, achievable only by reaching full independence from state actors, the US opened the discussion to reform ICANN in 2014 (National Telecommunications and Information Administration 2014). In order to avoid the handover of ICANN to an intergovernmental body that would have threatened the independency of ICANN, one of the conditions set by the US Department of Commerce was that IANA would be transferred to a multistakeholder community. Following three years of international negotiations, in October 2016 the IANA functioning was successfully transferred to the Public Technical Identifiers (PTI), a legally independent body of ICANN. The so-called 'IANA transition' offered a new opportunity to further reinforce the multistakeholder model in the governance of the internet, and the withdrawal of the US from ICANN.

A Gramscian reading of multistakeholderism

Since the WSIS, the debate on the multistakeholder approach has monopolised most of the disputes around the governance of the internet. Multistakeholderism may be seen as largely rhetorical, inasmuch as it has often reduced attention to the challenges associated with the constant expansion of internet connectivity and the evolution of technology, including the emerging concerns related to safety and security of the internet. However, following the initial enthusiasm, multistakeholderism has also raised some concerns about its efficacy, and a variety of criticisms can be detected.

First of all, we lack evidence that multistakeholderism has actually democratised the governance of the internet. Some claim that it has not removed power inequalities in decision-making processes over the governance of the internet (Franklin 2013). In contrast, it has reinforced the capacity of a limited number of actors to be more influential than others (Carr 2016). From this perspective, multistakeholderism is perceived to be a model generating consensus, instead of developing a genuine debate among stakeholders involved (Franklin 2013). Whether or not this is the case, power inequalities between states, industry and civil society in international cooperation developed in setting the internet governance agenda still exist.

Carr (2015) approaches the topic from a Gramscian perspective, arguing that multistakeholderism has offered the opportunity to legitimise what Gramsci (1948) defines as a hegemonic power. From this perspective, the implementation of this model is only useful for the agenda-setters to gain legitimacy rather than welcome criticism (Carr 2015). In other words, looking at multistakeholderism from a Gramscian hegemonic power perspective, the voice of stakeholders with limited influential capacity over the governance of the internet has little chance to impact on the final outcome of the negotiations, despite the false perception of decentred influence. At the same time, with their simple involvement in the process, they legitimise a process driven by those imposing their agenda. In this context, a critical contribution to internet governance negotiations could be more powerful and effective if expressed without constraints imposed by procedural processes outside the institutionalised platforms. This interpretation is also in line with the observation that the multistakeholder approach is traditionally adopted to respond to the crisis of legitimacy experienced by international political institutions (Cammaerts 2011). This interpretation sees the inclusion of diverse stakeholders in formal processes as a tool to neutralise their criticism and legitimise rule makers. In other words, this perspective considers inclusiveness as more of an ideological concept adopted to legitimise the hegemony of influential actors in setting the internet governance agenda, rather than a practice creating a truly transparent distribution of responsibilities across stakeholders.

This critical perspective on multistakeholderism is also useful to interpret the success and failure of various internet governance initiatives aimed at expanding the debate on internet governance, facilitating an open and inclusive debate. As discussed above, the IGF itself was, and still is, the ad-hoc forum launched to turn multistakeholderism into practice. However, the IGF does not have any formally recognised legitimacy to take action impacting on internet regulation. Although the IGF still offers the best opportunity to gather a variety of diverse actors with the goal of addressing the challenges of transnational governance collectively, its annual agenda does not go beyond the exchange of ideas and confrontation on procedures. Because of this, scepticism of the role and utility of the IGF itself have emerged, leading a growing body of governments to launch alternative initiatives with the ambition of overcoming the lack of implementation capacity of the IGF. In particular, several governments have launched their own international internet governance venue with the ambition of replacing the IGF, notably, the Freedom Online Coalition (FOC), a consortium of countries worldwide launched by the Dutch minister of foreign affairs, the Stockholm Internet Forum created by the Swedish Foreign Minister Carl Bildt, and the NetMundial, launched by the Brazilian government in 2014, in order to identify new directions in internet governance in the coming years. However, these initiatives have not replaced the IGF but have created parallel venues for discussion with the very same limitations of not holding any regulatory capacity and legitimacy. The proliferation of multiple parallel spaces for discussion on internet governance could be interpreted as a good opportunity to give voice to the increasing number of stakeholders globally and to exchange knowledge on the complexity of the internet governance debate among broader sets of representatives, with the overall result making global internet policy more transparent and inclusive of previously peripheral actors. However, this is a misleading interpretation.

The proliferation of internet governance fora has filled the calendar with a high number of events distributed worldwide, a phenomenon that has potentially jeopardised actors' efforts to contribute to the debate. Given the dense internet governance agenda and consequent travelling involved, only a limited number of actors have the resources to take part in all these events around the globe. Given the resource-intensive element of this decentred global activity, civil society is the stakeholder most penalised by this proliferation of internet governance venues. At the same time, we have witnessed a clash of foreign policy agendas which has also contributed to the proliferation of parallel debates creating a cacophonic approach to challenges more than the identification of a coherent transnational approach. Moreover, given the ambitions of various governments to appear as leading actors in diplomatic narratives around internet governance, they have limited motivation to attend events organised by other state actors, as this could be interpreted as a legitimation of other governments' efforts to increase their diplomatic leadership in the field. As a result of this, in contrast with the original goal of creating an inclusive transnational debate about the cyber domain, where all actors had the opportunity to contribute thanks to the multiple channels opened via the proliferation of events addressing the issue, the multiplicity of conferences risks weakening international efforts in the field. Finally, representatives of internet giants are the actors who benefit the most from this current situation, given their capability to contribute and participate in all events, further accelerating their legitimacy and influential capacity in internet governance debates.

A Gramscian perspective on the issue can be adopted in this case too, given that we have still limited evidence that the creation of many open and inclusive internet governance fora has contributed to democratise the debate or distribute the responsibility of the governance of the internet. In contrast, this dispersed modality has further supported the construction of hegemonic power, where internet giants that have the capacity to attend and influence most events have therefore had the opportunity to be more vocal than any other actors and gain further influential capacity vis-à-vis other stakeholders.

From internet governance to cybersecurity

In recent years, international cooperation in the cyber domain has shifted the primary concerns with internet governance to increasingly prioritising security driven responses to digitalisation of critical infrastructure (Mueller 2017). As a result of this, cybersecurity has attracted more interest from international organizations and has emerged as central in states' foreign policy.

Following years of efforts to expand digital infrastructure and narrow the digital divide, concerns now emerge as to how to protect the economy and society from cyber threats. Cyber threats are increasingly perceived as an attack on states and their sovereignty, causing cybersecurity to fall into the domain of state security. For this reason, narratives, negotiations and communities involved in setting cybersecurity agendas are often different from those engaged in talks around internet governance (Dunn-Cavelty 2008). Cybersecurity is approached as a matter for states' military and policing capacities, and it is managed accordingly. As a result of this, while as was discussed above, internet governance is historically characterised by an inclusive debate, the cybersecurity debate is instead characterised by state actors gaining a central role and assuming responsibility (Calderaro and Craig 2020). With the shift of priority from internet governance to cybersecurity in recent years it seems clear that due to significant state security concerns, the narrative on cybersecurity is set by actors that differ from those traditionally involved in internet governance venues. In line with the traditional state responsibility to develop state and military security, governments also have the leading role in governing and developing cybersecurity initiatives, and in negotiating these in international fora. Debates on cybersecurity are rarely open for public consultation, and the initial transnational negotiations of cybersecurity norms that we are witnessing in recent years emerge mostly in intergovernmental venues, where a multilateral formula is the standard approach. Governments mostly develop their national cybersecurity strategy as a matter of national security, coordinating their efforts as a complementary approach to national military capacity. International cooperation in the cybersecurity domain involves a dialogue among states, with limited involvement of other actors. Notably, the United Nations has established the UN Group of Governmental Experts (UNGGE) on Developments in the Field of Information and Telecommunications in the Context of International Security, through which it has the ambition of framing a transnational approach to cybersecurity by hosting negotiations addressing norms and principles in the cyber domain (United Nations 2015). Mostly relevant for the analysis we proposed here, the central role of the UN in setting an international agenda in the domain of cybersecurity means a return to state responsibility in the cyber domain. Although in some cases, civil society consultation is requested, we are far from the multistakeholder approach that has characterised most of the discussion on internet governance. This is the case of the United Nations Open-Ended Working Group (OEWG) that the UN launched in 2018, serving as the first ever multistakeholder consultation on cybersecurity stability, complementary to the UN GGE. Between 2018 and 2021, in addition to diplomats representing UN State Members, the OEWG involved actors from industry and civil society, including non-governmental organisations and academia. Hosted by the UN, representatives of the multistakeholder community of the OEWG regularly met to negotiate principles of international cooperation towards an "open, secure, stable, accessible and peaceful ICT environment", a process finalized in March 2021 with the release of the "UN OEWG Final Substantive Report" (United Nations 2021). This final report was adopted by consensus and concluded the OEWG 2018-2021 process, which had offered non-state actors the opportunity to provide their perspectives on negotiations taking place between UN members. However, their tangible impact and the long-term implications of this process remain uncertain. Nonetheless, although cyber stability of the cyber domain is increasingly identified as a shared responsibility between states, industry and civil society, the central role of international organizations reinforces rather than modifies the dominant role of state actors in governing the cyber domain.

Conclusion

This chapter has addressed how the ambition of distributing responsibilities of the governance of the internet across a variety of actors by maintaining an open, transparent and inclusive multistakeholder governance model has defined international negotiations in the internet governance domain from the beginning. The debate over who is responsible for governing the internet and in what manner this is done has evolved over time along with technological developments and the arrival of new actors. How responsibility is taken or allocated is a normative issue to which multistakeholderism appears to provide a democratic and legitimacy-enhancing solution. However, as argued, multistakeholderism has primarily generated an illusion of inclusiveness, rather than an effective governance model. The lack of a leading actor has carried the risk of somewhat weakening the development of a coherent and effective transnational approach to the governance of the internet. We have observed how the lack of rules has offered the industry the opportunity to increase their hegemonic power over states and civil society by developing business strategies without significant constraints, in line with the self-regulatory spirit that inspired the development of the internet itself (compare the chapter by Schlag in this volume). At the same time, the current ongoing change of agenda in the domain of cyber*security* governance is limiting the responsibility of civil society, putting the state back at the centre of internet governance. The return of the state that we are witnessing in recent years with the increasing priority on cybersecurity is marking this major shift, with the consequent wane of multistakeholderism, and turning responsibilities in the transnational governance of the cyber domain. The interlinkages between developments in this sector and broader trends in global governance, remain to be explored to a fuller extent.

Notes

1 Contrary to wide-spread popular believe, the US Department of Defence was only involved in the development of the ARPANET, with which the concept of the internet was launched. Given the implementation of a long series of protocols, already in the early 70s' ARPANET turned to be the internet that we know today. The US Department of defence stopped their initial economic support, and the internet developed its commercial nature.
2 PRISM is not an acronym but a code name for the surveillance programme.

References

Abbate, J. (2000). *Inventing the Internet*. Cambridge, MA: The MIT Press.
Barlow, J. P. (1996). *A Declaration of Independence of Cyberspace*. https://projects.eff.org/~barlow/Declaration-Final.html.
Breton, T. (2019). *Hearing of Thierry Breton, Commissioner-Designate, Internal Market: Opening Statement*. Brussels: European Commission.
Brousseau, E., and Marzouki, M. (2013). "Internet Governance: Old Issues, New Framings, Uncertain Implications." In Brousseau, E., Marzouki, M., and Méadel, C., eds. *Governance, Regulations and Powers on the Internet*. Cambridge: Cambridge University Press.
Brown, I., and Marsden, C.T. (2013). *Regulating Code: Good Governance and Better Regulation in the Information Age*. Cambridge, MA: MIT Press.
Calderaro, A. (2014). "Internet Politics Beyond the Digital Divide. A Comparative Perspective on Internet Politics across Political Systems." In Pătruţ, B., and Pătruţ, M., eds. *Social Media in Politics*: 3–17. New York, NY: Springer International Publishing.
Calderaro, A., and Craig J. S. A. (2020). "Transnational Governance of Cybersecurity: Policy Challenges and Global Inequalities in Cyber Capacity Building." *Third World Quarterly* 41(6): 917–38.
Calderaro, A., and Kavada, A. (2013). "Challenges and Opportunities of Online Collective Action for Policy Change." *Policy & Internet*, 5(1): 1–6.
Cammaerts, B. (2011). "Power Dynamics in Multi-Stakeholder Policy Processes and Intra-Civil Society Networking." In Mansell, R., and Raboy, M., eds. *The Handbook of Global Media and Communication Policy*: 129–146. Oxford: Blackwell.
Carr, M. (2015). "Power Plays in Global Internet Governance." *Millennium - Journal of International Relations*, 43(2): 640–659.
Carr, M. (2016). *US Power and the Internet in International Relations: The Irony of the Information Age*. Basingstoke: Palgrave Macmillan.
Christou, G., and Simpson, S. (2011). "The European Union, Multilateralism and the Global Governance of the Internet." *Journal of European Public Policy*, 18(2): 241–257.
De La Chapelle, B. (2009). "Towards Multi-Stakeholder Governance – The Internet Governance Forum as Laboratory." In Bygrave, L. A., and Bing, J., eds. *Internet Governance Infrastructure and Institutions*. Oxford: Oxford University Press.
Deibert, R. J. (2013). *Black Code: Inside the Battle for Cyberspace*. Toronto: McClelland & Steward.
Deibert, R. J., and Crete-Nishihata, M. (2012). "Global Governance and the Spread of Cyberspace Controls." *Global Governance: A Review of Multilateralism and International Organizations*, 18(3): 339–361.
DeNardis, L. (2013). "The Emerging Field of Internet Governance." In Dutton, W.H., ed., *The Oxford Handbook of Internet Studies*. Oxford: Oxford University Press.
DeNardis, L., and Raymond, M. (2013). *Thinking Clearly About Multistakeholder Internet Governance*. Rochester, NY: Social Science Research Network. SSRN Scholarly Paper.
Drake, W. (1993). "Territoriality and Intangibility." In Nordenstreng, K. and Schiller, H.I., eds., *Beyond National Sovereignty International Communication in the 1990s*. Norwood, NJ: Ablex Pub. Co.
Drezner, D. W. (2008). *All Politics Is Global. Explaining International Regulatory Regimes*. Princeton, NJ: Princeton University Press.

Dunn-Cavelty, M. (2008). *Cyber-Security and Threat Politics: US Efforts to Secure the Information Age*. New York, NY: Routledge.

Eriksson, J., and Giacomello, G. (2009). "Who Controls the Internet? Beyond the Obstinacy or Obsolescence of the State." *International Studies Review*, 11(1): 205–230.

Franklin, M. (2013). *Digital Dilemmas: Power, Resistance, and the Internet*. Oxford: Oxford University Press.

GAC (2017). "Operating Principles." https://gac.icann.org/operating-principles/operating-principles-june-2017.

Gramsci, A. (1948). *Quaderni Del Carcere*. Torino: Giulio Einaudi Editore.

Howard, P. N. (2010). *The Digital Origins of Dictatorship and Democracy: Information Technology and Political Islam*. New York, NY: Oxford University Press.

Klein, H. (2004). "Understanding WSIS: An Institutional Analysis of the UN World Summit on the Information Society." *The Massachusetts Institute of Technology*, 1(3–4): 3–13.

Livingston, S. (2014). *Bits and Atoms: Information and Communication Technology in Areas of Limited Statehood*. Oxford: Oxford University Press.

Merkel, A. (2019). *German Chancellor's Remarks to the IGF 2019*. Berlin: Internet Governance Forum.

Mueller, M. (1999). "ICANN and Internet Governance: Sorting through the Debris of 'Self-regulation.'" *Info*, 1(6): 497–520.

Mueller, M. (2008). "Governments, ICANN and the JPA (Part 2)." *Internet Governance Project*. https://www.internetgovernance.org/2008/01/29/governments-icann-and-the-jpa-part-2/

Mueller, M. (2010). *Networks and States the Global Politics of Internet Governance*. Cambridge, MA: MIT Press.

Mueller, M. (2017). "Is Cybersecurity Eating Internet Governance? Causes and Consequences of Alternative Framings." *Digital Policy, Regulation and Governance*, 19(6): 415–428.

National Telecommunications and Information Administration (1998a). "Improvement of Technical Management of Internet Names and Addresses." https://www.ntia.doc.gov/federal-register-notice/1998/improvement-technical-management-internet-names-and-addresses-proposed-

National Telecommunications and Information Administration (1998b). "Statement of Policy on the Management of Internet Names and Addresses." https://www.ntia.doc.gov/federal-register-notice/1998/statement-policy-management-internet-names-and-addresses

National Telecommunications and Information Administration (2014). "NTIA Announces Intent to Transition Key Internet Domain Name Functions." https://www.ntia.doc.gov/press-release/2014/ntia-announces-intent-transition-key-internet-domain-name-functions

Padovani, C. (2005). "Debating Communication Imbalances from the MacBride Report to the World Summit on the Information Society: An Analysis of a Changing Discourse." *Global Media and Communication*, 1(3): 3–13.

Radu, R. (2019). *Negotiating Internet Governance*. Oxford and New York: Oxford University Press.

Scholte, J. A. (2004). "Civil Society and Democratically Accountable Global Governance." *Government and Opposition*, 39(2): 211–33.

Scholte, J. A. (2005). *Globalization: A Critical Introduction*. New York, NY: Red Globe Press.

United Nations (2015). "Consensus Report from the Group of Governmental Experts on Developments in the Field of Information and Telecommunications in the Context of International Security." https://www.un.org/ga/search/view_doc.asp?symbol=A/70/174.

United Nations (2021). "Open-Ended Working Group on developments in the field of information and telecommunications in the context of international security - Final Substantive Report." https://front.un-arm.org/wp-content/uploads/2021/03/Final-report-A-AC.290-2021-CRP.2.pdf

Working Group on Internet Governance [WGIG] (2005). *Report of the Working Group on Internet Governance*. Château de Bossey: WGIG.

Yu, P. K. (2003). "The Neverending CCTLD Story." In Wass, E. S., ed. *Addressing the World: National Identity and Internet Country Code*: 1–16. Lanham, MD: Rowman & Littlefield.

Zürn, Michael. (2018). *A Theory of Global Governance: Authority, Legitimacy, and Contestation*. Oxford: Oxford University Press.

PART V

Critical reflections and theoretical debates

30
FRAMING RESPONSIBILITY RESEARCH IN INTERNATIONAL RELATIONS

Antje Wiener

Introduction

Responsibility has become a widely used principle in everyday practice and policies in international relations. It is frequently addressed in conjunction with the related principle of 'accountability' in the governance or public administration literature, yet, the latter is the more systematically studied term (Bovens 2007). For International Relations (IR) theorists, the principle has achieved most leverage with the constitution of the Responsibility to Protect (R2P) in 2001 which generated a plethora of research projects and publications (for many, see Ainley 2015; Bellamy 2008; Bellamy and McLoughlin 2019; Brunnée and Toope 2006, 2010; Erskine 2014, 2015; Gholiagha 2016; Welsh 2013, 2019) including a new academic journal on the principle.[1] Despite the expanding interest in studying 'responsibility' as a 'principle' and/or as a 'norm' in IR theory, the concept of 'responsibility' remains often elusive. Pending on the respective epistemological perspective, to some, the concept represents a value-based fundamental principle, to others, the fact-based organising quality is key. As this chapter seeks to demonstrate, with reference to central tools of critical norms research, these distinct takes of responsibility often imply that researchers talk past each other.

The point is demonstrated with reference to the R2P literature (compare also the respective chapters by Burai, Sienknecht and Niemann in this volume). The leading question that guides the argument is whether R2P is an ethical value or a social norm, or both? The following addresses this conceptual gap. To that end, it turns to the practicalities of studying responsibility. The argument is developed against the background of practice-based approach to norms research. Accordingly, responsibility is addressed with reference to first, the norm typology, and second, following the "dual quality" of norms assumption, i.e. a norm entails both constructed and structuring qualities. The key to identifying "meanings-in-use" of a norm with reference to individual "background knowledge" therefore lies in the practice (see for many, Adler 2019, Ch 4; Hofius 2016; Hofius et al. 2014; Milliken 1999; Wiener 2007, 2009). The chapter proposes two dimensions along which responsibility research may helpfully be operationalised: first, the *practical dimension* including research objective, question, methodology and method, and second, the *conceptual dimension* which involves ordering practices of contestation, negotiation, validation and constitution. They are guided by the ethics of knowledge production (*practical* dimension) as well as the underlying principal contestedness of norms in global society (*conceptual* dimension). Both highlight the dynamics of reflexive theorising as a process involving value-based critical reflection of the everyday practice (i.e. doing) in international relations in relation with International Relations (IR) theory-building.

The framework has been devised by the *critical constructivist norms* literature. As such, it works with a reflexive methodology that relies on interpretative discourse analysis, practice theory, ethnography and public philosophy. The latter is key to the chapter's central argument about the interrelation between norms as social facts and norms as ethical values. As Jonathan Havercroft and Toni Erskine have argued, for example, in the absence of a concise reference to a theory of ethics, any claim about the moral validity of a norm rests on shallow ethical grounds (Havercroft 2018, Erskine 2015; both develop a quite devastating critique of liberal constructivists' claims to the contrary, especially in Price 2008). With this in mind, the chapter is mindful of Hamati-Ataya's two meanings of a *reflexive approach*, i.e. 'reflective' and 'reflexive'. As she notes, "I use the terms 'reflective' and 'reflexive' to convey the two meanings of 'reflection': the subject is *reflective of* external structures (like a mirror is of light) and is reflexive when she *reflects on* her own thought" (Hamati-Ataya 2010, 1080). As she rightly concludes, when applied consequently, this approach leads to this leading question for IR scholars: "Among the many reflexive questions scholars may ask, the ultimate interrogation that concerns IR is the following: *how is theory itself affected by the cultural, normative, and material characteristics of the international system, and the position of IR theorists within it?*" (Hamati-Ataya 2010, 1100-01, emphasis in original text).

Against this backdrop, active IR scholarship involves ongoing reflection of a researcher's own location in global society and the contingency this implies for the use of academic resources and the contribution to IR theory. The approach then understands IR scholarship as responsible academic intervention by scholars who share a "cognitive endeavor and scholarly ethos as knowledge-producers and social agents" (Hamati-Ataya 2011, 206). The approach echoes the 'reflexive' strand of IR theory which gathered momentum with constructivism's turn to 'the social' as an under-researched yet influential dimension of international relations (Adler 1987; Katzenstein 1996) related with a move to "the midst" of intersubjective interactions and practices (Kratochwil 2018; Kurowska 2020). In the subsequent emergence of the now well-established field of norms research,[2] especially, critical norms research – with a 'c' – applying a reflexive methodology has been successful in identifying methods to study the social. Here, taking account of and better understanding "background knowledge" and "everyday cultural capabilities" as the socio-cultural contingencies that matter with regard to "unearthing" normative meanings-in-use (Hofius 2016; Walker 2017) have been centrally addressed and refined.

The recourse to the concepts of norms, practices, structures and processes has generated insights into contingencies of international relations that have remained invisible to IR theory (Giddens 1979; Bourdieu 1993; Milliken 1999). Along this line, *feminist IR scholars* contributed to the concern about 'practicalities' of research organisation with a call to enhance visibility, especially in the "global context in which power is both visible and invisible, often concealed by the structures that normalize potentially oppressive practices and values" (Ackerly and True 2008, 693; compare also the chapter by Ackerly in this volume). To counter this invisibility, they propose a new "research ethic (a set of questioning practices) that has implications for the research process and that can function as a compass when any international studies researcher, feminist or not, faces dilemmas in research" (Ackerly and True 2008, 693). In a similar vein, practice-based norms research has targeted the practicalities by developing framing tools to locate and evaluate norm contestation. For example, to facilitate zooming in on contestations (doing) in order to evaluate access to contestation (shaping). The frames enabled researchers to distinguish "meanings-in-use" of global norms with reference to their local practices of (re-)enaction.[3]

Section *one* presents the argument for framing value-based norms research and introduces the two central tools of the framework (norm-typology and the cycle-grid model). Section *two* details the use of the norm-typology with reference to the R2P norm. And section *three* addresses the empirical mapping and staging of contestations with reference to the responsibility of protect (R2P) norm drawing. The summary argument holds that using the framework offers an interface for reflexive research engagement that helps avoiding responsibility researchers to talk past each other despite taking distinct and often mutually exclusive epistemological standpoints on responsibility.

Framing norms research

The following addresses the practicalities of studying responsibility by asking a number of *leading questions* which range from the very basic, yet key, definition of responsibility: for example, do we conceive of responsibility as a policy-based principle that triggers distinct strategic mechanisms of action, or do we conceive of responsibility as a broader ethical value that guides that policy action? And if both roles apply, which takes prevalence and when? How do we know? To address these questions, the following picks up from the long-standing challenges that have arisen with IR scholars with regard to the impact and effect of 'values' and 'ethics' in international relations. Against the long-standing 'value-problem' in IR, i.e. the bracketing of value-based research while emphasising so-called fact-based analysis (Ackerly and True 2010; Hamati-Ataya 2011; Havercroft 2018; Steele and Heinze 2018),[4] addressing 'responsibility' calls for redressing that research gap. This chapter undertakes this task along the practical and conceptual dimensions based on the illustrative case scenario of R2P as a contested norm. It suggests that the norm's contestedness is highlighted by the rapidly expanding literature on the R2P norm. The concept of responsibility remains contested: pending on the perspective vis-à-vis the 'value-problem', the glass is either half-full or half-empty, as it were. The former follows from the – *de jure* – expectation that R2P lacks the formal back-up of an international legal norm, and the latter rests on the – *de facto* – expectation that R2P offers a novel pathway for responsible agents to identify a political strategy backed by relevant policy instruments. As this section seeks to demonstrate, reference to a *norm typology* that distinguishes three types of norms with regard to their expected degree of contestation and, relatedly, a *cycle-grid model* that allows for value-based evaluation of these contestations, is able to give credit to both perspectives (compare Figure 30.1). Taken together the typology and the model offer a framework that allows research to "follow the conflict" (Marcus 1995) and identify access to distinct practices of contestation (reactive and proactive) and validation of norms. In short, it sheds light on conditions of agency for the governed.

The following addresses the value-problem by taking account of two distinct intrinsically related dimensions of norms which Jonathan Havercroft has discussed by distinguishing 'norms as ethical values' from 'norms as social facts' (Havercroft 2018, 116). This being a handbook and not a Special Issue or edited collection with a given framework, some contributions have a particular approach. But some can be read as covering that nexus between the societal and the ethical dimensions. This contribution addresses that nexus especially. As Erskine argues, "somebody needs to defend evaluative criteria (however grounded) for moral judgment if there is any hope of the happy marriage between the ethical and the empirical in IR envisaged in this volume" (Erskine 2012, 458–9; referring to Price 2008). Having taken this call seriously in my earlier critical constructivist research on norms, I argue that the effect of applying responsibility in global governance depends on the relational quality of responsibility as a value *and* as a fact. The former

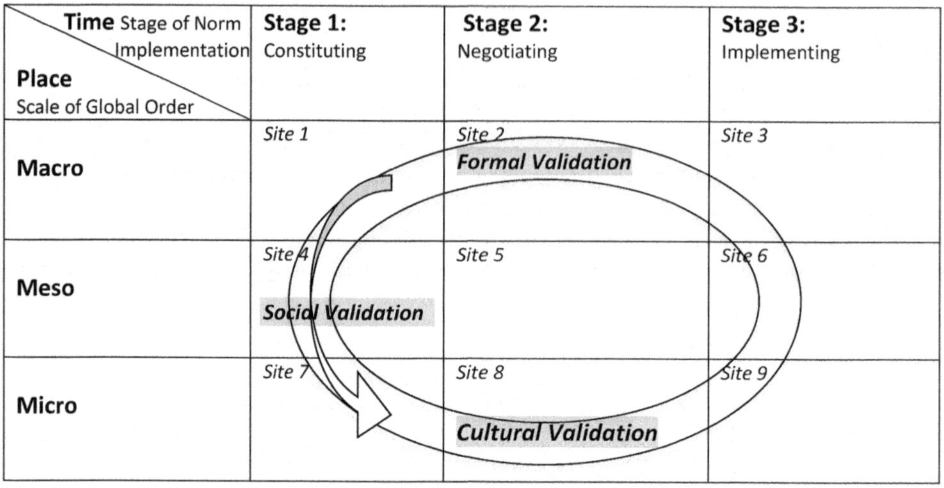

Time Stage of Norm Implementation / Place Scale of Global Order	Stage 1: Constituting	Stage 2: Negotiating	Stage 3: Implementing
Macro	Site 1	Site 2 **Formal Validation**	Site 3
Meso	Site 4 **Social Validation**	Site 5	Site 6
Micro	Site 7	Site 8 **Cultural Validation**	Site 9

Figure 30.1 Cycle-grid model: sites of contestation and practices of validation.

Source: Adaption from Wiener 2014, 21, Figure 2.1; 2017b.

enables agents to weigh in considerations about the legitimacy of responsibility in reply to the question why is responsibility a 'good' norm (compare Ackerly in this Handbook)? In turn, the latter provides insights into the local meanings-in-use which are contingent on the societal context in which norms are enacted guided by the question why should responsibility matter to 'me'.[5] The reflexive methodology is applied to bring the nexus more clearly to the fore. Both dimensions are reflected by the Handbook contributions that discuss the normative substance with reference to fundamental ethical principles that define responsibility in global governance and strategies of implementing responsibility in distinct policy areas of global governance ranging from security via climate change to corporate policy.

The framework brings these dimensions together. To that end, this section advances *two methodological steps* that draw on practice and contestation theory, respectively. The *first* conceives 'norms as social facts'. It consists in mapping responsibility contestations on local sites. Studying local 'responsibility contestations' serves as an indicator of (a) the societal conditions that frame engagement about responsibility norms in a given specific context: these include the 'rules of engagement' which are set by (b) the formal 'normative opportunity structure' (i.e. formal agreements like constitutions, treaties and conventions) on the one hand, and the social habits and customs (i.e. background knowledge and capabilities generated through group interaction and individual everyday experience) on the other. The *second* emphasises 'norms as ethical values'. Against the *critical norms research* literature, it is defined as access to agency for affected stakeholders pending on conditions that are set by local 'normative opportunity structures' (Wiener 2018; compare also Lantis and Wunderlich 2018). The following elaborates on both when detailing the practicality of studying responsibility in world politics.

Norm typology

In light of endless misunderstandings about what a norm is and which type of norm they are talking about, I have suggested elsewhere to refer to a norm typology that does not distinguish between legal, social, cultural or other norms, but which distinguishes types of norms with reference to their respective moral reach instead (Wiener 2008, 2014, 2018). The typology builds on James Tully's *Public Philosophy* which rests on a central concern about access to contestation beyond the limits of civil order (Tully 2008). To facilitate this access, Tully incorporates the wide range of practices summarised as civic activities which are part of the larger ongoing 'struggle' for 'civic freedoms' (Tully 2002, 2008; see also Owen 2019). Against this ethical background – which cannot be elaborated in detail given the limits of this handbook chapter – it now becomes possible to assess the distinct quality of a norm type with regard to two principal questions. First, what is the moral reach of a norm, i.e. does the norm reflect a widely shared belief in global society. And, second, what degree of contestation is expected with regard to this norm. Here, two practices of contestation are distinguished. First, objection to norm-violation or compliance with a norm (*reactive contestation*). Second, critical engagement with a norm in order to identify strategies and criteria for implementation (*proactive contestation*).

The typology therefore allows researchers to bring ethical values to bear when studying the power and meaning-in-use of a norm on the one hand, and to map contestations at local sites of engagement, on the other. The mapping is facilitated by the cycle-grid model which is presented in section "Mapping and staging responsibility contestations on the cycle-grid". The concept of *contestation of norms* was developed against the wave of liberal constructivism and, relatedly, the compliance literature in international law and international relations in the 1990s. The normative concern arose from political situations of 'contested compliance' when predominantly 'Eastern' or 'Southern' groups of states were not convinced about the moral validity of the international liberal order's norms and refused compliance (Wiener 2004). Subsequent research built on this observation and sought to critically challenge explanatory norms research that aimed to identify mechanisms of compliance or to solve issues of non-compliance while leaving the moral question of norm-ownership or moral validity to one side. That is, the compliance literature predominantly considers norms as 'good' prescriptive rules of the given liberal world order that are to be implemented because they are part of that order (Checkel 1999; Koh 1997; Risse et al. 1999). In the absence of highlighting ethical reasons for a norm's goodness, this leads to 'cryptonormativity' however (Havercroft 2018). That is, why should a norm which is followed by many, be considered as 'good'? The 'multiplicity' of local cultures in a global world, emphasises this misperception.

In turn, *critical norms research* would argue that only a contested norm can ever be a good norm. For normative legitimacy requires 'contestation all the way' (Tully 2002). Therefore, the critical norms literature focuses on explorative research in order to identify, map and evaluate distinct meanings of norms that are generated through practice. *Practice* plays a key role here, for it is only through identifying distinct practices of contestation that we are able to 'follow the conflict' and study the effect of practice on norms. The leading questions then become:

- How do norms and their meanings change through interaction?
- And how does that effect the order in world society?

The framework allows norms scholars to operating from the same page, as it were: the reference to the norm-typology allows for three leading assumptions. First, given the broad moral reach and high recognition, *type 1* norms generate low reactive and high proactive contestation. Second, given their origin in shared practices of politics and/or policy-making, *type 2* norms are shared by a group, the degree of reactive and proactive contestation is balanced. And, third, given their high degree of formalisation and thin moral reach, *type 3* norms generate high reactive contestation and low proactive contestation. In addition, the *theory of contestation* distinguishes three segments of norms that indicate the reference to their context of origin in practice, and the material form in which they become visible in the global order. They include first, "formal validity" with reference to official documents such as constitutions, treaties or agreements that are

Table 30.1 Three segments of norms

Segments	References	Form
Formal validity	Official document	Law, law-like
Social recognition	Social group	Unwritten, law-like
Cultural validation	Individual experience	Socio-cultural, informal

Source: (Wiener 2014, 20).

part of the law or have a law-like prescriptive effect; second, "social recognition" with reference to iterated practices that are constitutive for social groups and also have a law-like prescriptive effect although they are unwritten; and third, "cultural validation" as background knowledge generated through individual everyday practice (compare Wiener 2014, 20, Table 30.1).

This table represents norms that have been allocated following the two questions regarding 'moral reach' and 'expected contestation' (compare Table 30.2; Wiener 2018, Ch. 3). The table distinguishes between norms that are presented first, as "prototypes" (see column 2). These norms have been studied by the constructivist norms literature in IR. And second, it includes norms that

Table 30.2 The norm typology

Norm type	Examples: prototype	Examples: case scenarios	Scale	Moral reach	Reactive contestation	Proactive contestation
Fundamental Type 1	*Core Constitutional Norms*: Rule of Law, Democracy, Human Rights, Citizenship *Thick Taken for Granted Norms*: Sustainability	Fundamental Rights of Individuals, Legality, Torture Prohibition, Culture of Impunity, Sexual Violence Prohibition, Universal Jurisdiction	Macro	Wide	Low	High
Organizing Principle Type 2	*Practice-based Norms*: Common but Differentiated Responsibility; Responsibility to Protect (R2P); Rule of Law Mechanism (EU); Total Allowable Catch Annual Percentage Allocation	'Solange Principle'; Right to Fair Trial; Office of the Ombudsperson; 'Sexual Violence is a Security Matter'; 'Documenting Detail matters more than Victory in Court'	Meso	Medium	Medium	Medium
Standardised Procedures, Regulations Type 3	*Fixed Regulatory Standards*: CO_2 Emission Standards; R2P Pillars; Electoral Rules; Rule of Law Mechanism	International Law Procedure; Smart Sanctions; Blacklisting; Web-listing; Torture standards	Micro	Narrow	High	Low

Source: Adapted from Wiener (2008, 66) and Wiener (2017c).★

★I thank Andrea Liese and Georg Nolte for helpful comments on the norm typology which were offered following the presentation of the research project 'International Law and International Relations: Divided by a Common Language' at the Kolleg-Forschergruppe *Rule of Law*, Free University, Berlin, 9 April 2018.

are presented as "illustrative cases" (see column 3). These norms have been identified by applying the critical norms framework as "illustrative cases" (compare Table 30.2; Wiener 2018, Ch. 3; for more case study devised norms compare also True and Wiener 2019, xx). While Erskine finds, that "(W)hat is crucial is that *a yardstick for evaluating particular moral norms* as just or unjust, progressive or regressive, moral or immoral, *is not somehow inherent in constructivism*" (Erskine 2012, 458; emphasis added AW), I would hold that critical constructivists have made quite significant inroad in mending the gaping abyss between studying norms as mere social facts, on the one hand, and taking care to evaluate norms with regard to their moral reach, ethical value and perceived legitimacy, on the other.

Studying R2P

"Agreement on the responsibility to protect is a central element of the 2005 Summit Outcome Document, inasmuch as it is the only fundamental normative innovation agreed upon by the member states during this round of UN reform. (…) The ICISS mandate explicitly included a goal to foster normative development in relation to the use of force to protect human rights" (Brunnée and Toope 2006, 123, 132). How does the framework then work with regard to allocating the R2P norm? Following an approach that brackets ethics – as Erskine convincingly demonstrates, *liberal constructivists* tend to do – the distinction between types hardly matters, for liberal constructivists do not raise the question of 'moral reach'. As Erskine notes, "*(S)ocial constructivism*, as a school of thought and an important theoretical approach to world politics in the discipline of IR, *cannot yield a single, substantive set of ethical prescriptions or evaluative statements* such as 'we have a duty to respect and promote basic human rights', 'slavery (in all its forms) should be abolished', and 'torture is immoral'" (Erskine 2012, 457; emphasis added AW). And, while one could rightly argue that liberal constructivists do study contestation, scrutiny quickly reveals that their concern is not an ethical one, i.e. who has and ought to have access to contestation in order to partake in processes of critical engagement about the legitimate meanings-in-use of the norms. The condition arising for IR constructivists is therefore, where to look for an ethics-based approach outside IR that enables them to evaluate norms: "A self-sufficient 'constructivist ethics', or one that relies on constructivism's empirical strengths and interpretive methodology to arrive at a critical, evaluative criterion for making moral judgments, is an intriguing possibility. Yet, this possibility is itself revealed through direct engagement with other approaches" (Erskine 2012, 466).

By contrast, *critical norms research* is less interested in the question of whether a norm is "robust" but instead asks about the perceived "legality" (Brunnée and Toope 2012, 2019) and/or "legitimacy" of a norm (Hofius et al. 2014; Wiener 2014, 2018). This question requires zooming in on practices of contestation, asking whether access to these practices is warranted to those affected by the norm, and pending on the conditions of access, they evaluate access conditions and seek to enhance them if that is needed. As Brunnée and Toope show, R2P has been devised through a period of interaction among the affected – if privileged – stakeholders involved in the practices of constructing the norm, noting "(A)s set out by the ICISS, the responsibility to protect was a conscious attempt to cut through what had become the 'Gordian knot of humanitarian intervention'. The responsibility to protect was not about rights at all, but about duties. The primary-duty holder was the sovereign state which should offer security and protection to its own citizens" (Brunnée and Toope 2006, 123). And they add, "(B)ut it also offered a set of carefully crafted threshold-criteria for recourse to collective military action where there was 'serious and irreparable harm occurring to human beings, or imminently likely to occur.' The triggering events were 'large scale loss of life … with genocidal intent or not, which [was] the product either of deliberate state action, or state neglect, or inability to act, or a failed state situation,' or 'large scale ethnic cleansing'" (Ibid. 124).

R2P thus emerged as an organising principle (i.e. a *type 2* norm) from a process that involved proactive contestation over a period of time. While clearly bringing to bear moral standards, the process sought to bring together a toolbox of sorts in order to address the question of who has the duty to intervene, when, how and under which conditions. As a result, "R2P and the ICC seem to have galvanized, or perhaps even generated, *some* political will to act on humanitarian and justice norms" (Ainley 2015, 51; emphasis in original text). "Although the member states could not agree on a definition of terrorism or on a set of criteria for the authorization of military force by the Security Council, they did agree on one normative innovation that has the potential for transformative impact in international law and politics: the responsibility to protect" (Brunnée and Toope 2006, 122). And against that backdrop they add, "the 'responsibility to protect' could well be of a different order. It could entail a fundamental conceptual shift, rooted in prior developments, but going much further and calling upon states to re-consider the essentials of their role and powers. Unlike trading regimes rooted in reciprocity, and unlike environmental regimes based on imperatives of collective action, the responsibility to protect creates a – generalized set of interlocking obligations owed to states and to persons" (Brunnée and Toope 2006, 128).

To summarise, from the literature, it is quite obvious that there is some scholarly contention about whether R2P ought to be allocated in the top line, i.e. as a fundamental *type 1* norm, or, whether it would be more appropriate to allocate the norm in the medium line, i.e. as an organising principle or a *type 2* norm. The above paragraphs highlighted these contentions by spelling out the effect of the gap that is constituted by the value-problem in IR with reference to liberal and critical constructivism, respectively.

Mapping and staging responsibility contestations on the cycle-grid

If the quality of norms depends on how agents engage about their meanings-in-use (Puetter and Wiener 2009), how do we identify that quality? Responsibility has become a central if highly contested reference concept in IR theory and in global governance, especially in the aftermath of the ICISS report that established the concept in 2001.[6] As Ainley summarises, "the gradual diffusion of the R2P norm through international governance discourse and institutions following the publication of the ICISS report in 2001, and the entering into force of the Rome Statute that established the ICC in 2002, were judged by many, particularly in UN bureaucracies and the NGO sphere, to be game-changing in their challenge to power politics and state sovereignty" (Ainley 2015, 37).

Notably, the majority of research on the R2P principle is dedicated to addressing the central question of political decision-making processes in the United Nations Security Council (UNSC) and related committees and government offices with regard to whether, and if so, how to implement the principle with recourse to the fundamental norm of 'humanitarian intervention'. The most well-known cases in this regard, i.e. Kosovo, Libya and Syria brought the deeply contested views on how to implement the principle to the fore (Gholiagha 2016). They demonstrate that while by and large broadly conceived as a norm, R2P does not offer a straight-forward action manual. Instead, however, these practices reveal that it does offer a *reference frame* for common action along two dimensions: it reconciles the moral agreement that those with a share in the global order share the responsibility to act in certain situations with the preparedness to engage in discussions regarding how to proceed with respect to given cases together with those other 'shareholders' in the global order (compare also Owen 2019).

A facilitative space, linking facts and values

Understood in this way, R2P frames the practices towards implementing the norm by signposting how to proceed in each specific case while taking case-specific conditions (i.e. rules of engagement) into account. Implementing R2P therefore implies understanding its principled ethical values and its practical social facts. It is therefore best defined as an organising principle that works at the meso-scale of the global order. As such it provides a 'space' that facilitates linking *ethical values* (or fundamental norms) with *social facts* through mutual engagement about 'facts' that is informed by underlying 'values'. To understand how this space works a simple three-by-three table is helpful (compare Figure 30.1).

The horizontal rows represent the declining impact of ethical values over three typical stages that range from norm constitution via negotiation to implementation. The vertical boxes indicate the location within scales of order ranging from macro via meso to micro representing the declining power potential at the respective scales. It follows that *site one* of the grid represents the location where affected stakeholders enjoy the highest access to influencing the meanings-in-use of a norm. Access to site one therefore implies the highest potential for agency in international relations as affected stakeholders are enabled to practice both reactive and proactive contestation, and bring the three practices of validation (formal, social and cultural) to bear. Conversely, *site nine* represents the location with the lowest power potential. On this site, agency is limited to practice reactive contestation (i.e. objection against norm compliance or norm violation) bringing cultural validation (i.e. individual background knowledge) to bear.

Balancing reactive and proactive contestation

With its three pillars and underlying ethical values, and through its application in multiple recurring cases, R2P has come to represent an organising principle, a pattern that provides guidance with regard to identifying specific strategies and procedures in each case. The grid allows for mapping the conditions under which the meanings-in-use of a norm are generated through local practice (i.e. doings) thereby taking into account the 'normative opportunity structure' (i.e. the conventions, agreements or constitutions) on that local site. As the grid implies, moving along vertically from the macro- towards the micro-scale of global order, that normative opportunity structure becomes more diverse. This enhances the probable conflicts about meanings-in-use of the norm and their shared legitimacy. Conversely, this raises the probability of local contestations. Similarly, when moving along horizontally from site 1, the possibility to proactively take part in coining a norm's meaning shrinks as we move along from the stages of norm constitution towards the stage of implementation. This again, suggests a growing probability of reactive norm contestation.

A *central question with regard to a norm's legitimacy* then arises, namely, how to reverse the probability of objection while reconciling the dynamics of contestation? In a global order that is framed by a community ontology, the question is less obvious, because the order and the norms that constitute it are taken-for-granted, norm-following represents a top-down dynamic. In turn, when the global order is framed by a diversity ontology, the challenge becomes one of establishing legitimacy from the bottom-up (compare Table 30.3).

The conceptualisation of contestation as a two-fold either reactive or proactive practice allows for distinguishing affected stakeholders' access to agency. That is, while contestation is always political, its potential with regard to facilitating political agency is distinguished by differentiated access conditions that allow either mere reaction (doing) or proaction (shaping). 'Reactive' contestation is limited to the practice of objecting, for example, opposing acts of norm violation,

Table 30.3 Two ontologies: Community versus diversity

Perspective	Community ontology	Diversity ontology
State plus	(1) Conventional constructivist	(3) Regimes
	Norms *structure* state behaviour	Norms *are the glue* of regimes
Global	(2) Global governance	(4) Critical/consistent constructivist
	Norms *guide and control* multiple actors	Norms *form part of* the normative structure of meaning-in-use

or, undertaking the act of contesting compliance with a norm. By contrast, 'proactive' contestation represents a stakeholder's access to critical engagement with a norm and its meanings. As the cycle-grid model demonstrates, *site one* represents the location with the highest power potential, in turn, *site nine* represents the location with the lowest power potential. While all nine sites represent typical locations where affected stakeholders engage in norm contestation, their potential political agency is therefore restricted by differentiated conditions of access to reactive and proactive contestation, respectively. Following any given norm conflict to the site of contestation serves to identify these conditions with reference to the respective normative opportunity structure (i.e. the political and legal institutions that set the rules of engagement). Taking into account the *quod omnes tangit* principle (what touches all must be approved by all), it follows that while shared recognition of a norm indicates common practice, establishing legitimacy of a norm among plural agents who do *not* share everyday practices through everyday interaction within a stable social context, requires facilitating engagement about a norm for those who are affected by it. If only a contested norm can ever be a good norm this highlights the challenge of where to stage this engagement. According to the grid, the central site (i.e. *site 5*) offers the place for such interaction.

Conclusion

This chapter asked two principal questions with regard to the practicalities of responsibility research: first, do we conceive of responsibility as a policy-based principle that triggers distinct strategic mechanisms of action, or do we conceive of responsibility as a broader ethical value that guides that policy action? And, second, if both roles apply, which takes prevalence and when, how do we know? With recourse to the norm typology offered by *critical norms research*, the chapter first argued that responsibility research crucially must be mindful of the norm's value-based roots in addition to its workings as a social fact. As the chapter has argued this two-fold understanding of a norm as carriers of both social fact and ethical values is vital in order to generate meaningful scholarly engagement about specific responsibility norms, such as, for example, the R2P.

To sustain the point, the chapter recalled the emergence of the R2P norm through a process of interactive engagement among policy-makers, high-level officials and experts over a prolonged period of time. That is, the norm has been constituted through iterated social interaction at the meso-scale of global order. The chapter then moved on to the practicalities of studying the workings of the R2P norm with reference to the cycle-grid model as the second tool of *critical norms research*. To that end, it demonstrated how following the conflict and mapping distinct practices of norm contestation (reactive, proactive) and norm validation (formal, social, cultural) on the cycle-grid facilitate locating affected stakeholders on the grid's *sites*. The mapping takes into account the three typical scales of order, i.e. macro, meso and micro on the one hand, and the three typical stages of the norm-implementing process, i.e. constituting, negotiating and implementing. In the R2P case, the norm generative practices centre on the negotiating stage at the meso-scale. Here, the stakeholders take part in negotiating the detailed measures and instruments to facilitate norm implementation and identify the principles that frame the relevant deliberations within the UNSC and related committees (compare Ainley 2015; Brunnée and Toope 2006).

As wide-ranging accounts documenting the complexities of implementing R2P show, most cases reveal a general pattern insofar as they left scholars and politicians alike with the recurring challenge of identifying 'their' definition of the concept. The range of definitions spans from the R2P's three pillars as an action manual of sorts on the one hand, and the definition of R2P as an ethical value of international politics, on the other. Between these to signposts, a variety of definitions distinguishes R2P. Politicians pressed for decisions about how to implement the norm have been cast back to square one in order to devise a common strategy. By contrast, for academics, the multiple interpretations of the R2P norm and its meaning have revealed considerable mismatches between two quite distinct strands of constructivist norm scholarship, one – the liberal strand – is literally unable (if not entirely unprepared) to apply a value-based approach to norms drawing on external theories of ethics.

In turn, the other has begun to constructively address the value-problem in norms research by drawing on public philosophy, or indeed, de-colonial studies. As this chapter sought to demonstrated, critical norms research has taken up this principled approach and advanced towards operationalising empirical fieldwork. Thus, according to the norm-typology, in the R2P case, norm implementation is likely to generate balanced contestation, centring on *site five* with input from the neighbouring sites on the cycle-grid. That is, it is expected both reactive contestation (objection to the norm, especially with regard to concern about sovereignty) and proactive contestation (critical engagement with the norm, for example, with regard to identifying the degree of emergency, and the use of the relevant instruments) in order to come to an agreement about whether and how to implement the norm. Both suggest identifying the norm as balanced with regard to the expected degree of contestation, and privileged because of the depicted means of procedure in situations that suggest the duty to intervene by humanitarian intervention. Whether or not that duty is shared, remains to be established on a case by case basis.

Notes

1 GR2P (Global Responsibility to Protect), see: https://brill.com/view/journals/gr2p/gr2p-overview.xml?language=en
2 For many, see Kratochwil and Ruggie (1986), Katzenstein (1996), Klotz (1995), Finnemore and Sikkink (1998), March and Olsen (1998), Risse et al. (1999, 2013), Acharya (2004), Puetter and Wiener (2009), Zimmermann (2017), Wiener (2004, 2007, 2008, 2018), Deitelhoff and Zimmermann (2019), Stimmer and Wisken (2019), and Lantis and Wunderlich (2018).
3 See e.g. Acharya (2004), Wolff and Zimmermann (2016), Niemann and Schillinger (2016), and Wiener (2008, 2009).
4 Compare for example, Hamati-Ataya's observation that while often dismissed as 'marginal', 'the "problem of values" is inscribed in most of its disciplinary debates, and the properly moral dilemmas that IR scholarship faces today have been equally – if not more violently – present in its disciplinary past'. (Hamati-Ataya 2011, 260).
5 Compare Busser in this Handbook, p. 2 quoting O'Neill (2016, 10) 'In my view', Onora O'Neill has written, 'we do not take rights seriously unless we seek to show *who* ought to do *what* for *whom*'.
6 See: International Commission on Intervention and State Sovereignty (2001).

References

Acharya, A. (2004). "How ideas spread: Whose norms matter? Norm localization and institutional change in Asian Regionalism." *International Organization*, 58(2): 239–275.

Ackerly, B., and True, J. (2008). "Reflexivity in practice: Power and ethics in feminist research on international relations." *International Studies Review*, 10(4): 693–707.

Ackerly, B., and True, J. (2010). *Doing Feminist Research in Political and Social Science*. London: Red Globe Press.

Adler, E. (1987). *The Power of Ideology: The Quest for Technological Autonomy in Argentina and Brazil*. Berkeley and Los Angeles: University of California Press.

Adler, E. (2019). *World Ordering: A Social Theory of Cognitive Evolution*. Cambridge: Cambridge University Press.

Ainley, K. (2015). "The responsibility to protect and the international criminal court: counteracting the crisis." *International Affairs*, 91(1): 37–54.

Bellamy, A.J. (2008). "The Responsibility to Protect and the problem of military intervention." *International Affairs*, 84(4): 615–639.

Bellamy, A.J., and McLoughlin, S. (2019). "Human protection and the politics of armed intervention: With responsibility comes accountability." *Global Responsibility to Protect*, 11(3): 333–361.

Bovens, M. (2007). "New forms of accountability and EU-governance." In Wiener, A., Puetter, U., and Begg, I., eds., Special Issue: Contested meanings of norms – the challenge of democratic governance beyond the State". Comparative European Politics, 5(1): 104–120.

Bourdieu, P. (1993). *Sociology in Question*. London: Sage.

Brunnée, J., and Toope. S.J. (2006). "Norms, institutions and UN reform: The Responsibility to Protect." *Journal of International Law and International Relations*, 2(1): 121–137.

Brunnée, J. and Toope, S.J. (2010). *Legitimacy and Legality in International Law: An Interactional Account*. Cambridge: Cambridge University Press.

Brunnée, J., and Toope, S.J. (2012). "Constructivism and International Law." in Dunoff, J., and Pollack, M.A., eds., *Interdisciplinary Perspectives on International Law and International Relations: The State of the Art*. New York: Cambridge University Press.

Brunnée, J., and Toope, S.J. (2019). "Norm robustness and contestation in international law: Self-defense against nonstate actors." *Journal of Global Security Studies*, 4(1): 73–87.

Checkel, Jeffrey T. (1999) "Norms, institutions, and national identity in contemporary Europe." *International Studies Quarterly* 43(1): 83–114.

Deitelhoff, N., and Zimmermann, L. (2019). "Norms under challenge: Unpacking the dynamics of norm robustness." *Journal of Global Security Studies*, 4(1): 2–17.

Erskine, T. (2012). "Whose progress, which morals? Constructivism, normative IR theory and the limits and possibilities of studying ethics in world politics." *International Theory*, 4(3): 449–468.

Erskine, T. (2014). "Coalitions of the willing and responsibilities to protect: Informal associations, enhanced capacities, and shared moral burdens". *Ethics & International Affairs*, 28(1): 115–145.

Erskine, T. (2015). "'Coalitions of the Willing' and the Shared Responsibility to Protect." In Nollkaemper, A., and Jacobs, D., eds. *Distribution of Responsibilities in International Law*: 227–264. Cambridge: Cambridge University Press.

Finnemore, M., and Sikkink, K. (1998). "International norm dynamics and political change." *International Organization*, 52(4): 887–917.

Gholiagha, S. (2016). *The humanization of international relations—Prosecution, protecting, and killing* (Doctoral dissertation), University of Hamburg, Hamburg, Germany.

Giddens, A. (1979). *Central Problems in Social Theory: Action, Structure, and Contradiction in Social Analysis*. Berkeley and Los Angeles: University of California Press.

Hamati-Ataya, I. (2010). "Knowing and judging in International Relations theory: realism and the reflexive challenge." *Review of International Studies*, 36(4): 1079–1101.

Hamati-Ataya, I. (2011). "The 'problem of values' and international relations scholarship: From applied reflexivity to reflexivism." *International Studies Review*, 13(2): 259–287.

Havercroft, J. (2018). "Social Constructivism and International Ethics". In Steele, B.J. and Heinze, E.A., eds., *Routledge Handbook of Ethics & International Relations*: 116–129. London and New York: Routledge.

Hofius, M. (2016). "Community at the border or the boundaries of community? The case of EU field diplomats." *Review of International Studies*, 42(5): 939–967.

Hofius, M., Wilkens, J., Hansen-Magnusson, H., and Gholiagha, S. (2014). "Den Schleier lichten? Kritische Normenforschung, Freiheit und Gleichberechtigung im Kontext des 'Arabischen Frühlings'." *ZIB – Zeitschrift für Internationale Beziehungen*, 21(2): 85–105.

International Commission on Intervention and State Sovereignty (2001). "The Responsibility to Protect". Ottawa: International Development Research Center.

Katzenstein, P.J., ed. (1996). *The Culture of National Security: Norms and Identity in World Politics*. New York: Columbia University Press.

Klotz, A. (1995). "Norms reconstituting interests: Global racial equality and US sanctions against South Africa". *International Organization*, 49(3): 451–478.

Koh, Harold Hongju. (1997). "Why do Nations Obey International Law? Review Essay." The Yale Law Journals 106: 2599–2659.

Kratochwil, F. (2018) *Praxis: On acting and knowing*. Cambridge: Cambridge University Press.

Kratochwil, F., and Ruggie, J.G. (1986). "International organization: A state of the art on an art of the state." *International Organization*, 40(4): 753–775.

Kurowska, X. (2020). "Politics as *Realitätsprinzip* in the debate on constitutions and fragmented orders: remarks on meditation 3 "On constitutions and fragmented orders", *International Theory* 13 (1): 1–8, FirstView. DOI: https://doi.org/10.1017/S1752971920000573

Lantis, J.S., and Wunderlich, C. (2018). "Resiliency dynamics of norm clusters: Norm contestation and international cooperation." *Review of International Studies*, 44(3): 570–593.

March, J.G., and Olsen, J.O. (1998). "The institutional dynamics of international political orders." *International Organization*, 52(4): 943–969.

Marcus, G.E. (1995). "Ethnography in/of the world system: The emergence of multi-sited ethnography." *Annual Review of Anthropology*, 24(1): 95–117.

Milliken, J. (1999). "The study of discourse in international relations: A critique of research and methods." *European Journal of International Relations*, 5(2): 225–254.

Niemann, H., and Schillinger, H. (2016). "Contestation 'all the way down'? The grammar of contestation in norm research." *Review of International Studies*, 43(1): 29–49.

O'Neill, O. (2016). *Justice across Boundaries: Whose Obligations?* Cambridge: Cambridge University Press.

Owen, D. (2019). Untitled, Input at Workshop 'Democracy & its Futures' at University of Victoria, Canada, March 21-22, 2019, https://bit.ly/2VKAV1K.

Price, R. (2008). "The Ethics of Constructivism". In Reus-Smit, C., and Snidal, D., eds., *The Oxford Handbook of International Relations*: 317–326. Oxford and New York: Oxford University Press.

Puetter, U., and Wiener, A. (2009). "The quality of norms is what actors make of it: Critical constructivist research on norms". *Journal of International Law and International Relations*, 5(1): 1–16.

Risse, T., Ropp, S.C., and Sikkink, K., eds. (1999). *The Power of Human Rights: International Norms and Domestic Change*. Cambridge: Cambridge University Press.

Steele, B.J., and Heinze, E.A., eds. (2018). *Routledge Handbook of Ethics and International Relations*. London and New York: Routledge.

Stimmer, A., and Wisken, L. (2019). "The dynamics of dissent: when actions are louder than words." *International Affairs*, 95(3): 515–533.

True, J., and Wiener, A. (2019). "Everyone wants (a) peace: The dynamics of rhetoric and practice on 'Women, Peace and Security'." *International Affairs*, 95(3): 553–574.

Tully, J. (2002). "The unfreedom of the moderns in comparison to their ideals of constitutional democracy." *The Modern Law Review*, 65(2): 204–228.

Tully, J. (2008). *Public Philosophy in a New Key: Volume 1, Democracy and Civic Freedom*. Cambridge: Cambridge University Press.

Walker, N. (2017). "Constitutionalism and Pluralism". In Lang, A., and Wiener, A., eds., *Handbook on Global Constitutionalism*: 433–444. Cheltenham: Edward Elgar Publishing.

Welsh, J.M. (2013). "Norm contestation and the responsibility to protect". *Global Responsibility to Protect*, 5(4): 365–396.

Welsh, J.M. (2019). "Norm robustness and the responsibility to protect." *Journal of Global Security Studies*, 4(1): 53–72.

Wiener, A. (2004). "Contested compliance: Interventions on the normative structure of world politics." *European Journal of International Relations*, 10(2): 189–234.

Wiener, A. (2007). "Contested meanings of norms: A research framework." *Comparative European Politics*, 5(1): 1–17.

Wiener, A. (2008). *The Invisible Constitution of Politics: Contested Norms and International Encounters*. Cambridge: Cambridge University Press.

Wiener, A. (2009). "Enacting meaning-in-use: qualitative research on norms and international relations." *Review of International Studies*, 35(1): 175–193.

Wiener, A. (2014). *A Theory of Contestation*. Berlin: Springer.

Wiener, A. (2018). *Contestation and Constitution of Norms in Global International Relations*. Cambridge: Cambridge University Press.

Wolff, J., and Zimmermann, L. (2016). "Between Banyans and battle scenes: Liberal norms, contestation, and the limits of critique." *Review of International Studies*, 42(3): 513–534.

Zimmermann, L. (2017). *Global Norms with a Local Face: Rule-of-Law Promotion and Norm Translation*. Cambridge: Cambridge University Press.

31
ACADEMIC RESPONSIBILITY IN THE FACE OF CLIMATE CHANGE

Patrick Thaddeus Jackson

Introduction[1]

Greta Thunberg, as most readers of this chapter are probably aware, is a 16-year-old Swedish student who began a "school strike" in 2018 in order to protest the inaction of the Swedish government on climate change. Instead of attending her classes, she sat outside the Swedish parliament with a sign reading "School Strike for Climate"[2] every weekday from 20 August until 7 September, and every Friday thereafter. Her efforts inspired the FridaysForFuture movement (fridaysforfuture.org), which incorporates and coordinates worldwide student activism on the issue of climate change. Thunberg herself has been the public face of the movement, addressing the European Parliament, the United Nations, the US Congress, and the World Economic Forum, and speaking at dozens of other public venues. When she does so, she does not mince words, taking world leaders to task for not treating climate change as a pressing crisis and a state of emergency: "I am here to say our house is on fire," she began a 2019 speech to the World Economic Forum, before castigating "all political movements in their present form" for having failed to acknowledge both the problem and the solution:

> The main solution however is so simple that even a small child can understand it. We have to stop the emissions of greenhouse gases. And either we do that or we don't. You say nothing in life is black or white but that is a lie, a very dangerous lie. Either we prevent a 1.5 degree of warming or we don't. Either we avoid setting off that irreversible chain reaction beyond the human control, or we don't. Either we choose to go on as a civilization or we don't. That is as black or white as it gets.
>
> There are no gray areas when it comes to survival.
>
> *(Thunberg 2019a)*

Thunberg is of course not the first or the only popular climate change activist, but the spectacle of a young girl taking political leaders to task is especially intriguing for a consideration of political responsibility. A child not even of voting age has no electoral power, so her appeals are at best only indirectly based on notions of accountability to voters; she and the students she inspires can't vote the politicians out of office. She is also not appealing to notions of power and interest; indeed, when addressing the US Congress, she was quite scornful of the US's departure from the Paris climate accords because "it was a bad deal for the USA" (Thunberg 2019c). Instead, Thunberg's appeals operate in two registers *distinct from* partisan politics: a scientific or epistemic register, in which non-partisan facts command the assent of all political elites regardless of party; and an ethical register, in which adult leaders are accused of risking their children's futures and rich countries are accused of failing to take responsibility for their role in producing climate change. She does not present herself as a politician, and instead of making specific policy recommendations, Thunberg urges her audiences to "unite behind the science"—not to turn policymaking over to the scientists, but to conduct ourselves in a way that takes the facts into account and enacts changes that are likely to avoid the worst of the climate forecasts.

To explore Thunberg's appeal, I first turn to Max Weber's account of a "politics of responsibility." Weber suggested that responsibility—he uses the word *Verantwortungsgefühl*, literally a feeling of being answerable to—is one of the three "decisive" qualities for an authentic politician, along with passion and a sense of proportion (Weber 1994, 73–74). Without this sense of responsibility, a politician is ineffectual, because their passion for some cause doesn't serve to animate and direct their actions, and their sense of measured proportion simply devolves into a calculating adaptation to existing realities. The cause that a politician serves gives political successes their meaning and purpose (*ibid.*, 76), and the politician's sense of responsibility to their cause, whatever that cause is, allows them to endure the "strong slow boring of hard boards, with a mixture of passion and proportion at the same time" that constitutes, for Weber, the truest vocation for politics (*ibid.*, 88, translation modified; compare also the respective chapters by Busser, Baron, and Beardsworth in this volume).

But Weber's reflections need to be supplemented by an appreciation of the ways that a figure like Greta Thunberg calls a public constituency into being through her public actions; Thunberg is deliberately *not* working through established political institutions, but issuing a set of claims from outside that system which serve to mobilize people demanding action, as well as providing an ethical context to which politicians are expected to conform. To help conceptualize this, I next turn to John Dewey's classic work *The Public and Its Problems*. Thunberg operates like the kind of agent that Dewey called for in that work: she is constituting a public by showing that its members share a common concern. That process, in turn, involves locating the moral cosmology underpinning ethical appeals not so much in formal theological reasoning (which is the only place Weber identifies in his discussion as giving rise to binding ethical imperatives) as in a broader notion of the world as a meaningful place. A constituency taking to the streets (and boycotting their classes) in order to demand climate justice is working in the gap between an ethical expectation about what the world ought to be like and the concrete actuality of what it is like; their common concern is less a technical problem in need of solution, and more a sense that the world is, so to speak, out of joint.

In other words, Greta Thunberg is operating as a *public intellectual*, holding politicians to account and calling on them to act responsibly, which she can do precisely by not being one of them.

Weber and the vocation for politics

In his "Politics as a Vocation" lecture, Max Weber's greatest fear is that a politician will succumb to either pure passion or pure calculation, and thus forego their actual vocation in favor of either a vainglorious pursuit of power for its own sake rather than for its utility in achieving an publicly desirable end, or an "ethics of conviction" that refuses to take consequences seriously. Losing a sense of responsibility to a cause is what produces the former outcome, because without a morally praiseworthy purpose, all that remains is the ambition to control the machinery of the state—and to do so for one's own private purposes and benefit. No sense of the public good is possible in such circumstances, because the politician's only guiding light is their own enrichment. On the other hand, when a politician ignores the tragic necessity of using the unethical means of state coercion to achieve *any* end, even the most ethically praiseworthy, we have the opposite error:

> Can the ethical demands on politics really be indifferent to the fact that politics works with a specific means: power, behind which stands *violence*? Don't we see that the Bolshevist and Spartacist ideologues are achieving the *same* results as any militaristic dictator precisely because they are using this tool of politics?...How are we to distinguish between the polemics of most of the representatives of the supposedly new ethics against their opponents, and those of any other demagogue? By their noble intentions! we are told. Good. But here we are talking about means,[3] and the nobility of ultimate intentions is also claimed by their opponents with just as much sincerity.
>
> *(ibid., 78)*

Because of the necessity to use coercive force in political action, Weber argues, a politician *can't* follow an ethics of conviction in which the ethical desirability or value of the goal gives the politician license to ignore the "(foreseeable) *results*" of their actions (*ibid.*, 79)—because that road leads either to abandoning political action altogether because of its unethical means, or to justifying any and every action in terms of the goal pursued. Either way, the specific responsibility of the politician both *to* their cause and *for* the consequences of their actions—the unity of passion and a sense of proportion—is sacrificed. Even though Weber also notes that it is "authentically human and moving" when a responsible politician reaches a point where they adopt an ethics of conviction to say, after Martin Luther, "here I stand, I can do no other" (*ibid.*, 86), it is clear that for Weber, this is an extreme limit to political action rather than its core.

The vocation for politics, then, is to be suspended between two imperatives: the ethical imperative to do what is right, and the consequentialist imperative (so to speak) to do what is effective.[4] It would thus appear that a Weberian politician needs to know two things in order to properly exercise this vocation.[5] On one hand, they need to be able to foresee the consequences of their actions—not perfectly, but in a way that allows a deliberate consideration of what particular courses of action might lead to. On the other hand, they need a grounding in some vision of the goal to be achieved, an ethically compelling cause that can anchor their actions and give them meaning and purpose. Logically speaking, neither of these kinds of knowledge can be generated from within the sphere of politics, where the pursuit of power is the continual means; both ethical and consequential knowledge have to serve as a check on that pursuit, and as such need to emanate from somewhere *beyond* politics. A politician who simply announced a cause or produced their own forecast of outcomes would, and quite rightly, be quickly accused of inventing something that served their own interests rather than the ends explicitly promulgated. The very grammar (in the sense of Wittgenstein 1958) of such claims—claims about the ethical desirability of a cause, and claims about the validity of a forecast—is that they are evaluable in terms of standard other than the question of whether they serve the political interests of one or another politician or political faction. To put this a little differently, they can't be *political* claims, lest they lose any of their influence in politics.

Weber's account of where these claims come from is quite narrow and specific. Compelling ethical causes in Weber's account come from religious or quasi-religious sets of transcendental values, which provide an overall account of the world as a meaningful place and locate human action within an ordered cosmos. It is not an accident that his recurrent example is the Sermon on the Mount, a core component of Christian doctrine; for Weber's audience, this is a readily recognizable set of ethical imperatives, and one might imagine that had Weber not been talking to an audience of German students, he might have chosen a different religious example. But as it is, he looks to the Christian New Testament for his primary examples of absolute duty, such as the duty to tell the truth. This duty is "unconditional" as an ethical imperative, regardless of the consequences, even if those consequences involve a "confession of guilt, one-sided, unconditional" resulting from a decontextualized misuse of, say, official government documents (Weber 1994, 79).[6] It is fair to say that for Weber, the source of the highest values in a given culture is a *religious* source, even and perhaps especially if the imperatives of that religious source have been more or less thoroughly rationalized into the practical ethics of everyday social and economic life; such a rationalization and a routinization depends, at least implicitly, on a meaning-full cosmology that gives those ethical precepts their imperative force.[7]

As for valid forecasts of likely outcomes, the source of those lies in the topic of Weber's *other* celebrated lecture, "Science as a Vocation," and particularly in those sciences which place causality as the irreducible core of knowledge in a disenchanted world. Causal explanation, for Weber, is a considerably broader notion than the "subsumption under an empirically general law" conception we find prominently on display in contemporary neopositivism, and rests on identifying those combinations of factors that combine and concatenate to generate particular outcomes in specific cases (Jackson 2017). This broadly "manipulationist" account of causality (Woodward 2005) aims to provide precisely the kind of knowledge that a politician needs in order to make a particular outcome happen, or at least to make that politician aware of the likely consequences of specific actions they might choose to undertake. In his lecture, Weber takes great care in distinguishing this scholarly, *wissenschaftlich*, enterprise from ethical pronouncements on the desirability or relative value of particular outcomes, both in causal scholarship which would restrict itself to systematically explaining how initial conditions brought about those outcomes, and—to a lesser extent—in interpretive or hermeneutic scholarship which has as its end the systematic explication of a system of value-commitments. In neither case do scholarly conclusions provide anything like the necessary imperative quality that can serve as a standard for right action; showing that some action is a means to an end doesn't justify the end, and showing that some system of values would judge an end to be good doesn't make that end good. Scholarship, for Weber, is thus a distinctly limited and bounded enterprise, contemplative rather than operational.

The vocation for politics thus stands *between* ethics and scholarship, with the authentically responsible politician suspended between the meaningful cosmos of transcendental values and the recognition, based on the most sustained scholarly reflection, that coercion and violence is the indispensable means of politics—even to achieve desirable ends. Remove either side of this tension, and responsible politics disappears, devolving into either private instrumentality or the imposition of values at any cost. Politics won't save us, but perhaps it might be prevented from destroying us.

Dewey and the constitution of the public

I have been operating with the deliberately narrow Weberian definition of "politics" here, restricting that term to the operation of the machinery of state coercion. But even if we don't operate with such a bleakly "realist" understanding of politics, the same dual need for both ethical imperatives and valid forecasts shows itself. As an illustration, consider pragmatist thinking about the state, which is directed *against* the notion that the distinguishing characteristic of the state is its employment of coercive violence. John Dewey argued in *The Public and its Problems* that we should not understand rules of law as coercive commands, but as "the institution of conditions under which persons make their arrangements with one another": as "structures which canalize action," laws are "active forces only as are banks which confine the flow of a stream, and are commands only in the sense in which the banks command the current" (Dewey 1985, 295). On

Dewey's account, this introduces a very different set of standards to use in evaluating laws and other state policies: not whether those state actions are *legitimate*, but whether they are *effective*—and not effective in promoting the narrow interests of the politician, but effective in channeling the subsequent action of the citizens in a way that resolves practical problems.

For Dewey, political activity is about coordinating and organizing rather than commanding and coercing. The challenges of politics are "a practical problem of human beings living in association with one another" (*ibid.*, 255) and Dewey's emphasis is on the nature of those problems rather than on the character of the officials who play a role in solving those problems. The public, for Dewey, "consists of all those who are affected by the indirect consequences of transactions to such an extent that it is deemed necessary to have those consequences systematically cared for" (*ibid.*, 245). Those indirect consequences—where, for example, a commercial exchange between you and me, say when I hire you to build a fence to keep my cattle from wandering off, prevents other people from bringing *their* cattle to the water-source now enclosed with a fence—are what call for regulation, by producing a public composed of people who are being affected by something they had no part in bringing about. Precisely *how* that problem is to be solved is less important to Dewey than recalling *that* the problem is what called for regulation and government in the first place:

> Means of transit and communication affect not only those who utilize them but all who are dependent in any way upon what is transported, whether as producers or consumers. The increase of easy and rapid intercommunication means that production takes place more and more for distant markets and it puts a premium upon mass-production. Thus it becomes a disputed question whether railroads as well as highways should not be administered by public officials, and in any case some measure of official regulation is instituted, as they become settled bases of social life.
>
> (*ibid.*, 273)

Indeed, Dewey suggests that solutions to problems like this—whether railroads and roads need public officials to administer them, given the indirect effects of actions like building a road or laying railroad tracks—can only be ascertained in practice, experimentally, through "continuous inquiry, continuous in the sense of being connected as well as persistent" which "can provide the material of enduring opinion about public matters" (*ibid.*, 346). There is no *ex ante* solution to an actual problem, and no way to decide in advance of practical engagement in the situation whether (e.g.) publicly administering roads is better than letting private owners do so.

There is thus little or no coercion in Dewey's account of political life. This is likely due to Dewey's understanding of a public as something that is generated more or less automatically because of indirect consequences: a public exists whenever such consequences exist. The problem, though, which even Dewey recognizes, is that the factual *existence* of a public—which, in virtue of the common problem faced by all of its members, has an interest in solving that problem—isn't always enough to actually *produce* that public in a politically relevant way.

> Indirect, extensive, enduring and serious consequences of conjoint and interacting behavior call a public into existence having a common interest in controlling these consequences. But the machine age has so enormously expanded, multiplied, intensified and complicated the scope of the indirect consequences, has formed such immense and consolidated unions in action, on an impersonal rather than a community basis, that the resultant public cannot identify and distinguish itself. And this discovery is obviously an antecedent condition of any effective organization on its part.
>
> (*ibid.*, 314)

So it is possible to *know* that a public exists even if that public *does not know itself to be a public*. This in turn sets up what Dewey calls the "prime difficulty...of discovering the means by which a scattered, mobile and manifold public may so recognize itself as to define and express its interests" (*ibid.*, 327). By Dewey's own logic, this can't be a means that comes into being by the same channels as a public does. A public, for Dewey, is a constellation of people united by their commonly being subject to a set of effects, whether they realize it or not; the common interest that they have is in regulating those effects, not in constituting themselves as a public. Despite some trenchant observations about the role of communication in producing a community (*ibid.*, 329–331), there is a gap in Dewey's account between the existence of a public and the constitution of that public.

The bridging of that gap involves the active production of a public by demonstrating to the relevant people that they *do in fact constitute a public*. Dewey has great confidence in the capacity of artists to do this—"Artists have always been the real purveyors of news, for it is not the outward happening in itself which is new, but the kindling by it of emotion, perception and appreciation" (*ibid.*, 350)—but especially given the technical complexity of life in industrialized societies, he envisions a role for other kinds of detached observers too.[8] Observers who could trace out the complex consequences of various configurations and arrangements of action, and thus generate awareness of a need to regulate and coordinate them. Clearly such observations would need a standard of validity that couldn't be reduced to solving a problem that *the observers* were facing and trying to solve; otherwise publics would be produced as a byproduct of other processes and as a solution to other problems, and not because the members of that public themselves were facing problems. Dewey's answer to this conundrum presumes that people are engaged in "continuous inquiry" (*ibid.*, 346) so that they will recognize valid arguments about indirect consequences when they hear them, but even he admits that "[i]nquiry, indeed, is a work which devolves upon experts" (*ibid.*, 365) and not on every person equally.[9]

Despite immense differences in how they understand political action, Weber and Dewey agree that responsible political action involves some set of inputs from outside of political action, adhering to standards of validity that cannot be simply reduced to the political power of their advocates. Someone has to *know* that a group of people form a public, because they share an interest in solving a particular problem affecting them all, and that knowledge can't simply be a political claim. Then someone needs to *practically constitute* that public in a politically relevant way, making its members aware of their shared interest and concerned enough about it to do something; characterizing some effect as a problem in need of solution requires evaluating that effect in terms of whether it is acceptable or not, and is thus something of an ethical enterprise. Appropriate political action will follow from the recognition by members of that public of their shared interest, and as the public is constituted in a politically relevant way, it can present its claims to the politicians and demand that solutions be provided. In this way, the voice of the public functions much like the ethical inputs to Weber's responsible politicians, presenting a goal that the politicians are imperatively enjoined to pursue; scholars figure into this process both in initially delineating the factual existence of the relevant public, and in providing the politicians with potential solutions to the problems identified. Once again, the politicians themselves stand *between* an ethical imperative and a factual forecast of likely outcomes, and while Dewey is less convinced than Weber of the inescapably coercive character of the use of state power to produce such outcomes, the overall relationship between politics, ethics, and causal knowledge remains much the same.[10]

In this light, for both Weber and Dewey, there is a positive political value to epistemic claims that are *not* political, claims that results from an investigation where the goal is *not* to immediately produce a practical effect, but to generate a depiction that can fuel future action precisely in virtue of its general, abstract form. As I argued above, Weber calls this *Wissenschaft*, "scholarship"; Dewey calls it "abstraction," and notes that it is a kind of "liberation": "abstraction means that something has been released from one experience for transfer to another....The more theoretical, the more abstract, an abstraction, or the farther away it is from anything experienced in its concreteness, the better fitted it is to deal with any one of the indefinite variety of things that may later present themselves" (Dewey 1978, 166). And for both Weber and Dewey, the place where such claims come from is the academy, a space provisionally separated out from the hustle and bustle of everyday life to provide the opportunity for contemplation and reflection. The vocation for scholarship, as Weber pointed out, is to be wholly devoted to one's subject, to "serve only the thing" (Weber 1994, 7). When we focus on other things, we are not, in the strict sense, acting *as scholars*. And nothing hampers the role that scholarly knowledge can play in politics more than the suspicion that the claims in question are *not* valid in an abstract sense, but are merely partisan posturing. If scholarly knowledge is to play the role that both Weber and Dewey think it can and should, then the first responsibility of scholars is to protect and preserve the *nonpartisan* character of their inquiries.

But while this might exhaust academic responsibility for Weber, it does not exhaust academic responsibility for Dewey. Weber does not give scholars any specific role in producing the ethical inputs to the political process, in part because ethical imperatives for him are in important ways reducible to *religious* imperatives. Dewey, who generally thinks of ethics as practical knowledge that arises the same way that any other kind of practical knowledge arises—which is to say, through practical experimentation—is far less austere on this score, and indeed he would not be consistently able to derive ethical imperatives from any source outside of practical knowledge. So a public, animated by a sense of moral outrage at some problem its members face (and the very notion that a problem is a *problem* in need of solution relies, at least implicitly, on some value-laden judgment, which is in turn logically if not substantively dependent on a set of moral principles delineating good from bad outcomes), is in a sense bringing its own ethical imperatives into the very process of calling on politicians to act. Constituting that public in a politically relevant way thus involves not merely instructing its members on the causal chains that are producing discomfort, but also more broadly educating the members of the public about the commitments that they hold or should hold. Here we might adduce two additional roles for scholars, who are—at least in the academic form of life as we have inherited it—also *teachers*, and as such work with students both directly in their classes, and indirectly by producing the abstract conceptual tools that future action might well depend on when they leave the academy and turn or return to more direct work in the world. Constituting the public is a kind of *pedagogical* activity.

Public intellectuals and the constitution of publics

We can be more precise about this. A spatial mapping of conceptual distinctions can be very helpful here, inasmuch as the notion of responsible politics that emerges from both Weber and Dewey is connected to the relations between the scholarly sphere of the academy and the political realm; the question is how to concretely illustrate the ways that those relations might play out. Following Andrew Abbott (2001), we might take a cue from his insight that dichotomies—like scholarship/politics—have a tendency to "fractally" reproduce themselves at different levels of resolution, such that a split along one such dichotomy can very easily give rise to further splits *within* each of the resulting camps along self-similar lines. One result of this kind of fractalization is that inside of each of the main camps we can find, in effect, a version of the other camp, and this kind of internal other, or mutual imbrication, can help elucidate points of connection and crossover not readily apparent from the initial dichotomy itself.[11]

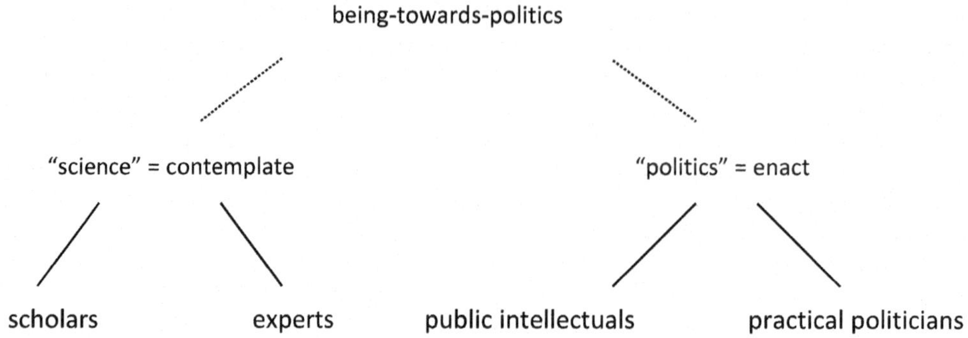

```
                          being-towards-politics
                         /                    \
              "science" = contemplate      "politics" = enact
                /        \                   /         \
         scholars      experts    public intellectuals   practical politicians
```

Figure 31.1 Orientations towards politics[12]

If we apply this to Weber's distinction, we end up with *four*, not two, positions (see Figure 31.1).

Weber's distinction between scholarship and politics is, at heart, a distinction between contemplating and enacting as vocational forms of life. Scholarship is about *knowing* as the goal, where politics is about *doing*, bringing about, making things happen.[13] If we replicate the contemplating/enacting binary within each camp, at the outer edges of the resulting diagram we find the "pure" contemplative scholars and the "pure" practical politicians, as well as two other intermediate positions. Within the scholarship camp, close to the pole of "pure" contemplation, but taking on board more of an orientation toward enacting, we have *experts*: knowing in order to do, producing knowledge that will be useful in making things happen. This is the pathway over which, Weber and Dewey would agree, causal knowledge about likely consequences would move, as academics with the situational capacity to produce compelling, well-vetted accounts turn their efforts toward making practical politicians understand their actual options. For Dewey, that kind of expert knowledge can also be helpful in constituting a public, insofar as it can help people to recognize that they do in fact form a public that shares an interest, but this runs into a problem of communicating specialized knowledge to a lay audience that is not in form dissimilar to the problem of "bridging the gap" (George 1993) between academics and policymakers.

This is where the fourth position, the *public intellectual*, really comes into its own. As an enactor first, the public intellectual is not in the first instance a scholar, but a practitioner: a role that is primarily focused on making things happen. Unlike the "pure" practical politician, however, the public intellectual is more directly connected to the world of scholarship; they might be a reflective practitioner, using scholarship to help elucidate and clarify practice, or a scholar-activist, drawing on scholarly conceptualizations to catalyze political activity. All four of these positions are roles, not concrete individuals; they delineate orientations and lines of action, and actual people might move more or less easily between them over time. As such it is entirely possible for someone who is a scholar sometimes to be a public intellectual at other times, and even a practical politician or an expert at other times. The point of the mapping is simply to differentiate between ways, or logics, of relating to the issues involved in both contemplating politics and enacting political programs. In many cases, it may be easier for a public intellectual to *also*, at other times, act as a scholar, so that she is in touch with contemporary academic discussions and can use them more effectively, but this is less a requirement than an "accidental" (from the perspective of the ideal-typical mapping) combination. Likewise, an expert need not *also* be a scholar, although many are.

The primary difference between the public intellectual and the expert lies in their respective relations to the two "pure" poles. The expert draws on scholarly knowledge and *tells* the practical politician what their options are, and the likely outcomes of each option; this is a vector for Weber's knowledge of consequences. The public intellectual draws on scholarly knowledge to help to constitute a public, performing the role that Dewey suggests is often fulfilled by artists; having done so, the active public can then issue demands which, I have argued, can complement the formally religious sources that Weber looks to in order to provide the ethical knowledge needed to prevent practical politicians from succumbing to the pursuit of power merely for its own sake. Experts can talk to practical politicians because they are the relative enactors of their groups; public intellectuals can talk to practical politicians, *and* to people in their everyday lives, inasmuch as they are all concerned with getting something done about a problem that they are facing. As such, the public intellectual constitutes a relevant public not simply as an intellectual exercise, but as connected to practical politicians—and, in particular, as connected to them as bearers of an ethical imperative to which the practical politicians must then respond. Constituting a Deweyian public means producing a vehicle for an ethical input into the political process, which the public intellectual herself might then serve as the spokesperson for.

Such is clearly the case with Ms. Thunberg, whose invitations to speak in global public fora and to a variety of world leaders is rather obviously related not simply to her notoriety as the originator of the school strike, but as the public face and inspirational leader of a global movement of social activists. Her constant refrain—"unite behind the science"—both establishes her as not a "pure" practical politician because of her expressed indebtedness to scholarly knowledge, and establishes her as not a "pure" scholar because she is, after all, a student and not a professional climate scientist. She is very clear about this:

> Some people say that I should be in school instead. Some people say that I should study to become a climate scientist so that I can "solve the climate crisis". But the climate crisis has already been solved. We already have all the facts and solutions.
>
> And why should I be studying for a future that soon may be no more, when no one is doing anything to save that future? And what is the point of learning facts when the most important facts clearly means nothing to our society?
>
> *(Thunberg 2019b)*

Elsewhere, Thunberg muses: "You say you hear us and that you understand the urgency. But no matter how sad and angry I am, I do not want to believe that. Because if you really understood the situation and still kept on failing to act, then you would be evil. And that I refuse to believe" (Thunberg 2019). Casting the issue as one of factual misunderstanding allows her to make an ethical claim without having to explicitly spell out an ethical position; the distinction she draws is between understanding the facts and being evil, and in (claiming to) "refuse to believe" that politicians are evil, she invokes, albeit tacitly and ambiguously, a morally ordered cosmos in which those politicians would not simply refuse to address the climate crisis, remaining instead narrowly focused on their partisan interests. In her speech to the US Congress, Thunberg cleverly combines a nod to the "American dream" with an invocation of what is perhaps Martin Luther King Jr.'s most well-known public address:

> I also have a dream: that governments, political parties and corporations grasp the urgency of the climate and ecological crisis and come together despite their differences – as you would in an emergency – and take the measures required to safeguard the conditions for a dignified life for everybody on earth.
>
> Because then – we millions of school striking youth – could go back to school.
>
> *(Thunberg 2019c)*.[14]

Rhetorically, such an appeal only has traction if the target audience can be swayed, either through the unlikely mechanism of persuasion, or the more plausible mechanism of "rhetorical coercion" (Krebs and Jackson 2007)—and rhetorical coercion, in turn, relies on a public that can police the boundaries of acceptable action and compel policymakers to respond to them. Respond to, and not stay within, precisely because a responsible politics does *not* require that ethical imperatives be precisely and narrowly enacted; indeed, that would be irresponsible politics, sacrificing an awareness of the tragic necessities of political action in favor of a false purity. The call to do something dramatic to address the climate crisis in its urgency doesn't immediately point to specific courses of action; it only puts an ethical demand on the table: *do something*.

Thunberg's speeches also feature no specific policy proposals, and the call to "unite behind the science" is less about accepting *particular* pieces of expert advice and more about accepting, as a non-political starting-point, the scientific *consensus* about the urgency of climate change. The ensuing politics would then have to be about sorting out which solution(s) to implement, and enforcing that decision. While it is likely that whatever policies emerged from such a process would not perfectly implement either the science or the ethical demand—they might not go far enough, they might feature compromises that water them down, they would certainly have to involve the use of coercive force against resistance, so the "dignified life for everybody on earth" would come at the cost of denying at least some people (and some lifeforms)[15] some of what they understand to be their rights and privileges and just desserts—that is just what Weber and Dewey would say is *always* true of responsible politics. By not acting as an expert, Thunberg is able both to call on politicians to listen to the experts, and to call into existence a public that can anchor an ethical demand for action.

Conclusion

Of course, Thunberg alone is not the sole cause or generator of the global movements around climate change. Innumerable academic experts have been communicating their findings and recommendations for decades, both in terms of specific policy proposals and, more broadly, in calls to alter our ways of being-on-the-planet in order to accord with one or another set of epistemic findings. This is the case, I would say, even for those speculative realisms and new materialisms that explicitly align themselves *against* the notion of "epistemic findings," seeking instead to base thinking on the wild provocations of "those more subtle connections or resonances whose effects are felt but not discrete" (Grove 2019, pt. 1498) and relying on neuroscientific and evolutionary-biological accounts to displace older, anthropocentric ontologies. If successful, such a project would close the gap between the two knowledges that produce a responsible politics, replacing ethical imperatives with an "ethic of cultivation" that "taps into contingent strains of attachment and presumptive generosity that are already there, seeking to amplify them and to adjust them to situations that sometimes change significantly" (Connolly 2017, 57). But I think this is a somewhat disingenuous hope, which fails to take seriously enough the ways that our knowledge *invariably* separates into distinct registers, a separation marked by the very grammar of ethical imperatives from epistemic facts: facts only have implications for action because we bring them into conversation with something else, some kind of purpose or intent that *discloses* the world rather than being a part of it.[16] Materialisms old and new join with various other sciences in generating, not ethical instructions, but factual baselines,[17] and while this is an important component of responsible political action, it cannot suffice on its own.

After all, scholarly expertise—the communication of epistemic findings about who we are and what kinds of effects we are having on the planet—can't *responsibly* dictate political outcomes. Here are the facts, the expert says, as they have been generated by our best scholarly efforts to produce valid knowledge. Here we stand, and we can do no other—in particular, what to do with those facts is not a call for a scholar or an expert to make. Instead, the ethical injunctions of a mobilized public or an elaborated theology (perhaps both) lay down a set of imperative demands for politicians to wrestle with. Perhaps the members of the public, or those who mobilize and effectively constitute the public, came to know those ethical injunctions from sitting in our classrooms or reading our elaborations of ethical perspectives and positions. Indeed, it would be *responsible* of us as teachers to make sure that our students were brought to encounter just these questions and just these issues. If we want politicians and, more broadly, citizens who are capable of responsible action, we should heed the calls issued by both Dewey and Weber—calls to us, calls to our scholarly natures, calls to our academic way of life—and recognize ourselves as a public united by an interest in making space for responsible politics by limiting our roles and separating our vocations. So that a little child may lead them, we need to get out of the way, and restrict ourselves to a supporting, or even to a backstage, role.

Notes

1. Thanks to all participants in the Münster workshop for helpful feedback on an earlier version. Constructive engagement welcome: ptjack@american.edu.
2. In Swedish, obviously, not in English.
3. In the German, *Mittel*, the same word translated "tool" above.
4. I hesitate over the term "consequentialist," because the term seems very close to the kind of ethical consequentialism often juxtaposed to a deontological ethics. Weber's point, however, is not that these are different ethical positions, but that a focus exclusively on outcomes and consequences is an *absence* of an ethical position.
5. "Properly" is key here, but also ambiguous, in terms of the very distinctions that Weber is drawing in these lectures. Indeed, I will argue that in delivering these lectures, Weber is occupying another category; the lectures are neither scholarship (which is how I will translate *Wissenschaft* in this essay) nor politics, but the public-constituting performances of a scholar-activist or a reflective practitioner. See below.
6. Weber refers here to the "war guilt" clause (article 231) of the Versailles Treaty concluding the First World War. The cause of truth, he suggests, would have been better served by a "all-around systematic inquiry by nonpartisans" than by a declaration based on simply reading German documents without context.
7. This is, of course, the thesis that Weber advances in *The Protestant Ethic and the "Spirit" of Capitalism*: the imperative quality of "working in a calling" comes from its linkage to notions of predestination and election, and even if we no longer remember that linkage, our everyday economic practices *presuppose* that linkage.
8. In this light, consider Walters and D'Aoust's (2015, 66) example of the role played by "Anarchopanda" in producing the public protesting in Montreal in 2012. Not coincidentally, perhaps, the character of Anarchopanda was played by an academic.
9. Along these lines, Dewey's often-misunderstood comment that "The man who wears the shoe knows best that it pinches and where it pinches, even if the expert shoemaker is the best judge of how the trouble is to be remedied" (Dewey 1985, 364) isn't a dismissal of expertise so much as its contextualization. In this respect, the implication that we have to "include others outside the academy in the process of knowledge production" (Abraham and Abramson 2017, 41) seems a little lacking in nuance. There are a lot of ways to include the community in the process of knowledge-production, and not all of them involve dissolving the boundaries of academia as a form of life.
10. Indeed, the differences between Dewey and Weber on this point seem comparatively minor. If there are different potential solutions to a problem, and if those solutions have different distributional consequences, even the politician in Dewey's account would have to decide which solution to implement, and then enforce that solution with state power if necessary. Dewey simply doesn't seem as *worried* about that use of coercive power as Weber is.
11. It is not necessary to decide in advance whether this is *always* the case—whether *every* self contains an internal other—in order to appreciate the insight that, at least some of the time, there is chocolate in the peanut butter and vice versa. In this case, I would argue, there most definitely is.

12 Variants of this figure have appeared in some of my previous writing, e.g. my contribution to (Hom 2017).
13 Yes, obviously Marx's infamous dictum in his eleventh thesis on Feuerbach speaks to this. But the kind of change that Marx is hoping for derives from a fairly sophisticated kind of scholarly knowledge about social relations, knowledge that comes from just the kind of mere interpretation that he wants to move beyond. So there's a place for Marx in this mapping as well: as a purveyor of the kind of expert knowledge that can advise political actors.
14 Here we might also pause to consider the powerful *imagery* of Thunberg's appeals: a young student, who "should" be in school, addressing rooms full of powerful men (and some women), and also addressing large crowds, *shaming* the adults by invoking a narrative of spoiled childhood innocence. In this way, Thunberg's physical bearing and presence tie her claims together in a way that positions her especially well to constitute an engaged public.
15 On the tensions in the era of the Anthropocene between safeguarding human life and safeguarding life more generally, see especially (Burke et al. 2016).
16 Wittgenstein: "the sense of the world must lie outside the world" (1961, para. 6.41).
17 Of course, one could also read the various strains of new materialism not as epistemic *sciences*, but as elaborations of ethical perspectives. That would make them exercises in (to follow McFague 1993 in drawing this distinction) the theology of nature, rather than the kinds of (atheistic) natural theologies they often purport to be. My suspicion is that as ethical tracts, they have a considerably smaller audience than more traditional theologies would and do, with a correspondingly smaller likelihood of producing a responsible political outcome.

References

Abbott, A. (2001). *Chaos of Disciplines*. Chicago: University of Chicago Press.
Abraham, K. J., and Abramson, Y. (2017). "A Pragmatist Vocation for International Relations: The (Global) Public and Its Problems." *European Journal of International Relations*, 23(1): 26–48.
Burke, A., Fishel, S., Mitchell, A., Dalby, S., and Levine, D. J. (2016). "Planet Politics: A Manifesto from the End of IR." *Millennium: Journal of International Studies*, 44(3): 499–523.
Connolly, W. (2017). *Facing the Planetary: Entangled Humanism and the Politics of Swarming*. Durham, NC: Duke University Press.
Dewey, J. (1978). *Reconstruction in Philosophy*. Electronic Edition. The Middle Works of John Dewey, 1899–1924, Volume 12, 1920. Carbondale and Edwardsville: Southern Illinois University Press.
Dewey, J. (1985). *The Public and its Problems*. Electronic Edition. The Later Works of John Dewey, 1925–1953, Volume 2, 1925–1927. Carbondale and Edwardsville: Southern Illinois University Press.
George, A. L. (1993). *Bridging the Gap: Theory and Practice in Foreign Policy*. Washington, DC: United States Institute of Peace Press.
Grove, J. V. (2019). *Savage Ecology*. Kindle edition. Durham, NC: Duke University Press.
Hom, Andrew R. (2017). "Forum: 'A Bridge Too Far'? On the Impact of Worldly Relevance on International Relations." *International Studies Review* 19(4): 692–721. https://doi.org/10.1093/isr/vix008.
Jackson, P. T. (2016). *The Conduct of Inquiry in International Relations*. 2nd ed. London: Routledge.
Jackson, P. T. (2017). "Causal Claims and Causal Explanation in International Studies." *Journal of International Relations and Development*, 20(4): 689–716.
Krebs, R. R., and Jackson, P. T. (2007). "Twisting Tongues and Twisting Arms: The Power of Political Rhetoric." *European Journal of International Relations*, 13(1): 35–66.
McFague, S. (1993). *The Body of God: An Ecological Theology*. Minneapolis, MN: Fortress Press.
Thunberg, G. (2019a). "Our House Is on Fire: Speech to the 2019 World Economic Forum, Davos, Switzerland." Greta-Speeches – FridaysForFuture. 2019. https://www.fridaysforfuture.org/greta-speeches.
Thunberg, G. (2019b). "Our Leaders Behave Like Children: Speech to the UN Secretary General, Katowice, Poland, 3 December 2018." Greta-Speeches – FridaysForFuture. 2019. https://www.fridaysforfuture.org/greta-speeches.
Thunberg, G. (2019c). "I Have a Dream That the Powerful Will Take the Climate Crisis Seriously." The Independent. September 19, 2019. https://www.independent.co.uk/voices/greta-thunberg-congress-speech-climate-change-crisis-dream-a9112151.html.

Thunberg, G. (2019). "Transcript: Greta Thunberg's Speech At The U.N. Climate Action Summit." NPR.Org. September 23, 2019. https://www.npr.org/2019/09/23/763452863/transcript-greta-thunbergs-speech-at-the-u-n-climate-action-summit.

Walters, W., and D'Aoust, A.-M. (2015). "Bringing Publics into Critical Security Studies: Notes for a Research Strategy." *Millennium: Journal of International Relations*, 44(1): 45–68.

Weber, M. (1994). *Wissenschaft Als Beruf - Politik Als Beruf*. Edited by W.J. Mommsen and W. Schluchter. Tübingen: J. C. B. Mohr.

Wittgenstein, L. (1958). *Philosophical Investigations*. Second. Oxford: Blackwell.

Wittgenstein, L. (1961). *Tractatus Logico-Philosophicus*. London: Routledge.

Woodward, J. (2005). *Making Things Happen: A Theory of Causal Explanation*. New York; Oxford: Oxford University Press.

32
RESPONSIBILITY AS POLITICAL BEAUTY?
Derrida's ethics of decision and the politics of responding to others
Stephan Engelkamp

Introduction[1]

In Summer 2015, the German Federal Government decided to suspend the so-called Dublin regulation, which stipulates that migrants need to apply for asylum in the EU country they first entered, and thus to effectively 'open'[2] German borders for refugees who were stuck in Hungary and other Central European countries. Roughly one million people eventually made it to German train stations in South Germany, from where they were then distributed to cities and villages all over the country. German Chancellor Angela Merkel later justified her decision to suspend the Dublin regulation as an exceptional humanitarian response to the concrete suffering of refugees. Initially, this response was met with an astonishing domestic support across the political spectrum, which manifested in a display of what was then termed 'welcoming culture'. Asked later about possible fears of German citizens faced with more than one million migrants from mostly Muslim societies and how she would accommodate such fears, Merkel responded that 'if we now have to start excusing ourselves for showing a friendly face in emergency situations, then this is no longer my country' (Mushaben 2017, 281). Her decision was even more noteworthy given the previous German policy of continuous neglect towards the growing refugee crisis at the EU's Southern borders. At the same time, a record number of more than 5,000 people have been lost in the Mediterranean Sea in 2016, making it the deadliest year on record according to the United Nations Refugee Agency (UNHCR 2016).

The German (and European) responses to the so-called refugee crisis in 2015 explicitly addresses the issue of taking responsibility towards others. This question confronts us with a political and moral dilemma: given constrained time and resources, how and to whom does one respond? Where does one's responsibility towards others begin, and where does it end, if at all? In this chapter, I shall argue that in order to address these questions, we need to take into account the interplay between narratives of responsibility, one's relationship with the other, and the ethics of decision underlying responsibility. How these elements interrelate will be reconstructed through an analysis of a guerilla campaign of the German performative art group *Center for Political Beauty*. I argue that this activist group transgressed conventional boundaries of political activism by playfully engaging the relationship between norms, facts, and fiction. However, their performances also demonstrate the limits of demanding an ethical response, as will become clearer by looking at the example of Merkel's political decisions to effectively 'open' borders and the German governments subsequent hardening of asylum policies.

The need to respond to the suffering of refugees and the politics of granting asylum highlight larger moral and political dilemmas of acting responsively: it confronts the self with the other who requires an immediate answer to her suffering. Jacques Derrida (1993; 1994; 1995) famously described this dilemma as an aporia, an impossible way with no easy or immediate solution, which nevertheless demands a decision, a response. I will draw on Derridean ethics to enquire the political and moral implications of the problem of responsibility, understood as a political and moral duty of care towards the suffering of the other. The case of the 2015 refugee crisis will serve as a heuristic to illustrate the larger aporias of taking responsibility. I am not suggesting Derrida's account are necessarily the only critical way to study the relationship between ethics and responsibility but his liminal approach makes some of the underlying ambiguities particularly visible (Campbell 1994).

My argument develops in three steps. The first part of this chapter starts with article 1 of the German State's basic law, which specifies the fundamental norm of protecting human dignity as a *duty* for German state authority. How migration and refugees are governed addresses the problem of human dignity and responsibility most explicitly. In this section, I shall discuss the problem of making a decision when faced with competing responsibilities through Mervyn Frost's discussion of ethical decisions as a dilemma between national citizen rights and universal human rights (Frost 1996; 2003). While the German basic law establishes the duty to respond firmly as a governmental duty, Frost conceives of the obligation to respond as an ethical decision of a (global) civil society, hence includes the individual citizen as a bearer of universal human rights. In a final step, I discuss how Frost's *solution* to the problem is complicated, but ultimately mirrored by a Derridean reading of responsibility as an aporic, impossible *decision to respond* which is bound in a double bind between different others.

The second part of this chapter presents the example of a German performance art group that engages the relationship between the moral demand to take responsibility, the politics of visibility and the ethics of making a decision. Drawing on a campaign enacted by the *Center for Political Beauty*, I shall illustrate how the problem of responsibility is represented through a performance that firstly makes the political dimension of taking a decision visible (Ansems de Vries and Guild 2019; Danewid 2017) and secondly seeks to link the moral dimension of the decision to a particular understanding of German historic responsibility. The activist group seeks to perform what they call acts of political beauty in order to reframe the problem of responding to others in a way that demands a political decision, both at state and the individual level. Consciously transgressing the boundary between fact and fiction, the purpose of their performances is to disrupt normal political discourse in order to advance a moral decision. While the campaign seems to offer a limited response, I argue that this cannot solve the aporic structure of making a responsible decision.[3]

In the third and concluding part of this paper, I critically enquire the sustainability of the German response towards refugees. Here, I note how – somewhat paradoxically – a reconfigured narrative of responsibility may sustain policies that contradict the initial moral demands towards the other. I close with the observation that the ethics of decision and the responsibility narrative perversely helped to enable legitimating the effective closure of German borders. The aporic moment of responding to others seems to be difficult to sustain, and a discussion of its political implications has been largely avoided in the case of the German response to the refugee crisis. I conclude that the responsiveness towards refugees is fragile, it is a contested terrain and always susceptible to becoming reincorporated into normal politics.[4]

The problem of responding to others

Article 1 of the Basic Law for the Federal Republic of Germany states:

1. *Human dignity shall be inviolable. To respect and protect it shall be the duty of all state authority.*
2. *The German people therefore acknowledge inviolable and inalienable human rights as the basis of every community, of peace and of justice in the world.*
3. *The following basic rights shall bind the legislature, the executive and the judiciary as directly applicable law.*

Article 1 seems to be straight forward in grounding all practices and policies of state authority in human dignity as a norm which is deemed fundamental and universal. It lays out the foundation of a moral and political responsibility on the part of the German State as it identifies 'state authority' as the actor which is obligated to respond to violations of human dignity. The fundamental value of human dignity for the German basic law is, of course, rooted in the extraordinary violence committed by Germany during the Nazi period. The responsibility of the state to respect and protect human dignity is the direct result of the German past, a moral obligation that seeks to redeem German statehood as part of a liberal and modern 'audience of normals' (Adler-Nissen 2014; see also Engelkamp and Offermann 2012). It is the fundamental political value of German politics that renders all other norms meaningful in the first place.

Article 1 does not, however, specify the contours or limits of German responsibility. In the ensuing part of this section, I discuss Mervyn Frost's writing on universal ethics and human rights who seems to offer a mechanism of how to arrive at an ethically informed decision in international politics. In the next subsection, I will then use Derrida's writings on responsibility in order to critically engage with Frost's approach. I argue that both arrive at a precarious 'solution' to the moral perils of making a decision by establishing a moral hierarchy among competing others.

Frost: hierarchies of responsibility

In his work on international ethics, Mervyn Frost (2003) addresses the problem of how to make an ethical decision explicitly; his key question is: how do we respond to the world out there if faced with competing demands of acting responsively? One of his empirical examples concerns the question of what one's moral obligations to strangers are. He is interested in formulating a response to the problem how to square competing responsibilities towards one's own society as a member of a national community vis-à-vis one's obligation as a citizen of the world and bearer of universal human rights. Ultimately, he arrives at a possible solution by establishing a hierarchy of values between the two competing sets of obligations. For Frost (2003), the rights one exercises as a citizen of a nation-state are dependent on the more fundamental universal rights one holds as a human being (compare the respective chapters by Busser, Sutch, and Beardsworth in this volume). From this perspective, an infringement on the latter rights, for example, human rights abuses, wherever they may take place, are a direct assault on one's universal rights as a human being. As a result, an ethical response to the dilemma of mutual and possibly contradictory obligations is for the individual to advocate for the more fundamental human rights within the nation-state (see also Markus Kornprobst's chapter in this volume).

This solution is informed by Frost's interpretive and practice-based approach: he begins his ethical approach towards responsibility by noting what is accepted practice in international politics, and also by reflecting on his own normative understandings that follow from his personal situation as a citizen and as a bearer of universal rights. At the same time, the limits of responding to others are defined by the norms accepted as universal and binding by the global community of citizens. For example, in the case of the refugee crisis, this would entail that others have the fundamental right to move wherever they wish, thereby transgress national borders and seek asylum. It does not follow, however, that the rights of citizens should be limited or curtailed. It could be still possible, for example, to deny refugees socio-economic benefits that are reserved for the community of citizens of a nation-state. At the same time, once people were granted the right to live within a community of citizens, they should have the right to join this community at some point in time (Frost 2003).

There are several problems with Frost's constitutive approach. While it is consistent from a liberal and ethical point of view and informed by an understanding of ethics that derives from social and normative practice (Erskine 2013), the question remains open how the actual decision to respond is actually to be made, especially in cases where parts of the host society are divided about the moral reasoning about how to act (Campbell 1994). And even if there were a social consensus about the moral principle, it is still unclear how this obligation could or should be translated into political practice at governmental level. His approach does not consider the possibility of an aporic dilemma that may arise in practice when it comes to making or implementing an ethical decision. An apparently alternative approach to the problem of responsibility has been formulated in Derrida's work on the ethics on decision, in which his understanding of aporias is instrumental.

Derrida: responsibility as sacrifice and gift relation

Are there limits to our duty to respond to others, and if so, where does it end? How to respond morally to the suffering of others? This dilemma has been spelled out most clearly in Jacques Derrida's writings about ethics. Derrida maintains that responsibility entails an impossible path, what he terms an aporic situation. Rather than leaving the responsible person with a good conscience (Butler 2004; Zehfuss 2004, 2007), acting responsible, for Derrida, demands making a decision between bad alternatives. Responding to strangers illustrates this dilemma particularly well. The example of European refugee policy seems to highlight the moral and political dilemmas of adjudicating between competing sets of responsibility. For instance, the responsibility one owes towards one's own society as a citizen may at some point clash with the responsibility toward the other, here the refugee, or, more precisely, towards a fundamental set of norms that define one as bearer of universal human rights. Derrida conceptualizes this dilemma in terms of a sacrifice which eventually constitutes a gift-relationship.

According to Derrida (1995, 25), '[i]n order to be responsible it is necessary to respond to or to answer to what being responsible means'. For if the concept of responsibility implies involvement in action, 'a *praxis*, a *decision* that exceeds simple conscience or simple theoretical understanding' (ibid), this requires a decision, responsible action, to answer *consciously*. Therefore, in debates concerning responsibility one must always take into account this original and irreducible complexity that links theoretical consciousness to practical conscience (ethical, legal, political), if only to avoid 'the arrogance of so many "clean consciences"' (Derrida 1995, 25).

To illustrate this point, Derrida (1995) refers to the biblical example of Abraham, who is asked by God to sacrifice his son Isaac. This request puts Abraham in an impossible situation, as he may not explain the reasons why he agrees to obey to God's demand and sacrifice his son: this puts himself in an unsolvable conflict with the competing duties that he aims responding to. In responding to God, he must disregard all human ethics. The example of Abraham's sacrifice characterizes for Derrida the main conceptual feature of responsibility. The aporic situation is nothing other than sacrifice, the 'revelation of conceptual thinking at its limit' (Derrida 1995, 68). Here, we find the relationship between a singular, absolute duty, which the responsibility towards an absolute Other, e.g. God, the Good, or a loved One, and the general duty towards human ethics, the responsibility towards all other others, e.g. society, social norms, even the law. In the event of an aporic decision, human ethics needs to be sacrificed in the name of absolute responsibility (Derrida 1995, 66-67). For Derrida, this example illustrates the conceptual structure of responsibility as a social relationship: it constitutes a double bind. Responsibility binds one to the singular, absolute Other, in his example, God. But at the same time, one is also bound to others, to the multitude of other people, as the duty to respect the ethical order is also a general and universal responsibility. Derrida's point is that Abraham, in the moment he decides to sacrifice his own son to obey his duty to God, he also sacrifices his ethics, but this decision would be itself the result of an ethical decision. He would betray his duty to social ethics out of duty to an absolute Other.

Irresponsibility occurs if demands of responsibility are not contextualised in a discussion of what responsibility means. At the same time, the activating of responsibility in an act, a praxis or a decision will always take place before and beyond any theoretical or thematic determination (Derrida 1995, 26). Hence, there are no short-cuts to identify what responsible action may mean in practice. For Derrida, it all comes down to the act of responding, to answering to the other, irrespective of the fact if the actual decision leaves one guilty. While this entails submitting oneself to the other's gaze, responsibility paradoxically also contains the structure of a secret (Derrida 1995, 27). Derrida refers to the metaphor of a gift that needs to be kept secret in order to truly remain a gift. The gift needs to abnegate itself, the true gift requires to sacrifice itself, it needs to be kept secret as it would otherwise create a relationship of mutual dependency (Derrida 1995, 29-31). Abraham does not know why God demands him to sacrifice his son. Once he is decided to obey to God, he still cannot be sure if God will intervene and release him from his duty. His God does it, of course, the sacrifice of Isaac in a *holocaust* [sic] is stopped by godly intervention and Abraham is allowed to sacrifice a lamb instead. What is important to note here is how Abraham's willingness to sacrifice his son establishes the absolute gift-relationship with God, the absolute Other.

Derrida presents the story of Abraham as a model case for an aporic moment of taking responsibility. Abraham needs to enter into a relation with singularity, in this case God, but it could be as well the Good, the State, or a loved one. In each case, the moment of decision puts the one who takes responsibility in a liminal situation, where she has to decide between the duty to a singular Other and the responsibility towards the more general others, the multitude of others, society, the moral order. Derrida's more general point here is that the structure of responsibility is ultimately predicated on this liminal, aporic experience of decision. This makes truly acting responsibly (for most of us) impossible, as embracing one form of responsibility makes us fail embracing the other dimension. The problem of ir/responsibility is that it necessarily leaves one guilty. One can never conform to all others who may merit one's response, still, one needs to decide whom to respond to. This double bind is, for Derrida, impossible to resolve in any ethically satisfiable way.

Discussing Derrida's approach to the ethics of responsibility may require a justification as it appears to be quite fatalistic and extremely pessimist. Utilitarian, Cosmopolitan and feminist thinkers, for instance, may disagree with his conclusion that ethical decisions are ultimately impossible in principle. However, the theoretical benefit of a Derridean approach lies in its liminality – it discusses the moral implications of responsible decision-making at its limits. His example of Abraham's predicament is constructed to make the fallacies of decision visible. But moreover, Derridean ethics do not stop at a single aporic moment in time. The point is to recognize that human suffering is a persistent condition of life and that responding to it remains a moral duty. While we may be bound to fail in our attempts to live up to the demands of the Other, we still have to try and make our decisions.

Derrida's example of Abraham's sacrifice does however seem to be predicated on a solution to the problem of the aporic decision. Abraham's dilemma is eventually resolved when he acknowledges that his obligation to God does not, in fact, contradict his obligations to family and society.[5] The obligation to God rather renders his other obligations possible in the first place. Obeying to God's demand, Abraham realizes, is what renders all other social and moral responsibilities meaningful in the first place. Thus, it is through establishing a moral hierarchy between his competing obligations that Abraham manages to arrive at the morally 'right' response – and is redeemed by God, who then refrains from his demand of a human sacrifice.

This example seems to show that there may be a way to accommodate the problem of making a responsible decision once a hierarchy of values can be established between competing and possibly contradicting ethical demands. Interestingly, Frost arrives at a similar solution to the problem of adjudicating between competing sets of responsibilities when he argues that it is the universality of human rights that render all rights as bearer of national citizenship meaningful. The actual process to arrive at such a hierarchy may be highly contested, however, as the case of the German response to the refugee crisis in 2015 seems to illustrate; and it may very well fail. Before I turn to this example, however, I shall illustrate how the underlying dilemma to act responsibly has been performed in activist art which suggests a performative way to establish 'political beauty' through making an ethical decision.

Responding to others as political beauty

The *Center for Political Beauty* is a German group of political activists that uses forms of performance art to advocate humanitarian aims in German and international politics. Since 2009, the group addressed a variety of controversial political issues, ranging from denouncing German weapon sales to Saudi-Arabia, to the criticism of UN and Western failure to prevent the massacres of Srebrenica, to their most elaborated campaign of advocating for a more liberal and open European migration policy. Presenting themselves as an 'assault team' for the advocacy of 'political beauty' and 'human greatness' (Ruch 2015a, 120ff.; Center for Political Beauty 2017), the group explicitly links its political action to the memory and historic background of the Shoa. From this, they argue, should not only follow a sensibility or critical engagement of the past on the part of German society (*Vergangenheitsbewältigung*), but a moral responsibility to take political action today and respond to human suffering through more humanitarian policies (see also Geis and Pfeifer 2017).

The concept of political beauty relates to a utopian understanding of politics as an epic drama around the formulation and enactment of great humanitarian ideas (Debord 1996; Ruch 2015b). Faced with an affluent society which would – in theory – have the means to prevent genocide, global hunger or humanitarian crises, but lacks the political will to act, the *Center for Political Beauty* aims to disrupt what they perceive as a state of political apathy through spectacular art performances (Ruch 2015a,b).

The activist group uses three main discursive strategies to advance its political message: First, they use performance art to disrupt ritualized forms of remembrance in order to politicize memory. Seeking to avoid narrative closure through a ritual construction of a good conscience, their performances aim at addressing the aporic dimension of responsibility in the face of the German Nazi past by re-configuring the meaning of such rituals (Laudenbach 2015). Second, overstepping symbolic and material borders is a key discursive strategy to disrupt normalised meanings of the relationship between self and other (Rauterberg 2015; Süddeutsche Zeitung

2014; ZEIT 2014b). Recognising the power of borders for constructing identities and legitimating identity-based policies, the violation of borders serves to highlight the symbolic and actual violence which these borders exercise (Shapiro 1997; Jacobsen 2015). Third, the *Center for Political Beauty* engages in a politics of visibility through performative art by blending facts and fiction with the aim of making the suffering of others visible and the hypocrisies of political structures explicit (Popp 2014). Together, these strategies aim at politicising a discourse about the meaning of German (and European) responsibility, stigmatising the cynicism of political apathy within society and politics.

The following example illustrates one of these strategies, the politics of visibility, through a study of a performance that seeks to expose and subvert the moral underpinnings of the discourse about migration and German responsibility in the so-called refugee crisis. While there have been several campaigns since 2014, I focus on the '*Kindertransporthilfe*' campaign as it exposes a key aspect of the German response to refugees, namely the attempt to determine the limits of responsibility through quantifiable means and thus enable a limited response to a supposedly global refugee crisis. I enquire the utopian potential of their campaign but also raise more critical questions about its potential limits.

Faking (and remembering) a rescue operation

In May 2014, a website went online that asked German families to volunteer as foster families for children from Syria in acute need of help during the ongoing civil war. The so-called '*Kindertransporthilfe des Bundes*' website (federal children transportation help, '1aus100' 2014) purported to be an Emergency Program initiated by the German Federal Ministry of Family Affairs, which would admit 55,000 Syrian children to Germany on a temporary basis. This number would amount to one percent of all Syrian children in danger. The initiative was said to be predicated on the British rescue of Jewish children from Nazi Germany ('*Kindertransporte*') during the 1930s. Once the website went online and was promoted in several leading German newspapers, hundreds of German families actually volunteered to take in refugee children from Syria. The only problem was that the German government never initiated this program in the first place.

The initiative was developed by the *Center for Political Beauty* as a ready-to-use emergency programme for the German Federal Government. The webpage was designed in a highly professional manner, quoting the legal foundations of the program, advertising video clips and showing iconic pictures of brown-haired Syrian children holding signs of then-Minister for Family Affairs, Manuela Schwesig (SPD), thanking her for 'saving' them. It was accompanied by a booklet issuing a welcoming speech by Schwesig and advertisements for media outlets. The resulting public attention put the Ministry in a very awkward position, as it was required to publicly distance itself from the campaign. The government eventually invited representatives of the *Center*, joined by two survivors of the historic British project to save Jewish children, to a meeting in the Federal Chancellery (Pantel 2014; ZEIT 2014a).

While the German government had in fact agreed to admit 10,000 Syrian refugees from the civil war, arguing that 'Germany is already doing what it can', a debate about the limits of German responsibility towards Syrian children ensued quickly. The quantitative dimension of the government's response to the Syrian civil war was highlighted through the activists' justification of the number of Syrian children that could be 'saved': while UNICEF estimated 5.5 million children were in acute danger, the website somewhat bluntly declared that 'we cannot help all the people in Syria who deserve aid. But as a society we can help one in a hundred children.' (1aus100 2014).

The next phase of the campaign carried the exposition of the ethical dilemma of this logic to extremes. The group performed an X Factor-style selection process with purportedly real photographs of Syrian children at risk to determine which children would be rescued. The audience was asked to join a tele-voting process to cast their vote for their favorites. Asked about the cynicism of their performance, the campaign organizer, Philipp Ruch, responded that saving 55,000 children would be less cynical than doing nothing. However, 'helping people entails making a choice. This leaves one dirty but one needs to take the risk' (Thimm 2014, my translation).

The cynical performance of making a decision in terms of a numbers game, enacted as a tele-voting may reduce the children to the state of victims, affirming their status as mere extras in an art performance. This aspect has been widely criticized in German media (e.g. Lemke-Matwey 2017). On the other hand, the performance raises a set of serious questions about the actual response of the German government towards the humanitarian crisis in Syria. By deliberately transgressing the symbolic borders of ethical conventions within the discourse on Germany's refugee and asylum policy, the activists demonstrated the inherent aporia of formulating a limited response to the situation of refugees. At the same time, the campaign exposed the German policy of accepting 10,000 children from Syria as a cynical fix to a more fundamental ethical problem. However, as Derrida noted, if one cannot respond to all others, one still needs to make a decision in responding. This decision will not leave one with a good conscience. In fact, what is performed here, the attempt to arrive at a quantifiable response to human suffering which is 'better than doing nothing', is eventually an impossible decision to make.

Through the historical analogy of the British initiative to save Jewish children, the performance attempted to connect the current situation in Syria with the memory of and international response to the Shoa, thus critically politicizing the particular way Germany had previously responded to the human suffering in Syria. This framing of the performance creates a direct link to a historic period in time which is instrumental for the identity-formation of the Federal Republic as a moral community and which eventually led to the paramount importance of human dignity for the German basic law. By strategically reframing the context of historical memory, the performance makes the aporic character of taking responsibility visible. At the same time, however, it suggests a limited solution to the ethical dilemma of responding. The historical analogy points towards the possibility of arriving at a limited response in the face of structural violence. While an important moral response, the British rescue of German children was limited, of course, as, the performance suggests, would be the German response to help Syrian children. Nevertheless, even a limited response would constitute an act of political beauty, in spite of the fact that it is ultimately irresponsible.

The performance shares some similarities with Derrida's example of Abraham's sacrifice discussed above. While it highlights the moral dilemma of selecting children to be saved, the structure of the example is different in one notable aspect. While Abraham was asked to sacrifice his son, German society was asked to select one in a hundred Syrian children to be saved while the others would be left in danger. But in contrast to Abraham, who would be spared by God to actually sacrifice his son once he made the 'right decision', the art performance can only avoid the ethical aporia if all children would eventually be saved, which would constitute the ultimate gift, an absolute (and possibly utopian) act of political beauty.

What were the effects of this performance? To what extent, if any, did the campaign succeed in sparking a larger debate about the moral and possibly aporic implications of responding to others? In fact, there was surprisingly little discussion in Germany about the ethical ramifications of the initial German response to the Syrian refugee 'problem', taking in 10,000 refugees following international legal regulations. The performance raised attention to the German response and forced the government to explain its policy in public. At the same time, the *Center of Political Beauty* demonstrated that individual citizens would be willing to take personal responsibility by acting as foster families, which is quite remarkable in its own right. However, the debate about the art performance was soon overtaken by real events. Looking at the example of the actual German (and European) response to the so-called refugee crisis during the summer of 2015 points to the limits of making a responsible decision and, possibly, the utopian idea of ir/responsibility as 'political beauty'.

The fragility of responsibility

When Chancellor Merkel and the German government decided to allow refugees to come to Germany in one summer in 2015, this was framed as a moral response in a context of exceptional politics. Merkel later justified her decision to suspend the Dublin convention and 'open the borders' as an exceptional humanitarian response to the concrete suffering of refugees. Initially, this response was met with overwhelming support from German society, which manifested in an unlikely display of what was then termed 'welcoming culture' (Mushaben 2017). People lined up at train stations to assist newly arriving refugees, cheering and applauding to amazed migrants. Chancellor Merkel's decision has been heralded by many as having 'saved the soul of Europe' (Kehlmann 2016; Lebor 2015). At the same time, she confronted stern criticism from right-wing populists and conservatives in Germany and abroad. While the German chancellor's decision was also met with critique, the dominant international response was over-all positive. Following the election of Donald Trump as US president, some international media even hailed her as the new 'leader of the free world', who saved 'Western conscience' (Lebor 2015).

At the same time, however, the German government was one of the key actors within the European Union pushing for a deal with the Turkish government which eventually led to the effective closing of flight paths for refugees. While the German government lobbied – largely without success – for a European regime to redistribute refugees across the continent, Germany quietly benefitted from the gradual closing of borders in Central European countries, leading eventually to a steep drop in numbers of refugees arriving in Germany and other West European countries (Kenan 2016, 2018). Two years after the summer of 2015, Germany was again effectively isolated from refugees, who are, once again, forced to attempt to choose the most dangerous routes via the Mediterranean Sea or end up in camps in Turkey, Greece or elsewhere in Central Europe (Danewid 2017; Trilling 2018).

The discursive strategy of the *Center for Political Beauty* aimed at exposing the aporia of trying to quantify, and hence limit, the response to the suffering of others. With hindsight, one needs to conclude that this strategy did not succeed. In contrast, the political debate about the summer of 2015 revolved around attempts at arriving at a fixed number of refugees Germany would be able to accept. Especially Horst Seehofer (CSU), the leader of the Christian Social Democrats, the Bavarian coalition partner of Merkel's Christian Democrats, made the case of pressing Merkel to accept an upper limit of refugees (*Obergrenze*). Merkel responded to such attempts by basically avoiding the debate and deferring the question altogether by quoting international and European legal obligations. After pointedly dropping her by now famous slogan 'wir schaffen das' ('we can do this'), relating to an optimism that Germany can succeed in managing the refugee crisis and integrating one million people into German society, she now maintains that 'immigration cannot take place beyond sustainable limits' and that Germany and the EU need to address supposed root causes of migration. At the same time, her government's practical policies worked to effectively limit the numbers of refugees able to reach German borders.

In fact, it even seems that the narrative about Germany's moral decision paradoxically worked to legitimize Germany's and the EU's ensuing hardening of border policies which helped to limit the flow of migrants to Europe. The migration deal with Turkey took place in a context of growing domestic unease following the summer of 2015. Since then, German asylum laws have hardened more and more, partly as a result of sexual assaults from men of supposedly North African descent and first instances of migrants committing terrorist acts within Germany. While this seems to point to a retour of the securitization discourse around migration (Aradau 2004; Aradau, Huysmans, and Squire 2010; Huysmans 2000, 2006; van Munster 2010; Waever 1995), especially from predominantly Muslim-majority countries, the overall narrative stays intact. Germany still poses as a champion of a liberal immigration policy in Europe, which is in principle open to refugees. However, after having acted responsibly, now it is argued that Germany needs to make a decision to effectively limit the number of refugees in the name of social coherence and security.

This is the opposite of Derridean ethics: it leaves one with a good conscience, while the actual practices, structures and policies of the German government rather point towards a reversal of the initial welcoming culture. The difficult ethical question about the limits and effects of one's responsibility gets, again, deferred and depoliticized through an approach of governing migration at a distance (the Turkey deal, hot spots, FRONTEX, see e.g. Ansems de Vries and Guild 2019; Carling and Hernández-Carretero 2011; Neal 2009). While this set of policies is presented as an ethical decision, protecting the supposed coherence and security of 'Germany', it appears as a reversal of the ethical decision, as laid out by Derrida or demanded by the activists of the *Center for Political Beauty*. Ironically, this turn of the narrative is further *sustained* through the background of the previous decision to open borders.

It appears to me that the German government faced an aporic moment in the summer of 2015. After a brief moment of responding unconditionally towards the other, actual political practice soon transformed this response into a more pragmatic and limited approach, turning the ethical dilemma into a technical problem of governing others (Bigo 2001, 2002). To some extent, a hierarchy of values has been re-configured, now valuing the 'coherence' and 'security' of 'Germany' as supreme, again avoiding the duty to respond to the problem of the human dignity of others. While this assessment is not meant to dismiss the events and decisions taken in 2015 as meaningless, it is notable that there has been no larger debate about the ethics of decision and the meaning of German (and European) ir/responsibility.

Conclusion

This chapter has argued that making a responsible decision may entail implications that are highly ambiguous from a moral and political perspective. The approaches to international ethics that have been discussed in this chapter, both Mervyn Frost's take on global human rights and Jacques Derrida's aporic perspective on responding to others, at some point tend to reconcile these tensions by establishing a specific hierarchy of values that provide some form of solution to this dilemma. What this may entail in practice has been illustrated by a case study on performance art in the German context.

What are the effects or possibilities of forms of 'artivism' as displayed by groups like the *Center for Political Beauty*? Can art incite a debate about the aporias of responsibility at all? The idea of political beauty, which is very close to Frost's hierarchy of universal values, is designed to provoke and subvert political apathy. It may function as an important discursive resource for raising awareness and sympathy towards the suffering of others in the short-term but is possibly not enough to sustain responsible decisions in Derrida's sense. This would require a continuous engagement with the other, what Derrida termed a continuous work of mourning, and a larger societal debate about structural forms of violence and German and European ir/responsibility (Derrida 1993, 1995). From Frost's perspective (2003), this would have been a requirement, as well, for individual citizens of a global civil society to recognize how the fundamental importance of global human rights requires them to respond to the suffering of distant others. However, this debate never really took place. Rather, the German response followed, somewhat paradoxically, the logic of the *Kindernothilfe* program: the effective opening of German borders is presented as an exceptional and effectively limited response to an emergency situation, as a supplement. The larger ethical questions of what it means to respond to others that may have followed from this decision has been deferred, in fact quietly abandoned, without engaging the dilemma of its possibly irresponsible dimension. Ironically, the German response, taking in the refugees who were very visibly already at the border in order to avoid an imminent human catastrophe, seems to have been accepted as exceptional and then turned into a discursive resource for a responsibility-with-a-good-conscience (Zehfuss 2004, 2007).

Derrida proposed to conceptualize responsibility as a sacrifice, situated between the need to respond to a singular other, and the responsibility toward a multitude of others. This places the individual who wants to act responsibly in an impossible situation: one is bound to fail in the act/practice of (not) responding. To some extent, this is what we can see in the political response to the European refugee crisis: in an aporic moment in Summer 2015, the German government responded to the humanitarian crisis with an exceptional decision. This created a narrative about German responsibility towards refugees which left the audience with a good conscience. The good conscience of having responded ethically even helped to legitimate the effective closing of borders. Rather than sustaining the work of mourning and politicizing the individual act of making responsible (if impossible) decisions, responsibility was turned into a program: Germany took in a million refugees, but then needed to find a technical solution to the problem. However, if Germany's absolute other is the responsibility to defend the principle of respecting human dignity, as stipulated in article 1 of the basic law, then it failed in the moment when the German government went back to normal politics of governing migration as a security issue.

Notes

1 Earlier versions of this draft have been presented at the EWIS workshop on 'Responsibility in International Relations Theory' in Cardiff (June 2017), at the EISA conference in Barcelona (September 2017) and the BISA workshop on Pessimism in IR in London (October 2017). The author wishes to thank all participants as well as the authors and editors of this volume for their valuable comments.
2 The idea of 'opening' borders is more of a figure of speech here. Borders remained open throughout the so-called 'refugee crisis' – however, the Dublin regulation made it practically impossible for most refugees to reach countries such as Germany.
3 Note that I do not make a causal claim about the effects of the art group's performances and the subsequent political decision of the German government to open the borders for refugees in summer 2015, thereby also changing the narrative towards refugees and German responsibility. I argue, instead, that both instances are predicated on a similar, constitutive relationship between responsibility, visibility, and the ethics of decision.
4 A note about my ethical stand is in order here, as it informs my speaking position and hence should be made explicit and reflected upon critically (Ackerly and True 2008). I agree with Frost (2003) to the extent that the normative dilemma of being both a citizen of a nation-state, and hence being responsible for the well-being of one's society, and being a bearer of what some call universal and indivisible human rights cannot absolve the citizen from responding to the suffering of others in a humanitarian way. This normative position makes me a critic of the European Union's (and the German government's) stance towards refugees and asylum. I am not convinced that an affluent society can or should limit its response towards refugees through policies such as the current regime of border management, which entails the

fortification of borders, the criminalization of migrants or the creation of hot-spots to keep away people who want to enter Europe. Hence, I share many of the political assumptions of the *Center of Political Beauty*, even though I am more skeptical about some of the means they employ, and the effects their performance may have, as will become more evident in the following.

5 I would like to thank David Karp for making this point clearer to me.

References

Ackerly, B., and True, J. (2008). "Reflexivity in Practice: Power and Ethics in Feminist Research on International Relations." *International Studies Perspectives*, 10(4): 693–707.

Adler-Nissen, R. (2014). "Stigma Management in International Relations: Transgressive Identities, Norms and Order in International Society." *International Organization*, 68(4): 143–176.

Ansems de Vries, L., and Guild, E. (2019). "Seeking Refuge in Europe: Spaces of Transit and the Violence of Migration Management." *Journal of Ethnic and Migration Studies*, 45(12): 2156–2166.

Aradau, C. (2004). "The Perverse Politics of Four-Letter Words: Risk and Pity in the Securitization of Human Trafficking." *Millennium: Journal of International Studies*, 33(2): 251–277.

Aradau, C., Huysmans, J., and Squire, V. (2010). "Acts of European Citizenship: A Political Sociology of Mobility." *Journal of Common Market Studies*, 48(4): 945–965.

Bigo, D. (2001). "Migration and Security." In Guiraudon, V., and Joppke, C., eds., *Controlling a New Migration World*: 121–149. London: Routledge.

Bigo, D. (2002). "Security and Immigration. Toward a Critique of the Governmentality of Unease." *Alternatives: Global - Local - Political*, 27(1): 63–92.

Butler, J. (2004). *Precarious Life: The Power of Mourning and Violence*. London and New York: Verso.

Campbell, D. (1994). The Deterritorialization of Responsibility: Lavinas, Derrida, and Ethics After the End of Philosophy. *Alternatives: Global - Local - Political*, 19(4): 455–484.

Carling, J., and Hernández-Carretero, M. (2011). "Protecting Europe and Protecting Migrants? Strategies for Managing Unauthorised Migration from Africa." *British Journal of Politics & International Relations*, 13(1): 42–58.

Danewid, I. (2017). "White Innocence in the Black Mediterranean: Hospitality and the Erasure of History." *Third World Quarterly*, 38(7): 1647–1689.

Debord, G. (1996). *Die Gesellschaft des Spektakels*. Berlin: Edition Tiamat.

Derrida, J. (1993). *Aporias*. Stanford: Stanford University Press.

Derrida, J. (1994). *Specters of Marx: The State of the Debt, the Work of Mourning and the New International*. New York: Routledge.

Derrida, J. (1995). *The Gift of Death*. Chicago: University of Chicago Press.

Engelkamp, S., and Offermann, P. (2012). "It's a Family Affair: Germany as a Responsible Actor in Popular Culture Discourse." *International Studies Perspectives*, 13(3): 235–253.

Erskine, T. (2013). "Normative International Relations Theory." In Dunne, T., Kurki, M., and Smith, S., eds., *International Relations Theories. Discipline and Diversity*: 36–58. Oxford: Oxford University Press.

Frost, M. (1996). *Ethics in International Relations*. Cambridge: Cambridge University Press.

Frost, M. (2003). *Constituting Human Rights. Global Civil Society and the Society of Democratic States*. New York: Routledge.

Geis, A. and Pfeifer, H. (2017). "Deutsche Verantwortung in der "Mitte der Gesellschaft" aushandeln? Über Politisierung und Entpolitisierung der deutschen Außenpolitik." *Politische Vierteljahresschrift, Sonderheft*, 52: 218–243.

Huysmans, J. (2000). "The European Union and the Securitization of Migration." *Journal of Common Market Studies*, 38(5): 751–777.

Huysmans, J. (2006). *The Politics of Insecurity: Fear, Migration and Asylum in the EU*. London: Routledge.

Jacobsen, L. (2015). "Und in Berlin fällt ein Zaun um." *ZEIT ONLINE*, June 21, 2015. http://www.zeit.de/kultur/2015-06/fluechtinge-leichen-zentrum-fuer-politische-schoenheit-berlin (accessed May 29, 2017).

Kehlmann, D. (2016). "Angela Merkel's Unpopular Goodness." *The New York Times*, April 1, 2016. https://www.nytimes.com/2016/04/02/opinion/angela-merkels-unpopular-goodness.html?mcubz=3 (accessed September 8, 2017).

Kenan, M. (2016). "Europe's Immigration Bind: How to Act Morally While Heeding the Will of Its People." *The Guardian*, January 31, 2016. https://www.theguardian.com/commentisfree/2016/jan/31/europe-bind-act-morally-on-immigrants-heed-its-citizens (accessed June 12, 2018).

Kenan, M. (2018). "How We Colluded in Fortress Europe." *The Guardian*, June 10, 2018. https://www.theguardian.com/commentisfree/2018/jun/10/sunday-essay-how-we-colluded-in-fortress-europe-immigration?CMP=share_btn_fb (accessed June 12, 2018).

Laudenbach, P. (2015). "Tote Flüchtlinge, mitten in Berlin." *Süddeutsche Zeitung Online*, June 15, 2015. http://www.sueddeutsche.de/kultur/umstrittene-kunstaktion-tote-fluechtlinge-mitten-in-berlin-1.2521823 (accessed May 29, 2017).

Lebor, A. (2015). "Angela Merkel: Europe's Conscience in the Face of a Refugee Crisis." *Newsweek*, September 5, 2015. http://www.newsweek.com/2015/09/18/angela-merkel-europe-refugee-crisis-conscience-369053.html (accessed September 8, 2017).

Lemke-Matwey, C. (2017). "Verkauft uns nicht für dumm!" *ZEIT ONLINE*, January 23, 2017. http://www.zeit.de/2017/02/kunst-politik-krisen-aesthetik-politisierung/komplettansicht (accessed May 29, 2017).

Mushaben, J. M. (2017). *Becoming Madam Chancellor: Angela Merkel and the Berlin Republic*. Cambridge: Cambridge University Press.

Neal, A. W. (2009). "Securitization and Risk at the Border: The Origins of FRONTEX." *Journal of Common Market Studies*, 47(2): 333–356.

Pantel, N. (2014). "Danke, Manuela Schwesig" *Süddeutsche Zeitung*, Online May 15, 2014. http://www.sueddeutsche.de/politik/fingierte-hilfsaktion-danke-manuela-schwesig-1.1959503 (accessed May 29, 2017).

Popp, M. (2014). "Europe's Deadly Borders. An Inside Look at EU's Shameful Immigration Policy" *Spiegel*, Online September 11, 2014. http://www.spiegel.de/international/europe/europe-tightens-borders-and-fails-to-protect-people-a-989502.html (accessed June 12, 2018).

Rauterberg, H. (2015). "In den Fallen der Freiheit." *ZEIT ONLINE*, (ZEIT 27/2015) July 18, 2015. http://www.zeit.de/2015/27/politik-kunst-zentrum-fuer-politische-schoenheit/ komplettansicht (accessed May 29, 2017).

Ruch, P. (2015a). *Wenn nicht wir, wer dann? Ein politisches Manifest*. München: Ludwig Verlag.

Ruch, P. (2015b). "Unsere Waffen sind Ideen." *ZEIT ONLINE*, (ZEIT 52/2015) December 23, 2015. http://www.zeit.de/2015/52/zentrum-fuer-politische-schoenheit-philipp-ruch/ komplettansicht (accessed May 29, 2017).

Shapiro, M. (1997). "Narrating the Nation, Unwelcoming the Stranger." *Alternatives: Global – Local – Political*, 22(1): 1–34.

Süddeutsche Zeitung (2014). "Aktivisten entfernen Gedenkkreuze für Mauertote." *Süddeutsche Zeitung*, Online November 3, 2014. http://www.sueddeutsche.de/politik/neue-aktion-des-zentrums-fuer-politische-schoenheit-aktivisten-entfernen-gedenkkreuze-fuer-mauertote-1.2202632 (accessed May 29, 2017).

Thimm, T. (2014). "Schön politisch." *ZEIT ONLINE* (ZEIT 23/2014), May 28, 2014. http://www.zeit.de/2014/23/kuenstlergruppe-berlin-rettung-syrische-kinder (accessed May 29, 2017).

Trilling, D. (2018). "Five Myths About the Refugee Crisis." *The Guardian*, June 5, 2018. https://www.theguardian.com/news/2018/jun/05/five-myths-about-the-refugee-crisis (accessed June 12, 2018).

UNHCR (2016). "Mediterranean death toll soars, 2016 is deadliest year yet." http://www.unhcr.org/news/briefing/2016/12/585ce804105/mediterranean-sea-100-people-reported-dead-yesterday-bringing-year-total.html (accessed June 3, 2017).

van Munster, R. (2010). *Securitising Immigration. The Politics of Risk in the EU*. Basingstoke: Palgrave.

Waever, O. (1995). "Securitization and Desecuritization." In Lipschutz, R., ed., *On Security*: 46–86. New York: Columbia University Press.

Zehfuss, M. (2004). "Writing War, Against Good Conscience." *Millennium: Journal of International Studies*, 33(1): 91–121.

Zehfuss, M. (2007). *Wounds of Memory: The Politics of War in Germany*. Cambridge: Cambridge University Press.

ZEIT (2014a). "Pseudo-Hilfsaktion bringt Schwesig in Bedrängnis." *ZEIT ONLINE*, May 13, 2014. http://www.zeit.de/politik/deutschland/2014-05/syrien-kunstaktion-schwesig (accessed May 29, 2017).

ZEIT (2014b). "Flüchtlingsaktivisten entfernen Berliner Mauerkreuze." *ZEIT ONLINE*, November 3, 2014. http://www.zeit.de/politik/deutschland/2014-11/kreuze-berliner-mauer-fluechtlinge-europa-aussengrenzen (accessed May 29, 2017).

'1aus100' (2014). "Soforthilfeprogramm des Bundes." Website, Center for Political Beauty, May 2014. http://http://www.1aus100.de/ (accessed May 29, 2017).

33
ON POTENTIAL AND LIMITS OF THE CONCEPT OF RESPONSIBILITY AS A REFERENCE POINT FOR THE USE OF PRACTICAL REASON

Sergio Dellavalle

Introduction: from duties to responsibilities?

First and foremost, in order to address correctly the relationship between the notions of responsibility, obligation and duty, a conceptual clarification is needed. While *duty* is used to describe what we mutually ought to do in order to implement the rights of others, *responsibility* is referred to forms of commitment to action which are not necessarily related to recognizing rights to its addressees. Thus, responsibility is centred on the subjective approach of the agent to the situation as well as on the specific context of the envisaged action and may be influenced by prudential choices and opportunities. Finally, obligation is understood in its most general connotation, as a self-imposed commitment to action, or as an external – more or less strictly binding – request to perform it. Such commitments or requests might originate from quite different sources of justification, such as agreements, customs, personal feelings of solidarity or responsibility towards individuals, social groups and communities, or even moral duties. Consequently, the reference to an obligation can indicate, in the following, an ought that derives from the acknowledgement of rights, so that the normative content of an obligation, in these circumstances, is essentially equivalent to that of a duty. Obligation, however, can also be referred to non-rights-related commitments or requests, such as those which are grounded on responsibility.

Given this premise, it is quite uncontroversial that the idea of the correct use of practical reason that characterized the Western Modern Ages – which necessarily included a certain understanding of what an obligation should be – left little room for the attitude that we generally call *responsibility*. Indeed, according to the main strand of modern philosophy, *obligations* have to be understood as *duties*, which are strictly related to non-alienable rights of the addressees of obligations. Insofar as rights were seen as essentially non-negotiable, the definition of obligations had also to rule out prudential considerations almost completely.

This approach was the result of a paradigmatic revolution from an essentially holistic view of the world to the primacy of the individuals, which marked the beginning of the modern era. According to the individualistic paradigm that framed, in the Modern Ages, first the epistemology and then the idea of social, political and legal order, true knowledge and just action are exclusively based on the correct use of reason made by the individual agent. This utterly solipsistic understanding of truth and justice may lead to an unhistorical view of knowledge as well as to paradoxical results in the field of moral decisions. No less problematic, however, are the consequences that arise for the conception of social, political and legal order.

Against the background of the deficits deriving from the individualistic concept of the use of reason, an alternative – and even opposite – idea was developed, namely that the search for truth should be understood as a social phenomenon and that action should not be guided by solipsistically developed individual convictions, but essentially focus on considerations regarding the effects that actions may have. This is the intellectual atmosphere in which the concept of responsibility was developed. Besides allowing to take the consequences of action into due account, the focus on responsibility had a further advantage. Indeed, the modern idea of the practical use of reason was characterized by the almost perfect identification of the subjects of obligations with the objects of obligations, so that only those consequences of action had to be taken into consideration, which were assumed to have an impact on entities capable of rationally justified decisions, actually on rational human beings. The only exception to this rule was made with regard to immature or intellectually impaired humans, who were implicitly seen as being part of the community of the objects of obligations because of their sharing of the *imago hominis*. By distinguishing between the subjects of obligations and the objects of obligations and by extending the range of the latter ensemble much farther than the former, the concept of responsibility makes it possible to concentrate on the impact of action on entities such as non-human animals, the biosphere, the global environment, as well as historically or aesthetically significant landscapes.

Yet, the problems that arise from the substitution of the individualistic perspective on moral action with the focus on responsibility are at least as important as its advantages. In particular, the fact that the community of the subjects of obligations should no longer reflexively coincide with the community of the objects of obligations necessarily leads to the assumption that some privileged observer may have the competence to decide on which entity should deserve being the addressee of responsibility. The almost inevitable consequence, from a political point of view, is a shift from the democratic self-government of the community to a paternalistic technocracy. Given these premises, the question is whether it is possible to figure out a conceptual constellation in which the extension of the set of those entities that are assumed to be addressees of obligations, as well as the flexibilization of the ways in which obligations are implemented, can be maintained without giving up the idea that the moral and legal community is grounded on the mutual recognition of the free and equal. Put differently, can we uphold the positive novelties introduced by the turn to responsibility, while retaining at the same time one of the most important and commendable achievements of the modern idea of social, political and legal order?

Starting from these overall considerations, the next section shows how the idea of obligations as *duties* emerged from the transition – in Western society as well as in the political philosophy that contributed to shape it – from a *holistic* to an *individualistic* understanding of social order. As a result, obligations are seen as mutual commitments agreed upon by the members of the community of the free and equal in order to protect their fundamental rights (section "Obligations as mutual duties: modern individualism and the community of the free and equal as the basis of the social, political and legal order"). Although the transition from holism to individualism can be regarded as one of the most outstanding achievements of Western thinking, it did not happen without raising some significant problems. The third section "The weaknesses of the individualistic paradigm and the turn to responsibility" analyses how the unresolved questions triggered the development of the concept of *responsibility* as a possible answer. However, while the notion of responsibility seems to facilitate the overcoming of some deficits of the theory of obligations as duties, the difficulties created in case that preference is granted to a non-rights-related understanding of obligations are no less deep-going (section "The blind spots of responsibility"). Therefore, since the notion of obligations as rights-related duties shows weaknesses, but the solution offered by a non-rights-related concept of responsibility is even more flawed, the fifth section "Towards a redefinition of obligations" explores a possible solution through the expansion of the moral and legal community of the free and equal in space, time, composition and contents, so that the tenet of mutual recognition is maintained, yet in a way that includes the most justified issues addressed by the increased attention to responsibility. Finally, the last section "Conclusion: does the use of the concept of responsibility make any sense?" is dedicated to some concluding remarks.

Obligations as mutual duties: modern individualism and the community of the free and equal as the basis of the social, political and legal order

In the premodern Western world, human knowledge was regarded as inherently true because an osmosis was implicitly presupposed between the knowing subject and the reality outside. In other words, the uninterrupted continuity that was assumed to exist between the subject and the world, as well as the unquestioned conviction that both belonged to a meaningful whole (*holon*), was the guarantee that the subject's utterances had a truth content. In the same vein, if we move from the theoretical to the practical use of reason, the individuals were seen as part of a broader community, the value of which was regarded as superior to the value of each community member or even to the total sum of them. Therefore, according to the *holistic* paradigm of social, political and legal order, the obligations that the individuals were assumed to have towards society were surely not duties – in the previously explained meaning – but could rather be compared to what we now call 'responsibility', although the term was not in use before the modern era and it took even more time to acquire its present connotation. In the holistic perspective, in fact, individuals are presumed to have more obligations than those which they owe to their fellow humans or citizens as rights holders.

Given that a *paradigm* can be defined as the set of fundamental concepts that essentially shape how theoretical and practical reason is used in a certain period of time and with reference to a specific field of knowledge and action, the beginning of the Modern Ages saw the transition from the *holistic* to the *individualistic* paradigm. The paradigmatic revolution from holism to individualism took hold first in the theory of knowledge. In particular, it was René Descartes who took up the challenge of developing a theory of knowledge that was based on the very *individual* capacity of questioning generally established theories and of creating new ones by means of the unprejudiced, purely rational thinking of the knowing subject (Descartes 1637; 1641; 1644). By doing this, he put the guarantee of the truth content of knowledge for the first time in the hand of the individuals and, more specifically, in their right use of reason. Shortly afterwards, the priority of the individual was extended by Thomas Hobbes to the field of political philosophy (Hobbes 1642; 1651). More explicitly, Hobbes introduced a veritable 'Copernican revolution' insofar as he turned the traditional centre-periphery relationship between community and individuals upside down (Bobbio 1990, 45, 121). Indeed, in his political theory it is not the community that is put at the centre, but the individuals with their rights and interests, as well as with their capacity to be guided by reason. The community – now transformed from the star of the system to a planet that shines of reflected light – does not entail some added value if compared with the worth of the sum of its members. Put differently, it should not be seen as having a worth in itself which is not rooted in the value of the citizens or, more generally, of the human beings who constitute it. Rather, the social community as a whole has its only justification in the safeguard of the entitlements of its members.

Hobbes's 'Copernican revolution' lies at the basis of the contract theory of state (Locke 1690; Rousseau 1762), namely of that understanding of the political community according to which public power is only justified if it is legitimated 'bottom-up' by those who have to abide by the law. The conceptual framework of this idea of political autonomy – i.e., that a polity is well-ordered if it arises from the mutual recognition of the free and equal – was then applied by Immanuel Kant to a project for the transformation of moral philosophy. In Kant's work, the notion of autonomy serves, in first place, to support a theory of moral obligations, which only in a second step becomes a political conception (Kant 1785; 1788; 1797). Therefore, following the probably most influential strand of modern philosophy, the moral and legal community is grounded on the individuals as endowed with inherent rights, as well as with interests and the capacity of rational judgement as its core element. On that basis, the individuals – supposed to be originally free and equal – grant each other a set of essential rights as the formalization of the inescapable rules and principles of a social life based on mutual acknowledgement, autonomy and legitimacy. As a result, not only the definition of rights and their protection are fundamental for the establishment of legitimate institutions but it is also assumed that no obligations are given except those which correspond to the safeguard of related rights on the other side. Put differently, I have obligations – or, in an even more explicit sense, I have duties – to the extent that someone else is acknowledged as having corresponding rights. Moreover, obligations do not need any further form of specific motivation but the acknowledgement that the addressees of the action are endowed with rights.

It is hardly possible to overestimate the importance of the historical achievements that were fostered – if not even made possible – by the development of the idea that the social, political and legal community is made of free and equal individuals, that these are endowed with inherent rights, and that the obligations that we owe to society are strictly defined through, limited by and dependent on the rights of our community members. Without ignoring the many unfulfilled promises that have accompanied its way through history, it is no exaggeration to say that this idea is one of the greatest gifts that Western thought has made to humanity in its entirety – if not the greatest at all. From the Mayflower Compact of 1620 – which anticipated by roughly a generation the philosophical elaboration of the fundamental principles of the individualistic paradigm of order in Hobbes's *De Cive* of 1642 – to the great documents of the American and French Revolutions; from the struggles for the recognition of social rights in the nineteenth and twentieth centuries to those for the overcoming of racism and colonialism; and from the fight for women's rights to the acknowledgement of the requests of the LGBTQ+ community – the insistence on the central importance of individual rights has accompanied all most remarkable stages of the enhancement of freedom and justice, first in the Western world and then everywhere else. Indeed, every step on this path can be interpreted as an enlargement of the community of the right bearers – with the consequence that the number of the addressees of obligations, and thus their range of application, also increased – or as an expansion of the catalogue of the acknowledged rights. Both developments were generally triggered by claims brought forward by strong social movements initiated by formerly discriminated social groups. Yet, although the merits of the individualistic paradigm and of its idea of obligations as duties corresponding to rights are undisputable, some shortcomings are also quite evident – and it is with reference to these deficits that the notion of responsibility comes into play.

The weaknesses of the individualistic paradigm and the turn to responsibility

The long-lasting dominance of the individualistic paradigm in the fields related to the theoretical use of reason led to a solipsistic and mentalistic understanding of knowledge. Since true and universal knowledge was considered achievable on the only basis of the correct implementation of the individual rational capacities, the intersubjective and social dimension of the development of science ended up being utterly and constantly neglected. In fact, it was not before the twentieth century – and more decisively in the second half of it – that voices were raised claiming the social component of the search for truth and of scientific experience (Wittgenstein 1953; Kuhn 1962; Habermas 1984, 127; Habermas 1999). Leaving apart the paradigmatic evolution of the theoretical use of reason and getting back to the centrepiece of this contribution, namely to the use of practical reason and, more specifically, to how obligations can be justified, the deficits of the individualistic approach were met by introducing the new concept of *responsibility*.

To be precise, the term of 'responsibility' was already in use since the second half of the eighteenth century, yet with a meaning which was slightly different from what it took later as a reaction to the perceived insufficiencies of the modern theory of moral and legal obligations. Indeed, when it made its first appearance, responsibility' – which is originally derived from the Latin word *responsum* (reply, answer) – was essentially a synonym for 'accountability', thus describing a condition in which someone is regarded as accountable for having performed or omitted an action the justification of which, however, is left outside the contextual dispute. In other words, if understood in this sense, 'responsibility' refers to the conditions under which someone can be held accountable for what she/he has done (or not done), while the justifications why this action should have been done (or not done) are simply not addressed. Though being still present in the current debate with prominent contributions (Raz 2012), the meaning of 'responsibility' as accountability has given progressively way to a different understanding, according to which the notion is used as a justification for action that is explicitly in alternative to the identification of obligations with duties deriving from corresponding rights. Therefore, responsibility has become the concept that should be used to substantiate non-duties-connected and non-rights-related obligations, so that some scholars are even speaking of a new era of responsibility as opposed to – and/or as a possible replacement of – the former era of rights (Shadmy 2016).

Basically, switching to responsibility is thought to overcome two main deficits of the rights-and-duties-related theory of obligations: first, it should make the implementation of obligations more flexible and context-dependent; and, second, it should increase the number and differentiate the nature of their addressees. Let us start with the first aspect. An obligation, if it is meant as a duty, entails a very limited range of flexibility. Indeed, what we are obliged to do as a duty is quite precisely determined by the content of the right which constitutes its counterpart after having been acknowledged on a reciprocal basis by the members of the moral and legal community. Kant described this condition, in his *Grundlegung zur Metaphysik der Sitten* (*Fundamental Principles of the Metaphysic of Morals*), as the 'kingdom of ends' (*Reich der Zwecke*), in which every human being – as a member of this 'kingdom' – is regarded as an end (*Zweck*) in her- or himself, and not as means (Kant 1785, 72; English: 56). Being an 'end' means that every human is recognized as a rights holder and that every fellow human should uncompromisingly act in defence of those rights. Kant admitted that the 'kingdom of ends' is not a real condition, but a fictional reality (*mundus intelligibilis*) or a thought experiment. Nonetheless, 'every rational being must so act as if he (or she) were by his (or her) maxims in every case a legislating member in the universal kingdom of ends' (Kant 1785, 72; English: 57). Therefore, if we want the society to be ruled by reason and the mutual recognition of rights, our actions must inevitably have the character of non-negotiable duties. Yet, such an adamant understanding of the nature of obligations, though fascinating, also raises some significant doubts. Even if we recognize that cheating is an offence against fellow humans since it does not essentially respect them as rational beings, what about the cases in which lying might avoid suffering or, in the most dramatic cases, even save lives? And, although it has to be generally acknowledged that every reasonable measure should be taken to tackle oppressive regimes, what should be done if an intervention to save the lives and dignity of a certain number of individuals who are persecuted by one of those regimes could end up endangering life and dignity of many more? Indeed, there might be situations in which a nuanced approach turns out to be the most reasonable solution. Sometimes prudence appears to be a more valuable and viable way to address a problem than insisting on a deontological stance and on the idea of obligations as non-negotiable duties. It was Max Weber who highlighted the question by providing a new conceptual instrument. In his speech on *Politik als Beruf* (*Politics as a Vocation*) of 1919, he contrasted the ethics of responsibility (*Verantwortungsethik*) with the ethics of conviction (*Gesinnungsethik*) (Weber [1919] 2004, 83) (compare chapter by Jackson in this volume). According to the latter – which is largely tailored on the predominant individualism of modern moral philosophy, in general, and on Kant's approach in particular – moral agents act on the basis of their personal persuasion about what is true and just. The ethics of responsibility suggests instead that moral agents should primarily focus on the consequences of their actions. From Weber's analysis on, the concept of responsibility has been applied to describe a justification of obligations which – unlike the concept of duty – includes a broad margin of prudential appreciation with reference to both whether and how to implement the action in question.

Two uses of 'responsibility' have been introduced in recent years, which can be led back to Weber's original argument that, under certain circumstances, actions must be judged more on the basis of their consequences than of their original deontological motivation. The first is the so-called *responsibility to protect*, which means the obligation by the international community to take measures – under the regime of international law – in order to protect essential rights of individuals, as well as of ethnic, religious, social and national groups (Pellet 2010; Benvenisti 2013; Byers 2015; Bellamy and Dunne 2016). In particular, the endangered groups should be protected 'from genocide, war crimes, ethnic cleansing and crimes against humanity' (United Nations General Assembly, 2005, para. 138). The fact that, to refer to this kind of obligations, the concept of 'responsibility' has been preferred to 'duty' implicitly weakens the compulsory dimension of the required actions, making them more depending on contextual conditions and the evaluation of possible outcomes. The second use of 'responsibility' in the sense of an instrument which is not compelling and of a justification of action which refrains from any reference to duties is Corporate Social Responsibility (CSR). The notion has been created to describe the voluntary initiatives taken by private economic actors to limit the negative impact that the production of goods, the markets and the financial transactions may have on the ecological and social equilibrium, in particular in view of the evident incapacity or unwillingness of states and international organizations to address the issue with the necessary vigour by means of public law (Mareş 2008). Opting for a conceptual framework that suggests high flexibility guarantees to the corporate actors an almost unrestrained blank check in determining range and quality of the measures to be taken, while justifying the independence of their choices as well as the alleged superfluousness of any public power's intervention.

The second main deficit of the rights-and-duties-related theory of obligations that should be overcome by the introduction of the notion of responsibility regards the number and nature of the addressees of obligations. Indeed, in modern philosophy, belonging to the moral and legal community is considered to be depending on individuals being capable of claiming their rights and interests in a propositional way. In other words, to be members of that community, individuals must be able to articulate what they reasonably believe to be their entitlements and priorities by means of understandable utterances within an open and fair discourse. Putting it even more concretely, the members of the community must possess a sufficient awareness of themselves as well as of the other participants in the interaction, and they must be endowed with the capacity to speak. Under these premises, the personal autonomy that is expressed through my own claim to rights and defence of interests is transformed into a collective autonomy by implementing the conditions of a fair discursive interaction. Through the open-minded exchange of arguments on rights and interests, and the mutual recognition which is implied hereby, a society constitutes itself as a community of free and equal rights holders.

Yet, such an understanding of the social and legal community of the free and equal as the rightful addressees of obligations, if taken literally, ends up precluding participation to a significant number of subjects or entities which are intuitively perceived as worthy of protection. The most evident case is provided by those members of the human community, such as little children as well as persons affected by mental disability or dementia, who are unable to express their needs by understandable linguistic means. Their case, however, is not only the most evident but also the easiest to solve insofar as their inclusion in the community of the addressees of obligation is guaranteed by resorting to the shared *imago Dei* (or *hominis*) and/or to the concept of *human dignity* – as vague as this concept may be (Dellavalle 2013). Anyway, responsibility is generally not brought into play with reference to this issue since immature and impaired human beings are considered full rights holders. There are, however, much more complex questions, in which it is quite difficult to recognize entities deserving protection as autonomous rights holders, so that it is precisely here that responsibility enters the debate. The first example is given by non-human animals. There can be no doubt that non-human animals do not even have the most abstract potentiality to enter the discursive interaction as a result of the barrier between species and of different, largely incommensurable forms of communication. Yet, the division line that was created to separate humans from non-human animals has become increasingly untenable because of growing evidences of surprising similarities. Some animals, for instance, are capable of behaviours which show signs of germinal morality, or display emotional reactions which are comparable to human feelings, such as love and empathy (De Waal 1996). Some may be regarded as 'subject-of-a-life' (Regan 1983), and, in any case, many are sentient beings who can feel pain and suffer (Singer 1975; Francione 2000; Francione 2008; Aaltola 2012). Thus, because a continuum can be detected in many fields of experience between human and non-human animals, the latter ones should be regarded – even if not as moral *agents* – at least as moral *patients* who can be severely affected by our actions. As a result, we do bear responsibility towards them.

A second example regards our obligations towards past and future generations. Indeed, we have inherited works of art and landscapes from past generations, and we have to pass them on to the future generations – along with a natural environment in which decent living conditions are possible. Obviously, fellow humans of past or future generations cannot be part of the actual community of the free and equal. Nonetheless, it can be hardly denied that we owe respect to those who created the world of culture into which we were born, as well as towards those who will live after us and deserve to experience natural and spiritual conditions which, at least, should not be worse – and possibly better – than ours (Saugstad 1994). If we limit the proper range of the application of duties only to the rights bearers as members of the community based on mutual recognition – as stated in the modern individualistic understanding of moral obligations – then we need the notion of responsibility to come to our aid in order to justify that broadening of perspective which is intuitively felt as indispensable.

The third – and last – example is related to the use of responsibility with reference to obligations towards entities such as nature as a whole, the environment (Jonas 1979), the world of the living creatures (Taylor 1981), and a specific cultural tradition or language (compare the respective chapters by Busser and Baron in this volume). In all these cases, the addressees of obligations are not individuals – be they actual human beings, members of past and future generations, or even sentient animals – but rather indistinct components of the real world which are nonetheless supposed to have an inherent value. These elements – which can correspond to a form of social interaction, for instance a specific language or culture, but also to non-social entities, the *holon* of nature or of the living world – are ontologized and transformed into supposedly specific beings, with a 'separate and distinct existence and objective or conceptual reality' (according to the definition of 'entity' in the Merriam-Webster Dictionary). As such, they are considered worthy of being respected in their own right.

In conclusion, the assertion that we are entering the era of responsibility, in particular in international law, may be indeed a kind of exaggeration (Crawford and Watkins 2010; Murphy 2010; Roeben 2012). Nonetheless, it seems that the reference to responsibility corrects some weaknesses of the traditional idea of the moral and legal community, as composed of human individuals who are able to mutually acknowledge one another and to express their claims through meaningful utterances. In fact, it would broaden the horizon of our obligations, extending them also to addressees who cannot explicitly express their claims, but nevertheless have to be regarded as rightful beneficiaries of our interventions. Yet, some disadvantages that derive from stressing the responsibility approach are no less significant than the advantages and, to some extent, even outweigh them.

The blind spots of responsibility

The less convincing argument in favour of the introduction of the concept of responsibility focuses on the alleged one-sidedness of the human rights discourse. More specifically, the debate on rights would only draw attention to the entitlements of the individuals, thus forgetting to put the due emphasis on their no less essential obligations with regard to the wellbeing of the community (Glendon 1991; Dyck 2005; Posner 2014). Instead, the discourse on responsibility would bring a more balanced approach into the debate. However, what seems to be a reasonable claim at first sight, turns out to be simply redundant on closer inspection. In fact, insisting on the importance of responsibility as the driving force behind the fulfilling of obligations only shifts the perspective from the addressee of the action to the agent, without adding any new content. In fact, in a moral and legal community of free and equal people, we ought to act with responsibility simply because we recognize that the counterparts are rights holders themselves. From the point of view of the moral agent, therefore, the recognition of rights must always correspond to the establishment of obligations, at least from the moment when we transform inherent but abstract individual rights into enforceable legal entitlements as a consequence of the implementation of the social contract derived from consent. For that reason, the recent tendency of an impoverished human rights discourse that aims almost exclusively at enforcing individual preferences, with little or no interest in even minimal standards of national or international social and ecological justice, should not be regarded as the coherent result of the intrinsic deficits of the human rights idea (Moyn 2012; 2016). Rather, it should be interpreted as pathological corruption within a context of unfettered selfishness. Nor is the present blindness of some advocates for the centrality of human rights towards the issue of economic inequality – which has been correctly criticized (Moyn 2018) – to be justified on the basis of the assumption that rights are rooted in mutual recognition. On the contrary, it is instead arguable that it is precisely a correct understanding of the concept of mutual recognition that requires a substantial limitation of inequality (Habermas 1992, 151; Rawls 1972, 57, 263).

Though not devoid of content, a second use of the concept of responsibility raises profound normative concerns. This is the case when responsibility is regarded as a 'virtue', (Williams 2008) aiming at implementing goods, and not at protecting rights. According to this interpretation, responsibility is the attitude that we display when it comes to the realization and protection of values which are considered to be essential for a specific idea of the common good

(MacIntyre 1981; 1984), such as a certain conception of what is thought to be a good way of life, a good society, or, more generally, a decent being-in-the-world. As a result, because responsibility according to this view is virtue-related and not depending on rights, obligations must be identified which do not correspond to mirror-inverted rights, provided that the discourse on responsibility is to have some specific added value. Accordingly, we would have justifiable obligations towards someone or something who or which is not generally acknowledged as a rights holder – or, at least, not as a holder of entitlements on equal footing.

Two consequences – both highly questionable – are generated by this approach. First, we would be forced to admit that the social and political community as a whole can be a source of obligations not rooted in individual rights, which actually amounts to a rejection of one of the most essential tenets of modern political philosophy. Second, insofar as I am supposed to have obligations towards someone regardless of the rights that we can mutually claim, these obligations must be generated by the specific and privileged social position of that person. This guarantees that she or he stands out from the populace. As a result, obligations must be grounded not in mutual commitment, but in hardly justifiable hierarchy and social status, which – once again – goes counter to the social contract of democratic communities. According to the idea of the democratic social contract, authority is generated from an original condition of equality and can be legitimated only through bottom-up deliberative procedures (Dellavalle 2011).

Sometimes, the appeal to responsibility seems to be a volatile attempt to lower the normative standards. This happens, for instance, when it is claimed that CSR should – and could – downright replace the intervention of public powers. This claim is not convincing for two main reasons. The first is the evident risk that CSR turns out to be a mere choosing and picking by the corporate actors, limiting the intervention to the fields where costs are low and media impact is high. The second reason for scepticism is even more substantial: if the contents of the standards introduced by the CSR codes are to be understood as having general validity, then they should also be broadly protected by law and not left to the arbitrary initiative of private actors.

Apart from these three applications of the notion of responsibility, which appear to be hardly justifiable from the very outset, it has been claimed above that in two main cases the concept of responsibility *does* touch upon unresolved problems of the theory of obligations as duties. In these cases too, however, caution is advised. Starting with what has been presented as the opportune extension of the community of the addressees of obligations, it should be always kept in mind what we have gained by grounding moral and legal obligations on the mutual and reflexive recognition of rights – and what we risk losing by abandoning this principle. First, in the social and political community corresponding to the individualistic paradigm of order, all human beings are assumed to be free, equal and independent of predetermined hierarchies. Second, individual rights cannot be fully alienated through the establishment of the political community. Third, public power originates from the reflexive and conscious will of those individuals who are united to form a people. Fourth, and last, the institutions established by the covenant that creates the political community have only the task to protect the rights of its members. These tenets characterize all most essential documents that paved the way to the establishment of modern liberal democracies. The most reasonable suggestion that we can draw from this evidence is that the idea of the moral and political community consisting of free and equal individuals, who are able to assert their rights and recognize them to one another on the basis of rational arguments, represents the core of a political system in which the safeguard of human rights, popular sovereignty and the rule of law can find their best implementation. More concretely, the protection of human rights is nothing but the guarantee that the fundamental conditions of interaction within a community of free and equal are realized. Furthermore, democratic participation expresses the involvement of the members of the community in the decisions on common concerns. Finally, the rule of law is the warrant that the rules of interaction within the community are respected. Can we really afford to jeopardize these conquests by carelessly undermining their fundaments?

Furthermore, such a step would also imply a significant epistemological problem. Indeed, how can we determine which rights should be protected? Or, beyond the rights-centred approach, how can our obligations be specified? If we assume the perspective of the self-reflexive community of autonomous individuals, the question is easy to answer: it is all members of the community who claim their rights and, after a deliberative process based on mutual recognition, establish together with their fellow citizens which entitlements are worthy of protection. Yet, in cases in which responsibility is applied, some addressees of obligations cannot claim their rights, so that is up to the agent to decide what should be done. The interpretation implies that agents can take the so-called position of the privileged observer, or in other words, a standpoint from which – due to their alleged superior knowledge – they are assumed to be able to know from the outside what are the essential interests of those who are involved, but are not in the position to speak out on their needs. Such an understanding, however, always encourages a patronizing attitude and an opinionated overestimation of the competences of those who are in charge of authority.

As specified above, the second situation in which the introduction of responsibility appears to be justified regards the possibility to make the implementations of obligations more flexible and to draw more attention to their consequences. As Weber implicitly suggested, shifting from 'conviction' to 'responsibility' always requires the identification of a specific community of reference which enables the agents to calibrate their actions on the basis of its visible and evaluable outcomes. Put differently, in order to take the consequences of their actions into due account, agents must have the possibility to refer them to a definite, specific and perceivable community. It is not by chance that responsibility has been, and still is, most commonly used with reference to the most immediately perceivable of all social communities, namely the family. Yet, if responsibility is so closely tied to the identification of a specific community of reference, then a significant difficulty arises when it comes to its possible application to more-than-particularistic contexts. Thus, the question is whether responsibility, in principle, is suitable to a universalistic approach. Following these considerations, it can be argued that resorting to responsibility runs the risk to roll-back, for the second time, the historical development of the paradigms of social, political and legal order. It has already been pointed out that, by moving away from the idea of the community of the self-reflexive free and equal as the basis for obligations, the concept of responsibility hardly disguises a certain nostalgia for premodern holism as opposed to modern individualism. But paradigms of order are made up not only by a claim regarding the ontological basis of the well-ordered society – traditionally, the holistic community *or* the individual – but also by assertions with reference to the possible extension of order and to its unitary or post-unitary structure. Leaving aside this last claim, which is not relevant to the question of the recent rise of the concept of responsibility, it is worth remembering that the *first paradigmatic revolution* – which happened more than two thousand years ago – marked the transition from particularism to universalism, ushering in a new era in which the realization of a well-ordered society was deemed possible not only within the limited range of the single political communities, each of them with its own idiosyncratic order, but on a cosmopolitan scale. Against this background, the new trend towards responsibility could quite unintendedly contribute – with its tendency to focus rather on clearly identifiable and short-ranged forms of social obligations – to challenge or even to reverse one of the most remarkable steps forwards of human thinking.

Towards a redefinition of obligations

On the basis of the pros and cons that have been listed in the previous sections, we come face-to-face with a dilemma. On the one hand, responsibility broadens the horizon of the use of practical reason and the domain of the addressees of obligations. According to this view, responsibility appears to be intuitively correct when compared to the rather limited range of the moral and legal community based on autonomy. On the other hand, however, the abandonment of the centrality of the moral and legal community grounded on self-rule has consequences which are anything but convincing. Furthermore, every attempt to justify the application of responsibility to universalistic contexts by resorting to some kind of holistic ontology is worryingly feeble. A way out of the impasse can be found by resorting to the conceptual organon of the communicative paradigm of social order (Apel 1973; 1990; Habermas 1981). The communicative understanding of the well-ordered society maintains one of the most essential tenets of modern subjectivism, namely the idea that the core of the social bond consists of the individuals with their endowment of reason and interests, and not of a predetermined vision of the common good, of self-reproducing functional systems, or of particularistic narrations. In contrast to modern individualism, however, the communicative paradigm of order does not assume that true, or at least correct, results of the use of theoretical and practical reason can be achieved on the basis of solipsistic mental processes. Rather, the search for truth and justice is the task of intersubjective procedures of communication consisting in the exchange of arguments within the context of mutual recognition.

As a result of the procedures of argumentative interaction, a communication community is established which provides the epistemological foundation of what has been defined, in the former sections, as the moral and legal community of the free and equal. In fact, the communication community recognizes rights and duties on the basis of claims expressed through meaningful propositions and their mutual acceptance. Yet, this is precisely the definition of obligations which is regarded as insufficient by the supporters of the introduction of the reference to responsibility. And, following their critical diagnosis, it is the concept of responsibility that should take on the task of expanding the concept of obligations so as to address issues which require our justifiable intervention. Therefore, the question is whether – and, if so, how – the idea of the communication community can integrate the issues raised by the discourse on responsibility in its conceptual framework, specifically as regards the extension of the domain of the addressees of obligations as well as the need for more flexibility under specific circumstances. It is possible to respond positively to these challenges if we introduce a distinction between the *real* communication community and its *ideal* counterpart (Apel 1973, vol. II, 358). The former describes the factual social context in which arguments are exchanged, while the latter indicates the most inclusive composition of the communication community, beyond the limitations of the real social contexts. We have to ascribe to the ideal communication community all beings whose claims can be reasonably considered overlapping or analogous to those explicitly expressed by the real participants in the argumentative interaction. In principle, therefore, it is possible to include into this community rational as well as non-rational beings, presently living individuals along with those who lived in the past or will live in the future, and persons who are able to express themselves in a propositional way as well as those who are not. This can be done, however, only under the condition that their claims are equivalent to those of the active members of the community of argumentative interaction. Because the discourse within the real communication community should always take all reasonable arguments into account, the real participants can achieve normatively acceptable solutions only if they always keep the situation and claims of all possible members of the ideal communication community in mind. Concretely, those who cannot participate at present always have to rely on someone making arguments on their behalf; yet, the decisions taken by the existing communication community have an adequate normative content only under the condition that the rights and interests of the potential members of the communication community are considered as valuable as those brought forward by the real participants in the discussion.

By shifting the focus from the real to the ideal communication community, the moral and legal community is expanded in space, time, composition and contents. Against this conceptual background, it is necessary to specify under which conditions and to what extent those individuals – human or even non-human beings – that are identified as reasonable addressees of obligations and responsibility can be integrated into the communication community. Only then can they be regarded as members of the moral and legal community. A quite easy challenge is posed by children or by people affected by mental disease or dementia. In fact, even if they cannot express their claims in a propositional way, children are destined to become fully-fledged members of the moral and legal community in the future, while elderly patients with dementia have been part of it in the past. Furthermore, people with mental diseases could have been members in their own rights, if only some circumstances would have been less negative. Therefore, we can reasonably assume that their claims are analogous to those of the active participants in the communication community, if these only were in the same situation. In fact, no one can raise serious doubts on the membership of children and mentally impaired persons in the community of the rights holders and addressees of duties. A similar argument can also be applied to the obligations towards those who, being hindered from participating in the discourse by political violence and social discrimination, are entitled to receive support from the international community in the sense of what has been defined as the 'responsibility to protect'. In this case as well, the addressees of obligations can be presumed to have claims which are the same as those of the active members of the communication community in a comparable situation. Thus, the obligations which the active members of the moral and legal community have towards them do not come from some kind of undetermined responsibility; they are simply duties and so is the responsibility to protect, too, the restriction of which can be justified only if their fulfilment would imply an even greater danger for the protection of other rights.

While the argument of analogy can also apply to the obligations towards past and future generations, the question is more difficult when it comes to the situation of non-human animals. In their case, we cannot simply presuppose a similarity of claims because of the interspecific barrier. Does a non-human animal have an interest to live? Or to be free? It is problematic for us to presume what they need because we cannot take on their position. Furthermore, there may be differences between species. There is at least one element, however, that we have in common with many non-human animals: the capacity to feel pain and to suffer. On the basis of this consideration, non-human animals can be included into the moral and legal community, at least in a non-reciprocal condition of moral patients and rights holders (Habermas 1991, 219). But this inclusion must rest on the partial redefinition of the epistemological fundament of the communication community, which should not be confined to the level of the exchange of rational arguments. Rather, to include sentient beings and also expand the range and meaning of communication, the exchange of rational arguments should be seen as the instrument to mutually avoid pain and suffering. On the contrary, no possibility is given to bring non-individual beings, such as the ecosystem or the world of living creatures as a whole, in the communication community. Their safeguard can nevertheless be justified as a duty towards those individuals whose right is recognized to enjoy the beauty of the world and decent living conditions also in the near and far future.

It is therefore possible, by slightly modifying the accentuation of the communication community, to include in the moral and legal community also those addressees of obligations who seemed to have to rely on the exercise of responsibility – and not on the fulfilment of duties – because of their apparent extraneity to the reason-and-autonomy-based pact of the free and equal. The dialectic between the real communication community and its ideal counterpart also accounts for that recourse to the concept of responsibility which points out its allegedly superior flexibility as regards the choice of the instruments of action. In the ideal communication community, duties would perfectly correspond to rights so that when a right is acknowledged, an immediate and uncompromising action should be implemented to protect it. Yet, we do not live in a perfect communication community, but only in a real one, in which sometimes a more prudential attitude is required (Apel 1990, 179). This means that, under certain circumstances, we are allowed to decide not to protect – at least not immediately and without compromise – right holders from the harm that is currently done to them. Nonetheless, the consequence should not be drawn that a duty to safeguard essential human rights has to be replaced by an arbitrary attitude, which we may call responsibility. The duty remains undiminished in its fundamental content, even if we have to acknowledge that its fulfilment in that specific situation would bring more harm than relief. Understood this way, refraining from action is not an alternative to the accomplishment of duties, based on a different, not deontological but strictly contextual approach. Rather, it may be sometimes justified, but only if action would bring even more damage to the safeguard of rights. Furthermore, compromises may be necessary in the real world; nonetheless, they are acceptable only to the condition that the concession leads to a middle- or long-term improvement of the protection of rights, and that the essential content of rights is not explicitly denied by our action or omission.

Conclusion: does the use of the concept of responsibility make any sense?

The claim that we are facing a change of paradigm – from the era of rights to the era of responsibility – is difficult to substantiate and, even if it were true, it could hardly be welcomed. Indeed, obligations with a relevant social impact cannot but be duties which correspond to mirror-inverted rights. Although we are allowed, under certain circumstances, to perform a duty with justifiable graduations of completeness, this concession does not have any consequence for the conceptual core of a convincing theory about the correct use of practical reason. However, we should not infer from these considerations that the notion of responsibility is useless and that it should be abandoned. First, its application makes sense insofar as it describes obligations located in the private domain, for example towards family members or friends, which derive from personal commitment or solidarity and cannot be considered related to rights and duties. Second, even with regard to issues of public relevance, responsibility can be reasonably referred to in order to address obligations which do not correspond to claims explicitly made by rights holders. These are duties indeed, but duties of a specific kind insofar as they imply an extension of the autonomous communication community from the real to the ideal level. Third, the notion of responsibility is characterized by a specific capacity to address the personal motivations of actions. Strong arguments tell us that obligations – at least in the public domain – are grounded in duties, but duties seem sometimes to be cold and distant, so that we need a driving force which is closer to our deepest sentiments. The appeal to responsibility may help to bring duties closer to our heart.

References

Aaltola, E. (2012). *Animal Suffering*. Basingstoke/New York: Palgrave Macmillan.
Apel, K.-O. (1973). *Transformation der Philosophie*. Frankfurt a. M.: Suhrkamp.

Apel, K.-O. (1990). *Diskurs und Verantwortung*. Frankfurt a. M.: Suhrkamp.
Bellamy, A, and Dunne, T., eds. (2016). *The Oxford Handbook of the Responsibility to Protect*. Oxford/New York: Oxford University Press.
Benvenisti, E. (2013). "Sovereigns as Trustees of Humanity: On the Accountability of States to Foreign Stakeholders." *The American Journal of International Law*, 107(2): 295–333.
Bobbio, N. (1990). *L'età dei diritti*, Torino: Einaudi.
Byers, M. (2015). "International Law and the Responsibility to Protect." In Chinkin, C., and Baetens, F., eds. *Sovereignty, Statehood, and State Responsibility*: 23–50. Cambridge/New York: Cambridge University Press.
Crawford, J., and Watkins, J. (2010). "International Responsibility." In Besson, S., and Tasioulas, J., eds. *The Philosophy of International Law*: 283–298. Oxford/New York: Oxford University Press.
Dellavalle, S. (2011). "'From Above', Or 'From the Bottom Up'?: The Protection of Human Rights Between Descending and Ascending Interpretations." In Council of Europe, ed., *Definition and Development of Human Rights and Popular Sovereignty in Europe*: 91–113. Strasbourg: Council of Europe Publishing.
Dellavalle, S. (2013). "From Imago Dei to Mutual Recognition: The Evolution of the Concept of Human Dignity in the Light of the Defence of Religious Freedom." In McCrudden, C., ed., *Understanding Human Dignity*: 435–449. Oxford: The British Academy by Oxford University.
Descartes, R. ([1637] 2001). *Discours de la Méthode*. Stuttgart: Reclam.
Descartes, R. ([1641] 1986). *Meditationes de Prima Philosophia*. Stuttgart: Reclam.
Descartes, R. ([1644] 1672). *Principia philosophiae*. Amsterdam: Elzevir.
De Waal, F. ([1996] 2003). *Good Natured*. Cambridge (MA)/London: Harvard University Press.
Dyck, A. J. (2005). *Rethinking Rights and Responsibilities: The Moral Bonds of Community*. Washington, DC: Georgetown University Press.
Francione, G. L. (2000). *Introduction to Animal Rights*. Philadelphia: Temple University Press.
Francione, G. L. (2008). *Animals as Persons*. New York: Columbia University Press.
Glendon, M. A. (1991). *Rights Talk: The Impoverishment of Political Discourse*. New York: Simon & Schuster.
Habermas, J. (1981). *Theorie des kommunikativen Handelns*. Frankfurt a. M.: Suhrkamp.
Habermas, J. (1984). *Vorstudien und Ergänzungen zur Theorie des kommunikativen Handelns*. Frankfurt a. M.: Suhrkamp.
Habermas, J. (1991). *Erläuterungen zur Diskursethik*. Frankfurt a. M.: Suhrkamp.
Habermas, J. (1992). *Faktizität und Geltung: Beiträge zur Diskurstheorie des Rechts und des demokratischen Rechtsstaats*. Frankfurt a. M.: Suhrkamp.
Habermas, J. (1999). *Wahrheit und Rechtfertigung*. Frankfurt a. M.: Suhrkamp.
Hobbes, T. ([1642] 1651). *De Cive*. London: Royston.
Hobbes, T. (1651). *Leviathan, or the Matter, Form, and Power of a Commonwealth Ecclesiastical and Civil*. London: Crooke.
Jonas, H. ([1979] 1984). *Das Prinzip Verantwortung*. Frankfurt a. M.: Suhrkamp.
Kant, I. ([1785] 1977). "Grundlegung zur Metaphysik der Sitten." In Kant, I., Wilhelm Weischedel, eds. *Werkausgabe*: Vol. VII, 9–102. Frankfurt a. M.: Suhrkamp (English translation by Thomas Kingsmill Abbott: "Fundamental Principles of the Metaphysic of Morals." In Kant, Immanuel, 1898, *Critique of Practical reason and Other Works*, 1–84, London/New York: Longmans, Green and Co.).
Kant, I. ([1788] 1977). "Kritik der praktischen Vernunft." In Kant, I., Wilhelm Weischedel, eds. *Werkausgabe*: Vol. VII, 105–302. Frankfurt a. M.: Suhrkamp.
Kant, Immanuel. [1797] 1977. "Die Metaphysik der Sitten." In Kant, Immanuel, Wilhelm Weischedel, eds. *Werkausgabe*: Vol. VIII, 309–634. Frankfurt a. M.: Suhrkamp.
Kuhn, T. ([1962] 1996). *The Structure of Scientific Revolutions*. Chicago: University of Chicago Press.
Locke, J. ([1690] 1698). *Two Treatises of Government*. London Awnsham-Churchill.
MacIntyre, A. (1981). *After Virtue*. Notre Dame, IN: University of Notre Dame Press.
MacIntyre, A. (1984). "Is Patriotism a Virtue?." The Lindley Lecture, University of Kansas, Dept. of Philosophy.
Mareş, R. (2008). *The Dynamics of Corporate Social Responsibilities*. Leiden/Boston: Martinus Nijhoff.
Moyn, S. (2012). *The Last Utopia*. Cambridge, MA: Belknap Press of Harvard University Press.
Moyn, S. (2016). *Rights vs. Duties: Reclaiming Civic Balance*. Boston Review, May 16, 2016, http://bostonreview.net/books-ideas/samuel-moyn-rights-duties (accessed March 31, 2021).
Moyn, S. (2018). *Not Enough: Human Rights in an Unequal World*. Cambridge, MA: Belknap Press of Harvard University Press.
Murphy, L. (2010). "International Responsibility." In Besson, S., and Tasioulas, J., eds. *The Philosophy of International Law*: 299–315. Oxford/New York: Oxford University Press.

Pellet, A. (2010). "The Definition of Responsibility in International Law." In Crawford, J., Pellet, A., and Olleson, S., eds. *The Law of International Responsibility*: 3–16. Oxford/New York: Oxford University Press.
Posner, E. A. (2014). *The Twilight of Human Rights Law*. Oxford/New York: Oxford University Press.
Rawls, J. (1972). *A Theory of Justice*. Cambridge, MA: Harvard University Press.
Raz, J. (2012). *From Normativity to Responsibility*. Oxford/New York: Oxford University Press.
Regan, T. ([1983] 2004). *The Case for Animal Rights*. Berkeley/Los Angeles, CA: University of California Press.
Roeben, V. (2012). "Responsibility in International Law." *Max Planck Yearbook of United Nations Law*, 16: 99–158.
Rousseau, J.-J. ([1762] 1966). *Du contract social, ou principes du droit politique*. Paris: Garnier-Flammarion.
Saugstad, J. (1994). "Moral Responsibility towards Future Generations of People." Lecture at University of Oslo (June 17, 1994). http://folk.uio.no/jenssa/Future%20Generations.htm.
Singer, P. ([1975] 2009). *Animal Liberation*. New York: HarperCollins.
Shadmy, T. (2016). "The Rising of Human Rights Responsibilities: R2P and CSR – Different Forms of the Same New Dialect." GlobalTrust Working Paper 2016/6. https://papers.ssrn.com/sol3/papers.cfm?abstract_id=3047021.
Taylor, P. W. (1981). "The Ethics of Respect for Nature." *Environmental Ethics*, 3: 197–218.
United Nations General Assembly (2005). *2005 World Summit Outcome*, A/RES/60/ 1, https://www.un.org/en/development/desa/population/migration/generalassembly/docs/globalcompact/A_RES_60_1.pdf (accessed March 31, 2021).
Weber, M. ([1919] 2004). "Politics as a Vocation." In Weber, M. (2004), *The Vocation Lectures*, edited by Owen, D. and Strong, T.B., translated by R. Livingstone, 32–94. Indianapolis (IN)/Cambridge: Hackett (German original: Politik als Beruf. Stuttgart: Reclam [1919] 1992).
Williams, G. (2008). "Responsibility as a Virtue." *Ethical Theory and Moral Practice*, 11(4): 455–470.
Wittgenstein, L. ([1953] 1984). "Philosophische Untersuchungen." In Wittgenstein, L. *Werkausgabe*, Vol. I, 225–580. Frankfurt a. M: Suhrkamp.

INDEX

Note: *Italicized* page numbers refer to figures, **bold** page numbers refer to tables

A5+5 375
Abbott, Andrew 429
Abdel-Nour, Farid 33
ABNJ (areas beyond national jurisdiction) 21, 358, 362, 364–365
Abraham 439–441
academic responsibility 132–133, 424–433
accountability 10, 318–319; drone accountability regime (DAR) 90–91; independent accountability mechanisms (IAMs) 20, 228–229, 293–294; of international organizations (IOs) 291–294; of Internet Communication Technology (ICT) companies 331–332; market 322; of multilateral development banks (MDBs) 291–294; online content moderation 331–332; of social media actors 331–332
Acharya, Amitav 232
Acharya, Viryal 385
Ackerly, Brooke 14, 58–66
Adler, Emanuel 85
Advanced Targeting and Lethality Automated System (ATLAS) program 177
African Development Bank 288
African Union (AU) 196
agency, double autonomy in 273
Agenda 21 110
Agreement for the Establishment of the Asia-Pacific Fishery Commission (1948) 351
Agreement on Conservation of Polar Bears 370
Agreement on Cooperation on Aeronautical and Maritime Search and Rescue in the Arctic 375
Agreement on Cooperation on Marine Oil Pollution Preparedness and Response in the Arctic 375
Agreement on Enhancing International Arctic Scientific Cooperation 375
Agreement to Prevent Unregulated High Seas Fisheries in the Central Arctic Ocean (CAOF Agreement) 375
Agreement to Promote Compliance with International Conservation and Management Measures by Fishing Vessels on the High Seas (1993) 373
agri-food system 16–17, 153–161; corporate actors in 157–158; food loss 158–159; food waste reduction 157–158; spatially differentiated notions of responsibility in 158–160
Ainley, Kirsten 416
Albert, Mathias 21, 369–377
algorithms 339
Allan, John A. 242
Allouche, Jeremy 246
AlphaGo 180
Alter, Karen 374
Amoore, Louise 339
Angola 262
Annan, Kofi 193, 197
Antarctic Treaty 376
Arbenz, Jacobo 321
Arbour, Louise 195
Arctic 369–377, 376–377; bazaar governance 374–376; and black carbon emission reductions 371; deglaciation 369–370; description of 371; and global warming 369, 371; as a globally embedded space 370; as a governance object 371–373; Ilulissat Declaration 374; regime complexity 374–376; responsibility 374–376; and UNCLOS 372
Arctic Council 371–372, 374–375
Arctic governance 22
Arctic paradox 371

Index

areas beyond national jurisdiction (ABNJ) 21, 358, 362, 364–365
Arendt, Hannah 4, 32, 34, 35–36, 39
Aristotle 320
Armed Activities on the Territory of the Congo (Democratic Republic of Congo v. Rwanda) (Armed Activities Case) 93
Arnold, Patricia 385
artificial intelligence (AI) 177, 339
Asian Development Bank (ADB) 247, 288
Asian Infrastructure Investment Bank (AIIB) 232, 238, 252
association principle 102; *see also* obligations
AU (African Union) 196
authority 11–12, 47; contracted 116; definition of 116; epistemic 120; in global governance 114–122; inscribed 116–117; of international organizations 115–117; legitimacy of 116; reflexive 117; sources of 116
autonomous systems 179–182
autonomy: of intelligent machines 182–183; in military systems 179–180; strategic 236; in technology 179–180

Balkans 274
Ban Ki-moon 192
Bangladesh 234
Bank of America 383
Bank of England 387
Barclays 383
Barkin, J. Samuel 21, 141, 347–357
Baron, Ilan Zvi 31–41
Barry, Christian 12, 100, 101
Barth, Mary 385
Barzani, Masoud 280
Barzani, Mustafa 279, 280
Basel Accord 388
BCIM (Bangladesh, China, India, Myanmar Economic Corridor) 238
Beardsworth, Richard 15, 71–83
Beck, Ulrich 389
Being and Time (Heidegger) 38
Beitz, Charles 86–93
Belarus 371
Belt and Road Initiative (BRI) 233, 237–238, 243, 251–252
Ben-Artzi, Ruth 293
beneficiary principle 12, 101–102
Benmelech, Efraim 385
Bernstein, Steven 16, 139–150
Bickert, Monica 337–338
Big Brother Watch 185
Bildt, Carl 401
BIMSTEC 235
Bio Bio river (Chile) 294–297
Biodiversity Convention 143

biodiversity in areas beyond national jurisdiction (BBNJ) 21, 358–366; agenda formation stage 362, **364**; institutional dynamics 361–362; negotiation stage 363–365, **364**; ocean protection 359–361; operationalization stage **364**; overview 358–359; regime effectiveness 361–362; responsibility for areas where nobody responsible 360–362
Biswas, Shampa 169
Bjola, Corneliu 219
black carbon (BC) 371–372
Blake, Michael 84
Bolsanaro, Jair 31
Brandt Report (1980) 219
Brazil 233, 237, 238
Breton, Thierry 395
Brexit referendum 109
BRICS countries 11, 13, 232, 238
Brock, Gillian 103
Brown, Chris 103, 131
Brundtland Commission 142
Brundtland Report (1987) 7, 219
Brunée, Jutta 92
Bryson, Joanna 187
Buber, Martin 32
Buchanan, Allen 86–92
Bukovansky 130
Bull, Hedley 129, 130, 133, 166, 222, 225–226
Burai, Erna 17, 192–199
Bureau of Flood Control for the Basin 246
Bush, George W. 168
Busser, Mark 15, 96–110
bystander duties 97, 99, 108

calculable risk 387
Calderaro, Andrea 22, 394–404
Callières, François D. 222
Cambodia 246, 247
Cambridge Analytica data scandal 43–55, 339
Canada 371, 374
CAOF Agreement (Agreement to Prevent Unregulated High Seas Fisheries in the Central Arctic Ocean) 375
capacity principle 12, 99–100; *see also* obligations
capital accumulation 76
carbon dioxide emissions 79, 358
carbon lock-in 149
care 38, 54, 100, 111, 115–116, 118, 121, 155–156, 159–161, 186, 319, 327, 338
Caribbean 209
Carr, Edward Hallet 102
Carr, Madeline 401
Catalonia 275
causal ineffectuality, thesis of 101, 103
causal responsibility 7, 145–146
Center for Political Beauty 23, 436, 441–445
Central African Republic 262

Central Intelligence Agency (CIA) 321
Challenge Program on Water and Food (CPWF) 250
Chandler, David 198, 210
Chang, Yung-Yung 19, 242–253
Chen, Tzu-Yin 383
Chih, Hsiang-Hsuan 383
Chih, Hsiang-Lin 383
Chile 20, 294–297
China 18–19, 231, 233; and Arctic governance 375; autonomous weapon systems 177, 179; Belt and Road Initiative 237–238; black carbon emissions from 371; BRICS summits 238; hydropower development 249–251; Internet governance 399; involvement in Mekong institutions 248; nuclear responsibility 167; water governance in Mekong region 242–253
Church of England Pensions Board 384
Ciepley, David 382
Circumpolar Conference 6
Clark, Ian 128, 129
Clausewitz, 225
climate change 6, 11, 16, 23, 65, 72, 76–77, 84, 110, 139–146, 148–149, 224, 233–235, 237, 262–264, 359, 369, 423–424
coalitions of the willing 10
Cognizant 337
Colander, David 386
Cold War 71, 119, 127, 231
Collective Responsibility (Arendt) 35
collective security arrangements 225
Colombia 361
colonial governance 20, 169
colonialism 12, 321, **323**
Commission on Security and Cooperation in Europe (CSCE) 119
Committee of Experts on the Application of Conventions and Recommendations (CEACR) 301, 304
Commodity Futures Trading Commission 382
common but differentiated responsibility and respective capabilities (CBDR) 139, 142–144
common heritage 139, 146
Communications Decency Act 334–335
communitarian principle 102
communitarianism 91–93
communities of fate 102
community ontology 417–418, **418**
compliance 20, 117, 210, 258, 261, 284–285, 289, 293–298, 301–302, 334, 363, 365, 413, 417–418
Compliance Advisor/Ombudsman (CAO) 294–297
compromise, and diplomatic peace 225
compulsory labor 303
Conca, Ken 145
Conference of the Parties 144
Congress of Verona 128

connectedness principle 12
Connolly, William 32, 37
consequential duties 97, 99, 108
consequentialism 319, **320**
Considine, Laura 17, 164–173
conspiracy theories 109–110
contestations: community ontology 417–418, **418**; diversity ontology 417–418, **418**; of norms 413; proactive 417–418; reactive 417–418
contracted authority 116
contribution principle 12, 100–102; *see also* obligations
Convention for the Conservation of Antarctic Marine Living Resources (CCAMLR) 354
Convention for the Prevention of Pollution from Ships (MARPOL) 360
Convention on Conventional Weapons (CCW) 187–188
Convention on North Sea Overfishing (1882) 351
Convention on the Elimination of All Forms of Discrimination Against Women 223
Convention on the Elimination of All Forms of Racial Discrimination (CERD) 223
Convention on the Prevention of Marine Pollution by Dumping of Wastes and Other Matter (London Convention) 352–353, 360, 361, 372
Convention on the Rights of Persons with Disabilities (CRPD) 62, 223
Convention on the Rights of the Child 223
Convention to Combat Desertification 143
Conventions and the Platforms for Action of the UN 62
Copernican revolution 451–452
core labor standards (CLS) 302, 304–305
corporate actors 157–158
corporate social responsibility (CSR) 4, 149, 153, 309, 322, 331, 334, 383–384, 454, 457
corrective obligations 99
Corry, Olaf 372
cosmopolitan responsibilities 132
cosmopolitanism 86–87, 91–93
Costanza, Robert 359
Cote d'Ivoire 262
CPWF (Challenge Program on Water and Food) 250
crazy religion diplomacy 222
critical constructivist norms 410
critical function 179
critical norms research 413, 415
CSCE (Commission on Security and Cooperation in Europe) 119
cultural validation **414**, 414
Cupac, Jelena 15–16, 114–122
Curran, Dean 389
cybersecurity 402–403
Cyclone Nargis 145, 198, 259

Index

Dabbashi, Ibrahim 227
Darfur 198
De Cive (Hobbes) 452
De Santo, Elizabeth 21, 358–366
de Waal, Alex 198
Decent Work Agenda (DWA) 302
Declaration on Fundamental Principles and Rights at Work (1998) 302, 304
Declaration on Social Justice for a Fair Globalization (2008) 302
decolonization 117, 321
deglaciation 369–370
Dellavalle, Sergio 24, 449–461
Democratic Republic of Congo 262
Deng, Francis 197
Denmark 371, 374
deontology 319, **320**
Derrida, Jacques 23, 437, 439–441
Descartes, Rene 451
DeSombre, Elizabeth R. 21, 141, 347–357
Deudney, Daniel 170, 171, 172
Deutsche Bank 383
developed countries 77–78
developing countries 77–78
Dewey, John 23, 424, 426–429, 430–431
dialogical responsibility 49
dialogue 225–226
Diesel scandal 5–6
digital sovereignty 395
Dinar, Ariel 246
diplomacy 219–228; and diplomatic peace 225–227; and international law 222–223; literature on 220–222; and national interests 224, 226–227; overview 219–220; responsible judgments in 226–227
Diplomacy: The Dialogue Between States (Watson) 221–222
diplomatic peace 225–227
disarmament 225
disaster management 203–214; diffusion of responsibility in 205–207; rebuilding 208–211; resilience 208–211; risk reduction 208–211; vulnerable entities and situations 211–212
discourse ethics 319, **320**
discourse level, responsibility to protect (R2P) 194
discretionary duties 319
discretionary responsibility 131
diversity ontology 417–418, **418**
Dlugosz, Jennifer 385
Doha Round 233
Dolsak, Nives 242
Domain Names System (DNS) 395–396
domination 76, 172
Downing, Theodore 295
Doyle, Thomas 171, 172–173
drone accountability regime (DAR) 90–91
Drubel, Julia 301–312

Dublin regulation 436
dumb public diplomacy 222
Dunne, Tim 59
duties 44, 46, 449, 454
duty of care 46, 166, 195, 437

Early Harvest Project 249
earth 126–128
Earth Summit (1992) 141–142
earthquakes 203, 207, 208
East India Company 321
eBay 336
Economic Community of West African States (ECOWAS) 193
ECOSOC 303
Eichmann in Jerusalem (Arendt) 36
El Salvador 361
Elhance, Alessandro P. 243
Empresa Nacional de Electricidad S.A. (Endesa) 294–295
enabling clause 143
Engelkamp, Stephan 23, 436–445
England 349
English School 16, 125–134; academic responsibility 132–133; general responsibilities 126–128; overview 16, 125–126; responsibilities as moral and legal standards in 126–131; responsibilities in international society 130–131; responsibility as virtue 131–132; special responsibilities 128–130; status differentiation 128–130
enjoyment approach to human rights 60–63
Enlightenment 203
entitlements 59–60
epistemic authority 120
Eritrea 361
Erskine, Toni 32–33, 115, 118, 131, 273, 410, 411, 415
ethics of care 34
European Bank for Reconstruction and Development (EBRD) 288
European Union 371, 375, 397
exclusive economic zones (EEZs) 349, 350–351, 353, 360
extended producer responsibility (EPR) 153
external recognition of responsibility 272, 276–278

Facebook 21, 43–55, 331–332, 332, 335; algorithms 339; approach to content moderation 336–339; community operations escalation 338; community standards 336–337; moderators 338; review and moderation policies 337–338; terms of service 336–337; users 338
Falkner, Robert 128
Fama, Eugene 382
Feedback 159
Feinberg, Joel 46

Feldman, Philip 187
Fichte, Johanne Gottlieb 39
fiduciary responsibility 381–382
Financial Crisis Inquiry Commission (FCIC) 389–390
Financial Crisis Inquiry Report 389–390
financial fraud 382–383
financial responsibility 380–390; calculable risk 387; and corporate social responsibility 383–384; in crisis 384–385; fiduciary responsibility 381–382; and financial fraud 382–383; and limits of personal responsibility 386–388; overview 380; rational control 388; and responsible corporate officer doctrine 382–383; and shareholder value 381–382; and socially responsible investing 383–384; unified individual agent 387–388
Finland 371, 375
First Amendment 335
First World War 127
Fischer, John 182
Fish Stock Agreement (FSA) 361, 373
flag of convenience states 351
Fletcher, S. 359–360
FOCEM regional development fund 237
fog of war 183
Food and Agriculture Organization (FAO) 157–158, 373
food loss 158–159
food system 153–161; corporate actors in 157–158; food loss 158–159; food waste reduction 157–158; moral geographies of responsibility in 154–157; spatially differentiated notions of responsibility in 158–160
food waste 157–159
forced labor: and capitalism 307; in concentration camps 303; definition of 301; within the global economy 305–308; people affected by **306**; prohibition of 302–305; and restrictive migration policies 307
Forced Labour Protocol 210, 305
formal validity 413–414, **414**
Founding Fathers 75
France 236; autonomous weapon systems 177, 179
fraud 382–383
freedom of expression 334–335
Frey, Raymond G. 35
FridaysForFuture movement 423
Friedman, Viktor 16, 125–136
Frost, Mervyn 437, 438–439
Fuchs, Doris 16–17, 153–161
Fundamental Principles of the Metaphysic of Morals (Kant) 453

G20 summits 232
Gabel, Friedrich 18, 203–214
Gaddafi, Muammar 227
Gaskarth, Jamie 132, 197

General Agreement on Tariffs and Trade (GATT) 143, 233
General Data Protection Regulation (GDPR) 395
genocide 5, 198
Georgia 198
German Network Enforcement Act (NetzDG) 333
Germany 436–438, 441–445
Glanville, Luke 196
Global Advisory Committee (GAC) 397
global agrifood system 153–161; corporate actors in 157–158; food loss 158–159; food waste reduction 157–158; moral geographies of responsibility in 154–157; spatially differentiated notions of responsibility in 158–160
Global Climate Action portal 148
global collective actions 71
global environmental governance 139–150; assigning of responsibility in 140–144; de-centering of state responsibility in 144–146; downloading and diffusing responsibility in 146–148; shared responsibility 139–150; trajectories of environmental responsibility in 144–148
global governance 5–6, 20, 71, 322, **323**; authority in 114–122; responsibility in 114–122
global justice 102–104
global public goods 71
global responsibility 15
Global South 158, 160
global warming 369, 371
globalization 232; demonization of 109; and forced labor 305–308
Goertzel, Ted 110
Goldman Sachs 383
Goodin, Robert 46
Google 331–332, 335
governance 43–55; transnational responsibility scheme of 48–52
Gramsci, Antonio 400–402
Grant, Ruth 289
great powers: duties and responsibilities of 129–130; hegemony 130
Greater Mekong Subregion Economic Cooperation Program (GMS) 247–248
greedy company diplomacy 222
Green, Leslie 74
Green Paper 396–397
Greenhill, Kelly 110
Greenland 371
Grimson, Olafur Ragnar 375
Groceries Supply Code of Practice 159
Grocery Code Adjudicator (GCA) 159
Grotius, Hugo 349, 359
Group of Friends of the Responsibility to Protect 194
Grupo de Accion por el Bibio (GABB) 295
Guiding Principles on Business and Human Rights 44–45

Gumbert, Tobias 16–17, 153–161
Gunkel, David 180
Gurria, Angel 384
Gusterson, Hugh 169
Guterres, António 263

Hair, Jay 295
Halabja chemical attack 281
Haldane, Andew 387
Hamati-Ataya, Inanna. 410
Hansen-Magnusson, Hannes 1–27, 118, 332
Hart, H.L.A. 7, 46, 319
hate speech 335
Havercroft, Jonathan 410, 411
hegemony 130
Heiddeger, Martin 37–38
Heidegger's Children (Wolin) 38
Held, David 102
Hellstroem, Thomas 183
Helsinki Final Act 119
Helsinki Rules on the Uses of the Waters of International Rivers 243–244
Herzberg, Elaine 184
Herzig, Christian 384
Heyns, Christof 178, 181, 186–187
high seas 347–357; definition of 349; as global commons 348–349; marine living resources 351–352; mining 353–354; ocean pollution 352–353; overview 347–348; and UNCLOS III 350–351
Hirsch, Philip 248
Hmmarskjöld, Dag 117
Hobbes, Thomas 117, 451–452
Holder, Eric 383
holism 451
Holland 349
Holocaust 35, 333, 440
Hopkins, Nick 336
hostages 171
human dignity 455
human rights 6, 58–66; businesses' responsibility for 318–328; differences and debates 63–65; elements of 58; as enjoyment 60–63; as entitlements 59–60; and online content moderation 334; overview 58–59; UN Guiding Principles on Business and Human Rights 323–328
Human Rights Council 145
Humanitarian Initiative on Nuclear Weapons (HINW) 165, 168, 169
humanitarian military interventions 73, 89–90, 127–128, 235, 416
Hungary 436
Hurd, Ian 116–117
Hurricane Katrina 205
Hussein, Saddam 282
hydro-hegemony 245

hydro-politics 243
Hyogo Framework for Action 204, 206–207, 208, 210

IANA (Internet Assignment Number Authority) 397
ICANN (Internet Corporation for Assigned Names and Numbers) 395–397, 400
Iceland 371, 375
ICT (Internet Communication Technology) companies 331–332; accountability of 331–332; corporate social responsibility 334; liability of 331–332; responsibility of 331–332
idealpolitik 18, 227
identity 36–37
Ikenberry, John 232
illegal, unreported, and unregulated (IUU) fishing 352
Ilulissat Declaration 374
imago Dei 455
imago hominos 455
immoral threats 171
The Imperative of Responsibility (Jonas) 38–39
independent accountability mechanisms (IAMs) 20, 228–229, 293–294
India 18, 231, 233; BRICS summits 238; globalization policies 237; Look East initiative 237; nuclear responsibility 167–168, 169; provision of public goods 233–235; responsibility as a rising power 233–236; responsibility in world affairs 236–237
Indian Ocean Naval Symposium (IONS) 236
individualism 25, 451–452; weaknesses of 452–456
inscribed authority 116–117
institutional layering 361
institutional moral agents 273
institutionalization level, responsibility to protect (R2P) 194–195
Inter-American Commission on Human Rights 6
Inter-American Development Banks (IDB) 288
internal claim of responsibility 272, 275–276
International Atomic Energy Agency (IAEA) 167
International Authority and the Responsibility to Protect (Oxford) 117
International Coalition for the Responsibility to Protect 194
International Code for Ships operating in Polar Waters (Polar Code) 373
International Commission on Intervention and State Sovereignty (ICISS) 31–41, 193–194, 197, 415
International Convention for the Northwest Atlantic Fisheries (1949) 351
International Convention for the Prevention of Pollution from Ships (1973/1978) 353

International Convention for the Protection of Marine Pollution from Ships (MARPOL) 372
International Convention for the Regulation of Whaling (ICRW) 351, 356
International Convention for the Safety of Life at Sea (SOLAS) 361, 372
International Convention on Oil Pollution Preparedness, Response and Co-operation (OPRC) 373
International Court of Justice (ICJ) 93
International Covenant on Civil and Political Rights (ICCPR) 6, 223
International Covenant on Economic, Social and Cultural Rights (ICESCR) 6, 223
International Criminal Court (ICC) 84
International Finance Corporation (IFC) 20, 288–289, 294–297
international human rights law (IHRL): and cosmopolitan responsibilities 87–89, 91–92; egalitarianism in 93; moral commitments in 86
international humanitarian law (IHL) 178, 181
International Labour Conference (ILC) 301
International Labour Organization (ILO) 20, 128, 301–312; legal responsibility 310–311; places of responsibility 308–310; prohibition of forced labor in 302–305; responsibility 307; topology of responsibility 308–311
international law 9, 15, 20, 51, 222–224; and cosmopolitanism 85–87; and diplomacy 222–224; foundation of 92; and global environmental governance 140–141; and great powers 12; hierarchisation of 92; and high seas 349, 354; moral theory of 93; objects of 71; and parochialism objection 89; and polluter pays principle 353; and prohibition of forced labor 308; and resources 222–224; and responsibility 45–46; and responsibility to protect 454; standards of civilization 127
International Law Commission (ILC) 145
international liberalism 73, 413
International Maritime Organization (IMO) 352, 372
international organizations (IOs) 288–298; authority of 115–117; limited immunity 288; overview 288–289; public accountability of 291–294; responsibility of 114–116, 289–291
international political theory (IPT) 85
International Red Cross 206
international relations (IR) 9, 11–12, 231; and Arctic governance 376–377; framing responsibility research in 409–419
international responsibility 15, 71–74, 101, 132, 235, 374
International Seabed Authority (ISA) 141, 354
international society 71, 91, 126–128; and diplomacy 221–222; English School 125; and great powers 197; norms on practices of 133; responsibilities of 129–131, 144

international system 126
International Telecommunication Union (ITU) 398, 399–400
Internet Assignment Number Authority (IANA) 397
Internet Communication Technology (ICT) companies 331–332; accountability of 331–332; corporate social responsibility 334; liability of 331–332; responsibility of 331–332
Internet Corporation for Assigned Names and Numbers (ICANN) 395–397, 400
Internet governance 22–23, 331, 394–404; and cybersecurity 402–403; definition of 394; dichotomous approach to governance of 397–399; early public-private partnership 395–397; and ICANN 395–397, 400; inclusion of civil society 397–399; multilateral approach to 399–400; multistakeholderism 397–402; overview 394–395
Internet Governance Forum (IGF) 398
intersubjectivity 36–37
intrastate conflicts 271–285
investment banks 383
Iran: earthquake 209; Internet governance 399; Kurds in 279; and UNCLOS 361
Iran–Iraq war (1980–1988) 280
Iraq: implementation of no-fly zone 281; Kurds in 279–283
Iraqi National Congress (INC) 281–282
Islamic State of Iraq and Syria (ISIS) 282–283
ISO Standards on Social Responsibility 44–45
Israel 31, 179

Jackson, Patrick Th. 23, 424–433
Jackson, Robert H. 128, 131, 132, 133
Jain, Neha 183
Jaishankar, Subrahmanyam 236
Jam v. IFC 288
Japan 234, 303; CAOF Agreement 375; marine resources 351
Jensen, Kurt Mørck 248
Joint Declaration of Principles for Utilization of the Waters of the Lower Mekong Basin 246
joint responsibility 129
Jonas, Hans 32, 37–38
Jones, Alex 110
Joshi, D.K. 236
JP Morgan Chase 383, 388
jurisdiction without territory 376
jus cogens theory 93
Just and Unjust Wars (Walzer) 89
just war tradition 178
justice 128

kafala system 307
Kagan, Shelley 35
Kant, Immanuel 75, 452, 452–456

Index

Karp, David 20, 147, 318–328
Kautilya 220
Kaye, David 334, 336
Kazakhstan 371
Kemper, Alison 386
Keohane, Robert 88, 289
killer robots 179–182
Kindertransporte 442
Kindertransporthilfe des Bundes campaign 442
King, Martin Luther, Jr. 431
Kissinger, Henry 221
Klinsky, Sonja 145
Klonick, Kate 336
Knecht, Sebastian 21, 369–377
Knox, John H. 6
Kopra, Sanna 129
Kornprobst, Markus 18, 219–228
Kosovo 193, 259, 274, 416
Kosovo crisis (1999) 131
Kosovo Liberation Army (KLA) 272
Kramarz, Teresa 290
Kratochwil, Friedrich 132
Krüger, Marco 18, 203–214
Ku Klux Klan 336
Kurdi, Alan 110
Kurdish Regional Government (KRG) 282–283
Kurdistan autonomous region 281
Kurdistan Democratic Party (KDP) 279–280, 281–282
Kurds 19, 275
Kurds in Iraq 279–283; Al-Anfal campaign against 280; establishment of governance structures 281–282; Halabja chemical attack against 289
Kyoto Protocol 142, 143

Lake, David 116
Lancang-Mekong Cooperation (LMC) 243, 247–249, 251–252
Landsman, Wayne 385
Laos 246, 247
Law of the Sea 139
League of Nations 303
Lee, Stan 51
Lee, Steven 171
legal standards, responsibilities as 126–128
legitimacy 11–12, 116
lethal autonomous weapons systems (LAWS) 17, 177, 179–182; commanding officers 186–187; criticisms of 180–181; designer 185–186; and human dignity 181; military users 186–187; moral agency 182–183; moral case for 180; programmer 185–186; technological risks 183–184
Lévinas, Emmanuel 32, 38, 53
Li Keqiang 252
liberal democracy 170–171
liberalism 73, 75, 86, 171, 413

Liberation Tigers of Tamil Eelam (LTTE) 272, 278
Liberia 193, 262
Libya 195, 416
linearity 160
Linklater, Andrew 128, 133
Lisbon earthquake (1755) 18, 203, 207
Lisbon Principles 359
Liu, Hin-Yan 186
Lluiya, Saul Luciano 6
Lockwood, Erin 22, 380–390
London Convention (Convention on the Prevention of Marine Pollution by Dumping of Wastes and Other Matter) 352–353, 360, 361, 372
London Whale trades 388
Long, Roderick 46
Lower Mekong 250–251
Lower Mekong states 246
Lowi, Miriam 242
Lula da Silva, Luíz Inácio 237
Luther, Martin 425

Machiavelli 39–40, 75, 220
Macron, Emmanuel 332
Malaysia 306
Manila Principles on Intermediary Liability 333
Mare Liberumi (Grotius) 349, 359
marine citizenship 359–360
marine living resources 351–352
Maritain, Jacques 63, 66
market accountability 322
Markowitz, Linda 384
MARPOL (International Convention for the Protection of Marine Pollution from Ships) 372
Marquis de Pombal 203, 205
Marshall, Charles Burton 79
Martin, Roger 386
Marx, Groucho 37–39
Master Plan on ASEAN Connectivity (MPAC) 252
material capacity 9
Mathur, Ritu 169
Matthias, Andreas 185
May, Larry 33
Mayflower Compact of 1620 452
McKinley, Emma 359–360
Mekong Agreement (1995) 246–247
Mekong Committee 247, 249
Mekong Forum on Water, Food and Energy 250
Mekong region 19, 242–253; and Belt and Road Initiative 251–252; description of 245; development of cooperation in 246–247; institutional development for managing water resources of 247–248; sustainable management 252–253
Mekong River 246
Men in Groups: Collective Responsibility for Rape (May and Strikwerda) 33

Index

Mendenhall, Elizabeth 21, 358–366
Menwan Dam 250
Merkel, Angela 395, 436, 444
Meunier, Sophie 374
Middleton, Carl 246
Millennium Development Goals (MDGs) 77, 147–148
Miller, David 96, 105, 115
Miller, Sarah Clark 34
Minamata Convention on Mercury (2013) 143, 373
mining 353–354
MINUSTAH peace mission 237
mission-adaptation 121
mission-creeping 121
Modi, Narendra 231, 234, 237
Moldova 371
Monitoring and Reporting Mechanism (MRM) 261
Montreal Protocol 142–143, 361
Moon, Jeremy 384
moral agency 154, 182–183
moral agents: and concept of responsibility 454; institutional 273
moral duties 154
moral geographies of responsibility 154–157
moral responsibility 84–94; and communitarianism 91–93; and cosmopolitanism 86–87, 91–93; and humanitarian military intervention 89–90; and international human rights law 87–89; in war 177–188; in world politics 273
moral standards, responsibilities as 126–128
Morgan Stanley 383
Morgenthau, Hans 32, 39–40, 220–221, 224
motivated moral reasoning, overview 15
multilateral development banks (MDBs) 20; overview 288–289; public accountability of 291–294
Multilateral Investment Guarantee Agency (MIGA) 294–297
Multilateral Ozone Fund 142–143
multinational corporations (MNCs) 5
multinodality 232
multiplex world 232
multipolarity 231
multistakeholderism 397–402
Muppidi, Himadeep 169
Myanmar 73, 145, 198, 247

Nagel, Thomas 98, 103–104, 108–109, 388
Nairobi Ministerial Conference (2015) 143
Nardin, Terry 103
Narlikar, Amrita 18–19, 231–240
national interest 77, 224, 226–227
national responsibility 132
national security 77
National Telecommunications and Information Administration (NTIA) 396

nations 126–128
NAZCA 148
Nazi Germany 324, 442
Nazis and Nazism 336
NEC 185
NeoFace Watch 185
neo-liberal governance 20
neoliberalism 322, **323**
Netanyahu, Benjamin 31
Netherlands 194
NetMundial 401
New Development Bank (NDB) 238
New International Economic Order (NIEO) 140
New Quad 233
New World Order 110
Niemann, Holger 19, 257–267
Nike 322
no-fly zone 281
Non Alignment Movement 234
non-discretionary duties 319
non-nuclear weapon state (NNWS) 165, 167
Non-Proliferation Treaty (1968) 164, 167, 168
normative basis 11–12
North Atlantic Treaty Organization (NATO) 193, 195
North Pacific Fur Seal Convention of 1911 351
North Somalia 272
North-South conflict 19
Northwest Atlantic Fisheries Organization (NAFO) 354
Norway 371, 374
nuclear deterrence 171
Nuclear Nonproliferation Treaty (1968) 17
nuclear reclusion 170
nuclear responsibility: asserting 167–168; common 166–167; conflicting 172–173; critiques of 169–170; institutionalized 165–166; special 166–167
nuclear sovereigns 166; conflicting nuclear responsibilities 172–173; hostage-holding 171; immoral threats 171; irresponsibilities 170–173; and liberal democracy 170–171; subjection to arbitrary power 171–172
nuclear weapon state (NWS) 165, 167
nuclear weapons 17, 76, 164–173; common responsibilities 166–167; overview 164–165; special responsibilities 166–167; state responsibilities 165–168
Nunn, Sam 221
Nyman, Elizabeth 21, 358–366

Obama, Barack 79, 166
object of responsibility 10–11
obligations 44, 46; association principle 102; capacity principle 99–100; contribution principle 100–102; definition of 449; as mutual duties 451–452; principles for distributing 99–102; redefinition of 459–461; rights-and-duties-related theory of 453–456

ocean governance 21
ocean protection: human responsibility 359–361; responsibility for areas wehere nobody responsible 360–362
offshoring 306
Old Quad 233
Olsthoorn, P. 187
O'Neill, Onora 97
online content moderation 331–335; accountability 331–332; and corporate social responsibility 334; and freedom of expression 334–335; and human rights 334; liability 331–332; responsibility 331–332
Operation Desert Storm 281
Operation Provide Comfort/Comfort II 281
OPRC (International Convention on Oil Pollution Preparedness, Response and Co-operation) 373
Orbán, Viktor 31
Orford, Anne 117
Organization for Economic Cooperation and Development (OECD) 322, 353
Ostrom, Elinor 242, 322
Ottoman Empire 279
outsourcing 306
overfishing 359
Owen, David 40

Palme Report (1982) 219
panarchy 211
Pangue Dam 20, 294–297
paradigm 451
Parekh, Serena 33
Paris Agreement (2015) 79, 140, 144, 148, 236, 369
Park, Susan 20, 288–298, 290
Parks, Bradley C. 65
Partnoy, Frank 385
Patriotic Union of Kurdistan (PUK) 280, 281–282
Pattison, James 197
peacekeeping 195
peer accountability 322
Pehuen Foundation 295
Pengue Dam 294–297
permafrost 369–370
Perry, William 221
Peru 159
Peshmerga 279
Pettit, Philip 171
Philosophical Investigations (Wittgenstein) 32
PhotoDNA 333, 339
Plagemann, Johannes 18–19, 231–240
plural theory of responsibility 31–41; causal and liable account 35; identity 36–37; intersubjectivity 36–37; non-causal/non-liable mod 35–36; ontological account 37–39; overview 34; political ethics 39–40
Pogge, Thomas 86–88, 92, 100

Polar Code 373
political authority 75; definition of 120; legitimacy of 76
political beauty 441–444
political conception 103
political ethics 39–40
political freedom 75
political responsibility 71–80; causal and liable 35; gap between the national and the international/global' 75–78; identity 36–37; intersubjectivity 36–37; non-causal/non-liable 35–36; ontological account 37–39; plural theory 31–41; and political ethics 39–40; as responsible government 74–75; as responsible leadership 78–80
Politics among Nations (Morgenthau) 220
"Politics as a Vocation" lecture (Weber) 424–425, 454
politics of responsibility 424
polluter pays principle 353
polylogue 225–226
Pombaline architecture 209
populism 77
Portugal 349
post-colonialism 19
Postel, John 396
post-truth era 109
power asymmetry 242
principled communitarianism, thesis of 101
principles of justice 101
proactive contestations 417–418; *see also* contestations
procedural responsibility 131–132
prospective responsibility 46
prudential responsibility 131–132
The Public and Its Problems (Dewey) 424, 426–429
public conscience 128
public intellectuals 424, 429–432
Public Philosophy (Tully) 413
Public Technical Identifiers (PTI) 400
public-reputational accountability 322

Qatar 307
Quad initiative 238

raison de système 18, 221, 222, 223, 224, 225, 227
raison d'état 18, 221, 222, 224, 227
Raley, Rita 339
Ramsey, Paul 171
Rapoport, Anatol 225
rational control 388
Ravizza, Mark 182
Rawanduz 280
Rawls, John 103, 103–104, 170
reactive contestations 417–418; *see also* contestations
realism 9
realpolitik 18, 221, 227
reason, use of 450

rebel responsibility 271–285; establishment of governance structures 281–282; and external recognition of responsibility by international community 276–278; in instrastate conflicts 274–279; internal claim of responsibility 275–276; Kurds in Iraq 279–283; overview 271–273; and security politics 278–279
Red Crescent Movement 206
referent objects 118
reflexive authority 117
reflexive methodology 410, 412
refugees 436–445; as weapons 110
Regional Fisheries Management Organizations (RFMOs) 351–352, 354–355, 373
regulatory instruments 44–45
relationship principle 102
remedial responsibility 7, 96
Remengesau, Tommy, Jr. 358
respondeo 34
responding to others 436–445; faking rescue operations 442–444; and fragility of responsibility 444–445; and hierarchies of responsibility 438–439; as political beauty 441–444; problem of 438–441; responsibility as sacrifice and gift relation 439–441
responsibility 154, 282–283; academic 132–133, 424–433; blind spots of 456–458; definition of 449, 453; English School 125–134; in global governance 114–122; as global scheme of governance 43–55; human rights approach to 58–66; of international organizations 114–116; jurisprudential interpretations 45–48; as moral and legal standards 126–131; moral geographies of 154–157; as moral practice 257–258; object of 10–11; plural theory of 31–41; potential and limits of 449–461; power relations of holding-responsible 105–108; principles for attributing 51–52; shift from individualistic paradigm to the concept of 452–456; as a signifier 32–34; subject of 8–10; as virtue 131–132; in world politics 3–7
responsibility gap 389
responsibility on the high seas 347–357; evolution of 349–350; and global commons 348–349; implementing 354–356; marine living resources 351–352; and mining 353–354; and ocean pollution 352–353; overview 347–348; and UNCLOS III 350–351
responsibility relations 7–13
responsibility research 409–419; conceptual dimension 409–410; critical constructivist norms 410; critical norms research 413, 415; framing norms research 411–416; mapping and staging responsibility contestations on the cycle-grid 416–418; norms typology 412–415, **414**; overview 409–411; practical dimension 409; responsibility contestations 416–418; responsibility to protect 415–416

Responsibility to Protect Doctrine 48, 50, 52, 72–73, 84, 145
responsibility to protect (R2P) 6–7, 15, 17–18, 23, 45, 84, 117, 118, 192–199, 195, 259–260, 454; contestations 417–418; discourse level 194; institutionalization level 194–195; in instrastate conflicts 271; level of collective expectations 195–197; level of justifications for state action 197–198; and normative conundrums of protection 193; norms 415–416; overview 192
responsibility triangles: complementarity in 278–279; in instrastate conflicts 277; Kurdish, international rejection of 282–283; and security politics 278–279; in world politics 273–274, *274*
responsibility while protecting (RWP) 195, 233
responsibilization 19; field of *8*
responsible corporate officer (RCO) doctrine 382; *see also* financial responsibility
responsible government 74–75
responsible nuclear sovereignty 166–167
responsible parties 45
responsible sovereignty 166
restraint, and diplomatic peace 225
retaliation 225
retrospective responsibility 7
Reus-Smit, Christian 92
Revelli, Christophe 382
Richardson, Matthew 385
Right of Humanitarian Intervention to Responsibility to Protect 48
Rio Declaration on Environment and Development (1992) 140, 142, 144, 353
rising powers 18, 231, 231–298; India 233–236; responsibility in world affairs 236–238
risk principle 101
Robeco 384
Roberts, J. Timmons 65
Robyn Eckersley 65
rogue state diplomacy 222
role responsibility 46
Rosanvallon, Pierre 74
Rousseau, Jean-Jacques 75, 203
Royakkers, L. 187
Royal Dutch Shell 384
Ruch, Philipp 443
Ruggie Principles 309
Russia: Arctic governance 371, 374; autonomous weapon systems 177, 179; and BBNJ regime 363; BRICS summits 238; Internet governance 399; marine resources 351; responsibility to protect 198
Ruzicka, Jan 168
Rwanda 193, 194, 259, 274
RWE 6, 12, 146

Safety of Life at Sea Treaty (SOLAS) 361, 373
Sagan, Scott 167

Sarbanes-Oxley Act (2002) 382
Sardo, Michael Christopher 22, 380–390
SAVE FOOD initiative 157
Scarry, Elaine 171, 172
Scharre, Paul 179
Schiff, Jade 32, 35
Schlag, Gabi 20–21, 331–343
Schlag, Pierre 331–340
Schmidt, Carl 117
Schroeder, Paul 221
Schuck, Christina M. 382–383
Schwarz, Elke 17, 177–191
Schwesig, Manuela 442
"Science as a Vocation" lecture (Weber) 426
Scientific Committee of Antarctic Research (SCAR) 376
search for truth 450
Securities and Exchange Commission (SEC) 382
Security Council 19, 121, 131, 145, 196–197; accountability mechanisms 265–266; anticipatory practices 266; counterterrorism 262; implications of responsibilization 263–267; Monitoring and Reporting Mechanism (MRM) 261; new subjects of responsibility 260–262; P4 veto 89–90; Resolution 1973 5; resolutions 260–261; responsibility as moral practice 257–258; responsibility for transnational security threats 262–263; responsibility to protect (R2P) contestations 416; responsibilization of 257–267; routinizing responsibility 264–265; segmenting objects of responsibility 264; sovereignty as responsibility 259–260
Seehofer, Horst 444
self-driving cars 184
Sendai Framework for Disaster Risk Reduction (SFDRR) 203, 206–207, 211, 211–212
Senegal 159
Sepinwall, Amy J. 382–383
September 11 attacks (2001) 262
Serbia 272
Sermon on the Mount 425
Serrano, Mónica 197
Shadmy, Tomer 14, 43–55
Shame and Necessity (Williams) 33
Shapiro, Oam 59
shared responsibility 139, 159
shareholder value 381–382; *see also* financial responsibility
Sharkey, Noel 181, 185
Sharp, Paul 222
Shen, Chung-Hua 384
Shue, Henry 99, 101, 103, 171
Shultz, George P. 221
Sienknecht, Mitja 19, 271–285
Sierra Leone 193, 262
Silver, Ellen 337–338
Simpson, Gerry J. 129

Singer, Peter 100, 154
Singh, Manmohan 168
Skinner, Quentin 75
slave trade 128
Slavery Convention (1926) 303
social expectations 9–10
social media 21
social media actors 331–340; accountability of 331–332; corporate social responsibility 334; liability of 331–332; online content moderation 331–335; overview 331–332; responsibility of 331–332
social purpose 121
social recognition 414, **414**
social security 77
socially responsible investing (SRI) 383–384
Solar Alliance 236
SOLAS (International Convention for the Safety of Life at Sea) 361, 372
Somali National Movement (SNM) 272, 276
Somalia 193
Somaliland 276
Soros, George 110
Souter, James 17, 164–173
South Africa 159, 233, 238
South Asian Association for Regional Cooperation (SAARC) 234
South Korea: and Arctic governance 375; autonomous weapon systems 179
South Sudan 275, 278, 279
sovereignty as responsibility 194
sovereignty model 321, **323**
sovereignty-based governance 20
Spain 275, 349
Sparrow, Robert 181–182, 183
speaker, position of 3
special responsibilities: nuclear weapons 166–167; status differentiation 128–130
Spiderman (film) 51
Srebrenica 259
Sri Lanka 234, 272, 278
standards of civilization 127
state responsibility: consequences for non-citizens 78; de-centering of 144–146; and nuclear weapons 165–168
status differentiation 128–130
Stimson, Henry 165
Stockholm Convention on Persistent Organic Pollutants (2001) 143, 373
Stockholm Declaration on the Human Environment (1972) 139, 140, 142, 144
Straddling Stocks Agreement (1995) 141, 351
strategic autonomy 236; *see also* autonomy
Strikwerda. Robert 33
Strong, Tracy 40
subject of responsibility 8–10
Sudan 198, 275, 279

Index

Sudan People's Liberation Army (SPLA) 279
Summit Outcome Document (2005) 415
sustainable development 21, 77–78, 142–145, 243, 246–249, 358, 370, 372
Sustainable Development Agenda 15, 77–79, 110
Sustainable Development Goals 140, 147–148, 157, 210, 305
Sutch, Peter 15, 84–95
Sweden 371, 375
Syria 73, 279, 416, 442–443

Talabani, Jalal 280
Task Force on Arctic Marine Cooperation (TFAMC) 374–375
Taylor, Charles 32, 36–37
technological risks 183–184
Teitel, Ruti 92
territorial sea 350
Tesco 159
Tesla cars 184
Thailand 246, 247
theory of contestation 413–414
A Theory of Global Governance: Authority, Legitimacy and Contestation (Zürn) 78–79
thesis of causal ineffectuality 101, 103
thesis of principled communitarianism 101
Thunberg, Greta 80, 423–424, 431
Tierney, Kathleen 209
Tiller, Rachel 21, 358–366, 366
Tokyo Round 143
Toope, Stephen 92
transboundary water management 243–245
transnational corporations (TNCs) 160, 302, 305, 306
transnational responsibilities 48; dialogical responsibility 49; obligations as 52–54; prospective responsibility 48–49
Treaty of Lausanne (1923) 279
Treaty of Sevres (1920) 279
Treaty on the Non-Proliferation of Nuclear Weapons (1968) 164, 165
Treaty on the Prohibition of Nuclear Weapons (2017) 17, 164, 168, 170
Truman, Harry 165
Truman Proclamation of 1945 350
Trump, Donald 31, 79, 109, 236, 238
Tully, James 413
Turkey 275, 279, 361, 445
Twitter 331–332, 335

Uber car, self-driving 184
Ukraine 371
Uludong, Ngedikes Olai 358
unfair trading practices (UTPs) 160
unified individual agent 387–388
unipolar moment 231
United Fruit Company 321

United Kingdom 263; autonomous weapon systems 177; marine resources 351
United Nations Charter: Charter I 223; Preamble 223
United Nations Conference of the Parties (2009) 79
United Nations Convention on Conventional Weapons 187–188
United Nations Convention on the Law of the Non-navigational Uses of International Watercourses 244
United Nations Convention on the Law of the Sea (UNCLOS) 350–351, 360–362; and the Arctic 372; Part XII of 141
United Nations Declaration of Human Rights 334
United Nations Declaration on the Rights of Indigenous Peoples (UNDRIP) 145
United Nations Disaster Relief Office (UNDRO) 205–206, 209
United Nations Economic Commission for Asia and the Far East (ECAFE) 246
United Nations Educational, Scientific and Cultural Organization (UNESCO) 223
United Nations Framework Convention on Climate Change (UNFCCC) 142, 373
United Nations Global Compact (UNGC) 324
United Nations Group of Governmental Experts (UNGGE) 403
United Nations Guiding Principles on Business and Human Rights (UNGPs) 20, 147, 318, 323–328, 334
United Nations International Strategy for Disaster Reduction (UNISDR) 211–212
United Nations International Strategy on Disaster Reduction (UNISDR) 206
United Nations Open-Ended Working Group (OEWG) 403
United Nations Trust Fund for Disaster Reduction 206–207
United States: and Arctic states 371, 374; autonomous weapon systems 177, 179, 179–182; foreign policy 13; marine resources 351; nuclear responsibility 167–168, 169
United States v. Dotterweich 382
Universal Declaration of Human Rights (UDHR) 6, 66, 223; Article 28 86–87; Article 29(2) 62; Preamble 60–61
universalism 458
upload filters 339
Upper Mekong 250
US-Indian Civil Nuclear Agreement 168

Vanderheiden, Steve 387
veto players 232
Vetterlein, Antje 1–27, 318–319, 332
Vienna Convention on Diplomatic Relations 223
Vienna Convention on the Law of Treaties 92
Vietnam 234, 246, 247
Vietnam War 39, 40

Vincent, Raymond John 59, 127, 128, 133
virtue ethics 319, **320**
Viviani, Jean-Laurent 382, 384
The Vocation of Politics (Weber) 39
Volkswagen 5
Voltaire 203

Waldron, Jeremy 94
Walker, William 166–167, 168, 169
Waltz, Kenneth 169
Walzer, Michael 89, 91–92
war: and killer robots 179–182; lethal autonomous weapons systems in 177–188; moral responsibility in 177–188
Warner, Jeroen 244, 245
Warsaw International Mechanism for Loss and Damage 66
water governance 242–253
water wars 244
Waterbury, J. 242
Watercourses Convention 244
Watson, Adam 221–222, 225–226
Weber, Max 23, 32, 39–40, 116, 424–426, 428–429, 430, 453
Westphalian sovereignty 232
Wheeler, Nicholas J. 59, 127, 133, 166–167, 169
Wiener, Antje 23, 409–419
Wiener, Norbert 177-178
Wight, Martin 131, 133
Williams, Bernard 33
Williams, Garrath 46
Willner, Dave 336
Wissenschaft 429
Wittgenstein, Ludwig 32, 425
Womack, Brantly 232

Working Group on Children and Armed Conflict 261
Working Group on Internet Governance (WGIG) 398
World Bank (WB) 20, 288; Inspection Panel 293–295; limits of accountability 293–294
World Conference on International Telecommunications (WCIT) 399
World Conference on National Disaster Reduction 206
World Health Organization 121
world politics 3–7
world society 125–128, 130–132, 284, 413
World Summit on the Information Society (WSIS) 398
World Summit Outcome Document (WSOD) 48, 195, 196, 259
World Trade Organization (WTO) 76, 87–89, 233
World Wide Web 331
Wu, Meng-Wen 384

Xi Jinping 79, 231, 237

Yemen 73
Yokohama Strategy 204, 206, 208, 209–210
Youde, Jeremy 128
Young, Iris Marion 32, 35–36, 101, 107, 156, 204, 333, 386
YouTube 331–332, 335
Yugoslavia 209

Zeitoun, Mark 242, 244, 245
Zionists 110
Zuckerberg, Mark 43, 331, 332, 337
Zürn, Michael 5, 15–16, 78–79, 114–122

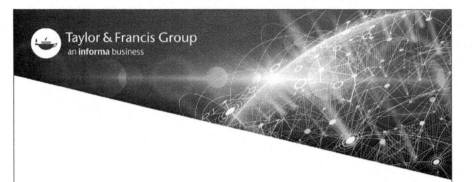